PSYCHOPATHOLOGY

A Competency-Based Assessment Model for Social Workers

 Brooks/Cole Empowerment Series

THIRD EDITION

Susan W. Gray

Barry University
Ellen Whiteside McDonnell School of
Social Work

Marilyn R. Zide

Barry University
Ellen Whiteside McDonnell School of
Social Work

BROOKS/COLE
CENGAGE Learning·

Australia • Brazil • Japan • Korea • Mexico • Singapore • Spain • United Kingdom • United States

BROOKS/COLE
CENGAGE Learning

Psychopathology: A Competency-Based Assessment Model for Social Workers, Third Edition
Susan W. Gray with Marilyn R. Zide

Publisher: Jon-David Hague

Acquisitions Editor: Seth Dobrin

Media Editor: Elizabeth Momb

Marketing Program Manager: Tami Strang

Editorial Assistant: Suzanna Kincaid

Art and Cover Direction, Production Management, Text Researcher, and Composition: PreMediaGlobal

Manufacturing Planner: Judy Inouye

Rights Acquisitions Specialist: Dean Dauphinais

Cover Image: © Robert Robinson/iStockphoto

For product information and technology assistance, contact us at
Cengage Learning Customer & Sales Support, 1-800-354-9706

For permission to use material from this text or product, submit all requests online at **www.cengage.com/permissions**
Further permissions questions can be e-mailed to
permissionrequest@cengage.com

Library of Congress Control Number: 2012935027

ISBN-13: 978-0-8400-2915-7

ISBN-10: 0-8400-2915-2

Brooks/Cole
20 Davis Drive
Belmont, CA 94002-3098
USA

Cengage Learning is a leading provider of customized learning solutions with office locations around the globe, including Singapore, the United Kingdom, Australia, Mexico, Brazil, and Japan. Locate your local office at **www.cengage.com/global**

Cengage Learning products are represented in Canada by Nelson Education, Ltd.

To learn more about Brooks/Cole, visit **www.cengage.com/brookscole**

Purchase any of our products at your local college store or at our preferred online store **www.cengagebrain.com**

Printed in the United States of America
1 2 3 4 5 6 7 16 15 14 13 12

To my beloved husband,
Kenneth E. Gray, JD
… you are my inspiration.

Contents

PREFACE

INTRODUCTION

An estimated 60 million people in the United States suffer from some type of mental disorder, 17 million of which are labeled "severe" (Pace, 2011). Kessler, Chiu, Demler, and Walters (2005) found approximately 46 per cent of all Americans have experienced some type of a mental disorder. Further, half of all cases reported onset by age 14 and three-quarters by age 24 (Kessler et al., 2005). What should we make of these numbers? In any given year, mental illness will more than likely be the most common problem you can expect to encounter in your practice. Social workers have been recognized as primarily responsible for providing mental health services in the United States, including assessment, and this trend is expected to continue (Pace, 2008; Thyer & Wodarski, 2007). The U.S. Department of Labor projects that the jobs available for social workers in mental health (including substance abuse) will rise from 137,300 in 2008 to 164,000 in 2018 (Bureau of Labor Statistics, 2011). Looking to the future, it is anticipated that the number of social workers will grow by almost 20 percent over the next 5 to 7 years.

Despite our presence in the mental health field of practice, there are still reservations about working with "those people." As I write this preface, I am reminded of an earlier experience with one of my former students. At the time I was teaching an introductory course in social work entitled, "Social Welfare as a Social Institution." I had decided that the best way to make the abstract and theoretical ideas about social welfare institutions to come to life was to visit a social welfare organization so that my students could see course concepts in action. We took a field trip to an agency serving the severely and persistently mentally ill that provided services organized around the clubhouse model of psychosocial rehabilitation (Farrell & Deeds, 1997). As we walked up the front steps of the building one of the clients was at the front door. He greeted us with a big smile and proudly announced, "Hi, I'm Danny and I have schizophrenia. Welcome to our clubhouse. I can't wait to show you around." When we returned to campus and talked about our impressions of the visit, my student revealed that she was scared about going to an agency that serves the mentally ill. She didn't know what to expect from "all those crazy people." Having an opportunity to talk first hand with someone living with mental illness changed her perspective. She added, "My heart just melted when I met Danny. The first thing I saw was somebody who was so proud to show us a place that meant so much to him." She realized that her misconceptions about mental illness got in her way of seeing the real person who also happens to have a diagnosable disorder. Unfortunately, stigmatizing and negative attitudes about those living with severe mental illnesses are still prevalent (Covarrubias & Han, 2011). Much like my student's initial impressions, negative assumptions about the functioning and behavior of those with a mental illness tend to get in the way of learning about the whole person where mental illness is but a part of their identity. The genesis of this book was to find a way to help students to move away from characterizing a person as a "diagnosis" and capturing the unique experiences of living with mental illness. The competency-based assessment is intended to provide a model to balance the disease orientation inherent in using the Diagnostic and Statistical Manual, or DSM, and formulate an assessment grounded in strengths and resilience that considers all aspects of a client's life.

The DSM is considered to be the gold standard for diagnosing mental illness, and there are a number of advantages and limitations to its use in social work practice. On the one hand, the DSM offers social workers a language with which to communicate with other professionals in the mental health field, but on the other hand, its focus remains on psychopathology, or what is wrong with the person. Missing is a recognition of an individual's strengths and resilience as he or she struggles with a mental disorder. Establishing a diagnosis is a critically important process, and it can set the stage for longer-term consequences. The day-to-day realities of a person's life are more complex than their diagnosis. A major challenge to formulating the DSM diagnosis is to factor in the totality of the individual's life events or circumstances. Missing from a diagnosis are the subtleties and nuances of the client's experience of his or her world. By combining the competency-based assessment with the DSM, the social worker incorporates a strengths-based approach to the diagnosis of specific disorders by encompassing the biopsychosocial, cultural, spiritual, and political aspects of the client's life. The practitioner recognizes the resources found within the individual, his or her family, and the community. In this way, the social worker keeps the whole person in perspective.

The competency-based assessment highlights a wider range of diagnostic considerations aimed at better understanding the interaction of stressors *and* resources in the client's life—for example, the client's values and beliefs, family connections, and social networks. The competency-based assessment looks to how a person copes with and rebounds from the challenges of living with a mental disorder. This perspective balances psychopathology with a parallel appreciation of factors related to strengths and resiliency. Not to address these aspects of the client's life can potentially limit or distort one's understanding of the client's experience of living with a mental illness. It goes without saying that using the DSM requires skill in order to be able to distinguish the client's symptom picture. The competency-based assessment looks beyond a list of symptoms to consider how a mental disorder is experienced, how it is expressed, and also how symptoms are interpreted by the person with a specific diagnosis. The competency-based assessment explores the client's subjective experiences of living with mental illness.

The intent of the competency-based assessment is to advance the assessment process as one that recognizes the person's uniqueness rather than to focus solely on the diagnostic label. In this way, the clinical social work practitioner formulates a more accurate diagnosis by understanding an individual's biopsychosocial makeup, cultural and political influences, coping methods, and factors that are a basis of strengths, resiliency, and resources. The process of diagnosing a mental disorder and related relationship problems includes equal attention to understanding a person's personal and environmental strengths as well as positive coping skills. From this perspective, the practitioner assumes that all people have strengths and resources regardless of their diagnosis. The competency-based assessment is not intended as the final word on understanding someone's experiences living with a mental illness. However, it is a first step toward a systematic assessment that provides a more complete understanding of an individual's uniqueness. In this way, the individual moves into the foreground, and categorization of their disorder shifts into the background. This is a good "fit" with social work's traditional perspective on the person-environment interaction and biopsychosocial approaches that frame practice within strengths and resilience. The aim of this book is to integrate the social work perspective with the traditional biomedical model of mental health as found in the DSM.

THE BOOK'S ORGANIZATION

The book outlines an eco-systems approach to assessment supported by systems theory, the person-in-environment perspective, and a strengths-based resilience approach to emphasize the multiple dimensions of the competency-based assessment in mental health practice. In this third edition, every effort has been made to retain the qualities that users of the prior editions found helpful—in particular, the succinct overview of each of the major disorders, case illustrations from real practice experiences, the straightforward and personal style, and the focus on a competency-based assessment. Students consistently tell me how helpful the case vignettes are to remember the DSM disorders within the competency-based framework. As commonly seen in social work practice, the cases illustrate the biological, psychological, social, political, and environmental aspects of mental illness and provide opportunities to examine a client's story from this range of perspectives. For example, the case of Louie Dessaint describes the story of a youngster who immigrated to the United States after the 2010 earthquake in Haiti. As a consequence of this natural disaster, Louie's life changes dramatically. He and his mother, his only surviving relative, are forced to leave their familiar small town of Jacmel in Haiti for the large metropolitan city of Miami, Florida. Shortly after his arrival, Louie is enrolled in school. His isolation is further increased since he speaks no English. Shortly thereafter Louie's teacher reports that he shows symptoms of attention deficit hyperactivity disorder (ADHD). The reader is called upon to discern the symptom picture of ADHD as described in the DSM while taking into account his mother's interpretation of her son's behavior. As a part of the competency-based assessment picture, additional factors to consider when formulating the diagnosis are Louie's immigration experience, the sudden death of his father, losing aunts, uncles, and cousins in the earthquake, and American expectations of acceptable classroom behavior.

As with prior editions, I hope you will continue to find the book clear and logical. The first chapter introduces the competency-based assessment model, along with supporting theories and perspectives familiar to social workers. Basic information about the *Diagnostic and Statistical Manual of Mental Disorders* is also included. In this way, the competency-based assessment model, consisting of biological, psychological and social variables, adds to the DSM multiaxial system rather than providing a substitute assessment framework. Sample questions are included that support the competency-based assessment model. Throughout the book, a visual diagram of the model is presented to further clarify the assessment process.

The remaining chapters are devoted to discussion of specific diagnostic categories that correspond to specific sections of the DSM. The major disorders are presented, but there are some that have been omitted—for example, learning disorders, sexual and gender identity disorders, sleep disorders, impulse-control disorders, and disorders due to general medical conditions. This decision allows for a more extensive and cogent discussion of each of the major adult disorders and disorders typically first seen in infancy, childhood, and adolescence. Each chapter is organized around a similar format beginning with a brief history and description of the diagnostic category. Next, specific disorders are reviewed, prevailing patterns are identified, and case vignettes are presented. They are followed by assessment summaries that take into account possible alternative diagnoses. Each assessment summary concludes with a multiaxial diagnosis for the preceding case vignette and the competency-based assessment so that readers become familiar with the process of distinguishing symptoms and client competencies in reality-based situations. In this way, readers may learn to take the client's "whole person" into account when making a diagnosis of mental illness. The chapter on substance-related disorders varies slightly due to its presentation in the DSM. Each chapter concludes with a series of practitioner reflections aimed at fostering critical thinking and discussion activities that can be used in a classroom setting.

INTRODUCTION TO ENHANCED CONTENT

An entirely new chapter on the disorders in infancy, childhood, or adolescence has been added to this edition. It is structured around the same format found in chapters 2 through 11; that is, you will find a review of the specific childhood disorder followed by a discussion of prevailing patterns, a case vignette, and a concluding assessment summary. To remain consistent with the prior editions, all of the chapters focusing on specific disorders have been ordered around how they appear in the DSM. Some instructors prefer to teach content about a particular disorder in a different sequence than presented in this book. To facilitate an individual instructor's preference, each chapter is designed to stand alone. That way, an instructor may choose to present the material that best fits his or her particular requirements.

You will also find a number of changes in each of the chapters. There is added material on the anticipated DSM – 5 changes. In addition, selected content has been streamlined, and excessive and extraneous discussion has been removed. The citations have been updated and new references added.

This third edition of the book is part of the Brooks/Cole Cengage Learning Empowerment Series and attends to the Educational Policy and Accreditation Standards (EPAS) established by the Council on Social Work Education (CSWE) in 2008. The EPAS represent a shift in teaching that moves away from a content-based curriculum to a competency-focused curriculum. This emphasis on student competencies has changed how we teach professional skills by focusing on what we do in practice or on an outcomes performance-based orientation. Instructors are challenged to answer the question, "What do we want our students to be able to do at the end of their educational program?" This perspective emphasizes educational practices that link theory and action. Learning is no longer considered to be a passive activity wherein students memorize or analyze information; students are now called upon to apply ideas to real-life situations. This perspective, with its emphasis on real-life case examples, supports the orientation of this book with the newly added Empowerment Series.

CSWE has identified 10 core competencies that are operationalized by 41 specific practice behaviors in the foundation year and 43 practice behaviors in advanced clinical practice. You will find a "Helping Hands" icon throughout this book to show the linkage between content specific competencies and practice behaviors. Each icon is labeled with the specific competency or practice behavior that relates to the content. For example, in Chapter 3 you will find an icon labeled EP (or Educational Policy) 2.1.3, which is the competency "apply critical thinking to inform and communicate professional judgment" (CSWE, 2008). For all icons, "competency notes" are provided at the end of each chapter. These competency notes explain the relationship between chapter content and CSWE's competencies and practice behaviors. They also indicate the page where the icons are located. A summary chart of the icons' locations in all chapters and the respective competency or practice behavior is placed in the front of the book.

A new Practice Behaviors Workbook accompanies the book that includes practice exercises linked to the EPAS recommended practice behaviors. The workbook is intended to help better prepare students for competent social work practice. It is possible to package the workbook together with the text. Instructors can work with their local Brooks/Cole Cengage Learning representative to receive a sample copy of the Practice Behaviors Workbook or request a bundle ISBN so that the text and workbook come packaged together at the bookstore.

TECHNOLOGY ENHANCEMENTS TO THE THIRD EDITION

Cengage Learning provides a CourseMate Web site that brings course concepts to life for students with interactive learning, study, and exam preparation tools that support the printed text. The CourseMate Web site includes an integrated eBook, quizzes, flashcards, videos, and more, and Engagement Tracker, a first-of-its-kind tool that monitors student engagement in the course. Students can access Course-Mate by going to www.cengagebrain.com.

A DVD featuring the same video clips that are available on the CourseMate Web site is also available. The video clips are of real people talking about their experiences living with a particular disorder. Students have the opportunity to observe actual clients talking about their disorder. Also included on the DVD is a set of PDFs that include reflective questions about the videos. These documents are included in an effort to ensure that readers move beyond looking at the symptom picture of particular mental disorders and never lose sight of the real people who struggle to live with these disorders. The reflective questions may be used by instructors for homework assignments or classroom activities.

The online Instructor's Manual providing useful information for faculty has been expanded. A complete chapter-by-chapter outline has been included. In addition, a complete set of Power Point lecture slides have been added that are available for download. The electronic test bank has been expanded to include questions for the chapter new to this edition. As before, the test questions can be used "as is" or adapted as needed. These supplements can be accessed by going to cengage.com/login.

This book is ideal for graduate students in a psychopathology, human behavior, or practice course. It is also helpful as a quick reference for social work practitioners, for those who want to review the basics of psychopathology, or to prepare for a state licensure exam. Supervisors will find it a useful reference for psychiatric diagnoses. The case studies are drawn from real practice experiences, and I hope you will find the diversity reflective of contemporary practice. They can be used by instructors or supervisors as part of a homework assignment, to supplement lectures, or can be adapted to provide evidence of students' understanding of the assessment process in practice.

ACKNOWLEDGEMENTS

Once again, I have worked on this book alone. I very quickly came to the realization that a project like this cannot be accomplished without help. I am grateful for all the helping hands behind the scenes that stood by me and worked so diligently to make this book a reality. Looking back on this undertaking, I find it hard to believe that 10 years have passed since the first edition of this text was published. I never anticipated that I would be writing the third edition and am appreciative of the positive feedback about the competency-based assessment. Since that time I have accumulated additional case stories from my students and colleagues. I have also continued to hear about the practice challenges from my students. They have reminded me that maintaining the values of our profession and applying social work values in contemporary practice is an ongoing struggle. Diagnosing a client is not an easy task. Over and over again my students have communicated that this textbook, with its real-life cases, has helped them to learn psychopathology in a way that keeps in mind a person's struggles associated with living with a mental disorder. I wish to thank my students for sharing their successes and challenges. I especially appreciate the assistance of one of my graduate students, Brandie Chandler. Her contributions in the later stages of this third edition were extremely helpful.

I wish to thank Seth Dobrin, Acquisition Editor, for his help on this third edition. He was easy to work with and very supportive, and he provided the impetus for including this edition of the book in the Cengage Learning Empowerment Series. His Assistant Editor, Alicia McLaughlin, was equally helpful. I was sorry when Alicia left Cengage but delighted to learn that she was moving on to her dream job in teaching. I would especially like to acknowledge all of the assistance on the production phase of the book, including Suzanna Kincaid, Assistant Editor for Social Work and Counseling; Elizabeth Momb, Associate Media Editor for Early Childhood Education, Counseling, and Social Work; Shawn De Jong, Permissions Project Manager; and Lindsay Bethoney, Project Manager, PreMedia Global. I recognize that there are many others on the publishing team who have worked quietly behind the scenes, and I do want to acknowledge their contributions.

I appreciate the comments of the reviewers who provided thoughtful feedback on the first edition and offered suggestions about what should be included in this third edition. In particular, I would like to thank Kim Andreaus, Wake Technical Community College; Margaret Arnd-Caddigan, East Carolina University; Elizabeth Danto, Hunter College; Elizabeth Pomeroy, University of Texas at Austin; Anne Petrovich, California State University, Fresno; Amanda Randall University of Nebraska at Omaha.

Finally, I would like to tell my husband, Kenneth, how much I appreciate his inspiration and support. After all these years of witnessing my involvement in social work, he still insists that he knows nothing about the profession but somehow always manages to say the right thing at the right time and finds the words of encouragement when I am up against the brick wall of having so much to do in so little time. It has been easier to complete the revisions for this third edition knowing that he is right there cheering me on. Thus far, he has seen me through the writing of three books without a complaint when we skip a meal, have lunch at odd hours, or grab some fast food instead of a delicious home-cooked dinner. As always, I am grateful for his continuing love, patience, and encouragement. His faith in me remains constant, and he is really something special.

REFERENCES

Bureau of Labor Statistics, U.S. Department of Labor, *Occupational Outlook Handbook, 2010–11 Edition*, Social Workers, Retrieved on November 20, 2011 from: http://www.bls.gov/oco/ocos060.htm

Council on Social Work Education. (2008). *Educational policy and accreditation standards*. Washington, DC: Council on Social Work Education.

Covarrubias, I., & Han, M. (2011). Mental health stigma about serious mental illness among MSW students: Social contact and attitude. *Social Work, 56*(4), 317–325.

Farrell, S. P., & Deeds, E. S. (1997). The clubhouse model as exemplar: Merging psychiatric nursing and psychosocial rehabilitation. *Journal of Psychosocial Nursing and Mental Health Services, 35*(1), 27–34.

Kessler, R. C., Berglund, P., Demler, O., Jin, R., Merikangas, K. R., & Walters, E. E. (June 2005). Lifetime prevalence and age-of-onset distributions of *DSM-IV* disorders in the National Comorbidity Survey Replication. *Archives of General Psychiatry, 62,* 593–602.

Kessler, R. C., Chiu. W. T., Demler, O., & Walters, E. E. (2005). Prevalence, severity, and comorbidity of 12-month *DSM-IV* disorders in the National Comorbidity Survey Replication. *Archives of General Psychiatry, 62,* 617–627.

Pace, P. R. (2008, January). Evidence-based practice moves ahead. *NASW News, 53*(1): 4.

Pace, P. R. (2011, July). Briefing weighs NIMH budget. *NASW News, 56*(2), 1–8.

Thyer, B. A., & Wodarski, J. S., (Eds.). (2007). *Social work in mental health: An evidence-based approach.* Hoboken, NJ: Wiley.

ABOUT THE AUTHORS

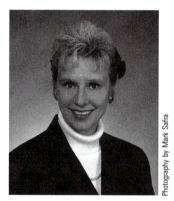

Photography by Mark Safra

Susan W. Gray is a professor in the Ellen Whiteside McDonnell School of Social Work at Barry University, Miami Shores, Florida. She earned her baccalaureate from Caldwell College for Women, her master's degree from Rutgers – the State University of New Jersey, a doctorate in education from Nova Southeastern University, and a doctorate in social work from Barry University. Having taught and supervised students for 30 years, she is known as an energetic, humorous, and yet challenging instructor. In addition to this text, she co-authored *Psychopathology: A Competency-Based Treatment Model for Social Workers* and authored *Competency-Based Assessments in Mental Health Practice: Cases and Practical Applications.* Her recent contributions include *Advanced Social Work Practice in Clinical Social Work* for the Council on Social Work Education, delineating advanced practice level standards for the 2008 Educational Policy and Accreditation Standards. She has also written extensively on a range of professional interests including clinical supervision, professional regulation and licensure, rural practice, bereavement groups, intergenerational family assessment tools, the brief solution-focused model of practice, methods of classroom teaching, and aspects of cultural diversity. Dr. Gray is active in the professional community and continues her work with a community mental health center, hospice, nursing association, senior citizens foundation, marine institute, and the Florida Keys Area Health Education Center. She is an active leader in in state and national professional organizations. Recognized as an engaging and informative speaker, Dr. Gray has presented numerous papers and workshops on the local, state, national, and international levels.

Marilyn R. Zide, late of Barry University, Ellen Whiteside McDonnell School of Social Work, earned her baccalaureate from Barry College, and her master's and doctorate degrees in social work from Barry University. She has made numerous contributions to the mental health field, both as a supervisor and as a unit director. She has also presented a number of scholarly papers at the local, state, national, and international levels, and has authored or co-authored numerous articles on a wide range of professional interests. In her last posting as an associate professor at Barry University School of Social Work, she taught courses on human behavior in the social environment as well as on methods of direct practice.

An Introduction to the Competency-Based Assessment Model

CHAPTER I

INTRODUCTION

The now century-old tradition of psychiatric social work was one of several specializations, including medical social work and child welfare, that emerged during the early part of the twentieth century. While the field of psychiatric social work grew during the 1900s, social workers struggled when seeking employment because of negative professional attitudes directed toward them. French (1940) identified some of the problems associated with early psychiatric social work positions such as large caseloads, low pay, and in some cases requirements to live on the institution's premises and perform nonprofessional duties within the institution.

The profession changed over time and the last part of the twentieth century documents social workers serving all areas of the public and private mental health sectors (see for example Abramson & Mizrahi, 1996, 1997; Berkman, 1996; Ell, 1996; Netting & Williams, 1996, 1997). During the past five decades, social workers have had considerable flexibility in assessing clients, with the choice of using diagnostic categories found in various editions of the *Diagnostic and Statistical Manual of Mental Disorders* (DSM-IV-TR) (American Psychiatric Association, 2000) or other psychosocial or behavioral criteria. Looking at practice in the twenty-first century, some of the ways social workers have historically studied clients is in jeopardy, especially regarding specific diagnostic descriptions and interventions based on presenting symptoms. In an effort to make the profession a convincing competitor in the marketplace, accountability is considered one of the central themes for contemporary social work practice. The DSM classification system is often used to meet these accountability requirements and for third-party payments. As a consequence, social workers are called upon to balance the profession's traditional focus on client strengths and resilience with the symptom-based orientation found in the DSM.

Looking to the future, managed care, changes in the service delivery structure of agencies, significant cost containment efforts, and the federal health reforms enacted in 2010 have moved the profession toward a further reevaluation of the assessment in clinical social work practice. The full extent of the repercussions of the overhaul of the American health care system is unknown. The push toward reform of the private health insurance market and proposals to provide better coverage for those with pre-existing conditions has set the stage for questions about spiraling medical expenses emerging in the form of increased costs for employee insurance coverage, as well as care for the poor and uninsured who currently seek medical treatment at emergency rooms and public clinics. Nevertheless, the implications of these initiatives are the merging of public and private services; the shifting of financial risk to service providers; the development of community-based service alternatives; and an increased emphasis on client strengths and social supports. Organized around theoretical underpinnings familiar to our profession, this book is about a competency-based assessment model that keeps sight of the complexities of life in vulnerable populations such as the mentally ill while formulating a differential diagnosis using the classification system found in the DSM.

Mental disorders are common and about 46 percent of all Americans are reported to have experienced a mental illness at some point in their life (Kessler, Berglund, Demler, Jin, Merikangas, & Walters, 2005). Looking to the rates of mental illness in children, approximately 7 percent of a preschool pediatric sample were given a psychiatric diagnosis in one study and approximately 10 percent of 1- and 2-year-olds receiving developmental screening were assessed as having significant emotional/behavioral problems (Carter, Briggs-Gowan, & Davis, 2004). Despite one's career direction within the field of social work, practitioners are more than likely to encounter clients with mental illness. Those who work with individuals considered mentally ill realize the need to learn how to decipher the DSM format. Part of the problem in using the manual is that one might come away from it questioning how the diagnostic criteria presented translate to the real-life clients seen in practice. Social workers must know not only how to assess individuals effectively but also how to develop an effective intervention plan that addresses clients' needs.

The DSM format is not for amateurs and should not be considered a substitute for professional training in assessment or the other skills needed to work with clients. For example, tasks such as performing mental status exams and monitoring of medication (historically the sole domain of psychiatrists) are now routinely handled by social workers. It is important to recognize that using a classification system can never replace an assessment that considers "the basic fact that people are quintessentially social beings, existing with each other in symbiotic as well as parasitic relationships" (Gitterman & Germain, 2008a, p. 41). That is, the person is much more than his or her diagnosis. There have been a number of long-standing criticisms of the DSM (Dumont, 1987; Kirk & Kutchins, 1988, 1992, 1994; Kirk, Siporin, & Kutchins, 1989). Being a social work practitioner as well as an educator, my primary reason for writing this book is to help make the DSM format more understandable and accessible to other social workers. This book does not take a linear or traditional psychiatric approach; rather, it incorporates a competency-based assessment as a vehicle to support the profession's historical orientation to practice.

Developing a working knowledge of psychopathology is similar to mastering a foreign language; at first everything seems confusing, but gradually the language becomes understandable. Similarly, beginning social work students are often anxious when asked to formulate an initial diagnosis, feeling they are somehow perpetuating the tendency to pigeonhole, stereotype, or label people. The process is complicated because most textbooks about mental disorders are written by psychiatrists or psychologists and tend to be biased toward their authors' own professional alliances (Austrian, 2005). I recognize that using the DSM format has been a longstanding and controversial topic within social work practice (e.g., see Kirk & Kutchins, 1992; Kirk et al., 1989; Kutchins & Kirk, 1987). Since its first introduction in the early 1950s, the manual has been used to describe and classify mental disorders. Admittedly, the DSM is an imperfect system, and it has the potential to stigmatize clients through labeling—however, despite its drawbacks, the manual continues to serve as the standard for evaluation and diagnosis. The aim in writing this book is not to reinvent the proverbial wheel by creating a "wannabe" mini-DSM. Rather, my concern for social work practitioners is that the emphasis that the DSM places on "disease" and "illness" obscures our profession's orientation, which centers on client strengths. While practicing from a strengths perspective, the social work practitioner does not ignore the hardships people living with a particular diagnosis must face. Schizophrenia, for example, presents some very real challenges. However, the competency-based assessment model expands the focus of the evaluation to include looking at a person's abilities, talents, possibilities, hopes, *and* competencies. Saleebey (2009) points out that people learn something valuable about themselves when they struggle with difficulty as they move through life. Although this book is organized around the DSM, I hope to simplify the language of psychopathology in a way that will help to influence the kinds of information gathered, how it is organized, and how it is interpreted. This interpretation includes looking at those strengths that would be useful to the person who struggles with mental illness and helps the social worker focus on the resourcefulness of a person, which is a beginning step in restoring hope (Saleebey, 2009). In essence, the social worker looks at how people survive and cope with a diagnosis of mental illness (Gitterman, 2001). A person's resourcefulness, strengths, and coping become a part of the assessment process, ensuring that the diagnosis does not become the center of his or her identity. The "whole story" of a person must include the parts of his or her struggle that have been useful to them and the positive information they have yielded.

THE MULTIAXIAL SYSTEM

Advanced
Clinical
EP 2.1.7 b

The competency-based assessment includes the ability to differentially apply knowledge of human behavior (specifically bio-psycho-social-spiritual theories) to better understand the client's current functioning. Familiarity with the DSM diagnostic classification system is considered to be a part of this comprehensive approach to the assessment process. A DSM evaluation involves making an assessment on five distinct dimensions or axes, each referring to a different domain of information that can be organized around the individual's competencies. Each axis should be completed even if no disorder is diagnosed, because leaving a blank in the evaluation makes it difficult to determine whether the practitioner "forgot" to enter a diagnosis or there was no diagnosis on that axis. An individual's behavior is divided into two distinct axes. Axis I, Clinical Disorders and Other Conditions That May Be a Focus of Clinical Attention, is used to denote all mental disorders except the personality disorders and mental retardation, which are only reported on Axis II. There is a distinction between the disorders considered for Axis I and those recorded on Axis II. Typically, the Axis I disorders are more evident during an assessment whereas the Axis II disorders are reserved for the personality disorders (or those long-standing personality defects ingrained in the developmental process of childhood that cause major, lifelong dysfunction in most aspects of the person's life). Mental retardation is also included on Axis II. When there is insufficient information to know whether or not a presenting problem can be attributed to an Axis I disorder, the practitioner records a "V code" indicating that the problem lies in "Other Conditions That May Be a Focus of Clinical Attention" (listed in the additional codes section of the DSM). If there is more than one Axis I disorder, the practitioner lists each individually in order of severity.

Axis II, Personality Disorders and Mental Retardation, is used to note various aspects of personality functioning and the presence of maladaptive personality features. It can also be used to note an individual's characteristic coping style—for example, the defense mechanisms of splitting, projection, or denial, or others, as appropriate. A diagnosis of mental retardation needs to be noted prior to age 18. A diagnosis of personality disorder is *never* assigned to anyone under the age of 18. The rationale for having both an Axis I and an Axis II diagnosis is to address the concern that practitioners might be tempted to give excessive attention to the more florid and dramatic Axis I disorders. By considering an Axis II diagnosis, the practitioner also pays attention to the less striking, longer lasting symptoms of mental retardation and especially to the personality disorders.

Axis III, General Medical Conditions, includes all general medical diseases or conditions that may be clinically relevant to the mental disorders reported on Axis I and Axis II. Axis III encourages the practitioner to conduct a thorough evaluation of the client and to consider the influence of a medical condition on the diagnosis. Any disorder listed on Axis III by a mental health professional who is not a physician should be qualified with "As reported by..." and the evaluator's name.

It is not unusual for someone with a problem to first seek help from his or her family physician. Many psychiatric symptoms may, on careful physical examination, have a clear relationship with a medical condition. For example, cancer or infectious diseases such as AIDS may produce symptoms consistent with depression. Thyroid disease may appear as a mood disorder. An overactive thyroid gland (hypothyroidism) might mimic certain anxiety disorders such as generalized anxiety disorder. This close linkage between medical and psychiatric symptoms creates opportunities for collaboration—and tapping into the expertise of other professionals improves the quality of assessments. Barlow and Durand (2012) suggest that any suspected medical condition should be thoroughly evaluated as a part of the assessment process.

Advanced Clinical EP 2.1.7 c

There are instances when social workers are called upon to consult with other professionals, as needed, as a part of the assessment process, and since the early days of the profession, practitioners have collaborated with other disciplines. The general medical conditions found on Axis III may complicate a client's mental health symptoms and, when coupled with social and environmental problems (indicated on Axis IV), the expertise from diverse professional backgrounds becomes increasingly important. Care is generally provided in a variety of mental health settings such as psychiatric hospitals, psychiatric units located in general hospitals, residential treatment centers, or outpatient clinics. **Interprofessional collaboration,** defined as "an effective interpersonal process that facilitates the achievement of goals that cannot be reached when individual professionals act on their own" (Bronstein, 2003, p. 299), is commonly found in many of these mental health settings. Social workers often function as part of an interdisciplinary team along with psychologists, nurses, physicians, psychiatrists, or neurologists—all of whom provide perspectives based on their unique knowledge and skills (Kirst-Ashman & Hull, 2008; Miley, O'Melia, & DuBois, 2010). The physician, for example, draws on chemistry, physiology, biology and other basic sciences in contrast to social workers, who are trained in the humanistic tradition and draw on their knowledge of the social sciences (Barnes, Carpenter, & Dickinson, 2000; Mizrahi & Abramson, 2000). Consulting with a medical professional, as needed, can help to confirm a diagnosis. In this way, Axis III encourages the practitioner to conduct a thorough evaluation of the client, and opportunities for collaboration among the various treatment providers increases. The assessment process in social work is ongoing, which means that the practitioner is taking note of, for example, changing medical circumstances or medications. Examples of the general medical conditions found on Axis III are: infectious and parasitic diseases; neoplasms (or tumors); endocrine, nutritional, and metabolic diseases and immunity disorders; diseases of the blood and blood-forming organs; diseases of the nervous system and sense organs; diseases of the circulatory system; diseases of the respiratory system; diseases of the digestive system; diseases of the genitourinary system; complications of pregnancy, childbirth, and the puerperium (the time immediately after the delivery of a baby); diseases of the skin and subcutaneous (just beneath the skin) tissue; diseases of the musculoskeletal system and connective tissue; congenital anomalies; certain conditions originating in the perinatal period; symptoms, signs, and ill-defined conditions; and injury and poisoning (American Psychiatric Association, 2000).

Axis IV, Psychosocial and Environmental Problems, calls attention to clinically relevant psychosocial and environmental issues found in many of the DSM disorders. This category includes problems or difficulties associated with the client's primary support group, social environment, or other interpersonal factors. Axis IV is intended to uncover those stressors that may be contributing to the "development of a new mental disorder," "the recurrence of a prior mental disorder," or "the exacerbation of an already existing mental disorder" (American Psychiatric Association, 2000, p. 31). Some examples might be: problems with primary support group such as divorce or physical abuse; problems related to the social environment such as the death of a friend; educational, occupational, housing, and economic problems; access to health care services such as inadequate insurance; problems related to interaction with the legal system and crime such serving time in jail; or other psychosocial and environmental problems such as not getting along with nonfamily caregivers or the social worker or physician (American Psychiatric Association, 2000).

Axis V, or the Global Assessment of Functioning (GAF) Scale, is used to assess the individual's overall psychological, occupational, and social functioning (American Psychiatric Association, 2000). Although a person's diagnosis is listed on Axis I or II, a diagnosis alone does not indicate the severity of the problem. The GAF rating provides a numerical indicator of a person's level of functioning and helps the practitioner clarify the areas in which the person is functioning well, thus highlighting the person's strengths. Axis V is particularly useful in tracking the individual's clinical progress. Scores may be assigned at the time of admission and/or at the time the client ends treatment. The GAF score can also be assigned during other time periods, for example, in the course of the client's highest level of functioning during the past 6 months.

The GAF Scale and the relative meanings of the scores are as follows:

- 100 = superior
- 90 = absent or minimal symptoms
- 80 = transient symptoms
- 70 = mild symptoms
- 60 = moderate symptoms
- 50 = serious symptoms
- 40 = some impairment in reality testing
- 30 = behavior that is considerably influenced by delusions or hallucinations; or serious impairment in communication/judgment; or inability to function in almost all areas
- 20 = danger of hurting self; or occasional failure to maintain minimal personal hygiene; or gross impairment in communication
- 10 = persistent danger of severely hurting self or others; or inability to maintain minimal personal hygiene; or serious suicidal act with clear expectation of death
- 0 = insufficient information

The practitioner uses intermediate codes, when appropriate such as a 35, 58 or a 72. In practice, the GAF score tends to be variable because each social worker's assessment of the client's situation is subjective. Despite this drawback, the GAF Scale provides a common language for clinicians. In sum, a score of 100 indicates optimal functioning, while the lower scores of 10 or below denote extreme danger that the client will hurt him- or herself or others. The DSM multiaxial system has been criticized as being too categorical when classifying mental disorders, and there have been a number of alternative diagnostic systems and approaches developed (Eriksen & Kress, 2005). Professionals have long debated whether mental disorders are discrete or continuous and whether they can be separated from relational or contextual factors (Shankman & Klein, 2002). Perhaps the alternative diagnostic model most familiar to social workers is the Person-in-Environment (PIE) system for describing, classifying, and coding the problems of social functioning of adult clients (Karls & Wandrei, 1994). Developed under a grant from the National Association of Social Workers (NASW), PIE provides a system of uniform descriptions of the client's interpersonal, environmental, mental, and physical problems. Also included is an assessment of the client's ability to deal with these problems. This classification system aims to balance the client's problems and strengths. A formal diagnosis is not made. Instead, the practitioner attempts to identify, describe, and classify the problems brought to their attention by the client.

Despite alternatives to formulating a diagnosis, the DSM multiaxial system remains the standard assessment tool. It is considered to be the shorthand that facilitates communication among professionals in the field of mental health. When used along with the competency-based assessment, the DSM becomes a means of organizing and gathering information that supports the client's strengths *while* also making a diagnosis. That is, the practitioner considers factors above and beyond diagnostic signs and symptoms. Clients do not exist in a vacuum. There is more to a person and his or her life story than a description of symptoms. The partnership between the DSM classification format and the competency-based assessment individualizes clients, looks at the full range of factors affecting their lives, examines the lack of "fit" between individuals and their environments, and extends the practitioner's understanding of psychopathology. Social workers who assess a client's condition solely in terms of whether the DSM criteria are met fail to appreciate the ways that clients cope with their particular life challenges, influencing factors, and available supports. **Competency-based practice** emphasizes the importance of identifying client competencies, and it focuses on assets instead of deficits. More precisely, it strives to build and enhance the client's own skills as they attempt to deal with life conditions.

Looking to the upcoming DSM-5, there are a number of changes proposed for the multiaxial system. One proposal is to collapse Axes I, II, and III into one axis that will contain all psychiatric and general medical conditions. This proposed change will make the DSM-5 classification system more compatible with the single-axis approach found in the International Classification of Diseases (ICD). The DSM-5 may also make the codes listed on Axis IV more compatible with the ICD as well. There may also be changes in Axis V aimed at better assessing a person's disability and distress.

The mental disorders found in the DSM will be presented here from a social work perspective. Sometimes interesting historical information will be included; at other times editorial asides about exploration and assessment will be offered. In most cases, a clinical case vignette is presented to help the reader keep in mind the major features of assessment. Above all, the intent is to provide what social workers need in a format that will prove clinically relevant, understandable, and practitioner-friendly.

This book is not intended to address all of the specific DSM classifications, nor does it include all specific disorders. It is anticipated that assessment criteria will be advanced from a social work perspective while balancing the tensions inherent in the medical model. The competency-based assessment encompasses an ecological approach, the strengths perspective, and systems theory to determine what biopsychosocial factors contribute to the client's problems, as well as factors that may be useful in intervention planning. The struggle is to shift the lens away from defining pathology and toward focusing on internal processes in which all of the social and environmental factors that influence functioning are considered. Many current textbooks are starting to move away from terminology describing those considered mentally ill as "patients." The DSM format has also moved away from such negative descriptions, but it remains to be seen how much of the rest of the literature follows suit. The ultimate challenge is to know how and when the DSM is effective and useful—and how and when to keep its classification system in perspective.

THE COMPETENCY-BASED ASSESSMENT MODEL

EP 2.1.7 a

A **competency-based assessment** provides a conceptual framework using bio-psycho-social-spiritual theories and the DSM multiaxial classification system to guide the process of assessment. In this way, the practitioner systematically reviews and understands an individual's past in order to distinguish among and interpret presenting concerns. By looking at a person's history, the social worker gains a greater insight into his or her current functioning. Attention is focused on examining biological, psychological (including cognitive), and social systems variables. In his classic article, Bronfenbrenner (1979) suggests that practitioners who do not consider all the various environmental influences lose the breadth and depth of the client's life experiences. The biopsychosocial framework, together with an ecological approach, the strengths perspective, and systems theory, explicates this competency-based assessment model. The **biopsychosocial framework** validates the potential importance of biogenetic, psychological, social, and environmental factors in understanding human behavior; the **ecological perspective** draws attention to the client's multiple interactions with his or her environment; the **strengths perspective** draws attention to the attributes, capacities, experiences, and resources in a person's life that contribute to a positive and satisfying life and effective social functioning; and **systems theory** integrates these principles. Individualizing how *this* person is affected by the "illness" is at the heart of this conceptualization.

Here is a brief overview of the components comprising the competency-based assessment model.

THE BIOPSYCHOSOCIAL FRAMEWORK

George Engel (1977, 1980, 1997) is considered the leading proponent of the biopsychosocial framework. According to Engel, the biological component addresses relationships among factors that include normal biology, disease processes, genetic influences, and their relationship to the person's biological functioning. The psychological component refers to such factors as thoughts, feelings, perceptions, motivation, and reaction to "illness." The social component examines cultural, environmental, and familial influences. According to Bandura (1969, 1977), reciprocal interactions are assumed between a person's behavior and his or her environment. Understanding the client's functioning at all levels helps provide a more complete clinical picture—one that identifies competencies that may be built upon. This biopsychosocial concept makes it essential to discern the client's medical status, individual psychology, and sociocultural factors affecting behavior.

Historically, there have been two major models explaining behavior: one is the biomedical model and the other is the psychodynamic model. The

biomedical model delineates diagnostic criteria, whereas the **psychodynamic model** focuses on symptoms, behaviors, and underlying psychological processes. Stoudemire (1998) observes that these two models, when integrated, form a biopsychosocial framework. This framework for assessment considers (a) genetic and biological factors in the pathogenesis of certain disorders (such as schizophrenia and mood disorders); (b) developmental experiences and/or conflicted family and social relationships (some individuals may be more vulnerable to certain types of illness); (c) current life stresses (which may precipitate the onset of certain psychiatric disorders and symptoms or contribute to the relapse of preexisting conditions).

The biopsychosocial framework supports the competency-based assessment model in several ways. First, the significance of understanding the client's present functioning and its relationship to past events underscores the need for fully understanding each client's unique history. Second, this model relies on a thorough assessment and prioritizing of problems. Third, it pays attention to the multiple systems that affect the client, such as the biological, psychological, social, and cultural aspects of the client's life. A fourth characteristic is the focus on positive behaviors and events in the client's life rather than on deficits. Finally, a competency-based assessment focuses on the relationship between behavior and surrounding events—that is, those events that can either elicit or maintain problematic behaviors. This framework helps the client and family maintain an identity apart from the "illness." Applying a competency-based assessment model underscores the importance of evaluating all aspects of the client's difficulties while looking for strengths.

The second element important to discussion of the competency-based assessment model incorporates an ecological perspective.

THE ECOLOGICAL PERSPECTIVE

Advanced
Clinical
EP 2.1.1 d

The competency-based assessment looks to therapeutic relationships with clients within the person-in-environment perspective. More than 30 years ago, Germain (1973) introduced the "ecological metaphor" as a way to expand the focus of social work practice by emphasizing the interaction between people and their environment. This orientation draws attention to both the internal as well as external factors in a client's life. The ecological perspective primarily focuses on human ecology—the way human beings and their environments accommodate each other (Germain, 1991; Gitterman & Germain, 2008b). This interaction is considered dynamic; that is, the goodness of "fit" between individuals and their surroundings is achieved through mutual interaction, negotiation, and compromise. In essence, people are seen as being involved in dynamic and reciprocal interactions with their environment. Sheafor and Horejsi (2010) highlight the importance of understanding clients through an ecological point of view:

> It should be apparent that there is not always a good fit between concepts borrowed from another field, like ecology, and the values and purposes of the social work profession. Nevertheless, these ideas stretch our thinking and encourage us to view human behavior and problems and consider planned change in ways that are new and fresh.

Above all else, ecology teaches us that people are shaped and influenced by their environment and, in turn, the environment is shaped and changed by humans (p. 63)

The mental disorders in the DSM describe disease processes, not people; individuals with the same diagnosis often look very different from one another in terms of behaviors, personality, life experiences, or problems in living. Depending on the diagnostic criteria offered, clients may have remarkably different life experiences. While the DSM may be recognized as a useful diagnostic tool, it tells the practitioner little or nothing about the "why's" of mental illness—and it does not address client individuality.

One of the strengths of the ecological perspective is that it draws attention to each person's unique history and takes into account the complexities of the human experience. Some of the more salient concepts of the ecological perspective take into consideration are the following:

- **Person: environment fit**—This is viewed as the actual congruence or "fit" between an individual's or a group's needs and their surroundings. Considered a defining characteristic of social work practice, the person: environment fit requires an assessment that encompasses the person, their environment, and the interactions between them.
- **Adaptations**—Adaptations are regarded as the continuous, change-oriented, cognitive, sensory-perceptual, and behavioral processes people use to sustain or improve the fit between themselves and their environment.
- **Life stressors**—Life stressors include difficult social or developmental transitions, traumatic life events, or other issues that disturb the existing fit between people and their environments.
- **Stress**—Stress is considered the response to life stressors; stress is characterized by troubled emotional or physiological states (or both). It may be characterized by anxiety, guilt, anger, fear, depression, helplessness, or despair.
- **Coping measures**—Any efforts to regulate negative feelings about changes in the environment may be considered coping measures.

According to Antonovsky (1980), the most basic category of coping resources consists of beliefs and attitudes toward life. Other coping mechanisms relate to a person's knowledge of and successful experiences with life tasks; cognitive capacities and ability to reason; ability to control and use emotional affective responses to stress; and skills to carry out planned action, which usually come from past successful experiences.

The ecological perspective views individuals as moving through a series of life transitions that require environmental supports and coping skills. Stress may result if there is not a good fit between internal and external demands and available resources (Gitterman & Germain, 2008a). The practitioner looks at those transactions that either promote or inhibit growth and development. In addition, this perspective helps the practitioner to work collaboratively with clients to mobilize strengths and coping skills, locate resources, and explore opportunities within the client's environment that may pave the way for the client to achieve success rather than leave him or her feeling powerless or disenfranchised.

The third aspect integral to the competency-based assessment is the strengths perspective.

THE STRENGTHS PERSPECTIVE

**Advanced
Clinical
EP 2.1.3 b**

As a part of the competency-based assessment, social workers are called upon to identify and articulate the client's strengths as well as vulnerabilities. The strengths perspective provides an avenue for the practitioner to identify and build upon client strengths. Strengths can be seen as any client resources, capabilities, knowledge, abilities, motivation, experience, intelligence or other positive qualities that can play a role in solving problems and pursuing positive and satisfying life experiences (Blundo, 2008). This perspective serves to counterbalance the deficit oriented approach so often associated with an assessment of pathology. Rather than solely focusing on what is wrong in a person's life, the strengths perspective looks to a consideration of the positive and functional aspects of behaviors and situations (Glicken, 2004). The strengths perspective does not ignore the reality that a psychiatric diagnosis may impose limitations on a person's functioning but looks to those experiences as a potential source of strength and opportunity.

As a part of the competency-based assessment, the practitioner's focus shifts to an exploration of each person's unique experience with the challenges associated with mental illness. The strengths perspective presumes that every person has strengths, even when some of the behaviors associated with a particular diagnosis are seriously dysfunctional. The practitioner assumes that strengths can be found in all environments, no matter how difficult they might seem (Rapp & Guscha, 2006). As such, the practitioner looks for something positive and important that the client is doing, can do, or wants to do. Saleebey (2009) identifies the following principles that are the underpinnings of the strengths perspective:

- Every individual, group, family, and community has strengths.
- Trauma and abuse, illness and struggle may be injurious but they may also be sources of challenge and opportunity.
- Assume that you do not know the upper limits of the capacity to grow and change and take individual, group, and community aspirations seriously.
- We best serve clients by collaborating with them.
- Every environment is full of resources (pp. 15–18).

In summary, the strengths perspective provides the structure to look for those capabilities and resources that differentiate each client's experience with mental illness.

The fourth and last element comprising the competency-based assessment model is systems theory.

SYSTEMS THEORY

Systems theory was developed during the 1940s and 1950s by Ludwig von Bertalanffy (1968) as an approach to understanding the interconnectedness of the various relationships within a person's life. From its beginning, systems theory postulated that the behavior of any living system could be influenced by other conditions. Bertalanffy suggested that all social sciences can be integrated by using systems as the unit of analysis—that is, the biological system, the personality system, and the social system.

Systems theory organizes the practitioner's understanding of human development. The theory does not attempt to explain human behavior, but asserts that human behavior is viewed through three distinct frames of reference: biological, psychological, and social. Systems theory clarifies the person: situation gestalt by conceptualizing the client's world. It moves away from a linear explanation of cause and effect to appreciate the complex interactions between the individual and all aspects of their biopsychosocial system. In other words, the true role of systems theory is to help the social worker pay attention to those complex interactions between clients and their environment. The competency-based assessment complements using the DSM for assessing mental illness. This systems approach to assessment includes exploring how the client's current thoughts and feelings *as well as* environmental factors relate to functioning versus looking only at behavior as a sign of intrapersonal or personal concerns. Using the biopsychosocial framework fosters an evaluation based on "behaviors in situations" rather than on behaviors or situations alone. The competency-based assessment also considers capacities, motivation, and environmental qualities as components of ecological competence for the multiple transactions between people and their social environments. This approach changes the type of assessment questions asked—the social worker is more interested in finding out what is *right* about the client rather than focusing solely on what is *wrong*. This summary of the central ideas supporting the competency-based assessment model sets the stage for the constructs discussed in the following chapters.

Assessment is an ongoing process with a focus toward valuing client strengths. Sheafor and Horejsi (2012) distinguish the assessment from diagnosis in a number of ways:

> In direct practice with individuals, families, and small groups, the social worker's data gathering and assessment will be shaped and guided by the person-in-environment framework. In other words, attention is given to the client as a unique and whole person as well as the demands and constraints placed on the client by the context or environment in which he or she must function (p. 172).

The competency-based assessment changes the emphasis in the questions a practitioner asks. The practitioner gives some attention to all dimensions of the whole person and considers any factors that may affect his or her social functioning. For example, when working with a client who is socially isolated and may be depressed, asking a question about how he or she manages to get through the day shifts the focus away from pathology and toward the client's own competency. This then provides the foundation for examining effective problem solving, self-change, viable alternatives, and solutions. From this example, using a wide-angle lens in formulating the assessment provides the opportunity to gather data that focuses on the client's experiences in coping with depression. The biological, psychological, and social elements found in the competency-based assessment, when merged with the DSM multiaxial classification system, provide an individualized way of looking at clients and their social contexts.

Systems theory supports the competency-based assessment and helps to inform interprofessional collaboration. Systems theory, for example, provides a perspective that helps practitioners better understand how assessment and related services are

Advanced
Clinical
EP 2.1.7 c

linked together. The social worker may consult with other professional disciplines to confirm a diagnosis or to monitor a client's medication. When professionals from different disciplines work together, they have the opportunity to formulate a diagnosis more accurately and deepen their understanding of a person's symptoms than when they conduct assessments independently. Seeking the advice and counsel of other professionals is integral to the competency-based assessment process and is supported by the Code of Ethics (National Association of Social Work, 1999). The Code specifically notes that social workers should put personal biases aside and act on behalf of clients based on professional social work knowledge, skills, and values to the best of their ability and in the client's best interest. This requires social workers to define what is unique about their professional perspective, have a solid professional identity, and know what falls outside their purview (Reamer, 2006). Interprofessional collaboration includes upholding the values and ethics of social work, respect for professional colleagues, an ecological holistic view of practice, and a perspective that is similar or complementary to the collaborators' perspectives (Bronstein, 2003).

In subsequent chapters, the connections among the biological, psychological, and social factors are presented. Figure 1.1 is a graphic representation of this approach. This pedagogical feature is repeated throughout the book, each time focusing on the specific disorder under discussion. The case illustrations are not to be considered as the final word, but seen as representations of assessment data. By envisioning the convergence of these perspectives, I hope that the practitioner will get a fuller picture of assessing for competence (those skills that enable the client to function effectively) and the client's unique experience with mental disorders. The competency-based assessment is the process of clarifying competence within the client system, the unique features of the client's environment, the goodness of fit between the client and his or her environment, and the impact of mental illness. Gitterman and Germain (2008a) note,

> By immersing ourselves in clients' stories and environments, social workers are in a natural position to describe adaptive and dysfunctional patterns, as well as processes of change. Through detailed and rich descriptions, including direct quotes from clients and significant environmental figures, we capture the whole person within a life course and ecological perspective (p. 129).

Our clients are seen as active, striving human beings who are capable of organizing their lives and realizing their potentialities, as long as they have appropriate resources that can be located in the family, their community, or the environment. The competency-based assessment is directed toward finding ways to support the client's strengths and coping strategies. The competency-based assessment model provides a framework for understanding persons with mental illness as unique and fosters the consideration of not only a person's illness but of his or her capacity to grow in relationships. The social worker, in collaboration with the client system, focuses on social adaptation, coping skills development, and empowerment. In addition, the practitioner identifies and amplifies the client's existing capacities in order to resolve problems and improve quality of life. The competency-based approach to the assessment can be seen as respectful toward and empowering of oppressed and vulnerable people such as those with mental illness (Werner, 2000).

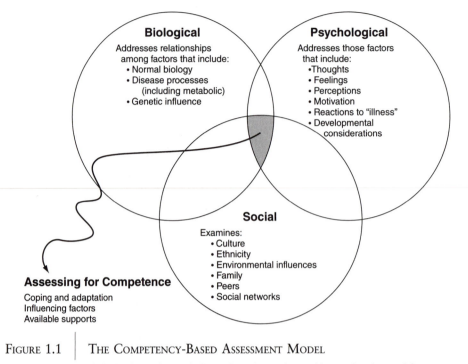

FIGURE 1.1 | THE COMPETENCY-BASED ASSESSMENT MODEL

The interactions of the biological, psychological, and social variables in the client's life.

© Cengage Learning

THE SOCIAL WORKER'S ROLE

A basic premise of the competency-based assessment is that an effective assessment depends on the engagement of the client in a working relationship. This can be challenged by the reality that persons with a mental illness may lose some of their capacity for relationships because of cognitive or mood impairments. The individual may experience social disconnections such as the hallucinations or delusions seen in schizophrenia, and their ability to engage in social situations is compromised. The social worker may be further challenged to connect with inarticulate, ambivalent, paranoid, or otherwise socially detached clients.

In addition, clients may have a range of needs that may include but not be limited to housing, income support, medical care, job training, recreation, living skills development, counseling, and medication. Meeting these needs can be challenged by the client who is occasionally hospitalized or experiences crisis intervention episodes. Although the social worker's activities may differ somewhat depending on the setting, the following roles are fundamental to practice in mental health (Bentley, 2002):

- *Crisis counselor*—As crisis counselor, the social worker provides emergency interventions for individuals who experience sudden or abrupt situations where there is an imminent risk of harm; for example suicide, violence toward others or impaired judgment to the extent where the person is endangered (i.e.: delirium, dementia, an acute psychotic episode, or severe dissociative state to name a few).

- *Therapist*—The social worker, as therapist, works with individuals, their families and groups using the techniques, strategies, skills and resources aimed at helping these client systems to achieve desired outcomes.
- *Mediator*—As a mediator, the social worker is a neutral and impartial third party who helps to facilitate a mutually agreeable resolution to a dispute by following the structured process known as mediation.
- *Educator*—As an educator, the social worker is involved in the dissemination and exchange of information with clients (and families).
- *Skills trainer*—As a skills trainer, the social worker engages in two areas of skills training—one domain applies to the wide range of challenges facing someone with a mental illness and offers training, usually organized around a specific curriculum or program, in the key areas of communication, problem solving and assertiveness; the second domain is more population-specific and targets training about those skills relevant to a particular problem or clinical population—for example, someone with an anxiety disorder might benefit from social skills training.
- *Case manager*—Looking to the many problems and issues faced by those with mental illness, the social worker's role as case manager involves coordinating services, advocating for clients and, on some occasions, controlling resources and purchases services for his or her client.
- *Medication facilitator*—Traditionally referred to as a medication manager, the social worker's role as medication facilitator refers to collaborating with clients, their family, and other providers to address and help resolve the dilemmas and issues related to taking psychotropic medications.
- *Consultant*—As consultant, the social worker collaborates with his or her clients to address questions and concerns related to living with mental illness. Family members of someone with a mental illness may also turn to the social worker with questions and concerns. As a family consultant, the practitioner collaborates with the family to arrive at options for addressing or resolving these issues.
- *Collaborator on interagency and interdisciplinary teams*—Working with clients diagnosed with mental illness often involves many different professionals, agencies, and groups. As a collaborator in this realm, the practitioner interacts with members of these constituencies in shared activities and partnerships.
- *Advocate and community organizer*—As advocate, the social worker champions the rights of individuals or communities through direct intervention or through empowerment. In the role of community organizer, the social worker acts as facilitator of planned efforts to achieve specified goals in the development of a group, neighborhood, constituency or other community. Both advocacy and community organizing roles are aimed at helping to achieve social justice, economic or social developments or other improvements.
- *Program evaluator and researcher*—In this role, the social worker (sometimes in collaboration with others) designs and constructs studies to evaluate programs, clinical activities, and services across a wide range of mental health problems and populations.

- *Administrator and policy analyst in mental health settings*—As an agency administrator, the social worker analyzes policy in terms of how it will impact their particular organization. The role of a policy analyst, in contrast, is to recommend or analyze legislation (or the administrative rules) from the larger perspective of the public good. The policy analyst explains the advantages and disadvantages of competing policy alternatives and how these alternatives will differentially affect various stakeholders.

Taking on the different roles associated with practicing in the field of mental health does not necessarily make one a good practitioner. Gerdes and Segal (2011) examined the characteristic of empathy and its connection to working effectively with clients. They found that "empathic social work practitioners are more effective and can balance their roles better" (p. 141). In addition to empathy, Bentley (2002) delineates a number of other characteristics attributed to effective mental health practitioners. They are:

- *Committed*—The social worker is personally invested in working across system levels; for example individuals, families, groups, and communities.
- *Collaborative*—This means having the ability to relate to clients, families, and other providers in a way that conveys respect and appreciation for their legitimacy and perspectives.
- *Creative*—Creativity involves the ability to use one's professional imagination and clinical judgment to apply knowledge or skills to each unique and different client situation.
- *Competent*—Competency is characterized by having the power to perform and the internal and external resources to act.

EP 2.1.1 c

To summarize, practitioners should know what they are doing and the way they are doing it. At all times, social workers are attentive to professional roles and boundaries when working with others. The competency-based assessment encompasses the practitioner's multiple roles by looking to find ways to reduce the risks found in the lives of those (and their families) with mental illness, build on strengths, and ensure access to programs and services as well as the availability of adequate and appropriate resources and policies. Social work practitioners may not be experts in the multiple roles spanning the various client system levels (i.e., individual, family, groups, and communities) but they must be committed to an assessment that considers each of these aspects in the life of a client who struggles with mental illness (Corcoran & Nichols-Casebolt, 2004).

UNDERSTANDING THE CLIENT

EP 2.1.7 b

Competent social work practice includes the ability to critique and apply knowledge of human behavior in order to fully understand the client's presenting problems and the environmental interplay. Shulman (2009) distinguishes social work practice as viewing the client as being in a reciprocal relationship with his or her social surroundings. The individual and his or her environment are mutually interdependent, but sometimes obstacles get in the way of the person's social functioning. The assessment should be guided by obtaining relevant information and understanding of the client's circumstances, which then informs the development of intervention strategies. Assessment should ask, "What's the matter?" instead of the more deficit-oriented focus of "What is wrong *with you*?"–especially since the person is coping as best as he or she can under current circumstances or events. Unlike the model borrowed from medicine where the focus is on examining how past events have affected individuals, it is important to understand the context of current issues. To be representative of the competency-based assessment, major assessment categories were adapted from a range of authors, including, for example, Compton, Galaway, and Cournoyer (2004); de Jong and Berg (1998); Gitterman and Germain (2008a); Jordan and Franklin (2003); Shulman (2009); and Woods and Hollis (2000). These categories include the nature of the presenting problem; the client's current life situation, including intrapersonal (or personal) issues and interpersonal concerns such as family, work or school, and peers; context and social support networks; relevant historical data; and sociocultural factors. This is not intended to be a comprehensive list but a beginning outline for systematically exploring presenting concerns with the client. The specific information elicited about the nature of the presenting problem is summarized on Table 1.1.

TABLE 1.1	THE NATURE OF THE PRESENTING PROBLEM

Identify the reason for referral:

What made the client seek help now and not before?

How has the client sought to solve the problem previously including other therapy (and with what results)?

What is the client's ability to identify and define problems, or to discuss probable causative factors?

Describe the events leading up to the referral or other factors precipitating the referral.

Identify the contributing conditions and components of the problem:

History

    When did the problem first occur?

    Is this a long-standing unresolved problem, or a recent one?

Duration

    How long has the problem been going on?

Frequency

    How often does the problem occur?

Magnitude

    What is the intensity of the problem?

Antecedents

    What happens immediately before the problem occurs?

Consequences

    What happens immediately after the problem occurs?

(continued)

TABLE 1.1 | CONTINUED

Clarify the client's competence:

What are the unique capacities, skills, attitudes, motivations, strengths, and potentialities of the client?

What are the particular areas of coping strengths?

What are indicators of resilience in the person?

Which areas of competence need to be reinforced or supported?

Which life experiences can be mobilized to stimulate or support the process of change?

What client resources are available for solving the problem?

How does the client relate to the worker and demonstrate the ability to use help?

What is the social worker's perception of the problem?

How much agreement is there between the worker and the client concerning these problems?

Are there other difficulties associated with (or in addition to) the problem?

© Cengage Learning

Formulating a competency-based assessment is more than relying on gut feelings or worker intuition. This is not to say that clinical judgment is unimportant, only that effective judgments concerning clients must instead be grounded in empirical observations and documentation of client characteristics. In the author's experience, there is a temptation for practitioners to diagnose first and then ask questions to support this clinical picture. Typically, the social worker should look at the multiple influences in the client's life, for example, intrapersonal issues, patterns of interpersonal relationships, social context, and support networks. Table 1.2 provides suggestions for examining biopsychosocial functioning and areas that delineate the fit between the person and his or her social networks.

TABLE 1.2 | THE CLIENT'S CURRENT LIFE SITUATION

I. Intrapersonal (or personal) issues:

Cognitive functioning

What is the client's perception of the problem?

Is there evidence of the client's capacity to solve problems?

Is there evidence of rational (versus irrational) thoughts?

Emotional functioning

Describe the client's affect.

Is there evidence of appropriate (versus inappropriate) affect?

Has the client had difficulty managing any recent stresses or pressures?

Behavioral functioning

What is the client's physical appearance?

TABLE 1.2 | CONTINUED

Does the client have any distinctive mannerisms?

Does the client have any disabilities?

Physiologic functioning

Has the client been seen medically during the past year?

If so, what are the results?

Has the client had any recent illnesses or surgery?

Is there evidence of drug and/or alcohol usage?

Is the client taking any medications?

Describe diet, caffeine use, nicotine use, etc.

Mental status

Note any of the following:

Disturbances in appearance, dress, or posture.

Disturbance in thoughts (such as hallucinations or delusions).

Disturbances in level of awareness (such as memory, attention).

Disturbances in emotional tone (deviations in affect or discrepancies between the client's verbal report of mood/affect and practitioner observation).

Degree of client awareness of the nature of the problem and need for treatment.

Client roles and role performance

What roles does the client perform (such as spouse or parent)?

Are the client's issues related to role performance?

Are the client's issues related to role satisfaction or dissatisfaction?

Are there any serious problems with children, marriage, and/or other close relationships?

Developmental considerations

Trace the birth, developmental history (including the mother's pregnancy), developmental milestones, or illnesses.

Explore sexual, marital, and family history (such as domestic violence, abuse).

Is there a legal history?

What has family life been like for the client?

Does the client recall any specific events while growing up (such as a parent's death or a divorce)?

II. Interpersonal family issues:

What is each family member's perception of the problem(s)?

Client's marital/partner status

What is the client's sexual, dating, partner, or marital history?

What is the quality of the client's intimate relationships?

At what age (or ages) did the client marry (or engage in a partner relationship)?

How many marriages (or partner relationships) has the client had?

(continued)

TABLE 1.2 | CONTINUED

Family structure

What is the quality of the client's family interactions?

Describe the family system, including composition, structure, boundaries, cohesion, flexibility, rules, family alliances, family power, negotiation, family decision making, problem solving, and communication patterns.

Has there been any recent serious illness or death in the client's family?

How does the client describe his or her parents and/or siblings (if any)?

III. **Interpersonal work or school issues:**

What is the client's occupation or grade in school?

How satisfied is the client with work/school?

Are there indicators of successful achievement in this setting?

Are there issues related to grades, performance, pay, or promotions?

Describe the client's relationships with colleagues/peers.

Does the presenting problem(s) occur in this setting?

If so, does it affect the client's ability to get along with peers, teachers, bosses, or other authority figures?

What is the client's academic/work history?

Is the client having any problems with money or with employment?

Is the client in debt?

IV. **Interpersonal issues with peers:**

Does the client have friends?

What is the quality of these relationships?

Is the client satisfied with his or her peer relationships?

Advanced Clinical EP 2.1.2 d

As a part of the competency-based assessment, social work professionals recognize and manage their personal biases as they influence the relationship and assessment process. Practitioners are knowledgeable about the shifting societal mores and how they can potentially affect a client's well-being. This orientation to the assessment includes an exploration of the client's context and social support networks (see Table 1.3). This includes culture and ethnicity, which are an integral part of one's identity. It is important to explore the extent to which these factors can affect a person with a mental illness. Along with respect for these considerations, the practitioner must remember to take into account his or her own attitudes and biases as they affect the assessment process and the therapeutic relationship (Comstock, 2005; Lum, 2004, 2010; Thyer, Wodarski, Myers, & Harrison, 2010).

TABLE 1.3	THE CLIENT'S CONTEXT AND SOCIAL SUPPORT NETWORKS

Clarify the environmental characteristics that influence coping and adaptive patterns of the client:

What environmental resources does the client have?

How adequate are the client's material circumstances—for example, housing, transportation, food?

What does the client know about community resources and how to use them?

What actual or potential supports are available in the environment?

Does the client have access to family or peer supports or support from agencies in the neighborhood that are not being used?

What are the risks and vulnerabilities in the client system?

What blocks, obstacles, and/or deficits interfere with the client's life processes and adaptive strivings?

What is the goodness of "fit" between the client system and his or her environment?

Are there any ethnic/cultural considerations for the client?

What is the client's ethnic or cultural group and is this a source of stress or support?

What is the degree of acculturation?

Is there evidence of prejudice or discrimination by others toward the client?

To what extent is there isolation from (or participation in) extra-familial groups and associations, such as ethnic or cultural groups?

What is the client's perception of the effect ethnic/cultural group identification has had?

How do sociocultural factors (such as racism, sexism, cultural values) affect the client's functioning?

Does the client experience any social and/or economic injustice?

Can the client draw from the resources of his or her culture or ethnic group?

© Cengage Learning

SUMMARY

The competency-based assessment model translates the process of summarizing, prioritizing, and classifying the information found in the DSM into a format that is more familiar to social work practitioners. However, the practitioner looks for strengths and resources in the individual and his or her related social systems that can be developed and supported. Additionally, individual, family, and socio-environmental systems in the client's life are reviewed. A thorough understanding of the client's problems often demystifies using a diagnostic label and provides clinical insight into what seems to be a complicated symptom picture (Gray, 2006, 2011). The worker must be knowledgeable about many factors related to presenting issues. Therefore, familiarity with the diagnostic conditions and the ability to apply them correctly is important to the competency-based assessment for social workers. While readers may regard this orientation as simply good old-fashioned social work practice, the competency-based perspective advances professional clinical social work practice by suggesting that an assessment grounded in strengths and possibilities increases the opportunities to serve those who seek help.

Recent legislative initiatives and managed care have transformed the landscape of mental health practice, and it is becoming increasingly necessary to conduct the kind of assessment that provides accurate information about a person's complex mental health symptoms. The need for interprofessional collaboration is becoming increasingly apparent as professionals are pressed to "justify themselves by advocates and by the public at-large" (Allen-Meares & Garvin, 2000, p. 448). Social work practice in the twenty-first century has become more complicated and underscores the growing need for interprofessional collaboration, which draws upon the knowledge of other disciplines and professionals (Weinstein, Whittington, & Lieba, 2003). There are a number of benefits to interprofessional collaboration. Merging the expertise and knowledge from different disciplines maximizes the creativity needed for fully understanding the symptoms experienced by those who are struggling with mental illness (Bronstein, 2003).

A crucial component of the competency-based assessment is its client-centered focus that values the unique strengths and perspectives of people who are struggling with mental illness. An important social work value relates to appreciating human worth and respecting dignity. We often see people who are not at their best. It goes without saying that the profession is committed to helping people who are oppressed and disempowered. The social worker focuses on the strengths of the person, thereby promoting both personal and societal competence despite the obstacles associated with mental illness. As a matter of fact, well over 30 years ago, Siporin (1975) recognized that "a chief mandate of the social work profession is

to work with people who are disenfranchised and oppressed" (p. 4). Social work values both the strengths and vulnerabilities of people. These values are integral to the competency-based assessment model, which incorporates both biopsychosocial factors *and* the relationship between the client's behavior and his or her context. This perspective provides a complete picture describing the individual's functioning at all levels. Social workers have also traditionally been concerned with social justice, and this perspective has encouraged practitioners to look beyond a client's mental health diagnosis and consider the broader issues of a person's welfare such as what it is like to live with a diagnosis. The competency-based assessment helps the practitioner to understand *both* a client's diagnosis and to consider the experience and impact of this diagnosis on his or her family, community, and social environment (Gray, 2006, 2011). This requires an understanding of the social and environmental contributors to mental illness, such as family welfare, housing, income security, and community or a sense of belonging somewhere.

In sum, the competency-based assessment focuses on relationships between behavior and surrounding events—those events that elicit or maintain problematic behaviors. The individual's present functioning is examined in relationship to past events, while considering biopsychosocial factors as well as environmental systems. The focus is on client strengths rather than deficits. Integral to the competency-based assessment is the assumption that clients have the capability to reorganize their lives as long as they have appropriate family, community, societal, and environmental resources and supports.

COMPETENCY NOTES

EP 2.1.1 c: Attend to professional roles and boundaries (p. 16): Social workers serve as representatives of the profession, its mission, and its core values.

EP Advanced Clinical 2.1.1 d: Develop, manage, and maintain therapeutic relationships with clients within the person-in-environment and strengths perspective (p. 9): Advanced practitioners in clinical social work

recognize the importance of the therapeutic relationship, the person-in-environment and strengths perspectives, the professional use of self with clients, and adherence to ethical guidelines of professional behavior.

EP Advanced Clinical 2.1.2 d: Recognize and manage personal biases as they affect the therapeutic

relationship (p. 20): Advanced practitioners in clinical social work are knowledgeable about ethical issues, legal parameters, and shifting societal mores that affect the therapeutic relationship.

EP Advanced Clinical 2.1.3 b: Identify and articulate clients' strengths and vulnerabilities (p. 11): Advanced practitioners understand and differentiate the strengths and limitations of multiple practice theories and methods, clinical processes, and technical tools, including the differential diagnosis.

EP 2.1.7 a: Use conceptual frameworks to guide the processes of assessment, intervention, and evaluation (p. 8): Social workers are knowledgeable about human behavior across the life course, the range of social systems in which people live, and the ways social systems promote or deter people in maintaining or achieving health and well-being.

EP 2.1.7 b: Critique and apply knowledge to understand person and environment (p. 16): Social workers apply theories and knowledge from the liberal arts to understand biological, social, cultural, psychological, and spiritual development.

EP Advanced Clinical 2.1.7 b: Use bio-psycho-social-spiritual theories and multiaxial diagnostic classification systems in formulation of comprehensive assessments (p. 3): Advanced practitioners are familiar with diagnostic classification systems used in the formulation of a comprehensive assessment.

EP Advanced Clinical 2.1.7 c: Consult with medical professionals, as needed, to confirm diagnosis and/or to monitor medication in the treatment process (pp. 5, 13): Advanced practitioners are familiar with diagnostic classification systems used in the formulation of a comprehensive assessment.

REFERENCES

Abramson, J., & Mizrahi, T. (1996). When social workers and physicians collaborate: Positive and negative interdisciplinary experiences. *Social Work, 41,* 270–281.

Abramson, J., & Mizrahi, T. (1997). Models of effective collaboration between social workers and physicians: A typology. Paper presented at the Annual Program Meeting of the Council of Social Work Education, Chicago, IL.

Allen-Meares, P., & Garvin, C. (Eds.) (2000). *The handbook of social work direct practice.* Thousand Oaks, CA: Sage.

American Psychiatric Association. (2000). *Diagnostic and statistical manual of mental disorders* (4th ed. text revision). Washington, DC: Author.

Antonovsky, A. (1980). *Health, stress, and coping.* San Francisco: Jossey-Bass.

Austrian, S. G. (2005). *Mental disorders, medications, and clinical social work* (3rd ed.). New York: Columbia University Press.

Bandura, A. (1969). *Principles of behavior modification.* New York: Holt, Rinehart & Winston.

Bandura, A. (1977). *Social learning theory.* Englewood Cliffs, NJ: Prentice Hall.

Barlow, D. H., & Durand, V. M. (2012). *Abnormal psychology: An integrative approach.* Belmont, CA: Wadsworth Cengage Learning.

Barnes, D., Carpenter, J., & Dickinson, C. (2000). Interprofessional education for community mental health: Attitudes to community care and professional stereotypes. *Social Work Education, 19* (6), 565–583.

Bentley, K. J. (Ed.). (2002). *Social work practice in mental health: Contemporary roles, tasks, and techniques.* Belmont, CA: Brooks/Cole Thomson Learning.

Berkman, B. (1996). The emerging health care world: Implications for social work practice and education. *Social Work, 41,* 541–551.

Bertalanffy, L. von (1968). General system theory: A critical review. In W. Buckley (Ed.), *Modern systems research for the behavioral scientist* (pp. 11–30). Chicago: Aldine.

Blundo, R. (2008). Strengths-based framework. In T. Mizrahi & L. E. Davis (Eds.), *Encyclopedia of social work* (20th ed., Vol. 4, pp. 173–177). Washington DC: National Association of Social Workers and Oxford University Press.

Bronfenbrenner, U. (1979). *The etiology of human development: Experiments by nature and design.* Cambridge, MA: Harvard University Press.

Bronstein, L. R. (2003). A model for interdisciplinary collaboration. *Social Work, 48* (3), 297–306.

Carter, A. S., Briggs-Gowan, M. J., & Davis, N. O. (January 2004). Assessment of young children's social-emotional development and psychopathology: Recent advances and recommendations for practice. *Journal of Child Psychology and Psychiatry, 45* (1), 109–134.

Compton, B. R., Galaway, B. & Cournoyer, B. R. (2004). *Social work processes* (7th ed.). Pacific Grove, CA: Brooks/Cole Thomson Learning.

Comstock, D. (Ed.). (2005). *Diversity and development: Critical contexts that shape our lives and relationships*. Belmont, CA: Brooks/Cole Thomson.

Corcoran, J., & Nichols-Casebolt, A. (2004). Risk and resilience ecological framework for assessment and goal formulation. *Child and Adolescent Social Work, 21,* 211–235.

de Jong, P., & Berg, I. K. (1998). *Interviewing for solutions.* Pacific Grove, CA: Brooks/Cole Thomson Learning Wadsworth.

Dumont, M. P. (1987). A diagnosis parable. *Readings, 2* (4), 9–12.

Ell, K. (1996). Social work and health care practice and policy: A psychosocial research agenda. *Social Work, 41,* 583–592.

Engel, G. L. (1977). The need for a new medical model: A challenge for biomedicine. *Science, 196,* 120–136.

Engel, G. L. (1980). The clinical application of the biopsychosocial model. *American Journal of Psychiatry, 137,* 535.

Engel, G. L. (1997). From biomedical to biopsychosocial: Being scientific in the human domain. *Psychosomatics, 38* (6), 521–528.

Eriksen, K., & Kress, V. E. (2005). *Beyond the DSM story: Ethical quandaries, challenges, and best practices.* Thousand Oaks, CA: Sage.

French, L. M. (1940). *Psychiatric social work.* New York: The Commonwealth Fund.

Gerdes, K. E., & Segal, E. (2011). Importance of empathy for social work practice: Integrating new science. *Social Work, 56* (2), 141–148.

Germain, C. B. (1973). An ecological perspective in casework practice. *Social Casework, 54,* 323–330.

Germain, C. B. (1991). *Human behavior in the social environment: An ecological view.* New York: Columbia University Press.

Gitterman, A. (2001). *Handbook of social work practice with vulnerable and resilient populations* (2nd ed.). New York: Columbia University Press.

Gitterman, A., &. Germain, C. B. (2008a). *The life model of social work practice* (3rd ed.). New York: Columbia University Press.

Gitterman, A., & Germain, C. B. (2008b). Ecological Framework. In T. Mizrahi & L. E. Davis, (Eds.), Encyclopedia of Social Work (*e-reference edition*). National Association of Social Workers and Oxford University Press. Retrieved on May 5, 2011 from: http://www.oxford-naswsocialwork.com/entry?entry=t203.e118

Glicken, M. (2004). *Using the strengths perspective in social work practice.* Boston: Allyn and Bacon.

Gray, S. W. (with Zide, M. R.) (2006). *Psychopathology: A competency-based treatment model for social workers.* Pacific Grove, CA: Brooks/Cole Thomson Learning.

Gray, S. W. (2011). *Competency-based assessments in mental health practice: Cases and practical applications.* Hoboken, NJ: John Wiley and Sons.

Jordan, C., & Franklin, C. (2003). *Clinical assessment for social workers: Quantitative and qualitative methods* (2nd ed.). Chicago: Lyceum Books.

Karls, J. M., & Wandrei, K. E. (1994). *Person-in-environment system: The PIE classification system for social functioning problems.* Washington DC: NASW Press.

Kessler, R. C., Berglund, P., Demler, O., Jin, R., Merikangas, K. R., & Walters, E. E. (June 2005). Lifetime prevalence and age-of-onset distributions of DSM-IV disorders in the National Comorbidity Survey Replication. *Archives of General Psychiatry, 62* (6), 593–602.

Kirk, S. A., & Kutchins, H. (1988). Deliberate misdiagnosis in mental health practice. *Social Service Review, 62,* 225–237.

Kirk, S. A., & Kutchins, H. (1992). *The selling of DSM: The rhetoric of science in psychiatry.* New York: Aldine de Gruyer.

Kirk, S. A., & Kutchins, H. (1994, June 20). Is bad writing a mental disorder? *New York Times,* p. A17.

Kirk, S. A., Siporin, M., & Kutchins, H. (1989). The prognosis for social work diagnosis. *Social Casework, 70,* 295–304.

Kirst-Ashman, K. K., & Hull, G. H. (2008). *Understanding generalist practice* (5th ed.). Belmont, CA: Brooks/Cole Cengage Learning.

Kutchins, H., & Kirk, S. A. (1987). DSM-III and social work malpractice. *Social Work, 32,* 205–211.

Lum, D. (Ed.). (2004). *Cultural competence, practice stages, and client systems: A case study approach.* Belmont, CA: Thompson Brooks/Cole.

Lum, D. (2010). *Culturally competent practice: A framework for understanding diverse groups and justice issues* (4th ed.). Belmont, CA: Brooks/Cole Cengage Learning.

Miley, K. K., O'Melia, M., & Dubois, B. (2010). *Generalist social work practice: An empowering approach* (6th ed.). Upper Saddle River, NJ: Prentice Hall.

Mizrahi, T., & Abramson, J. S. (2000). Collaboration between social workers and physicians: Perspectives on a shared case. *Social Work in Health Care, 31* (3), 1–24.

National Association of Social Work. (1999). *Code of Ethics.* Washington, DC: NASW Press.

Netting, F. E., & Williams, F. G. (1996). Case management–physician collaboration: Implications for professional identification, roles, and relationships. *Health & Social Work, 21,* 216–224.

Netting, F. E., & Williams, F. G. (1997, March). Preparing the next generation of geriatric social workers to collaborate with primary care physicians. Paper presented at the Annual Program Meeting of the Council on Social Work Education, Chicago, IL.

Rapp, C., & Guscha, R. (2006). *The strengths model.* (2nd ed.). New York: Oxford University Press.

Reamer, F. (2006). *Ethical standards in social work* (2nd ed.). Washington DC: NASW Press.

Saleebey, D. (Ed.) (2009). *The strengths perspective in social work practice* (5th ed.). Boston: Allyn and Bacon.

Shankman, S. A., & Klein, D. N. (2002). Dimensional diagnosis of depression: Adding the dimension of course severity, and comparison to the DSM. *Comprehensive Psychiatry 43,* 420–426.

Sheafor, B. W., & Horejsi, C. J. (2010). *Techniques and guidelines for social work practice* (9th ed.). Boston: Allyn and Bacon.

Shulman, L. (2009). *The skills of helping individuals, families, groups, and communities* (6th ed.). Belmont, CA: Brooks/Cole Cengage Learning.

Siporin, M. (1975). *Introduction to social work practice.* New York: Macmillan.

Stoudemire, A. (1998). *Clinical psychiatry for medical students* (3rd ed.). Philadelphia: Lippincott Williams and Wilkins.

Thyer, B. A., Wodarski, J. S., Myers, L. L., & Harrison, D. F. (2010). *Cultural diversity and social work practice* (3rd ed.). Springfield, IL: Charles C. Thomas.

Weinstein, J., Whittington, C., & Lieba, T. (2003). *Collaboration in social work practice.* London: Jessica Kingsley Publishers.

Werner, E. (2000). Protective factors and individual resilience. In J. Shonoff & S. Meisels (Eds.), *Handbook of early childhood intervention* (2nd ed., pp. 115–133). Cambridge, MA: Cambridge University Press.

Woods, M. E., & Hollis, F. (2000). *Casework: A psychosocial therapy* (5th ed.). New York: McGraw-Hill.

CHAPTER 2

DISORDERS OF INFANCY, CHILDHOOD, OR ADOLESCENCE

INTRODUCTION

Most of us remember childhood as a carefree and easygoing period in our lives. Ideally, this is a time for children to imagine, play, learn, and develop in an environment characterized by safety and love. This is the stage of life distinguished by significant social, emotional, and cognitive changes. This transformation generally follows a pattern in which the child develops one skill and then moves ahead to acquire another. For the child who struggles with a mental health disorder, their experience is quite different. These children do not smoothly progress through life and its related challenges. For example, a child diagnosed with autism struggles with social relationships. They may not be able to form a meaningful relationship with their parents and may have a difficult time learning how to communicate with others. They may not even want to talk to other people at all. The author remembers a recent news story about a young boy with autism who was lost in the woods for several days. When found, he did not talk to any of his rescuers. Approximately 12 to 22 percent of all children under age 18 in the United States are in need of services for mental, emotional, or behavioral problems (Latest Findings in Children's Mental Health, 2004).

Advanced Clinical EP 2.1.10 (b) c

A child's behavior is affected by a number of factors such as family and home life, spiritual influences, culture, community, and economic issues as well as inborn characteristics, such as genetic makeup (Ashford, LeCroy, & Lortie, 2005). The development of mental health disorders in children is influenced by the interaction of these complex psychosocial and biological features. A child diagnosed with a mental disorder is set apart from other children by significant deviations from developmentally appropriate behaviors, emotions, or relationships (Webb, 2003).

This underscores the comprehensive approach of the competency-based assessment model that keeps the whole child in perspective as the practitioner participates in assigning a DSM diagnosis. Paying attention to the child's contexts and sources of strength and resilience becomes a part of the diagnostic process and serves to reinforce and improve adaptation.

In most instances, the child can be seen as the proverbial involuntary client since it is usually a parent or another adult in the child's life who identifies a problem. It is this adult who takes the first step toward getting help. Unfortunately, the stigma associated with having a child who struggles with a mental disorder and related behaviors may prevent some parents from reaching out for assistance (Kataoka, Zhang, & Wells, 2002). When that happens, they are more likely to look to informal resources such as extended family, friends, neighbors, and clergy (Pumariega, 2003). Access to help can be further complicated by the harsh realities of poverty, language barriers, the lack of insurance, or differences in cultural values about what is a sign of mental illness (Moniz & Gorin, 2003). In reality, children with mental health disorders often receive services from agencies whose primary focus is something other than treating mental health problems. This includes settings such as schools, child welfare, juvenile justice, or general health clinics. For example, one study found that 63 percent of male and 71 percent of female juvenile detainees had a mental health disorder (Teplin, Abram, McClelland, Dulcan, & Mericle, 2002).

We now turn to an overview of cultural perspectives and their interplay with the exploration of a child's mental illness.

CULTURAL PERSPECTIVES

EP 2.1.4 c

Ethnicity and culture affect what behaviors parents perceive as "normal" versus "abnormal" behavior in their child (Slade, 2004). It is important for the practitioner to recognize the importance of difference in shaping the child's life experiences and to be able to communicate this understanding to those who are a part of the child's life. For example, what the parent thinks about the child's behavior and their parenting efforts play a role in the assessment process. Surprisingly, there are no generally available assessment guidelines beyond the Appendix on Cultural Formulations in the DSM (Rousseau, Measham, & Bathiche-Suidan, 2008). It falls upon the practitioner to differentiate between what may appear as illness behaviors as specified in the DSM and those behaviors inherent in specific cultural beliefs and practices. Two fundamental questions come to mind:

- Are the child's behaviors functional and adaptive or do they produce conflict?
- Do these behaviors cause distress?

Canino and Alegria (2008) point out that a child's cultural background influences every facet of the illness experience and should always be taken into account in order to fully understand a child's symptoms of mental illness. The competency-based assessment looks beyond dysfunctional behaviors and explores strengths and coping. To avoid prematurely labeling particular behaviors as a mental disorder, the degree to which a child's emotional and behavioral problems fall along a continuum of adjustment and resilience within a specific culture is considered. It is helpful for the practitioner to explore whether the child's behaviors are adaptive, as opposed to producing conflict and suffering or distress.

From the competency-based perspective, the practitioner asks about everyday activities as well as relationships with the family (and peers), and looks into the attitudes and feelings that others in the child's life may have about the symptom picture (Lewis-Fernandez et al., 2002). The practitioner elicits both the child's and the parents' view of the problem, expectations of help, and prior experiences with services (Staudt, 2003). The competency-based approach to the assessment process also includes a review of the daily stresses associated with a child's problematic behavior and the practical problems encountered when trying to manage a troubled child (Dixon, 2002). It is helpful to keep in mind that each cultural and ethnic group will differ with regard to practices and activities related to adaptation and survival.

Organized around the competency-based assessment, there are several guidelines aimed at fully exploring the extent to which culture affects how symptoms and the specific syndromes are shown in children. They are:

EP 2.1.7 b

- *Assess lifestyle behaviors, expected standards of behavior, and everyday activities relevant for cultural adaptation and survival.* Ask about everyday activities, peer relationships, and family routines in order to better understand the symptom picture within the context of the child's culture. The assessment of lifestyle and daily activities helps the practitioner to determine what is considered to be pathological versus what is regarded as normal and expected in the child's environment.

- *Comprehend meanings, labels, and interpretations commonly used to describe a child's behavior or emotional problems.* Attempt to understand the child's culture, related terminology, and commonly regarded symptoms of distress or pathology. Before labeling a particular behavior as a psychiatric symptom (or disorder), identify the specific words used to label the child's problematic behaviors or emotions in order to distinguish how people in a specific culture know that the child has a problem. Recognition of symptoms and the labeling of distress as being either deviant or pathological depend on the norms of behavior accepted in the child's particular culture.

- *Evaluate the cultural context of what appears as illness behaviors to determine whether they support the DSM diagnostic criteria for a mental illness diagnosis.* Consider whether the child's behavior is functional and adaptive or if it produces conflict and causes distress or suffering for others. Find out if these behaviors and symptoms influence what the child does, his or her personal identity, or how others perceive him or her (Kleinman & Benson, 2006). Further, ask both the child and the parents about what they are afraid would happen if these behaviors and symptoms had any special significance if seen as a psychiatric illness.

- *Determine whether the DSM diagnostic criteria for specific disorders are valid for the specific population to be assessed.* Consider if the specific symptoms of a particular disorder (e.g., worrying more than usual) have the same meaning or relevance for certain cultures. Cauce and colleagues (2002) point out that asking parents (or a child) whether behaviors occur more or less often than in a typical similar-aged child might be hard to answer when the parents (or child) do not share the DSM diagnostic concept of typical behavior. However, a psychiatric illness would not be automatically ruled out just because the parents struggle to respond to the practitioner's questions about the child's symptoms. Alegria and McGuire (2003) highlight the example of anorexia; that is, certain cultures may not recognize extreme weight loss as a problem. Therefore, within that cultural context, getting accurate feedback about pathological weight loss would be unlikely, but the diagnostic picture that characterizes anorexia remains.

- *Consider the child's and the parents' threshold of stress (and that of significant others in the child's life) and how they cope with the child's behavioral problems.* Determine if the parents (or others in the child's life) are under stress themselves; if so, determine how this affects their response to the child. Consider the influence of culture on the types of problems that parents (or significant others) regard as serious. The practitioner evaluates whether the parents have a high tolerance for certain behavioral problems while, conversely, the child sees them as problematic (Roberts, Alegria, Roberts, & Chen, 2005). Also take into account the child who may have a high distress threshold and might be reluctant to talk about certain symptoms or traumatic events.

- *Recognize how the client perceives the practitioner's social position.* Acknowledge that the assessment process can be influenced by the identity and social positioning of the practitioner and the client (Groleau, Young, & Kirmayer, 2006). The practitioner, as a first step, strives to establish an atmosphere of trust and explains what information is or is not disclosed (confidentiality). The practitioner takes into account for example, the family's social position, religion, education, national origin, sexual orientation, immigration history, and integration into the community as well as intergenerational conflicts in the family, to list a few factors.

- *Show self-awareness.* Remember that the practitioner needs to ask him- or herself if they are generalizing the child's behaviors or symptoms and not paying full attention to the child's (or family's) specific cultural background. Avoid the temptation to stereotype, especially when little is known about a client's specific culture or context (Hwang, 2006).

We now explore the influence of the child's stage of development on the assessment process.

THE CHILD'S STAGES OF DEVELOPMENT

EP 2.1.7 b

Children are not little adults but unique individuals with distinctive qualities, characteristics, and needs. The child's stage of development offers another level of understanding of the child's presenting symptoms. Some behaviors or emotions are normally expected at a certain age and are not necessarily symptoms of pathological deviations, whereas at another age they would be considered age-inappropriate. For instance, the temper tantrums seen in a 2-year-old are not unusual and are popularized as the "terrible twos." However, if these same behaviors are seen in an older child, they could be a problem. While each of the disorders seen in infancy, childhood, and adolescence has a different set of symptoms, all indicate some type of adaptational failure, that is, the inability to meet the challenges associated with a particular developmental milestone. These are the youngsters who are somehow set apart from other children of the same developmental stage. The competency-based assessment considers the child's developmental course and the challenges associated with each life stage along with a parallel assessment of strengths and coping. From this perspective, the practitioner critiques and applies knowledge of the various theories of childhood development in order to better understand the interaction between a particular child's development and his or her situation.

MENTAL RETARDATION

Intellectual disability, or **mental retardation**, is primarily a physical and mental condition rather than a psychiatric illness (Noble, Maluccio, Whittaker, & Jones, 2008). The social worker does not play a central role in formulating the diagnosis and therefore the symptoms will not be highlighted in this chapter. Mental retardation is commonly associated with a number of factors, including prenatal damage due to toxins, deprivation of nurturance or stimulation, fetal malnutrition, premature birth, viral infections during the mother's pregnancy, childhood infections, injuries, or poisonings. In order to make a definitive diagnosis, information is gathered from a number of sources such as intelligence tests, classroom evaluations, and developmental and medical history. There are also a number of scales developed to assess the child's adaptive functioning. The DSM-5 proposes changing the name of this diagnosis from mental retardation to intellectual disability to be more congruent with terminology used by other professionals.

DISORDERS SEEN IN INFANCY, CHILDHOOD, AND ADOLESCENCE

Many disorders can start in childhood or adolescence, but they may not be formally diagnosed until much later in adulthood. However, for diagnostic convenience the DSM provides a separate section for disorders diagnosed in infancy, childhood, and adolescence. The DSM diagnoses can be characterized as **uncontrolled behaviors** in which the child lacks or has insufficient control over his or her behavior. These include the autism spectrum disorders (ASD), in particular, the diagnoses of autism, Asperger's, and pervasive developmental disorder not otherwise specified (NOS), followed by the more common attention deficit and disruptive behavior disorders. Uncontrolled behaviors also include Rett's disorder and childhood disintegrative disorder.

The second grouping of DSM disorders is the **overcontrolled behaviors** or the disorders that tend to create more problems for the child than for others. Separation anxiety, one of the anxiety disorders that apply solely to children and adolescents who have experienced some form of life stress or trauma, will be highlighted.

To complete our discussion, a third group of disorders that are considered rare, or are ones in which the practitioner does not play a central role in the diagnostic process, will be briefly reviewed to extend the social worker's understanding of the child's difficulties. In many instances social workers are involved in the problems these syndromes create for the child and his or her family. Included are the feeding and eating disorders of infancy or early childhood, tic disorders, elimination disorders, and a group of other disorders loosely identified as selective mutism, reactive attachment disorder, stereotypic movement disorder, and disorder of infancy, childhood, or adolescence NOS.

We now turn to an overview of the key features of the autism spectrum disorders.

AUTISM SPECTRUM DISORDERS

The terms **autism spectrum disorders (ASD)** and pervasive developmental disorders (PDD) are often used interchangeably. Overall, PDD, sometimes simply referred to as the autistic disorders, is one of a distinct group of congenital-neurological conditions that are characterized by a constellation of symptoms. They are: atypical communication, social impairments including atypical social interactions, and atypical responses to social and perceptual stimuli in the environment. Following is a summary of the major characteristics of PDD.

- *Communication.* The child's speech pattern may consist of repeating phrases spoken to them (echolalia), using phrases in unusual ways, saying the same phrases over and over again (perseveration), and reversing pronouns (for example, saying something like "You want toy" when it is really the child who wants the toy).
- *Social interactions.* The child shows an impaired ability to perceive events around them and to accurately interpret communications from others. Unusual and unexpected responses, including a tendency to interact less with others, can be seen in social interactions. In other words, this is the youngster who may make less eye contact, including when spoken to, or may avoid eye contact altogether. This is the child who may seem to have less interest in sharing with others, show little emotion, and prefer to focus on an object rather than to show it to the parent. There is an overall less reciprocal giving and taking of objects.
- *Restricted behaviors.* The child with PDD may have unusual interests and their play may appear to be less imaginative and more repetitive. For instance, rather than playing with a doll, the child may be more interested in simply taking the doll's shoes off and then putting them back on over and over. They might show an attachment to odd items, such as being attached to a plastic cup and keeping it nearby instead of behaving like most children who form attachments to a favorite blanket or soft cuddly toy. Other unusual behaviors that might be seen are walking on toes, hand flapping, repetitive spinning, or other movements that appear to have no purpose.

Some of the very early diagnostic signs the practitioner can expect to find in the child's history are failures in the development of the paralinguistic signaling system (or nonverbal communications) characterized by poor eye contact, failure to develop a **protodeclarative point** (pointing to show something such as when a child points his finger to show his dad an airplane), and the lack of facial affect that demonstrates reciprocal engagement or shared attention (Harris, 2000). There is a common set of symptoms comprising the diagnostic criteria for autistic disorder, as well as Asperger's and pervasive developmental disorder—not otherwise specified (PDD-NOS) that fall within the autistic spectrum disorders. Each will be reviewed with respect to how it is associated with altered perception or the processing of specific types of social or environmental stimuli.

Autism

The diagnosis of **autism** is considered to be the most serious of the pervasive developmental disorders. The essential feature of autistic disorder is the child's markedly abnormal or impaired development in social interaction and communication, and a markedly restricted repertoire of activity and interests. This is the child who behaves in bizarre, unusual and often puzzling ways.

Prevailing Pattern

The Centers for Disease Control and Prevention (CDC) released a study indicating that autism affects 1 in every 110 children in the United States. The rate among boys is 1 of 70 children (CDC, 2009). Earlier prevalence rates were somewhat lower, showing that autism affected about 1 of every 150 children. Government statistics suggest that the rate of autism is increasing 10 to 17 percent annually, making this diagnosis more common than thought earlier. The reason for the increase is unclear but may be attributed to a better understanding of the diagnosis.

DIFFERENTIAL ASSESSMENT

EP 2.1.10
(b) a

Children diagnosed with autism show delays in normal functioning or show abnormal functioning before 3 years of age but the extent of these delays can vary. Social interaction, communication, and restricted repetitive and stereotyped patterns of behavior are the most impaired. Problems with social interaction are considered the hallmark feature of autism, as the child appears uninterested in reciprocity, playing with others, peer relationships, sharing, or even eye contact. Most children struggle with conversation with others. Also, children with autism can show behavioral problems, including aggression, self-injury, self-stimulation (such as rocking), and preoccupation with parts of inanimate objects (such as the wheels of a toy truck).

The diagnosis requires a total of six (or more) items from the following three categories:

- *Impaired social interaction.* Use of many nonverbal behaviors in social interaction (for example, eye-to-eye gaze, facial expression, body posture, gestures); failure to develop peer relationships; lack of spontaneous enjoyment or interests with others; lack of reciprocity. At least two are required from this category.
- *Impaired communication.* Delay in or total lack of spoken language; difficulty initiating or maintaining a conversation with others; impaired ability to converse with others; if language is used, speaking in ways that are difficult to understand (for example, echolalia, or repeating words one has heard; and

pronoun reversal, or use of the word "you" instead of "I"); lack of spontaneous play. At least one is required from this category.

- *Restricted repetitive and stereotyped patterns of behavior, interests and activities.* Restricted interests; adherence to specific and nonfunctional routines; repetitive mannerisms; preoccupation with parts of objects. At least one is required from this category.

We now turn to the case of Chris Wells to illustrate autism.

CASE | THE CASE OF CHRIS WELLS

Chris Wells, age 3½, was referred to the Children's Rehabilitation Center by his family pediatrician for a complete evaluation. The center uses a team to do the evaluation, consisting of medical doctors, psychiatrists, social workers, nurses, and audiologists, as well as occupational, physical, and recreational therapists. The family had been concerned about their son for some time. The social worker on the team was assigned to conduct the social history. Following is the parents' story.

Mrs. Wells began, "Looking back, I didn't consider my pregnancy with Chris difficult. Well, there were some moments like when I didn't gain weight in the first trimester. Actually, I lost weight. Chris is my second child so I really didn't become too alarmed since I also lost a few pounds in my first pregnancy. I just figured it was part of 'morning sickness' and, like before, it would pass. By the fifth month I started to gain weight and continued to gain monthly so I figured all was fine. Let me tell you though. That last month was a bummer. Chris was really active when he was inside me. Seemed like my ribs and pelvic bone were getting a workout from all his hyperactivity. I couldn't wait to deliver! Then I went into premature labor. I went to the hospital and the labor was stopped by the use of some kind of IV medication to relax my muscles. I think they took the medication off the market since then but I'm sure you'll find the details in my medical records. Finally, I had Chris by a C-section, just like my first one. I was so relieved when he arrived very healthy and hearty. They could hear him cry from the delivery room all the way down to the other end of the hall."

Mrs. Wells continued, "Chris seemed to develop okay. Almost from the beginning he could hold up his head and by 10 months he was climbing out of his crib. On the other hand he did have some

peculiarities. Right from the start, Chris did not especially like to be cuddled and he didn't like to be rocked to sleep. He never even held out his hands for me to pick him up. Even now, he doesn't look at you. It's like he's in his own little world. Chris slept through the night right away so when I couldn't get him to nap during the day I wasn't really too worried. Now traveling with him was another story. My oldest would fall asleep as soon as the car started but not Chris. He would cry and scream for the entire trip. It didn't matter if we were going around the block or if it was an hour drive. Nothing could console him. Chris was ready to walk by about 10 months but he couldn't. This was because he refused to put his whole foot on the floor. Instead, he could curl up his toes and walked on the tops of them. My husband reassured me that we probably had a budding basketball star but I still worried. Took him about 6 months to walk normally with his whole foot on the floor. But he still isn't talking."

Mr. Wells interjected, "At first we thought maybe he was deaf but all tests indicated normal physical functioning. While Chris didn't speak, he would make soft sounds. Seemed like they made sense only to him though. Odd, but Chris made no effort to communicate with us and often seemed oblivious to other people in the room. We sort of worked around it but now that he's in pre-kindergarten class, his behavior is more obvious. We thought it might be good for Chris to be with other children his age. Well, that's not really working out and I'm afraid that maybe we made a mistake by pushing him too hard to socialize with other kids. The teacher tells us that he has absolutely no friends and really seems to be in his own world. She tries to get him interested in the toys but he just doesn't seem to want to get involved. He loves his toy trains,

continued

| CASE | THE CASE OF CHRIS WELLS *continued* |

though. Chris will spend hours just spinning the wheels over and over and over. If you try to take his trains away he just screams until you give them back." Mrs. Wells nodded her head in agreement and Mr. Wells continued, "Seems Chris is more interested in his trains than people. When I was little I remember that I was interested in trains, too. But not like this. Seems he's more fascinated with the wheels rather than the whole train. Come to think of it, everybody told me stories about how I couldn't be separated from my special blanket. Chris? He loves those hard metal train wheels. He has to have all his train wheels lined up just so, too. If not, he has a fit. Odd, don't you think? We're here to do whatever it takes to get him to be more like other kids. His older brother loves him, though I don't know why. They have so little in common.

My older boy, though he's only 7, already wants to be on a baseball team. Can't start them too early, you know."

Mrs. Wells continued, "Chris is still not talking and I hope you can find out why. At first our pediatrician reassured us that Chris would grow out of it but with no progress, he finally referred us here. Oh, and let me tell you about his motor skills. Like all babies he would reach for your glasses or jewelry. Well, Chris would go a step further. He would grab my husband's glasses and in 2 seconds flat would fling them across the room before you even realized it! I stopped wearing jewelry because he would do the same with me. Don't know where he inherited that aggressive streak. Not from us. Sometimes I'm afraid it will just get worse when he gets older. What do you think?"

Advanced Clinical EP 2.1.7 c

ASSESSMENT SUMMARY The rehabilitation center where Chris was seen uses a team approach to determine the final diagnosis. As such, Chris will be seen by other professionals at the agency. The advanced clinical social work practitioner working in a setting like this one checks with other medical professionals, as needed, in order to confirm Chris's diagnosis. As part of the diagnostic workup, this vignette highlights Chris Wells's developmental history, which supports a symptom picture of autism. From the very beginning, Mrs. Wells describes her son as somehow "different." He did not like to be cuddled, did not reach out for attention or affection, and did not even look at his parents. In fact, when Chris was held as an infant, he would aggressively grab his father's glasses and fling them across the room.

Adjusting to new circumstances also seemed difficult. For instance, Chris was described as being upset when taking car trips, no matter how long; that is, he would cry the entire time. In addition to delays in talking, Chris did not walk right away though his parents saw him as "ready" at 10 months of age. This was because of his peculiar way of curling up his toes and walking on the tops of them.

Chris's play was described as odd; that is, he would focus on his toy train wheels and was constantly spinning them. He would be upset if any of his trains were not lined up in precise order. Social interaction was further impaired. For example, Chris was described as unable to make friends in preschool. Further, Chris showed no enjoyment in the toys in the classroom. At the time he was referred to the rehabilitation center, Chris was still not talking, which further impaired his ability to socialize. He was characterized as being "in his own world."

Mr. and Mrs. Wells are concerned about their son and willing to do "whatever it takes" to help him. The causes of autism are unclear and the clinic takes a comprehensive approach to the assessment in order to determine the final diagnosis. This includes input from medical doctors, psychiatrists, social workers, nurses, audiologists, and occupational, physical, and recreational therapists. Chris has already had his hearing evaluated before coming to the center and no abnormalities were found. In addition, the pediatrician found Chris to be in good health, thus ruling out any medically based explanation for his behavior. Therefore, the pediatrician referred the Wells family to the center for a complete evaluation. Figure 2.1 shows the interactions of the biological, psychological, and social variables in Chris Well's life.

CHRIS WELLS'S DSM MULTIAXIAL DIAGNOSIS IS AS FOLLOWS:

Axis I	299.00 Autistic Disorder
Axis II	V71.09 (No diagnosis)
Axis III	None
Axis IV	Adjusting to preschool
Axis V	GAF = 55 (on admission)

© Cengage Learning 2013

We now turn to Asperger's disorder.

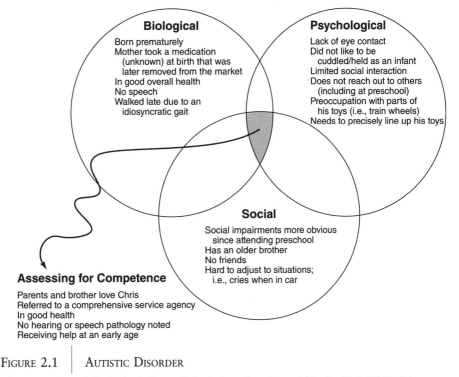

Biological
Born prematurely
Mother took a medication
  (unknown) at birth that was
  later removed from the market
In good overall health
No speech
Walked late due to an
  idiosyncratic gait

Psychological
Lack of eye contact
Did not like to be
  cuddled/held as an infant
Limited social interaction
Does not reach out to others
  (including at preschool)
Preoccupation with parts of
  his toys (i.e., train wheels)
Needs to precisely line up his toys

Social
Social impairments more obvious
  since attending preschool
Has an older brother
No friends
Hard to adjust to situations;
  i.e., cries when in car

Assessing for Competence
Parents and brother love Chris
Referred to a comprehensive service agency
In good health
No hearing or speech pathology noted
Receiving help at an early age

FIGURE 2.1 | AUTISTIC DISORDER

The interaction of the biological, psychological, and social variables in Chris Well's life.

© Cengage Learning 2013

ASPERGER'S DISORDER

**EP 2.1.10
(b) a**

Considered one of the autism spectrum disorders, **Asperger's disorder** (AD) is similar to autism in that both involve severe impairment in social interaction and bizarre behavior patterns. This similarity underscores the practitioner's skill in being able to carefully collect, organize, and interpret assessment data. Asperger's disorder is distinguished by the child's significant difficulties in social interaction and by unusual patterns of interest and behavior (Klin, Volkmar, & Sparrow, 2000). These children generally show relatively intact cognitive and communication skills. Toddlers with AD may be hyper-verbal, labeling everything in their world, and weaving words into sentences at a very young age. Yet they struggle to make friends and have a limited ability to show empathy. These children have few interests and when they do, they are highly focused and intense. Children with AD also do not have the adaptive delays seen in autism. They do not have trouble dressing themselves, using utensils, or understanding community expectations such as looking both ways before crossing the street.

Children with Asperger's tend to retain their early language skills, often having large vocabularies for their age. Compared to the other PDDs, these children tend not to experience severe intellectual impairments. Intelligence levels fall in the normal to superior range. A very small number of children may show exceptional talents, referred to as **splinter abilities** (Melvin, 2002), in some areas such as math or art. Despite severe social problems, these individuals are often able to make great intellectual contributions (Brasic, 2011). Albert Einstein, for example, was lauded for his highly developed mathematical skills but he was also seen as being unaware of social norms and insensitive to the emotional needs of his family and friends.

It is not uncommon for a parent (or caregiver) to notice that something is unusual by the child's third birthday, although some children may show symptomatic behavior as early as infancy. AD is commonly detected in the early school years and less frequently in early childhood or later on in adulthood. Some of the indicators to look for are the child who may have difficulty crawling, may walk late, and is seen as clumsy. Difficulties with clumsiness can be found in a variety of areas such as locomotion, basic motor skills (throwing and kicking), balance, manual dexterity (such as handwriting), being unable to take a deliberate and considered approach to activities, and rhythm.

PREVAILING PATTERN

The incidence of AD has not been well established (Frombonne & Tidmarsh, 2003). One reason is that family and friends might excuse the child's diagnostic symptoms as simply a quirk or an eccentric behavior. Various studies indicate rates ranging from 1 in 250 children to as low as 1 in 10,000 (Brasic, 2011). A large number of children are diagnosed after age 3, with most diagnosed between the ages of 5 and 9. While there are some reports of girls diagnosed with AD, boys are significantly more likely to be affected (Mattila et al., 2007).

DIFFERENTIAL ASSESSMENT

Making the diagnosis for AD is similar in many ways to the symptoms of autistic disorder, except that the communication problems are seen less frequently. Although some children may show communication difficulties, including poor non-verbal communication and/or **pedantic speech** (academic, or a bookish type of speech), many have good verbal skills. When assessing for AD, the practitioner looks for impaired social interactions marked by at least two of the following:

- Impaired use of multiple nonverbal behaviors such as eye-to-eye gaze, facial expression, body postures, and gestures to regulate social interaction.
- Failure to develop peer relationships appropriate to developmental level, and lack of spontaneous seeking to share enjoyment, interests, or achievements with other people.
- Lack of social or emotional reciprocity.

The child also shows restricted repetitive and stereotyped patterns of behavior, interests, and activities as shown by at least one of the following:

- Encompassing preoccupation with one or more stereotyped and restricted patterns of interest that are abnormal either in intensity or focus.
- Apparently inflexible adherence to specific, nonfunctional routines or rituals.
- Stereotyped and repetitive motor mannerisms—for example, hand or finger flapping or twisting or complex whole-body movements.
- Persistent preoccupation with parts of objects.

The child also shows significant impairments in his or her social life or other important areas of functioning. However, there are no clinically significant delays in the youngster's language; for example, single words are used by age 2 and entire phrases by 3 years of age. As well, there is no clinically significant delay in cognitive development or in the development of age-appropriate self-help skills, adaptive behavior (other than social interaction), and curiosity about the environment. The child does not show symptoms that meet criteria for another specific pervasive developmental disorder or schizophrenia.

Adolescents with AD may show major problems in daily life such as poor personal hygiene and dressing. For instance they might refuse to wash, bathe, shower, or brush their teeth, complaining that the water, soap, shampoo, or toothpaste just does not "feel right." Clothes or shoes may be worn for days, weeks, or even months at a time. These adolescents may also be choosy about food preferences due to sensory integration issues in which not only the taste but the temperature and texture of the food become an issue.

As expected, children with AD may be vulnerable to co-occurring diagnoses. Often the symptoms of these other disorders will go unnoticed until the child grows older. For example, adolescence can be a challenging time for any young person. As will be seen in Bobby Owens's story, he begins to feel stressed out and anxious as he deals with peer pressure and increasing academic requirements. Another challenge adolescents typically face is the physical changes happening to their bodies. For someone with AD, their feelings about these changes can be exacerbated by a growing awareness that they are somehow different from their peers.

Depression and anxiety might be seen when the child is unable to handle normal changes in school and at home. Alternatively, AD may mask some of the signs of anxiety or depression. Many children struggle with obsessive-compulsive disorder and substance use disorders. Because of a similar symptom picture, children with AD are sometimes misdiagnosed with attention deficit hyperactivity disorder (Harchik & Solotar, 2009).

We now turn to the case of Robert "Bobby" Owens to illustrate the symptom picture of AD.

CASE | THE CASE OF ROBERT "BOBBY" OWENS

"Don't get me wrong," started Mrs. Owens. "I love my son but from the very first I thought something was 'off' with him. He was just so different from his brother, who is 20 months older." I asked Mrs. Owens to continue. "Bobby is 11 years old now but he has always been …," she paused and continued, "well, a little different. He doesn't seem to get the give-and-take of social interaction." Mrs. Owens stated that Bobby has a hard time understanding other people's perspectives and that he will speak impulsively. I asked her what she meant and Mrs. Owens indicated that Bobby just blurts out whatever he is thinking. "I remember once when we were in the grocery store and a rather heavyset woman was putting a huge box of cookies in her cart. Bobby just went up to her and announced that fat people should eat vegetables. I was so embarrassed but Bobby just couldn't see what was wrong. You might say he has a hard time appreciating what other people might think."

Mrs. Owens added that her son stands out in a group of children. "Bobby loves to read DC comic books. You know, Batman, Superman, and all those superheroes. He can tell you all about them in the minutest detail. All he wants to do is talk about those comic book stories and he can't seem to tell when you're bored. He just goes on and on and on. You might say Bobby has a narrow interest in things. Most of the boys in his class are involved in some kind of sport but Bobby just isn't interested. He would rather be reading his comic books, so it's tough for him to make friends."

I noticed that Mrs. Owens looked a little uncomfortable at this point, but she insisted that I needed to understand what was going on with her son. She continued, "Now that Bobby's in middle school he started showing some really serious behavior problems. It all began the past summer with his anger outbursts. I'm afraid that if we don't do something he'll be put in one of those special classes. That's why I came here. I'm hoping you can suggest some kind of program to help Bobby get along in school."

The social worker asked about Bobby's developmental history, and Mrs. Owens described it as unremarkable. However, she described her son as having a number of what she called "quirky" behaviors. Mrs. Owens stated, "For instance, things had to be a certain way for Bobby and you could not convince him otherwise. Like needing to eat from the same bowl, line up his toys in exact order, and travel the same way home. And then there were the issues with his clothes. All the tags had to be removed and for the longest time he wanted to wear his underwear inside out. If things were not the way he thought they should be then he would have a fit. You might say there were a lot of meltdowns in our house." The social worker reflected, "So that's what rigidly holding on to specific and nonfunctional routines looks like." Mrs. Owens continued, "It was like you were dealing with a two-year-old. You know, the 'terrible twos,' but only Bobby is much too old now for that kind of behavior. I thought maybe he had allergies or something so I took him to the doctor for a check-up. He told me that he didn't think Bobby was 'that bad.' All he said was Bobby was just immature for his age and then ran a bunch of tests. I don't think he had a clue about what could be wrong." The social worker noted that no medical problems were found that might better explain Bobby's behavior.

Mrs. Owens indicated that she had hoped her son would grow out of his behaviors. She added, "What with all his temper outbursts this past summer I finally came to the realization that my son is turning into a different person." About a month into summer vacation she noticed that Bobby was getting more and more upset. Mrs. Owens added that unstructured time was generally hard for Bobby, and he needed everything to be planned, with no deviation in his schedule. As the summer progressed, Bobby became more and more agitated and withdrawn. Then he started yelling at everyone who tried to talk to him. Mrs. Owens added, "Things started going from bad to worse. He began to say that everyone hated him. My heart sank when he said that I hated him. I just didn't know what to do for him and he was so unhappy. You never knew what to expect next. All those days of yelling and worrying were taking a toll on everybody in the family. We couldn't go to the store, shopping, or even to the movies. Bobby just couldn't get along with anybody. I thought that things would get better when school started back up. Boy was I wrong on that one," said Mrs. Owens.

Bobby started the sixth grade, and for the first time he was going to middle school. It was a new school for him and much larger than his elementary school. He also had all new teachers. "Those teachers decided to treat Bobby as if he was 'choosing' his behaviors. Bobby always had bad handwriting but his teachers seemed to think he wasn't trying hard enough. No one seemed to care about him, and on most days he would be in tears in the vice principal's office. He started to go into his own world and block everyone completely out. He would not listen. He would just stare right through you as if you weren't there. Then there were the anger issues. It got so that Bobby had alienated all the kids he knew from elementary school. And if that wasn't bad enough, I just learned a couple of weeks ago about the bullies who were tormenting Bobby. He doesn't know how to stand up for himself. My husband and I complained to the school but nothing was done. To make matters worse, those bullies were smart enough to not get caught. Since Bobby was seen as so explosive by the teachers, if something did happen, it was seen as his fault. Right there and then my husband and I decided we needed help. That's why we're here." said Mrs. Owens.

ROBERT "BOBBY" OWENS DSM MULTIAXIAL DIAGNOSIS IS AS FOLLOWS:

Axis I	299.80 Asperger's Disorder
Axis II	V71.09 (No diagnosis)
Axis III	None
Axis IV	Attends new school
Axis V	GAF = 60 (current)

ASSESSMENT SUMMARY   The vignette illustrates Bobby Owens' struggle with Asperger's disorder. Almost since birth Bobby's mother noticed that her son's behavior was not quite right. Difficulty making friends emerges as a consistent theme for Bobby while growing up, and he shows a lack in the give-and-take of social relationships or reciprocity. Mrs. Owens recounts the time in the supermarket when Bobby told a heavyset stranger who was putting cookies into her cart that she needed to be eating vegetables instead. Bobby was described as showing a deep and narrow interest in DC comics and being unable to discern when others would get bored when he talked about the comic book heroes.

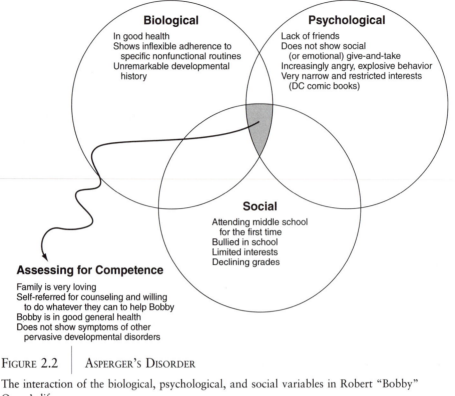

Biological

In good health
Shows inflexible adherence to
    specific nonfunctional routines
Unremarkable developmental
    history

Psychological

Lack of friends
Does not show social
    (or emotional) give-and-take
Increasingly angry, explosive behavior
Very narrow and restricted interests
    (DC comic books)

Social

Attending middle school
    for the first time
Bullied in school
Limited interests
Declining grades

Assessing for Competence

Family is very loving
Self-referred for counseling and willing
    to do whatever they can to help Bobby
Bobby is in good general health
Does not show symptoms of other
    pervasive developmental disorders

FIGURE 2.2 | ASPERGER'S DISORDER

The interaction of the biological, psychological, and social variables in Robert "Bobby" Owen's life.

© Cengage Learning 2013

Mrs. Owens indicated that she maintained the hope that Bobby would eventually change. She describes Bobby's odd behaviors as quirks; for instance, things had to be a certain way for him, such as eating from the same bowl or wearing his underwear inside out. When Bobby entered middle school his behavior became more aggressive and disruptive. His school work was not reported as problematic in elementary school but since entering middle school it has declined. Teachers were described as characterizing Bobby as "choosing" his classroom behaviors. His social relationships suffered and he alienated the few friends he had since elementary school. Bobby also became the target for bullying. According to Mrs. Owens, her son spent many hours in the vice principal's office and she was afraid Bobby would be placed in special classes.

Using the competency-based assessment, the advanced clinical practitioner does a parallel assessment of a client's coping strategies that may serve to reinforce and improve adaptation. In this case story, Bobby is reported to be in good overall health and does not show signs of any of the other pervasive developmental disorders or schizophrenia. Though stressed by Bobby's explosive behavior, his family seems to love him very much and to want to do whatever they can to get help for him. Aside from a recent decline in his grades, he is reported as an overall good student. Figure 2.2 shows the interactions of the biological, psychological, and social variables in Robert "Bobby" Owen's life.

**Advanced
Clinical
EP 2.1.10
(b) c**

Two additional disorders complete the PDD picture. They are Rett's disorder and childhood disintegrative disorder. Since they are rare and highly unlikely to be seen by the practitioner, they are summarized as follows:

- *Rett's disorder*—Commonly seen in girls, those with Rett's experience normal development for the first 6 months to a year and then begin to decline; for example, stereotyped hand movements, loss of social interaction, poorly coordinated gait, and impaired language develop, and the increase in head circumference decelerates.
- **Childhood disintegrative disorder**—This is a disorder in which the child shows a significant loss of previously acquired skills before age 10. Areas affected are language, social skills, bowel or bladder control, play, and motor skills.

Pervasive developmental disorder not otherwise specified (NOS), also called atypical autism, completes the diagnostic picture for PDD. Considered a threshold condition, this diagnosis is used when some but not all the features of autism or another explicitly identified PDD are seen.

We now turn to a review of attention deficit hyperactivity disorder.

ATTENTION DEFICIT HYPERACTIVITY DISORDER

Attention deficit hyperactivity disorder (ADHD) has warranted considerable attention given its importance in a child's school performance and school adjustment. This is the child who cannot seem to sit still, has trouble concentrating, starts something and then cannot seem to finish it, and simply cannot pay attention when someone else is talking to him or her. ADHD is one of the most common reasons children are referred for help in the United States (Durand, 2011). Polanczyk and colleagues (2007) estimate that between 3 and 7 percent of school-age children are diagnosed with ADHD.

PREVAILING PATTERN

Boys are three times more likely than girls to be diagnosed with ADHD (Spencer, Biederman, & Mick, 2007). Little is known about why boys are diagnosed more often than girls. One possible explanation is that boys tend to be more aggressive in contrast to girls with ADHD, who seem to display less obvious behaviors such as anxiety and depression (Mick et al., 2011). Parents first notice their child's behavior around the age of 3 or 4; for example, the child is characterized as active, slow to toilet train, or oppositional. Despite expectations that the child will outgrow these behaviors, McGlough (2005) points out that half of the children diagnosed with ADHD experience ongoing problems well into adulthood. Noble and Jones (2006) point to environmental toxins, drug exposure in utero, and a history of child abuse and multiple foster care placements as being associated with the ADHD diagnosis.

DIFFERENTIAL ASSESSMENT

EP 2.1.10
(b) a

Diagnosing children with ADHD is complicated by the reality that up to 80 percent of children also show symptoms of one or more other diagnoses (Brown, 2009). This underscores the practitioner's skill in collecting, organizing and interpreting assessment data. Commonly co-occurring disorders are anxiety, depression, and disruptive behavior. According to Durand (2011), at least half of those children with ADHD also show symptoms of oppositional defiant disorder (ODD). Similarly, conduct disorder, a precursor to antisocial personality disorder, is also commonly seen (Nock, Kazdin, Hiripi, & Kessler, 2006).

The essential feature of ADHD is the child's struggle with either with a lack of attention *or* hyperactivity that is more frequently shown and more severe than is typical for other children at a comparable developmental level. For a diagnosis, some interfering symptoms must be present before the age of 7 years that must be shown in two or more settings, and a significant impairment in functioning must be present. Symptoms characterizing *lack of attention* may include: inattention, does not seem to listen, does not follow through on instructions, avoids (or struggles with) tasks that require sustained mental effort, loses things, is easily distracted, and is forgetful. Those symptoms characterizing *hyperactivity* are: fidgeting, leaving his or her seat, running around or climbing about, difficulty playing quietly, often "on the go," and excessive talking. Those characterizing *impulsivity* are: difficulty waiting, and interrupts or intrudes on others.

A diagnosis of ADHD requires that the child's symptoms are not better explained by another disorder and are not seen during the course of a pervasive developmental disorder, schizophrenia, or other psychotic disorder. The presence of a medical condition should also be ruled out. Subtypes include predominately inattentive, predominately hyperactive-impulsive, and combined. Attention deficit hyperactivity disorder NOS is used when the child does not meet all of the criteria for attention deficit hyperactivity disorder. For example, the symptoms may have emerged after 7 years of age.

We now turn to the case story of Louie Dessaint.

CASE | ## THE CASE OF LOUIE DESSAINT

Louie Dessaint was 8 years old when he was referred to the Children's Center by the school social worker. Although Louie had been attending his neighborhood school for almost a year, the social worker noticed that he was not communicating in English. The school social worker suspected that Louie might have been abused but she was not able to support her suspicions. "To be on the safe side, I think it's best to refer him for a complete workup," reflected the social worker. Ms. Dessaint did not seem to understand what was wrong with Louie's behavior in school but was receptive to the referral to the Children's Center and readily agreed to follow up on the evaluation of her son.

The intake worker at the Center noted on the referral form that Louie's classroom teacher described him as being socially isolated from the other children. Although he seemed bright, he was not progressing academically and did little work in class. He rarely listened to the teacher and did not pay attention. He needed constant reminders to stay on task. The report noted that Louie would forget to do what he was told and seemed overwhelmed if given detailed instructions. He would easily become distracted, lose his concentration, and give up. He did not stay in his seat but tended to wander around the classroom. Because of his behavior, the other children stayed away from Louie or they would make fun of him.

When Louie and his mother arrived at the Center for their appointment, the social worker noticed the both of them sitting in the corner of the room looking scared. Ms. Dessaint stared at her hands, and Louie was in constant motion, fidgeting in his chair next to hers. It seemed impossible for him to sit still. The Center had a corner with toys and books but nothing seemed to interest Louie. The receptionist at the front desk noticed that Ms. Dessaint would whisper something to Louie. She recognized it was in Creole and that Ms. Dessaint was telling Louie to behave—but he just didn't seem to listen. The longer he waited, the more he fidgeted. Then Louie started to leave his seat and wander around the waiting room, climbing over empty seats.

The social worker assigned to see Ms. Dessaint explained that Louie was also was being seen by another social worker during the same time as their appointment. She added that the purpose of today's session was to learn more about Louie's background in order to find out how the Center could be of help. Despite the social worker's attempts to put Ms. Dessaint at ease, she still looked uncomfortable. Reluctantly, Ms. Dessaint began, "We Haitians are a very private people but I will try to answer what you ask of me for the sake of my son. He is all I have left. The school thinks he has very big problems. Education is important to me so I will do everything I can to improve Louie's school work." Though cooperative, it was clear that it was hard for Ms. Dessaint to talk about Louie's psychosocial history. "I wonder if she's just a very private person or if something else is going on. I guess maybe it's just cultural," mused the social worker.

Ms. Dessaint shared that the family had experienced a number of traumas before coming to the United States. She did not tell anyone at the school about the details because she did not want Louie to be stigmatized. Louie's father died suddenly. He had been killed in the 2010 earthquake in in Haiti. "I will never forget the day it happened," said Ms. Dessaint. "At the time we lived in Jacmel just outside of Port au Prince. I remembered the trembling but thought nothing of it. At the time Louie was in the bedroom with his father. When it started to get worse, he came out to where I was in the kitchen. Next thing I know there was darkness everywhere and all we could hear was Louie's father moaning— then it was quiet. Louie wanted to go back to his father but I said we must leave. I remember looking back and all I could see was my husband's bloody hand sticking out from under what was left of our

roof. I would not let Louie look but I am sure he saw …" Her voice trailed off and then she resumed. "We lost many relatives. All of my sisters and their families and my parents died, too. In the nights following the earthquake we slept on the pavement. There was nowhere else to go. Everything was destroyed. The Catholic Relief Services helped us to move here to the United States. Louie was used to growing up with his cousins. Now we are here. I mean it is safe and all but we are so alone." Ms. Dessaint looked visibly shaken and I asked if she would like a drink of water. "No," she answered, "Haitians are a strong people. I will get through this for the sake of my Louie."

The psychosocial history revealed that Louie had no opportunity to learn English before entering school in the United States. Developmental milestones were unremarkable but Louie was described as having been an active and agitated child ever since he was a toddler. Some of Ms. Dessaint's family members thought that Louie's behaviors were due to evil spirits. "… but the mambo helps," added Ms. Dessaint. The social worker was puzzled and said, "Ms. Dessaint, I have been asking you a lot of questions about how we can help Louie but it looks like you are already getting some help. I don't know about a mambo. Can you help me understand?" Ms. Dessaint explained that she had consulted with a mambo, a female voodoo priest, who advised her to set out a white candle with a clear glass of water and to say certain prayers on a particular saint's day to ward off the evil spirits.

The social worker who saw Louie individually noted that he easily separated from his mother and seemed cooperative throughout the interview. At first, Louie was somewhat reserved. He said very little beyond pointing to the toys in the play corner of the social worker's office. The social worker indicated it was alright for Louie to play with the toys, and his solemn demeanor brightened as he examined several of the toys. The social worker observed that Louie was unable to sustain an interest in any one item for very long. He was easily distracted and it was hard for him to sit still. Louie lost interest in the games that required concentration and gravitated toward the soft, cuddly toy animals. At the end of the session Louie forgot the social worker's earlier instructions to put away the toys when he was finished. When

continued

reminded, he was cooperative and carefully tried to put things in their place. The task seemed to take his full attention. Though he struggled, Louie seemed eager to please. The social worker thought, "He's a likeable kid, but his behaviors somehow just seem to get in his way. I think we have some programs that can help."

The Center conducted a full educational assessment and found Louie's IQ to be in the normal range; no learning difficulties were noted. A speech and language assessment found no abnormalities. The pediatrician's report indicated Louie was in good overall health. What is your assessment of Louie Dessaint?

Advanced Clinical EP 2.1.4 a

ASSESSMENT SUMMARY   The vignette illustrates some of the challenges assessing ADHD, especially in a transcultural context. Beyond simply understanding diversity, the practitioner was called upon to apply her knowledge of the Haitian culture in order to find ways to enhance Louie's and his mother's well-being. The competency-based assessment provides a vehicle to explore the wide range of factors and in this case vignette. The diagnostic process was complicated by a number of factors, including how Ms. Dessaint saw Louie's problems (being caused by evil spirits), and a premigratory history of trauma. In particular, before coming to the United States Louie had been exposed to the violent death of his father and the loss of his extended family in a devastating earthquake. He was currently faced with adapting to a new culture, including learning a new language. Louie was used to being surrounded by all of his cousins in his small town in Haiti but currently he and his mother live in isolation. In addition, his mother is trying to cope with Louie's difficulties in school, but she has a limited understanding of what was causing her son's problems. Relatives attributed Louie's behavior to evil spirits and so Ms. Dessaint consulted a culturally familiar source of help; specifically, a mambo (female voodoo priest) who prescribed certain rituals. Mrs. Dessaint seems to love her son and followed through with the referral to the Children's' Center although she does not fully understand his problems. It was difficult for Ms. Dessaint to share family history due to her Haitian culture of being "very private." She also did not want her son stigmatized at his school, so she withheld some information.

In addition to the symptoms of inattentive type ADHD exhibited in school and at home (i.e.: inattentive, distracted, not paying attention, not listening, not following through on detailed instructions, forgetful), Louie also showed a number of other problems, such as difficulties in learning and in making friends. Louie shows some symptoms of hyperactivity and impulsivity but not to the extent to assign the ADHD subtype of predominantly hyperactive-impulsive (i.e.: fidgets, leaves his seat, climbing about). His experiences in school seemed to further complicate adjusting to a new life in the United States. Unfortunately, this contributed to a picture of a little boy with low self-esteem, a common struggle for youngsters with ADHD (Anastopoulos, Sommer, & Shatz, 2009).

Advanced Clinical EP 2.1.9 a

The cultural context also plays a role in ascertaining Louie's diagnosis: his mother did not see any problems as he was growing up (though she mentioned symptomatic hyperactive/impulsive behaviors when Louie was a toddler). It was important for the practitioner to be able to assess Louie's interactions within his different social contexts. For example, his behavior seemed problematic to his mother only after she migrated to the United States and Louie entered the American classroom. Timmini and Taylor (2004) point to Western society's intolerance for certain behaviors, and the pressure to conform academically, that highlight ADHD.

The competency-based assessment provides a framework to take into account the broad range of factors that are continuously interacting with one another as the child develops. Included is attention to the child's cultural identity, language, and spiritual beliefs. Risks for developing disorders are also considered; for instance, a child such as Louie, who is living in relative isolation and has experienced the trauma of losing his father and all of his relatives in a devastating earthquake before migrating to the United States. The competency-based assessment also looks to strengths and resources such as a caring parent, supportive schools, and appropriate services. Figure 2.3 shows the interactionx of the biological, psychological, and social variables in Louie Dessaint's life.

Louie Dessaint's DSM Multiaxial Diagnosis Is as Follows:

Axis I	314.00 Attention Deficit Hyperactivity Disorder Predominantly Inattentive Type
Axis II	V71.09 (No diagnosis)
Axis III	None
Axis IV	Migrated to the United States
Axis V	GAF = 70 (on admission)

© Cengage Learning 2013

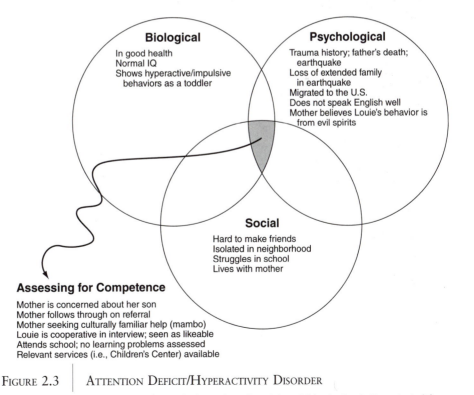

FIGURE 2.3 | Attention Deficit/Hyperactivity Disorder

The interaction of the biological, psychological, and social variables in Louie Dessaint's life.

Attention deficit hyperactivity disorder and conduct disorder are found to be common among children who have been maltreated; have lost a family member to death, military deployment, or incarceration; or have witnessed violence (Noble & Jones, 2006). Louie Dessaint's story highlights his losses and the related trauma associated with his father's death along with those of most of the members of his family.

We not turn to an overview of the disruptive behavior disorders in childhood beginning with conduct disorder.

CONDUCT DISORDER

Conduct disorder (CD) can be seen in children who have experienced inconsistent child-rearing practices such as harsh discipline, a lack of supervision, maternal smoking during pregnancy, and exposure to violence (Noble & Jones, 2006). The essential feature of this disorder is a consistent pattern of violating the rights of others or violating major age-appropriate societal norms or rules (Henggeler & Sheidow, 2003). Studies have shown that those with conduct problems during childhood or adolescence are at a higher risk for other mental disorders, legal problems, and premature mortality (Kim-Cohen et al., 2003; Simonoff et al., 2004). Unfortunately, children who are diagnosed with CD report higher levels of distress and impairment in virtually all areas of living than youth with other mental disorders (Lambert, Wahler, Andrade, & Bickman, 2001).

PREVAILING PATTERN

Estimates for the lifetime prevalence of CD in the United States population are between 6 percent to 16 percent for males and 2 percent to 9 percent for females (Loeber, Green, Lahey, Frick, & McBurnett, 2000; Maughan, Rowe, Messer, Goodman, & Meltzer, 2004). The symptoms for CD tend to be seen before age 16 and are believed to be influenced by environmental as well as genetic factors. The median age of onset is approximately age 11 (Nock, Kazdin, Hiripi, & Kessler, 2006).

DIFFERENTIAL ASSESSMENT

EP 2.1.10
(b) a

The diagnosis of CD requires the presence of any 3 of the following 15 symptoms for at least 12 months and at least 1 symptom over the past 6 months. They include:

- Bullying, threatening, or intimidating others.
- Starting fights.
- Using a weapon.
- Being physically cruel to people.
- Being physically cruel to animals.
- Stealing while confronting the person (i.e.: mugging, purse snatching, extortion, armed robbery).
- Committing sexual assault.
- Setting fires with the intention of causing serious damage.
- Destroying property.
- Breaking into another's property.

- Lying.
- Stealing without confronting the person (i.e.: shoplifting or forgery).
- Staying out at night.
- Running away from home.
- Refusing to attend school.

As the practitioner is completing the competency-based assessment it may be easier to organize data by remembering that these behaviors can be grouped into four major categories as follows: aggression to people and animals, destruction of property, deceitfulness or theft, and serious violations of the rules. The practitioner specifies childhood onset when symptoms are present before 10 years and specifies adolescent onset when symptoms are seen after 10 years of age. Severity of CD may be noted as mild, moderate, or severe.

The diagnosis for CD indicates significant social, school, or work problems. Behaviors typically seen in boys are fighting, stealing, vandalizing property, and breaking school rules. Girls with CD are more likely to lie, run away from home, be truant, use drugs, and become involved in prostitution. Both boys and girls can show little empathy and concern for others, callousness, lack of guilt and remorse, low self-esteem, irritability, poor frustration tolerance, recklessness, and high levels of aggression. Overall, these children (and adolescents) are also more likely than their peers to engage in early sexual behaviors, smoking, drinking, drug use, fighting, reckless acts, and gang-related activity. They are more likely to contract sexually transmitted diseases, become pregnant, or get injured from accidents or fighting.

The case of Norman Gibson illustrates the symptom picture for CD.

| CASE | THE CASE OF NORMAN GIBSON |

After his most recent arrest, Norman Gibson, a 15-year-old male, was referred to the Guidance Clinic by his juvenile probation officer. Norman was scheduled to appear before a judge for his most recent charges. Since this was his second arrest in less than a year, there was a good chance that he might receive a stronger sentence. Norman's father was motivated to get help for his son, indicating, "Maybe the judge will go easier on the boy since we're in family counseling this time around."

At the very beginning of the interview with Norman, he was belligerent and dismissive. He sat with his leg swung over the side of the chair and announced, "Call me Namron. You see Norman is my slave name." He went on to say that he would not answer any questions that "I don't feel like answering." The social worker's first thought was that she really didn't like this youngster but then remembered the first thing she learned in graduate school about the social worker's role. In order to be a professional, she had to be nonjudgmental and offer unconditional positive regard. "Well, this is going to be tough," reflected the social worker. Gently, she asked Namron about why he thought he was here. His response was confrontational as he began, "Well just ask me all your f_ _ kin, questions so we can get this over with and I can get out of here. I got better things to do." The social worker was surprised by Norman's response and found she was feeling a little angry. "This is really not professional and I'd better watch my behavior. If I had my druthers, I would just tell this kid off," she thought.

The social worker remembered the intake report described a history of problems. Specifically, a year ago almost to the day of the intake, Norman was arrested for vandalism at his local high school. He and a group of his friends were caught on security camera videos breaking windows, spray painting

continued

graffiti on the walls, and trashing several of the class-rooms. Since this was his first offence, Norman was placed on probation for 6 months. When the social worker asked about the charges, Norman just laughed. "Hell, that's only half of what I've done." He went on to describe several shoplifting sprees with his friends, missing school, and smoking marijuana. "But I only smoke on the weekends," he added with a wink in her direction. "Good grief! This kid is a sarcastic little bugger," thought the social worker. His record indicated missing school for 61 days—just about one third of the school year.

The social worker asked Norman what had happened that brought him to the clinic. He described his recent arrest 4 months ago for torturing and killing raccoons that were eating food from the garbage bins located behind a local grocery store. For several months, Norman, along with several of his friends, started hanging out at night behind the store. They would usually drink or get high, and then they noticed the raccoons. At first, the boys started taunting the animals, but then one thing led to another. "Those raccoons were a nuisance so what do I care? I was doing that store a favor. Then some goody two-shoes animal rights idiot comes along and reports us. I'm pretty sure I know who it was, too. It's that skinny old grey-haired bum who feeds the cats in the front of the store every day. People who shop there even give him money to buy more cat food. What a bunch of jerks!" said Norman. "We'll take care of him," he added ominously. "Was this a threat?" wondered the social worker. She thought, "I also need to explore the extent of his drug use. I think he'll be more honest with me once we develop a relationship."

Norman was the only one who was caught, and he blamed his friends for leaving him behind. "But I'm not going to rat on my friends. It's against the code," he said. At that point, the social worker noticed that Norman wore his baseball cap backwards and had a red bandanna hanging out of his left side back pocket. She recognized these as the markings of a local gang and wondered if Norman was a member. She made a mental note to explore this further. "He's so belligerent and confrontational right now, so this might take a little time. And I've got to get my negative feelings toward this kid in check, too. I hope it doesn't show right now," she reflected.

The social worker asked Norman about his goals for the future. He immediately responded that he didn't think much was going to come out of his upcoming court appearance. "The judge is such a f_ _ king a_ _ hole," he said adding that several of his friends had been in court with this judge and "all they got was community service." Norman was indifferent about school and brushed off the social worker's suggestions for work-study or part-time programs. Emphatically he stated, "Look lady. I can take care of myself. I've been doing it for most of my life. The old man is always working and never seems to have time for me. Forced me to look out for 'number one.' That would be me, in case you're wondering … and I've been doing okay in that department." As the session drew to a close, Norman stood up, and on his way out the door, he abruptly turned around and stated, "Look lady, thanks for all your sweet talk but I really don't care what happens to me." The social worker was surprised when Norman went on to add that he really didn't like himself very much anymore.

Mr. Gibson was also interviewed. The social worker had the impression that while Mr. Gibson was cooperative, he was also careful to justify his actions as a parent. "My wife left me a while back and then 3 years ago she dumped Norman back on me. Norman has always been in good health but she started saying he was too much for her to handle. Claimed he didn't get along with her latest boyfriend and the baby. Whatever that means. Since he's been with me she doesn't even call let alone remember the boy on Christmas. No wonder he has problems," added Mr. Gibson.

As a single parent, Mr. Gibson claimed that he had to work a lot and admitted his son was alone for most of the day. He seemed unaware of what Norman did and guessed that his son was either on the computer or hanging out with his friends. The social worker had the impression that their relationship was cordial, but distant. Mr. Gibson said, "The boy and I have a good relationship and I want to get help for him. Norman just needs someone to get through to him and get him back on track. Since you're the professionals, I hope you know the right way to get some sense into him. You can't depend on the school. After all, nobody even let me know about all his absences until it was too late. Now he'll probably be suspended big time. Frankly, I think he was the one arrested this time around instead of the other boys because he got off so easy with the vandalism stuff. You see we live in a small town and the school resource officer is married to the police chief. So she

tells her husband about what happened at the school and next thing you know, Norman gets arrested for the supermarket episode. I think the police had it in for Norman all along. They were just waiting for the right opportunity to arrest him."

The social worker scheduled up follow-up appointments and asked for consent to contact the school counselor, the juvenile probation officer, and his mother. She wanted to get a bigger picture of Norman's behavior in other contexts.

ASSESSMENT SUMMARY   The vignette illustrates one of the central features of CD seen in Norman's persistent pattern of behavior in which the rights of others are ignored and age appropriate societal rules are broken. Over the past year, Norman described shoplifting, missing school, and smoking marijuana. While we do not know the details of his academic performance, the social worker did ask for consent to contact the school counselor to further clarify Norman's status. In addition, he was arrested for destroying school property and more recently for torturing and killing raccoons behind a local supermarket. Because this is the first known episode of cruelty to animals and Norman has not harmed any animals in recent months, his CD is rated as moderate.

Norman was sent to live with his father 3 years ago because his mother was reported to have been unable to handle him. Therefore the social worker has no history of symptoms before age 10; as such, the diagnosis of CD would be adolescent onset. The social worker did request permission to talk with Norman's mother, thus underscoring the value of obtaining information from different sources about his behavior. However, the assessment focuses on Norman's current and most problematic behaviors; that is, his recent legal charges for animal cruelty. Several areas emerged for further exploration; namely, his school academic performance, gang membership, and the extent of Norman's substance use.

EP 2.1.1 d

Norman's behavior toward the social worker was belligerent, confrontational, and challenging. Clients such as this young man can challenge any practitioner's ability to demonstrate professional demeanor in behavior, appearance, and communication. Norman used foul language and was, at times, sarcastic. He evoked reactions of fear and hostility in the social worker. His sarcasm was evident when he gave the social worker a knowing wink as he described his substance use. The social worker's struggle "to be professional" can be seen when she reflected her concern that her negativity would not be conspicuous.

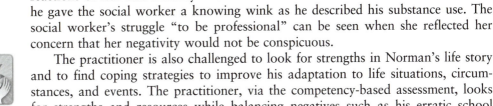

Advanced
Clinical EP
2.1.10 (b) c

The practitioner is also challenged to look for strengths in Norman's life story and to find coping strategies to improve his adaptation to life situations, circumstances, and events. The practitioner, via the competency-based assessment, looks for strengths and resources while balancing negatives such as his erratic school attendance, legal charges, shoplifting, animal cruelty, and an overall belligerent and hostile attitude. In addition, Norman's mother is absent and his father appears minimally involved in his son's life. However, Mr. Gibson did follow up on the probation officer's referral for counseling. While not directly stating that he wants to be involved in family counseling, Norman's father did express the hope of getting help for his son in order to improve his son's life. As the social worker's interview ended with Norman, he was able to admit not liking himself anymore. Hopefully this recognition of low self-esteem can set the stage for a working relationship aimed at making positive changes in his life. Figure 2.4 shows the interactions of the biological, psychological, and social variables in Norman Gibson's life.

NORMAN GIBSON'S DSM MULTIAXIAL DIAGNOSIS IS AS FOLLOWS:

Axis I	312.82 Conduct Disorder Adolescent Onset Type Moderate
Axis II	V71.09 (No diagnosis)
Axis III	None
Axis IV	On probation Current legal charges
Axis V	GAF 65 (on admission)

© Cengage Learning 2013

We now turn our attention to oppositional defiant disorder, the major reason children are referred for mental health services.

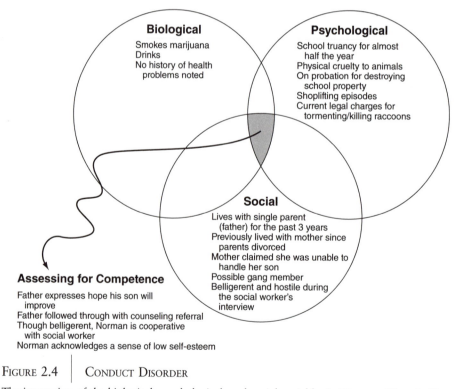

FIGURE 2.4 | CONDUCT DISORDER

The interaction of the biological, psychological, and social variables in Norman Gibson's life.

© Cengage Learning 2013

OPPOSITIONAL DEFIANT DISORDER

Oppositional defiant disorder (ODD) can be found in children who have a history of a succession of different caregivers or who live in families with harsh, inconsistent, neglectful child-rearing practices (Noble & Jones, 2006).

PREVAILING PATTERN

Common features of ODD include excessive, often persistent anger, frequent temper tantrums or angry outbursts, and disregard for authority. The lifetime prevalence of ODD is estimated to be 10.2 percent of the United States population (Nock, Kazdin, Hiripi, & Kessler, 2007). Of those, the greater percentage are males. ODD is a common child- and adolescent-onset disorder associated with substantial risk of secondary mood (45.8 percent), anxiety (62.3 percent), impulse-control (68.2 percent), and substance use (47.2 percent) disorders.

DIFFERENTIAL ASSESSMENT

ODD is characterized as an ongoing pattern of disobedient, hostile, and defiant behavior toward authority figures that goes beyond the bounds of normal childhood behavior. Children and adolescents who have it may appear very stubborn and angry. The essential feature of ODD is the recurrent pattern of negativistic, defiant, disobedient, and hostile behavior toward authority figures that lasts for at least 6 months. In order to meet criteria for a diagnosis, the child must show four of eight symptoms. These include: frequent loss of temper, arguing with adults, noncompliance, annoying others, blaming others for mistakes or misbehavior, over-sensitive to the behavior of others, angry and resentful, and vindictive. All of these behaviors occur more frequently than in most children of a comparable age. In addition, the child's behaviors must cause some level of impairment in key areas of functioning such as interpersonal relationships or in school.

The case of Jerry Sheppard illustrates ODD.

| CASE | THE CASE OF JERRY SHEPPARD |

Mrs. Sheppard showed up for the intake interview with her 12-year-old son, Jerry. Mrs. Sheppard was seen first. She explained that she had contacted the counseling center based on the advice of her AA sponsor. The intake form noted that Mrs. Sheppard was reportedly having a lot of trouble controlling her son lately. He was constantly getting into trouble and increasingly defiant toward Mrs. Sheppard. In addition, the family was recently in turmoil over Mr. Sheppard's incarceration. Now that he was out of the house, the level of fighting between Jerry and his mother was becoming intolerable. According to Mrs.

Sheppard, "Therapy might be a good way of getting things on track with Jerry." She added, "I'm in recovery and doing okay for the first time in my life so I guess its Jerry's turn."

Mrs. Sheppard made it clear to the intake worker that if her husband, Frank, was not in jail she was sure he would have come in. Since her husband's incarceration, Mrs. Sheppard had started working part-time to help out with the financial strain on the family made worse by her husband's absence. She added, "Sometimes Frank's a little hard on Jerry but I know he loves him. We don't always agree on

continued

what's right for the boy but that's all Frank knows. My husband had a hard childhood himself." Mrs. Sheppard explained that she disagreed with her husband about how to discipline Jerry and this led to inconsistent punishment. Mr. Sheppard preferred corporal punishment, in contrast to Mrs. Sheppard, who tried to negotiate with her son and reward good behavior. "That's when I wasn't drinking," added Mrs. Sheppard. "You might say I just wasn't there for Jerry. Guess he just about raised himself. Now that I'm sober I want to be there for him. I have a lot of missed time to make up for. Like I said, most of the time when Jerry was growing up I was battling my addiction." She continued, "On top of that, we struggled financially, too. Frank always had a hard time keeping a job. He drank too, but not like me. Seems like we were always a paycheck away from being homeless. Whenever Frank was laid off, I had to apply for food stamps. When Frank had a job, he worked long hours. He didn't have much education so he usually found unskilled work. He had to work a couple of jobs and was not home a lot," she said. Mrs. Sheppard was insistent that her husband loved Jerry "in his own way."

Last year in the sixth grade, Jerry was suspended from school for several days each month; some of the reasons included talking back to his teacher, another time for showing a poor attitude, and yet another for throwing a temper tantrum. Finally the school principal and Jerry's teacher requested a meeting with Mr. and Mrs. Sheppard. During this meeting, Mrs. Sheppard learned that Jerry had a long-standing pattern of misbehavior in the classroom. He argued with the teacher and annoyed his classmates by teasing them every chance he could. This had been going on for most of the school year. She added that Jerry constantly argues with her when she's home but she

just locks herself in her room. "It beats arguments with him that go nowhere. Besides, I'm afraid I might do the wrong thing. Jerry usually cools down and I spend a lot of time in my room. I don't know what happened. He just seems so angry all the time," said Mrs. Sheppard.

Mrs. Sheppard indicated she had no birth problems with Jerry, and developmental milestones occurred within normal limits. He is in good overall health. However, Mrs. Sheppard admitted to being at a loss to understand her son's behavior. She added that she was becoming increasingly concerned about her ability to manage her son now that he was almost a teenager. At the point of the school meeting, Jerry was refusing to do most of his school work and his grades were poor. With signed consent, the social worker contacted the school, and Mrs. Sheppard's account of Jerry's behavior and poor academic performance was confirmed.

After battling an addiction to drugs for more than 10 years, Mrs. Sheppard found inspiration from a social worker who spoke at a drug and alcohol support group meeting she started attending after her discharge from rehab. "Somehow we just seemed to connect," said Mrs. Shepard. "She sort of took me under her wing. She saw potential in me to go on and get better. That's why I came here. I'm hoping one of your social workers will be able to hit it off with my Jerry," she added. "Do you have somebody like that here?" asked Mrs. Sheppard. The social worker remembered reading the report of Jerry's intake session with another social worker on staff and said to herself, "I sure hope so." The report noted that Jerry was sullen and uncooperative. He challenged the other social worker to explain why he needed to come in and then abruptly walked out after 20 minutes.

ASSESSMENT SUMMARY   As Jerry's mother describes her son's behavior in this vignette, highlighted are the key features of ODD. Jerry demonstrates an ongoing pattern of negative, defiant, argumentative, disobedient, and hostile behavior. School reports indicate that Jerry argues with his teacher, annoys his classmates, loses his temper even to the point of being suspended, and constantly argues with his mother at home. He is seen as defiant and angry just about all the time. When seen during the intake interview, Jerry was hostile and uncooperative.

**Advanced
Clinical
EP 2.1.10
(b) c**

Using the competency-based assessment, the social worker is able to assess Jerry's coping strategies. Hopefully they will set the stage to reinforce and improve his adaptation to life situations, circumstances, and events. Despite a history of neglectful and harsh child-rearing often found in children with ODD, there are a number of parallel strengths in Jerry's life. His mother is making a serious attempt at her own recovery and wants to be more available to raise her son. Mrs. Sheppard also reports that her husband loves Jerry "in his own way." Although Jerry's school grades and behavior are problematic, he does attend school and no learning problems are noted. Mrs. Sheppard followed through on the school referral, and her motivation is to learn how to better manage his behavior. Figure 2.5 shows the interactions of the biological, psychological, and social variables in Jerry Sheppard's life.

JERRY SHEPPARD'S DSM MULTIAXIAL DIAGNOSIS IS AS FOLLOWS:

Axis I	313.81 Oppositional Defiant Disorder
Axis II	V71.09 (No diagnosis)
Axis III	None
Axis IV	School difficulties
Axis V	GAF = 70 (on admission)

© Cengage Learning 2013

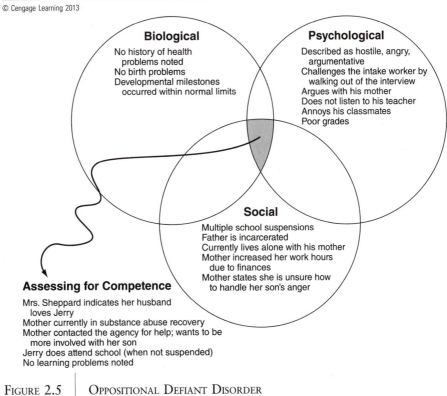

FIGURE 2.5 | OPPOSITIONAL DEFIANT DISORDER

The interaction of the biological, psychological, and social variables in Jerry Sheppard's life.

© Cengage Learning 2013

Disruptive disorder NOS is used for patterns of behavior that do not fit the diagnostic classifications for conduct disorder or oppositional defiant disorder. In this case, the child has symptoms of both disorders, but not to the extent to be as troubled as Norman Gibson, who is diagnosed with conduct disorder, or Jerry Sheppard, who has a diagnosis of oppositional defiant disorder. Disruptive disorder NOS is also used when there is not enough information about the child's situation.

We now turn to one of the overcontrolled behaviors found in the DSM disorders, separation anxiety.

SEPARATION ANXIETY

Separation anxiety is normal part of a child's development, but when it persists past a certain age or has a significant impact on life and activities, it can be a problem. Most children tend to be minimally affected by separation anxiety by age 5. Separation anxiety disorder (SAD) is characterized by an extreme fear and significant distress about being away from home and family to the extent that it affects a child's ability to function socially and academically. For example, they may worry about being kidnapped or getting lost.

These children have a great need to stay home or be close to their parents, and they worry excessively when they are apart. The author remembers a close friend complaining that her 2-year-old would not fall asleep unless she was nearby. Every night they had to check her closet and under the bed for monsters. My friend added that she just couldn't wait for her little one to outgrow these night fears and be able to go to bed like everybody else in the house. Unlike these mild worries a child may feel at times of separation, SAD affects the child's ability to engage in ordinary activities. This is the child who when faced with separation shows panic or tantrums well beyond what is expected for the child's age.

Prevailing Pattern

While the cause of separation anxiety is unknown, there are number of risk factors that contribute to its development. For example, children and adolescents who have experienced some form of significant stress such as a stay in the hospital, the death of a loved one or pet, or a change in environment are at a higher risk for developing the disorder. Even moving to another house or a change of schools can lead to separation anxiety. Trauma, such as physical or sexual assault, can also be a contributing factor. This disorder is often seen in children when they first begin attending school, but can occur at all ages and in many situations. The lifetime prevalence of childhood SAD is estimated to be 4.1 percent of the general population and is equally distributed between boys and girls (Shear, Jin, Ruscio, Walters, & Kessler, 2006).

Differential Assessment

EP 2.1.10
(b) a

SAD should not be confused with the normally occurring separation anxiety seen in children between 18 months and 3 years of age, or stranger anxiety, which is typically seen at 7 to 11 months of age. Being able to differentiate between normal age-appropriate behavior and the symptoms of SAD underscores the social worker's skill in collecting, organizing, and interpreting client data. The main differences between healthy separation anxiety and SAD are the intensity of the child's fears, and whether these fears keep him or her from normal activities. Children with SAD may become agitated at just the thought of being away from a parent, and may complain of sickness to avoid playing with friends or attending school.

To reach the diagnostic threshold for this disorder, the child's anxiety or fear must cause distress or affect social, or academic functioning and must last at least 1 month. Symptoms are seen before 18 years of age, and early onset can be specified if SAD occurs before age 6. Children with separation anxiety may cling to their parent and have difficulty falling asleep alone at night. The most common fear a child with SAD experiences is the worry that harm will come to a loved one in the child's absence. They worry that some unpredicted event may happen which would lead to permanent separation. When separated, the child may be afraid that his or her parent will be involved in an accident, become gravely ill, or in some other way be "lost" to the child forever. They may also worry about being kidnapped or getting lost. The need to stay close to their parents or home may make it difficult for the child to attend school or camp, stay at friends' houses, or be in a room alone. Some children may even have repeated nightmares or scary dreams about separation. The child may complain of headaches or stomachaches. An intense fear of separation can lead to dizziness, nausea, or palpitations (Barlow, Pincus, Heinrichs, & Choate, 2003).

Patty Nemeth's vignette highlights the behaviors that illustrate the symptom picture for SAD. Since we do not know the details of her family life, the competency-based assessment is not included.

| CASE | THE CASE OF PATTY NEMETH |

Patty Nemeth is a 7-year-old girl who lives with both of her parents. She has two older sisters, Myra and Kimberly. Ever since kindergarten, Patty has missed several days of school each month. Mrs. Nemeth had not experienced any of these problems with her other two daughters, and she hoped Patty would grow out of this behavior. Unfortunately, Patty's fears about going to school only seem to have gotten worse. For the past 4 weeks, Patty has become even more upset about going to school. Patty tells her mother that she is afraid "something bad" will happen to her family if she leaves them. Her mother wonders if all the recent news on the television about the tornadoes in the Midwest has something to do with Patty's fears.

At any rate, Patty has temper tantrums and screams to be allowed to stay home. It's hard for Mrs. Nemeth to see her daughter so upset, and she struggles not to give in. This behavior usually happens on a Monday. On the other days when Patty does go to school, she insists that her mom stay close by for at least an hour. Mrs. Nemeth worked out an arrangement with Patty's teacher to leave the classroom door open so Patty can see her. After about an hour of checking the door, Patty seems okay with her mother leaving. After Mrs. Nemeth leaves, the school counselor checks in on Patty just before lunch, or more often if the teacher notices Patty starts to worry that something bad has happened to her mother on the way home. Mrs. Nemeth stays near her cell phone just in case the school calls. Patty insists that her mother be either on time or early in picking her up after school. If Mrs. Nemeth is even a little late, Patty threatens not to go to school the next day.

To make matters worse, Patty started having nightmares about being kidnapped by strangers who would come in her bedroom window to get her and take her away. She even refused to go on a recent school trip unless her mother went along. When she is at home, Patty wants her mother in sight at all times. Patty also worries about her mother having a terrible accident.

ASSESSMENT SUMMARY   The most outstanding feature of Patty Nemeth's behavior is her persistent reluctance to go to school starting as early as kindergarten. The early start of these behaviors warrants adding the specifier of early onset to Patty's DSM diagnosis of SAD. Patty's mother had hoped her daughter would outgrow this behavior but for the past month it has only gotten worse. The fears of separating from mother are beyond what could be reasonably expected for a 7-year-old. Patty's refusal to go to school typically starts on a Monday. When she does go to school, Mrs. Nemeth, along with the teacher's assistance, developed an elaborate plan to separate Patty from her mother; that is, Mrs. Nemeth stays outside the classroom door for at least an hour, allowing Patty to check on her mother. After Mrs. Nemeth leaves, the school counselor checks in on Patty. At the end of the school day, Patty insists that her mother pick her up early or on time. Patty also expresses the fear that something "bad" will happen to her family. In addition, Patty has started to have nightmares and refused to go on a recent school trip unless her mother went along. When she is at home, Patty insists on keeping her mother in sight at all times.

It is interesting to note that the vignette makes no reference to the Nemeth family seeking counseling for Patty's behaviors. Unfortunately, this is typical for a number of families struggling with a child with SAD. Instead, Mrs. Nemeth worked out an elaborate plan with the teacher to facilitate her being able to leave Patty at school. The school counselor intervenes only to check on the status of Patty's fears and call Mrs. Nemeth to pick up her daughter, if needed.

In summary, all children experience some anxiety around separation from significant caregivers to some extent but this fear usually diminishes as the child grows older. Separation anxiety, as seen in Patty Nemeth's vignette, qualifies as a diagnosis when it is greater than would be expected of a child of her age. Unfortunately, there is evidence that separation anxiety, if not treated, can extend into adulthood in about a third of cases (Shear, Jin, Ruscio, Walters, & Kessler, 2006).

PATTY NEMETH'S DSM MULTIAXIAL DIAGNOSIS IS AS FOLLOWS:

Axis I	309.21 Separation Anxiety Disorder Early Onset
Axis II	V71.09 (No diagnosis)
Axis III	None
Axis IV	Missing school
Axis V	GAF = 60 (current)

© Cengage Learning 2013

OTHER DISORDERS OF INFANCY, CHILDHOOD, AND ADOLESCENCE

There are a number of disorders of infancy, childhood, and adolescence that are relatively rare or in which the practitioner plays a less significant role in the diagnostic process. To complete the practitioner's diagnostic understanding, they are summarized beginning with the feeding and eating disorders of infancy or early childhood.

- *Pica*—Pica is typically defined as the persistent ingestion of nonnutritive substances for a period of at least 1 month. This happens at an age where this behavior is considered to be developmentally inappropriate. For example, eating nonnutritive substances is common and not considered pathological for the child who is 18 months to 2 years of age. Additionally, the child's eating behavior is not considered to be part of a culturally sanctioned practice. The two main signs of pica are the craving and eating of non-food substances. Pica is most frequently seen in children and it appears more commonly in those with developmental disabilities (Young, Wilson, Miller, & Hillier, 2008). Infants commonly ingest paint, plaster, string, hair, and cloth, while the older child tends to consume animal droppings, sand, insects, leaves, pebbles, and cigarette butts. Very often, pica is discovered only after a health problem; for example, the child who suffers from intestinal blockage, intestinal perforation, poisoning, and/or parasitic infection. Not surprisingly, these children may have severe tooth abrasion, small cracks or notches on the teeth, or surface tooth loss (Johnson, Shynett, Dosch, & Paulson, 2007).

- *Rumination disorder*—Rumination disorder involves the repetitive regurgitation of undigested food (or rumination) after the start of a meal occurring for at least 6 weeks within the past 12 months. Onset is usually seen before the child's first birthday. The regurgitation begins within 30 minutes of the completion of a meal and stops within 90 minutes or when the regurgitated food becomes acidic. Sometimes the child spits food out but in other cases it is re-chewed and re-swallowed. Symptoms are not the result of some type of medical condition such as an obstruction or gastroesophageal reflux disease. Regurgitation primarily affects infants, young children, and people with cognitive disabilities such as mental retardation (Chial, Camileri, Williams, Litzinger, & Perrault, 2003; Talley, 2011). The typical age of onset for children is from 3 to 12 months of age, and adolescent onset is at about 12 years of age (Olden, 2001).

We now turn to an overview of the tic disorders.

- *Tic disorders*—The tic disorders are characterized by sudden, repetitive, and non-rhythmic motor movements. Symptoms must be seen before the age of 18, and they cannot result from ingestion of substances like stimulants or from a general medical condition like Huntington's disease. Some tics are invisible to others, such as abdominal tensing or toe crunching. They may also consist of phonic productions such as eye blinking and throat clearing (Malone & Pandya, 2006). Phonic tics may also involve grunting, whistling, or the repetition of complete words or phrases. These tics are also referred to as verbal tics or vocal tics. The most common are facial tics (Kesaree, 2003). Just before onset, most individuals feel an urge that is similar to the need to yawn, blink, sneeze, or scratch. Tics increase in stressful situations—even if they are positive, such as getting excited about a vacation. At other times tics can be seen when the child is relaxed; for example, watching TV. Tics seem to worsen during adolescence, and the symptoms become more unpredictable. There are four types of tics occurring along a continuum from the least to the most severe in terms of impairment in the child's social and interpersonal functioning. The least severe is a **transient tic** that consists of multiple motor and/or phonic tics lasting at least 4 weeks but less than 12 months. Next along the continuum of severity is the **chronic tic,** seen as either single or multiple motor or phonic tics (but not both) and are present for more than 1 year. The most severe is **Tourette's,** which consists of both motor and phonic tics lasting for more than 1 year. The fourth type of tic disorder is referred to as **tic disorder NOS.** This is considered when tics are present but do not meet criteria for any of the more specific tic disorders.

The elimination disorders are reviewed next beginning with encopresis.

- *Encopresis*—Encopresis describes the child who cannot control his or her bowel movements so they pass these bowel movements in their underwear. In most situations, encopresis develops as a result of long-standing constipation. Common symptoms are loose watery stools; involuntary stooling or the need to have a bowel movement with little or no warning, which may cause the child to soil their underwear if they cannot get to the bathroom soon enough; scratching or rubbing the anal area due to irritation; withdrawal from friends, school and/or family; and hiding underwear. The DSM specifies two specific types: with constipation and overflow incontinence, and without constipation and overflow incontinence.
- *Enuresis*—Enuresis is characterized by the involuntary discharge of urine either during the day or at night. Usually the child cannot control the discharge, but in some cases it may be intentional. Much like encopresis, this condition is stressful for both the child and his or her family. Boys are more commonly affected, especially among younger school-age children. Enuresis declines as the child matures, and most children eventually stop bed-wetting on their own. There are three subtypes. The first is nocturnal only. This is seen as the most common, wherein the child wets only during sleep or at night. The second is diurnal in which the passage of urine occurs during the waking hours, most often in the early afternoons on school days. The third subtype is nocturnal and diurnal, which is the combination of both day and night patterns.

There are a number of diagnoses categorized by the DSM as other disorders of infancy, childhood, or adolescence. We begin with selective mutism.

- *Selective mutism*—Selective mutism, formerly known as elective mutism, is characterized by the child's inability to speak in certain settings where speaking is expected while they are able to speak in other settings. For instance, the child may not talk at school but speak freely at home. In some instances, the child may not speak to specific people. These children are often extremely shy. The pattern is serious enough to interfere with school or with social communication, lasting for at least a month but not limited to the first month of school. In addition, this inability to speak is not due to a lack of knowledge of or discomfort with the language required in a social situation.
- *Reactive attachment disorder*—Reactive attachment disorder, sometimes referred to as attachment disorder, is a rare disorder and a fairly new addition to the DSM. This disorder is seen before the age of 5, usually starting in infancy. A key feature is that the child has not bonded to an adult and is unable to trust. Essentially, the child has learned that the adults in his or her

life are untrustworthy. The child's basic needs for comfort, affection, and nurturing have not been met, and loving, caring attachments with others were never established. The child may show markedly disturbed and developmentally inappropriate ways of relating socially in most contexts. This is the child who may watch others closely but does not engage in social interactions or withdraws from others. Alternatively, they may show indiscriminate sociability or be unable to show appropriate selective attachments. In other words, this is the youngster who shows excessive familiarity with virtual strangers by asking if they could hold their hand or go home with them. Children separated, ignored, or neglected by their birth parents (or primary caretakers), and placed in multiple foster homes, or traumatized by physical, sexual, or emotional abuse are at higher risk for developing this disorder. Symptoms begin before age 5 and usually can be seen while still an infant (Boris, Zeanah, & Work Group on Quality Issues, 2005). As children with reactive attachment grow older, they may develop either inhibited or disinhibited types of behavior patterns. Children with inhibited behavior may avoid relationships and attachments to just about everyone. Children with disinhibited behavior will seek attention from just about everyone, including strangers.

- *Stereotypic movement disorder*—Stereotypic movement disorder is distinguished by the child's repeated, rhythmic, purposeless movements such as nail biting, head banging, or body rocking. These movements may ultimately injure the child or interfere with normal activities. Other movements may include playing with the hair (but not to the extent of pulling hair as seen in **trichotillomania**), nose picking, thumb sucking, hand flapping, or self-biting. While stereotypic movements can be seen at any age, they are most common in infants and toddlers. Symptoms must last for at least 4 weeks and cannot be better explained by an anxiety disorder, use of substances, or a medical condition.

- *Disorder of infancy, childhood, or adolescence NOS*—This diagnostic category is used when it is clear that some disorder of infancy, childhood, or adolescence is present but the practitioner does not have enough information to make a more specific diagnosis. As more information becomes available, a more specific diagnosis can be made.

SUMMARY

This chapter looks at the disorders of childhood that the practitioner will most likely encounter in mental health practice. They are:

- *Autism*—A pervasive developmental disorder with onset usually before 3 years of age, autism is characterized by impaired social interaction and communication, and restricted behavior. Children with this diagnosis also show a restricted and limited repertoire of activities and interests.

- *Asperger's disorder*—Asperger's disorder is characterized by autistic-like behaviors wherein the child shows severe defects in social and communication skills that may be accompanied by high intelligence and hyperfocusing on one particular area of interest.

- *Attention deficit hyperactivity disorder*—This disorder characterizes a child who has an unusually high activity level and short attention span. The child may act impulsively and may have behavior and/or learning problems.

- *Conduct disorder*—Children with conduct disorder act inappropriately, infringe on the rights of others, and violate the behavioral expectations of others.
- *Oppositional defiant disorder*—Oppositional defiant disorder characterizes a child who shows a recurring pattern of negative, hostile, disobedient, and defiant behavior that lasts for at least 6 months. The absence of a serious violation of the basic rights of others distinguishes this disorder from conduct disorder.
- *Separation anxiety disorder*—Separation anxiety disorder characterizes a child who has experienced prolonged, developmentally inappropriate, and excessive anxiety and distress regarding removal from parents, home, or familiar surroundings.

The disorders in which the social worker does not play a central role in the diagnostic process or are considered to be extremely rare and more than likely will not be seen in the average social worker's mental health practice have been summarized. They are: Rett's disorder, childhood disintegrative disorder, pervasive developmental disorder NOS, the feeding and eating disorders of infancy or early childhood, tic disorders, elimination disorders, and the category of other disorders such as selective mutism, reactive attachment disorder, stereotypic movement disorder, and disorder of infancy, childhood, or adolescence NOS.

In regard to the DSM-5, one proposal is to develop a single diagnostic category of autism spectrum disorder (ASD) that will incorporate the current diagnoses of autistic disorder, Asperger's disorder, childhood disintegrative disorder, and pervasive developmental disorder (not otherwise specified). Under the proposed new classification, the practitioner would rate the severity of ASD as severe, moderate, or mild. Another proposal is related to attention deficit hyperactivity disorder and is intended to increase the diagnostic criteria for the age when symptoms are present from 7 years to 12 years of age. There are also recommended changes for oppositional defiant disorder. One is to divide the eight symptoms into the following categories: angry/irritable mood, defiant/headstrong behavior, and vindictiveness. The minimum of four symptoms required to meet diagnostic criteria can come from all or just one or two of the proposed categories.

Practitioner's Reflections

The disorders discussed in this chapter represent a broad spectrum of problems for children. These youngsters suffer many problems on a daily basis and often rely on others for help. They might act out in the supermarket or movie theatre, or you might be sitting next to them on an airplane. Perhaps you might be annoyed and start to wonder why the parents do not control their child. This chapter points to the possibilities that a parent might be trying to address a child with more severe disorder such as ADHD or severe disruptive behavior. The next time you see a child being troublesome in public, remember the disorders discussed in this chapter and begin asking yourself what really might be causing this behavior.

Activities

EP 2.1.10
(b) a

1. Sometimes there is a fine line between what might be considered normal behavior and those behaviors that support a DSM diagnosis. This underscores the practitioner's skill in collecting, organizing and interpreting client data. Looking back at the case story of Louie Dessaint, how do you think his behaviors differ from a typical child? Given his life story, can you see any of

Louie's behaviors that might seem normal for a child his age?

2. Children, regardless of their mental status or diagnosis, eventually grow up and mature into adulthood. Do you think persons with pervasive developmental disorders should marry and have children of their own? Explain why or why not.

3. Explain why you think that many of the disorders discussed in this chapter are more commonly found in boys than in girls. How might parents (and teachers) deal differently with boys and girls?

4. Select any one of the case stories representing the disruptive behavior disorders (such as Norman Dixon, diagnosed with conduct disorder, or Jerry Sheppard, diagnosed with oppositional defiant disorder) and discuss with another colleague or your supervisor what challenges you might encounter developing, managing, and maintaining a professional relationship with these clients. Keep in mind the person-in-environment and strengths perspectives as you identify the relationship challenges.

Advanced
Clinical
EP 2.1.1 d

COMPETENCY NOTES

EP 2.1.1 d: Demonstrate professional demeanor in behavior, appearance, and communication (p. 49): Social workers are representative of the profession and commit themselves to the profession's enhancement and to their own professional conduct and growth.

EP Advanced Clinical 2.1.1 d: Develop, manage, and maintain therapeutic relationships with clients within the person-in-environment and strengths perspectives (p. 61): Advanced clinical social work practitioners recognize the importance of the therapeutic relationship and the person-in-environment and strengths perspectives.

EP 2.1.4 c: Recognize and communicate understanding of the importance of difference in shaping life experiences (p. 27): Social workers understand how diversity characterizes and shapes the human experience and how it is critical to the formation of identity.

EP Advanced Clinical 2.1.4 a: Research and apply knowledge of diverse populations to enhance client well-being (p. 44): Advanced clinical practitioners are knowledgeable about the ways in which various dimensions of diversity affect explanations of illness, help-seeking behaviors, and healing practices.

EP 2.1.7 b: Critique and apply knowledge to understand person and environment (pp. 28, 29): Social workers are knowledgeable about human behavior across the life course, the range of social systems in which people live, and the ways social systems promote or deter people in maintaining or achieving health and well-being.

EP Advanced Clinical 2.1.7 c: Consult with medical professionals, as needed, to confirm diagnosis and/or to monitor medication in the treatment process (p. 34): Advanced practitioners understand how to synthesize and differentially apply the theories of human behavior and the social environment (biological, developmental, psychological, social, cultural, and spiritual).

EP Advanced Clinical 2.1.9 a: Assess the quality of clients' interactions within their social contexts (p. 44): Advanced clinical social work practitioners are knowledgeable about how different relational, organizational, and community systems may impact clients.

EP 2.1.10 (b) a: Collect, organize, and interpret client data (pp. 32, 36, 42, 46, 54, 60): Social workers have the knowledge and skills to practice with individuals, families, groups, organizations, and communities.

EP Advanced Clinical 2.1.10 (b) c: Assess client coping strategies to reinforce and improve adaptation to life situations, circumstances, and events (pp. 26, 40, 49, 53): Clinical social work practice involves the dynamic, interactive, and reciprocal processes of therapeutic engagement, multidimensional assessment, clinical intervention, and practice evaluation at multiple levels.

REFERENCES

Alegria, M., & McGuire, T. (2003). Rethinking a universal framework in the psychiatric symptom-disorder relationship. *Journal of Health and Social Behavior*, 44, 257–274.

American Psychiatric Association. (2000). *Diagnostic and statistical manual of mental disorders*, (4th ed., text revision). Washington, DC: Author.

Anastopoulos, A., Sommer, J., & Shatz, N. (2009). ADHD and family functioning. *Current Attention Disorders Reports*, 1 (4), 167–170.

Ashford, J. B., LeCroy, C. W., & Lortie, K. L. (2005). *Human behavior in the social environment: A multidimensional perspective*, (3rd ed.). Pacific Grove, CA: Brooks/Cole.

Barlow, D. H., Pincus, D. B., Heinrichs, N., & Choate, N. (2003). Anxiety disorders: A lifespan developmental perspective. In I. Weiner, (Ed.), *Comprehensive handbook of psychology*, (Vol. 8), (pp. 119–147). New York, NY: John Wiley.

Boris, N. W., Zeanah, C. H., & Work Group on Quality Issues. (2005). Practice parameter for the assessment and treatment of children and adolescents with reactive attachment disorder of infancy and early childhood. *Journal of the American Academy of Child and Adolescent Psychiatry*, 44 (11), 1206–1219.

Brasic, J. R. (2011). Pervasive developmental disorder: Asperger syndrome. Retrieved September 20, 2011, from: http://emedicine.medscape.com/article/912296-overview

Brown, T. E. (Ed.). (2009). *ADHD comorbidities: Handbook for ADHD complications in children and adults*. Arlington, VA: American Psychiatric Publishing.

Canino, G., & Alegria, M. (2008). Psychiatric diagnosis—is it universal or relative to culture? *Journal of Child Psychology and Psychiatry*, 49 (3), 237–250.

Cauce, A., Rodriguez, M., Paradise, M., Cochran, B., Shea, J., Srebink, D., & Baydar, N. (2002). Cultural and contextual influences in mental health help seeking: A focus on ethnic minority youth. *Journal of Clinical Psychology*, 70, 44–55.

Centers for Disease Control and Prevention (CDC). (Summer 2009). Prevalence of autism spectrum disorders—Autism and Developmental Disabilities Monitoring Network, United States, 2006. Morbidity and Mortality Weekly Report (MMWR) Surveillance Summaries, 58 (No SS-10).

Chial, H. J., Camileri, M., Williams, D. E., Litzinger, K., & Perrault, J. (2003). Rumination syndrome in children and adolescents: Diagnosis, treatment, and prognosis. *Pediatrics*, 111 (1), 158–162.

Dixon, A. (2002). Culturally competent practices with children and youth who have serious emotional disturbance. In D. T. Marsh & M. A. Fristad, (Eds.), *Handbook of serious emotional disturbance in children and adolescents*, (pp. 77–92). New York, NY: John Wiley and Sons.

Durand, V. M. (2011). Disorders of development. In D. H. Barlow, (Ed.), *Oxford handbook of clinical psychology*, (pp. 551–573). New York, NY: Oxford University.

Frombonne, E., & Tidmarsh, C. (2003). Epidemiologic data on Asperger disorder. *Children and Adolescent Psychiatric Clinics of North America*, 12 (1), 15–21.

Groleau, D., Young, A., & Kirmayer, L. (2006). The McGill Illness Narrative interview (MINI): An interview schedule to elicit meanings and modes of reasoning related to illness experience. *Transcultural Psychiatry*, 43, 671–691.

Harchik, A., & Solotar, L. (2009). Asperger syndrome and the difficulties of diagnosing and treating related conditions. *Exceptional Parent Magazine*, 58, 56–59.

Harris, S. L. (2000). Pervasive developmental disorders. The spectrum of autism. In M. Hersen & R. T. Ammerman, (Eds.), *Advanced abnormal child psychology*, (2nd ed., pp. 357–370). Mahwah, NJ: Erlbaum.

Henggeler, S. W., & Sheidow, A, J. (2003). Conduct disorder and delinquency. *Journal of Marital and Family Therapy*, 29, 505–522.

Hwang, W. (2006). The psychotherapy adaptation and modification framework. *American Psychologist*, 61, 702–715.

Johnson, C. D., Shynett, B., Dosch, R., & Paulson, R. (2007). An unusual case of tooth loss, abrasion, and erosion associated with culturally accepted habit. *General Dentistry*, 55 (5), 445–448.

Kataoka, S. H., Zhang, L., & Wells, K. B. (2002). Unmet need for mental health care among U. S. children: Variation by ethnicity and insurance status. *American Journal of Psychiatry*, 159, 1548–1555.

Kesaree, N. (2003). Tic disorders. In G. P. Matur & S. Mathur, (Eds.), *Movement disorders in children and adolescents*, (pp. 69–74). New Delhi, India: Jypee.

Kim-Cohen, J., Caspi, A., Moffitt, T. E., Harrington, H., Milne, B. J., & Poulton, R. (2003). Prior juvenile diagnoses in adults with mental disorder: developmental follow-back of a prospective-longitudinal cohort. *Archives of General Psychiatry, 60* (7), 709–717.

Kleinman, A., & Benson, P. (2006). Anthropology in the clinic: The problem of cultural competency and how to fix it. *Public Library of Science Medicine, 3,* 1673–1676.

Klin, A., Volkmar, F. R., & Sparrow, S. S. (2000). *Asperger Syndrome.* New York. NY: Guilford Press.

Lambert, E. W., Wahler, R. G., Andrade, A. R., & Bickman, L. (2001). Looking for the disorder in conduct disorder. *Journal of Abnormal Psychology, 110* (1), 110–123.

Latest Findings in Children's Mental Health. (2004). Institute for Health Care Polity, and Aging Research. Rutgers University. Retrieved September 1, 2011 from: http://www.ihhcpar.rutgers.edu

Lewis-Fernandez, R., Guarnaccia, P. J., Martinez, I. E., Salman, E., Schmidt, A., & Liebowitz, M. (2002). Comparative phenomenology of ataques de nervios, panic attacks, and panic disorder. *Culture, Medicine and Psychiatry, 26,* 199–223.

Loeber, R., Green, S. M., Lahey, B. B., Frick, P. J., & McBurnett, K. (2000). Findings on disruptive behavior disorders from the first decade of the Developmental Trends Study. *Clinical Child and Family Psychology Review, 3* (1), 37–60.

Malone, D. A., & Pandya, M. M. (2006). Behavioral neurosurgery. *Advances in Neurology, 99,* 241–247.

Mattila, M. L., Kielinen, M., Jussila, K., Linna, S. L., Bloigu, R., Ebeling, H., & Moilanen, I. (2007). An epidemiological and diagnostic study of Asperger syndrome according to four sets of diagnostic criteria. *Journal of the American Academy of Child and Adolescent Psychiatry, 46* (5), 636–646.

Maughan, B., Rowe, R., Messer, J., Goodman, R., & Meltzer, H. (2004). Conduct disorder and oppositional defiant disorder in a national sample: developmental epidemiology. *Journal of Child Psychology and Psychiatry, 45* (3), 609–621.

McGlough, J. J. (2005). Adult manifestations of attention-deficit/hyperactivity disorder. In B. J. Sadock & V. A. Sadock, (Eds.), *Kaplan & Sadock's*

comprehensive textbook of psychiatry, (pp. 3198–3204). Philadelphia, PA: Lippincott, Williams and Wilkins.

Melvin, L., (Ed.). (2002). *Child and adolescent psychiatry: A comprehensive textbook,* (3rd ed.). Philadelphia: Lippincott, Williams and Wilkins.

Mick, E., Byrne, D., Fried, R., Monuteaux, M., Faraone, S., & Biederman, J. (2011). Predictors of ADHD persistence in girls at 5-year follow-up. *Journal of Attention Disorders, 15,* 183–192.

Moniz, C., & Gorin, S. (2003). *Health and health care policy: A social work perspective.* Boston: Allyn and Bacon.

Noble, D. N., & Jones, S. H. (2006). Mental health issues affecting urban children. In N. K. Phillips & S. L. Straussner, (Eds.), *Children in the urban environment: Linking social policy and clinical practice,* (2nd ed., pp. 97–121). Springfield, IL: Thomas.

Noble, D. N., Maluccio, A. N., Whittaker, J. K., & Jones, B. L. (2008). Children. In T. Mizrahi & L. E. Davis, (Eds.)., *Encyclopedia of social work (e-reference edition).* Washington DC: NASW Press and New York: Oxford University Press. Retrieved on September 1, 2011 from: http://www.oxford-nasawsocialwork.com

Nock, M. K., Kazdin, A. E., Hiripi, E., & Kessler, R. C. (2006). Prevalence, subtypes, and correlates of DSM-IV conduct disorder in the National Comorbidity Survey Replication. *Psychological Medicine, 36* (5), 699–710.

Nock, M. K., Kazdin, A. E., Hiripi, E., & Kessler, R. C. (2007). Lifetime prevalence, correlates, and persistence of oppositional defiant disorder: results from the National Comorbidity Survey Replication. *Journal of Child Psychology and Psychiatry, 48* (7), 703–713.

Olden, K. W. (2001). Rumination. *Current Treatment Options in Gastroenterology, 4* (4), 351–358.

Polanczyk, G., de Lima, M. S., Horta, B. L., Biederman, J., & Rhode, L. A. (2007). The worldwide prevalence of ADHD: A systematic review and metaregression analysis. *American Journal of Psychiatry, 164,* 942–948.

Pumariega, A. J. (2003). Cultural competence in systems of care for children's mental health. In A. J. Pumariega & N. C.Winters, (Eds.), *The handbook of child and adolescent systems of care,* (pp. 82–104). San Francisco, CA: Jossey-Bass.

Roberts, R., Alegria, M., Roberts, C., & Chen, I. (2005). Concordance of reports of mental health functioning by adolescents and their caregivers: A comparison of European, African and Latino Americans. *Journal of Nervous and Mental Disease*, *193*, 528–534.

Rousseau, C., Measham, T., & Bathiche-Suidan, M. (2008). DSM-IV, culture and child psychiatry. *Journal of the Canadian Academy of Child and Adolescent Psychiatry*, *17* (2), 69–75.

Shear, K., Jin, R., Ruscio, A. M., Walters, E. E., & Kessler, R. C. (2006). Prevalence and correlates of estimated DSM-IV child and adult separation anxiety disorder in the National Comorbidity Survey. *American Journal of Psychiatry*, *163*, 1074–1083.

Simonoff, E., Elander, J., Holmshaw, J., Pickles, A., Murray, R., & Rutter, M. (2004). Predictors of antisocial personality. Continuities from childhood to adult life. *British Journal of Psychiatry*, *184*, 118–127.

Slade, E. P. (2004). Racial/ethnic disparities in parent perception of child need for mental health care following school disciplinary events. *Mental Health Services Research*, *6*, 75–92.

Spencer, T. J., Biederman, J., & Mick, E. (2007). Attention deficit/hyperactivity disorder: Diagnosis,

lifespan, comorbidities, and neurobiology. *Ambulatory Pediatrics*, *7* (1, Suppl. 1), 71–81.

Staudt, M. M. (2003). Helping children access and use services: A review. *Journal of Child and Family Studies*, *12*, 49–60.

Talley, N. J. (2011). Rumination syndrome. *Gastroenterology and Hepatology*, *7* (2), 117–118.

Teplin, L. A., Abram, K. M., McClelland, G. M., Dulcan, M. K., & Mericle, A. A. (2002). Psychiatric disorders in youth in juvenile detention. *Archives of General Psychiatry*, *59*, 1133–1143.

Timmini, S., & Taylor, E. (2004). ADHD is best understood as a cultural construct. *British Journal of Psychiatry*, *184*, 8–9.

Webb, N. B. (2003). *Social work practice with children*. New York, NY: Guilford.

Young, S. S., Wilson, M. J., Miller, D., & Hillier, S. (2008). Toward a comprehensive approach to the collection and analysis of pica substances, with emphasis on geophagic materials. *PLoS ONE*, *3* (9), e3147.

Cognitive Disorders: Delirium and Dementia

CHAPTER 3

INTRODUCTION

It is well known that people today are living longer, and it is not uncommon to find 80-, 90-, and 100-year-olds living active and productive lives. The author's 95-year-old aunt looked forward to her hundredth birthday so that she could get a free hearing aid from her audiologist. How old is old? What does the concept of chronological age really mean? When are people no longer deemed productive or valuable? "Beliefs about aging are maintained by language. Expressions often reserved for older people can be found in metaphors such as the "autumn years" or the "twilight of one's life." Popular characterizations are less favorable terms like "old codger," "curmudgeon," "doddering," or "senile." People today seem more impressed with looking young, staying healthy, and maintaining their productivity. This is often characterized as the search for the proverbial Fountain of Youth. We can find an array of lotions, crèmes, and surgeries all aimed at reversing the aging process. Instead of seeing aging as a normal part of the life cycle, aging is seen as something to be cured. This chapter will review the three classes of disorders that develop much later in life; they are delirium, dementia, and amnestic disorders (amnesia). We begin with a discussion of delirium.

Delirium is characterized as a temporary condition that often follows a short and fluctuating course. People affected with delirium cannot think or reason clearly and consequently lose contact with the world around them. It includes prominent disturbances in alertness, meaning that the individual is confused and disoriented. Those suffering from delirium generally do not know what day it is or where they are. They might be able to focus on one thing, but this focus only lasts a few moments. Additionally, individuals with delirium cannot relate their present situation to anything they experienced in the past—in other words, their thinking is disconnected. One of the ways to recognize the presence of delirium is the person's tendency toward restlessness, agitated behavior, and constant moving around without purpose. This behavior is recognized by others as unusual for that person. Delirium can occur at any age, and under many different circumstances. Its effects are almost always time-limited. Once we saw it as a temporary condition, but we are now finding that the effects of delirium for some individuals can be longer lasting (Cole, Ciampi, Belzile, & Zhong, 2009).

The various types of delirium listed in the DSM-IV-TR (American Psychiatric Association, 2000) are those that are due to a general medical condition, may be substance-induced (including complications from prescribed medication), and have multiple etiologies. Delirium is estimated to be found in as many as 30 percent of older adults admitted to acute care facilities such as hospital emergency rooms (Fearing & Inouye, 2009). This chapter focuses on substance-induced delirium as it is commonly seen by the practitioner in hospital or other medically related settings.

Dementia is an advancing, progressive, and degenerative condition that is marked by a gradual deterioration of a broad range of cognitive abilities. As people age, they continue to develop—and they experience many changes both individually and in their relationships. Their rich personal histories and experiences are a part of their "life story." During the latter part of the aging process, adults will retire from the workforce and may face the loss of support for their role identity. Friends and/or family have either died or moved away, prompting the loss of family relationships and friendships. As health declines, the older person is confronted with the gradual erosion of functioning. Being able to do things that one once did at a younger age becomes a source of pride. Some cultures view the aged as productive members throughout their entire lives and treat them as treasured jewels. Others regard the aged as inconvenient burdens or nuisances.

The population is graying rapidly, and the "very old" is the fastest growing group in the United States. The 2005 U.S. Census Bureau report notes that the population age 65 and older is projected to double in size to about 72 million within the next 25 years (He, Sengupta, Welkoff, & DeBarros, 2005). A little more than 5 percent of people older than 65 in the United states will struggle with dementia, and the rate increases to 20 percent to 40 percent for those who are older than 85 (Richards & Sweet, 2009). Those who are 85 years of age and older are now the fastest-growing segment of the population. It is expected that the number may quadruple by the year 2050 (Brookmeyer, Johnson, Ziegler-Graham, & Arrighi, 2007). Nearly half will have Alzheimer's disease (National Institute on Aging, 2005).

Dementias are characterized by prominent memory disturbances and central nervous system (CNS) damage, and a dementia is likely to have a protracted course. Unlike those with delirium, people with dementia are not disoriented or confused in the early stages. Over time, individuals with dementia experience a global deterioration in their intellectual, emotional, and cognitive abilities. They experience a great deal of difficulty performing tasks that require them to remember or learn things or to use information they once knew. A person with dementia finds it increasingly difficult to maintain attention and sustain this attention. A gradual decline in the normal richness of their thought process takes place.

Dementia has many causes and the various types included in the DSM-IV-TR are:

- Dementia of the Alzheimer's type;
- Vascular dementia;
- Dementia due to HIV, head trauma, Parkinson's disease, Huntington's disease, Pick's disease, Creutzfeldt-Jakob disease, or other general medical disorder;
- Substance-induced persisting dementia due to multiple etiologies.

The competency-based assessment is especially suited to working with people suffering from dementia and their families because of the integration of biological, psychological, social, environmental, and economic concerns. This integration emphasizes individuals and their multiple interactions with their environments. In terms of financial cost, dementia is an extremely expensive disorder because of the use of formal services. This chapter will focus on dementia of Alzheimer's type to underscore the importance of looking at its medical underpinnings.

Like delirium or dementia, **amnestic disorders** are characterized by prominent memory disturbances and complications in level of alertness or other cognitive functions. However, the primary characteristic in this disorder is the individual's inability to remember and perceive things. Typically, the person has difficulty using both short-term and long-term memory. For example, the individual might have an easier time remembering something that happened to them 50 years ago than remembering what they ate for breakfast yesterday. The term "amnestic disorder" is meant to describe a specific defect involving the loss of memory rather than a pattern featuring multiple cognitive impairments. It should be noted that the competency-based assessment of amnestic disorder rules out other symptoms such as **executive functioning** (difficulty in making decisions) or **agnosia** (the failure to recognize family or friends). Features associated with amnestic disorders include disorientation, **confabulation** (filling in memory gaps with invented information), emotional blandness, and apathy. The DSM-IV-TR notes three types of amnestic disorders: (1) amnestic disorder due to a general medical condition; (2) substance-induced persisting amnestic disorder; and (3) amnestic disorder due to multiple etiologies.

Cognitive disorders are characterized by syndromes of delirium, dementia, and amnesia—all of which are caused by either a general medical condition, substance use (both prescribed and illicit, and including alcohol), or a combination of these factors. Disturbances in cognition involve mental confusion, memory impairment, problems maintaining attention, difficulty thinking, and the inability to plan or engage in self-actualized daily living. We begin with a discussion of delirium and how it affects individuals.

DELIRIUM

Delirium is one of the first mental disorders to be documented in history. People with these symptoms are described in writings more than 2,500 years old. Over time, delirium has been known by many different names, including acute confusional state, toxic psychosis, acute brain syndrome, and metabolic encephalopathy. Although the brain may be directly involved (as in the case of a seizure disorder), the actual cause of delirium is usually a process initiated outside the central nervous system. Delirium is known to have many causative factors, including fevers, drug allergies, chemotherapy, anesthesia, and/or the effects of drug use or an overdose of drugs. The delirium process can include effects from hypo- or hyperactive endocrine dysfunction (thyroid disease); infections (meningitis); liver disease (hepatic encephalopathy); renal disease (uremic encephalopathy); vitamin deficiency diseases (thiamine, folic acid, nicotine acid); drug withdrawal or toxicity (anti-cholinergic agents, antipsychotic drugs, and others); poisons (carbon monoxide); and the effects of postoperative states (anesthesia).

These multiple factors highlight the interplay between cognitive functioning and biological influences and underscore the importance of making the competency-based assessment. Of particular importance to the practitioner is a thorough exploration of biological factors. For example, the practitioner considers that those who have high fevers are taking certain medications or are undergoing a surgical procedure. Because delirium can be brought on by the improper use of medications, this diagnosis can be difficult to make in older people because they are likely to be taking prescription medications more than any other age group (Cole, 2004). Most of the medical conditions are potentially treatable; therefore, delirium can often be reversed in a relatively short period of time. Delirium should be thought of as a syndrome and not a disease.

PREVAILING PATTERN

Advanced Clinical EP 2.1.7 c

The characteristic features of delirium underscore the importance of consulting with medical professionals, as needed, to confirm the diagnosis. The disorder is characterized by impaired consciousness and cognition during the course of several hours or several days (Conn & Lieff, 2001; Rahkonen et al., 2000). Perhaps because of its transient nature (i.e., it can occur and then resolve itself quickly), delirium has been difficult to study. Estimates are lacking of the actual number of people affected. However, Barlow and Durand (2012) suggest that delirium is a common disorder and most prevalent in those who undergo general surgical procedures, cancer patients, and people with acquired immune deficiency syndrome (AIDS). Many medical conditions have been linked to the onset of delirium, including intoxication from drugs, toxins, and poisons; withdrawal from drugs; infections; head injuries; and various other types of trauma to the brain. Delirium often signals the presence of a medical situation or a medical emergency that is causing brain dysfunction; thus, it behooves the practitioner to intervene as soon as possible. The pattern of delirium is typically short term, and it is this feature that helps to distinguish it from the other cognitive disorders, particularly dementia. Delirium tends to develop quickly, and its course can vary over the day. Symptoms of delirium tend to worsen during early evening hours or at night (known as **sundowning**), seen as the result of fatigue or a disturbance in the brain's biological clock (Lemay & Landreville, 2010). This sundowner syndrome can also be seen when the person is in an unfamiliar and unstructured environment.

The competency-based assessment pays particular attention to the person's mental status, including **clouding of consciousness** (the inability to focus, sustain, or shift attention). Individuals appear confused, bewildered, or alarmed—and they may have difficulty responding to reassurance or in following directions. Impaired cognition often includes a marked disturbance of recent memory, and the individual may be unable to provide meaningful psychosocial history. They may be disoriented to time and place; their speech may have a rambling or incoherent quality; they may have trouble finding words, or identifying commonly recognized objects or people. Perceptual disturbances may also be present and may include illusions and visual hallucinations. Often, actual perceptions are misinterpreted, and ordinary noises or objects can be perceived as dangerous, threatening, and disturbing. Persecutory delusions based on sensory misperceptions are fairly common. However, once the causative factor is eliminated, the individual gradually returns to his or her prior (or premorbid) level of functioning. Delirium has a short and fluctuating course in contrast to the gradual cognitive decline that characterizes dementia. Associated features include the following:

- *Disturbance in the sleep-wake cycle*—The individual sleeps during the day and remains awake and agitated at night.
- *Disturbance in psychomotor behavior*—The person may appear disorganized, with purposeless movements, or have increased or decreased psychomotor activity.
- *Emotional disturbances*—Periods of irritability (the individual striking out), belligerence (attempting to flee), or euphoria (resulting in being injured, for example, falling out of a bed) can also occur.

The following case vignette is an example of delirium.

| CASE | THE CASE OF SALVADOR CULLOTTO |

Adeline Cullotto brought her husband Salvador to Memorial General Hospital's emergency room. She entered the reception area pleading, "Please, please can someone help my husband? He's talking out of his head, and I don't know where else to go!" The social worker on duty attempted to calm down Mrs. Cullotto, and asked, "Can you tell me what's been happening to your husband?"

Mrs. Cullotto responded, "Well, Sal doesn't know his name, he doesn't know who I am, and he's talking out of his head. He seems very confused. On top of all that, he has not slept a wink all night. I'm really so worried about him. He's terribly frail right now. Do you think he's becoming senile?" The social worker said he needed more information and asked Mrs. Cullotto, "What has been happening recently or differently that might explain your husband's current behavior?"

She replied, "Well, Sal does have some anemia—you know, low blood counts." After a moment of thought, she replied, "Oh you mean like Sal having chemotherapy treatments for leukemia? Now that you mention it, Sal's doctor changed his treatment several days ago, but Sal never had any problems before with medication changes. You know, come to think of it Sal is really out of it. While we were driving over here, he whispered to me, 'The doctor is taking blood out of one arm and putting it right back into my other arm.' Sal made me promise to tell the proper authorities—whoever that is—he says to me not to let them charge us double."

The social worker asked Mrs. Cullotto to explain further. Shaking her head, she continued, "Sal insists that the doctor is selling his blood back. He takes blood from one arm and then puts it right back into the other arm. He doesn't want to let him get away with that." She sighed, "I've never seen Sal like this before. That's really a screwy idea, and I don't know what's gotten into him. He absolutely loves Dr. Canner. He's been taking care of Sal for years." Mrs. Cullotto shared that she and Sal had been married

continued

for 55 years, both are retired (she was a hairdresser, and he was a factory worker). They have one son who lives nearby.

When the emergency room social worker turned to Mr. Cullotto, he asked a series of questions about Mr. Cullotto's memory and orientation. "Sir, what is your name? Do you know where you are right now? Do you know what today's date is? How old are you? What is your wife's name? Do you know what you ate for breakfast this morning? How are you feeling?" The social worker wrote in his progress notes, "Mr. Cullotto appears unable to focus, sustain, or shift his attention enough to answer the questions posed to him. His attention wanders, and he is distracted by room sounds around him. He is unable to follow instructions, complete a thought, or reply fully to questions posed to him.

His speech has a rambling quality and is difficult to follow."

The emergency room social worker reassured Mrs. Cullotto and promised to speak with Mr. Cullotto's doctor. Mr. Cullotto was subsequently hospitalized. When the social worker followed up with the Cullottos after admission, he learned that Mr. Cullotto's chemotherapy protocol had indeed been changed. Two days after admission, Mr. Cullotto's symptoms began to lessen, and he was discharged 3 days later. Upon discharge, Mrs. Cullotto was overheard commenting to her husband, "Sal, it's just so wonderful to see you back to your usual self. You really weren't you, and I was really scared that you were starting to get Alzheimer's disease. Let's go home and order a pizza! Maybe we'll rent that Bruce Willis movie you wanted to see."

EP 2.1.10
(b) a

ASSESSMENT SUMMARY   The practitioner collects, organizes, and interprets a range of client data in order to assess for delirium. The key assessment issue is the recognition of causative factors. (The vignette is intended to illustrate the presenting symptoms of delirium and thus interactions of the biological, psychological, and social elements in Sal Cullotto's life are not illustrated.) A case in point is when the social worker asked Mrs. Cullotto about the strength of her husband's belief that his blood was being sold back to him. The features of Mr. Cullotto's delirium—features in contrast to those of dementia—were that they had an acute beginning, a relatively brief duration, and the minute-to-minute shifting of his mental status. Barlow and Durand (2012) observe, "Concern by medical professionals is increasing—perhaps because of the increased number of adults living longer—leading some to recommend that delirium be included as one of the 'vital signs' (along with heart-beat, breathing rate, temperature, and blood pressure) that physicians routinely check when seeing older adults" (p. 536). Unfortunately, the diagnosis of delirium is all too often missed in medical settings, especially in those individuals who are quiet and subdued as opposed to those who are agitated.

Dementia can be distinguished from delirium by the absence of confusion, but the two conditions may occur concurrently. Assessment for delirium should distinguish it from other mental disorders that present with similar features (e.g., confusion, disorientation, and perceptual disturbances). Intoxication or withdrawal from many drugs of abuse can also cause these symptoms, but the assessment of substance-induced delirium should not be made unless the symptoms exceed those that would be expected during typical intoxication or withdrawal. When schizophrenia is present, the individual's hallucinations and apparent confusion can resemble a delirium, but the individual does not have the disorientation, memory loss, and (daily) sleep disturbance seen in delirium. Those with generalized anxiety disorder may present with agitation, but it is without disorientation, confusion, and memory loss. The specific coding noted in the DSM determines the differentiation:

- Due to a General Medical Condition (293.0) (List/indicate the general medical condition.)
- Substance Intoxication Delirium (291.0) (Code based on the substance used.)
  - 291.0 includes alcohol, amphetamine or amphetamine-like substance.
  - 292.81 includes cannabis, cocaine, hallucinogen, inhalant, opioid, phencyclidine or phencyclidine-like substance, sedative, hypnotic, or anxiolytic, other, or unknown substance.
- Substance Withdrawal Delirium (Code based on specific substance.)
- Delirium Due to Multiple Etiologies (Code based on specific etiology.)
- Delirium Not Otherwise Specified (NOS) (780.09)

If the delirium is caused by a general medical condition, the practitioner should note both the delirium (Axis I) and the identified general medical condition (Axis III) that is judged to be causing the disturbance. For example, if a client has delirium due to congestive heart failure, it would first be noted on Axis I as Delirium Due to Congestive Heart Failure (293.0) and then on Axis III as Congestive Heart Failure (428.9). The practitioner should be certain to record all causative agents on Axis III, as in the case of Mr. Cullotto's chemotherapy.

MR. CULLOTTO'S DSM MULTIAXIAL DIAGNOSIS IS AS FOLLOWS:

Axis I	293.0 Delirium Due to Chemotherapy
Axis II	V71.09 (No diagnosis)
Axis III	208.10 Chronic Lymphocytic Leukemia
	280.9 Anemia
Axis IV	Retired
Axis V	GAF = 35 (on admission), 65 (on discharge)

© Cengage Learning

EP 2.1.10
(b) a

The competency-based assessment model provides a framework to collect, organize, and interpret client data. In this vignette, the practitioner focuses on underlying causative factors as well as the client's environment in order to determine the necessary steps to reverse and correct his or her condition. The challenge for practitioners is to be sure to assess for delirium—if left unrecognized, delirium can often result in serious medical complications or irreversible cognitive impairments. The vignette illustrates questions about Mr. Cullotto's memory and orientation as a part of the assessment process, but it is also helpful for practitioners to gather data from collateral sources such as family members or friends. For example, Mrs. Cullotto was the first one who noticed sudden and observable changes in her husband; that is, she noticed Sal was confused, disoriented, and illogical. Ultimately, Mr. Cullotto experienced a substance-induced delirium in reaction to his new chemotherapy treatment. Once his treatment was adjusted, Sal returned to his prior level of functioning.

DEMENTIA

ALZHEIMER'S-TYPE DEMENTIA

When German psychiatrist Alois Alzheimer first described this disease in 1906, it was considered to be relatively rare. Perhaps this was because life expectancy at the turn of the century was 47 years as opposed to the current figure of 77 years. Of those with dementia, half are found to have **Alzheimer's-type dementia,** which translates to more than 5 million Americans (Alzheimer's Association, 2010). In some forms, people who are in their 40s or 50s can be affected; sometimes referred to as pre-senile dementia. However, Alzheimer's disease usually appears in individuals who are in their 60s and 70s. The disease is more prevalent among women and can be found in all ethnic groups, with slightly lower rates seen among American Indians (Craig & Murphy, 2009; Weiner, Hynan, Beckly, Koepsell, & Kukull, 2007).

There is no foolproof way to diagnose Alzheimer's disease, other than perhaps after death at autopsy, but medical science has made several critical discoveries about how the disease affects and destroys the brain. For instance, a project called the Alzheimer's Disease Neuroimaging Initiative or ADNI uses sophisticated brain scans along with new chemical tracers to help clinicians identify the disease before the significant declines in cognitive abilities become evident (Weiner et al., 2010).

The amyloid cascade hypothesis provides a biological explanation of Alzheimer's disease. Similar to the way cholesterol builds up on the walls of blood vessels and restricts blood supply, deposits of amyloid proteins are believed to cause cell death associated with Alzheimer's (Bourgeois, Seaman, & Servis, 2003). During the late 1980s, scientists isolated and identified a molecule called amyloid precursor protein (APP), which is a normal protein produced by healthy neurons. The human body produces at least three enzymes—dubbed alpha, beta, and gamma secretase—that eventually cleave APP into shorter forms. The exact purpose of these enzymes is not yet known and their specific function remains to be demonstrated conclusively (Nunan & Small, 2000). What is clear is that these secretase inhibitors can build up in the fluid surrounding neurons to form plaques. At one time, the medical community believed that individuals with Alzheimer's disease produced too many of the enzymes known as A-beta, but that has not proved to be the case; in fact, people with Alzheimer's disease produce A-beta at the same rate as healthy people.

Researchers reexamined the issue and found it was not the process of buildup in the fluid surrounding the neurons, but a matter of how these fluids are disposed. In a healthy person, A-beta usually dissolves after it drifts away from the cell—but scientists now find that sometimes A-beta folds into insoluble forms called fibrils, which stick together and form plaques. We all produce some plaques as we go through the aging process. However, problems begin when these plaques trigger an inflammatory response in the brain, generating toxic agents called free radicals, which fight off infections. The free radicals kill off indiscriminately both the fibrils and healthy neurons. Much of the current work in Alzheimer's research involves looking at how a host of agents (such as enzymes, vitamins, heredity, environmental factors, the use of anti-inflammatory drugs, and hormones) play a role in the onset of this disease. Treatment is aimed at preventing the destruction of healthy neurons while stalling the production of A-beta enzymes.

EP 2.1.7 b

Dementia is frequently confused with organic mental syndrome, chronic organic brain disorder, rapid-onset brain syndrome, slow-onset brain syndrome, amnestic disorder (amnesia), and delirium. Perhaps no other mental disorder has been surrounded by such a confusion of inaccurate terminology and interchangeable names, thus underscoring the importance of the practitioner's ability to understand and critically evaluate a person's level of cognitive functioning and environmental influences.

The term dementia is derived from a combination of Latin fragments—*de*, meaning "out of," plus *mens*, meaning "mind," plus *ia*, meaning "state of"—and ends up suggesting that the person is deprived of his or her mind. Recent research regarding brain functioning suggests that several important mental functions are localized in specific areas of the brain and that injury to these areas can result in certain types of cognitive impairment. Our understanding of the brain has greatly improved. We know the brain is divided into many different components, but in order to do its job it must function as a well-integrated system. Clearly, Alzheimer's disease disrupts that functioning. The essential feature of the resulting dementia is deterioration of memory, awareness, thought, and perception—which affects how a person remembers and understands language and how they learn. When that happens, the person loses interest in others and becomes more socially isolated. As the disease progresses, a person can become agitated or confused, depressed, anxious, or even combative. The overall impact on a person's life is tremendous.

The practitioner should consider dementia when the cognitive decline has been present for at least several months and has been shown not to be a manifestation of a fluctuating course of delirium (discussed earlier). Conditions such as Alzheimer's disease often cause degeneration across many areas of the brain, producing a mosaic of cognitive problems. A 1996 Consensus Conference, cosponsored by the National Institute on Aging and the Reagan Institute of the Alzheimer's Association, recommended uniform evaluation procedures and diagnostic assessment for Alzheimer's disease (Wisniewski & Silverman, 1997).

Age-related cognitive decline is important to consider when making a competency-based assessment, in part because many diseases that cause brain deterioration more than likely affect the elderly. In addition to memory loss, at least *one* of the following must be present for a diagnosis of Alzheimer's:

- *Agnosia*—The failure to recognize familiar friends, family members, or commonly used objects (such as eating utensils).
- *Aphasia*—The inability to understand written language, while comprehending speech.
- *Apraxia*—Difficulty coordinating motor behaviors despite intact motor functions and the physical capacity to perform these motor behaviors.
- *Loss of **executive functioning***—Judgment and impulse control are affected, and the ability to analyze, understand, and adapt to new situations is impaired.
- *Other cognitive impairments*—Inability to remember events (even those happening minutes earlier), the loss of appropriate judgment about behavior, confusion and disorientation, and/or difficulties in accurately perceiving spatial arrangements.

As discussed above, the three A's—agnosia, aphasia, and apraxia—are most commonly seen in dementia. They are also most likely to occur later on in a person's dementia experience. Dementia is the reduction or impairment of intellect, emotion, and behavioral functioning severe enough to be detrimental in social, occupational, and other important areas in life. It is almost as if the person has lost his or her "road map of life." The individual experiences difficulty with short-term memory and, to a lesser degree, long-term memory. For example, when short-term memory problems occur, people forget where they left their purse or wallet, forget to turn off the stove (sometimes when the food has been completely cooked), or forget to lock the doors before going to bed. Problems experienced with long-term memory are considered less severe; for example, they cannot remember where they live or how to get home.

Family members or others who are close to a person with Alzheimer's may speak about personality changes which may manifest in a number of ways such as a lack of appropriate grooming. The individual might begin to wear clothing inside out (or no clothing at all), display a major decline in personal hygiene including bowel and urinary incontinence, cease oral care or shaving, and overall be unable to care for him- or herself. It is generally this loss of "good judgment" and lapse of previously "normal" behavior that prompts family members to seek help. In one of the authors' clinical practice, a family member described her loved one in the following manner: "My mother once could vie for the regalness of being the Queen of England. She always had such impeccable table manners and social graces. Now mother eats butter with her fingers, and throws the bread on the floor or tries to stuff peas up her nose." It is often this heartbreak of seeing loved ones unable to sustain their former standard of behavior that is so difficult for the family to endure. Family members often describe the heartbreak of losing their loved one while witnessing the progressive decay of his or her appropriate judgment. In some cases, a person once described as easygoing and friendly may become extremely rigid, anxious, hostile, or aggressive.

Social work practitioners often encounter families struggling with caring for their loved one at home. Having to make the difficult decision to institutionalize a beloved family member with dementia usually occurs when there is an excessive amount of nighttime activity, a history of falls and injuries, immobility or difficulty in walking, incontinence, and a situation of being cared for by a female, usually a relative, who is not physically able to handle someone with limited capacities. Other difficulties encountered by caretakers can include depression, emotional distress, financial worries, loss of work, and family conflict.

Alzheimer's-type dementia will undoubtedly increase in older adults as a result of the increase of "baby boomers" entering the ranks of the elderly (Hebert, Scherr, Bienias, Bennett, & Evans, 2003). Making a competency-based assessment is vitally important to both clients and their families in helping to understand the "personality changes" that will occur. Even though only one person in a marital relationship is likely to have dementia at any given time, the disease has two or more victims—the affected spouse, the caretaker spouse, and the family.

During the early and later stages of Alzheimer's, a person's cognitive deterioration is slow, but it is more rapid during the middle stages (Richards & Sweet,

2009). Practitioners must be able to recognize the various warning signs of Alzheimer's:

The Early Stage

- Memory loss (recent) begins to affect the individual's performance
- Loss of initiative
- Mood or personality changes (e.g., avoiding family or friends)
- Confusion about current circumstances (e.g., being at home)
- Difficulty performing usual chores

The Middle Stage

- Increasing problems recognizing family and/or friends
- Escalating memory loss and confusion
- Increase in making repetitive statements
- Occasional muscle jerking or twitching
- Difficulty in reading, writing, or understanding numbers
- Problems thinking logically
- Difficulty finding "the right words"
- Needs close supervision (e.g., may wander away from home)
- Becomes suspicious, irritable, or restless
- Difficulty with bathing and/or self-care

The Late Stage

- Difficulty swallowing/feeding self and maintaining weight
- Does not recognize family members or lifelong friends
- Does not distinguish familiar everyday objects (e.g., how to use a fork or spoon)
- Becomes incontinent (unable to control bladder and/or bowels)
- Unable to care for self
- Difficulty communicating (e.g., cannot speak or respond to others)

The following vignette illustrates one case of dementia, Alzheimer's type.

CASE | THE CASE OF ZELDA "JEAN" PFOHL

"Mr. Pfohl, why don't you follow me and I'll show you our nursing home facility," said the social worker.

"You know, I'm still not so sure about putting Jean in here," Mr. Pfohl responded. "Actually, I'm really sick about it. This June we'll be married 55 years. You know a lot of people can't say that these days." Mr. Pfohl followed the social worker down a hallway. "Jean and I promised each other if ever the other one should ever 'get so bad' as to need a nursing home—well, we just wouldn't do it. We promised we'd do everything in our power to stay at home

together, but—" Mr. Pfohl started to cry. "Things are just so terrible right now ... I hired a very nice woman who took wonderful care of my wife 6 days a week. She'd cook meals, bathe Jean—she provided 24-hour care—but then one of her own relatives got sick, and she. ... I just can't take care of Jean by myself. I can't even lift her in or out of the bathtub." He stopped walking and braced himself on the handrail. Looking at the floor, he continued in a softer voice. "But the worst part was changing her diapers. I mean, how much can a person deal with? I can't stand to see the one person I love most

continued

in this world reduced to being … a baby. It's just too much … just too much. She's not the Jean I knew. She doesn't recognize our children, the grandchildren, her only great-grandchild—sometimes she doesn't even know ME!"

The social worker found a quiet corner in the home's formal parlor away from the activity of the residents and staff. She invited Mr. Pfohl to sit down and asked him to talk about what made him decide to visit the nursing home.

Mr. Pfohl related, "We had it pretty good for many years. Sure, we had rough times, but mostly times were good for us. We were just two young kids when we married in 1929. Neither one of us finished high school, but not many people did in those days. I left school, got a job—and a model-T Ford—in that order," he chuckled, as his eyes brightened. "Jean was the only girl in her family, and the third of four children. She was like a mother to the other kids. Their parents died with the swine flu epidemic in 1918— Jean was still a baby herself, but she was determined that she and her brothers wouldn't be separated—and by golly they weren't! Once she made up her mind, everybody better watch out."

The social worker listened attentively, and encouraged Mr. Pfohl to go on.

"We've been married 55 years, and for the most part it's been a good marriage. We have two wonderful children. They both live nearby. Our daughter is divorced, but she's doing okay. She has three grown children of her own—and just last summer finished her master's degree in teaching. On top of that, she's a world-class musician." Mr. Pfohl beamed. "We've always been proud of her accomplishments."

The social worker asked about the Pfohls' other children.

"Our son is a doctor, who married his high school sweetheart. At first, we didn't approve of their relationship, but as time went on we could see they really were meant for each other. Now they've got three children and are also doing very well. Since Jean's been having problems, the daughter-in-law has been very helpful bringing food over and whatnot, but how much can we expect her to take care of us? Our grandchildren are wonderful, too—but everybody's got their own lives to live."

The issue of the Pfohls' financial situation had not been mentioned, so the social worker inquired.

"I forgot to mention that Jean got a real estate broker's license after the kids were grown and out of the house. I won't lie, I wasn't too thrilled with her working outside of the home. You know, in those days … but she was stubborn about this. She said she was tired of cleaning the house, and she only wanted to sell real estate for pin money. Ha!" Mr. Pfohl laughed. "She did a pretty good job, too. In a few years, Jean had three or four other people working for her. She'd buy fixer-uppers, do whatever was needed to make them nice, then she'd sell them for a nice tidy profit. Her commissions always went back into buying other houses. I tell you, she had some nose for business. We're lucky we don't have any financial worries, but that's because of Jean—it sure isn't because of what I earned in my seat cover business. She's the brains in our family." He lowered his head, and his voice followed. "That's why her being this way is so hard for me."

After a few moments, Mr. Pfohl said softly, "These were supposed to be our golden years. We used to have lots of friends, and we went out a couple of times a week. I guess I really don't blame anybody, it's just. …"

Sensing a need to explore other areas, the social worker gently shifted the conversation to the kinds of things that told Mr. Pfohl something was happening with his wife—something that was different from her usual behavior.

"I guess I knew things weren't going right when Jean forgot where she left her purse, or when she left the stove on. Five or six years ago, I didn't think too much of it, but then it got worse. A couple of times she almost burned the house down! After that, I wouldn't let her cook anymore." He removed his glasses and wiped his hand across his eyes. "She'd forget who she was talking to on the telephone, or else didn't remember how to get home when she went out on errands. Two times the police picked her up for driving crazy. I had to promise them I wouldn't let her drive anymore. Sometimes I think I was wrong for trying to let her continue to be normal. She's used to going out to show houses and all that—and even after she realized she couldn't do that anymore, sometimes I'd just give her the car keys and hope for the best. I just didn't want to face the truth that she was changing. She isn't the Jean I knew—I've lost my best friend."

The social worker waited a moment for Mr. Pfohl to gather himself, then asked him to describe his wife's behavior in a little more detail.

"Sometimes she's as placid as a lamb, and other times she gets so agitated that she physically lashes out at others trying to help bathe or take care of her. A couple of times she accused me of stealing her money. A few times she got so riled up that I'd give her a little change purse filled with dollar bills. Just being able to touch or feel the money seemed to calm her down. Now, if she tells me I took her money, I show her the change purse and she quiets right down again." Mr. Pfohl's eyes again filled with tears, and he again took his glasses off, this time to clean them with a well-worn wrinkled handkerchief.

"We used to go to all the spring training baseball games; we knew all the players—especially the rookies. We'd do all the typical things, you know, eat hot dogs, drink soda pop, sing along with 'Take Me Out to the Ball Game.' Jean sure loved going to those games. Sometimes we'd take a glove with us to try to catch pop flies. One time we actually caught a ball and gave it to our youngest grandson, Kenny." Mr. Pfohl paused, and said to the social worker, "I feel like I'm about to talk your ears off. I guess I've needed someone to talk to. Am I taking up too much of your time? Do you have someone else you need to see?"

The social worker reassured Mr. Pfohl that she really wanted to hear about what had been happening to him and his wife, and added, "I have as much time as you need. You're my only priority right now."

He continued, "Jean keeps me up at night. Several times she started to open the front door and wander away. I have to watch her real close. I used to let her dress herself, but she'd get things on backwards. Now sometimes she'll just sit naked until I dress her. Until recently, she was able to walk around our condo, but she fell a couple of times—then 3 months ago she broke her arm. Let me tell you, it was no picnic taking care of her with a full arm cast. More times than not, I use a wheelchair to get her around just because she's so unsteady on her feet. It just seems easier than letting her walk. I got one of those gizmos that fits on the back of my car so it makes using a wheelchair easier. But nothing is really easy."

Mr. Pfohl sat quietly, struggling to keep his composure. He was visibly upset, and the social worker reassured him that what he is experiencing is very normal.

"Yeah, that's what everyone says. What I'm feeling is very normal, but it doesn't help when I have to break my promise and put Jean in a nursing home because I'm too weak to take care of her. I used to think of myself as a rock, a strong man—but not anymore." He looked defeated. "I guess that's the real problem of getting old. You start having health problems, financial problems, and problems with things you used to be able to do easy. I haven't had a good night's sleep in months. Jean is really restless, especially at night, and she keeps me up half the night. That's when I knew I had to hire someone to help me take care of her. Now I'm in a real bind because I don't want to put her in a nursing home, but I don't seem to have much choice. Thankfully, money's not an issue. I feel like I've betrayed her somehow, but if I don't get some relief this thing is going to kill us both. I've always heard people say that getting old with the one you love is what it's all about. Well, if you ask me, getting old is really just an awful experience—especially when you have to do it without your best friend."

ASSESSMENT SUMMARY Assessing Alzheimer's-type dementia with accuracy requires the practitioner to first rule out potential medical and neurological explanations. In the usual course of events, the nursing home social worker is among the last professionals to be consulted—and, as happened in the vignette, despite Jean's fall and broken arm, her complete medical and neurological evaluations were not mentioned, thus preventing the social worker from ruling out other general medical problems.

There are several ways to code dementia of the Alzheimer's type, depending on the age of onset and the various accompanying signs and symptoms, such as "uncomplicated, with delusions," "with depressed mood," and "with delirium." A differentiation between early onset (under 65) and late onset (over 65) is particularly important.

An assessment of dementia, at least in an overall sense, is usually not difficult to make—except in the very early stages. Because effects of delirium present with features similar to dementia (disorientation and memory loss), dementia cannot be assessed until after the delirium clears. In addition, agnosia, aphasia, and apraxia are much more common in Alzheimer's dementia than in delirium.

MRS. JEAN PFOHL'S DSM MULTIAXIAL DESIGNATION WOULD BE:

Axis I	294.10 Alzheimer's Dementia, late onset, uncomplicated
Axis II	V71.09 (No diagnosis)
Axis III	331.0 Alzheimer's Disease
	733.10 Fractured left arm
Axis IV	None
Axis V	GAF = Deferred

© Cengage Learning

Advanced Clinical EP 2.1.3 b

In looking at Jean's past and present history, the practitioner can gain a greater insight into her strengths and vulnerabilities. Looking at her current functioning, specific attention focuses on understanding variables in biological, psychological (including cognitive), and social systems. The competency-based assessment notes that Jean has a very strong support system in her husband, Harry, and in her children, who live nearby. Mr. Pfohl is currently in a crisis himself. However, he is very resilient in that he is able to talk openly with the social worker about his feelings and seeks outside assistance. While Mrs. Pfohl is the "identified client," in actuality it is Mr. Pfohl who becomes the focus of the assessment. Several key competencies include his role as the sole caretaker, a strong desire to keep his family together, and his intention to maintain a normal lifestyle. Figure 3.1 shows the interactions of the biological, psychological, and social variables in Zelda Jean Pfohl's life.

VASCULAR DEMENTIA

The second most common type of dementia the social worker may find in practice is vascular dementia, sometimes referred to as multi-infarct dementia. Vascular dementia is caused by at least one stroke and possibly is the result of a series of strokes. Risk factors include diabetes, hypertension (high blood pressure), heart disease, and medical disorders that lead to cerebral emboli. The precise relationship between a cerebral infarct and manifesting dementia requires further research, but such an association has been found (Rubin, 1997).

The differential diagnosis for vascular dementia is that the person's condition worsens in a series of small debilitating steps (as these strokes occur), whereas the deterioration of function is more gradual with Alzheimer's-type dementia.

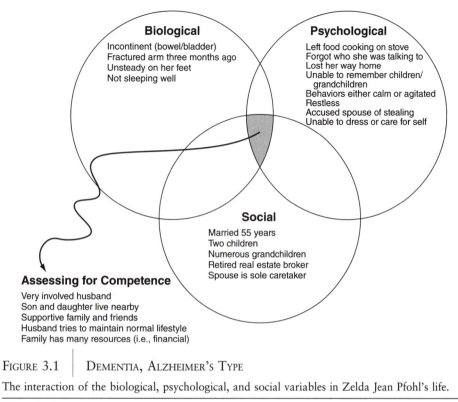

Biological

Incontinent (bowel/bladder)
Fractured arm three months ago
Unsteady on her feet
Not sleeping well

Psychological

Left food cooking on stove
Forgot who she was talking to
Lost her way home
Unable to remember children/
    grandchildren
Behaviors either calm or agitated
Restless
Accused spouse of stealing
Unable to dress or care for self

Social

Married 55 years
Two children
Numerous grandchildren
Retired real estate broker
Spouse is sole caretaker

Assessing for Competence

Very involved husband
Son and daughter live nearby
Supportive family and friends
Husband tries to maintain normal lifestyle
Family has many resources (i.e., financial)

FIGURE 3.1 | DEMENTIA, ALZHEIMER'S TYPE

The interaction of the biological, psychological, and social variables in Zelda Jean Pfohl's life.

© Cengage Learning

DEMENTIAS DUE TO DISEASES OTHER THAN ALZHEIMER'S

Parkinson's disease (with dementia) is a slow and progressive neurological condition characterized by tremors, rigidity, involuntary and rhythmic movements of extremities, motor restlessness, and posturing instability.

Pick's disease usually occurs between ages 45 and 50. Impairments are in memory, concentration, abstract thinking, and speech, along with disorientation and apathy. Pick's is considered a degenerative disease, particularly of the frontal and temporal lobes of the brain.

Creutzfeldt-Jakob disease is a rare illness believed to be caused by a recently discovered agent known as a prion. Individuals lose their mental alertness (often leading to a misdiagnosis of Alzheimer's disease), experience memory loss, and are disoriented. A distinctive feature of this disease is myoclonus, a shock-like contraction of muscles. Myoclonus is not unique to Creutzfeldt-Jakob disease, but, when it is present (in combination with the signs of mental deterioration), it can serve as an indicator of what is happening to an individual.

Huntington's disease is inherited through a single dominant gene, and it is a progressive and degenerative disease that includes difficulties in cognition, emotion, and movement. Symptoms generally begin between 30 and 50 years of age, and death usually occurs within 10 to 20 years of its onset. The individual exhibits involuntary tremors and twitching of the head, torso, and extremities, a lurching gait, and explosive speech. Huntington's is usually associated with excessive levels of dopamine, deficient GABA (or gamma-aminobutyric acid, which functions as the major inhibitory neurotransmitter in the brain), and atrophy in the caudate nucleus and frontal-temporal lobes of the brain.

AMNESTIC DISORDER (AMNESIA)

Although this disorder is relatively uncommon, distinguishing its symptoms from those of delirium and dementia is important. The individual should be described as having an amnestic syndrome when loss of memory is severe and is the most outstanding defect noted. At this point, we know very little about the successful management of persons with amnestic disorders (Burke & Bohac, 2001). However, the competency-based assessment helps the practitioner discern differences between problems that may be psychological in origin and those that might involve organic processes.

There are multiple amnestic syndromes, but the differences among them revolve mainly around what individuals can and cannot remember. The most common example of the amnestic disorder is alcoholic Korsakoff syndrome (also referred to as **Korsakoff psychosis**). This disorder is characterized by the individual's striking inability to form new memories, with subsequent "blank spots," often filled in with confabulation. If amnesia is not detected, the person may suffer residual disabilities and the family may experience unnecessary frustration.

SUMMARY

Delirium can be recognized by its acute onset and its brief duration. Dementia is a more insidious and progressively deteriorating process. Dementia of the Alzheimer's type has been called "the longest good-bye" because its features can last 10 or more years. The person is present in the lives of loved ones but his or her memory and distinctive personality gradually fade away over time. Amnestic disorder is fairly well circumscribed and thus easier to diagnose than delirium or dementia. Recent memory is extremely damaged. However, the individual is able to deal with an immediate situation or problem. This inability to remember underscores the importance of gathering information from collateral sources who know the individual. Chronic alcohol use (Korsakoff syndrome) with insufficient thiamine (vitamin B1) is the most frequent cause of amnestic disorders. Associated features include confusion and disorientation, confabulation (or imagining events), and subtle emotional changes. Two of

the most frequently undetected disorders in the clinical setting are delirium and dementia. While delirium can occur at any age, dementia is generally associated with those over 55. In contrast, the less common disorder, amnesia, is the inability (commonly caused by chronic alcohol use) to learn new information or to recall previously learned material. Table 3.1 summarizes the differential features between delirium and dementia.

Looking to the DSM-5, it is proposed that the label "delirium" is to remain the same but will be combined with the other cognitive disorders, such as dementia and amnestic disorders, and called the neurocognitive disorders. Their dimensions are expected to be specified as either the major or the minor subtype. These proposed changes may be the outcome of the overlap of the different types of dementia and amnestic disorder found in people; that is, one individual may actually be diagnosed with multiple types of neurocognitive problems (Sweet, 2009).

TABLE 3.1 | The Differential Features Between Delirium and Dementia

Characteristics	Delirium	Dementia
Onset	Sudden/acute. Occurs at any age	Insidious. Generally occurs after 55 years of age
Duration	Fluctuates, lasting hours to weeks	Long term; months to years ("the longest good-bye")
Prevailing Pattern	Temporary reversible condition while "causative factors exist." Examples: drug allergies, chemotherapy, anesthesia, substance use	Permanent, irreversible condition
Attention	Lack of direction, distractibility, fluctuates during the day	Relatively unaffected
Speech	Incoherent	Confabulates
Personality Changes	No long-standing change	Person is "shell" of former self
Environment	Difficulties generally do not arise due to short-term nature of syndrome	Interpersonal difficulties. Examples: Caregiver stress, financial worries
Common Features	Memory loss	Memory loss
	Confusion	Confusion
	Decreased alertness and orientation	Decreased alertness and orientation
	Problem with perception, mood, and behavior	Problem with perception, mood, and behavior

© Cengage Learning

Practitioner's Reflections

One of the key challenges the practitioner faces is knowing how to differentiate between delirium and dementia or the related cognitive disorders. The competency-based assessment underscores the importance of exploring biological, psychological, and social influences.

Activities

Advanced Clinical EP 2.1.1 b

Advanced Clinical EP 2.1.4 d

1. As you think about the professional relationship with clients, describe the challenges to a social worker's professional demeanor in behavior and communication when interviewing a client like Mr. Sal Cullotto.

2. Diversity plays a role in working with others. Early research suggests that certain populations, such as the Amish or Native Americans, were less likely to be affected with dementia of the Alzheimer's type (Pericak-Vance et al., 1996; Rosenberg et al., 1996). However, these differences may have actually been related to differences in those who seek assistance, which can be considered unacceptable in some cultural groups. Identify how you would go about engaging someone from another culture to teach you specific perspectives on seeking help for delirium and dementia.

Advanced
Clinical
EP 2.1.7 c

3. Practitioners often are called upon to consult with other medical professionals. Imagine for a moment that you are referring one of your clients with dementia-like symptoms to a neurologist to confirm the diagnosis. How would you present your case?

Advanced
Clinical
EP 2.1.7 b

4. If you were interviewing a family member or someone close to your client who presents with a delirium-like picture, what kinds of questions would you ask to determine the presence of the disorder? Would you interview the client? Explain why or why not.

5. List all of the problems, obstacles, and challenges that you anticipate that Zelda Jean Pfohl and her family (i.e., her husband, their children) might encounter given Zelda's diagnosis of Alzheimer's dementia.

6. Access the CourseMate website at www.cengagebrain.com where the case of "Mike" is highlighted. He is struggling with memory loss after being involved in an accident. Although his work has been affected, notice that he has a number of supports in his life to help him cope with his memory problems. Identify the specific coping strategies that Mike is using to improve his adaptation to living with his memory loss.

Advanced
Clinical
EP 2.1.9 a

Advanced
Clinical
EP 2.1.10
(b) c

COMPETENCY NOTES

EP Advanced Clinical 2.1.1 b: Demonstrate professional use of self with client(s) (p. 81): Advanced practitioners in clinical social work recognize the importance of the therapeutic relationship, the person-in-environment and strengths perspectives, the professional use of self with clients, and adherence to ethical guidelines of professional behavior.

EP Advanced Clinical 2.1.3 b: Identify and articulate clients' strengths and vulnerabilities (p. 78): Advanced practitioners understand and differentiate the strengths and limitations of multiple practice theories and methods, clinical processes, and technical tools, including differential diagnosis.

EP Advanced Clinical 2.1.4 d: Social workers view themselves as learners and engage those with whom they work as informants (p. 81): Social workers understand how diversity characterizes and shapes the human experience and is critical to the formation of identity.

EP Advanced Clinical 2.1.7 b: Critique and apply knowledge to understand person and environment (pp. 73, 82): Social workers are knowledgeable about human behavior across the life course, the range of social systems in which people live, and the ways social systems promote or deter people in maintaining or achieving health and well-being.

EP Advanced Clinical 2.1.7 c: Consult with medical professionals, as needed, to confirm diagnosis and/or to monitor medication in the treatment process (pp. 68, 82): Advanced practitioners understand how to synthesize and differentially apply the theories of human behavior and the social environment (biological, developmental, psychological, social, cultural, and spiritual).

EP Advanced Clinical 2.1.9 a: Assess the quality of clients' interactions within their social contexts (p. 82): Advanced practitioners in clinical social work are knowledgeable about how relational, organizational, and community systems may impact clients.

EP 2.1.10 (b) a: Collect, organize, and interpret client data (pp. 70, 71): Social workers have the knowledge and skills to practice with individuals, families, groups, organizations, and communities.

EP Advanced Clinical 2.1.10 (b) c: Assess client coping strategies to reinforce and improve adaptation to life situations, circumstances, and events (p. 82): Clinical social work practice involves the dynamic, interactive, and reciprocal processes of therapeutic engagement, multidimensional assessment, clinical intervention, and practice evaluation at multiple levels.

REFERENCES

Alzheimer's Association. (2010). Alzheimer's disease facts and figures. *Alzheimer's and Dementia* (Vol. 6). Chicago, IL: Alzheimer's Association.

American Psychiatric Association. (2000). *Diagnostic and statistical manual of mental disorders* (4th ed., text revision). Washington, DC: Author.

Barlow, D. H., & Durand, V. M. (2012). *Abnormal psychology: An integrative approach* (6th ed.) Belmont, CA: Wadsworth Cengage Learning.

Bourgeois, J. A., Seaman, J. S., & Servis, M. E. (2003). Delirium, dementia, and amnestic disorders. In R. E. Hales & S. C. Yudofsky (Eds.), *Textbook of clinical psychiatry* (4th ed., pp. 259–308). Washington, DC: American Psychiatric Press.

Brookmeyer, R., Johnson, E., Ziegler-Graham, K., & Arrighi, M. H. (2007). Forecasting the global burden of Alzheimer's disease. *Alzheimer's and Dementia, 3* (3), 186–191.

Burke, W. J., & Bohac, D. L. (2001). Amnestic disorder due to a general medical condition and amnestic disorder not otherwise specified. In G. O. Gabbard (Ed.), *Treatment of psychiatric disorder*, Vol. *1* (3rd ed., pp. 609–624). Washington, DC: American Psychiatric Press.

Cole, M. G. (2004). Delirium in elderly patients. *American Journal of Geriatric Psychiatry 12*, 7–21.

Cole, M. G., Ciampi, A., Belzile, E., & Zhong, K., (2009). Persistent delirium in older hospital patients: A systematic review of frequency and prognosis. *Age and Aging, 38* (1), 19–26.

Conn, D. K., & Lieff, S. (2001). Diagnosing and managing delirium in the elderly. *Canadian Family Physician, 47*, 101–108.

Craig, M. C., & Murphy, D. G. M. (2009). Alzheimer's disease in women. *Best Practice and Research Clinical Obstetrics and Gynecology, 23* (1), 53–61.

Fearing, M. A., & Inouye, S. K. (2009). Delirium. In D. G. Blazer & D. C. Steffens (Eds.), *The American Psychiatric Publishing textbook of geriatric psychiatry* (4th ed., pp. 229–242). Arlington, VA: American Psychiatric Publishing.

He, W., Sengupta, M., Welkoff, V. A., & DeBarros, K. A. (2005). *65 + in the United States: 2005. U. S. Census Bureau Current Population Reports.* Washington DC: U.S. Government Printing Office, 23–209.

Hebert, L. E., Scherr, P. A., Bienias, J. L., Bennett, D. A., & Evans, D. A. (2003). Alzheimer disease in the U.S.

population: Prevalence estimates using the 2000 census. *Archive of Neurology, 60*, 1119–1122.

Lemay, M., & Landreville, P. (2010). Verbal agitation in dementia: The role of discomfort. *American Journal of Alzheimer's Disease and Other Dementias, 25* (3), 193–201.

National Institute on Aging. (2005). *Alzheimer's disease fact sheet.* Washington, DC: National Institutes of Health.

Nunan, J., & Small, D. H. (October 13, 2000). Regulation of APP cleavage by alpha-, beta-, and gamma-secretases. *Federation of European Biochemical Sciences Letters, 483* (1), 6–10.

Pericak-Vance, M. A., Johnson, C. C., Rimmler, J. B., Saunders, A. M., Robinson, L. C., D'Hondt, E. G., ... Haines, J. I. (1996). Alzheimer's disease and apolipoprotein E-4 allele in an Amish population. *Annals of Neurology, 39*, 700–704.

Rahkonen, T., Makela, H., Pannila, S., Halonen, P., Sivenius, J., & Sulkava, R. (2000). Delirium in elderly people without severe predisposing disorders: Etiology and 1-year prognosis after discharge. *International Psychogeriatrics 12* (4), 473–481.

Richards, S. S., & Sweet, R. A. (2009). Dementia. In B. J. Sadock, V. A. Sadock, & P. Ruiz (Eds.), *Kaplan and Sadock's comprehensive textbook of psychiatry* (9th ed., Vol. I, pp. 1167–1198). Philadelphia: Lippincott Williams and Wilkins.

Rosenberg, R. N., Richter, R. W., Risser, R. C., Taubman, K., Prado-Farmer, I., Dbalo, E., ... Schellenberg, G. D. (1996). Genetic factors for the development of Alzheimer's disease in the Cherokee Indian. *Archives of Neurology, 53*, 997–1000.

Rubin, E. H. (1997). Cognitive disorder: Dementias. In S. B. Guze (Ed.), *Adult psychiatry* (pp. 197–210). St. Louis, MO: Mosby-Year Book.

Sweet, R. A. (2009). Cognitive disorders: Introduction. In B. J. Sadock, V. A. Sadock, & P. Ruiz (Eds.), *Kaplan and Sadock comprehensive textbook of psychiatry* (19th ed., Vol. I, pp. 1152–1153). Philadelphia: Lippincott Williams and Wilkins.

Weiner, M. F., Hynan, L. S., Beckly, D., Koepsell, T. D., & Kukull, W. A. (2007). Comparison of Alzheimer's disease in American Indians, whites, and African Americans. *Alzheimer's and Dementia, 3* (3), 211–216.

Weiner, M. W., Aisen, P. S., Jack, C. R. Jr., Jagust, W. J., Trojanowski, J. Q., Shaw, L., ... Schmidt, M. (2010). The Alzheimer's Disease Neuroimaging Initiative: Progress report and future plans. *Alzheimer's and Dementia, 6* (3), 202–211, e207.

Wisniewski, H. M., & Silverman, W. (1997). Diagnostic criteria for the neuropathological assessment of Alzheimer's disease: Current status and major issues. *Neurobiology of Aging, 18* (4 Suppl.), S43–S50.

SUBSTANCE-RELATED DISORDERS | CHAPTER 4

INTRODUCTION

Drug abuse and addiction is one of our most challenging public health problems. The total overall costs of substance abuse in the United States, including productivity and health, and crime-related costs are estimated to be over $600 billion annually. This includes approximately $181 billion for illicit drugs (Office of National Drug Control Policy, 2004), $193 billion for tobacco (Centers for Disease Control and Prevention, 2007), and $235 billion for alcohol (Rehm et al., 2009). Most of us have used psychoactive substances (which alter mood and/or behavior) at one time or another. For instance, most of us start the day with a cup of coffee to help us wake up; or maybe we have an alcoholic drink in the evening with friends to socialize and relax. Some of us smoke "grass" (marijuana), snort some "candy" (cocaine), or swallow a little "black beauty" (amphetamine) occasionally. We rationalize that it's all right as long as it does not interfere with our job or relationships with others. Most of us do not abuse drugs. However, some people do abuse drugs or use them illegally—conservative political radio talk show host Rush Limbaugh made headlines over illicit drug use. In early 2006, Limbaugh accepted a plea bargain for charges of "doctor shopping." He agreed to submit to periodic drug testing and treatment as a part of the agreement. A few months later, Limbaugh was detained at the Palm Beach, Florida airport for carrying unlabeled prescription drugs, which turned out to be Viagra (to treat erectile dysfunction), and did not have his name on the label in an effort to protect his privacy. Limbaugh's very public struggle with substance use raises an interesting question: Are people increasingly turning to drugs to solve their problems?

In 1992, Congress established the Substance Abuse and Mental Health Services Administration (SAMHSA) under the Department of Health and Human Services in order to collect, analyze, and disseminate public health data. Estimates of current trends show that through 2009, 19 million Americans had used an illicit substance at least once during their lifetime, representing an almost 12 percent increase since 2002 (SAMHSA, 2009). That represents a large percentage of the U.S. population—making illicit drugs a part of the lives of a lot of people. Further, an estimated 22 million Americans age 12 and over used illegal drugs at least once a month in 2009. In addition, between 20 percent and 50 percent of all hospital admissions are related to the effects of alcohol abuse and/or addiction (Galanter & Kleber, 2008; McKay, Koranda, & Axen, 2004).

The critical question is: Who among those who use drugs is likely to become dependent on them or addicted to them? Looking at drug habits as defined by the *Diagnostic and Statistical Manual* (DSM), Wilens (2004, 2006) suggests that between 10 percent and 30 percent of adults in the United States have a **substance use disorder**. Unfortunately, drug abuse and dependence represent a major public health problem affecting many people from all walks of life. Among the U.S. population, 35 percent of men and 18 percent of women are predicted to develop a substance use disorder at some point in their lives (Rhee et al., 2003). The use of chemicals alters the way we feel and see things, and a person may not want to stop using them, even when they cause serious physical and social problems. A person can become addicted to legal drugs prescribed by a physician just as readily as they can to illegal drugs. Many people become addicted to things (such as alcohol, cigarettes, or smokeless tobacco) that they don't even think of as drugs. Some may be surprised to learn that nicotine is rated ahead of methamphetamine and crack cocaine as the most addictive of drugs. Then, there are all the legal substances that, when used improperly, can become addictive (e.g., inhalants like nail polish, certain types of glue, or gasoline).

THE ESSENTIAL FEATURES OF SUBSTANCE-RELATED DISORDERS

The DSM-IV-TR (American Psychiatric Association, 2000) section dealing with substances is structured differently from other sections we have covered; therefore this chapter is organized in a way that differs from the previous chapters. The DSM describes 11 classes of substances and polysubstances, but there is not a discrete diagnosis for each class of substance. (Refer to Table 4.1.) Notice that the DSM section for Substance-Related Disorders is first divided on the basis of the nature of the disorder—that is, the problems either arise from *use* of the substance (e.g., alcohol) or are *induced* by the substance (e.g., amphetamine-induced auditory hallucinations). Then, for those disorders related to the use of a substance, there are two descriptive categories to choose from in making a diagnosis: dependence or abuse. Likewise, for those disorders induced by a substance, there are two categories describing the effect: intoxication or withdrawal.

The process of making a diagnosis, then, begins with the name of the substance followed by the related syndrome or set of symptoms (i.e., dependence, abuse, intoxication, or withdrawal). For example, if someone were compulsively using cocaine to the point that it was causing significant problems in his or her life, then the diagnosis would be cocaine dependence. In order to refine a diagnosis even further, the DSM then adds any specifiers that may apply. Say the person who has been diagnosed as cocaine-dependent is now in the early stages of recovery, still

TABLE 4.1 | OVERVIEW OF THE DSM-IV-TR ORGANIZATION OF THE SUBSTANCE-RELATED DISORDERS

The Eleven Classes of Substances

Alcohol
Amphetamines
Caffeine
Cannabis
Hallucinogens

Inhalants

Nicotine
Opioids
Phencyclidine
Sedatives/Hypnotics/Anxiolytics
Polysubstance (3 or more
    substances used)

The Specifiers

Early Full Remission
Early Partial Remission
Sustained Full Remission
Sustained Partial Remission

Substance Use Disorders

Dependence (3 in 12 months)

Tolerance
Withdrawal
Use more than planned
Enduring desire/unsuccessful
    in reducing use
Time devoted to substance-
    related activities
Minimal/reduced involvement
    in career/leisure activities
Continued use despite
    negative impact

Abuse (at least 1)

Impaired primary roles
Recurrent use of drugs/
    alcohol in hazardous
    situations
Substance-related legal
    problems
Continued substance
    use despite knowing
    it has negative impact

Substance-Induced Disorders

Intoxication

Develop reversible
    substance-specific
    syndrome
Maladaptive behavior
    or psychological
    changes
Symptoms not due
    to a general medical
    condition or other
    mental disorder

Withdrawal

Develop substance-specific
    syndrome due to stopping
    or reducing heavy
    substance use
This substance-specific
    syndrome causes distress
    or impairment (i.e.:
    social, work)
Symptoms not due to a
    medical condition or
    other mental disorder

© Cengage Learning

having some lingering problems (i.e., has used cocaine within the previous 12 months), but has not used cocaine for at least one month. Then the specifier would be noted as early partial remission. This is often referred to as the "mix and match approach." Later in this chapter, two case studies, one for each of the two categories of substance-related disorders, will be presented to facilitate understanding the key symptomatic features of substance use and applying the competency-based assessment model.

ORGANIZATION OF SUBSTANCE USE DISORDERS

The **substance use disorders** are characterized either by dependence or by abuse. **Substance dependence** involves continued use, craving, and other cognitive, behavioral, and physiological symptoms that occur through the use of certain drugs, alcohol, medications, and toxins. Dependence is often referred to as addiction. **Substance abuse** is the excessive use of a drug or its use for purposes not medically intended. It is a pattern of substance use that results in recurrent and significant adverse consequences associated with frequent use of substances (e.g., drinking alcohol in the morning to reduce a hangover or just to help start the day—and that hangover might be the upshot of a weekend of binge drinking).

DEPENDENCE SPECIFIERS   Where a diagnosis of substance dependence is considered, the nature of that dependence must be determined. The DSM specifiers are "with physiological dependence" or "without physiological dependence"—and the distinction between the two is revealed in the presence or absence of symptoms of tolerance or withdrawal (American Psychiatric Association, 2000):

- *With physiological dependence*—This specifier is used when substance dependence is accompanied by evidence of **tolerance** (defined as either the need for markedly increased amounts of the substance to achieve intoxication/ desired effect, a markedly diminished effect with continued use of the same amount of the substance) or **withdrawal** (defined as the development of a substance-specific syndrome due to the cessation of or reduction in substance use that has been heavy and prolonged. The substance-specific syndrome causes clinically significant distress or impairment in social, occupational, or other important areas of functioning). Alternatively, the same (or closely related) substance is taken to relieve or avoid withdrawal symptoms. Tolerance or withdrawal from a substance may be associated with a greater risk for medical problems and relapse.
- *Without physiological dependence*—This specifier should be used when there is *no* evidence of tolerance or withdrawal, rather the individual's substance dependence is exhibited in a pattern of compulsive use characterized by at least *three* of the following features:
  - The substance is often taken in larger amounts or over a longer period of time than was intended.
  - There is a persistent and/or unsuccessful desire to cut down or control use of the substance.
  - A great deal of time is spent in activities necessary either to obtain the substance (such as visiting multiple doctors or driving long distances), to use the substance (such as chain smoking), or to recover from its effects.

- Important social, occupational, or recreational activities are given up or reduced because of substance use.
- The substance use is continued despite knowledge of having a persistent or recurrent physical or psychological problem that is likely to have been caused or exacerbated by the substance (e.g., continuing to drink alcohol despite knowing that a stomach ulcer will be aggravated by it).

COURSE OF DEPENDENCE OR ABUSE   The first year following a diagnosis is when a person is at a particularly high risk for relapse, so the DSM allows for the complexities often seen in the person's remission and recovery. The course of an individual's substance dependence or abuse is described in terms of remission, and is specified in one of the following four ways:

- *Early full remission*—This is used if no criteria for dependence or abuse have been met for at least 1 month, but for less than 12 months.
- *Early partial remission*—This is used if, for at least 1 month but less than 12 months, one or more criteria for dependence or abuse have been met (but the full criteria for dependence have not been met).
- *Sustained full remission*—This specifier is used if none of the criteria for dependence or abuse have been met at any time during a period of 12 months or longer.
- *Sustained partial remission*—This is used if full criteria for dependence have not been met for a period of 12 months or longer; however, one or more criteria for dependence or abuse have been met.

TREATMENT SPECIFIERS   There are two additional variables that may apply in making an accurate diagnosis for substance dependence or abuse: whether the person is on agonist therapy or in a controlled environment.

- *On agonist therapy*—This specifier is used if the person is on a prescribed **agonist** medication (a substance that acts to "trick" the body into reacting as if the endogeneous chemical were present) such as methadone and no criteria for dependence or abuse have been met for that particular class of medication for at least the past month (except tolerance to, or withdrawal from, the agonist). This category also applies to those being treated for dependence using a partial agonist or an agonist/antagonist (a substance that essentially blocks the effects of a chemical already working within the body).
- *In a controlled environment*—This is used if the person is in an environment (e.g., a therapeutic community or locked hospital unit) where access to alcohol and controlled substances is restricted and no criteria for dependence or abuse have been met for at least the past month.

ORGANIZATION OF SUBSTANCE-INDUCED DISORDERS

The substance-induced disorders are categorized in the DSM according to the manifested effect of the substance on the individual. They are:

- **Substance intoxication**—This refers to the occurrence of a reversible substance-specific syndrome due to recent ingestion or exposure to a substance.

TABLE 4.2 | SUBSTANCE-INDUCED DISORDERS IN OTHER SECTIONS OF THE DSM

Substance-Induced Disorder	Diagnostic Classification Section
Delirium	Delirium, Dementia, and Amnestic and Other Cognitive Disorders
Persisting Dementia	Delirium, Dementia, and Amnestic and Other Cognitive Disorders
Persisting Amnestic Disorder	Delirium, Dementia, and Amnestic and Other Cognitive Disorders
Psychotic Disorder	Schizophrenia and Other Psychotic Disorders
Mood Disorder	Mood Disorders
Anxiety Disorder	Anxiety Disorders
Sexual Dysfunction	Sexual and Gender Identity Disorders
Sleep Disorder	Sleep Disorders

© Cengage Learning

- **Substance withdrawal**—Withdrawal is manifested as a substance-specific maladaptive behavior change with both physiological and cognitive elements that are due to the cessation or reduction of heavy and prolonged substance use.

Some substance-induced disorders can cause symptoms that are characteristic of other disorders (e.g., taking certain medications can cause delirium). When that is the case, the disorder is not diagnosed as substance-related but according to the class of Delirium, Dementia, and Amnestic and Other Cognitive Disorders. Table 4.2 summarizes the substance-induced mental disorders that are more appropriately classified in other sections of the DSM-IV-TR.

The symptoms of substance-induced disorders are specified according to the conditions present at onset (American Psychiatric Association, 2000):

- *With onset during intoxication*—If a symptom arises while taking a substance and then gradually abates after dosing stops, it is likely to be part of intoxication.
- *With onset during withdrawal*—If the symptom arises after stopping the substance, or reducing its use, it is likely to be part of withdrawal.

POLYSUBSTANCE-RELATED DISORDER

Earlier, Grant and Pickering (1996) conducted a longitudinal study of alcohol use and found that 23 percent of respondents with a lifetime alcohol use disorder also had another drug use disorder. More recent studies continue to describe polysubstance use among those who struggle with alcohol dependence (Staines, Magura, Foote, Deluca, & Kosanke, 2001). Practitioners increasingly find that many of their clients are using multiple substances instead of using only one. The DSM now provides a diagnostic category called **polysubstance dependence**. In order to make this diagnosis, the person must be using (or abusing) at least three groups of substances (excluding caffeine and nicotine). Although polysubstance use is considered to be a problem, little is known at present about how various substances are used with one another (Barrett, Darredeau, & Pihl, 2006) or how they interact with one another (Barrett, Gross, Garand, & Pihl, 2005; Cole, Sumnall, Smith, & Rostami-Hodjegan, 2005).

OTHER DIAGNOSTIC CONSIDERATIONS

In some situations a person may have other mental problems in tandem with the substance-related disorders, and that individual is given a dual diagnosis. An example of such a case appears later in this chapter—the case of Chris Oghia describes someone suspected of having an avoidant personality disorder in addition to being alcohol dependent; however, at the time the diagnosis was made, the social worker had not been able to distinguish all of the symptoms of a comorbid disorder, so it was listed as "rule out avoidant personality disorder" on Axis II.

ORGANIZATION OF SUBSTANCES   In the interest of simplicity, the 11 classes of substances listed in the DSM have been organized in this chapter into the five basic categories that practitioners encounter most frequently in practice. They are:

1. *Depressants*—includes alcohol and sedatives, hypnotics and anxiolytics.
2. *Stimulants*—includes amphetamines, cocaine, nicotine, and caffeine.
3. *Opioids*—includes heroin, opium, codeine, and morphine.
4. *Hallucinogens*—includes marijuana/cannabis, LSD, and others.
5. *Other drugs*—includes inhalants and phencyclidine.

SOME KEY CONCEPTS   There is a unique language used by those who practice in the field of substance-related disorders. Diagnosing someone and attempting to classify their use of chemicals with varying intensity is challenging; therefore, a common language to describe drug abuse and dependence problems is helpful. We have already touched briefly on these key terms, but their importance in this chapter and in the diagnostic process can benefit from elaboration.

- *Abuse*—This occurs when a person uses a drug without a legitimate medical need to do so. Alcohol is a little different; abuse can be defined as drinking in excess of accepted social standards. Barker (2003) characterizes substance abuse as a maladaptive pattern of using certain drugs, alcohol, medications, and toxins despite their adverse consequences. As such, substance abuse is considered less problematic than substance dependence in that tolerance and withdrawal symptoms have not yet occurred.
- *Dependence*—While there is some disagreement about how to define addiction or substance dependence (Strain, 2009), it is generally seen as the continued use; craving; and other cognitive, behavioral, and physiological symptoms that occur through the use of certain drugs, alcohol, medications, and toxins. Symptoms may include preoccupation about the substance; taking greater amounts than intended; persistent efforts to control its use; reducing occupational or social activities; and continued use despite recognizing that it is causing recurrent physical, psychological, or social problems.

Dependence is characterized by impaired control over taking a substance, a preoccupation with the substance despite adverse consequences, and distortions in thinking.

- *Intoxication*—Intoxication is characterized by specific behavioral patterns and symptoms; these may include cognitive impairment, emotional lability, belligerence, impaired judgment, and poor social or occupational functioning due to recent use of a drug, alcohol, medication, or toxin.
- *Withdrawal*—Substance withdrawal is typified by significant patterns of physical discomfort and emotional distress, cognitive impairment, emotional lability, belligerence, impaired judgment, and poor social or occupational functioning. These behaviors are a consequence of the person's reduced or discontinued use of a specific drug, alcohol, medication, or toxin.

EP 2.1.3 a

Diagnosing someone with a substance-related disorder is difficult, and critical thinking plays an essential role in the diagnostic process as the social worker distinguishes, evaluates, and integrates multiple sources of information, including both research-based and practice wisdom. In sum, the competency-based assessment helps the practitioner to look at the full range of the person's experiences with a particular drug (legal and illegal), alcohol, medication, and/or toxin. The competency-based assessment provides a framework for the practitioner to take into account—in addition to the symptoms of the particular syndrome—the multiple personal, relational, social, medical, legal, financial, and/or occupational problems that are often at the center of the substance-related disorders.

Now that we have addressed the organization of substance-related disorders and introduced the language and key concepts used in their assessment and diagnosis, we will look at each topic and each of the five drug categories in turn. The discussion begins with an overview of the substance use disorders.

SUBSTANCE USE DISORDERS

The diagnostic class of substance use describes those disorders that are associated with the pathologic use of psychoactive substances where the person shows maladaptive behavioral changes. Typically described as addiction, dependence is often accompanied by the symptoms of tolerance and withdrawal. The defining characteristic is one of compulsive drug use that significantly interferes with the person's life. Substance abuse can be seen as a residual category in which maladaptive patterns of psychoactive substance use have never met the criteria for dependence. Intoxication is the physiological reaction to ingested substances (commonly known as getting "high"). Withdrawal happens when the person stops or reduces heavy and prolonged substance use and is distinguished by changes in behavior along with physical and cognitive changes.

PREVAILING PATTERN

The use of substances is widespread and generally on the rise. The Substance Abuse and Mental Health Services Administration (SAMHSA) surveyed the use and frequency of the consumption of alcoholic beverages and other drugs and found that the rate of alcohol use as well as the number of drinkers in the general population has steadily increased since 1997. Results from the 2008 National Survey on Drug Use and Health (SAMHSA, 2009) reported that over 205 million or 82.2 percent of the general population over age 12 reported ever using alcohol; over 17 million were heavy users (or 6.9 percent). In the past year, slightly over 25 million persons (10.3 percent) reported using marijuana, followed by 5.26 million using cocaine (2.1 percent), 1.11 million using crack (0.4 percent), and 453 thousand (0.2 percent) using heroin. In essence, alcohol remains the most used and abused substance in the United States, followed by marijuana. Overall, these statistics point to the pervasiveness of substance use in our society.

According to the American Psychiatric Association (2000), "Individuals between ages 18 and 24 have relatively high prevalence rates for the use of virtually every substance, including alcohol" (p. 205). The typical age of onset for a substance use disorder is during late adolescence or early adulthood (Corcoran & Walsh, 2006), and individuals who develop a substance use disorder in adolescence are at a higher risk to continue it into adulthood (Brook, Brook, Zhang, Cohen, & Whiteman, 2002; Rohde, Lewinsohn, Kahler, Seeley, & Brown, 2001). Some people do develop a substance use disorder in middle age or even late adulthood (Mirin et al., 2002). There is no clear-cut relationship between the development of dependence and abuse; for example, it has been found that only a minority of alcohol abusers (30 percent) will eventually meet criteria for dependence (Corcoran & Walsh).

Advanced
Clinical
EP 2.1.7 b

In order to fully appreciate the many factors related to developing a substance use disorder, the competency-based assessment organizes the practitioner's understanding of the interplay of theories of human behavior and the client's social environment. For example, there is growing evidence that suggests genetic factors contribute between 50 percent and 60 percent of vulnerability to alcoholism (Foroud, Edenberg, & Crabbe, 2010). While genetic predisposition does seem to play some role, the process is a lot more complex than originally thought. The substance use disorders cannot be linked definitively to a specific gene—however, a person with a family history of substance use is at higher risk for developing a substance use disorder.

EP 2.1.9 a

Social workers are also aware of contexts that shape practice. In particular, practitioners attend to the social factors that have been identified as contributors to the development of substance disorders. For example, drug-addicted parents spend less time monitoring their children than parents without drug problems, and this seems to be an important contribution to early substance use in adolescents (Barnes, Hoffman, Wolfe, Farrell, & Dintcheff, 2006). To some extent, all psychoactive drugs provide a pleasurable experience and the social contexts for drug taking may also encourage its use (Strain, 2009). Looking at development over the lifespan, alcohol affects people differently at different life stages. For example, we do know that the brains of adolescents continue developing into young adulthood and they also tend to engage in risky behaviors, such as alcohol and drug use. Windle and Zucker (2010) observe that adolescents tend to experience the effects of alcohol differently from adults; that is, they are less sensitive to the negative effects of drinking such as sleepiness but are more likely to have trouble with more complex tasks such as driving.

Similarly, neurobiological influences play a role in the substance-related disorders. The pleasurable experience in taking psychoactive substances helps to explain why some people continue to use them (Strain, 2009). The pleasure center in the brain is believed to include the dopaminergic system and its opioid-releasing neurons, which begin in the midbrain ventral tegmental area and then work their way forward through the nucleus accumbens and then on to the frontal cortex (Strain, 2009). Researchers are only beginning to understand how different drugs affect different neurotransmitter systems that converge to activate the pleasure pathway, which is primarily made up of dopamine-sensitive neurons.

Temperament has also been considered as a factor in the etiology of substance abuse and addiction. One personality trait closely related to the substance disorders is impulsivity; generally referred to as risk-taking, lack of planning, chaotic lifestyle, desire for immediate gratification, and explosiveness (Ivanov, Schultz, London, & Newcorn, 2008). Research has found that measures of impulsivity can be found in people with substance dependence, craving, and withdrawal symptoms (Moeller et al., 2001; Petry, 2001).

EP 2.1.4 c

Diversity shapes the client's experience, and the social worker understands its importance in shaping the client's life experiences. Gender, for example, plays a role. Corcoran and Corcoran (2001) found that gender rather than race (African American and Caucasian) was the determining factor in starting substance use. Women are more apt than men to start abusing substances because of problems with coping (e.g., many women with substance use disorders have a history of physical or sexual abuse, both as children and as adults). Orwin, Miranda, and Brady (2001) studied the impact of prior physical and sexual victimization on substance abuse treatment and found that 42 percent of the women in their research sample had been sexually abused. Women also develop substance use problems in the context of their relationships. Ashley, Marsden, and Brady (2003) found that many have become involved with drugs or alcohol through their partner. Women also tend to bear the burden of family responsibilities.

Sociocultural factors also play a role in influencing attitudes toward substance use. The elderly, for example, present certain challenges for the practitioner. Many elderly people are at risk for developing polysubstance problems due to their misuse and abuse of alcohol in combination with prescription medications and over-the-counter remedies (Memmott, 2003). Observes Westermeyer (as cited in Castillo, 1997), "A person's decision to use a mood-altering substance is made within a sociocultural context. Each society has its own values, beliefs, and customs regarding the use of mood-altering substances, as well as differences in the availability" (p. 161). Cultural attitudes and beliefs also play a role when diagnosing substance use in the elderly. Vinton and Wambach (2005) observe that many health care providers are reluctant to bring up the issue of substance abuse with elderly clients because of the lack of a perceived benefit from treatment (such as rehab) or improvement in quality of life as a result of this kind of intervention. Further, who wants to entertain the thought that his or her grandparent is addicted to drugs and/or alcohol? Moreover, the reliability of an elder self-report may be questionable. It can be difficult to determine if the physical and cognitive problems found in the elderly are due to the normal process of aging or if they are the effects of consuming a substance. According to Corcoran and Walsh (2006), "denial, sense of stigma, social desirability effects (or the need to say the right thing), and memory loss can affect the accurate recollection or admission of alcohol problems among the elderly" (p. 310). It is anticipated that the number of adults who are over 50 and encounter problems with substance use will increase. The Woodstock generational cohort, popularly known as the baby boomers, is comfortable taking medications for a wide range of problems—and as a result, they are more vulnerable to abusing substances later in life. The 55-year-old celebrity Rush Limbaugh mentioned at the beginning of the chapter was legally charged with prescription drug fraud in connection with his addiction to painkillers. He is considered representative of the new kind of patient who is now showing up in treatment centers.

Other populations are also affected by substance use. Lesbian women, gay men, and bisexual and transsexual persons (LGBT) are at increased risk for substance abuse, primarily because one of the few legitimate places for meeting and socializing with others remains the gay bar scene, with its association with alcohol. The LGBT community is also vulnerable to the loss of friends and acquaintances, both inside and outside their support network. In addition, many LGBT individuals do not have the full range of support commonly found in family, friends, coworkers, and neighbors—which often leaves them feeling isolated and alone and may contribute to substance use as a way of coping.

The ecological factors of poverty and limited resources also tie in to the incidence of substance use. Wright (2001) describes the effects of cultural factors and poverty influencing substance abuse among African Americans. In addition, poor neighborhoods have a high concentration of liquor stores, thus making access to alcohol easier.

In sum, substance use disorders are associated with a wide range of factors in a person's life, including, for example, genetics, individual traits or temperament, gender, family history, sociocultural attitudes, and neighborhood. The competency-based assessment provides a framework for the practitioner to evaluate and understand the complicated reasons a person misuses drugs and alcohol. Drug dependence and drug abuse represent different ends of the same disease process.

SUBSTANCE DEPENDENCE

The DSM-IV-TR describes substance dependence as "a maladaptive pattern of substance use, leading to clinically significant impairment" (American Psychiatric Association, 2000, p. 197). The person continues to use drugs (or alcohol) even when substantial related problems have developed. Dependence is the body's physical need for, or addiction to, a specific agent. As mentioned earlier, the term *addiction* is used interchangeably with dependence. It is not unusual for the practitioner to work with clients who have addictions that are not related to drugs or alcohol (e.g., to chocolate, sex, gambling, television, or even shopping). The number of things that can be addictive highlights the role that culture plays in determining a person's addiction. For example, each society has its own values, beliefs, and customs regarding mood-altering substances. In some Islamic countries it is considered sinful and immoral to drink alcohol, while smoking hashish is acceptable behavior (Castillo, 1997). Without a doubt, just the opposite is true in the United States.

Tolerance and withdrawal are the two main features of substance dependence. Tolerance is the need for increased amounts of a substance to attain the desired effect—or a decreased effect from the amount of substance typically used. Withdrawal symptoms emerge with decreased use. The person is also deemed dependent when unsuccessful in trying to decrease use, and when he or she spends more and more time trying to obtain the substance. Substance-dependent individuals retreat from their usual social and recreational activities and continue to use the substance even when they know that physical or psychological problems can develop. People can even become dependent on over-the-counter drugs if they are abused. Over time, substance dependence can cause physical harm (such as deterioration in overall health), behavior problems (such as mood swings), and harmful changes in social interactions (such as neglecting family or friends to spend time with others who also abuse drugs).

Not all individuals who use and abuse substances become dependent on them. **Chipping** is a term used to describe a pattern of drug use in which the user is not physically dependent and is able to control his or her consumption of a drug (e.g., the person who uses substances for relaxation and not as an escape from facing a particular problem).

Substance dependence may be physical, psychological, or both. **Physical dependence** occurs when the person regularly uses drugs and his or her body becomes accustomed to its effects—consequently, the person must then continue to use the drug in order to feel "normal." Absence of the drug triggers symptoms of withdrawal and produces intense cravings, which are intensified by stress. **Psychological dependence** has developed when the habitual use of a drug results in the person becoming emotionally reliant on its effects, either to elicit pleasure or to relieve pain. In essence, the psychological dependence means that the person perceives him- or herself as incapable of functioning without the drug.

Addictive substances create a brief rush of euphoria, called a "high." Although this high may last only a few minutes, it produces longer-lasting effects in the brain. Addictions are understood as learned habits that, once established, become difficult to extinguish; the effects on the brain also play a role in dependence. Eventually, addiction takes on different dimensions: (1) the development of established and problematic behavior that is both pleasurable and reinforcing, (2) the presence of both physical and psychological components, and (3) the interactions among all of these aspects that sustain the addiction.

Essentially substance dependence is a cluster of cognitive, behavioral, and physiological symptoms that develop as an individual continues using the substance (or substances) despite significant substance-related problems. According to the DSM IV-TR (American Psychiatric Association, 2000), substance dependence is a maladaptive pattern of use leading to clinically significant impairment or distress as manifested by three (or more) of the following features occurring at any time in a 12-month period:

1. Signs of tolerance, as defined by either of the following:
   a. A need for markedly increased amounts of the substance to achieve intoxication or desired effect.
   b. Markedly diminished effect with continued use of the same amount of the substance.
2. Symptoms of withdrawal, as evidenced by either of the following:
   a. The characteristic withdrawal syndrome for the substance.
   b. The same (or closely related) substance is taken to relieve or avoid withdrawal symptoms.

3. Use of more of a substance than planned (e.g., when a person continues to drink until severely intoxicated despite having set a limit of only one drink). In other words, the substance is taken in larger amounts and/or over a longer period than was intended.

4. Continuing desire and/or unsuccessful efforts to cut down or control the use of the substance. Many people develop a history of unsuccessful attempts to decrease or discontinue use of a substance. (Note that *craving* is a commonly used term for a strong drive to use the substance, although it is not a specific criterion for substance dependence.)

5. More and more time invested in obtaining and using the substance, whether because of the need for visits to multiple doctors to get prescriptions, or to drive long distances to hook up with a supplier, or to set aside time to use the substance (e.g., chain smoking), or to require time to recover from its effects (e.g., hangovers). Virtually all of the person's daily activities revolve around the substance.

6. Giving up or reducing important social, occupational, or recreational activities (e.g., spending more time with substance-using friends, giving up hobbies, or withdrawing from family activities).

7. Failure to abstain from using the substance despite having evidence of the problems that it is causing (e.g., recurrent cocaine use despite knowledge of cocaine-induced depression, or continued alcohol use despite recognition that it exacerbates a gastric ulcer).

People can become dependent on every substance and class listed except caffeine. However, certain classes of substances cause symptoms that are less prominent than others, and in some instances not all symptoms apply—for example, withdrawal symptoms are not specified for hallucinogen dependence.

SUBSTANCE ABUSE

Abuse is the excessive use of a drug or using it for purposes for which it was not medically intended. All racial, economic, and cultural groups are affected. Substance abuse describes a pattern of use leading to significant problems or distress (e.g., suspension from school, erratic work performance, arguing or physically fighting with relatives or friends about the consequences of abusing a substance, neglecting one's children, arrest for disorderly conduct, or being in situations that are physically hazardous such as driving while impaired). Legal or illegal substances can be abused. Abuse simply refers to the intense desire to obtain increasing amounts of a substance (or substances) to the exclusion of everything else. Alcohol is the most common legal substance to be abused.

There are a number of behaviors that can indicate that someone is having a problem with substance abuse. Although each individual's experience may be different, practitioners should be alert to the following signs that a client may be abusing one or more substances:

- Attitude changes, such as becoming more irritable
- Secretive behavior or frequent trips to the bathroom and other private places
- Decline in physical appearance and hygiene

- Changes in how one dresses, such as constantly wearing sunglasses to hide dilated (or constricted) pupils or wearing long sleeves to hide injection marks
- Getting high on drugs or intoxicated with alcohol on a regular basis
- Lying, especially about how much of a substance one is using
- Avoiding family members and friends
- Withdrawal from responsibility
- Giving up activities that one enjoyed in the past
- Talking a lot about using drugs or alcohol
- Believing that one needs to drink or use a drug in order to have fun
- Pressuring others to drink or use drugs
- Having legal problems related to substance use (e.g., driving under the influence [DUI])
- Taking risks while under the influence of a drug, such as driving
- Declining work performance due to substance abuse (whether it occurs before, during, or after work)
- Missing work (e.g., calling in sick on a Monday) due to substance abuse
- Changing school performance (e.g., repeated absences or declining grades)
- Borrowing money frequently
- Stealing
- Feeling depressed, hopeless, or suicidal

Abuse is considered when the symptoms have never met the criteria for substance dependence.

The substances (listed from most frequently to least frequently abused) are (Nestler & Malenka, 2004):

- Alcohol
- Nicotine (in the form of tobacco, particularly cigarettes, but increasingly, chewing tobacco and snuff)
- Caffeine (such as coffee, tea, or caffeineated soda)
- Marijuana (cannabis, or the active ingredient THC [tetrahydrocannabinol])
- Hallucinogens (LSD, Mescaline, psilocybin [mushrooms], phencyclidine [PCP or Angel Dust])
- Cocaine
- Amphetamines
- Opiates and narcotics (such as heroin, opium, codeine, meperidine [Demerol], hydromorphone [Dilaudid], oxycontin)
- Anabolic steroids
- Barbiturates, tranquilizers
- Inhalants (such as hair spray, paint thinner, nail polish remover, glue, solvents, propellants, correction and lighter fluid, paint)

Onset of substance abuse is typically in late adolescence to early adulthood, but can occur later in life as well. MSNBC (2006) reported, for instance, that of the 495,859 emergency-room hospital visits in the United States in 2004 for the nonmedical use of pharmaceuticals, 32,556 visits were by people aged 55 to 64, and 31,203 were by people older than 65. In addition, many older people take multiple medications and consume alcohol, and adverse alcohol-drug interactions can put them in the hospital. It is not uncommon for the elderly to share drugs with one another, which contributes to use of unprescribed prescription drugs and/or use of drugs for unapproved purposes. In addition, the elderly are especially vulnerable to substance abuse because the aging process itself produces traumas (such as isolation or the death of friends and family) that place them at higher risk than would have been the case earlier in their lives.

In summary, the key features of substance abuse are the repeated negative consequences a person experiences resulting from a maladaptive pattern of substance use. The negative consequences can include multiple social, occupational, and legal problems. For diagnostic and assessment purposes, these problems must occur during a 12-month period.

The following vignette describes Chris Oghia's struggle with alcohol and illustrates the diagnosis of substance dependence.

| CASE | THE CASE OF CHRIS OGHIA |

It is Susan's last day on the job. She has been promoted to an administrative position in her agency and will no longer be seeing clients. As she cleans out her desk in preparation for moving upstairs, she spots a small crumpled piece of paper in the bottom of a drawer. It's a note she wrote almost a year and a half ago reminding her to call back a client by the name of Chris O. "Chris Oghia," she says softly, as the memories of the case flood back into her mind. It feels as if she saw him just yesterday.

Chris is not someone you can easily forget. He was always on time for his appointments, and (unlike many of her court-mandated clients) Chris seemed eager to work on his problems. He was articulate and reflective as he spoke about his struggles with alcohol and the problems they caused him.

At his first visit with Susan, Chris was a 32-year-old white male who was referred to the agency for counseling by the courts. He had been convicted for driving while intoxicated—apparently his car was weaving and crossing over the center line. Fortunately, it was late at night when there was hardly any traffic on the road. However, his erratic driving was noticed by a police officer who pulled Chris over.

"Do you know why I stopped you?" The officer shined his flashlight into the car, checking for any open alcohol bottles or cans. Chris's slurred speech added to the officer's suspicions, so Chris was asked to step out of the car. The dashboard camera in the patrol car later proved that Chris stumbled getting out of his car. With his unsteady gait and smelling

of alcohol, Chris did not even think to object to a roadside sobriety test. The video showed that he had a hard time walking a straight line, let alone putting his finger on his nose. The Breathalyzer showed an illegal level of intoxication, confirming the obvious. Chris was arrested immediately, his third for DUI.

When he went to court, the judge sentenced Chris to a 6-month work/release program and mandated therapy during that time. Chris had never had any type of counseling before.

During their first interview, Susan had taken Chris's psychosocial history, which revealed that Chris had started abusing alcohol when he was a freshman in high school. He had been drinking excessively ever since (almost 15 years at the time). Chris's father always said a real man could handle his liquor—and Chris had grown up watching his father and grandfather down a "couple of shots and a beer" together after work. To Chris, that kind of hard drinking was a sign of manhood.

After high school, Chris landed a good job in construction and then married his high school sweetheart, Katie Rose. They had two children right out of the box, but after 5 years the marriage ended in divorce—partly because Katie Rose couldn't tolerate Chris's drinking. The next 5 years were a blur. Chris loved his kids and tried to maintain contact with them. After the divorce, Katie Rose struggled to make ends meet—so it was understandable that she would get angry with Chris when support payments

continued

were either late or skipped entirely. Katie Rose would immediately petition the court; it had almost become a routine.

In the meantime, Chris was struggling to work his construction job and go to school at the same time. He realized that he was going to need a college degree if he wanted to support a family—and he had discovered pretty early during that first semester that he couldn't continue to drink the way he had been and "do school."

Chris hadn't had anything alcoholic to drink for about 6 months when he met Diane. She was fun and crazy, and she made Chris laugh—something he felt he deserved after everything that had happened. From Chris's point of view, everything finally seemed to be coming together for him. He and Diane got along great together, and gradually he started sharing a few beers with her at the end of the day. Chris really liked Diane's parents, too, and they made him feel just like family. Diane's Mom had trouble sleeping, so the doctor had prescribed some sleeping pills for her, which she usually swallowed with a cocktail (occasionally watered down with club soda). Diane's mother was usually "in the bag" by about ten in the evening. Her father got started much earlier in the day. He believed that a beer or two was the best way to kick back and relax—and he usually started relaxing right after breakfast. For Chris, things were starting to feel like home.

Chris had been fairly successful at keeping his drinking under control when he and Diane were first married, but after their daughter Sylvia was born he began to feel the pressure of being responsible for yet another child. For most of his life, Chris had felt like a failure. Even though he always loved his job in construction and had dreamed that maybe someday he could start his own company, he never really saw himself going any further in life—until college opened his eyes. With the encouragement of one of his professors, Chris discovered creative talents that he never knew he had.

Somehow, Chris eventually completed college and landed a job in a large advertising firm in New York City. Chris was quite talented and everyone at the agency could see that he had real potential. Over time, the office staff and assistants realized that

there were going to be some occasions when Chris needed them to "cover" for him—and nobody minded. Chris was a great guy. His bosses overlooked his slow starts at the beginning of the week, and, despite frequent absences (usually on a Monday after a weekend of heavy drinking), Chris had been steadily promoted. Seven years passed.

When Chris first came to see Susan, he was responsible for the national promotional campaign for a popular brand of wines, and was involved in designing the product displays you see in stores. He seemed to have a good eye for what would appeal to people. Chris consumed little alcohol during the day, but would begin drinking beer as soon as he got home from work (much as his father and grandfather had done). Chris readily admitted to Susan that there had been several weekend episodes of binge drinking as well as occasional blackouts. She remembered very clearly what Chris said in that first interview about his drinking. "When I drink, I don't have a care in the world. Nothing really bothers me. I'm on top of the world! It's when I'm not drinking that my troubles come back, so I drink again. You know, the problems will always be there, but when I'm drinking I don't have to think about them. That's why I drink."

Chris didn't seem to mind the hangovers. His solution was to have a little "hair o' the dog that bit him" (yet another drink to chase off the headache and grogginess). Diane had cut back on alcohol when she was pregnant, and then stopped drinking altogether shortly after Sylvia's arrival. Over the years, it had gotten so that Diane and Chris were not much company to each other. It seemed to Diane that he was drinking more and more, and they were arguing more and more—usually about his drinking. Chris made a rule that he would stop drinking by midnight, but Diane would often awaken in the wee hours and hear the ice tinkling in his glass downstairs.

They really had no social life. Chris pretty much just sat with his drink after work and on weekends, and he convinced himself that it was no big deal to Diane because she was always so absorbed with Sylvia. Diane worried about Chris's health. He started losing weight and gobbled down antacids like they were gumdrops. Chris would complain about a gnawing pain in his stomach between his breastbone and his navel. Sometimes the pain radiated to his back. After a particularly heavy bout of drinking, Chris experienced a bitter-tasting regurgitation. But he never complained, he just swallowed it back down.

Susan was packing some books into boxes as she recalled how Chris had described himself to her that first day as a "quiet guy." Susan smiled at the memory because, at the time, he was so sincere. "When things get really bad between me and Katie Rose—you know, my ex-wife—I just want to be by myself. I'll find some isolated place to go and just be alone. I'm a loner," he had said as if he believed it. However, he later admitted that he really enjoyed being around people. His friends from work all liked to stop off at a bar for a pick-me-up before going home. Chris's eyes literally sparkled as he recounted, "I'm usually the last guy to arrive because of my overseas phone calls and whatnot—and, I gotta say, it warms my heart to walk in the door and

have everybody yell out, 'Hey, Oggie's here! Set him up, Charlie.' Charlie's been the bartender there since the place opened—way before I moved here." Chris seemed to love the idea that there was a place where he felt welcome, no questions asked. He confessed, "Drinking helps me feel more like one of the guys. Let's face it, I'm a small-town guy … pretending to be a big shot in Manhattan. It's just a lot easier for me to make friends when I'm loosened up."

By the time Chris completed the mandated counseling program, he had not had a drink for one month. However, he told Susan at their last session, "I recognize I've got a lot of work to do. My relationship with Diane isn't great … I feel like I've neglected Sylvia … and I know I have to find a better way of dealing with Katie Rose and the kids."

Susan had been very encouraged when Chris said he'd decided to continue their counseling sessions on a voluntary basis.

Advanced Clinical EP 2.1.10 (b) c

ASSESSMENT SUMMARY   Although the focus of this case discussion revolves around Chris Oghia's struggle with alcohol, the discussion also points to his coping strategies and areas where the social worker might be able to help him improve his adaptation to life circumstances and events. When Chris was initially pulled over for erratic driving, he showed signs of alcohol intoxication. His recent ingestion of alcohol was evident by the "smell" of alcohol on his breath when the police officer approached him. Chris's speech was slurred, and when he got out of his car he was unsteady on his feet. The officer asked him to walk a straight line and then put his finger to his nose. Chris was not coordinated enough to do either, so he failed the roadside sobriety test. He was subsequently arrested.

Chris's pattern of drinking at the time appeared to be related to significant behavioral changes in his life; a prior divorce, responsibilities for three children, a stressed relationship with his current girlfriend (now wife), health problems, and legal charges for driving while intoxicated, to name a few. However, for almost 15 years, Chris had been suffering from alcohol dependence. Although Chris promised himself that he would stop drinking at midnight, it was usually in the predawn hours when he actually stopped or simply blacked out. He had been able to stay away from alcohol when he met his girlfriend, Diane, but 6 months later he returned to his prior drinking habits. Subsequently they both started to argue over his drinking. Chris had been married before and divorced his first wife due to his drinking. This relationship was currently troubled. His first wife routinely pressed charges against Chris for failure to provide support payments for the two children they had together. Chris also had several outstanding legal charges due to his drinking. By the time he was mandated to attend counseling, he had three convictions for driving while intoxicated. Remarkably, Chris was doing well on the job, although his superiors overlooked his frequent absences at the beginning of the week, usually on a Monday. Chris began to lose weight, complained of abdominal pain, and experienced waterbrash (or bitter regurgitation): all symptoms of a gastric ulcer. He chewed antacids with limited relief. Despite this discomfort, he continued to drink.

As is common for those with alcohol dependence, Chris reported a family history of substance use. His father and grandfather drank and conveyed to Chris that "real men" enjoyed a "shot and a beer" at the end of the day. Chris's drinking affected important interpersonal areas of his life. Relationships with his ex-wife and current wife were strained due to his drinking. He faced legal charges due to drinking while under the influence of alcohol. Although he wanted friends, Chris reported being a loner and described himself as shy. Drinking made him feel more confident and able to make friends, although these friends were much like him. An underlying disorder of avoidant personality disorder was considered. However, the practitioner deferred making this diagnosis until Chris experienced a period of time without alcohol in order to determine whether the symptoms of the personality disorder would emerge with abstinence.

The diagnosis of substance abuse would be made if Chris had not exhibited the full spectrum of compulsive alcohol use, indicating dependence. The criteria for substance abuse consider only the harmful consequences of repeated use rather

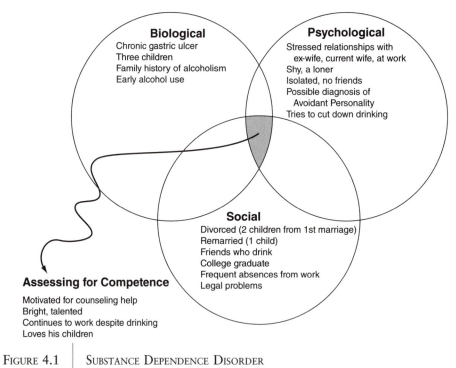

FIGURE 4.1 | SUBSTANCE DEPENDENCE DISORDER

The interactions of the biological, psychological and social variables in Chris Oghia's life.

than tolerance, withdrawal, or a pattern of compulsive use. Chris was starting to drink more. He tried to stop drinking by midnight but was really unable to stop until the predawn hours, and the relationship with Diane was becoming increasingly stressed due to his drinking.

Despite a pattern of alcohol dependence, Chris was able to work steadily and was even given the responsibility for major marketing campaigns. Although their relationship was troubled, Diane stayed with him. Chris also worked hard to remain connected to his children. When Chris completed the course of mandated counseling, he had not been drinking for at least 1 month but for less than a year. He recognized that he needed to address the other problems in his life related to alcohol and planned to continue seeing the social worker. At that point, the specifier, early partial remission, could be applied to his diagnosis. Figure 4.1 illustrates the interactions of the biological, psychological, and social variables in Chris Oghia's life. It also identifies the areas of competency Chris possesses—the strengths that he can draw on to succeed in his battle against alcohol dependence.

CHRIS OGHIA'S MULTIAXIAL DSM DIAGNOSIS IS AS FOLLOWS:

Axis I	303.90 Alcohol Dependence, Early Partial Remission
Axis II	V71.09 (No diagnosis)
	Rule out Avoidant Personality Disorder
Axis III	531.70 Ulcer gastric, chronic
Axis IV	Legal problems—DUI; failure to consistently pay child support
Axis V	GAF (on admission) 50

© Cengage Learning

SUBSTANCE-INDUCED DISORDERS

The substance-induced disorders are characterized by their development in connection with the use of particular substances, their presence only when the person uses substances, and the person's (supposed) improvement during the initial weeks of abstinence. However, research has shown that the substance-induced disorders tend to co-occur with other mental disorders, such as mood, anxiety, delirium, dementia, amnesia, psychosis, sexual dysfunction and/or a sleep disorder (Bakken, Landheim, & Vaglum, 2003). For example, de Graaf and colleagues (de Graaf, Bijl, Smit, Vollebergh, & Spijker, 2002) examined risk factor profiles of pure and comorbid mood, anxiety, and substance use disorder over a 12-month period in the general population and found high levels of comorbidity among the disorders. The assessment of the substance-induced disorders poses particular challenges for the practitioner. While making the distinction between substance-induced disorders and other mental disorders may not be particularly useful (Stefani, 2000), distinguishing between the symptoms of the co-occurring disorders and the symptoms of the substance-induced disorders has implications for assessment. For example, symptoms of substance-induced delirium are described (and coded) under the DSM category of the cognitive disorders.

SUBSTANCE INTOXICATION

The person with substance intoxication experiences impaired judgment, mood changes, and lowered motor ability, which creates problems with walking and even talking. The state of being intoxicated may appear different depending on the drug taken, how much is ingested, and the particular individual's biological reactions.

The key features of substance intoxication are clinically significant maladaptive behavioral or psychological changes resulting from ingestion of a specific substance. These maladaptive changes are found in social or occupational impairment, mood instability, cognitive impairment, or belligerence. Cognitive impairment can include changes in perception, wakefulness, attention, or judgment. These maladaptive changes must be present for the diagnosis of substance intoxication to be considered. This diagnostic category does not apply to nicotine.

SUBSTANCE WITHDRAWAL

Withdrawal is classified in the DSM-IV-TR as both a symptom of substance dependence and as a disorder on its own (American Psychiatric Association, 2000). Key features of the disorder of substance withdrawal are the cognitive, physiological, and behavioral changes that take place when bodily concentrations of a substance decline after one stops a pattern of prolonged use. The actual withdrawal symptoms vary according to the specific substance used. Most symptoms are the opposite of those seen in intoxication with the same substance. For example, someone who is loud-mouthed and aggressive with alcohol intoxication may become increasingly more subdued as he or she stops ingesting alcohol and withdraws from it.

The diagnosis of substance withdrawal is applied to the following groups of substances:

- Alcohol
- Amphetamines and related substances
- Cocaine
- Nicotine
- Opioids
- Sedatives, hypnotics, or anxiolytics

The following vignette describes Janet Sellar's struggles with repeatedly using four groups of substances (alcohol, amphetamines, sedatives, and hallucinogens) during the past 12-month period.

CASE | THE CASE OF JANET SELLAR

On the surface, Janet Sellar's life appears to be ideal. At age 42, she is the office manager for a busy medical practice where she is held in high esteem among the entire staff, especially by the doctors and nurses. She has this uncanny ability to work with just about everyone. Her husband, Jerry, is a very successful accountant who frequently keeps long hours in the office, particularly around tax time, when weeks can pass without the couple seeing each other at all. Their combined incomes make it possible for them to live in a gated community in west Kendall, a comfortable and affluent suburb south of Miami. The couple has three sons, Scott (9), Chris (12), and Mike (15). Janet had always wanted a girl, but was afraid to take a chance with another pregnancy after Scott was born. So she and Jerry adopted a Korean girl, Stephanie, who is the light of their lives. At age 5, Steph is an exotically beautiful and precocious child who is extremely popular in her kindergarten class.

Behind this picture-book façade, however, all is not as it seems. This successful middle-class family has a serious problem known only to Janet and a small number of her closest friends. The Sellars' difficulties developed gradually at first, but one day their lives would change dramatically and forever. Things had started to fall apart when Janet was diagnosed as being HIV-positive. When their oldest son, Mike, was born, she had developed some medical problems that required several blood transfusions—one of which, it turned out, was tainted. At this point in time, her CD4 counts are such that she does not have AIDS, but naturally she worries about the day when her disease progresses to the next stage. She does receive routine medical care to monitor her status, but not from any of the physicians she works for. Janet decided she wanted to, as she says, "keep the personal from the professional." Her current medications include protease inhibitors and anti-retrovirals for the HIV.

All seemed to be progressing until a recent incident. Janet had a setback with her HIV diagnosis and was afraid that she had developed full-blown AIDS. She began to feel depressed and described symptoms of major depression on one of her regular visits to her doctor. "I feel like I've lost all my energy—and it's getting harder and harder to get up and go to work. ...I've always loved my job but I just don't enjoy it anymore." Janet continued, "I feel worthless and tainted—what if I end up with AIDS?" The doctor asked if she was having any other problems, and Janet admitted that she had also started having problems falling asleep, and her appetite was spiraling out of control. She had started gaining weight. She tried to explain that she enjoys her home and is extremely proud of her children, but "lately nothing seems to give me pleasure." When Janet revealed that she was plagued with thoughts of suicide, her physician immediately referred her to a psychiatrist who prescribed the antidepressant Zoloft and Ambien, a sedative for sleep.

Janet begged her physician to prescribe some kind of diet pills for her, but he was reluctant to do so because of the antidepressant medication. He finally agreed on Didrex (benzphetamine), a medication related to the amphetamines but less addictive if taken as prescribed. However, working in a doctor's office, Janet knew that she could ask one of her employing doctors "for a favor" to prescribe the same diet pills. She was afraid of running out of pills, and this way she had a backup source to hold her over until her medical doctor would agree to write another prescription.

As happens with most antidepressant medications, results were painfully slow in surfacing. During the time she felt depressed, Janet stopped taking her HIV medications, fatalistically stating that she had no interest in "prolonging the inevitable." Janet also stopped believing that the Zoloft would ever work for her, and she made a mental note to be sure to tell her psychiatrist at the next appointment. Jerry didn't seem to be able to cope with the entire situation because it seemed to Janet that he was staying at the office later and later.

When her friends saw what was happening, they decided to try to cheer Janet up by taking her out to some of the hot spots where dancing and "being seen" were an important part of the evening. This seemed to lift her spirits a little at first—but it was during one of these girls' nights that Janet was introduced to the hallucinogenic drug, ecstasy. Her friends meant well and only intended to try and keep her spirits up. Soon, Janet started telling Jerry she was going out for "tea with the girls." That tea turned out to be cocktails—and more often than not, ecstasy. With the drugs in addition to the alcohol, Janet's mood certainly changed, but not in the direction that her friends had hoped. She began to show a severe and unpredictable temper.

She often took this explosive anger out on the boys by being verbally aggressive toward them. Sometimes she would scare them by becoming physically aggressive. She would punch doors or the kitchen counter with her fist. Janet's temper seemed to flare with greater frequency and intensity when she drank. Most evenings, Janet would drink to the point where her speech was slurred, she was unsteady on her feet, and she was forgetful. The boys tried to stay out of her way when she was like this. They usually retreated to their rooms to watch TV or play video

continued

games. Left alone, Janet found that a little "Adam" (ecstasy) would lift her spirits and give her a feeling of boundless energy. She tried not to take the whole pill because she was afraid she might grind her teeth. "How could I explain a broken tooth to Jerry?" she thought. When the effects started to wear off, it would sometimes be early in the morning, but then she had her sleeping pills to count on. After several days of drinking, ecstasy, and sedatives, Janet would be exhausted, so she depended on her diet pills to give her that needed boost of energy—and the cycle continued.

The day that changed Janet's life started out routinely enough. The previous evening she had worked very late at the office uploading files to the new computerized record-keeping system and teaching the rest of the staff how to use it. Janet arrived home, showered, and went straight to bed. She got up around mid-morning and prepared a breakfast for herself of toast slathered with lots of jelly. She also had a Bloody Mary for a pick-me-up. Stephanie was going directly from school to one of her friend's house for a sleepover, so she wasn't expected. But the boys came home at their usual time (by which point Janet had consumed about three ounces of alcohol).

While the boys were doing homework, Janet fixed a light dinner of fried chicken fingers for them and a salad for herself. She had another Bloody Mary and two rather large glasses of wine. Janet knew her middle son, Chris, needed a ride to baseball practice, so she decided to leave Mike home to look after Scott. Janet stashed a couple of ecstasy pills in her purse, "just in case," and left the house with Chris. Jerry was working late, as usual. If any of the boys had noticed how much Janet was drinking, no one said anything. They had learned lately to fear her temper. During the hour and a half of baseball practice, Janet left the ball field and went to a near-by sports lounge and continued to drink wine.

By this point, Janet should not have been allowed near the wheel of her car—but there was no one around to stop her from putting the keys in the ignition. She was driving her 4-wheel drive SUV about 60 miles an hour in a 35-mile-an-hour work zone. Janet's reflexes were slowed, so it seemed to her that the road turned very suddenly and sharply to detour traffic around

some heavy construction equipment. When Janet hit the brakes, it caused her SUV to veer sideways into a huge Royal Poinciana tree on the side of the road. (Fortunately, it was late in the day and no construction workers were standing there.) The car came to rest wrapped around the tree at about the midsection, between the front and back passenger side doors. Chris, who was sitting next to Janet in the front seat, was wearing his seatbelt and escaped with "just" a broken right arm and scratches on his face.

Janet, who was not wearing a seat belt, did not fare as well. When the SUV hit the tree, the windshield exploded in her face and she was tossed around like a rag doll before becoming trapped in the wreckage. The rescue team extricated Janet with the "jaws of life" and airlifted her to Jackson hospital's Ryder Trauma Center. On admission, Janet was diagnosed with a severe cerebral contusion with significant edema, multiple fractures of her facial bones, and a severe injury to her left eye. At this point Janet's chances for survival were slim.

Miraculously, Janet's cerebral edema did not progress, and after several days she began to emerge from her coma. Jerry stayed by her side constantly until she was out of danger. Janet was extubated after 2 weeks and transferred to a nearby rehabilitation hospital where she continued to improve. Janet was finally discharged back home.

Later, Janet was charged with driving while legally intoxicated. When her SUV was searched, the ecstasy she had hidden in her purse was found. Additional charges were brought against her for felony possession of illegal drugs. As a part of her sentence, Janet was placed under house arrest to be followed by a period of probation. She was also ordered to get counseling.

Jerry's punishment for Janet might be even harsher. "I want a divorce," he stated flatly after the first few weeks of shock had worn off. "How could you even dare to put our children in jeopardy? I'm so mad and I just want out of this mess." Over time, however, he seemed to soften a little. "Seeing you in the hospital, you looked so vulnerable. I remembered how much I love you. You are my wife, after all." Jerry ultimately decided his ambivalence must be a sign that he should do nothing, at least for the moment.

Janet contacted a local mental health agency that specializes in treating substance disorders in order to start her court-mandated counseling. As the social worker completed Janet's psychosocial history, she was struck by the thought that drug and alcohol use are not limited to a small minority of deviants. The social worker mused, "If it can happen to someone like Janet, it can happen to anybody. But where had the opportunities been missed to intervene and avoid Janet's tragedy? Here is somebody who has access to all kinds of help. What happened?" They scheduled their next appointment, and Janet left the office. The practitioner wandered over to the window and stared out at the searing South Florida sun. "I've worked with so many clients who used multiple substances, but this situation really stands out," she thought. "Or maybe this is just another case that fell through the cracks." The social worker turned and walked back to her desk. "Everyone involved with Janet was trying to help; yet the issue of her drinking and the multiple drugs that she was taking, the prescribed ones and the others, was never addressed. Not by her physician or by her psychiatrist or even her husband—it's clear that Janet's friends were uneasy about her depression and upset about her refusal to comply with her HIV regimen ... and I'm sure they feel guilty now for introducing Janet to ecstasy." The social worker shook her head slowly as she swiveled her chair idly. "And then there's Janet's husband ... he's devoted to his family, but he was away from home so much of the day and evening ... I guess he couldn't see what was happening. The poor kids just tried to cope by staying out of her way. Seems there was no one who could see the whole picture, no one suspected the extent of Janet's drug and alcohol use—or, worse yet, if they did know about it, they chose to ignore it. It took a near fatal accident for something to be done. Who is responsible?"

A light tap on the office door signaled the arrival of the social worker's next client.

Advanced Clinical EP 2.1.10 (b) c

ASSESSMENT SUMMARY The case discussion illustrates Janet Sellar's level of intoxication by alcohol and various drugs, some prescribed and some not. The case discussion also points to coping strategies that the social worker might tap into in order to improve Janet's adaption to her life situations and events. After the accident, Janet's medical diagnosis was alcohol intoxication—the legal assessment was driving under the influence and felony drug possession. The officer who searched her car and purse found her stash of ecstasy, which turned out to be a quantity that justified the charge of felony drug possession. Because Janet had no prior criminal record, she was placed under house arrest followed by probation and mandated treatment.

Prior to the day of the accident, Janet's behavior showed many signs of intoxication. The clinically significant maladaptive behavioral and psychological changes resulting from ingestion of specific substances could be seen in her erratic temper, slurred speech, unsteadiness on her feet, and forgetfulness. Janet's cognitive impairment included changes in perception and wakefulness, attention deficits, and compromised judgment. Her mood instability, cognitive impairment, and belligerence caused significant stress among family members. Although Janet has been diagnosed with HIV, this medical condition does not explain her behavioral changes. The case details show that "during this period, the dependence criteria were met for substances as a group, but not for any specific substance" (American Psychiatric Association, 2000, p. 93). Therefore, Janet's final diagnosis is one of polysubstance dependence.

The diagnosis of polysubstance dependence is made because Janet had repeatedly used four groups of substances: alcohol, sedatives (Ambien), amphetamines (Didrex, a benzphetamine), and hallucinogens (ecstasy). Having worked in a doctor's office for many years, Janet clearly understood the dangers of mixing her medications with alcohol or other drugs and of taking more than had been prescribed.

Janet is also diagnosed with major depression, single episode without psychotic features. After a setback with her HIV diagnosis, she felt worthless, had problems sleeping, showed a markedly diminished interest in enjoyable activities, and started gaining weight. Her suicidal ideation prompted the referral to the psychiatrist. The delay in treatment impact associated with antidepressant medications left Janet in a hellish limbo where she acted on her suicidal thoughts by stopping her medical regimen for the HIV diagnosis. Her well-meaning but misguided friends tried to "help" by introducing her to ecstasy and by enabling her heavy use of alcohol.

With this kind of pattern it is difficult to determine the extent to which Janet's alcohol and drug use added to her depression. It is not clear whether she ever received (or would have received) any benefit from Zoloft. However, this situation highlights the vulnerability of clients during the period of time it takes for any antidepressant to reach therapeutic levels. In order to fully and accurately understand Janet's depression, it is necessary to withdraw all substances. As such, the polysubstance diagnosis is listed first on Axis I followed by the diagnosis of her depression. Not complying with HIV treatment is listed as a V-code. Clearly, Janet's depression and use of multiple substances have complicated her diagnostic picture. Figure 4.2 summarizes the interactions of the biological, psychological, and social variables in Janet Sellar's life.

Janet Sellar's Multiaxial DSM Diagnosis Is as Follows:

Axis I	304.80 Polysubstance Dependence, Early Full Remission
	296.23 Major Depressive Disorder, Single Episode, Severe Without Psychotic Features
	V 15.81 Noncompliance with Treatment (HIV)
Axis II	V71.09 (No diagnosis)
Axis III	Human Immunodeficiency Virus (HIV)
	Injuries sustained from recent auto accident
Axis IV	Legal problems—DUI and felony possession of drugs
Axis V	GAF 50 (on admission)

UNDERSTANDING SPECIFIC SUBSTANCES

Substances have different effects on different people, and the effects of substances vary according to how they are used. Substances may be taken into the body in the following ways: oral ingestion (swallowing), inhalation (breathing in) or smoking, injection into the veins (shooting up), or depositing into the mucosa (moist skin) of the mouth or nose (snorting). The substance-related disorders can create problems in many aspects of people's lives (as well as for their families). Those with substance disorders usually seek help for a wide range of problems *other than* substance use—such as family conflict, depression, anxiety, financial and/or legal difficulties, and declining school or work performance, to name just a few.

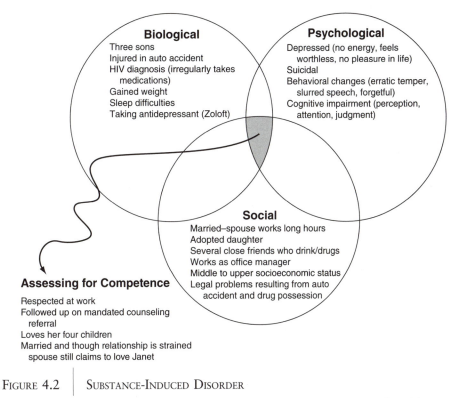

Biological
Three sons
Injured in auto accident
HIV diagnosis (irregularly takes
    medications)
Gained weight
Sleep difficulties
Taking antidepressant (Zoloft)

Psychological
Depressed (no energy, feels
    worthless, no pleasure in life)
Suicidal
Behavioral changes (erratic temper,
    slurred speech, forgetful)
Cognitive impairment (perception,
    attention, judgment)

Social
Married–spouse works long hours
Adopted daughter
Several close friends who drink/drugs
Works as office manager
Middle to upper socioeconomic status
Legal problems resulting from auto
    accident and drug possession

Assessing for Competence
Respected at work
Followed up on mandated counseling
    referral
Loves her four children
Married and though relationship is strained
    spouse still claims to love Janet

FIGURE 4.2 | SUBSTANCE-INDUCED DISORDER

The interactions of the biological, psychological, and social variables in Janet Sellar's life.

However, because the person rarely sees the use of substances as a problem, he or she may not "volunteer" information to the social worker about use of alcohol and/or other substances. As a part of the competency-based assessment process, it is helpful for the practitioner to be aware of the many ways substance use can manifest itself. An assessment for substance use must explore the following issues (American Psychiatric Association, 2000):

- *Route of administration*—How a substance is taken determines the effect it will have (e.g., people "snort" cocaine because the nasal mucosa absorb it more rapidly into the bloodstream than, say, by swallowing it; the more rapid absorption also results in a more intense high or intoxication).
- *Speed of onset within class of substance*—Some substances are faster-acting than others. For example, diazepam (Valium), a tranquilizer commonly prescribed to reduce anxiety, acts more quickly than phenobarbital (Nembutal), which is also prescribed for its sedative qualities.
- *Duration of effects*—Some substances are relatively short-acting (i.e., they leave the body quickly), and others linger in a person's system, dissipating very slowly.
- *Interactivity of multiple substances*—Substances may act in uncharacteristic ways when taken with other substances. Sometimes a person will use multiple

agents to achieve a desired effect; for example, one who is dependent on cocaine may also use sedating substances such as alcohol or marijuana to counteract the cocaine-induced anxiety.

- *Associated mental disorders*—The substance use disorders often co-occur with other disorders such as schizophrenia, mood, anxiety, or antisocial and borderline personality disorders. They may also be a factor in another disorder such as delirium. The effects of each substance may vary in the presence of each type of mental disorder.

Advanced
Clinical
EP 2.1.7 c

The practitioner may also consult with other health care or medical professionals to seek information, such as:

- *Associated laboratory findings*—Analysis of a person's blood or urine may be necessary to determine recent use of a substance. For example, it is possible for a person who chronically uses alcohol to be intoxicated without showing any overt signs of intoxication.
- *Associated physical exam*—A person's physical signs and symptoms may be the first indication of the presence of a substance; for example, the presence of needle marks on his or her arm as a consequence of injecting heroin.

As was mentioned in the introduction to this chapter, the DSM-IV-TR lists 11 classes of substances, but for our purposes (i.e., based on what practitioners commonly encounter in practice), the substances have been organized into the following five categories: depressants, stimulants, opioids, hallucinogens, and other drugs. We will cover each category in turn.

DEPRESSANTS

ALCOHOL

Alcohol is the most commonly used drug in the United States and is legal for anyone over the age of 21. Alcohol is not a product of modern decadence: it has been used throughout history, and there are reports of finding wine and mead (beer) in pottery jars at the site of a Sumerian trading post in western Iran dating back at least 6,000 years (Goodwin & Gabrielli, 2004).

Alcoholic beverages are created by capturing the ethanol produced by the action of yeast on sugars from grapes, grains, or berries, which is then distilled to liquids. The alcohol in this liquid form can be absorbed into the human bloodstream rather quickly—in 5 to 10 minutes—and can stay in the body for several hours. Alcohol is carried through the blood vessels into the stomach, internal organs, liver, kidneys, and muscles, or just about everywhere in the body.

Alcohol affects the human central nervous system and the brain. Although it is considered a **depressant** (a chemical agent that diminishes the function or activity of a specific part of the body), the initial effect on the user apparently is one of stimulation. A person who ingests alcoholic beverages generally experiences a sense of well-being, reduced inhibitions, and the ability or willingness to be more outgoing than he or she usually is. These effects are the result of the brain's inhibitory centers' being slowed down. Alcohol sensitizes NMDA (N-methyl-D-aspartate) receptors in the brain (important for the transmission of some aspects of pain in the central nervous system), making them more responsive to the excitatory neuro-transmitter glutamate, thus boosting brain activity. These effects are most pronounced in areas of the brain that are associated with thinking, memory, and pleasure. Low doses (one to two drinks) can lower a person's inhibitions and make him or her feel more comfortable; but for reasons not yet understood, some individuals become more aggressive than they would customarily be. With continued drinking, alcohol depresses more areas of the brain, which further impedes the ability to function properly. This increased amount of alcohol desensitizes the same brain receptors and activates the inhibitory GABA (gamma-aminobutyric acid) system. GABA's task is to calm the central nervous system and to promote sleep. Higher doses depress the central nervous system and initially produce a feeling of relaxation but then lead to "drunkenness" or intoxication characterized by poor physical coordination (staggering), memory loss, cognitive impairment (or becoming confused), slurred speech, and blurred vision. The individual's reaction time is slowed, and his or her ability to make judgments is reduced. Very high doses of alcohol can cause vomiting, coma, and even death.

ALCOHOL INTOXICATION   The criteria for alcohol intoxication include recent drinking and significant maladaptive behavioral or psychological changes—such as inappropriate sexual or aggressive behavior, mood lability, impaired judgment, and problems in social or work interactions that developed during or shortly after alcohol ingestion (American Psychiatric Association, 2000). In addition, the person shows one or more of the following signs: slurred speech, lack of physical coordination, unsteady gait, nystagmus (rapid involuntary movements of the eyes in a side-to-side or occasionally up-and-down direction, or "eye wiggles"), impairment in attention or memory, stupor, or coma. For an assessment of alcohol intoxication, these symptoms are not better explained by a general medical condition or another mental disorder.

The general rule of thumb is that an average person can process about one beer or one shot of liquor each hour. Any more than that and alcohol collects in the bloodstream and intoxication ensues. While this may be true for most people, a number of factors contribute to the rate at which alcohol is metabolized; for example, sex, size, genetics, and how frequently one drinks. This makes everyone's speed of metabolizing alcohol a little different. The contents of one's stomach, overall health, and efficiency of the liver (the main organ that metabolizes alcohol) will also play a determining role in metabolic rates. Binge drinking occurs when a person drinks a large amount in a short period of time, leading to intoxication. For men, this is five or more drinks at a time; for women, the amount is usually four or more.

ALCOHOL WITHDRAWAL   Long-term alcohol use can lead to serious liver, heart, and stomach problems. Alcohol dependence meets the criteria for substance dependence. Physiological dependence is indicated by tolerance or withdrawal symptoms. O'Neill and Sher (2000) conducted a longitudinal study of alcohol dependence and found that tolerance and withdrawal symptoms reported in early adulthood were associated with a substantial risk for later alcohol use disorder.

Severe reactions to withdrawing from alcohol dependence include convulsions, tremors, and mental confusion—also referred to as withdrawal delirium or delirium tremens (the DTs), which is why detoxification should occur in carefully monitored settings. The diagnostic criteria for alcohol withdrawal are stopping or reducing alcohol use that has been heavy or prolonged (American Psychiatric Association, 2000). Within several hours to a few days after stopping or reducing drinking, the person also develops two or more of the following symptoms: autonomic hyperactivity (such as sweating or a pulse rate greater than 100); increased hand tremor; insomnia; nausea or vomiting; transient visual, tactile, or auditory hallucinations or illusions; anxiety; and/or grand mal seizures. For an assessment of alcohol withdrawal, these symptoms must cause significant distress or impairment in social, work, or other important areas of one's functioning, and they cannot be better accounted for by another mental disorder or general medical condition.

Often the symptoms of withdrawal are so unpleasant that a person may continue to consume alcohol despite adverse consequences. Alcohol dependence is characterized by depression, blackouts, liver disease, and other sequelae such as seizures and hallucinations (American Psychiatric Association, 2000). Unfortunately, once a pattern of compulsive use develops, people with alcohol dependence may spend substantial periods of time obtaining and consuming alcoholic beverages.

Alcohol abuse is seen as less severe than alcohol dependence (American Psychiatric Association, 2000). However, social interactions and work performance may be adversely affected by alcohol abuse either from the aftereffects of drinking or actual intoxication while attempting to carry on with responsibilities. The consequences of alcohol abuse and dependence also may include injury or death from attempting to operate vehicles or machinery while intoxicated and/or legal difficulties because of public intoxication or drinking while driving.

LONG-TERM EFFECTS OF ALCOHOL DEPENDENCE   There are three types of brain damage associated with alcohol use: (1) Wernicke's encephalopathy, (2) Korsakoff's psychosis, and (3) alcoholic dementia.

Wernicke's encephalopathy was first described in 1881 and is now known to be caused by thiamine deficiency resulting from malnutrition usually brought on by chronic alcohol abuse. This condition is a degenerative disease of the brain and is characterized by abnormal eye movements, difficulties with muscle coordination, and confusion. It is almost always accompanied by or followed by Korsakoff's syndrome, also known as **Korsakoff psychosis** or amnesic-confabulatory syndrome. Korsakoff's syndrome is a neurological condition that involves impairment of memory and cognitive skills such as problem solving or learning. The most distinguishing symptom is confabulation (fabrication), where the person makes up detailed and believable stories about experiences or events in order to cover gaps in his or her memory. Wernicke's encephalopathy and Korsakoff's psychosis may occur independently or together; when they occur simultaneously, they are sometimes referred to as Wernicke-Korsakoff syndrome. This syndrome is also called **alcoholic dementia**—problems with memory and cognitive skills as a result of excessive drinking over a period of years.

OTHER ISSUES IN ALCOHOL DEPENDENCE   Many people who abuse alcohol or are dependent on it fluctuate between drinking heavily, drinking socially without negative effects, and not drinking at all (or being abstinent). About 20 percent of those with severe alcohol dependence can have a spontaneous remission or stop drinking on their own, and will not re-experience problems with drinking (Schuckit, 2009). Unfortunately, alcohol dependence and alcohol abuse are often associated with using (or abusing) other substances as well such as cannabis, cocaine, heroin, the amphetamines, sedatives, or nicotine (Gossop, Marsden, & Stewart, 2002). This combined substance use increases the risk for suicide, accidents, or violence (Canapary, Bongar, & Cleary, 2002; Stuart et al., 2003). As a matter of fact, 40 percent of people in the United States will experience an alcohol-related accident at some time in their lives (SAMHSA, 2004). Absenteeism from work, job-related accidents, and low employee productivity, all related to alcohol use, have been well documented (National Institute on Alcohol Abuse and Alcoholism, 2005).

Historically, women consume less alcohol than men, drink less frequently, and are less likely to develop alcohol-related problems. However, when women do develop problems related to drinking alcohol, those problems tend to be more severe (Paris & Bradley, 2001). For instance, women have been found to have a higher prevalence of the co-occurring problems of anxiety and depressive disorders (Williams & Cohen, 2000). Alcohol consumption has declined among white Americans since the mid-1980s, but ethnic and minority groups continue to be disproportionately affected by alcohol-related problems. Studies show an increase of alcohol-related difficulties among Blacks and Hispanics, and they tend to experience more negative health and social consequences of drinking such as unemployment, poor education outcomes, and legal problems connected to alcohol (Boyd, Phillips, & Dorsey, 2003).

SEDATIVES, HYPNOTICS, AND ANXIOLYTICS

This group of depressants includes substances that have similar but subtle differences in effect: the sedatives (which are calming), the hypnotics (which are sleep-inducing), and the anxiolytics (which are anxiety-reducing) (Mack, Franklin, & Frances, 2003). The benzodiazepines and barbiturates are also included in this sub-category. The benzodiazepines are considered to be safer than the barbiturates, which carry greater risk for abuse and dependence. They all are Schedule IV drugs under the Federal Controlled Substances Act (meaning that they are drugs with a currently accepted medical use and must be prescribed by a physician, physician's assistant, or nurse practitioner). These substances are used to reduce tension, irritability, agitation, and serious anxiety (or to prevent anxiety attacks).

The first benzodiazepine, chlordiazepoxide (Librium), was discovered in 1954 by an Austrian scientist named Dr. Leo Sternbach for the pharmaceutical company Hoffman-Laroche. He stopped his work on the drug but "rediscovered" it when an assistant was cleaning up the laboratory (Sternbach, 1972). Sternbach's further research revealed that the drug was a very effective tranquilizer. In 1963, government approval for use was given to diazepam (Valium), a simplified version of Librium, to offset anxiety symptoms. In 1965, nitrazepam (Mogadon) was introduced to treat sleep-related problems, and in 1973 flurazepam (Dalmane) was released (O'Brien, 2005). These drugs are usually prescribed for short-term relief of severe and debilitating anxiety. Although they have proven helpful in the treatment of the anxiety disorders, they do have the potential for abuse and may cause dependence or addiction when not used as medically prescribed. The benzodiazepines were at one time known as minor tranquilizers or antianxiety drugs. Physical dependence develops when these medications are used at high doses and/or for prolonged periods of time. Common withdrawal symptoms include anxiety, insomnia, restlessness, agitation, muscle tension, and irritability. Seizures and depression may sometimes occur. People can experience unpleasant withdrawal symptoms if they abruptly stop taking these medications.

The barbiturates (Amytal, Seconal, Nembutal) were first prescribed to help people sleep and replaced alcohol and opium. They were commonly used in the 1930s and 1940s, before their addictive properties were known—and by the 1950s they had become the most abused drugs in the United States. At low doses, the barbiturates relax muscles and produce a mild feeling of well-being. Larger doses can produce effects that resemble those of heavy drinking; in particular, slurred speech, problems with walking, and inability to concentrate. Extremely high doses can relax the diaphragm muscles to the point of causing death by suffocation. Barbiturate use has declined since the introduction of the benzodiazepines in the early 1960s.

The anxiolytics are generally divided into two groups: the benzodiazepines and non-benzodiazepines (Albers, Hahn, & Reist, 2001–2002). This category also includes herbs, such as St. John's Wort and Kava (Kava Kava); however, there is limited evidence available for their efficacy. In Europe, the root of the valerian is a popular anxiolytic. The group of anxiolytics known as the non-benzodiazepines lack the sedation and potential for dependence associated with the benzodiazepines. Buspirone (Buspar) is a new non-benzodiazepine anxiolytic agent and is described as a serotonin 1A agonist. Barbiturates and the sedative drug meprobamate (Miltown, Equanil, Meprin) have an anxiolytic effect, but the risk of abuse and addiction is high. However, they can be valuable for the short-term treatment of insomnia.

The most common anti-anxiety medications (followed by their brand name) include:

- Alprazolam (Xanax)
- Chlordiazepoxide (Librium)
- Clonazepam (Klonapin, Rivotril)
- Diazepam (Valium)
- Lorazepam (Ativan)
- Oxazepam (Serax)

Commonly prescribed medications with a hypnotic or sedative effect are:

- Flurazepam (Dalmane)
- Triazolam (Halcion)

The drug midazolam (Versed, Hypnovel) is mostly used as an intravenous injection for sedation before surgery or for emergency procedures such as intubation (a procedure for inserting a tube into the mouth or nose, which is then advanced into the airway when a person is not breathing).

The benzodiazepines are commonly divided into three groups: (1) short-acting compounds (for 6 hours or less), (2) intermediate compounds (lasting for 6 to 10 hours), and (3) long-acting compounds (with sedative effects that persist). However, with most of the benzodiazepines, noticeable effects usually wear off within a few hours. With frequent use, tolerance develops for many of the therapeutic effects of the benzodiazepines. Unlike tolerance to other drugs such as the opioids or stimulants, tolerance to the benzodiazepines can create an iatrogenic syndrome (or a spectrum of side effects that can be worse than the original condition). For that reason, the benzodiazepines are generally prescribed for a limited period of time (e.g., 2 to 4 weeks). Typically, tolerance to the hypnotic effects happens within days, and the anxiolytic effects usually do not last beyond a few months. Tolerance can cause a range of symptoms related to nervous system dysfunction, and they are the same as withdrawal symptoms. If a person abruptly stops taking the benzodiazepines, severe and unpleasant withdrawal symptoms may occur such as convulsions, confusion, psychosis, and effects similar to delirium tremens (see previous discussion of alcohol withdrawal). Therefore, it is recommended that the person who has been taking a benzodiazepine for a long period of time be weaned off the drug over a period of months.

CRITERIA FOR DEPENDENCE OR ABUSE   The DSM-IV-TR criteria for diagnosis of dependence on sedatives, hypnotics, and anxiolytics do not differ substantially from those for other substance dependence disorders (American Psychiatric Association, 2000). Both dependence on sedatives, hypnotics, and anxiolytics and their abuse involve maladaptive behavioral changes (e.g., sexual or aggressive behavior), mood changes, impaired judgment, impaired social or occupational functioning, impaired speech, coordination problems, and an unsteady gait. Diagnosing abuse follows the criteria for substance abuse. Abuse of this group of drugs may occur in conjunction with the use of other substances (e.g., a person might use intoxicating doses of a benzodiazepine to come down from a cocaine high).

INTOXICATION AND WITHDRAWAL   The specific criteria for sedative, hypnotic, or anxiolytic intoxication are the same as the symptoms for intoxication discussed earlier.

Withdrawal symptoms for the sedative, hypnotic, and anxiolytic drugs appear when dosage is either reduced or the person stops taking the drug entirely. A diagnosis of withdrawal from these drugs must include the development of two or more of the following symptoms within several hours to a few days: autonomic hyperactivity (such as sweating or a pulse rate greater than 100); increased hand tremor; insomnia; rebound REM (or dreaming) sleep; nausea that is sometimes accompanied by vomiting; transient visual, tactile, or auditory hallucinations or illusions; psychomotor agitation; anxiety (or panic attacks); and grand mal seizures. These symptoms are the opposite of the acute effects seen in the first-time user, who generally feels drowsy and uncoordinated. A general medical disorder or another mental disorder does not better account for these symptoms. The duration of the withdrawal syndrome is usually related to the half-life of the substance. Additional long-term but less intense symptoms may endure for several months (e.g., moodiness, anxiety, or problems sleeping) and could be incorrectly diagnosed as an anxiety or mood disorder.

STIMULANTS

AMPHETAMINES

The amphetamines, otherwise known as speed or pep pills, are central nervous system (CNS) stimulants that are usually synthetically made in illegal labs. Amphetamine was first synthesized in 1887 by the Romanian chemist Lazar Edeleneau at the University of Berlin. He called this new drug phenylisopropylamine. The experimental use of amphetamines in the United States began in the 1920s and was introduced in the form of the pharmaceutical called Benzedrine. At that time, the drug was used by the military, especially the Air Force, to fight fatigue and increase alertness. Pilots used amphetamines (Dexadrine) as stimulants, calling them go-pills. After completing a mission, the pilots were given a no-go-pill (Ambien or Temazepam) to help them sleep (Caldwell, Caldwell, & Darlington, 2003). Despite what we now know of the dangers of amphetamines, 65 percent of U.S. pilots in combat during the Desert Storm campaign of 1991 admitted to having used an amphetamine compound at least once (Emonson & Vanderbeek, 1995). Although military officials suspended the program in 1992, it was later reinstated with more strict medical regulations (Bonne, 2003).

In the mid-1950s, the amphetamines were limited to prescription use but illegal use was common. The drug became popular among truck drivers, construction workers, and factory workers whose jobs required long or irregular shift work or automatic repetitive tasks. Although it was popularized as a "redneck drug," college students who kept long hours studying also used the amphetamines in order to keep up their grades. President John F. Kennedy was rumored to have used methamphetamine during his term in office in the early 1960s (Owen, 2008). White-collar workers who tried to stay alert during long and busy days also used it.

The amphetamines are a class of synthetic drugs also used (and still used) as appetite suppressors. In the United States, the amphetamines are Schedule II controlled drugs, which means that they have a currently accepted medical use that is severely restricted, but also have a high potential for abuse. The amphetamines (and methamphetamines) are stimulants that cause a release of the neurotransmitters dopamine and noradrenaline (norepinephrine) from storage vesicles in the CNS (Sulzer, Sonders, Poulsen, & Galli, 2005). Here is a list of just some of the amphetamines and amphetamine derivatives along with their street names:

- Amphetamine (uppers, bennies, pep pills, black beauties, white bennies)
- Methamphetamine (speed, meth, chalk)
- Methamphetamine combined with marijuana and heroin (brown)
- Methamphetamine used with Viagra (Tina)
- Smokable methamphetamine (batu, crystal, crank, glass, ice)
- Dextroamphetamine (dexies, beans)

Amphetamines may come in the form of tablets and capsules. A recent appearance is Yaba, which in Thai means "crazy medicine." The tablets are sometimes flavored to taste like candy (grape, orange, or vanilla) and marketed to a young audience. The tablets may also be reddish-orange or green and shaped so that they fit inside the end of a drinking straw. The straws are marked with a variety of logos—WY is the most common. These drugs can also appear as powders, off-white crystals, or chunks that look like ice. The smokeable methamphetamine looks like shaved glass slivers or clear rock salt that can be swallowed (bomb), sniffed or snorted (ingested through the nose), or injected. A relatively rare method of ingestion involves rubbing the drug into the gums—this is known as dabbing.

When methamphetamine is either smoked or injected, the individual experiences an intense sense of euphoria (a "rush" or a "flash") that lasts only a few minutes. The effects of smokeable methamphetamine are comparable to those of crack cocaine in intensity—the high is reported to be too intense for the casual drug user. A practitioner known to the author shared a comment from a former client who said, "It was just like getting hit with a sledgehammer." Snorting produces effects within 3 to 5 minutes, but the high is not an intense rush. Oral ingestion produces effects within 15 to 20 minutes. The experience is variously described as speeding, tweaking (or tweaked), spinning (or spun), or up.

The amphetamines are available through a prescription by a medical doctor or from illegal sources that manufacture look-alike drugs synthetically in secret laboratories. Recipes are readily available on the Internet for anyone who wants to look, although some of the chemicals may be difficult to obtain. Crystal meth can easily be produced in small clandestine labs (even in a kitchen or bathroom) by mixing a cocktail of about 15 substances, including ammonia, paint thinner, ether, Drano, and the lithium from batteries. "Christmas tree meth" describes green methamphetamine produced using Drano crystal. "Bathtub crank" is the street term for a poor-quality methamphetamine that is literally produced in bathtubs. A "crankster" is someone who is known to manufacture (or use) methamphetamine, and "cooking" refers to the manufacturing process. This level of availability increases the risk of abuse and dependence for people of all ages.

Tolerance to amphetamines develops rapidly. As the person's body adapts to the drug, he or she needs larger doses to achieve the same effects. This means that the person uses more and more of the drug to achieve a high. After chronic use, even at low doses, a person can develop tolerance. The amphetamine user feels a sense of well-being and increased energy. The effects of the amphetamines are similar to the effects of cocaine, but last longer, so amphetamines are usually taken fewer times per day. As is true with cocaine dependence, a person may use amphetamines on a chronic or episodic basis with binges (speed runs) combined with brief periods of time where he or she may be entirely drug-free.

To make the diagnosis for amphetamine dependence the person must meet the criteria for substance dependence. Dependence on amphetamines can be both physical and psychological. Individuals who develop amphetamine dependence may show symptoms of restlessness, anxiety, depression, insomnia, and suicidal behavior. A person may also develop a psychological dependence on the drug in an effort to avoid the "down" feeling when the effects wear off. It is not uncommon for the practitioner to find that the person who is dependent on amphetamines also has a number of legal problems.

Amphetamine abuse follows the criteria for substance abuse. The person with amphetamine abuse may also be involved in illegal activities (e.g., stealing in order to obtain the drug), but this behavior is more commonly found in those who struggle with dependence.

AMPHETAMINE INTOXICATION   Amphetamine intoxication is characterized by the presence of significant maladaptive behavioral or psychological changes that develop during, or shortly after, the use of amphetamine or a related substance. The person manifests two or more of the following symptoms (American Psychiatric Association, 2000):

- Tachycardia (fast heart beat) or bradycardia (slow heart rate)
- Papillary dilation
- Elevated or lowered blood pressure
- Perspiration or chills
- Nausea or vomiting
- Evidence of weight loss
- Psychomotor agitation or retardation
- Muscular weakness, respiratory depression, chest pain, or cardiac arrhythmias (abnormal heart rhythm)
- Confusion, seizures, dyskinesias (impaired ability to control movement), dystonias (muscle spasms), or coma.

Intoxication usually begins with a "high" feeling followed by euphoria (intense feelings of joy or elation) with enhanced energy, gregariousness, hyperactivity, restlessness, hypervigilance, sensitivity to others, talkativeness, anxiety, tension, alertness, feelings of grandiosity, stereotypical and repetitive behavior, anger, fighting, and impaired judgment (American Psychiatric Association, 2000).

AMPHETAMINE WITHDRAWAL   Withdrawal symptoms occur when a person abruptly stops taking amphetamines. Onset of the symptoms begins within a few hours to several days, and they are generally the opposite of those seen during intoxication (e.g., the person may develop a dysphoric mood—exaggerated feeling of depression—instead of the euphoria of intoxication). Withdrawal can be an unpleasant experience. People who stop using amphetamines often experience the physical signs of paranoia, depression, difficulty breathing, dysphoria, stomach pain, and lethargy. The severity of these withdrawal symptoms depends on the degree of use/abuse. Crashing (marked withdrawal symptoms) often follows an episode of intense high doses (speed runs). However, there is considerable variation in people's sensitivity to the effects of the amphetamines (Doweiko, 2009). The short-term physical effects can include a decreased appetite; increased stamina and energy; increased sexual drive/ response; involuntary bodily movements; nystagmus; increased perspiration; hyperactivity; jitteriness; nausea; itchy, blotchy, or greasy skin; increased heart rate; irregular heart rate; increased blood pressure; sleep disturbance; and headaches. The short-term psychological effects may consist of alertness; a sense of euphoria; increased concentration; rapid talking; increased confidence; release of social inhibitions; feelings of cleverness, competence, and power; increased social responsiveness; and hallucinations.

The physical effects of long-term abuse of amphetamines may include tremor; restlessness; insomnia; drying of the skin and increased itchiness and/or obsessively picking at the skin (sometimes until it bleeds); hyperreflexia (overactive reflexes such as tremors); tachypnea (rapid breathing); gastrointestinal narrowing; weight loss; and a weakened immune system. Regular amphetamine use can lead to gingivitis (inflammation of the gums) (Hasan & Ciancio, 2004), and long-term use can result in dental caries (tooth rot) (Shaner, 2002). Erectile dysfunction; heart problems; stroke; and liver, kidney, and lung damage can result from prolonged use. When the drug is snorted, the person may experience a deterioration of the lining of the nostrils. The long-term psychological effects can include insomnia, mental states similar to schizophrenia, irritability, confusion, panic, and violent and aggressive behavior. More than any other drug, the amphetamines are associated with violence and antisocial behavior.

COCAINE

In the late nineteenth century, a gentleman by the name of John Stith-Pemberton developed a product in response to a decision by the city of Atlanta to prohibit the use of alcohol. He thought his product would be seen as the "temperance drink" (Martensen, 1996, p. 1615). The product contained 60 milligrams of cocaine per 8 ounce serving and later became known around the world as Coca-Cola (Gold & Miller, 2004). During this era, it was not uncommon to use drugs that were potentially addictive, and its use did later become regulated by the Pure Food and Drug Act of 1906. Cocaine once again became fashionable in the 1970s and 1980s as a popular recreational drug and currently remains a significant part of the drug-abuse problem in the United States (Gold & Miller, 2004). Results from the 2009 National Survey on Drug Use and Health report that more than 30 million people (14.7 percent) in the United States have used cocaine at least once in their lifetime, and current use over the past month is reported as 1.86 million people (0.7 percent) (SAMHSA, 2009).

How cocaine is produced has changed little. Cocaine comes from the leaves of the coca plant (*Erythroxylon coca*), a native of the eastern slopes of the Andes. The climate is well suited for the plant to grow. It is one of the most powerfully addictive drugs. Cocaine comes in two main forms. One is cocaine hydrochloride, a white crystalline powder that can be snorted into the nostrils or dissolved in water and injected. Snorting cocaine may cause erosion of the membranes inside the nose. Street names for cocaine in the powder form are coke, snow, candy, flake, blow, big C, lady, white, and snowbirds. The other form is crack cocaine hydrochloride that has been processed with ammonia or baking soda and water into a freebase cocaine, which makes it smokeable. The drug's appearance is in chips, chunks, or rocks. Smoking allows the cocaine to reach the brain very quickly and results in a rapid high. Heavy use of cocaine can produce hallucinations, paranoia, aggression, insomnia, and depression.

Cocaine is a very powerful stimulator of the central nervous system. A typical dose, about 50 to 100 milligrams, rapidly induces feelings of self-confidence, exhilaration, and energy that can last for about 15 to 45 minutes before giving way to fatigue and melancholy. Crack cocaine condenses these effects into a shorter and more intense high. The drug also increases heart rate and blood pressure, sometimes causing death. Very high doses can potentially lead to cardiac arrest and respiratory failure. The principal effect of cocaine is to block the re-uptake of dopamine, serotonin, and noradrenalin into neurons, leading to higher than normal levels of these neurotransmitters in the brain.

In small amounts, cocaine boosts a person's sense of self-esteem and optimism, increases mental and physical abilities, and conveys feelings of power. Extended use leads to a number of negative symptoms such as anxiety, depression, suicidal ideation, weight loss, aggressiveness, sexual dysfunction, sleeping problems, and paranoid delusions and hallucinations (Barlow & Durand, 2012). It is estimated that two-thirds or more of those individuals who are chronic cocaine abusers will develop a drug-induced psychosis that looks very much like paranoid schizophrenia, sometimes called coke paranoia (Kalayasiri et al., 2006).

Cocaine dependence follows the criteria for substance dependence. Cocaine abuse follows the criteria for substance abuse. To make the diagnosis of intoxication, the person must have recently used cocaine, and show clinically significant maladaptive behavioral changes (such as euphoria or affective blunting; changes in sociability; hypervigilance; interpersonal sensitivity; anxiety, tension, or anger; stereotyped behaviors; impaired judgment; or impaired social or occupational functioning) that developed during or shortly after cocaine use (American Psychiatric Association, 2000). As with amphetamine intoxication, the individual intoxicated with cocaine must show two (or more) of the following symptoms: tachycardia or bradycardia; pupillary dilation; elevated or lowered blood pressure; perspiration or chills; nausea or vomiting; evidence of weight loss; psychomotor agitation or retardation; muscular weakness, respiratory depression, chest pain, or cardiac arrhythmias; and confusion, seizures, dyskinesias, dystonias, or coma.

A diagnosis of cocaine withdrawal is made when the person stops or reduces cocaine use that has been heavy and prolonged. As well, the individual has a dysphoric mood and shows two (or more) of the following physiological changes within a few hours to several days: fatigue; vivid, unpleasant dreams; insomnia or hypersomnia; increased appetite; and psychomotor retardation or agitation (American Psychiatric Association, 2000). The symptoms cause the person distress or he or she may experience problems in social relationships, on the job, or in other important areas of life. The symptoms are not related to a general medical condition and not better explained by another mental disorder.

CAFFEINE

Coffee beans are indigenous to Ethiopia, and historical evidence has revealed that, in the period around 575 A.D., coffee beans had become a form of currency and were consumed as food (Nawrot et al., 2003). By the fourth century, coffee beans had been introduced to Arabia, where they were called "gahwah" (a poetic term for wine). The Turkish equivalent is "kahveh," which translates to "café" in French and "kaffee" in German (Burchfield, 2006). Coffee shops were fashionable in Europe as early as the seventeenth and eighteenth centuries. Some suggest that the Boston Tea Party of 1773 was the genesis of Americans' present-day coffee-drinking habits. Protesting against the excessive taxes on tea, the citizens of Boston boarded British ships and dumped their cargoes of tea overboard. Since that time, the United States has been considered a leader in coffee consumption. Almost a century later, in the 1880s, the first caffeinated soft drinks were created.

If you missed your cup of coffee this morning and now have a headache or are having difficulty concentrating, you could be experiencing caffeine withdrawal (a diagnostic category listed in the DSM IV-TR for further study). Juliano and Griffiths (2004) conducted a comprehensive review of the literature regarding caffeine withdrawal and identified the following symptoms: headache, fatigue, decreased energy/activity level, decreased alertness, drowsiness, decreased contentedness, depressed mood, difficulty concentrating, irritability, foggy/not clearheaded, and flu-like symptoms of nausea/vomiting and muscle pain/stiffness. According to the authors, these symptoms can be mild or severe—but about 13 percent of people who drink coffee develop symptoms so significant that they cannot do what they normally would do, such as leaving the house or performing on the job. Drinking as little as one cup of coffee—only 100 milligrams of caffeine—can cause these symptoms. Caffeine is absorbed into the bloodstream very quickly but takes a relatively long time to leave our bodies. Its effects can last from 12 to about 24 hours, which explains why starting the day with a cup of coffee is a morning ritual for so many people. Typically, the onset of withdrawal symptoms occurs 12 to 24 hours after abstinence and can last from 2 to 9 days.

Caffeine is a plant alkaloid that is naturally produced in the leaves, seeds, or fruits of many plants. The primary source of caffeine is the coffee bean (or seed of the coffee plant), from which coffee is brewed. Other less common sources of caffeine include the plants yerba mate and guarana, which are sometimes used in the preparation of teas and energy-boosting drinks. When caffeine is removed from the plant and reduced to its natural state, it forms a white powder. This powdered form of caffeine is bitter, which is probably why many beverages containing caffeine also have a lot of sugar or other sweeteners added. Caffeine can also be produced artificially.

Caffeine is considered a drug because it stimulates the central nervous system. It can be found in many beverages besides coffee and coffee-based drinks like latte. Caffeine is in many types of soda (also known as pop, soda pop, soft drink), many fizzy drinks, some teas, several energy drinks, chocolate (including hot chocolate), and some over-the-counter medications such as pep pills and cold and flu remedies such as Excedrin and NoDoz. Caffeine increases alertness, decreases fatigue, and improves muscle coordination. It is very similar in chemical structure to another substance in our bodies called adenosine, whose function is (among other things) to dilate blood vessels in the head. Caffeine blocks this dilation, causing a mild stimulating effect on the central nervous system. Because of its effect on arterial dilation, caffeine is commonly found in headache and migraine medications. It also has the ability to enhance the effects of aspirin.

In the United States, the average daily caffeine intake per person is about 280 milligrams—the equivalent of two mugs of coffee or three to five cans (or bottles) of soft drinks. The American Psychiatric Association (2000) estimates that up to 80 percent of Americans regularly use caffeine in any given year. Barlow and Durand (2012) place that estimate even higher, at approximately 90 percent. Caffeine is legal and considered generally safe, and thus it could be characterized as the most commonly used and least harmful psychoactive substance. It is readily available and inexpensive, and the need for it does not lead to the compulsive drug-seeking behaviors discussed in relation to other substances. It is possible to skip that cup of coffee in the morning. Nonetheless, there are some caffeine use disorders such as the following (American Psychiatric Association, 2000):

- Caffeine intoxication
- Caffeine-induced sleep disorder
- Caffeine-induced anxiety disorder

The DSM-IV-TR diagnostic guidelines define caffeine intoxication as the recent daily consumption of at least 250 milligrams of caffeine, or the equivalent of just two and a half cups of brewed coffee (American Psychiatric Association, 2000). Symptoms may develop during or shortly after caffeine use—and five or more of the following signs must be present for a diagnosis of intoxication: restlessness, nervousness, excitement, insomnia, flushed face, diuresis (removal of excess fluid from the body through increased urine output), gastrointestinal disturbance, muscle twitching, rambling flow of thought and speech, tachycardia or cardiac arrhythmia, periods of inexhaustibility, or psychomotor agitation.

It is unlikely, however, that the practitioner will encounter someone with caffeine intoxication in his or her practice. For example, Griffiths, Juliano, and Chausmer (2003) conducted a telephone survey and found that only 7 percent of current caffeine users met the DSM-IV-TR criteria for caffeine intoxication and experienced symptoms that interfered with their functioning at work, school, or home. Typically, a cup of coffee contains 150 milligrams of caffeine—enough to increase alertness and promote wakefulness, but not enough to result in intoxication.

Individuals with anxiety disorders are especially sensitive to the effects of caffeine but may not recognize the role that it plays in their anxiety symptoms. Caffeine disrupts sleep. When it is consumed just before bedtime (or continuously throughout the day), sleep onset may be delayed, total sleep time reduced, normal stages of sleep altered, and the overall quality of sleep diminished.

NICOTINE

Early Europeans, most notably Christopher Columbus, visiting the New World saw Native Americans smoking cigars and chewing tobacco. When the Spanish introduced tobacco to Europe in the early 1500s, it was thought to be of medicinal value and was used to treat diseases of the ear, eyes, nose, and mouth. Apparently, the treatment involved blowing smoke into all openings of the head.

Nicotine is a poisonous oily liquid that comes from the nightshade family (*Solanaceae*) of plants and is called *Nicotiana tabacum*. (This tobacco plant was named in honor of a French ambassador, Jean Nicot, who promoted it for its medicinal value.) Interestingly, small amounts of nicotine are found in foods of other plants in the nightshade family (e.g., tomatoes and eggplants). Nicotine is introduced into the body in various ways: via the smoke of cigarettes, cigars, and pipe tobacco; or through smokeless tobacco (for chewing) and snuff (finely ground tobacco that is "snuffed" into the nose or "dipped" and held in the cheek or lower lip). Manufacturers are increasingly prepackaging moist snuff into small paper or cloth packets to make the product more convenient. Cigarette smoking is the most popular form of nicotine ingestion—and nicotine is the substance in tobacco that causes dependence.

Fifty-five percent of people in the United States have tried smoking cigarettes. Approximately 22.8 percent of Americans are current smokers, and another 30 percent are ex-smokers. Male smokers outnumber female smokers, although the rates of smoking are decreasing more rapidly for males than females (Centers for Disease Control and Prevention, 2003). The incidence of tobacco use is higher for African Americans, for those with little education, and for those of low socio-economic status (Benowitz, 2002). Genetic factors play a role in nicotine dependence, and the risk of addiction for those with a first-degree relative who smokes is three times higher than for someone in a family of nonsmokers (Hughes, 2009).

Social and cultural influences also contribute to who uses nicotine. Teens are generally resistant to antismoking messages. Adolescent smokeless tobacco users are more likely than nonusers to become cigarette smokers (National Institute on Drug Abuse, 2005). The country singer Gretchen Wilson has helped to popularize smokeless tobacco through her 2005 record album *All Jacked Up*, which has a song entitled "Skoal Ring." (There is a smokeless tobacco product marketed under the brand name Skoal, and it is packaged in a round tin.) A self-declared "redneck woman," Wilson's song glamorizes the attributes of a man whose habit of carrying a can of chewing tobacco in the back pocket of his jeans produces a Skoal ring. Use of smokeless tobacco products also gets a boost from the fact that many professional baseball players chew tobacco or dip snuff—and, through the worshipful eyes of little boys just learning to love the sport, all of that chewin' and spittin' becomes just another one of the rituals, along with tugging on the bill of a cap or adjusting the fit of a glove.

Some drugs are more difficult to quit than others—and nicotine is rated by most experts as the most difficult to quit. Only about 4 percent to 7 percent of people are able to quit smoking on any given attempt without medicines or other help (American Cancer Society, 2011). Mark Twain was reported to have said, "To cease smoking is the easiest thing I ever did. I ought to know, because I've done it a thousand times." About 90 percent of smokers are persistent daily users and 55 percent become dependent. A small percentage (perhaps 5 percent to 10 percent) are not dependent. Those who are episodic nicotine users are known as "chippers" (Doweiko, 2009).

The nicotine in tobacco smoke rides on small particles of tar. American cigarettes contain about 9 milligrams of nicotine, but much of the nicotine is burned off. As a result, a smoker gets about 1 milligram of nicotine in every cigarette. The cigarette smoke with the nicotine/tar mixture is immediately absorbed by the lungs, and within seven seconds it reaches the smoker's brain (Gray with Zide, 2006). About 90 percent of inhaled nicotine is actually absorbed—making the cigarette a very efficient drug-delivery system. Neurochemical changes occur in the brain after just a few cigarettes, which suggests that a limited exposure to nicotine can initiate dependence (Mansvelder, Keath, & McGehee, 2002). Nicotine mimics the effect of acetylcholine (the neurotransmitter in the brain that appears to be involved in learning and memory), causing the release of acetylcholine and norepinephrine. The user experiences a sense of release from stress and even may experience feelings of euphoria. Additional physical effects may include increases in blood pressure and heart rate; faster respiration; constriction of arteries producing cool, pale skin; and stimulation of the central nervous system. At high doses, nicotine produces convulsions and death. Several years ago, the *New Straits Times* (1997) reported a "smoking contest" between two young men, ages 19 and 21. They were both farmers living in central China who apparently started smoking out of boredom. Encouraged by spectators, they tried to see who could smoke the most cigarettes in a single sitting. The result was devastating. The 19-year-old man died after smoking 100 cigarettes, and the 21-year-old young man was seriously poisoned after smoking 80 cigarettes.

Chronic use of nicotine leads to changes in the brain and therefore in behavior. One of the first changes is tolerance, or a decrease in the effects of nicotine. Tolerance occurs rapidly in response to some of the early unpleasant effects such as dizziness, nausea, and vomiting. As the unpleasant effects subside and the pleasurable effects of nicotine surface, the person continues with his or her further use of the drug. With the development of physical dependence, further nicotine use is necessary to avoid a physiological disturbance (i.e., nicotine withdrawal). Needless to say, nicotine is highly addictive, as it provides an almost immediate "kick" from the neurochemical changes in the brain (National Institute on Drug Abuse, 2005). Nicotine is not stored in the body, so its effects last only a few minutes. It is metabolized in the body fairly quickly and disappears within a few hours—therefore some tolerance is lost overnight when the person is sleeping. Those who smoke often comment that the first cigarette of the day is the strongest and the most satisfying. As the day continues and acute tolerance develops, the cigarettes have less of an effect. The person needs to absorb more and more nicotine to be able to experience effects.

For some people, handling the cigarette, the smell of it, and the ritual of lighting and actually smoking it are all part of the pleasant sensation. This can make withdrawal or craving worse. These rituals offer a sense of security and can contribute to a person's tendency to smoke when he or she is anxious or nervous (Doweiko, 2009). Many smokers come to associate having a cigarette with other pleasant activities such as having a cup of coffee or an alcoholic drink, or enjoying a good meal. Smoking can even be tied to having a good time with friends. For many, smoking requires taking a break from daily responsibilities. A colleague of the author routinely takes a break from meetings in order to smoke a cigarette. She returns feeling "refreshed." In other words, people may also learn to connect smoking with the temporary relief of tension, boredom, or fatigue. This is a habit that is easily reinforced. For instance, let's say smokers take an average of 10 puffs on each cigarette. If they smoke one pack a day, this amounts to 200 puffs (or "kicks") of nicotine a day—more than 72,000 puffs a year.

NICOTINE DEPENDENCE   Chronic exposure to nicotine results in dependence. Some of the signs of nicotine dependence that the practitioner might look for are a tobacco odor, cough, very wrinkled skin, and/or the medical diagnosis of chronic obstructive pulmonary disease. Anyone who has ever smoked knows how hard it is to quit. In 1988, C. Everett Koop, then the surgeon general of the United States, declared nicotine as addictive as either heroin or cocaine in his annual report to Congress. Fully 10 percent of those who smoke report wanting to quit, and 46 percent try to quit each year (Department of Health and Human Services, 1990). Of those who do manage to quit, only 5 percent to 7 percent of them are able to remain abstinent from smoking for an entire year (Hughes, 2009). In addition to nicotine's addictive qualities, the availability of cigarettes, the small number of legal and social consequences of tobacco use, and the sophisticated marketing and advertising methods used by tobacco companies all contribute to dependence.

Nicotine dependence is more prevalent in people with other mental disorders than in the general population. Based on a U.S. national survey of adults, Strat, Ramoz, and Gorwood (2010) found that nicotine dependence was seen in almost half (or 48 percent) of those diagnosed as alcohol-dependent. Another study by Meyer, Rumpf, and Hapke (2004) discovered increased rates of mental disorders among smokers, especially those diagnosed with depressive or anxiety disorders. Nicotine dependence is also common among those with the diagnosis of schizophrenia (American Psychiatric Association, 2000). According to the DSM-IV-TR, 55 percent to 90 percent of those with a mental disorder smoke compared with only 22 percent of the general population—meaning that people with mental illness are 2.5 to 4 times as likely to smoke. The reasons for this are unclear; practitioners often comment that smoking gives their clients something to do and provides a framework for organizing the day.

The diagnosis of nicotine dependence is considered when the person exhibits three or more of the following features: tolerance; withdrawal; uses more nicotine than intended; wants to or has tried to cut down; spends a great deal of time using nicotine (e.g., the person chain smokes); reduces important social or occupational activities because of tobacco use; and continues to use nicotine despite recurrent physical or psychological problems (e.g., continuing to smoke despite a diagnosis of high blood pressure) (American Psychiatric Association, 2000). In addition, the person's nicotine use may create negative interactions among friends or family members. The Fagerstrom Test for Nicotine Dependence (FTND) is a helpful tool for practitioners to assess nicotine dependence (Heatherton, Kozlowski, Frecker, & Fagerstrom, 1991). Two of the six questions on the test account for most of the person's score and help to determine total tobacco intake and craving. Those two questions are:

How many cigarettes per day do you smoke?

How soon after you wake up do you smoke your first cigarette?

If the person reports smoking more than 30 cigarettes a day and the time after getting up before smoking the first cigarette is less than 5 minutes, he or she can be considered highly nicotine-dependent. The mother of a very close friend of the author had the habit of smoking her first cigarette of the day as soon as she stepped into the shower.

NICOTINE WITHDRAWAL   Withdrawal symptoms result when a person tries to stop using nicotine—and these symptoms are unpleasant for the chronic user. Symptoms usually begin within 2 hours of the last use of tobacco, peak within 24 hours and then begin to decline over the next 10 days to several weeks (Hughes, 2009). For some, withdrawal discomfort and cravings continue for six months or longer. Although each person's symptoms may vary, withdrawal usually involves confusion, anxiety, irritability, impatience, difficulties in concentration, restlessness, drowsiness, dizziness, headache, nausea, disturbed sleep, increased eating and weight gain, and profound craving for tobacco (Hughes, 2009). Other symptoms might include depression, hostility, fatigue, feeling light-headed, a tingling sensation in the limbs, constipation, and increased coughing (Schmitz, Jarvik, & Schneider, 2004). The diagnosis of nicotine withdrawal is made when the person abruptly stops using nicotine, and within 24 hours they show four or more of the following symptoms: a depressed mood; insomnia; irritability, frustration, or anger; anxiety; difficulty concentrating; restlessness; decreased heart rate; or increased appetite or weight gain (American Psychiatric Association, 2000).

OPIOIDS

In the nineteenth century, the opioids were prescribed for a variety of medical conditions. Dr. H. H. Kane's textbook written in 1880, *The Hypodermic Injection of Morphia, Its History, Advantages, and Dangers, Based on Experience of 360 Physicians*, listed 54 diseases believed to benefit from morphine injections. They were diverse—anemia, angina pectoris, diabetes, insanity, nymphomania, tetanus, and vomiting from pregnancy. Physicians often referred to opium (or morphine) as G.O.M., or God's Own Medicine (Earle, 1880). Another commonly accepted practice during this era was to substitute opiates for alcohol. Dr. J. R. Black (1947), in a paper entitled "Advantages of Substituting the Morphia Habit for the Incurably Alcoholic," noted that it had a calming effect and led to a more healthy life for a person than one of alcohol use.

Currently, the **opioids** are widely used as strong pain relievers. Sometimes referred to as narcotics, they are a class of drugs that depress the central nervous system. The opioids have long been used to treat acute pain, like the kind experienced by individuals post-operatively. They have also been used in palliative care to alleviate the severe, chronic, and disabling pain of terminal conditions such as cancer. When used as prescribed by a physician, they are considered safe and generally do not lead to dependence—but unfortunately they have a high potential for abuse. The opioids include the naturally occurring alkaloids such as morphine, the main active ingredient of opium, and derivatives of these such as heroin and synthetic compounds such as methadone. Prescription opiates include morphine, meperidine (Demerol), methadone, codeine, and various opioid drugs for treating coughing and pain. They can come in a variety of forms including capsules, tablets, syrups, solutions, and suppositories.

Illicit opioids include heroin, whose street names include junk, smack, horse, boy, brown sugar, H, big H, skag, and dope. Heroin can be a white or brownish powder that is usually dissolved in water and then injected. Most street preparations of heroin are diluted (or "cut") with other substances such as sugar, starch, powdered milk, or quinine. Street heroin can also be cut with strychnine or other poisons. The term opioid is derived from opium, the narcotic resin extracted from the unripe seedpods of the opium poppy (*Papaver somniferum*). Opium appears as dark brown chunks or as a powder and is usually smoked or eaten.

The 2008 National Survey on Drug Use and Health estimated that 3.7 million people aged 12 or older had used heroin at some time in their lives, representing approximately 1.5 percent of the population (SAMHSA, 2009). A highly addictive substance, heroin is commonly described as a "downer" that affects the brain's pleasure systems and interferes with its ability to perceive pain. Heroin induces feelings of euphoria, a dreamy sense of drowsiness, and a general sense of well-being. Some have described the effects of injecting the drug as a "whole body orgasm," while others may experience unpleasant effects. It can also cause nausea, constipation, sweating, itchiness, and depressed breathing and heart rate. Sharing needles or syringes puts users at risk for infections such as hepatitis and HIV. High doses of the drug itself can cause death.

Heroin can be injected into a vein (called "mainlining") or into a muscle. Years ago, just the idea of using a needle kept many potential heroin users away from the drug; however, today it can be smoked through a water pipe or a standard pipe, mixed in a marijuana "joint" or cigarette, inhaled as smoke through a straw ("chasing the dragon"), or inhaled as powder through the nose. It is a fast-acting drug, especially when injected or smoked. Heroin users quickly develop tolerance and need more and more of the drug to achieve the same high.

The opiates tend to relax the user. The person may go "on the nod" or go back and forth from feeling alert to drowsy. Physical dangers associated with the opiates depend on the specific drug used, its source, the dose, and the way it is ingested. Most of the risks for the person who uses this drug are from using too much and becoming dependent upon it. Other hazards are related to using unsterile (or dirty) needles, contaminated drugs, or combining the drug with other substances. Infections from unsterile solutions, syringes, and needles can cause illnesses such as liver disease, tetanus, HIV, and hepatitis B and C. Chronic heroin injection can cause scarred and/or collapsed veins, bacterial infections of the blood vessels and heart valves, abscesses (boils) and other soft-tissue infections, as well as liver or kidney disease and congested lungs. These lung complications (including various types of pneumonia and tuberculosis) may be as much the result of the poor health of the user as of heroin's depressing effects on respiration. The most common adverse reactions include nausea and vomiting, drowsiness, dizziness, headache, orthostatic hypotension (decreased blood pressure when standing, which may result in fainting), itch, dry mouth, miosis (decreased pupil eye size), urinary retention, and constipation (Rossi, 2005). Chronic users may experience serious constipation that leads to bowel obstruction, fecal impaction, or paralytic ileus (loss of movement in the small intestine resulting in gas and fluid buildup).

Tolerance makes it necessary for the person to use ever-increasing doses of opioids in order to achieve the same effects and can be detected within 12 to 24 hours of taking the drug (Rang, Dale, Ritter, & Moore, 2003). Regular use of an opioid induces physical dependence, which becomes apparent with the symptoms of withdrawal when regular doses are abruptly discontinued or the dosage is rapidly reduced. Persons with the diagnosis of opioid dependence will have significant levels of tolerance and will experience withdrawal symptoms—with onset in a matter of minutes or up to several days after the last dose. The symptoms of withdrawal, as with other substances, are opposite to those of the drug when initially taken and include three or more of the following:

- Severe dysphoria
- Nausea or vomiting
- Muscle aches (cramps)

- Lacrimation or rhinorrea (runny eyes or nose)
- Papillary dilation, piloerection (goose bumps), or sweating (the combination of chills or cold flashes with goose bumps is referred to as "cold turkey")
- Diarrhea
- Yawning
- Fever
- Insomnia

Currently, the diagnosis of opioid dependence does not imply that a withdrawal syndrome is imminent if the opioids are discontinued. However, this nomenclature is being reconsidered for the DSM-5. The criteria for substance abuse are used to make the diagnosis of opioid abuse. Opioid intoxication is considered when the person has recently used an opioid and shows clinically significant maladaptive behavior or psychological changes (such as euphoria followed by apathy, dysphoria, agitation or psychomotor retardation, impaired judgment, or impaired social or occupational functioning) that develop during or shortly after opioid use (American Psychiatric Association, 2000). In addition, the person's pupils constrict (or dilate) and one (or more) of the following signs is present: drowsiness or coma, slurred speech, and impairment in attention or memory. Again, the diagnosis of opioid intoxication requires that symptoms cannot be better explained by a general medical condition or another mental disorder.

HALLUCINOGENS

The hallucinogens are a broad class of natural and synthetic compounds that alter a person's perception and consciousness. In the 1990s, the two most commonly used drugs of this class were LSD (acid) and MDMA or ecstasy (Adam) (American Psychiatric Association, 2000). The amphetamine derivative MDMA (3, 4-methylenedioxy-N-methylamphetamine) is sold as ecstasy on the street; however, the street version often contains no MDMA. Ecstasy is a synthetic drug that acts both as a stimulant and a hallucinogen. Technically known as a hallucinogenic amphetamine (or an empathogen), MDMA produces feelings of energy, empathy, openness (and a desire for physical contact), teeth clenching, plus mild visual and auditory hallucinations (Gray with Zide, 2006). Some individuals have been known to experience dangerous reactions such as jumping out of a window because they believe they can fly. A number of users describe a hangover the following day characterized by feelings of fatigue, drowsiness, and sore jaw muscles. The drug causes the brain to dump large amounts of serotonin into the synapses and raises dopamine levels. MDMA is not toxic, but it can cause death due to overheating and dehydration. It also inhibits the production of urine and can lead to a fatal buildup of fluid in the tissues.

Illegal drug manufacturing is a huge enterprise, and those involved in it have become very creative not only in making the drugs but also in making them available to the public. Green Hornet is a good example. This was a drug in liquid form that was marketed as an alternative for ecstasy sold on the street. Green Hornet could be found on the Internet, and it was promoted as the herbal version of ecstasy. It contained, among other things, the active ingredients of the over-the-counter drugs diphenhydramine and dextromethorphan. Two known manufacturers were Cytotec Solutions, Inc., a company in Tampa, Florida, and Kekio, Inc., located in Colorado Springs, Colorado. The U.S. Food and Drug Administration (USFDA) deemed their sales practices clearly illegal, and views any product promoted as a street drug alternative as an unapproved drug (USFDA, 2004 a, b).

The most widely used hallucinogens are the LSD group, including LSD (lysergic acid), LSA (d-lysergic acid amide), mescaline (found in the peyote cactus plant), DMT (dimethyltryptamine, found in ayahuasca), and psilocybin (the main active ingredient found in certain species of mushrooms; known by the street names shrooms or mushies). Ayahuasca has primarily been prepared for its folk-medicinal and religious purposes. Sections of a vine of the Virola tree found in South and Central America are ground up and boiled alone or with leaves from other plants, resulting in a brew with hallucinogenic effects.

LSD is considered the most common hallucinogen and is one of the most potent mood-changing chemicals. Made from lysergic acid, it is found in a fungus that grows on rye and other grains. Commonly referred to as "acid," LSD is sold illegally in tablet form, capsules, and occasionally as a liquid. It is odorless and colorless with a slightly bitter taste. The hallucinogenic experience is often referred to as a "trip," and adverse reactions are known as a "bad trip." After one has taken the drug, they may experience flashbacks and can be diagnosed as having **hallucinogen persisting perception disorder** (American Psychiatric Association, 2000). The essential feature is the transient recurrence of disturbances in a person's perception reminiscent of those experienced during one or more earlier episodes with the hallucinogenic. The diagnostic criteria for hallucinogen persisting perception disorder (or flashbacks) are:

*   After one stops taking the hallucinogen, he or she re-experiences one or more of the perceptual symptoms that were experienced while intoxicated (e.g., geometric hallucinations, false perceptions of movement in the peripheral visual fields, flashes of color, intensified colors, trails of images of moving objects, positive afterimages, halos around objects, **macropsia** (where objects look larger than they actually are), and **micropsia** (like the rear view mirror in your car where objects look smaller than they are in reality).
*   The symptoms cause significant distress or impairment in social, occupational, or other important areas of functioning.
*   The symptoms are not due to a general medical condition or better accounted for by another diagnosis (e.g., delirium, dementia, schizophrenia) or hypnopomic hallucinations (those that occur upon awakening, commonly seen in the neurologic sleep disturbance narcolepsy).

The causes of these flashbacks are unknown (Drummer & Odell, 2001). They may develop days, weeks, or months after the individual's last use of LSD. The majority of flashbacks consist of visual sensory distortion, but there are also somatic flashbacks that involve feelings of depersonalization and emotional flashbacks involving periods when the individual re-experiences distressing emotions felt during the active use of LSD (McDowell, 2005). Doweiko (2009) observes that seasoned LSD users seem to accept the occurrence of flashbacks much like chronic alcohol users accept a hangover as the price one pays for chemical use.

The DSM-IV-TR criteria for hallucinogen dependence are the same as those for substance dependence. Hallucinogen abuse follows the criteria for substance abuse. The diagnostic criteria for hallucinogen intoxication are similar to those of marijuana. The person experiences perceptual changes such as the subjective intensification of perceptions, depersonalization, derealization, illusions, hallucinations, and synesthesias (intersensory, intersensual associations—e.g., "Can't you just hear the changing colors on the trees?"). The physical symptoms of hallucinogen intoxication noted in the DSM-IV-TR (American Psychiatric Association, 2000) are papillary dilation, rapid heartbeat, sweating, palpitations, blurred vision, tremors, and lack of coordination. Tolerance develops quickly to a number of the hallucinogens (Pechnick & Ungerleider, 2004), and most people experience no withdrawal symptoms.

CANNABIS/MARIJUANA

Although cannabis can have hallucinogenic effects, it is discussed separately in the DSM-IV-TR because of differences in its other psychological and behavioral effects (American Psychiatric Association, 2000). Cannabis is the most routinely used illicit psychoactive substance in the United States. It comes from the leaves, buds, flowers, and resin of the cannabis plant (*Cannabis sativa* or *Cannabis indica*) native to Central Asia. Marijuana is the name given to these plant parts and because the plants tend to grow wild, it is also called weed (Iversen, 2000). There are more than 200 street names for marijuana, and they can vary from city to city and from neighborhood to neighborhood. Some of the most common names are pot, grass, herb, Mary Jane, reefer, skunk, boom, gangster, kif, chronic, and ganga (sometimes spelled ganja).

The plants contain a number of psychoactive compounds called **cannabinoids** that are believed to alter mood and behavior, the most potent of which is delta-9-tetrahydrocannabinol (THC). Cannabis is usually smoked in the form of dried leaves and buds or as dried resin (hashish). When smoked as a cigarette, it is commonly called a "joint"; and when made into cigars, they are called "blunts." Some users also mix marijuana into foods (e.g., brownies) or brew it as tea. The THC latches onto specific receptors in the brain known to be involved in appetite regulation and the perception of pain. Precisely how this process works is not fully understood.

Mood swings are the typical reaction to marijuana. Smoked in moderate amounts, cannabis produces a vague or fuzzy feeling many people describe as mellowness and a sense of general well-being. Others might enter a dreamlike state where time seems to stand still. For some people, it can interfere with memory and increase appetite (a condition popularly referred to as "the munchies"). However, more than any other drug, marijuana can cause some very different reactions in different people. Some individuals may experience nausea, anxiety, and paranoia. Iversen (2000) observes that the feeling of well-being evoked by a small dose of marijuana can change to paranoia, hallucinations, and dizziness when larger doses are taken. Coordination can be affected, which increases the risk of accidents. If eaten, the resin has a hallucinogenic effect. Those who are frequent long-term users of marijuana risk impairments of memory, concentration, motivation, and self-esteem, difficulties in relationships with others, and problems at work.

The diagnostic criteria for cannabis intoxication are (American Psychiatric Association, 2000):

- Recent use of cannabis
- Clinically maladaptive behavioral or psychological changes (such as impaired coordination, euphoria, anxiety, sensation of slowed time, impaired judgment, social withdrawal) that developed during or shortly after using cannabis
- Two or more of the following signs developing within 2 hours of cannabis use:
  - Conjunctival injection (or bloodshot eyes)
  - Increased appetite
  - Dry mouth
  - Tachycardia
- Symptoms are not due to a general medical condition and not better accounted for by another mental disorder

The diagnostic criteria for cannabis abuse follow the criteria for substance abuse. Typically, people who use cannabis value the relaxation, increased sensory awareness, and elevated mood it provides. The diagnostic criteria for cannabis dependence follow the criteria for dependence. Cannabis-dependent individuals compulsively use the drug and have the associated problems: they are often seen as passive; lacking in ambition; and prone to depression, suspiciousness, panic or anxiety attack, and impaired judgment.

OTHER DRUGS

INHALANTS

The **inhalants** are a chemically diverse group of psychoactive substances found in volatile solvents that can be breathed directly into the lungs. These substances are normally found in more than 1,000 ordinary household products—the most commonly abused of which are spray paint, paint thinner, gasoline, amyl nitrate, nitrous oxide (or laughing gas), nail polish remover, felt-tipped markers, airplane glue, contact cement, dry-cleaning fluid, and spot remover. According to the National Survey on Drug Use and Health, the primary users of inhalants are adolescents ranging in ages from 12 to 17 years of age, and in 2008 1.1 percent of this population reported use over the past month (SAMHSA, 2009). Sadly, the inhalants are readily available, inexpensive, and easy to conceal, thus making it easier to use them.

Although inhalant abusers tend to prefer one particular substance because of its smell or taste, a variety of substances may be used to achieve the same effects, due to availability and/or cost. Most inhalants act directly on the central nervous system (CNS) to produce psychoactive or mind-altering effects. Substances are inhaled and absorbed rapidly by the capillary surface of the lungs. This method of ingestion results in a rapid peak in blood levels. The substances enter the brain at such a rapid pace that the intensity resembles the effects that can be produced by an intravenous injection of other psychoactive drugs.

The most common form of ingestion involves sniffing the inhalant directly from an open container or "huffing" from a rag soaked in the substance and held to the face. Another method is to place an open container or a rag soaked in the substance in a bag where the vapors concentrate before being inhaled. This is called "bagging." In the 1996 movie *Citizen Ruth*, the character Ruth is seen huffing patio sealant from a paper bag. Inhalant abusers sometimes spray aerosols directly into the nose. The former *Howard Stern Show* cast member John Melendez would inhale the compressed nitrous oxide found in whipped cream cans ("whippits"). The use of inhalants can cause brain, nerve, liver, and other damage to the body. If the user is startled while high, he or she may go into cardiac arrest, an event known as Sudden Sniffing Death Syndrome.

Some of the effects of inhalants that the practitioner may encounter include: behavior that resembles alcohol inebriation; stimulation and a loss of inhibition that is followed by depression; euphoria; lethargy; distortion in perceptions of time and space; headache; nausea or vomiting; slurred speech; dizziness; loss of motor coordination; sneezing; or "glue sniffer's rash" around the nose and mouth. Most inhalants produce a rapid high that looks like alcohol intoxication with initial excitation, then drowsiness, disinhibition, lightheadedness, and agitation (American Psychiatric Association, 2000). If sufficient amounts are inhaled, nearly all solvents and gases can produce a loss of sensation, dulling of pain responses or anesthesia, and even loss of consciousness.

A person can develop dependence (and the diagnostic criteria follow substance dependence), abuse (following the diagnostic criteria for substance abuse), and intoxication. The physical symptoms for the diagnosis of intoxication that the practitioner might look for are (two or more): dizziness; nystagmus; lack of coordination; slurred speech; unsteady gait; lethargy; depressed reflexes; psychomotor retardation; tremor; generalized muscle weakness; blurred vision or diplopia (or double vision); stupor or coma; and euphoria (American Psychiatric Association, 2000).

Tolerance developing within several hours to a few days after use has been reported with heavy or sustained use of inhalants. The diagnosis of withdrawal is not included in the DSM. There are, however, a number of long-term health problems associated with inhalant use such as loss of hearing; brain and nervous system damage that could result in personality changes and learning disabilities; blood oxygen depletion; bone marrow damage; and heart, lungs, liver, and kidney damage (Sakai & Crowley, 2009).

PHENCYCLIDINES

This is a class of hallucinogenic drugs that produce feelings of depersonalization and detachment from reality, which are qualities with great appeal to recreational drug users who value escapism. It should come as no surprise that entrepreneurial chemists have been able to manipulate the chemical structure of known drugs of abuse and produce a seemingly endless lineup of new drugs. These "designer drugs" obviously are not listed as controlled substances by the Drug Enforcement Administration. Their street names vary from location to location and can change over time. The phencyclidines class of drugs includes phencyclidine (PCP, Sernylan) and ketamine (Ketalar, Ketaject), which is a derivative of cyclohexamine and phencyclidine. Ketamine is generally considered a chemical cousin to PCP. Another dissociative drug is dizocilpine (DZ, MK-801). The phencyclidines were first developed as dissociative anesthetics in the 1950s and became street drugs in the 1960s. They can be taken orally, intravenously, or smoked. A diagnosis of dependence, abuse, or intoxication can be considered, but withdrawal is not included in the DSM (American Psychiatric Association, 2000).

PCP   PCP is a white crystalline powder with a distinctively bitter chemical taste. It is a popular drug for illicit chemists to experiment with, and at least 30 forms of PCP have been identified (Doweiko, 2009). The forms of PCP on the illegal market are tablets, capsules, and colored powders, and they are known by a variety of names including PCE, TCP, PCC, Angel Dust, Hog, Trang, PeaCe Pill, wack, rocket fuel, and "Eu4ia" (an amphetamine-like drug synthesized from legally purchased over-the-counter chemicals). PCP can be snorted, smoked, or eaten. When smoked, PCP is often applied to tobacco or marijuana or to a leafy herb such as mint or parsley. When mixed with marijuana, PCP is called "crystal supergrass" and "killer joints."

Low doses of phencyclidine cause the user to experience dizziness, ataxia (or impairment in control of voluntary muscle coordination), nystagmus, mild hypertension, abnormal involuntary movements, slurred speech, nausea, weakness, slowed reaction times, euphoria or affective dulling, and lack of concern (American Psychiatric Association, 2000). Medium-sized doses of PCP produce reactions of disorganized thinking, changed body image and sensory perception, depersonalization, and feelings of unreality. At high doses, the user may experience amnesia and coma, with analgesic (decreased sensation of pain) effects sufficient for surgery. Seizures and respiratory depression can also occur at the highest doses. For individuals who also have a diagnosis of schizophrenia, their psychotic symptoms may be exacerbated. Peak effects usually occur about 2 hours after oral doses. A mild level of intoxication may resolve itself after 8 to 20 hours, whereas severe intoxication may last for several days.

KETAMINE   Ketamine is a surgical anesthetic, which, unlike some others, does not cause respiratory or cardiac depression (Walton, 2002). Liquid ketamine was developed in the early 1960s and was used on the battlefields in Vietnam. It has been useful in combat, natural disasters, and other situations when an emergency anesthetic is necessary (Schultz, 2002). Powdered ketamine first surfaced as a recreational drug in the 1970s and was known as Vitamin K or Super-K. It resurfaced in the 1990s with the rave scene and became known as Special K. Although ketamine can be manufactured in illicit laboratories, it is a difficult chemical process—so most of the drug found on the streets is diverted from human or veterinary supplies (Gahlinger, 2004). The drug is made by drying ketamine in a stove until it turns from a liquid into a powder.

The effects of ketamine kick in within 30 to 45 minutes, depending on the dose, and the high lasts anywhere from 30 minutes to 2 hours. Users of illicit drugs typically take a low dose and experience feelings of euphoria, visual hallucinations, a sense of unreality, depersonalization, and vivid dreams (Freese, Miotto, & Reback, 2002; Gahlinger, 2004). Some individuals report flashback experiences that occur days or even weeks after taking the drug (Gahlinger). An out-of-body experience has been described by some individuals who took high doses of ketamine. The person describes losing all sense of self and feeling a detachment of mind and body, leading to a trance-like state. In this trance, the person reports experiencing a "superior reality" filled with dazzling insights and visions. Some find this experience wonderful—others are frightened by it.

Long-term use, especially at high doses, may result in memory problems. This effect, coupled with its effectiveness at doses lower than those needed to produce anesthesia, has reportedly made ketamine popular as a date-rape drug (Gahlinger). The drug is usually inhaled through the nose (or snorted) but is sometimes sprinkled on tobacco or marijuana and smoked. Special K is frequently used in conjunction with other drugs such as ecstasy, heroin, or cocaine.

DIZOCILPINE Dizocilpine was originally developed for treating traumatic brain injury and neurodegenerative diseases such as Huntington's, Alzheimer's, and amyotrophic lateral sclerosis (ALS) or Lou Gehrig's disease. The drug is an anticonvulsant. It had a promising future until neurotoxic-like effects were seen in certain regions of the brain. When this occurred, the pharmaceutical company Merck stopped further legal development of the drug. Some recreational users report unpleasant experiences such as strong aural (or auditory) hallucinations.

PHENCYCLIDINE DEPENDENCE AND ABUSE Phencyclidine dependence is diagnosed using the criteria for substance dependence; however, some of the criteria for craving do not apply. Although some individuals with heavy use have reported cravings, the symptoms of tolerance and withdrawal are not clearly demonstrated (American Psychiatric Association, 2000). Phencyclidine is easy to obtain and individuals often use the drug several times a day, thus spending a significant part of their day using the substance. Some individuals may continue to use the drug, despite psychological problems (e.g., anxiety, rage, aggression, or flashbacks) or medical problems (e.g., hyperthermia, hypertension, seizures). Due to a lack of insight and judgment while intoxicated, a person might also get into situations (such as fighting) that can result in legal problems.

To diagnose abuse, the substance abuse criteria are applied. While the person uses the drug less often than someone with a diagnosis of dependence, he or she may still neglect obligations at home, work, or school. Legal problems are not uncommon, and the person's behavior while intoxicated may contribute to arguments or risky behaviors such as driving while under the influence of the drug. When considering intoxication, the practitioner looks for clinically significant behavior changes (e.g., belligerence, assaultiveness, impulsiveness, unpredictability, agitation, impaired judgment, or impaired social or occupational functioning) that develop during or shortly after phencyclidine use. Intoxication is also indicated when the user experiences two or more of the following symptoms within an hour (of swallowing the drug) or less (when smoked, snorted, or used intravenously): vertical or horizontal nystagmus; hypertension or tachycardia; numbness or diminished responsiveness to pain; ataxia; slurred speech; muscle rigidity; seizures or coma; or sensitivity to sound (American Psychiatric Association, 2000). The diagnosis of intoxication is made only if these symptoms are not associated with a general medical condition or better explained by another mental disorder.

SUMMARY

Taken together, the substance-related disorders are the most prevalent mental health issue, and more than likely practitioners can anticipate seeing someone struggling with drugs and/or alcohol at some time in their practice. In fact, at any given time in the United States, there are approximately 2 percent to 10 percent of adults who either abuse or are addicted to illegal drugs (Doweiko, 2009). There is no clear-cut cause of substance use, though many explanations have been offered. As the case studies in this chapter illustrate, persons with substance-related problems experience multiple medical, psychological, family, and social consequences.

EP 2.1.3 a

The competency-based assessment fosters the practitioner's critical thinking by exploring the multiple dimensions of a person's life and provides an avenue to truly grasp all aspects of a client's struggle with substances. Research, observation, and common sense have shown that there are many determinants of substance use and abuse. There are the intrapersonal or personal factors, such as genetics, temperament, or individual traits; interpersonal determinants, such as family history; and the community and environmental influences, such as cultural background and social attitudes—yet, none of this knowledge provides a clear-cut explanation or prediction for who will become substance-dependent and who will not.

The DSM-IV-TR classifies the substance-related disorders at the highest level as either problems of substance use or problems that are substance-induced. Within the group of disorders related to substance use, problems are further distinguished by being related either to substance dependence or to substance abuse. Within the group identified as substance-induced disorders, problems are deemed to be related to either substance intoxication or substance withdrawal. Polysubstance disorders apply to those who are using (or abusing) at least three groups of substances (excluding caffeine and nicotine).

The first part of this chapter provided the terminology that is commonly used in this field of practice as well as providing the organizational framework for the substance-related disorders. The second part of the chapter was devoted to the substances themselves. The 11 classes of substances presented in the DSM were organized into the five groups of drugs most commonly encountered by social workers in practice. They are the depressants, stimulants, opioids, hallucinogens, and other drugs. Each group was reviewed in order to provide knowledge and insight into why and how people use drugs. Many clients who come to the attention of the social worker are not motivated to change, even if their drug habits are self-destructive. Clients (and their families) are usually affected on multiple levels as a consequence of addictive behavior. Therefore, practitioners must become aware of all the various substances of use and abuse and develop a base of knowledge that will allow them to accurately assess the nature and severity of the client's needs and resources. This overview is intended to familiarize practitioners with substances as they are used in the real lives of our clients.

As we have seen in this chapter, the distinctions between substance abuse and dependence are not always clear. Looking to the DSM-5, it seems probable that both of these diagnostic categories will be subsumed within a general diagnosis called "substance use disorder" under an expanded addiction section that will include for the first time a behavior addiction, compulsive gambling.

PRACTITIONER'S REFLECTIONS

Sooner or later all practitioners will be confronted with the substance-related disorders. Despite massive efforts in the United States to eliminate recreational chemical abuse, it continues to be a major issue that results in a wide range of social, economic, and psychological problems—not just for the individual users, but for their families and communities as well. Social workers are among the "first responders" when drug- and alcohol-related problems are

destroying clients' lives. Thus, it is critical that practitioners know what to look for and be able to assess clients' situations for successful intervention.

ACTIVITIES

Advanced Clinical EP 2.1.1 d

1. Interview a friend or colleague who has given up an addiction to a legal substance such as alcohol, nicotine, or caffeine. Be sure to ask about what helped them to give up the addiction. Based on these experiences, what insights can you gain that will help you to develop, manage, and maintain a therapeutic relationship with your clients who struggle with the abuse of substances, both legal and illegal? Address the strengths and resources in the environment that helped your friend or colleague move through his or her addiction.

2. Reflect back on the experiences of one of your clients who has struggled with an addiction to an illegal substance. What insights can you learn from their experience that will help you to develop the therapeutic relationship with your own clients from a strengths perspective found in the competency-based assessment? (If you have not worked with a client with a substance-related problem, interview a colleague with expertise in this area, and ask about what insights they can share to help inform your practice.)

3. Having studied both, are there any differences between legal and illegal substance use?

4. People who abuse substances often cope by denial or deceit. If you were working with someone you suspect was abusing or was addicted to substances, what questions would you ask to determine if substance use was a problem?

EP 2.1.10 (b) a

a. After you have developed this list of questions, role-play an interview with a colleague using your questions in order to explore the suspected abuse (or addiction). Once

done, talk with your colleague about how he or she experienced these questions and what might have been "missing" in your approach. Alternatively, explore what you did well.

b. If you got stuck in the role play interview, describe how you would use supervision or consultation to improve your skills. Develop a specific list of questions for your supervisor or consultant.

EP 2.1.1 f

5. Find another colleague with whom to debate the following statement: "The difference between substance abuse and substance dependence is really not important." (As an alternative, discuss this statement with several colleagues who have experience in the field of substance use.) Reflect on how this debate helped you to distinguish, appraise, and integrate multiple sources of knowledge to inform your perspectives on the debate.

EP 2.1.3 a

6. People from all walks of life can be adversely affected by the use of substances. Imagine for a moment that you have been asked to develop a brochure for an agency waiting room that focuses on the prevention of substance use. Outline the key points that you would plan to cover in this preventive program. As a part of completing this "reflection," it might be helpful if you tailored this brochure to a specific agency.

7. Reflect on how people who are addicted to drugs and/or alcohol are portrayed in the popular media. Compare this image to your actual social work practice with people dependent on substances.

EP 2.1.4 b

If you are a professional who is not employed in the field of substance use, interview a colleague who works in this area for his or her opinion about how the media portrayal compares with their work experiences. What can you conclude about how people who struggle with substance use are commonly seen? List at least three ways that these media images may potentially influence your own (or other professional colleagues') personal biases and values when working with diverse clients.

8. Nicotine is considered to be high on the list of the most powerfully addictive substances, which helps to explain why so many smokers find it difficult or impossible to stop. Interview several people who regularly smoke, and ask them to support or refute the following statement: "Most smokers don't think of themselves as drug addicts." Based on the information they provide, what can be said about nicotine dependence?

9. Imagine that you are new to the field of working with people who struggle with substance use. After reading this chapter, you realize that you will need to have a great deal of medically oriented information in order to be effective with your clients. Develop a plan to increase your knowledge base in this area. Be as specific as you can (i.e.: Who would you talk with? What would you read? What courses or seminars would you take? What experiences would be useful?, etc.).

10. Access the CourseMate website at www. cengagebrain.com. Go to the case vignette that provides a series of reflective questions about Tim's struggles with a substance use disorder. He sees alcohol in his life as a positive, adding that nothing bothers him when he drinks. Apparently Tim's problems come back when he is not drinking. The case study is intended to help you identify the key criteria for a substance use disorder.

COMPETENCY NOTES

EP 2.1.1 f: Use supervision and consultation (p. 136): Social workers commit themselves to the profession's enhancement and to their own professional conduct and growth.

EP Advanced Clinical 2.1.1 d: Develop, manage, and maintain therapeutic relationships with clients within the person-in-environment and strengths perspectives (p. 136): Advanced practitioners in clinical social work recognize the importance of the therapeutic relationship, the person-in-environment and strengths perspectives, the professional use of self with clients, and adherence to ethical guidelines of professional behavior.

EP 2.1.3 a: Distinguish, appraise, and integrate multiple sources of knowledge, including research-based knowledge, and practice wisdom (pp. 92, 135, 136): Social workers are knowledgeable about the principles of logic, scientific inquiry, and reasoned discernment.

EP 2.1.4 b: Gain sufficient self-awareness to eliminate the influence of personal biases and values in working with diverse groups (p. 136): Social workers appreciate that, as a consequence of difference, a person's life may include oppression, poverty, marginalization, and alienation as well as privilege, power, and acclaim.

EP 2.1.4 c: Recognize and communicate understanding of the importance of difference in shaping life experiences (p. 94): Social workers understand how diversity characterizes and shapes the human experience and is critical to the formation of identity.

EP Advanced Clinical 2.1.7 b: Use bio-psycho-social-spiritual theories of human behavior and the social environment to guide clinical practice (p. 93): Advanced practitioners understand how to synthesize and differentially apply the theories of human behavior and the social environment (biological, developmental, psychological, social, cultural, and spiritual).

EP Advanced Clinical 2.1.7 c: Consult with medical professionals, as needed, to confirm diagnosis and/or to monitor medication in the treatment process (p. 110): Advanced practitioners understand how to synthesize and differentially apply the theories of human behavior and the social environment (biological, developmental, psychological, social, cultural, and spiritual).

EP 2.1.9 a: Continuously discover, appraise, and attend to changing locales, populations, scientific and technological developments, and emerging societal trends to provide relevant services (p. 93): Social workers recognize that the context of practice is dynamic.

EP 2.1.10 (b) a: Collect, organize, and interpret client data (p. 136): Social work practice involves the dynamic and interactive process of engagement with clients on multiple levels.

EP 2.1.10 (b) c: Assess client's coping strategies to reinforce and improve adaptation to life situations, circumstances, and events (pp. 101, 107): Advanced practitioners have a theoretically informed knowledge base so as to effectively practice with individuals, families, and groups.

REFERENCES

Albers, L., Hahn, R., & Reist, C. (2001–2002). *Handbook of psychiatric drugs*. Laguna Hills, CA: Current Clinical Strategies.

American Cancer Society. (2011). Guide to quitting smoking. Retrieved on May 29, 2011 from: http://www.cancer.org/Healthy/StayAwayfromTobacco/GuidetoQuittingSmoking/guide-to-quitting-smoking-success-rates

American Psychiatric Association. (2000). *Diagnostic and statistical manual of mental disorders* (4th ed., text revision). Washington, DC: Author.

Ashley, O., Marsden, M. E., & Brady, T. (2003). Effectiveness of substance abuse treatment programming for women: A review. *American Journal of Drug and Alcohol Abuse, 29,* 19–54.

Bakken, K., Landheim, A. S., & Vaglum, P. (2003). Primary and secondary substance misusers: Do they differ in substance-induced and substance-independent mental disorders? *Alcohol and Alcoholism, 38* (1), 54–59.

Barker, R. L. (2003). *The social work dictionary* (5th ed.) Washington, DC: NASW Press.

Barlow, D. H., & Durand, V. M. (2012). *Abnormal psychology: An integrative approach* (6th ed.). Belmont, CA: Wadsworth Cengage Learning.

Barnes, G. M., Hoffman, J. J., Wolfe, J. W., Farrell, M. P., & Dintcheff, B. A. (2006). Effects of parental monitoring and peer deviance on substance use and delinquency. *Journal of Marriage and the Family, 68,* 1084–1104.

Barrett, S. P., Darredeau, C., & Pihl, R. O. (2006). Patterns of simultaneous polysubstance use in drug-using university students. *Human Psychopharmacology: Clinical and Experimental, 21* (4), 255–263.

Barrett, S. P., Gross, S. R., Garand, I., & Pihl, R. O. (2005). Patterns of simultaneous polysubstance use in Canadian rave attendees. *Substance Use and Misuse, 40* (9–10), 1525–1537.

Benowitz, N. L. (2002). Smoking cessation trials targeted to racial and economic minority groups (Editorial). *Journal of the American Medical Association, 288,* 497–499.

Black, J. R. (1947). Advantages of substituting the morphia habit for the incurably alcoholic. *Cincinnati Lancet-Clinic* in A. R. Lindesmith, *Opiate addiction* (p. 183). Evanston, IL: Principia Press.

Bonne, J. (January 9, 2003). 'Go pills': A war on drugs? Air Force use of amphetamines raises questions. Retrieved on May 30, 2011 from: www.msnbc.msn.com/id/3071789/

Boyd, M. R., Phillips, K., & Dorsey, C. J. (2003). Alcohol and other drug disorders, comorbidity, and violence: Comparison of rural African-American and Caucasian women. *Archives of Psychiatric Nursing, 17,* 249–258.

Brook, D., Brook, J., Zhang, C., Cohen, P., & Whiteman, M. (2002). Drug use and the risk of major depressive disorder, alcohol dependence, and substance use disorders. *Archives of General Psychiatry, 39,* 1039–1044.

Burchfield, G. (2006). Caffeine. Retrieved on June 26, 2006 from: www.abc.net.au/quantum/poison/caffeine/about.htm

Caldwell, J. A., Caldwell, J. L., & Darlington, K. K. (2003). Utility of dextroamphetamine for attenuating the impact of sleep deprivation in pilots. *Aviation, Space, and Environmental Medicine, 74* (11), 1125–1134.

Canapary, D., Bongar, B., & Cleary, K. M. (2002). Assessing risk for completed suicide in patients with alcohol dependence: Clinicians' views of critical factors. *Professional Psychology: Research and Practice, 33* (5), 464–469.

Castillo, R. J. (1997). *Culture and mental illness: A client-centered approach*. Pacific Grove, CA: Brooks/Cole Thomson Learning.

Centers for Disease Control and Prevention (2003). Cigarette smoking among adults—United States,

2001. *Morbidity and Mortality Weekly Report, 52,* 953–956.

Centers for Disease Control and Prevention, National Center for Chronic Disease Prevention and Health Promotion, Office on Smoking and Health, U.S. Department of Health and Human Services. (2007). Best Practices for Comprehensive Tobacco Control Programs. Available at: http://www.cdc. gov/tobacco/stateandcommunity/best_practices/ pdfs/2007/bestpractices_complete.pdf

Cole, J. C., Sumnall, H. R., Smith, G. W., & Rostami-Hodjegan, A. (2005). Preliminary evidence of the cardiovascular effects of polysubstance misuse in nightclubs. *Journal of Psychopharmacology, 19* (1), 67–70.

Corcoran, J., & Walsh, J. (2006). *Clinical assessment and diagnosis in social work practice.* New York: Oxford University Press.

Corcoran, M., & Corcoran, J. (2001). Retrospective reasons for the initiation of substance abuse: Gender and ethnic effects. *Journal of Multicultural Social Work, 10,* 69–83.

de Graaf, R., Bijl, R. V., Smit, F., Vollebergh, W. A. M., & Spijker, J. (2002). Risk factors for 12-month comorbidity of mood, anxiety, and substance use disorders: Findings from the Netherlands mental health survey and incidence study. *American Journal of Psychiatry, 159,* 620–629.

Department of Health and Human Services. (1990). *The health benefits of smoking cessation: A report of the Surgeon General* (DHHS Publication No. CDC 90-8416). Washington, DC: U.S. Government Printing Office.

Doweiko, H. E. (2009). *Concepts of chemical dependency* (7th ed.). Belmont, CA: Brooks/Cole Cengage Learning.

Drummer, O. H., & Odell, M. (2001). *The forensic pharmacology of drugs of abuse.* New York: Oxford University Press.

Earle, C. W. (1880). The opium habit: A statistical and clinical lecture. *Chicago Medical Review, 2,* 442–446.

Emonson, D. L., & Vanderbeek, R. D. (1995). The use of amphetamines in the U.S. Air Force tactical operations during Desert Storm. *Aviation, Space, and Environmental Medicine, 66* (3), 260–263.

Foroud, T., Edenberg, H. J., & Crabbe, J. C. (2010). Genetic research: Who is at risk for alcholism? *Alcohol Research and Health, 33* (1 & 2), 64–75.

Freese, T. E., Miotto, K., & Reback, C. J. (2002). The effects and consequences of selected club drugs. *Journal of Substance Abuse Treatment, 23* (2), 151–156.

Gahlinger, P. M. (2004). Club drugs: MDMA, gamma-hydroxybutyrate (GHB), rohypnol, and ketamine. *American Family Physician, 69,* 2919–2927.

Galanter, M., & Kleber, H. D. (Eds.) (2008). *Textbook of substance abuse treatment* (4th ed.). Washington, DC: American Psychiatric Press.

Gold, M. S., & Miller, N. S. (2004). Cocaine (and crack): Neurobiology. In J. H. Lowinson, P. Ruiz, R. B. Millman, & J. G. Langrod (Eds.), *Substance abuse: A comprehensive textbook* (4th ed., pp. 166–180). New York: Lippincott Williams & Wilkins.

Goodwin, D. W., & Gabrielli, W. F. (2004). Alcohol: Clinical aspects. In J. H. Lowinson, P. Ruiz, R. B. Millman, & J. G. Langrod (Eds.), *Substance abuse: A comprehensive textbook* (4th ed., pp. 142–147). New York: Lippincott Williams & Wilkins.

Gossop, M., Marsden, J., & Stewart, D. (2002). Dual dependence: Assessment of dependence upon alcohol and illicit drugs, and the relationship of alcohol dependence among drug misusers to patterns of drinking, illicit drug use, and health problems. *Addiction, 97* (2), 169–178.

Grant, B. F., & Pickering, R. P. (1996). Comorbidity between DSM-IV alcohol and drug use disorders: Results from the national longitudinal alcohol epidemiologic survey. *Alcohol Health Research World, 20* (1), 67–72.

Gray, S. W. (with Zide, M. R.). (2006). *Psychopathology: A competency-based treatment model for social workers.* Pacific Grove, CA: Brooks/Cole Thomson Learning.

Griffiths, R. R., Juliano, L. M., & Chausmer, A. L. (2003). Caffeine pharmacology and clinical effects. In A. W. Graham, T. K. Schultz, M. F. Mayo-Smith, R. K. Ries, & B. B. Wilford (Eds.), *Principles of addiction medicine* (3rd ed., pp. 193–224). Chevy Chase, MD: American Society of Addiction.

Hasan, A. A., & Ciancio, S. (2004). Relationship between amphetamine ingestion and gingival enlargement. *Pediatric Dentistry, 26* (5), 396–400.

Heatherton, T. F., Kozlowski, L. T., Frecker, R. C., & Fagerstrom, K. O. (1991). The Fagerstrom test for nicotine dependence: A revision of the Fagerstrom tolerance questionnaire. *British Journal of Addiction, 86,* 1119–1127.

Hughes, J. R. (2009). Nicotine-related disorders. In B. J. Sadock, V. A. Sadock, & P. Ruiz (Eds.),

Kaplan and Sadock's comprehensive textbook of psychiatry (9th ed., Vol. I, pp. 1353–1359). Philadelphia: Lippincott Williams & Wilkins.

Ivanov, I., Schultz, K. P., London, E. D., & Newcorn, J. H. (2008). Inhibitory control deficits in childhood and risk for substance use disorders: A review. *American Journal of Drug and Alcohol Abuse, 34,* 239–258.

Iversen, L. L. (2000). *The science of marijuana.* New York: Oxford University Press.

Juliano, L. M., & Griffiths, R. R. (2004). A critical review of caffeine withdrawal: Empirical validation of symptoms and signs, incidence, severity, and associated features. *Psychopharmacology, 176* (1), 1–29.

Kalayasiri, R., Kranzler, H. R., Weiss, R., Brady, K., Gueorguirva, R., Panhuysen,C., & Malison, R. T. (2006). Risk factors for cocaine-induced paranoia in cocaine-dependent sibling pairs. *Drug and Alcohol Dependence, 84,* 77–84.

Kane, H. H. (1880). *The hypodermic injection of morphia. Its history, advantages, and dangers. Based on experience of 360 physicians.* New York: Chas L. Bermingham and Company.

Mack, A. H., Franklin, J. E., & Frances, R. J. (2003). Substance use disorders. In R. E. Hales & S. C. Yudofsky (Eds.), *Textbook of psychiatry* (4th ed., pp. 309–377). Washington, DC: American Psychiatric Press.

Mansvelder, H. D., Keath, J. R., & McGehee, D. S. (2002). Synaptic mechanisms underlie nicotine-induced excitability of brain/reward areas. *Neuron, 33,* 905–919.

Martensen, R. L. (1996). From Papal endorsement to southern vice. *Journal of the American Medical Association, 216,* 1615.

McDowell, D. (2005). Marijuana, hallucinogens, and club drugs. In R. J. Frances, S. I. Miller, & A. H. Mack (Eds.), *Clinical textbook of addictive disorders* (3rd ed., pp. 157–183). New York: Guilford.

McKay, A., Koranda, A., & Axen, D. (2004). Using a symptom-triggered approach to manage patients in acute alcohol withdrawal. *MEDSURG Nursing, 13* (1), 15–20, 31.

Memmott, J. L. (2003). Social work practice with the elderly substance abuser. *Journal of Social Work Practice in the Addictions, 3* (2), 85–103.

Meyer, J. U., Rumpf, H. J., & Hapke, U. (2004). Smoking, nicotine dependence, and psychiatric comorbidity—a population-based study including smoking cessation after three years. *Drug and Alcohol Dependence, 76* (3), 287–295.

Mirin, S., Batki, S. B., Bukstein, O., Isbell, P., Kleber, H., Schottenfeld, R., Weiss, R. D., & Yandow, V. W. (2002). Practice guideline for the treatment of patients with substance use disorders: Alcohol, cocaine, opioids. *American Psychiatric Association practice guidelines for the treatment of psychiatric disorders: Compendium 2002* (pp. 249–348). Washington, DC: American Psychiatric Press.

Moeller, F. G., Dougherty, D. M., Barratt, E. S., Schmitz, J. M., Swann, A. C., & Grabowski, J. (2001). The impact of impulsivity on cocaine use and retention in treatment. *Journal of Substance Abuse Treatment, 21,* 193–198.

MSNBC. (2006). U.S. face of drug abuse grows older. Retrieved on June 5, 2006 from: www.msnbc.msn.com/id/12839601/print/1/displaymode/1098

National Institute on Drug Abuse. (March 2005). Cigarettes and other nicotine products. *NIDA Info Facts.* NIF-010 National Institutes of Health—U.S. Department of Health and Human Services.

National Institute on Alcohol Abuse and Alcoholism. (July 2005). Brief interventions. *Alcohol Alert, 66,* 1–8.

Nawrot, P., Jordan, S., Eastwood, J., Rothstein, J., Hugenholtz, A., & Feeley, M. (2003). Effects of caffeine on human health. *Food Additives and Contaminants, 20* (1), 1–30.

Nestler, E., & Malenka, R. (March 2004) The addicted brain. *Scientific American,* 78–83.

New Straits Times. (August 11, 1997). Fatal smoking contest. Retrieved from: www.nstp.com.my

O'Brien, C. P. (2005). Benzodiazepine use, abuse, and dependence. *Journal of Clinical Psychiatry, 66* (Suppl. 2), 28–33.

Office of National Drug Control Policy. (2004). *The Economic costs of drug abuse in the United States, 1992–2002.* Washington, DC: Executive Office of the President (Publication No. 207303). Available at: www.ncjrs.gov/ondcppubs/publications/pdf/economic_costs.pdf

O'Neill, S. E., & Sher, K. J. (2000). Physiological alcohol dependence symptoms in early adulthood: A longitudinal perspective. *Experimental and Clinical Psychopharmacology, 8* (4), 493–508.

Orwin, R., Maranda, M., & Brady, T. (2001). *Impact of prior physical and sexual victimization on substance abuse treatment outcomes.* Fairfax, VA: Caliber Associates.

Owen, D. (2008). *In sickness and in power: Illnesses in heads of government during the last 100 years.* Westport, CT: Praeger.

Paris, R., & Bradley, C. L. (2001). The challenge of adversity: Three narratives of alcohol dependence, recovery, and adult development. *Qualitative Health Research, 11* (5), 647–667.

Pechnick, R. N., & Ungerleider, J. T. (2004). Hallucinogens. In J. H. Lowinson, P. Ruiz, R. B. Millman, & J. G. Langrod (Eds.), *Substance abuse: A comprehensive textbook* (4th ed., pp. 230–237). New York: Lippincott Williams & Wilkins.

Petry, N. M. (2001). Substance abuse, pathological gambling, and impulsivity. *Drug and Alcohol Dependence, 63,* 29–38.

Rang, H. P., Dale, M. M., Ritter, J. M., & Moore, P. K. (2003). *Pharmacology* (5th ed). Edinburgh: Churchill Livingstone.

Rehm, J., Mathers, C., Popova, S., Thavorncharoensap, M., Teerawattananon Y., & Patra, J. (2009). Global burden of disease and injury and economic cost attributable to alcohol use and alcohol-use disorders. *Lancet, 373* (9682), 2223–2233.

Rhee, S. H., Hewitt, J. K., Young, S. E., Corley, R. P., Crowley, T. J., & Stallings, M. C. (2003). Genetic and environmental influences on substance initiation, use, and problem use in adolescents. *Archives of General Psychiatry, 60,* 1256–1264.

Rohde, P., Lewinsohn, P., Kahler, C., Seeley, J., & Brown, R. (2001). Natural course of alcohol use disorders from adolescence to young adulthood. *Journal of the American Academy of Child and Adolescent Psychiatry, 40,* 83–90.

Rossi, S. (Ed.) (2005). *Australian medicines handbook 2005.* Adelaide: Australian Medicines Handbook.

Sakai, J. T., & Crowley, T. J. (2009). Inhalant-related disorders. In B. J. Sadock, V. A. Sadock, & P. Ruiz (Eds.), *Kaplan and Sadock's comprehensive textbook of psychiatry* (9th ed., Vol. I, pp. 1341–1353). Philadelphia: Lippincott Williams & Wilkins.

Schmitz, J. M., Jarvick, M. E., & Schneider, N. G. (2004). Nicotine. In J. H. Lowinson, P. Ruiz, R. B. Millman, & J. G. Langrod (Eds.), *Substance abuse: A comprehensive textbook* (4th ed., pp. 276–293). New York: Lippincott Williams & Wilkins.

Schuckit, M. A. (2009). Alcohol-related disorders. In B. J. Sadock, V. A. Sadock, & P. Ruiz (Eds.), *Kaplan and Sadock's comprehensive textbook of psychiatry* (9th ed., Vol. I, pp. 1268–1288). Philadelphia: Lippincott Williams & Wilkins.

Schultz, C. H. (2002). Earthquakes. In D. E. Hogan and J. L. Burstein (Eds.), *Disaster medicine.* New York: Lippincott Williams & Wilkins.

Shaner, J. W. (2002). Caries associated with methamphetamine abuse. *Journal of the Michigan Dental Association, 84* (9), 42–47.

Staines, G. L., Magura, S., Foote, J., Deluca, A., & Kosanke, N. (2001). Polysubstance use among alcoholics. *Journal of Addictive Diseases, 20* (4), 57–73.

Stefani, M. D. (2000). Institutional experiences in psychotic episodes with drug-addicted patients and their families: Substance, drug and group opiate-dependence dynamic. *Group Analysis, 33* (2), 289–294.

Sternbach, L. H. (1972). The discovery of Librium. *Agents Actions, 2,* 193–196.

Strain, E. C. (2009). Substance-related disorders. In B. J. Sadock, V. A. Sadock, & P. Ruiz (Eds.), *Kaplan and Sadock's comprehensive textbook of psychiatry* (9th ed., Vol. I, pp. 1237–1268). Philadelphia: Lippincott Williams & Wilkins.

Strat, Y. L., Ramoz, N., & Gorwood, P. (2010) In alcohol-dependent drinkers, what does the presence of nicotine dependence tell us about psychiatric and addictive disorders comorbidity? *Alcohol and Alcoholism, 45* (2), 167–172.

Stuart, G. L., Ramsey, S. E., Moore, T. M., Kahler, C. W., Farrell, L. E., Recupero, P. R., & Brown, R. A. (2003). Reductions in marital violence following treatment for alcohol dependence. *Journal of Interpersonal Violence, 18* (10), 1113–1131.

Substance Abuse and Mental Health Services Administration. (2004). *Results from the 2003 national survey on drug use and health: National finding.* (NSDUH Series H-25, DHHS Publication No. SMA 04-3964). Rockville, MD: Office of Applied Studies.

Substance Abuse and Mental Health Services Administration. (2009). *Results from the 2008 national survey on drug use and health: National findings* (NSDUH Series H-36, DHHS Publication No. (SMA) 09-4434). Rockville, MD: Office of Applied Studies.

Sulzer, D., Sonders, M. S., Poulsen, N. W., & Galli, A. (2005). Mechanisms of neurotransmitter release by amphetamines: A review. *Progress in Neurobiology, 75,* 406–433.

U.S. Food and Drug Administration. (2004a). FDA warns consumers not to purchase Green Hornet, promoted as herbal version of "ecstasy." Retrieved on September 20, 2006 from: www.fda.gov/bbs/topics/NEWS/2004//NEW01026.html

U.S. Food and Drug Administration. (2004b). FDA expands warning about "green hornet" to include all other products by Cytotec Solutions, Inc. Retrieved on September 20, 2006 from: www.fda.gov/bbs/topics/news/2004/NEW01049.html

Vinton, L., & Wambach, K. (2005). Alcohol and drug use among elderly people. In C. A. McNeese & D. DiNitto (Eds.), *Chemical dependency: A systems approach* (pp. 484–502). Boston: Pearson.

Walton, S. (2002). *Out of it: A cultural history of intoxication*. New York: Harmony Books.

Wilens, T. E. (2004). Attention deficit/hyperactivity disorder and the substance use disorders. The nature of the relationship, who is at risk, and treatment issues. *Primary Psychiatry, 11* (7), 63–70.

Wilens, T. E. (2006). Attention deficit/hyperactivity disorder and substance use disorders. The nature of the relationship, subtypes at risk, and treatment issues. *American Journal of Psychiatry, 163,* 2059–2063.

Williams, R., & Cohen, J. (2000). Substance use and misuse in psychiatric wards. *Psychiatric Bulletin, 24,* 43–46.

Windle, M., & Zucker, R. A. (2010). Reducing underage and young adult drinking: How to address critical drinking problems during this developmental period. *Alcohol Research and Health, 33* (1 & 2), 29–44.

Wright, E. M. (2001). Substance abuse in African American communities. In S. A. Ashenberg Strausser (Ed.), *Ethnocultural factors in substance abuse treatment* (pp. 31–51). New York: Guilford.

Schizophrenia and Other Psychotic Disorders

CHAPTER 5

INTRODUCTION

Dr. John Haslam, an early pioneer in the field of mental illness, wrote *Observations on Madness and Melancholy*, published in 1809. He conceptualized schizophrenia as "a form of insanity," stating:

> The sensibility appears to be considerably blunted; they do not bear the same affection towards their parents and relations; they become unfeeling to kindness, and careless of reproof.... I have painfully witnessed this hopeless and degrading change, which in a short time has transformed the most promising and vigorous intellect into a slavering and bloated idiot. (Haslam, 1809/1976, pp. 65–67)

Almost 50 years later, in 1860 a Belgian psychiatrist named Benedict Augustin Morel (1890) standardized and formally described symptoms of schizophrenia using the French terms *demence* (loss of mind) and *precoce* (early, premature).

The use of the term schizophrenia began in 1896 with Emil Kraepelin, a German professor of psychiatry who brought together under one heading several types of mental abnormalities previously viewed as separate and distinct disorders even though they shared similar underlying features. Kraepelin (1971) distinguished three subtypes and included them under the Latin term **dementia praecox**:

1. **Catatonia** (alternating immobility and excited agitation).
2. **Hebephrenia** (silly and immature emotionality).
3. **Paranoia** (delusions of grandeur or persecution).

Kraepelin postulated that, although clinical manifestations might differ, the central feature of the disorder was its early onset that ultimately developed into a "mental weakness." He went on to identify several features occurring in dementia praecox, such as hallucinations, delusions, and negativism. Further, Kraepelin believed that changes in the brain were of some importance in its cause. He was the first to suggest that dementia started in early adolescence and evolved into a long-term chronic course due to brain deterioration.

In 1911, Eugene Bleuler, a Swiss psychiatrist, differed from Kraepelin's conceptualizations and described a group of "different" schizophrenias characterized by disturbances of feelings, thinking, and relationships to the outside world. Bleuler (1926, 1950) believed that underneath the person's unusual behaviors was an "associative splitting" of the basic functions of personality. He felt the most prominent feature of schizophrenia was the tearing apart of the individual's psychic functions. This, he believed, was especially evident in inappropriate behavior, in the loosening of associations between ideas, and disorganization of thought, affect, and actions. He coined the term **schizophrenia** from the Greek word *skhizein*, meaning "split," and *phren*, meaning "mind" (Fusar-Poli & Politi, 2008). This new word replaced terms such as madness, lunacy, and dementia praecox. Bleuler did not intend to suggest that "split mindedness" represented two distinct personalities (as is found in the person with dissociative identity disorder), rather that it denoted a shattered personality. Bleuler believed the split referred to the widening gap between internal and external realities. This schism between thought, emotion, and behavior established what continues to remain as the most enduring description of schizophrenia. Bleuler isolated four fundamental diagnostic features, sometimes called "the four A's," to identify the splitting of external reality. They are:

- **Associations**—logical thought processes. When thought processes are altered, speech loses its coherence (associations are loosened) and connections among ideas are absent or obscure. Communication may become highly idiosyncratic and individualized; that is, the person may create his or her own words (**neologism**) according to some form of special symbolism. An example of a neologism would be, *"Every time I hear the clinks, snaps, and bangs on the grass, I guess, I think, I know that's where Jesus clicks and clocks."*
- **Affect**—observable manifestation of a person's mood or emotion. In schizophrenia this is characterized by diminished emotions (flat or blunted), feeling disconnected from surrounding events (impersonating or performing within a role), and/or emotional indifference to the surrounding world (reduction in pleasurable experiences).
- **Autism**—characterized by significant impairment in social interactions, communication, and restricted patterns of behavior, interest, or activity.
- **Ambivalence**—positive and negative values that exist simultaneously; they include uncertainty about taking a particular direction or vacillating between two different perspectives and/or courses of action.

In the 1930s, Kurt Schneider (1959) introduced the concept of first- and second-rank symptoms—now known as positive and negative symptoms—which have become a significant factor in assessing schizophrenia. Building on Schneider's first-rank symptoms, the positive symptoms are summarized in Table 5.1.

TABLE 5.1	POSITIVE SYMPTOMS (OR THE PRESENCE OF ALTERED BEHAVIORS) ADAPTED FROM SCHNEIDER'S FIRST-RANK CRITERIA

Disorganized thinking
- Disturbances of audible thoughts.
- Voices arguing.
- Voices commenting to each other.

Disorganized behavior
- Somatic passivity experiences or inertia.

Catatonic behavior
- Muscular rigidity and immobility.
- Stupor and negativism or state of excitement.

Delusions
- Thought withdrawal (e.g., believing thoughts have been removed by an outside force).
- Thought broadcasting (e.g., believing passages from books, television, and other environmental stimuli are specifically directed at oneself).

Hallucinations
- Delusional perceptions (can occur in any of the five senses, but auditory, such as hearing voices, is the most common).

Other
- All other experiences involving avolition (inability to initiate or participate in important activities).
- Unusual motor behavior (such as rocking or pacing).
- Depersonalization (or feeling detached).
- Derealization (or loss of one's sense of reality in the external world).
- Somatic preoccupations.

Source: Adapted from the American Psychiatric Association, *Diagnostic and statistical manual of mental disorders*, 4th ed., text revision. (Washington, DC: American Psychiatric Association, 2000), and from K. Schneider (M.W. Hamilton, Trans.) *Clinical psychology*. (London: Grune and Stratton, 1959).

The negative symptoms, including Schneider's contribution of second-rank symptoms, are described in Table 5.2.

UNDERSTANDING SCHIZOPHRENIA

The exact cause of schizophrenia is unknown, but there is growing support for the idea of genetic and biological factors being associated with its origin. Schizophrenia is characterized by a broad range of behaviors marked by a loss of the person's sense of self, significant impairment in reality testing, and disturbances in feeling, thinking, and behavior. The individuals affected are unable to distinguish the accuracy of their own perceptions and thoughts from external reality. Persons diagnosed with schizophrenia (as opposed to other psychiatric disorders) are often unaware of their symptoms or even may contest that they have them (Lysaker, France, Hunter, & Davis, 2005). The term **psychosis** is often used interchangeably with schizophrenia and refers to a group of incapacitating disorders traditionally defined as the loss of reality testing and the impairment of mental functioning

TABLE 5.2	NEGATIVE SYMPTOMS (OR THE LACK OF BEHAVIORS) ADAPTED FROM SCHNEIDER'S SECOND-RANK CRITERIA

Loss of feeling or an inability to experience pleasure (anhedonia)
- Disturbances of perception (the simple pleasures of life are no longer enjoyed).
- Lack of interest in social or recreational activities through failure to develop close relationships.

Poverty of speech (alogia)
- Amount of speech is greatly reduced and tends to be vague or repetitious.
- Perplexity, bewilderment, and confusion (being slow in responding to questions or does not respond at all).

Flat presentation (affective flattening)
- Depressive and euphoric mood changes.
- Unchanging facial expressions, poor or no eye contact, reduced body language, and decreased spontaneous movements.
- Stares vacantly into space and speaks in a flat, toneless voice.

Withdrawal, loss of motivation, and ambivalence (avolition)
- Feelings of emotional impoverishment or seeming lack of interest in what were usual activities.
- Inattentive to personal grooming, hygiene.
- Difficulty in persisting at work, school, or household chores.

Source: Adapted from the American Psychiatric Association, *Diagnostic and statistical manual of mental disorders*, 4th ed., text revision. (Washington, DC: American Psychiatric Association, 2000), and from K. Schneider (M.W. Hamilton, Trans.) *Clinical psychology*. (London: Grune and Stratton, 1959).

manifested by delusions (or irrational beliefs) and/ or hallucinations (or sensory experiences in the absence of external events), as well as confusion, impaired memory, and the inability to function within the interpersonal domain.

More narrowly defined, psychosis describes characteristics and behaviors involving delusions, prominent hallucinations, grossly disorganized or catatonic behavior, incoherent speech, aimless agitation (or total immobility), and an affect that ranges from apathy and withdrawal to incoherent thinking (Barlow & Durand, 2012). Complicating the practitioner's ability to understand this syndrome is the fact that many of the abovementioned features are not found in everyone with schizophrenia but *can* be found as a part of other mental disorders. To better understand an individual and his or her distinctive course of schizophrenia, the competency-based assessment encourages the practitioner to look at the person's capacity for interpersonal relationships, cultural influences, environmental and social factors, and coping resources.

Advanced
Clinical
EP 2.1.3 b

Despite the reality that some people with schizophrenia can function productively, the symptom picture remains misunderstood and it becomes important for the social worker to identify and articulate a client's strengths as well as recognize vulnerabilities. Attitudes about those with mental disorders have varied throughout history, but in all eras, people with schizophrenia have been maligned. For example, someone with schizophrenia is more likely to be harassed in public than a person without the diagnosis (Tarrier, Khan, Cater, & Picken, 2007). The diagnosis of schizophrenia burdens people who have to make their way in a society that views them as different or "of a less desirable kind" (Van Dorn, Swanson, Elbogen, & Swartz, 2005, p. 152). Popular books, movies, and television portrayals have exploited this illness and contribute to the misinformation about it. Newspaper headlines reading "Ex-Mental Patient Goes on Wild Shooting Spree" may be factually accurate, but they foster a false picture that all people with schizophrenia should be considered dangerous. These accounts help perpetuate a detrimental and negative picture of everyone who suffers with a mental illness.

Schizophrenia interferes with almost every aspect of a person's intrapersonal functioning and interpersonal world. It disrupts how they see their social environment, the manner in which they think, speak, and even move. The emotional as well as financial aspects of this diagnosis take a tremendous toll on the individual and his or her family. A complex symptom picture characterizes schizophrenia—but there are specific patterns or features that tend to appear together.

Schizophrenia has a chronic course, which generally includes three phases: a **prodromal** phase, an **active or acute phase** (characterized by delusions, hallucinations, or both), and a **residual phase** in which the prevailing features are in remission. In assessing for schizophrenia, the disorder must persist for at least 6 months and include at least 1 month of active phase symptoms (or less, if successfully treated)—which means two (or more) of the following symptoms are present: delusions, hallucinations, disorganized speech, grossly disorganized or catatonic behavior, and negative symptoms (American Psychiatric Association, 2000). In real life, people with schizophrenia do not always fit neatly into these specific subcategories, thus causing confusion among practitioners about the usefulness of their assessment guidelines.

CULTURAL CONSIDERATIONS

EP 2.1.4 a

Schizophrenia is known around the world and in most cultures and socioeconomic groups. Kearney and Trull (2012) observe that the diagnosis is more common in developing countries and in immigrants and migrant workers than in developed countries. When psychosis does occur, it is not viewed as a normal phenomenon and is always seen as an indication of some profound mental process. A cultural frame of reference expands the conceptualization of mental illness and sets the stage for biases when working with those diagnosed with schizophrenia. For example, mental illness can be conceived as resulting from "bad character," the way a person is raised, or God's will (Van Dorn et al., 2005). In some industrialized countries, researchers contend that schizophrenia is a culturally created label for those people who behave in ways that are outside accepted cultural norms (Barlow & Durand, 2012). Conversely, labeling someone may predispose them to display symptoms consistent with the disorder. Angermeyer and Schulze (2001) note that someone who was just diagnosed may withdraw from others to avoid discrimination, experience a lowered sense of self-esteem and quality of life, become depressed or angry, and act somewhat oddly. The practitioner pays attention to the extent to which the societal values may oppress, marginalize, or alienate his or her client. Additionally, as a consequence of being seen as somehow "different," clients may be misjudged and not seen as having their full potential.

As part of the competency-based assessment, the practitioner should take into consideration how mental illness is perceived within the person's culture of origin as well as how it is seen in the current culture and the diverse ways of understanding a diagnosis. Also helpful is to examine the composition, structure of social and family support, and level of social communication. There are cultural variations in how families react to a member with schizophrenia, but their reactions do not contribute to the cause of the disorder (Weisman de Mamani, Kymalainen, Rosales, & Armesto, 2007). Social support, particularly attachment to others and reassurance of worth, is the best protective factor in mental health, whereas critical and hostile environments provide additional stressors that can, in turn, contribute to more relapses (Caron, Latimer, & Tousignant, 2002; Caron, Lecompte, Stip, & Renaud, 2005, van Os & Allardyce, 2009). Given the symptom picture of schizophrenia, it is easy to understand how this person can challenge the resources of family members regardless of their culture and social structure. The case of Rudy Rosen presented later in this chapter illustrates some of these challenges.

PREVAILING PATTERN

One of the first tasks confronting the practitioner is to determine the extent of psychotic symptoms including inquiries into manic and/or depressive features (if they have ever been present).

For most people with schizophrenia, the symptoms come and go. The following three phases are indicative of the schizophrenic cycle:

1. The **prodromal phase** refers to the period before the features of schizophrenia become very apparent; this is the period of time during which the person's level of functioning deteriorates.
2. The active phase, wherein the disorder persists for at least 6 months with the individual exhibiting psychotic features (e.g., hallucinations, delusions, and grossly disorganized behavior and speech) or negative features such as flat affect for at least 1 month during that period.
3. The residual phase follows the active phase. This is sometimes considered a "filler" category because people have either been helped successfully or they have improved to the point where they no longer have enough features for the practitioner to ascertain the presence of schizophrenia.

The following metaphor may be helpful in visualizing the active and residual phases. Imagine for a moment that you have a full glass of milk in front of you. Everyone can easily identify it as a glass of milk because of its color, texture, smell, and taste. This could be considered analogous to the active phase of schizophrenia; that is, the individual has all the attributes characteristic of schizophrenia. Further imagine this glass of milk has now been emptied. Enough of a residue remains so that one can still identify its prior contents as milk. This residual phase suggests that the person has some remaining features but not to the extent that he or she could be fully assessed for schizophrenia.

Although at least 50 percent of individuals with schizophrenia improve significantly with treatment, some people experience the disorder as a chronic illness characterized by frequent hospitalizations and/or incarcerations—with attendant social and/or legal consequences. The overall course tends to be a progressive deterioration of functions, at least during the first few years. This includes both the exacerbations of symptoms and the partial remissions. It is this small group of chronic sufferers who often come to the practitioner's attention. The general outlook for these individuals tends to be guarded, as the disorder can be quite devastating in terms of impaired interpersonal and social functioning. Suicide, depression, substance abuse, and social withdrawal often coexist (Compton, Weiss, West, & Kaslow, 2005; Jobe & Harrow, 2005).

There are several factors that have some bearing on a person's prognosis. According to Caron, Mercier, Diaz, and Martin (2005), a negative predictor for someone's future adaptation is linked to hospitalization at a young age when the first diagnosis of schizophrenia has been made. Other factors related to a poorer prognosis are an insidious or slow onset of psychosis; poor insight; poor early adjustment; delusions; flat affect and other negative symptoms; and substantial impairment after the first episode of psychotic symptoms (Elmsley, Chiliza, & Schoerman, 2008; Ho, Nopoulos, Flaum, Arndt, & Andreasen, 2004; Malla & Payne, 2005). The outlook is brighter where the person receives effective treatment soon after an episode of strange behavior, has extensive social support, or when a person's cognitive functioning is still relatively good.

Features that suggest a chronic course with schizophrenia include an insidious onset; previous personal or family history of schizophrenia; evidence of social withdrawal; inappropriate or shallow affect; the prior assessment for schizoid, schizoaffective, schizophreniform, or schizotypal personality disorders; and difficulties conforming to treatment regimens. Veen (2005) notes that the apparent prevalence of schizophrenia rises over time in people with psychotic disorders, and they tend to retain the diagnosis of schizophrenia for a longer term.

Because of the limitations in subtyping schizophrenia, the DSM Task Force proposed a three-factor dimensional model to describe current and lifetime symptomatology for possible inclusion in the DSM-5. This proposal is tentative, but it is hoped that the proposed categories will provide a common language for researchers to help refine the diagnostic process. Briefly, the three proposed dimensions are:

- *Psychotic dimension*—the degree to which hallucinations or delusions have been present.
- *Disorganized dimension*—the degree to which disorganized speech, disorganized behavior, or inappropriate affect have been present.
- *Negative (deficit) dimension*—the degree to which negative symptoms (i.e., affective flattening, alogia or speech disturbance, and avolition or loss of goal-directed behavior) have been present. Note: Do not include symptoms that appear to be secondary to depression, medication side effects, or hallucinations or delusions (American Psychiatric Association, 2000, p. 766).

If these proposed subtypes are accepted, practitioners would evaluate the presence of these categories as they currently exist and over a person's lifetime.

UNDERSTANDING POSITIVE AND NEGATIVE SYMPTOMS

Some practitioners may find positive and negative categorizations of psychotic behaviors confusing, so here is another way to conceptualize them. Think of positive symptoms as those outward psychotic signs (delusions or hallucinations) that are *present* in the person with schizophrenia and absent in a person without psychosis. Negative symptoms are those that are *notably absent* in the person with schizophrenia (full range of emotions and affect), but usually present in people without the disease.

In terms of positive symptoms, there are several different types of delusions—grandeur, guilt, jealousy, persecution, and ideas of reference. The symptoms vary widely, and no single feature is common to everyone with schizophrenia. Individuals with a psychotic disorder must have at least one (or more) positive symptom. In addition to distortions in thought content (delusions), other positive symptoms include distortions in perception (hallucinations), language and thought process (disorganized speech), and either grossly disorganized behavior or catatonia.

Negative symptoms, as mentioned, are those characteristics that are notably absent even though they are normally present in people's experience. For example, the person with schizophrenia (a) has a blunted affect instead of the full range of emotions evident in someone without a diagnosis, (b) is emotionally withdrawn instead of socially connected, (c) has poor rapport with others instead of being able to relate easily, (d) shows difficulty in abstract thinking or stereotypical thinking instead of being oriented and "connected," (e) lacks spontaneity instead of relating freely, or (f) shows poor self-care instead of maintaining proper diet and hygiene. Speech and motivation are also features that are absent but should be present. For example, the person may show signs of **alogia** (lack of fluency and productivity of thought and speech) or **avolition** (a loss of goal-directed behavior). As well, the individual may be ambivalent about approaching social situations. Overall, negative symptoms severely reduce the singular characteristics of an individual's personality. An assessment for the presence of schizophrenia requires at least two negative features in the sensory areas of the body (sight, hearing, taste, smell, and touch). There is no universal agreement about which symptoms should be included in these categories.

A third dimension, disorganized symptoms, also appears to be an important aspect of schizophrenia (Ho, Black, & Andreasen, 2003). Disorganized symptoms include rambling speech, erratic behavior, and inappropriate affect.

A summary of both positive and negative symptoms follows.

Delusions   **Delusions** are false and fixed beliefs based on incorrect deductions or misrepresentations in a person's reality. These beliefs are not considered as normative within the individual's cultural or religious group. The two most common types are **delusions of grandeur** (belief that one is special, famous, or important) and **delusions of persecution** (belief that others intend harm). The practitioner can explore delusions by suggesting an alternative scenario to the individual, saying, for example, "Suppose those people who followed you were not going to harm you, but rather they were just going to the same place you were." If the individual cannot acknowledge the possibility of this alternative explanation, then chances are that the practitioner is seeing a delusion at work.

Delusions are of major importance in understanding schizophrenia. These delusional beliefs are firmly maintained by the individual, despite evidence to the contrary. Following is a representative sample of the types of delusions that the practitioner might encounter along with a series of questions aimed at exploring them further.

- *Delusions of Grandeur*
  - Do you think you have exceptional talents, unique powers, or mysterious abilities that no one else has?
  - (If YES) Could you describe them? Could you tell me more about this?
  - Do you possess these special abilities during special times?
- *Delusions of Persecution*
  - Do you think people are against you, following you, or are trying to hurt you?
  - (If YES) Could you tell me more about that?
  - Why do you think people are out to get you?
  - Are people plotting against you?
  - Do they want to hurt you?
  - (If YES) Why do you think someone would want to hurt you?
  - When you notice this happening to you, what do you think this means?
- ***Delusions of Reference***
  - When you are watching television, reading a newspaper, or listening to the radio, do you believe that "they" are referring specifically to you? Or that there are special messages intended just for you to see or hear?
  - (If YES) What kinds of things have you noticed?
  - What does this mean to you?
  - Do you think that strangers in stores, the mall, or in a movie theater take special notice of you or talk about you behind your back?
  - (If YES) How do you know this? What does this mean to you?
- ***Thought Broadcasting***
  - Have you ever thought about something so strong or hard that other people could hear your thoughts?
  - (If YES) Do you think people can hear what you are thinking, even if you don't say anything out loud?
  - How do you know this?
- ***Thought Insertion***
  - Are there thoughts inside your head that have been placed there by somebody from the outside? (Be sure to clarify that you are referring to thoughts inserted by others.)
  - (If YES) Could you tell me more about where these thoughts come from?
  - Have you noticed there is a special time or place when this happens?

HALLUCINATIONS **Hallucinations** are experiences of sensory events in the absence of environmental stimulation. For an assessment of schizophrenia, the hallucination must be considered prominent. **Auditory hallucinations** or hearing voices is considered the most common feature of schizophrenia. These auditory hallucinations may be present in other mental disorders, but in schizophrenia the person typically talks *about*, as well as *to*, the imagined individual. Often these voices sound so real to the person that he or she is convinced that they are coming from outside—from hidden microphones, for example. The voices are often described as abusive and critical in nature, or they command the person to perform unpleasant or harmful tasks.

Somatic or **tactile hallucinations** are considered the least common and include sensations similar to electrical tingling or burning sensations. I remember a former client who related feeling as if "a boa constrictor was slithering down inside my body. It went around my chest, and when it split in half one part went down my arms, and the other part went down my legs." Tactile and somatic hallucinations are important in the assessment process for schizophrenia because they occur in relatively few other psychiatric disorders.

DISORGANIZED SPEECH   **Disorganized speech** is not governed by logic. Sometimes it is exhibited in rhymes or puns; other times it may take the form of mimicking speech patterns of those around the person—he or she may copy the tone, words, or fragments of overheard conversations (**echolalia**). Other examples include condensing or combining words or inventing new words (neologism). Some may continuously repeat the same words or sentence (**perseveration**) or use rhyme or puns (**clanging**). Two other manifestations of disorganized speech include failure to answer specific questions (going off on a tangent) and the random or arbitrary leaping from topic to topic (**derailment**). Needless to say, these patterns of speech complicate the person's ability to communicate with others.

Alogia involves a speech disturbance in which there is either relative scarcity in the amount of speech or poverty in its content. It is important to note that only speech that is seriously disorganized and extremely difficult to understand and/or interpret should be considered a symptom of schizophrenia. Disorganized speech can be seen in other disorders such as delirium or dementia, and these other conditions must be ruled out. Alogia is derived from the Latin term alogiae meaning nonsense.

DISORGANIZED BEHAVIOR   **Disorganized behavior** involves physical actions that do not appear to be goal-directed—for example, taking off one's clothes in public, assuming or maintaining unusual postures, pacing excitedly, or moving fingers or extremities in idiosyncratic and repetitive ways. These forms of behavior are seen as severe and cause a great deal of impairment to the individual; they are not simply odd or eccentric as in a tic or compulsion. Similar to disorganized speech, disorganized behavior is seen in other disorders such as substance intoxication, and those other conditions must be ruled out.

OTHER POSSIBLE INDICATORS OF SCHIZOPHRENIA   **Flat affect** is exhibited by gazing with "vacant eyes." The individual is seemingly unaffected by what is going on around him or her and displays little change in facial expressions. Often, inappropriate affect is displayed by laughing or crying at incongruous times.

Bizarre behavior refers to a pattern of conduct or demeanor far removed from normal and expected experiences. Determining what is bizarre and what is not becomes especially important.

Avolition involves the inability to make goal-directed choices along with the expression of little or no interest in activities. The individual is generally disorganized, behaves inappropriately, and may be excessively controlled and rigid. Avolition is indifference and unresponsiveness to even the most basic everyday activities, such as maintaining personal hygiene, and the inability to independently sustain other important self-care activities. The term avolition was derived from the prefix *a*, meaning "without," and *volition*, meaning "an act of choosing, or deciding."

An easy way to summarize the diagnostic criteria for schizophrenia is in terms of the presence of (1) a psychotic factor, (2) a disorganized factor, and (3) a negative factor. For a significant portion of time since the onset of the disorder, one or more major areas of social functioning will have deteriorated, such as occupational, social, or self-care. Duration includes continuous signs and symptoms that must persist for at least 6 months. During this period, at least 1 month must include features of psychosis (or the active phase). Periods of either prodromal or residual traces are not enough to represent a full-blown episode of schizophrenia. Additionally, the person must display negative symptoms, and at least two other features, such as poor personal hygiene, plus an increased belief that people are talking about them behind their back.

DIFFERENTIAL ASSESSMENT

Schizophrenia affects about 1 percent of the world's population and it affects 3.2 million people in the United States (National Institute of Mental Health, 2005). Of that 3.2 million, 2.2 million are adults (18 or older), which constitutes 1.1 percent of the entire adult population of the United States. A diagnosis of schizophrenia costs the nation $32.5 billion annually but that number is estimated to be over $60 billion when factors such as family caregiving, lost wages, and treatment are included (Jablensky, 2009; Wu et al., 2005).

It has been suggested that schizophrenia affects men and women equally, but evidence indicates that it occurs slightly more often in men (Aleman, Kahn, & Selten, 2003; Luoma, Hakko, Ollinen, Jarvelin, & Lindeman, 2008). Additionally, important gender differences are noted in relation to the age of onset. In particular, males tend to have symptoms at a younger age than females. With an earlier start, this means that men will have more severe symptoms (Dickerson, 2007). It is not known why this happens. Although the disorder can occur at any age, the median age of onset is 22 years. To fully understand the symptom picture and the influence of the client's social environment, the competency-based assessment provides a framework for the social worker to take into account information about a client's biological, social, cultural, and psychological development.

FAMILIAL AND BIOLOGICAL/GENETIC CONSIDERATIONS

EP 2.1.7 b

Competent social work practitioners consider the many theories that explain a client's behavior across the life span. When considering schizophrenia, there is considerable debate among various professional disciplines regarding the validity of a schizophrenia-specific onset occurring in childhood. One prevalent explanation for how schizophrenia (and the other psychotic disorders) can develop is the neurodevelopmental hypothesis (Murray, Jones, Susser, van Os, & Cannon, 2003). This theory suggests that there is a subtle disease process that affects brain areas very early in life, possibly as early as the second trimester of the prenatal period, and gradually continues to the point where full-blown symptoms emerge. This hypothesis is supported by evidence that indicates early problems, and brain changes can show up as a child develops. For instance, children who show a decline in intelligence over time, lower tested intelligence scores, more repeated grades and trouble paying attention are found to be at a higher risk for developing schizophrenia (Maki et al., 2005). Children who ultimately develop schizophrenia tend to show more withdrawn, neurotic, depressive, solitary, aggressive, and disruptive behaviors (Niemi, Suvisaari, Tuulio-Henriksson, & Lonnqvist, 2003). Each family responds differently to someone with the disorder but these reactions in and of themselves do not cause schizophrenia (Weisman de Mamani, Kymalainen, Rosales, & Armesto, 2007). Nevertheless, if the home environment is hostile and critical this can create additional stressors that can, in turn, lead to greater struggles and possibly more relapses.

A family history of schizophrenia worsens the overall prognosis but there is no evidence to show that there is a single gene that causes schizophrenia. Instead, thousands of gene variances combine to produce vulnerability to having the disorder (Purcell et al., 2009; Wray & Visscher, 2010). Evidence of genetic transmission of the risk for schizophrenia has been widely accepted, and some twin and family studies further support the idea of a genetic component in schizophrenia. Studies comparing **monozygotic** (or identical) to **dizygotic** (or fraternal) twins confirm the hypothesis that genetics play a large role in the predisposition and vulnerability to schizophrenia. Several interesting findings emerged in a definitive study begun my Fischer (1971) and continued by Gottesman and Bertelsen (1989). Findings indicated that if one parent is an identical twin (monozygotic) with schizophrenia then his or her child has about a 17 percent chance of having the disorder. Additionally, the child's risks for schizophrenia remained at 17 percent when the parent was the identical twin without schizophrenia (and the co-twin had the disorder). Clearly, one can have genes that predispose a diagnosis of schizophrenia and not actually have the disorder but still pass on the genes. It was also found that if one parent of fraternal twins (dizygotic) has schizophrenia it followed that his or her child had about a 17 percent chance of having schizophrenia. Interestingly, when the parent did not have schizophrenia but the parent's fraternal twin did, then the child's risk for a diagnosis of schizophrenia was about 2 percent.

The risk of having schizophrenia varies according to how many genes an individual shares with someone who actually has the disorder. Gottesman (1991), in a classic analysis, looked at data from about 40 studies of schizophrenia and summarizes the disorder as follows: "While the genes are necessary for causing schizophrenia, they are not sufficient or adequate by themselves, and one or more environmental contributors are also necessary for schizophrenia but they are not specific to it" (p. 164). Nevertheless, there is sufficient and increasing evidence to support the fact that those with schizophrenia have a different biochemical makeup from the general population (Opler & Susser, 2005).

Magnetic resonance imaging, commonly referred to by the acronym MRI, provides a way to view the structure of the brain without the use of unnecessary radiation. In principle, an MRI is a noninvasive procedure that relies upon the interactions of magnetic fields and radio frequency radiation with body tissues to provide a three-dimensional view of internal organs and structures within the body. Current research suggests significant differences can be found in brain ventricle size, with a sizeable majority of people with schizophrenia showing abnormally large lateral ventricles (Shenton & Kubicki, 2009). Other investigations have compared brain structure among people with schizophrenia, their same-sex siblings who did not have schizophrenia, and healthy volunteers. Both those with schizophrenia and their otherwise unaffected siblings had enlargement of the third ventricle compared to the volunteers in the study, suggesting that the enlargement of ventricles may be related to susceptibility of schizophrenia (Staal et al., 2000). However, it seems that several brain sites are associated with the cognitive dysfunction seen in those with schizophrenia, especially the prefrontal cortex, various related cortical regions, and subcortical circuits, including the thalamus and the stratum (Shenton & Kubicki, 2009). Decreased brain volume in the temporal region suggests a relationship between the severity of auditory hallucinations and disorganized language (Gur & Pearlson, 1993) as well as blunted affect and motivation (Klausner, Sweeney, Deck, Hass, & Kelly, 1992). Other variations occur in areas pertaining to cognitive competency skills, levels of concentration, memory, and perception. Many practitioners continue to believe schizophrenia is a disorder of the brain; however, no evidence of brain abnormality (structure or function) has been found common to those who have schizophrenia.

Biochemical theories suggest that the presence of **neurotransmitters** in the brain is clearly involved in the pathophysiology of schizophrenia, but their specific role remains undetermined. Neurotransmitters are chemical substances (such as epinephrine or dopamine) that transmit nerve impulses across synapses to either inhibit or excite a target cell. Some researchers maintain schizophrenia may be caused by alterations in these neurochemical systems resulting from some other more fundamental pathophysiologic process occurring in four areas of the brain: limbic system, frontal lobes, temporal lobes, and basal ganglia. However, the association of a single area of the brain with the cause of this disorder is unlikely—the four areas are so interconnected that dysfunction in one area often causes primary pathology in another.

THE ROLE OF DOPAMINE

The role of the neurotransmitter **dopamine** remains the basis for one of the foremost and enduring biochemical theories regarding the etiology of schizophrenia. Because certain antipsychotic medications work by blocking the effect of the neurotransmitter dopamine, there has been much hypothesizing about it. The following discussion is a brief overview and is intended to familiarize the practitioner with the major concepts of the role of dopamine in schizophrenia.

The central nervous system depends on neurotransmitters to communicate— they are, in essence, chemical messengers. Through their effects on specific nerve circuits, these neurotransmitters can affect a person's mood, memory, and well-being. There are hundreds of substances known or suspected to be neurotransmitters, and one of the best-understood is dopamine (Wade & Tavris, 2010). There are several types of dopamine, whose effects are either excitatory (a voltage shift in a positive direction) or inhibitory (a voltage shift in a negative direction), depending on which receptor sites are activated. The simplest formulation of the dopamine hypothesis for schizophrenia points to the possibility that somehow the dopamine system is too active (or excitatory). Excessive dopamine may mediate the positive symptoms of auditory hallucinations or delusions, while deficient dopamine (which is inhibitory) in cortical regions of the brain may mediate the negative symptoms of schizophrenia (such as the emotional blunting, social withdrawal, apathy, and so forth). Research evidence leads us to believe that schizophrenia in certain people is partially attributable to excessive dopamine activity, especially involving the D2 receptors (the group of dopamine receptors that are typically inhibitory) (Laurelle, Kegeles, & Abi-Dargham, 2003).

Although some dopamine sites may be overactive, a second type—prefrontal D1 receptors—has captured the interest of researchers. This dopamine site is in the part of the brain used for thinking and reasoning and may account for other symptoms common in schizophrenia (Koh, Bergson, Undie, Goldman-Rakic, & Lidow, 2003). What seems clear is that dopamine's involvement in the development of schizophrenia is more complicated than once thought.

Briefly, the human brain is made up of billions of **neurons**, which all send or "fire" messages back and forth between each other. These messages are received from presynaptic neurons; they continue to cross over gaps and progress toward the **synapse**, moving onto a **receptor**, and finally are delivered to a postsynaptic neuron. The basic dopamine hypothesis does not really elaborate on whether dopaminergic hyperactivity is due to too much release of dopamine, too many dopamine receptors, hypersensitivity of the dopamine receptors to dopamine, or some combination of those mechanisms. Regardless of its role in schizophrenia, dopamine continues to be seen as an important neurotransmitter that is involved in the regulation of cognition, sensory processes, and mood.

There are two major limitations associated with the dopamine hypothesis. First, dopamine antagonists are effective in treating virtually all psychotic and severely agitated individuals, not just those diagnosed with schizophrenia. Other clinical investigations have been looking into several other neurotransmitters suspected of being involved in the pathophysiology of schizophrenia—for example, serotonin, acetylcholine, glutamate, and gamma aminobutyric acid (GABA). There is continued debate among some practitioners about whether the impact or presence of specific neurotransmitters can alone endorse an assessment of schizophrenia. There seems to be some evidence that dopaminergic hyperactivity is not seen uniquely in individuals with schizophrenia. The second major limitation associated with the dopamine hypothesis is that some electrophysiological data suggest that dopaminergic neurons may increase their firing rate in response to long-term exposure to antipsychotic drugs. A revised theory regarding dopamine is that the neurotransmitter itself is less important than is its role in helping to control information processing in the cortex (Murray, Lappin, & Di Forti, 2008).

Other neurotransmitters have been implicated in schizophrenia, including noradrenaline, serotonin, gamma aminobutyric acid, and glutamate (Carlsson, 2006; Craven, Priddle, Crow, & Esiri, 2005). Possibly these other neurotransmitters, especially serotonin, interact with dopamine, and deficits in key brain areas help produce the symptoms of schizophrenia. Others suggest that less serotonin in the frontal cortex leads to more activity in this brain area and thus more dopamine activity (Alex, Yavanian, McFarlane, Pluto, & Pehek, 2005).

SUICIDE, DEPRESSION, AND SUBSTANCE USE

Suicide is a profoundly serious complication associated with schizophrenia. Unfortunately, one in ten people with schizophrenia eventually commits suicide (National Institute of Mental Health, 2005). Often these individuals see suicide as the only reasonable alternative to living with this devastating and chronic disorder. People with schizophrenia often lead lonely, isolated lives, and the disorder itself makes them highly suspicious and/or ambivalent in their relationships with others. Their behavior appears erratic and inconsistent. They have major problems relating to others and have little insight into their problems (Caron, Mercier, Diaz, & Martin, 2005). They frequently demonstrate either a strong dependency on familiar people or become bothersome, annoying, or intrusive to strangers. Real friendships rarely exist. The content of their delusions and hallucinations usually frightens, estranges, or alienates others. Those at a higher risk for suicide tend to be single, unemployed, and socially isolated males (Hawton, Sutton, Haw, Sinclair, & Deeks, 2005; Palmer, Pankratz, & Bostwick, 2005; Pinikahana, Happell, & Keks, 2003).

Other disorders commonly associated with schizophrenia are mood, especially depression, and the substance-related disorders (Freudenreich, Holt, Cather, & Goff, 2007). Depression may develop either before or after someone is diagnosed with schizophrenia. When depression develops before the onset of schizophrenia, it may help to trigger psychotic symptoms. Alternatively, the onset of psychotic symptoms could lead to a downward spiral in a person's functioning involving problems such as losing his or her job that later cause them to become depressed (Rosen, Miller, D'Andrea, McGlashan, & Woods, 2006).

The presence of comorbid substance use disorders exacerbates problems already associated with the course of schizophrenia—including increased hospitalizations; homelessness; violence; family, emotional, and financial strain; and noncompliance with treatment modalities (Bentley & Walsh, 2006). Substance abuse among those with schizophrenia symptoms is common, but whether stressful life events and drug use trigger psychotic symptoms or whether the symptoms develop afterward is not clear. What we do know is that some may use marijuana or other drugs to cope with their psychotic symptoms (Henquet, Murray, Linszen, & van Os, 2005). "Schizophrenia is a complex syndrome that inevitably has a devastating effect on the lives of the person affected and on family members.... Society often devalues these individuals" (Barlow & Durand, 2012, p. 469). The prevailing consensus is that schizophrenia is more complicated than other disorders because of the combination of social and emotional factors that play a large role in determining its outcome.

A COMPETENCY-BASED ASSESSMENT OF SCHIZOPHRENIA AND OTHER PSYCHOTIC DISORDERS

The competency-based assessment involves a careful evaluation of the client by the practitioner and by what others in the client's social world have observed. The assessment carefully explores thoughts, speech, perception, affect, psychomotor activity, and interpersonal functioning. Other noteworthy areas to explore include the following:

- *Absence of insight*—The person is noncompliant in taking medications because he or she does not believe there is a problem.
- *Disturbance of sleep*—The person may experience trouble sleeping, especially when the onset of auditory hallucinations and delusions keeps him or her awake.
- *Dysphoric mood*—The individual exhibits anxiety, hypersensitivity, anger, and depression.

The assessment for schizophrenia must determine that, for much of the individual's time, the disorder substantially impairs his or her ability to socialize, work, or maintain some level of self-care. When this disorder develops during late childhood or adolescence, the person tends to fall short of realizing and achieving normative expected scholastic, social, and/or occupational status.

Distinguishing the diagnosis of schizophrenia from other disorders can be a challenge for the practitioner because some symptoms can closely resemble those found in other disorders. For example, a person with schizophrenia commonly experiences a mood disturbance that typifies the mood disorders. A diagnosis of schizophrenia is made when the client's symptoms are not due to the effects or use of a substance (e.g., abuse of a drug or prescription medication) and when they are not directly caused by a general medical condition, such as cerebrovascular disease, herpes encephalitis (herpes in the brain), **Wernicke encephalopathy** (vitamin deficiency of thiamine, which metabolizes poorly in heavy drinkers, resulting in confusion, loss of muscle coordination, and unintelligible speech), or **Korsakoff psychosis** (amnesic disorder caused by damage to the thalamus from chronic, heavy alcohol use). If the individual has had a past history of an autistic disorder or another type of pervasive developmental disorder, then schizophrenia is considered only if prominent and pronounced hallucinations or delusions are also present and last for a month or more (or less, if the individual has been treated successfully).

SCHIZOPHRENIA: THE FIVE SUBTYPES

The types of schizophrenia are not based on any understanding of the mechanisms of the disorder; they simply organize sets of symptoms that tend to appear together. The earlier historical discussion of Kraepelin's initial concept of schizophrenia outlined his formulations regarding some differences noted between various categories of schizophrenia, which he later identified as subtypes. Subsequent classification models identified specific divisions among these subtypes of schizophrenia. Although symptoms can cut across several subtypes, only one subtype can be assessed at any time. The five subtypes are **paranoid type, catatonic type, disorganized type, undifferentiated type,** and **residual type.** According to Ho, Black, and Andreasen (2003), research supports dividing schizophrenia into these subtypes because of the differences among them. In practice, however, people do not fit precisely into specific subcategories, because they generally do not remain "true" to just one subtype classification. What is known, though, is that people display defined patterns of features—schizophrenic features that can be divided into two specific types of symptoms, positive and negative (as discussed earlier in this chapter).

PARANOID-TYPE SCHIZOPHRENIA

In schizophrenia of paranoid type, persecutory delusions are present. For example, the person has delusions of grandeur, auditory hallucinations, or an unsubstantiated fear that he or she will be harmed or persecuted by others. The person does not display negative symptoms, such as disorganized speech or catatonic behavior. On the surface, he or she often seems to be almost "normal-appearing," despite psychotic ideation. The delusions are dominated by themes of persecution or grandiosity. This is frequently accompanied by auditory hallucinations related to these themes.

Individuals diagnosed with paranoid-type schizophrenia are generally older when they experience their first episode than those with other subtypes, and they are usually able to take care of their daily needs, even when most symptomatic. These individuals are characterized as tense, suspicious, guarded, reserved, hostile, or aggressive. It is helpful for the practitioner to explore the content of the individual's delusions, particularly if the theme is one of violence or aggression. This is even more important if the person incorporates the practitioner into his or her delusional, violent thoughts. Keeping in mind the safety of both client and practitioner, one should proceed slowly and respectfully during the interview while also providing detailed explanations for what is occurring.

The following vignette provides an opportunity to become familiar with the specific features of paranoid-type schizophrenia and is intended to help practitioners differentiate among the various subtypes. The case illustrates the influence of the multiple factors that help individualize Rudy Rosen's experience with schizophrenia. This vignette addresses how this disorder has also affected the client and his family, and the effects of frequent hospitalizations, medication, and chronic relapse.

CASE | THE CASE OF RUDY ROSEN

Rudy Rosen is a 76-year-old white male who is currently hospitalized because of a recent suicide attempt. Persecutory hallucinations are reflected in his statement to the social worker on admission: "My medication is poisoned by my wife." He was escorted to a large, metropolitan psychiatric hospital by a mobile crisis unit because he refused to admit himself voluntarily for observation.

During the intake process, Mr. Rosen's wife, Ruth, revealed a history that began approximately 25 years ago when her husband was first diagnosed with schizophrenia, paranoid type. "That statement changed my life," Mrs. Rosen told the social worker. At that time, Rudy had been employed as an auto mechanic. According to Ruth, one day he suddenly and without warning began to show some bizarre symptoms. Ruth remembered her husband saying, "Our home telephone is bugged, and the people at work tampered with it." Rudy accused some of the other mechanics of stealing his tools, and he claimed several people

continued

were following him home and plotting to harm him. His wife noted that soon after, Rudy began accusing her and their two children of plotting against him as well. However, his rationale for this blaming attitude remained vague. She went on, "Rudy ran around the house, screaming that I thought he was crazy, and that I am working with the police and his boss to put him in the 'crazy' hospital."

During Rudy's initial hospitalization 25 years ago, he had a difficult time understanding his illness or why he had been put in the "hospital for crazy people." Rudy did not believe what the psychiatrists, social workers, and his family were trying to tell him about his illness. He remained steadfastly convinced that people were plotting against him, his phone was bugged, and his medicine could not help him because "it's poisoned." Rudy began a 6-week trial course of Thorazine, his symptoms abated, and he was discharged from the hospital. Rudy did relatively well for a long period of time, although he did have several episodes of first-rank symptoms after he refused to take his medications. Whenever Rudy's symptoms became worse, his wife brought him to the hospital, where he was usually readmitted, particularly when he was actively suicidal.

The social worker reviewed Rudy's chart and found a family history noting that he was the youngest of five children. Three of his siblings are still living: a brother, Harry, aged 90 and two sisters, Natalie, 85, and Miriam, 87. The details about Rudy's oldest sister are vague; one sentence notes she died while hospitalized in a mental institution more than 50 years ago. Apparently, she had been hospitalized for what was termed "depression" following the birth of her only child. Further exploration of family history reveals that Rudy's mother was described by almost everyone in the family as being "very strange." His mother accused people of being against her, out to hurt her, and those around her reported that she "heard voices that were not heard by anyone else." Rudy's father and older siblings had raised him because the mother was considered "unfit and crazy." Of noteworthy physical importance, both of Rudy's eardrums were punctured from a serious infection when he was 5 years old. The etiology remains unknown; however, he was treated for many years, including several surgeries for chronic ear infections. This left Rudy with a very significant permanent hearing deficit. Rudy also had a history of rheumatoid heart disease as a youngster.

Rudy's wife reports that one of his sisters, Miriam, exhibits "bizarre-like" behavior. However, no diagnosis has been determined, and the 87-year-old sister remains under the care of a full-time paid nursing companion.

Rudy and Ruth have been married a little over 55 years, and they have two children—a daughter who is age 54 and a son who is 50. Both children are professionals, and they live in the same community with their parents. The Rosens have six grandchildren and one great-grandchild. Rudy is retired, with no outside hobbies, interests, or friends. He is in poor cardiac health, having had a quadruple heart bypass 5 years ago. In addition, he has a pacemaker, and suffers from congestive heart disease (CHD), cataracts, and chronic ear infections. Rudy experiences severe tardive dyskinesia (TD) from his many years of taking high doses of antipsychotic drugs. His symptoms include hand tremors, tongue thrusting, and unsteady gait. In addition, Rudy takes a cadre of daily medications including Coumadin (a blood thinner); Resperdal (for his psychosis); Valium (for sleep); Cogentin (for TD); Wellbutrin, Paxil, and Buspar (for his positive symptoms); and Synthroid (to treat his slow metabolism).

Ruth is a retired office manager. She looked quite tired and sad during the intake interview, and commented that she had retired to become "Rudy's full-time nurse, appointment keeper, and jailer." Although she and Rudy had a "good marriage" despite his illness, she had clung to the hope that their golden years would be filled with quality time spent together, with vacations, family activities, and fun. She always thought that if he took good care of himself and took his medications that the schizophrenia would abate. Instead, her days are spent driving Rudy from doctor to doctor, to the dentist, or to hearing aid technicians. His behavior makes it difficult for him to keep any one doctor for an extended period of time. With a sigh, Ruth explains that this is because he accuses them of "cheating, giving him the wrong medicine, or trying to kill him." Rudy changes doctors and dentists very often.

Ruth no longer allows him to take his medications without close supervision. She recently found evidence (pills on the bathroom floor) that he sometimes flushes his medications down the toilet. She is not sure how long this has been going on but suspects it is what led to his current hospitalization. He again began to have active signs and symptoms of delusions and hallucinations.

ASSESSMENT SUMMARY   Rudy's life, as depicted in this vignette, illustrates the signs and symptoms of paranoid-type schizophrenia. Although his initial onset occurred late in life, the course illustrated in this example is chronic. However, Rudy was able to have periods when he functioned fairly well. Research suggests that people with the paranoid subtype of schizophrenia may function better before and after paranoid episodes than those diagnosed with the other subtypes (Ho, Black, & Andreasen, 2003). Rudy's interpersonal and social functioning problems have been exacerbated over his lifetime, especially when he neglects taking his medication. It is important to note the impact this disorder has had on his family. Rudy's wife has borne the emotional and financial brunt of his illness over the past 25 years. While his children were growing up, they constantly had to cope with the loss of a meaningful parental relationship, with their father's bizarre behavior, and with his frequent hospitalizations.

THE MULTIAXIAL DSM DIAGNOSIS FOR RUDY ROSEN IS AS FOLLOWS:

AXIS I	295.30 Schizophrenia, Paranoid Type
Axis II	V71.09 (No diagnosis)
Axis III	366.9 Cataracts
	389.9 Hearing Loss
	333.82 Neuroleptic-induced Tardive Dyskinesia
	428.0 Congestive Heart Disease (pacemaker)
Axis IV	Deferred
Axis V	GAF = 25 (on admission), 50 (on discharge)

© Cengage Learning

Advanced Clinical EP 2.1.10 (b) c

This case vignette describes how a social worker would look to access coping strategies that serve to reinforce and improve Rudy's (as well as the family's) adaptation to life circumstance, situations, and events. The competency-based assessment examines effective problem solving and viable alternatives. What has helped Rudy cope with such a devastating mental disorder has been the devotion shown by his wife, Ruth. They have been married for 55 years and according to his wife, "It is a very good and satisfying marriage." In addition, Rudy is emotionally supported by his children and his grandchildren. There have been long periods of time when Rudy took his medication and experienced periods of remission. During those times, the family had a sense of cohesiveness, laying the foundation for a shared memory of "normalcy" that seemed helpful during the times when Rudy relapsed. Figure 5.1 illustrates the interaction of the biological, psychological, and social variables in Rudy Rosen's life.

CATATONIC-TYPE SCHIZOPHRENIA

People with catatonic-type schizophrenia exhibit many of the basic features mentioned previously. However, what distinguishes this type from the other four subtypes of schizophrenia is the person's abnormal and striking physical movements—or complete lack of physical movements. The practitioner likely will

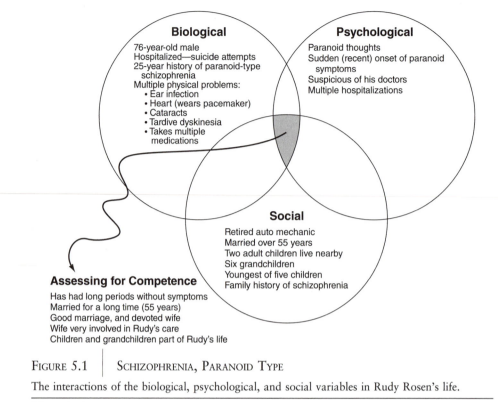

FIGURE 5.1 | SCHIZOPHRENIA, PARANOID TYPE

The interactions of the biological, psychological, and social variables in Rudy Rosen's life.

© Cengage Learning

easily recognize psychomotor disturbances, which alternate between the extremes of excitement and stupor. Because of this volatility, the person with the catatonic subtype may require medical supervision to prevent injury to him or her or to others. Clients with catatonic-type schizophrenia may be unable to eat or drink on their own—even the process of normal body elimination may require monitoring. In addition, these individuals may experience complications from untreated malnutrition, dehydration, electrolyte disturbances, or exhaustion.

At times, the person's physical motor activity may appear to be "speeded up," but the more typical catatonic behavior is a slow, retarded, or stupor-like state. The amount of activity generally ranges between extremes of seemingly driven agitation (as in an excited catatonic state) to a withdrawn and inactive state usually associated with catatonic stupor. Several characteristics usually dominate an individual's behavior. They may, for example, adopt and maintain rigid postures for hours at a time, assume bizarre positions, appear to be in a stupor, and/or become mute, which is a particularly common display. The person is seemingly oblivious to the external world, and he or she may resist being moved by others. Another pattern is rapid alternation between excitement and immobility.

The bearing and manner of the person with catatonic-type schizophrenia is often described as artificial and stilted. He or she will spontaneously pose or display bizarre, inappropriate silliness and "odd" mannerisms (for example, use facial grimaces or make silly faces). These strange postures can be held for very long periods of time, making the person look like a figure in a wax museum. This behavior is referred to as **catatonic posturing**. Someone else may try to manipulate or move the individual's limbs, but once moved the limbs can then remain fixed for hours or days. This is referred to as **waxy flexibility**. Such disturbances of volition include **negativism**, which is characterized by an almost mulish refusal to follow any course of action suggested or expected. This negativism is sometimes passive (e.g., if food is served to the person and they do not eat it or if someone asks a question and the person does not answer)—and at other times it may be active.

The person's negativism is characterized as active if, for example, he or she resists being moved out of a rigid posture. The person may also repeat or mimic spoken words of others (echolalia); for example, when asked a question, he or she repeats it over and over, which can sometimes go on for an hour or more. **Echopraxia** is mimicking the physical gestures and movements of others (similar to a pantomime). This behavior is not intended to mock and may continue long after the other person has left the room. Echolalia and echopraxia are seen as involuntary and meaningless repetitions of the words and actions of others.

Certain mannerisms connected to delusions or hallucinations often have special meaning to the catatonic individual. This may take the form of seemingly purposeless repetitive movements such as folding a piece of paper along the same creases until it disintegrates. These types of movement are referred to as **stereotypy** or stereotyped behaviors, and they commonly involve the entire body (the person may rock or sway, for example). Although these behaviors have some special significance to the client, the meaning is generally not discernible to others. When asked, "Why are you folding this piece of paper over and over again?" the person will offer no explanation. A client with catatonic-type schizophrenia may involuntarily repeat tasks over and over—such as answering a question repeatedly until asked to stop. This is referred to as perseveration (from the word *persevere*). We should note that using such filler words as "you know," "like," or "I mean" does not constitute perseveration.

An assessment for catatonic-type schizophrenia should include *at least two* of the following features:

- Stupor or motor immobility (**cataplexy**) or a sudden and transient episode of paralysis (with no loss of consciousness) that affects nearly all voluntary muscles; or waxy flexibility
- Hyperactivity that is not influenced by external stimuli
- Mutism (deficit of communication through speech or interaction with others) or marked negativism
- Peculiar or odd behaviors evidenced by posturing, stereotypes, or mannerisms

The following case vignette describes the important features of catatonic type schizophrenia, and the subsequent case discussion includes other conditions that may complicate the practitioner's ability to make an accurate assessment. As you read about Joey Esterson, think about how you would differentiate between features of catatonic-type schizophrenia on the one hand, and a general medical condition such as substance and/or alcohol abuse or other types of psychosis.

| The Case of Joey Esterson

Joey is a 20-year-old single man who has been admitted to a large metropolitan hospital's mental health service. He was not verbal and offered no chief complaint on admission. Joey's older cousin, Lenny Pasternak, brought him to the hospital and offered that "Joey is going crazy again. He probably needs to go back to the state hospital." Lenny is a poor historian and was able to provide very little coherent information about his cousin's background, except, "Joey is the middle child of three children. His older sister and younger brother both live in New York, but they don't have any contact with Joey. Joey's father died from a heart attack 5 years ago." The only other information provided was that Joey's father had been diagnosed with schizophrenia many years earlier. There was even less information regarding Joey's mother, who apparently had abandoned him and his siblings when they were young children.

Lenny described his cousin: "Joey always talked funny, even when he was 10 or 12 years old. He heard and saw things that nobody else did." Eventually, at the age of 17, Joey had been diagnosed with catatonic-type schizophrenia.

During the current episode, Lenny practically had to carry Joey into the hospital—Joey would only walk on the outside arches of his feet, and he refused to be moved. The social worker's notes describe Joey's appearance as that of a slightly built, disheveled young man who paid no attention to his current surroundings. During their initial meeting, he sat with his eyes shut tight, did not look up when spoken to, and did not answer questions directed to him. Joey refused to participate in a conversation with the social worker, and did not answer any questions.

Although it appeared that Joey understood things happening around him, he did not interact with anyone. He sporadically introduced phrases he had apparently heard before into his speech, and he accomplished this without opening his eyes or looking up. His speech was affected so that he sounded like a babbling child—he often spoke with a lisp or stammer, and occasionally burst forth with a fragment of a song. Joey made many facial grimaces and performed various other kinds of seemingly senseless physical movements. For example, he crossed his legs rigidly so that they were "assembled" in odd positions while his hands were in constant motion on top of his head.

The social worker attempted a mental status examination with the following results: Joey was admitted in a semi-mute state; and very little could be explored regarding his thought content, cognitive processes, insight, or judgment. Joey was retained at the hospital involuntarily for a 72-hour period. During that time, he remained essentially motionless, seated in a chair for many hours at a time. This practitioner noted Joey showed evidence of a noticeable tremor in his extremities, a common sign of agitation. In addition, when Joey's arms or legs were placed in any position (for example, extended straight out), he maintained this position for a long period of time—even after being told he could resume his former position. If others attempted to bend Joey's extremities, he resisted. If Joey was approached from one side of his body, he gradually would turn his head away in order to look in the opposite direction. In addition, Joey wrinkled his nose, made twitching movements with his mouth, and pursed his lips for no apparent reason. These purposeless movements often lasted over several seconds and were not accompanied by any other motions of the tongue, which might be indicative of the effects of tardive dyskinesia.

Assessment Summary　Joey exhibits classic features of catatonic-type schizophrenia. Once considered rare, it is often inadequately diagnosed. From this case discussion, it is clear that these features have persisted far longer than the required 6 months' duration.

Joey demonstrates other important characteristics such as muteness, negativism, catatonic excitement, posturing, waxy flexibility, and facial grimacing. An important distinction should be noted in that Joey was not considered stuporous (or in a daze) because he was alert enough to turn away from an approaching stimulus (negativism).

Advanced
Clinical
EP 2.1.7 c

In this case vignette, the practitioner's consultation with other medical professionals is underscored. The competency-based assessment model includes attention to ruling out general medical conditions when considering schizophrenia. In Joey's situation, there was no evidence of medical disorders (such as epilepsy and/or certain strokes) that could have produced or mimicked his catatonic behavior. The practitioner in this case referred Joey for a complete general medical and neurological evaluation to rule out other disorders. It is expected that a laboratory inquiry, including urine and blood analysis for toxic substances and drug(s) of abuse, will be conducted. There is one major source of support in Joey's social environment, his cousin Lenny. This relative not only brought Joey to the hospital but has also cared for him for most of his life. Despite being abandoned at an early age by his mother, Joey continues to be looked after by Lenny, who expresses concern and apparently cares for his cousin. Figure 5.2 shows the interactions of the biological, psychological, and social variables in Joey Esterson's life.

THE DSM MULTIAXIAL DIAGNOSIS FOR JOEY ESTERSON IS AS FOLLOWS:

Axis I	295.20 Schizophrenia, Catatonic Type
Axis II	V71.09 (No diagnosis)
Axis III	None
Axis IV	Problems related to the social environment
	Occupational problems
	Economic problems
	Problems with primary support group
Axis V	GAF = 20 (on admission), 50 (on discharge)

© Cengage Learning

DISORGANIZED-TYPE SCHIZOPHRENIA

In contrast to the paranoid-type schizophrenia, individuals with the disorganized type exhibit marked disruption in their speech patterns (disorganized speech) and behavior (disorganized behavior). They may display flat or inappropriate affect such as silliness or laughter without apparent reason. Incongruous grinning and facial grimacing are quite common. If hallucinations or delusions are present, they are not organized around a central theme as in the paranoid type—they are more fragmented and disjointed. This subtype was previously known as hebephrenia. Individuals diagnosed with disorganized-type schizophrenia show early signs of difficulty with life problems, and the course of the disease tends to be chronic.

The disorganized subtype of schizophrenia is characterized by marked regression toward primitive, disinhibited, and unorganized behavior, and the absence of

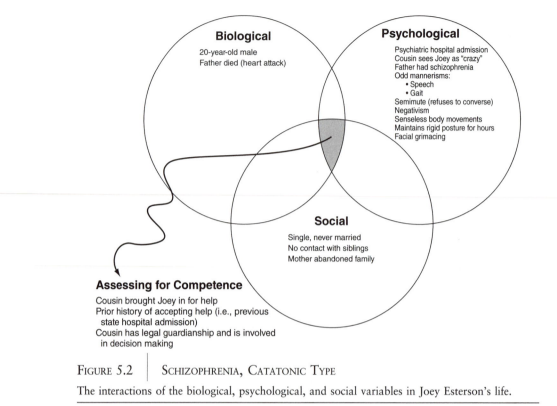

Biological
20-year-old male
Father died (heart attack)

Psychological
Psychiatric hospital admission
Cousin sees Joey as "crazy"
Father had schizophrenia
Odd mannerisms:
• Speech
• Gait
Semimute (refuses to converse)
Negativism
Senseless body movements
Maintains rigid posture for hours
Facial grimacing

Social
Single, never married
No contact with siblings
Mother abandoned family

Assessing for Competence
Cousin brought Joey in for help
Prior history of accepting help (i.e., previous
  state hospital admission)
Cousin has legal guardianship and is involved
  in decision making

FIGURE 5.2 | SCHIZOPHRENIA, CATATONIC TYPE

The interactions of the biological, psychological, and social variables in Joey Esterson's life.

© Cengage Learning

symptoms that meet the criteria for the catatonic type are notable. The early symptoms may be deterioration in personal grooming and inappropriate social behavior. Personal hygiene is often described as shabby or unkempt. Family and friends often are the first to observe these personality changes and often describe the person as "just not the same as they used to be."

These individuals are usually active, but in an aimless and unproductive manner. Their thought disorder is very pronounced, and their connection with reality is seen as limited. Their prognosis is generally poor—few have significant remissions.

The criteria for disorganized-type schizophrenia are disorganized behavior, disorganized speech, and flat or inappropriate affect. Individuals with this diagnosis tend to manifest signs of difficulty early, their problems are more than likely chronic, and they often lack the improvement of symptoms (remissions) that characterize the other forms of schizophrenia (Hardy-Bayle, Sarfati, & Passerieux, 2003). The following case vignette illustrates the signs and symptoms of disorganized-type schizophrenia. Pay particular attention to the onset and duration of symptoms.

CASE	THE CASE OF SARAH MACDONALD

Sarah is a 30-year-old African American woman who looks a lot younger than her stated age. She was brought to the hospital emergency room by her brother Jack, who was not sure how many times his sister had previously been admitted to the psychiatric unit, "but it's been a lot of times." Sarah has lived with her brother, his wife, and their two children during the past 10 years. Jack stated, "Most times things around the house are all right, but when Sarah starts her crazy stuff, things get pretty chaotic."

Jack added that recently he has become more fearful for the safety of his two children. He was unable to be specific, but claimed that "Sarah stays in her room banging her closets and dresser drawers open and closed all day. She throws things around, and it sounds like she's talking to somebody in her room—except she doesn't have a telephone and nobody ever visits her. My sister has never been very sociable, and we always thought of her as a loner even when she was little."

The social worker asked Jack if he could elaborate regarding her relationships with others. He continued, "My sister rarely laughs. She always seems distant, you know, almost unfeeling—and she never seems to enjoy anything very much."

When asked about Sarah's moods, Jack shook his head and said, "I tell you, Sarah's either angry at everybody or just giggling and carrying on. Sometimes she makes up words—you know, just silly stuff— but often as not her mood doesn't match up with what she's saying." He continued, "Sarah's really just like a child. She walks along a'bouncing and, you know, swinging her hips. I'm not sure what she's doing. She really acts silly and sometimes just breaks out in a fit of giggling for no reason I can make out."

Additional history provided by Jack confirms that Sarah abruptly stopped taking her medications 6 weeks ago; her prescriptions include clozapine (Clorazil), clonazepam (Klonopin), and alprazolam (Xanax). Soon after discontinuing her medication, she began to hear voices again, act bizarre, and neglect her physical appearance. She has sometimes disappeared from the house for weeks at a time, but eventually the police pick her up "wandering the street." There is no known history of drug or alcohol abuse or other general medical condition that might account for Sarah's appearance and behavior.

Sarah was first hospitalized when she was 18 years old. At that time she had been exhibiting a variety of psychotic symptoms that included disorganized speech and behavior. According to Jack, his sister never really attended school on a regular basis, nor was she able to maintain employment or live independently. During her initial hospitalization, Sarah had been successfully treated with antipsychotic drugs, and within several weeks her psychotic symptoms abated. She was discharged to the care of her brother. For the next few years, Sarah seemed to be getting along okay. That is, she attended a day care program and through that activity she made a few friends and enrolled in a restaurant worker program. She took her medication consistently and appeared to be coping well.

During the past 10 years, Sarah has had numerous hospitalizations, medication trials, and subsequent releases into her brother's care. Once Sarah was home, she would only sporadically take her medication, ultimately becoming symptomatic and disorganized again. During this current admission, Sarah's speech made little sense and was interspersed with frequent rhyming. Sometimes she would make sounds, rather than articulate specific or meaningful words. She was involuntarily admitted for 3 days, then discharged with medications and a scheduled follow-up visit in the hospital's outpatient department.

ASSESSMENT SUMMARY   Nothing in Sarah's history suggests a general medical condition. Although her affect had been described as flat, she does not exhibit anything remotely similar to the severely depressed mood of a major depressive disorder with psychotic features. Sarah has never expressed suicidal ideation, nor has she had any symptoms suggestive of manic-type features. The fact that these features have persisted longer than 6 months rules out schizophreniform disorder or brief psychotic disorder. Sarah's personal appearance, social behavior, pronounced thought disorder, negative symptoms, poor hygiene, social withdrawal, poor rapport, and emotional responses are seen as inappropriate—all of which contribute to the assessment of disorganized-type schizophrenia. The vignette describes behaviors that include incoherent speech, inappropriate affect, auditory hallucinations, grossly disorganized behavior, and an onset that occurred at an early age (she was 18 when first hospitalized).

Sarah MacDonald's DSM Multiaxial Diagnosis Is as Follows:

Axis I	295.10 Schizophrenia, Disorganized Type
Axis II	V71.09 (No diagnosis)
Axis III	None
Axis IV	Occupational problems with unemployment
	Occasionally homeless
	Problems with access to health care services
Axis V	GAF = 20 (on admission), 30 (on discharge)

© Cengage Learning

Advanced Clinical EP 2.1.10 (b) c

Despite Sarah's struggle with a serious diagnosis, the competency-based assessment explores potential strengths and resources. Figure 5.3 shows the interactions of the biological, psychological, and social variables in Sarah's life. The most important resource she has is her brother, who is involved actively in her life. Even though Jack is concerned for his own family's safety, he continues to take care of her. He provides her with housing, attempts to make sure she takes her medication on a regular basis, brings her to therapy appointments, and watches for possible signs of relapse.

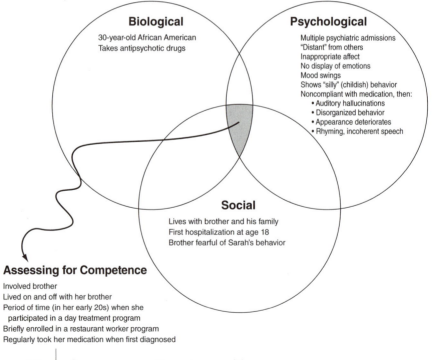

Biological
30-year-old African American
Takes antipsychotic drugs

Psychological
Multiple psychiatric admissions
"Distant" from others
Inappropriate affect
No display of emotions
Mood swings
Shows "silly" (childish) behavior
Noncompliant with medication, then:
• Auditory hallucinations
• Disorganized behavior
• Appearance deteriorates
• Rhyming, incoherent speech

Social
Lives with brother and his family
First hospitalization at age 18
Brother fearful of Sarah's behavior

Assessing for Competence
Involved brother
Lived on and off with her brother
Period of time (in her early 20s) when she
   participated in a day treatment program
Briefly enrolled in a restaurant worker program
Regularly took her medication when first diagnosed

Figure 5.3 | Schizophrenia, Disorganized Type

The interactions of the biological, psychological, and social variables in Sarah MacDonald's life.

© Cengage Learning

CASE	THE CASE OF SHAYLA PATTERSON

Shayla is a 20-year-old female who was born to a single teenage mother. Her father came from Trinidad; Shayla has never had contact with him. She was referred to the Bayside Community Mental Health Agency by her next-door neighbor who once attended a parenting group there. The neighbor told Shayla, "It's a real good place to go and get help, and besides the 'shrinks' are real nice."

Shayla and her mother, Beth Shafer, both attended the intake interview. Shayla is a petite young woman who exhibited poverty in the amount and content of her speech (alogia), and she appeared unkempt and disheveled (avolition). Shayla's mother seemed quite anxious, distraught. She urgently wanted someone to help her daughter. Mrs. Shafer described Shayla's childhood as one exemplified by a cadre of difficulties including poor school performance, aggressive behavior at home, speaking in "funny voices," hearing people talk back to her (not validated by others), and being in contact with "beings from outer space." Mrs. Shafer stated, "You know, Shayla's father used to talk to himself, too. He had to be put in a mental institution a time or two when he got too crazy." Mrs. Shafer was unable to provide reliable information regarding Shayla's father other than, "He was just a crazy old coot a lot of the time." She added, "I just love my baby, and I don't want anything to happen to her."

During the time of intake, the social worker carefully explored intrapersonal and interpersonal functioning. Shayla exhibits a variety of psychotic symptoms that include delusions. Shayla asserts that she is in contact with George Washington, Abraham Lincoln, and Cleopatra—and she is convinced that they talk back to her (auditory hallucinations). However, there are no clear systemized themes or patterns involved (which would suggest paranoid-type schizophrenia). There is no evidence of a mood disorder, specific organic factors, or drug and/or alcohol abuse. The social worker further noted that Shayla has been unable to keep any type of job, and her social functioning is described as very limited at best. As a next step, Shayla has been referred for a psychiatric evaluation.

UNDIFFERENTIATED-TYPE SCHIZOPHRENIA

Individuals who exhibit the major features of schizophrenia but have not met the full assessment distinctions for paranoid-, disorganized-, or catatonic-type are considered (not surprisingly) of undifferentiated type. The characteristics are virtually indistinguishable from the three other schizophrenia categories; essentially this determination is made of exclusion rather than being based entirely on symptomatology.

The process of making an assessment of undifferentiated-type schizophrenia is basically one of using what's left over. Some individuals do not quite fit into the previously reviewed subtypes. In other words, the person has met all the basic criteria for schizophrenia but has *not* met specific criteria for paranoid, catatonic, or disorganized types of schizophrenia. The case vignette of Shayla Patterson provides an opportunity to become acquainted with undifferentiated-type schizophrenia and what it might look like.

ASSESSMENT SUMMARY   Several features described in this vignette support making the assessment for undifferentiated-type schizophrenia. Contributing to this diagnosis was Shayla's extreme decline in functioning over a period of several years, her occasional delusions, and her many oddities of behavior and speech. There is no evidence of a mood disorder, a general medical condition, or substance abuse that could better account for these symptoms. The emergence of features during Shayla's middle adolescent years is noteworthy. Her delusions frequently have different themes as opposed to a specified pattern (i.e., they are not systematized), thereby ruling out the paranoid subtype. The absence of any notable or prominent catatonic features rules out the catatonic subtype. Although Shayla's speech is at times viewed as incoherent, her affect is unremarkable and not seen as particularly flat or grossly inappropriate, thereby ruling out the disorganized type. Thus, undifferentiated-type schizophrenia is left.

SHAYLA PATTERSON'S DSM MULTIAXIAL DIAGNOSIS IS AS FOLLOWS:

Axis I	295.90 Schizophrenia, Undifferentiated Type
Axis II	V71.09 (No diagnosis)
Axis III	None
Axis IV	None
Axis V	GAF = 35 (current)

© Cengage Learning

Advanced Clinical EP 2.1.10 (b) c

Formulating a correct diagnosis for Shayla requires that the practitioner be familiar with the information found in the DSM and be able to differentiate among the various subtypes of schizophrenia. However, the worker also looks for strengths and resources to improve a client's adaptation. In this case, Shayla's mother talked with others about getting help for her daughter and followed through with appropriate recommendations (e.g., going to the clinic). Additionally, the mother came to the intake appointment and appeared very supportive and nurturing. Figure 5.4 illustrates the interactions of the biological, psychological, and social variables in Shayla Patterson's life.

RESIDUAL-TYPE SCHIZOPHRENIA

Residual-type schizophrenia classification has changed very little over time. It describes circumstances and conditions of individuals who continue to exhibit a schizophrenic-like picture but with *no current active phase* in evidence. To consider the residual subtype, an individual must have had at least one episode of schizophrenia while not currently manifesting active symptoms. Even though there is no evidence of bizarre delusions or hallucinations, the person still exhibits remnants, or "leftovers," of previous active disease. Emotional blunting, social withdrawal, eccentric behavior, illogical thinking, and some loosening of associations are present. However, the symptoms are not as pronounced as they once were. Some fragmentary symptoms still exist, and the individual is seen by others as somewhat unusual, odd, or peculiar, but the person is able to maintain some level of social functioning.

This subtype serves essentially as a filler and is used infrequently in clinical practice. The residual category is addressed here because it underscores the importance of formulating an accurate clinical assessment. Unfortunately, little additional information is available regarding the prevalence or other important demographic

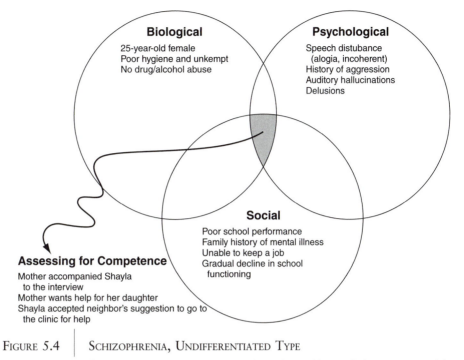

Biological

25-year-old female
Poor hygiene and unkempt
No drug/alcohol abuse

Psychological

Speech disturbance
  (alogia, incoherent)
History of aggression
Auditory hallucinations
Delusions

Social

Poor school performance
Family history of mental illness
Unable to keep a job
Gradual decline in school
  functioning

Assessing for Competence

Mother accompanied Shayla
  to the interview
Mother wants help for her daughter
Shayla accepted neighbor's suggestion to go to
  the clinic for help

FIGURE 5.4   SCHIZOPHRENIA, UNDIFFERENTIATED TYPE

The interactions of the biological, psychological, and social variables in Shalya Patterson's life.

© Cengage Learning

data concerning this subtype. Nevertheless, the following features are important to consider:

- The person has at one time met the specific criteria for one of the other four subtypes of schizophrenia—i.e., paranoid, catatonic, disorganized, or undifferentiated.
- The person no longer exhibits features of catatonic behavior, hallucinations, delusions, or disorganized behavior or speech.
- The person is still beset with any of the following specific features:
  - Flat affect, minimized speech, or lack of volition (negative symptoms)
  - A diminished pattern of at least two basic features of schizophrenia (e.g., odd beliefs, distorted perceptions, odd speech, or peculiar behavior)
  - Positive symptoms such as hearing one's thoughts spoken aloud or auditory hallucinations that comment on the individual's behavior. (Individuals self-report that either their thoughts are being controlled, they have the ability to extend their thoughts onto others, they experience delusions, or they feel others controlling or influencing them from the outside.)

In summary, a number of factors have been implicated in the causes of schizophrenia, including genetic influences, brain structure, neurotransmitter imbalances, and psychological stressors. Regardless of the various assumptions about the etiology of schizophrenia, it is clear that this disorder affects each individual differently. Each person may have the same set of symptoms, but their level of functioning may be very different. Thus, the competency-based assessment plays a vital role in diagnosing schizophrenia, because it examines the interplay of interpersonal, social, environmental, and cultural influences in the individual's life.

UNDERSTANDING OTHER PSYCHOTIC DISORDERS

SCHIZOPHRENIFORM DISORDER

Sometimes people display symptoms akin to schizophrenia, but not at the same level as those found in full-blown schizophrenia. Schizophreniform disorder presents, but differentiates from, the symptoms suggestive of schizophrenia—and, to complicate the clinical picture, these symptoms can disappear just as quickly as they appear, with no discernible explanation (except possibly treatment). An assessment for the presence of schizophreniform disorder requires that there be no detected organic cause of psychotic symptoms, the psychotic features must last *less than 6 months*, and the features must include a prodromal, active, and residual phase.

In schizophreniform disorder, it appears as if the person has schizophrenia, but he or she subsequently recovers completely with no residual effects. A particularly useful aspect of this provisional category is that it helps practitioners avoid coming to premature conclusions about a person's behavior. It may also serve as a warning that the underlying cause of a specific psychosis may not yet be determined. This in itself is a valuable tool.

Some practitioners find it quite confusing that the symptoms and criteria for schizophreniform disorder are identical to those of schizophrenia. The important distinctions are in duration and intensity. An easy way to distinguish between the two disorders is to remember that the duration of schizophrenia must be longer than 6 months, whereas schizophreniform symptoms must exist for at least a substantial part of 1 month (less, if successfully treated) but no longer than 6 months. If an assessment must be made without waiting for the required duration interval or possible recovery (which is sometimes the case), "schizophreniform, provisional" should be noted; if the person's recovery is complete within 6 months, this notation should be eliminated.

The following sample of a social work student's process recording illustrates the conversation between the intern and a client, Claudia Benjamin, who was involuntarily placed in a general medical hospital's psychiatric unit. The process recording includes both the word-for-word conversation and the student's reactions to the contents of the interaction. It is presented to demonstrate the schizophrenic-like picture a person with schizophreniform disorder may present and its subtle distinctions from schizophrenia. The biopsychosocial features are not illustrated in this case. The intent, instead, is to illustrate through the vignette how the symptom picture may emerge from the scope of the therapeutic conversation.

CASE	THE CASE OF CLAUDIA BENJAMIN

Ms. Benjamin is a 23-year-old Jamaican female who was brought to the hospital by the police, who found her wandering naked around 14th Street and Ocean Drive on South Beach. According to the police report, the woman appeared to be distraught and claimed, "My mother is coming from the moon to pick me up." The police officers felt the young woman was delusional and thought she was hallucinating at the time, so they decided to transport her to the hospital's emergency room. During transit, the police called their dispatcher to report their status, and they were informed of a missing person's bulletin describing the young woman they had just picked up. A social work intern was assigned to the emergency room as a part of her hospital rotation. Here is the transcript of their encounter:

Interview Content

> W: "Hi, Ms. Benjamin? I'd like to introduce myself. I'm a social work intern here at General. How are you feeling now?"
>
> CB: [The client shrugs her shoulders and begins to play with her hair and hum some kind of tune. There is no eye contact.]
>
> W: "Are you comfortable?"
>
> CB: "Get them away! Get them away!"
>
> W: "I'm not sure what you want me to get away from you. Could you be clearer?"
>
> CB: "Those things, things, that are after me."
>
> W: "Ms. Benjamin, what 'things' are you referring to? I'm not quite sure I understand what you want me to know. Could you be a bit clearer?"
>
> CB: [The client cocked her head to one side and closed her eyes very tightly. It appeared to me that she wasn't listening to me, but to another conversation ... inside her head.]

Social Worker's Reactions to the Interview Process

I'm really nervous about working with someone who might be psychotic.

I heard that no eye contact is bad.

I'm trying to make her like me, but I don't think I'm getting anywhere with her.

Oh, boy. This isn't going the way I want it to. What should I do now?

That sounds like paranoia, but is it enough paranoia? I'm confused whether she is having delusions or hallucinations. Oh, boy.

I haven't a clue as to what to do next.

At this point, I thought it was time to have a talk with my supervisor. I needed help in finding out what was going on for my client. Mary Jo Cringle, my field supervisor, suggested I talk with Claudia's family, who was sitting in the waiting room. As I spoke with the Benjamin family, the information they supplied helped to clear up some of my confusion.

According to Ms. Benjamin's mother, Claudia has been "acting this way" for only a few months. Her family told me that before this incident they cared for Claudia at home. After she wandered away from home today, they realized she needed more care than they could provide. Mrs. Benjamin said, "My daughter was a really good kid growing up. You know, it's very difficult to watch your own child talk to someone she thinks is there, but who really isn't. She thinks we are going to poison her food or harm her in some way." Mrs. Benjamin denied that Claudia ever experienced depressive or manic episodes, and she denied any medical problems or the use of substances ("Claudia doesn't even take aspirin"). "I just don't understand what happened to my wonderful daughter. She was all right up until just a few months ago and now this. Do you think you can help her?"

EP 2.1.1 d

ASSESSMENT SUMMARY   The purpose of this vignette is to look at the social worker's process rather than at the client's life story. The transcript describes the social work intern's uncomfortable feelings about the interview and illustrates how unsettling it can be for the beginning practitioner to attempt to relate to someone who is not responding "rationally." The student's struggles to maintain a professional demeanor while interviewing the client can be seen in the transcript. The client's odd mannerisms and delusions leave the social work intern frightened and confused. While the student valiantly attempts to understand the client's "reality," Claudia Benjamin's response leaves the student feeling bewildered and inept. The differential diagnosis of brief psychotic disorder was not considered in the above vignette because the duration of symptoms was more than 30 days. Schizophreniform disorder is regarded to have a more hopeful outlook than does schizophrenia. Some experience the symptoms of schizophreniform for a few months only and can usually resume normal lives. Relatively few studies have been conducted on this disorder, and therefore we know very little about key aspects of how people can be affected (Barlow & Durand, 2012). However, what we do know is that approximately two-thirds of those with schizophreniform disorder advance toward developing schizophrenia or schizoaffective disorder (Whitty et al., 2005).

THE DSM MULTIAXIAL DIAGNOSIS FOR CLAUDIA BENJAMIN IS AS FOLLOWS:

Axis I	295.40 Schizophreniform Disorder
Axis II	V71.09 (No diagnosis)
Axis III	None
Axis IV	Unknown
Axis V	GAF = 30 (on admission)

© Cengage Learning

SCHIZOAFFECTIVE DISORDER

Historically, individuals who showed symptoms of schizophrenia along with a mood disorder such as depression were grouped together under the umbrella of schizophrenia. This was often viewed as a mixed bag of problems for the practitioner who was attempting to sort through and understand these complex behaviors. Some practitioners suggest that schizoaffective disorder is either a mixture of a mood disorder and schizophrenia (*affect* refers to or is affiliated with mood) or a form of bipolar disorder (because individuals often respond well to medication, specifically lithium treatment). Others hold that this is an entirely separate type of psychosis. Still others believe this is simply a collection of confusing and contradictory symptoms. Complicating the symptom picture further is the fact that depression frequently accompanies schizophrenia, making it even more difficult to distinguish schizophrenia from schizoaffective disorder and other forms of mood disorders.

Schizoaffective disorder presents with features of both psychosis and mood disturbance. If the periods of depression or mania are brief in relation to schizophrenia, the presence of schizophrenia is taken into account; however, if they are lengthy, a mood disorder or schizoaffective disorder should be considered. (Refer to the chapter on mood disorders for a more detailed discussion.)

The competency-based assessment is helpful in making distinctions among a person with schizophrenia, someone with a mood disorder, or someone who has both conditions. In particular, practitioners should obtain pertinent intrapersonal information (including history of medical, neurological, or psychiatric problems) as well as pertinent family history. The prognosis for someone with schizoaffective disorder is better than for an individual with schizophrenia, but worse than someone having a mood disorder.

DIFFERENTIAL ASSESSMENT   There is relatively little data available on schizoaffective disorder, but what does exist indicates that it is less common than schizophrenia. To consider a diagnosis of schizoaffective disorder, both a mood episode and the psychotic features of schizophrenia (such as social impairment and poor self-hygiene) must be present *concurrently* for a substantial and uninterrupted period of time. During this same time, there must be *at least 2 weeks* of delusions or hallucinations in the absence of a mood episode. The person's mood is manifested as either a major depressive episode, manic episode, or mixed episode. For example, the person may be depressed for 2 weeks, or they may be depressed for 1 week and show manic symptoms for another week. The mood should be seen as a very significant part of the total clinical picture.

As a part of the competency-based assessment, the practitioner should carefully explore the client's history, looking for alternative explanations of their behavior (e.g., the presence of a general medical condition such as AIDS). This careful exploration of the client's life story helps the practitioner avoid coming to premature conclusions about what is already a confusing picture.

For the practitioner to establish a diagnosis, the person must exhibit all of the following features during a single and unremitting period:

- The basic requirements noted for schizophrenia (including delusions or hallucinations without a major mood disorder) in evidence for 2 or more weeks.
- The requirements for either major depressive disorder, manic disorder, or a mixed episode for at least 2 weeks.

The following case discussion of Sydney Sutherland shows the importance of thoroughly understanding the client's presenting concerns. Clients often come to the attention of the social worker when they are disoriented and unable to provide accurate information. This underscores the importance of talking with others who are close to the client (such as family or friends) and who may be able to provide reliable factual data.

CASE | THE CASE OF SYDNEY SUTHERLAND

Sydney Sutherland was rushed to the hospital after being found unconscious by her brother, Jerry Sutherland, in his home. Within her reach were an empty liquor bottle and an assortment of medicine bottles, including barbiturates, benzodiazepine-based tranquilizers, stimulants, painkillers, and a collection of unknown drugs. Sydney's condition was stabilized in the emergency room, and she was transferred to the psychiatric ward for observation.

The record room called to inform the social worker that, over the course of 10 years, Sydney had several prior admissions both to the psychiatric unit and to the acute medical hospital. The medical records also indicated Sydney had been treated for unspecified bacterial pneumonia just 3 months ago. The psychiatric records indicate she has a diagnosis of schizophrenia, paranoid type and is being followed by Dr. Irene Morrell. Sydney attends the day treatment program at Bethune Shores Mental Health Agency, and Mr. Sutherland thinks the name of his sister's social worker is either Lee or Leslie Wagner. This social worker will contact Bethune Shores to find out Ms. Sutherland's current status. Her brother was asked to sign a release of information form that will enable the social worker to contact both Dr. Morrell and the day treatment program.

continued

"Hello, this is Martina Lopez. I'm a social worker at Regional Hospital, psych unit. Is it possible to speak with a Lee or a Leslie Wagner?"

"Lee Wagner speaking. Can I help you?"

"I certainly hope so," Ms. Lopez replied. She introduced herself and assured Ms. Wagner that she had the necessary signed permission forms allowing her to inquire about Ms. Sutherland. Martina provided some of the current information on Sydney Sutherland and then asked if Ms. Wagner might be able to fill in some gaps. "I'd really appreciate anything you can tell me that will be more relevant about Ms. Sutherland's treatment."

Ms. Wagner responded, "Of course. I've seen Sydney on and off for the past 3 years. She's been pretty unreliable throughout the time that I've known her. Most of the time, she doesn't show up for appointments—and she doesn't like to take her meds." Ms. Wagner continued, "Sydney has been diagnosed with paranoid-type schizophrenia and pretty much stays in the active phase, at least since I've been seeing her. You know, she'd have a fair chance to go into some type of remission—but, as I said before, she won't stay on her meds. Whenever I ask her about it, she insists that we put poison in the pills because we want to kill her."

Thoughtful, Ms. Lopez asked, "Has Sydney ever shown evidence of having a depressed, manic, or mixed episode?"

"I can't remember her ever having a mood component to the psychosis," Ms. Wagner replied, "but that sure sounds like what's going on for her right now. Is that your thinking?"

"Yes, it seems that way to me," Ms. Lopez said, "but I also need to talk with her brother to see if he's noticed any changes in her behavior recently."

Lee Wagner ended the conversation by asking if she could be kept informed as to how Sydney was doing. Martina Lopez promised she would be in touch.

Soon after this telephone conversation, Martina Lopez spoke with Jerry Sutherland. They found a quiet corner in the day room to talk. He appeared to be in shock and blurted out, "Geez! I knew Syd was having mental problems, but I didn't think she'd try to kill herself." He ran his fingers through his hair in frustration. "Oh, man!"

Martina asked him what his impressions were of his sister's behavior over the past month or two—in particular, anything that may have been different, either worse or better than before.

"Well, you know she was always seeing things and talking to things that weren't there," Jerry said. "Sydney could never keep a job more than a day. Mostly she panhandled or hustled, you know, to earn money—but she didn't *have* to do that. Our parents are pretty well fixed and could easily take care of her. Mostly, she lived at Mom and Dad's, but once in awhile she'd come and stay a day or two at my condo. I tried to feed her a hot meal, give her a place to take a hot shower ..." Jerry lowered his head, "... but most of the time she just came by to borrow money."

Ms. Lopez sat silently while Mr. Sutherland seemed to be deep in thought.

"The only thing I noticed different about her was that the last month or so," he began, "Syd seemed really depressed. You know, like if she slept over my house, she couldn't drag herself out of bed until after 4:00 in the afternoon—and for her that was really unusual." He paused for a moment. "And she cried a lot ... more than I've ever seen her—yeah, now that you're asking, she told me a few times that things were hopeless and she wanted to die. But I didn't think she meant it! Hey, do you think this suicide attempt was my fault?"

Martina offered reassurance to Jerry, explaining that his sister was pretty troubled. "You couldn't possibly follow her around 24 hours a day to make sure she was okay," she pointed out. "I'm sure we can help Sydney. Let's just stay in close touch." After saying good-bye to Mr. Sutherland, Ms. Lopez made her way back to the psychiatric unit, wishing that she felt confident in what she had just told her client's brother.

EP 2.1.7 b

ASSESSMENT SUMMARY As a part of the competency-based assessment, the social worker, Martina Lopez, considers several theories about human behavior and the influence of the environment in order to better understand Sidney's struggles. For instance, Sydney Sutherland had been found unconscious with numerous medications and alcohol nearby. In addition, certain organic mental disorders often have signs and symptoms resembling schizophrenia, such as hallucinations, delusions, and incoherence. Thus, the competency-based assessment must rule out factors that might otherwise explain her behavior. An assessment of schizoaffective disorder should be made if the periods of depression or mania are brief in relation to the ongoing symptoms of schizophrenia. In the case vignette, Sydney has a long history of schizophrenia as reported both by her brother and by the social worker at the day care center (i.e., according to both sources, Sydney experiences auditory and visual hallucinations). However, within the last month she also began to show signs of major depression—sleeping all day, crying more than usual, confiding to her brother that things were hopeless and that she wanted to die. Because Sydney's depression is prolonged (lasting at least the past month or so), Martina Lopez concludes that a schizoaffective disorder should be considered. Figure 5.5 illustrates the interactions of the biological, psychological, and social variables in Sydney Sutherland's life.

THE DSM MULTIAXIAL DIAGNOSIS FOR SYDNEY SUTHERLAND IS AS FOLLOWS:

Axis I	295.70 Schizoaffective Disorder
Axis II	V71.09 (No diagnosis)
Axis III	482.9 Pneumonia, Unspecified Bacterial Infection
	970.9 Stimulants
	967.0 Barbiturates
	969.4 Benzodiazepine-Based Tranquilizers
Axis IV	Occupational problems
Axis V	GAF = 20 (on admission)

© Cengage Learning

BRIEF PSYCHOTIC DISORDER

Brief psychotic disorder is seldom assessed in clinical practice, and therefore has received minimal attention. We include it in this chapter to help the practitioner carefully explore all aspects of a client's life as a part of making the competency-based assessment. There is not a great deal of reliable information regarding the incidence, prevalence, sex ratio, average age of onset, or subsequent course of this disorder.

Typically, brief psychotic disorder *lasts more than one day, but less than 30 days*, and the individual eventually returns to his or her prior level of functioning. If these psychotic features persist beyond 30 days, the assessment would then have to suggest one of the other psychotic categories such as schizophreniform disorder. If a new mother, within 4 weeks of childbirth, threatens to

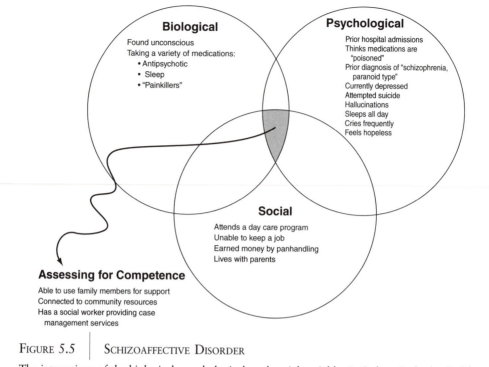

FIGURE 5.5 | SCHIZOAFFECTIVE DISORDER

The interactions of the biological, psychological, and social variables in Sydney Sutherland's life.

© Cengage Learning

harm or kill her infant, experiences bizarre delusions or hallucinations, or additionally exhibits disorganized speech or catatonic behavior, then the postpartum onset of psychosis should be specified. However, if the psychotic symptoms of bizarre delusions or hallucinations are culturally sanctioned (or are perceived as a normative coping response), then the practitioner would not necessarily consider using the diagnosis. For example, in some parts of the world, cultural schemas support the idea of being possessed by an evil spirit. Castillo (1997) points out that when individuals are "possessed," they may tear off their clothes, assault others, throw things, behave incoherently, and believe that they have supernatural powers that allow them to harm or even kill people. This same behavior in modern industrialized societies is seen as deviant and bizarre, and the diagnosis of brief psychotic disorder would most likely be considered the appropriate explanation of the person's behavior.

Features labeled brief psychotic disorder *always* include at least one major symptom of psychosis; it usually occurs with an abrupt onset, but does not always include the characteristic patterns seen in schizophrenia. For example, when a person experiences some extreme, traumatic, or overwhelming situation(s), he or she may display erratic emotions, screaming, muteness, impaired memory of recent events, and/or other eccentric behaviors. Situations such as the loss of a parent, a life-threatening accident, or even the birth of a child are the kind of major life events that would cause anyone significant emotional upheaval. Thus, practitioners should consider "the event" within the context of the stress it may cause, in addition to whether or not the client might derive any type of secondary gain or benefit from illness.

Overall, the outcome for people diagnosed with brief psychotic disorder is good—that is, they do not generally experience long-term major psychiatric problems. For practitioners, it is useful to include information gathered from the person's friends and family as a part of the competency-based assessment, particularly exploring the individual's prior level of intrapersonal functioning, past history regarding reactions to similar stressors, and the chronological relationship between the current life stressor and the onset of symptoms. Other differential assessment distinctions should include the consideration of factitious disorder, malingering, psychotic disorder due to a general medical condition (as in epilepsy or delirium), substance-induced psychotic disorder, dissociative identity disorder, and psychotic episodes associated with borderline and schizotypal personality disorders.

DELUSIONAL DISORDER

As the name implies, the central characteristic of **delusional disorder** is the person's persistent belief about something that is contrary to reality. The individual may imagine events that *could* be happening but, in fact, are not. At face value, the person's thoughts seem completely plausible (in that they are not bizarre). The individual with delusional disorder does not exhibit some of the other features commonly associated with schizophrenia, such as flat affect or other negative symptoms. Compared with some other disorders, the onset of delusional disorder is relatively late in life—usually beginning when the individual is between 40 and 49 years of age (Vahia & Cohen, 2009). It is not known why this disorder has such a late onset, but there is some speculation that perhaps these individuals lead otherwise relatively normal lives and do not feel the need to seek help. The person comes to the social worker's attention at the point when his or her symptoms become problematic and **ego-dystonic** (incompatible with the person's view of him- or herself).

When a practitioner is considering an assessment of delusional disorder, the individual in question must exhibit one or more positive symptoms of schizophrenia (often precipitated by stressful situations) lasting less than 1 month, *but at least for 1 day*. Unfortunately, as with other relatively rare disorders, little is known about the biopsychosocial influences on delusional disorder (Suvisaari et al., 2009). We really do not yet know, for example, the prevalence or course of the illness. What we can say is that it is seen more in women than in men and that it has a genetic component.

The practitioner must be mindful that several other disorders cause delusions, and those should be ruled out before making an assessment of delusional disorder. One rule of thumb is to always consider the use of substances such as alcohol and/ or illicit drugs prior to making a definitive assessment of delusional disorder. Brain tumors, vascular dementia, and cognitive-type dementia also can manifest similar features and must be discounted.

Shared Psychotic Disorder (Formerly Known as Folie à Deux)

The last of the psychotic disorders addressed in this chapter is known as **shared psychotic disorder**. When the practitioner evaluates the client's interpersonal relationships as a part of the competency-based assessment, he or she must always be alert to situations in which there is a "significant other person" who exerts undue influence in the client's life. The following discussion is intended to help the practitioner carefully explore the multiple features of the client's social world.

Relatively little is known about this rare and rather exotic disorder. The syndrome has been known by many different names—communicated insanity, infectious insanity, double insanity, and *folie à deux*. The term literally translates from the French language as "madness of two." It was introduced in 1897 to describe the occurrence of shared delusions of two (or more) people who live in close proximity and are relatively isolated from the outside world and its influences. It was thought to be common between a mother and her daughter or sister to sister pairs, but in actuality it can occur in a range of paired relationships (Shimizu, Kubota, Toichi, & Baba, 2007). Its main feature is the slow development of delusions that are the result of being in a symbiotic relationship with an "other." Typically, such a situation arises when one person is under the influence of another (more dominant) person who is having delusions—e.g., a long-standing submissive relationship between parent and child, husband and wife, or cult leader and acolyte. Usually, people who have cultivated a shared delusion live together in social isolation, and they move frequently to escape the difficulties associated with their delusional behaviors. Aside from their shared delusion, they typically do not exhibit any other associated psychotic features. The age of onset is variable. The development of these delusions is gradual, and the disorder usually remits spontaneously upon separation of the parties.

PROPOSED DIAGNOSTIC CATEGORIES

The DSM-IV Task Force (American Psychiatric Association, 2000) proposed two new categories of schizophrenia. Although there is not yet enough evidence to include them in the current DSM, they are reviewed here in order to help refine our understanding of the broad range of behaviors that characterize this complex syndrome.

The first of these proposed diagnostic categories is **postpsychotic depressive disorder** of schizophrenia. The essential feature is "a major depressive episode that is superimposed on and occurs during the residual phase of schizophrenia" (American Psychiatric Association, p. 767). The criteria for this disorder are also those an individual meets for a diagnosis of a major depressive episode that is superimposed on and occurs only during the residual phase of schizophrenia. The major depressive episode is not the result of the effects of a substance or a general medical condition.

The second proposed diagnostic category is **simple deteriorative disorder** or simple schizophrenia. "The essential feature is the development of prominent negative symptoms, which represent a clear change from a pre-established baseline. If positive psychotic symptoms … have ever been present, they have not been prominent" (American Psychiatric Association, 2000, p. 769). The criteria for this diagnosis are the progressive and marked decline in occupational or academic functioning; the gradual appearance of (and increase in) negative symptoms (e.g., affective flattening, alogia, and avolition); and poor interpersonal relationships, social isolation, or social withdrawal for a period of at least 1 year. Additionally, for an assessment of simple schizophrenia, Criterion A (positive and negative symptoms) for schizophrenia has not been met before, and the symptoms are not better accounted for by the diagnosis of one of the following: schizotypal or schizoid personality disorder, psychotic disorder, mood disorder, anxiety disorder, dementia, or mental retardation. In addition, the effects of a substance or a medical condition cannot account for the symptoms. While both of these proposed diagnoses require further study, they support using the competency-based assessment that provides a comprehensive framework for evaluating all aspects of a person's behavior and his or her environment.

In practice, it is sometimes difficult to differentiate among the different subtypes of schizophrenia discussed in this chapter. Additionally, a person's symptom picture may change over time. The DSM-5 is considering the possibility of removing the subtypes and adding a dimensional rating for some of the core symptoms of schizophrenia. For example, an individual may have (and be distressed by) the following dimensions: hallucinations, delusions, disorganized speech, abnormal psychomotor behavior, restricted emotional expression, avolition, impaired cognition, depression, and mania. At least one dimension should include delusions, hallucinations, or disorganized speech. It is anticipated that this approach to diagnosing schizophrenia will provide a fuller description of the multiple problems individuals encounter that are often unspecified by the diagnosis of a specific subtype.

SUMMARY

Although many persons with schizophrenia have some symptoms in common, each individual's course and outlook may be vastly different. This underscores the importance of the competency-based assessment, which examines the extent of the individual's coping, resources, capacity for interpersonal relationships, life stressors, cultural influences, and the impact of his or her social environment. Each variable plays an important part in the assessment process. Here is a summary of the major features of the disease:

- Schizophrenia is characterized by a wide spectrum of cognitive and emotional features including delusions, hallucinations, disorganized speech and behavior, and inappropriate emotions.
- Symptoms of schizophrenia are classified as either positive or negative.

- *Positive symptoms* refer to outward signs and symptoms, or those characteristics that are present but should be absent (i.e., abnormal behaviors such as delusions, hallucinations, and disorganized speech).
- *Negative symptoms* refer to inward signs and symptoms, or those characteristics that are absent but should be present. These involve deficits in normative behavior in the dimensions of affect, speech, and motivation.
- Schizophrenia is subdivided into five categories:
  - *Paranoid type*—The person has prominent delusions or hallucinations, while their cognitive skills and affect remain relatively intact.

- *Catatonic type*—Individuals have unusual and striking motor responses such as remaining in a fixed position (referred to as waxy flexibility), excessive activity, and being oppositional in remaining rigid. In addition, they display odd mannerisms with their bodies and faces, which often include grimacing.
- *Disorganized type*—Individuals exhibit marked disruption (disorganization) in their speech and behavior. They also display flat or inappropriate affect.
- *Undifferentiated type*—Individuals do not fit neatly into the other subtypes, yet they exhibit the major features of schizophrenia.
- *Residual type*—Individuals who have had at least one episode of schizophrenia but who no longer have the major symptoms of the disorder.
- Several other disorders characterized by psychotic-type behaviors (e.g., hallucinations and delusions) have been described and classified. These include:
  - *Schizophreniform disorder*—The individual has experienced symptoms of schizophrenia for less than 6 months.
  - *Schizoaffective disorder*—Individuals have symptoms of schizophrenia as well as the characteristics of mood disorders (i.e., major depressive disorder and bipolar affective disorder).
  - *Delusional disorder*—The individual has a persistent delusion or belief that is contrary to reality, but the other characteristics of schizophrenia are absent.
  - *Brief psychotic disorder*—The individual exhibits one or more positive symptoms (i.e., delusions, hallucinations, disorganized speech, or disorganized behavior) for a period lasting less than 1 month.
  - *Shared psychotic disorder*—Individuals who, by virtue of their intensely close relationship, come to share the same delusion(s).

PRACTITIONER'S REFLECTIONS

Knowing the various signs and symptoms of schizophrenia is, of course, necessary, but it is also essential for the practitioner to tune in to the client's "full story." People with schizophrenia and other psychotic disorders may, at times and in many ways, function productively. At other times, they may struggle with the broad range of their symptoms. The reflections or activities provided here are designed to help you consider the full range of the experience of a person with a diagnosis of schizophrenia.

ACTIVITIES

Advanced Clinical
EP 2.1.1 d

1. List all of the myths about and reactions to people diagnosed with schizophrenia that you (or others who you know) have heard about, seen in the media, or read about in books. The professional social worker develops relationships with clients within the person-in-environment and from a strengths perspective. How might these myths and reactions challenge a strengths-based professional relationship?

2. List all of the words you can think of associated with the word *psychotic*. Review this list and indicate how many of them have a positive connotation and how many are negative. What does this tell you about how people with psychotic disorders are perceived? Further, imagine for a moment that you overhear several of your colleagues in the cafeteria referring to

EP 2.1.1 d

their clients in some of these negative terms. What should you do?

3. Review the case of Joey Esterson. Identify the problems related to interviewing someone who is reticent and responds the way that Joey does. Clearly, this is a client who challenges the social worker's abilities to communicate. Role play the portion of the interview where the social worker attempts the mental status examination of Joey that illustrates your professional demeanor.

Advanced
Clinical
EP 2.1.3 b

4. Look over the case vignettes discussed in this chapter, and identify some of the obstacles each person may pose in developing a therapeutic relationship. Identify and make a list of each client's strengths and vulnerabilities.

5. Imagine that an appointment was made with you and the receptionist has just told you that Rudy Rosen is in the waiting room. You greet him, help him to get settled in your office, and exchange some general pleasantries. You are now ready to begin your first interview with him.

a. Write the first 4 to 5 minutes (8 to 10 exchanges) of your session as you imagine it to have happened. (Refer to the case of Claudia Benjamin for an example of what this process recording might look like.)

b. Look again at your process recording. What prompted you to say what you did and ask the questions you asked? How you were feeling at the time? Working with someone like Rudy can be frustrating at times. List the issues you would discuss with your supervisor.

EP 2.1.1 f

6. Access the CourseMate website at www.cengagebrain.com where the video, The Case of Etta is highlighted. Etta has been diagnosed with schizophrenia. In practice, she would be considered "low functioning." She had been characterized as "very sweet" before her diagnosis, but as you will see it is very difficult to communicate with her. The interview highlights her delusions. Note Etta's involuntary hand movements as they illustrate aspects of the body movements found in tardive dyskinesia. She also shows negative symptoms (i.e., blunted affect). Imagine that Etta is your client and describe the challenges she presents to conducting a professional interview with her.

Advanced
Clinical
EP 2.1.1 d

COMPETENCY NOTES

EP 2.1.1 d: Demonstrate professional demeanor in behavior, appearance, and communication (pp. 173, 182): Social workers commit themselves to the profession's enhancement and to their own professional conduct and growth.

EP Advanced Clinical 2.1.1 d: Develop, manage, and maintain therapeutic relationships with clients within the person-in-environment perspectives (pp. 182, 183): Advanced practitioners in clinical social work recognize the importance of the therapeutic relationship, the person-in-environment and strengths perspectives, the professional use of self with clients, and adherence to ethical guidelines of professional behavior.

EP 2.1.1 f: Use supervision and consultation (p. 183): Social workers commit themselves to the profession's enhancement and to their own professional conduct and growth.

EP Advanced Clinical 2.1.3 b: Identify and articulate clients' strengths and vulnerabilities (pp. 146, 183): Advanced practitioners understand and differentiate the strengths and limitations of multiple practice theories and methods, clinical processes, and technical tools, including differential diagnosis.

EP 2.1.4 a: Recognize the extent to which a culture's structures and values may oppress, marginalize, alienate, or create or enhance privilege and power

(p. 147): Social workers understand how diversity characterizes and shapes the human experience and is critical to the formation of identity.

EP 2.1.7 b: Critique and apply knowledge to understand person and environment (p. 153): Social workers are knowledgeable about human behavior across the life course, the range of social systems in which people live, and the ways social systems promote or deter people in maintaining or achieving health and well-being.

EP Advanced Clinical 2.1.7 c: Consult with medical professionals, as needed, to confirm diagnosis and/or to monitor medication in the treatment process (p. 164): Advanced practitioners understand how to synthesize and differentially apply the theories of human behavior and the social environment.

EP Advanced Clinical 2.1.10 (b) c: Assess client coping strategies to reinforce and improve adaptation to life situations, circumstances, and events (pp. 161, 168, 170): Clinical social work practice involves the dynamic, interactive, and reciprocal processes of therapeutic engagement, multidimensional assessment, clinical intervention, and practice evaluation at multiple levels.

REFERENCES

Aleman, A., Kahn, R. S., & Selten, J. P. (2003). Sex differences in the risk of schizophrenia: Evidence from meta-analysis. *Archives of General Psychiatry, 60*, 565–571.

Alex, K. D., Yavanian, G. J., McFarlane, H. G., Pluto, C. P., & Pehek, E. A. (2005). Modulation of dopamine release by striatal 5-HT2C receptors. *Synapse, 55*, 242–251.

American Psychiatric Association. (2000). *Diagnostic and statistical manual of mental disorders* (4th ed., text revision). Washington, DC: Author.

Angermeyer, M. C., & Schulze, B. (2001). Reducing the stigma of schizophrenia: Understanding the process and options for interventions. *Epidemiologia e Psichiatria Sociale, 10*, 1–10.

Barlow, D. H., & Durand, V. M. (2012). *Abnormal psychology* (6th ed.). Belmont, CA: Wadsworth Cengage Learning.

Bentley, K. J., & Walsh, J. (2006). *The social worker and psychotropic medication* (3rd ed.). Pacific Grove, CA: Brooks/Cole Thomson Learning.

Bleuler, E. (1926). *La schizophrenie. Rapport au Congrès des médecins alienistes et neurologistes de France et des pays de langue française. (Schizophrenia: Report to the congress of French and French-speaking alienists and neurologists).* 30th Session. Geneva. Lausanne, Paris: Masson.

Bleuler, E. (1950). *Dementia praecox or the group of schizophrenias.* Madison, CT: International Universities Press.

Carlsson, A. (2006). The neurochemical circuitry of schizophrenia. *Pharmacopsychiatry, 39* (Suppl. 1), S10–S14.

Caron, J., Latimer, E., & Tousignant, M. (2002). Predictors of psychological distress and quality of life in disadvantaged socioeconomic populations of Montreal. *Journal of Urban Health, 79* (Suppl. 1), S56–S60.

Caron, J., Lecompte, Y., Stip, E., & Renaud, S. (2005). Predictors of quality of life in schizophrenia. *Community Mental Health Journal 41* (4), 399–417.

Caron, J., Mercier, C., Diaz, P., & Martin, A. (2005). Sociodemographic and clinical predictors of quality of life in patients with schizophrenia or schizoaffective disorder. *Psychiatry Research 13* (3), 203–213.

Castillo, R. J. (1997). *Culture and mental illness: A client centered approach.* Pacific Grove, CA: Brooks/Cole Thomson Learning Wadsworth.

Compton, M. T., Weiss, P. S., West, J. C., & Kaslow, N. J. (2005). The association between substance use disorders, schizophrenia spectrum disorders, and Axis IV psychosocial problems. *Psychosocial Psychiatry and Psychiatric Epidemiology, 40*, 939–946.

Craven, R. M., Priddle, T. H., Crow, T. J., & Esiri, M. M. (2005). The locus coeruleus in schizophrenia: A postmortem study of noradrenergic neurones. *Neuropathology and Applied Neurobiology, 31*, 115–126.

Dickerson, F. B. (2007). Women, aging, and schizophrenia. *Journal of Women and Aging, 19*, 49–61.

Elmsley, R., Chiliza, B., & Schoerman, R. (2008). Predictors of long-term outcome in schizophrenia. *Current Opinion in Psychiatry, 27*, 173–177.

Fischer, M. (1971). Psychoses in the offspring of schizophrenic monozygotic twins and their normal co-twins. *British Journal of Psychiatry, 118*, 43–52.

Freudenreich, O., Holt, D. J., Cather, C., & Goff, D. C. (2007). The evaluation and management of patients with first-episode schizophrenia: A selective, clinical review of diagnosis, treatment, and prognosis. *Harvard Review of Psychiatry, 15,* 189–211.

Fusar-Poli, P., & Politi, P. (2008). Paul Eugen Bleuler and the birth of schizophrenia (1908). *American Journal of Psychiatry, 165* (11), 1407.

Gottesman, I. I., & Bertelsen, A. (1989). Confirming unexpressed genotypes for schizophrenia. Risks in the offspring of Fischer's Danish identical and fraternal discordant twins. *Archives of General Psychiatry, 46,* 867–872.

Gottesman, I. I. (1991). *Schizophrenia genesis: The origins of madness.* New York: Freeman.

Gur, R. E., & Pearlson, G. D. (1993). Neuroimaging in schizophrenia research. *Schizophrenia Bulletin, 19* (2), 337–353.

Hardy-Bayle, M. C., Sarfati, Y., & Passerieux, C. (2003). The cognitive basis of disorganization symptomatology in schizophrenia and its clinical correlate toward a pathogenic approach to disorganization. *Schizophrenia Bulletin, 29,* 459–471.

Haslam, J. (1976). *Observations on madness and melancholy.* Reprint edition. New York: Arno Press. (Original work published in 1809.)

Hawton, K., Sutton, L., Haw, C., Sinclair, J., & Deeks, J. J. (2005). Schizophrenia and suicide: Systematic review of risk factors. *British Journal of Psychiatry, 187,* 9–20.

Henquet, C., Murray, R., Linszen, D., & van Os, J. (2005). The environment and schizophrenia: The role of cannabis use. *Schizophrenia Bulletin, 31,* 608–612.

Ho, B. C., Black, D. W., & Andreasen, N. C. (2003). Schizophrenia and other psychotic disorders. In R. E. Hales & S. C. Yudofsky (Eds.), *Textbook of clinical psychiatry* (4th ed., pp. 379–438). Washington, DC: American Psychiatric Press.

Ho, B. C., Nopoulos, P., Flaum, M., Arndt, S., & Andreasen, N. C. (2004). Two-year outcome in first-episode schizophrenia. Predictive value of symptoms for quality of life. *Focus, 2,* 131–137.

Jablensky, A. (2009). Worldwide burden of schizophrenia. In B. J. Sadock, V. A. Sadock, & P. Ruiz (Eds.), *Kaplan and Sadock's comprehensive textbook of psychiatry (*9th ed., Vol. I,

pp. 1451–1462). Philadelphia: Lippincott Williams & Wilkins.

Jobe, T. H., & Harrow, M. (2005). Long-term outcome of patients with schizophrenia: A review. *Canadian Journal of Psychiatry, 50,* 892–900.

Kearney, C. A., & Trull, T. J. (2012). *Abnormal psychology and life: A dimensional approach.* Belmont, CA: Wadsworth Cengage Learning.

Klausner, J., Sweeney, J., Deck, M., Hass, G., & Kelly, A. B. (1992). Clinical correlates of cerebral ventricular enlargement on schizophrenia: Further evidence for frontal lobe disease. *Journal of Nervous and Mental Disease, 180,* 407–412.

Koh, P. O., Bergson, C., Undie, A. S., Goldman-Rakic, P. S., & Lidow, M. S. (2003). Up-regulation of the D1 dopamine receptor-interacting protein, calcyon, in patients with schizophrenia. *Archives of General Psychiatry, 60,* 311–319.

Kraepelin, E. (1971). *Dementia praecox and paraphrenia* (R. M. Barclay, Trans.). New York: Krieger. (Original work published 1919.)

Laurelle, M., Kegeles, L. S., & Abi-Dargham, A. (2003). Glutamate, dopamine, and schizophrenia: From pathophysiology to treatment. *Annals of the New York Academy of Sciences, 1003,* 138–158.

Luoma, S., Hakko, H., Ollinen, T., Jarvelin, M. R., & Lindeman, S. (2008). Association between age at onset and clinical features of schizophrenia: The Northern Finland 1966 birth cohort study. *European Psychiatry, 23,* 331–335.

Lysaker, P. H., France, C. M., Hunter, N. L., & Davis, L. (2005). Personal narratives of illness in schizophrenia: Associations with neurocognition and symptoms. *Psychiatry 68* (2), 140–151.

Maki, P., Veijola, J., Jones, P. B., Murray, G. K., Koponen, H., Tienari, P., … Isohanni, M. (2005). Predictors of schizophrenia: A review. *British Medical Bulletin, 73–74,* 1–15.

Malla, A., & Payne, J. (2005). First-episode psychosis: Psychopathology, quality of life, and functional outcome. *Schizophrenia Bulletin, 31,* 650–671.

Morel, B. A. (1890). *Traite des maladies mentales. (Treatise on mental illness).* Paris, France: Masson.

Murray, R. M., Jones, P. B., Susser, E., van Os, J., & Cannon, M. (2003). *The epidemiology of schizophrenia.* Cambridge, UK: Cambridge University Press.

Murray, R. M., Lappin, J., & Di Forti, M. (2008). Schizophrenia: From developmental deviance to dopamine dysregulation. *European Neuropsycho-pharmacology, 18* (Suppl. 3), S129–S134.

National Institute of Mental Health. (2005). *Schizophrenia.* Bethesda, MD: Author.

Niemi, L. T., Suvisaari, J. M., Tuulio-Henriksson, A., & Lonnqvist, J. K. (2003). Childhood developmental abnormalities in schizophrenia: Evidence from high-risk studies. *Schizophrenia Research, 60,* 239–258.

Opler, M. G. A., & Susser, E. S. (2005). Fetal environment and schizophrenia. *Environmental Perspectives 113* (9), 1239–1242.

Palmer, B. A., Pankratz, V. S., & Bostwick, J. M. (2005). The lifetime risk of suicide in schizophrenia: A reexamination. *Archives of General Psychiatry, 62,* 247–253.

Pinikahana, J., Happell, B., & Keks, N. A. (2003). Suicide and schizophrenia: A review of literature for the decade (1990–1999) and implications for mental health nursing. *Issues in Mental Health Nursing, 24,* 227–236.

Purcell, S., Wray, N., Stone, J., Visscher, P., O'Donovan, M., Sullivan, P., ... Morris, D. W. (2009). Common polygenic variation contributes to risk of schizophrenia and bipolar disorder. *Nature 460,* 748–752.

Rosen, J. L., Miller, T. J., D'Andrea, J. T., McGlashan, T. H., & Woods, S. W. (2006). Comorbid diagnoses in patients meeting criteria for the schizophrenia syndrome. *Schizophrenia Research, 85,* 124–131.

Schneider, K. (1959). *Clinical psychopathology.* (M. W. Hamilton, Trans.). London: Grune and Stratton.

Shenton, M. E., & Kubicki, M. (2009). Structural brain imaging in schizophrenia. In B. J. Sadock, V. A. Sadock, & P. Ruiz (Eds.), *Kaplan and Sadock's comprehensive textbook of psychiatry* (9th ed., Vol I, pp. 1494–1507). Philadelphia: Lippincott Williams & Wilkins.

Shimizu, M., Kubota, Y., Toichi, M., & Baba, G. (2007). Folie à deux and shared psychotic disorder. *Current Psychiatry Reports, 9* (3), 200–205.

Staal, W. G., Pol, H. E. H., Schnack, H. G., Hoogendoorn, M. L. C., Jellema, K., & Kahn, R. S. (2000). Structural brain abnormalities in patients with schizophrenia and their healthy siblings. *American Journal of Psychiatry, 157,* 416–421.

Suvisaari, J., Perala, J., Saarni, S., Juvonen, H., Tuulio-Henriksson, A., & Lonnqvist, J. (2009). The

epidemiology and descriptive and predictive validity of DSM-IV delusional disorder and subtypes of schizophrenia. *Clinical Schizophrenia and Related Psychoses, 2* (4), 289–297.

Tarrier, N., Khan, S., Cater, J., & Picken, A. (2007). The subjective consequences of suffering a first episode psychosis: Trauma and suicide behavior. *Social Psychiatry and Psychiatric Epidemiology, 42* (1), 29–35.

Vahia, I. V., & Cohen, C. I. (2009). Schizophrenia and delusional disorders. In B. J. Sadock, V. A. Sadock, & P. Ruiz (Eds.), *Kaplan and Sadock's comprehensive textbook of psychiatry (*9th ed., Vol I, pp. 4073–4081). Philadelphia: Lippincott Williams & Wilkins.

Van Dorn, R. A., Swanson, J. W., Elbogen, E. B., & Swartz, M. S. (2005). A comparison of stigmatizing attitudes toward persons with schizophrenia in four stakeholder groups: Perceived likelihood of violence and desire for social distance. *Psychiatry, 68* (2), 152–163.

van Os, J., & Allardyce, J. (2009). The clinical epidemiology of schizophrenia. In B. J. Sadock, V. A. Sadock, & P. Ruiz (Eds.), *Kaplan and Sadock's comprehensive textbook of psychiatry* (9th ed., Vol I, pp. 1475–1487). Philadelphia: Lippincott Williams & Wilkins.

Veen, N. D. (2005). People diagnosed with schizophrenia retain the diagnosis long term. *Evidence-Based Mental Health, 8* (3), 68–71.

Wade, C., & Tavris, C. (2010). *Psychology* (10th ed.). Upper Saddle River, NJ: Pearson Prentice Hall.

Weisman de Mamani, A. G., Kymalainen, J. A., Rosales, G. A., & Armesto, J. C. (2007). Expressed emotion and interdependence in white and Latino/Hispanic family members of patients with schizophrenia. *Psychiatry Research, 151,* 107–113.

Whitty, P., Clarke, M., McTigue, O., Browne, S., Kamali, M., Larkin, C., & O'Callaghan, E. (2005). Diagnostic stability four years after a first episode of psychosis. *Psychiatric Services, 36,* 1084–1088.

Wray, N. R., & Visscher, P. M. (2010). Narrowing the boundaries of the genetic architecture of schizophrenia. *Schizophrenia Bulletin, 36* (1), 14–23.

Wu, E., Birnbaum, H., Shi, L., Ball, D., Kessler, R., Moulis, M., & Aggarwal, J. (2005). The economic burden of schizophrenia in the United States in 2002. *Journal of Clinical Psychiatry, 68* (9), 1122–1129.

Mood Disorders

CHAPTER 6

INTRODUCTION

Depression has been described throughout the ages, and accounts of what are currently referred to as **mood disorders** can be found in many ancient documents. The DSM-IV (American Psychiatric Association, 1994) expanded in size by approximately 50 percent from its predecessor DSM-III-R (American Psychiatric Association, 1987), and the space allocated to mood disorders tripled in size. Mood disorders refer to a group of emotional disturbances characterized by serious and persistent difficulty maintaining an even, productive emotional state. The term *affective disorders,* although now considered somewhat dated, continues to be used interchangeably to describe these mood conditions. The DSM-IV-TR (American Psychiatric Association, 2000) attempts to define and differentiate between these two closely related concepts by offering the following in its glossary:

> **Affect** is a pattern of observable behaviors that is the expression of a subjectively experienced feeling state (emotion). Common examples of affect are sadness, elation, and anger. In contrast to mood, which refers to a more pervasive and sustained emotional "climate," affect refers to more fluctuating changes in emotional "weather." What is considered the normal range of the expression of affect varies considerably, both within and among different cultures. (p. 819)

A mood disorder generally involves varying degrees of depression, elation, or irritability. However, the presence of an altered mood is not sufficient to warrant the assessment of a mood disorder. In practice, the social worker may hear the person with a mood disorder say, "I just can't seem to get myself out of bed," or "When I try to remember anything, it's like trying to fight through a thick fog." The person's reduced interest, energy, and motivation begin to adversely have an impact on his or her interpersonal life. The person may have difficulty making normal everyday decisions, lose interest in pleasurable activities, have difficulty sleeping, and/or show decreased interest in sexual activities.

Negative ideation and low self-esteem characterize the intrapersonal or personal domain; they view themselves as worthless and valueless. Individuals with a mood disorder are generally pessimistic and possess little or no sense of hope for themselves or their future. They tend to "forget" about their accomplishments while fixating on their present failures, misdeeds, and flaws. The person may experience restless thoughts and complain of somatic ailments such as constipation, headaches, and menstruation irregularity. If left on their own, they may not bathe or change their clothing for days at a time. As a result, major depressive episodes often lead to interpersonal difficulties such as unemployment, scholastic failure, divorce, and social isolation.

The practitioner must always look for a mood disorder when a client comes in for help. The competency-based assessment underscores the need for a thorough investigation into the client's life and helps the practitioner look beyond the chief complaint. Over 10 years ago, Morrison (1995) noted that mood disorders account for almost half of a typical mental health practice and are found in all social classes, races, and cultural backgrounds—and this level of incidence is expected to continue. For example, Kessler and colleagues (2003, 2005) estimated that 16 percent of the population experiences a mood disorder at some point in their life. Approximately 6 percent have experienced a major depressive disorder in the last year (Hasin, Goodwin, Stinson, & Grant, 2005). While mood disorders have many different levels of severity, their identification can be reduced to a few main principles.

This chapter will pay particular attention to the two major mood disorders: (1) **major depression**, whose sufferers experience only depressive episodes (previously referred to as unipolar depression, which is not a DSM term), and (2) **bipolar disorder** (previously known as manic depression), whose sufferers either exhibit manic, euphoric, or heightened mood as well as depression, or manic episodes alone. We will also focus on two minor (i.e., less severe) forms of mood disorders: **dysthymia** (chronic in nature) and **cyclothymia** (fluctuating in nature). Although milder, these two disorders present many of the same symptoms as those found in major depressive disorder and bipolar disorder.

The DSM-IV-TR (American Psychiatric Association, 2000) defines mood as "a pervasive and sustained emotion that colors the perception of the world. Common examples of mood include depression, elation, anger, and anxiety" (p. 825). The mood disorders include four types of mood episodes that serve as the building blocks for the mood disorder diagnoses. (These episodes do not in themselves constitute diagnoses, and the DSM has no diagnostic code for them.) The four types of mood episodes are:

1. **Major depressive episode**—At least 2 weeks of depressed mood accompanied by a characteristic pattern of depressive symptoms.
2. **Manic episode**—At least 1 week of exhilarated, heightened, or irritable mood accompanied by a characteristic symptom pattern.
3. **Mixed episode**—At least 1 week of a combination of manic and depressive symptoms.
4. **Hypomanic episode**—At least 4 days of exhilarated, heightened, or irritable mood that is less extreme than a manic episode.

The competency-based assessment helps the practitioner to decipher the confusing symptoms of each type of mood episode and disorder—which is not an easy matter because they are not seen as separate disorders. For example, an individual's symptom presentation cannot legitimately be diagnosed as a manic episode unless it is considered within the larger context of the mood disorder.

Individuals diagnosed with depression usually report experiencing a dampening or lowering of mood. Many of us experience an occasional bad day, when for no apparent reason we feel glum, irritable, grumpy, or out of sorts—however, what is considered clinical depression lasts for more than a day or two. People who live with clinical depression do not bounce back; this down feeling consumes their entire lives to the extent that nothing is interesting or fun any more. In the same vein, many of us go through periods of elation or feeling as if we are floating on a cloud. These extremes of mood usually do not linger for an extended period of time—people usually bounce back and move on.

Experiences that would ordinarily be expected to raise someone's mood (e.g., spending a fun evening with a friend) do not seem to have any impact on the person who is depressed. A client once described his depression in the following way:

> "I just don't enjoy eating food, making love to my wife, sleeping, or spending time with friends anymore. I always feel either sluggish or restless. I can't concentrate, and making the smallest decision tends to paralyze me into inaction. Sometimes it takes me all day just to get out of bed, and then I sit out on the couch watching TV until it's time to go back to bed. That's no life."

Over 20 years ago, Gelman (1987) aptly dubbed depression as "the common cold of mental illness" (p. 7); unfortunately, unlike a cold, depression does not resolve itself after a few weeks. In summary, practitioners can differentiate between a person's experience of moods as a part of everyday life and the presence of depressive disorder in the following ways:

- The depressed mood is not temporary or easily shaken off, and it typically persists for weeks, months, or years.
- The depressive disorder is significant and severe enough to impair important areas of a person's interpersonal functioning.
- Depressed individuals exhibit both physical and behavioral signs and symptoms, such as sleep disturbance, loss of interest in pleasurable pursuits, and changes in appetite.

There are a number of problems related to defining who is depressed and how depression is shown. For example:

- Not all clients can accurately describe how they feel.
- Presenting symptoms of depression can vary greatly—one person might sleep too much, whereas another sleeps too little, or one eats too much and another cannot touch food.
- Practitioners may not fully appreciate the impact that culture plays on the assessment of depression.
- Mood disorders commonly occur as presenting features in a wide variety of other disorders such as the eating or anxiety disorders.

- The terms *affect* and *mood* continue to be used interchangeably, causing some confusion among practitioners.

THE MAJOR DEPRESSIVE DISORDERS

Major depressive disorder (most often referred to as major depression) is characterized by the presence of one (single episode) or more (recurrent) depressive episodes during an individual's life and includes many features in addition to feeling sad or blue. The language of the client may reflect other expressions of depression such as feelings of worthlessness, loss of energy, and a marked loss of ability to experience pleasure (**anhedonia**). Although all of these are important in assessing for depression, the presence of physical changes, referred to **vegetative features,** are critical to a determination of mood disorder, often serving as warning signals in the form of changes in sleep patterns, energy levels, or appetite fluctuations (Bech, 2009; Kessler & Wang, 2009). The vegetative features occur along with a person's behavioral and emotional shutdown.

EP 2.1.7 a

The competency-based assessment provides a framework for a systematic review of the various theories of human behavior and environmental influences to help the practitioner distinguish between what could be considered an expected sad reaction from the symptoms of depression. The core issue in looking for the presence of major depression is evaluating whether the presenting characteristics are the primary problem or are related to another disorder. This distinction is complicated by the fact that both situations tend to create problems in living for the individual. Almost everyone at some point in his or her life experiences feeling depressed—but the low that comes from a setback (e.g., losing one's job) is very different from having major depression. The competency-based assessment recognizes that getting a new job or moving on in life does not necessarily eliminate the feelings of sadness. The practitioner considers major depression when the following features have been present over a 2-week period of time and represent a change from the client's earlier ways of coping:

- Despondent mood most of the day, nearly every day.
- Markedly diminished interest or pleasure in most activities.
- Significant changes in weight (either gain or loss).
- Vegetative features such as insomnia (cannot sleep) or hypersomnia (sleeping too much).
- Psychomotor agitation or retardation (either hand wringing and restless pacing or slowness in activities such as walking or talking).
- Fatigue and/or loss of energy.
- Feeling worthless or experiencing excessive guilt.
- Inability to concentrate or think.
- Recurring thoughts of death, or suicidal ideation.
- Significant distress or impairment in social, occupational, or other important areas of interpersonal functioning.

Assessment of major depression requires the presence of *either* a depressed mood *or* a loss of interest or a loss of pleasure. Major depression is not caused by street drugs, medication, physical illness, or alcohol, and symptoms related to the bereavement process are not included in its diagnosis.

PREVAILING PATTERN

Major depression appears, in part, to be inherited and the prevalence is two to three times higher among parents, siblings, or offspring (first-degree relatives) of those who have suffered a major depressive episode than among the general population (Klein, Lewinsohn, Rhode, Seeley, & Durbin, 2002; Levinson, 2009). Major depression can start at any age but the mean age of onset is 30 years. The disorder presents itself in a variety of ways and exhibits itself in varying degrees of severity. The first episode usually develops gradually—commonly beginning during adolescence and becoming more prominent during the individual's mid-20s. Overall, the prevalence of mood disorders in prepubertal children occurs less often than in adults but rises dramatically in adolescence (Brent & Birmaher, 2009; Costello, Foley, & Angold, 2006; Garber & Carter, 2006; Garber et al., 2009; Rudolph, 2009). In rare instances, it may occur in early childhood or among children ages 2 to 5 (Garber et al., 2009). For older adults who are in the later stages of life, prevalence rates are about half that of the general population (Blazer & Hybels, 2009; Byers, Yaffe, Covinsky, Friedman, & Bruce, 2010; Fiske, Wetherell, & Gatz, 2009; Hasin, Goodwin, Stinson, & Grant, 2005).

Unfortunately, the occurrence of just one isolated depressive episode in a person's lifetime is rare (Judd, 2000; Solomon et al., 2000). More commonly, as many as 75 to 85 percent of people will have two or more incidences during their life span (Solomon et al., 2000). Sometimes an episode may not abate entirely, leaving the person with some residual symptoms. When that happens, the likelihood of another episode followed by another partial recovery is much higher (Boland & Keller, 2009).

Major depression generally occurs in specific episodes or in cycles; that is, individuals cycle down into and then back up from periods of depression. Exceptions do occur, but for the most part this periodic (or cycling) depressive process is what you can expect to see in clinical practice. Individuals who have a major depressive episode have a higher probability of recurrence, and each new episode carries renewed risks of psychosocial difficulties and suicide. In severe cases where an episode can last for 5 years or even longer, only about 35 percent of these individuals can be expected to eventually recover (Barlow & Durand, 2012). The length of each episode may vary from as little as 2 weeks to several years in severe cases—with the average duration of the first episode being 4 to 9 months if not treated (Kessler et al., 2003). A greater clinical uncertainty is whether an individual will experience new episodes, since there is no way to reliably predict the influence of the biological, psychological, and social factors in a person's life.

COMPLICATIONS ASSOCIATED WITH MAJOR DEPRESSION

Thoughts about killing oneself (or **suicidal ideation**) are almost always present, and often the risk is greatest when the individual begins to recover from the depression. While coming out of depressive fatigue, the person may acquire enough energy to carry out a suicide strategy. Suicide is often associated with other disorders, and some people may experience panic attacks or other problems such as obsessions or compulsions. In fact, more than 80 percent of people who actually kill themselves have a mood or other disorders such as substance use or impulse control disorders

(Berman, 2009; Joe, Baser, Breeden, Neighbors, & Jackson, 2006; Nock, Hwang, Sampson, & Kessler, 2009).

Complications typically center on interpersonal difficulties related to employment, relationships with others, marital discord, and substance abuse—thus, the practitioner should consider a client's use of any drug when assessing for a mood disorder (Akiskal, 2009). The following two cases illustrate different pictures of depression. The first vignette introduces Anita Richards, who experiences recurring episodes of major depression. In contrast, the subsequent case describes Alice Jackson, who is experiencing her first episode.

CASE | ## The Case of Anita Richards

Anita Richards was admitted to the hospital psychiatric unit after being brought in by the Mobile Crisis Unit (MCU), which responded to her suicide threat made over the telephone. The intake report notes that she threatened to slash her wrists with a razor blade. Anita Richards is a 38-year-old Hispanic divorced mother of four (ages 15, 12, 11, and 9). Ms. Richards has been hospitalized on three previous occasions. According to her medical records, she has been diagnosed with major depressive disorder, recurrent. Here is a partial account of the practitioner's interview.

The social worker enters Ms. Richards's hospital room and immediately notes her disheveled and unkempt appearance. Ms. Richards's hair is tousled and wild—her eyes are puffy and swollen. When she sees the social worker, Ms. Richards jumps right in.

"I've got lots and lots of problems that just don't seem to go away. My boss fired me 6 months ago and I haven't been able to find work since. Every time somebody calls him about me, he tells them not to hire me because I was always late to work. Sure I overslept a few times, but that's not enough to ruin my getting another job, is it? Because of him, I can't support my four kids. The oldest two live with their father out in Arizona, and I never see them. My younger two live with my mother. I'm going to get them back as soon as I can."

The social worker asks gently, "What happened to bring you back to the hospital this time?"

Ms. Richards begins to sob quietly. "I don't know what gets into me. I get into these crying jags, and I just can't seem to stop."

"Are you still taking the antidepressants prescribed during your last hospitalization?" the practitioner asks. Ms. Richards closes her eyes and becomes silent as she twists a tissue into shreds.

"I hated being so constipated all the time," she responds. "I gained 15 pounds and none of my clothes fit me…. I know I should take those damn pills! But after awhile I just didn't think they helped."

When Ms. Richards appears to have calmed down somewhat, the social worker asks, "What happens when you have one of those crying jags?"

"Oh, you know … I feel really rotten." Ms. Richards begins to cry again. "I hate myself, and I don't feel like I deserve to live anymore. I hate the way I look, hate the way I feel, I hate … [sobbing harder] … I hate … hate … I hate all of this. I just want it all to end." She dabs at her eyes with a new tissue and sniffles quietly.

The social worker leans over and gently suggests, "Perhaps you really don't want to end it all." (She is very aware that this is a tenuous moment in the interview. She knows she can't talk Anita out of wanting to commit suicide—that would be like just ignoring her feelings. Instead, at this point the practitioner decides to focus on Anita's other options for living and getting help.) She points out to Ms. Richards, "Deep down inside you want someone to help you find a way to get better. After all, you did reach out and make that phone call to MCU." There is a long pause, then the social worker asks, "What do you think about what I just said?"

The client nods her head slightly and says, "I just don't think anything in my life is ever going to get better. Jeez, you have no idea how tired I am of fighting life." She seems lost in thought and then continues, "I got busted by the cops 2 days ago for selling crack. I spent the whole night in jail because I didn't have the money to post bail. I called my mother, but she wouldn't help—some mother, huh?

I used my one phone call just to hear her tell me I got into trouble one too many times. She said, 'I hope the judge throws the book at you, and you rot in jail for 10 years.' I tried to tell her the whole deal wasn't my fault. How was I supposed to know the kid was a narc? He looked like he was about 12 years old, you know what I mean? He set me up. I don't use drugs, but I got to eat, don't I?" Anita continued, "My mother didn't want to tell my kids that I was in jail so she just took the easy way out and finally came up with the money to bail me out. I know I'll never hear the end of it. You know, what a screw-up I am!" Anita looks intently at the tissue in her lap and whispers almost as if she was talking to herself, "I'll never get my kids back."

The social worker asks about her suicidal call to MCU, and Ms. Richards responds, "Well, what do you expect? I don't have a job, I can't ever seem to get caught up, my no-good ex and my lousy mother are raising my kids—and, and, I can't eat, can't sleep, can't [she is sobbing] …"

When she calms down, the social worker asks her to describe what has been happening to her. "Well, it's just like the other times," Ms. Richards goes on. "I can't force myself to eat anything. I guess I've lost weight—at least my clothes fit me again." She tugs at the waist band of her jeans. "Actually, they kind of hang on me now, you know sorta baggy."

The social worker smiles at this, and then asks, "What about other problems? Is anything else going on?"

"I feel down in the dumps ALL the time," Ms. Richards replies. "I cry all the time, fall asleep for hours on end, but then I wake up feeling like I never slept at all. I just feel really blah…. I'm just tired of life, that's all there is to it. It's hopeless. I have nothing going for me. I'm a real loser. You know, there's absolutely nothing I like about living. I've tried to just hang on until the kids are grown up

and independent; then there won't be anything to hold me here." She relates this with a wistful half smile and tears streaming down her face.

"Anita, aren't there any times when you feel good? Do you ever feel up in the clouds or just really happy and full of energy?"

"No, I wish I did," she replies. "Maybe then I'd feel like there was at least something to keep me going."

As the conversation continues, Ms. Richards denies experiencing manic or psychotic behavior, and she has trouble accurately recounting when her last depressive episode occurred. Her hospital chart shows three previous admissions for major depression—all within the last 3 years. Her most recent admission was noted 5 months earlier.

The social worker tries to explore further. "What about your other relationships? Can you tell me what they are like?"

"I used to have a boyfriend, but he left me stranded." The client looked sadly at the floor. "Said I was a cold fish—just because I didn't want to have sex all the time. He's a jerk."

The social worker asks if Ms. Richards has any hobbies or special things she enjoys doing.

"When I was a kid I used to like to read," Anita offers. "Now I can't seem to concentrate—I can't get through two pages before I forget what I read. I guess that's why I don't watch much TV either."

As the interview continues, they discuss several questions about Ms. Richards's past and present medical history. She denies any medical or neurological problems—and she denies using alcohol or drugs. "I just sell them, I don't use them," Anita says. The practitioner notes this response and plans to explore this issue further.

Anita Richards was subsequently hospitalized for observation.

EP 2.1.10 (b) a

ASSESSMENT SUMMARY In this case vignette, the social worker needs to decide if Anita is currently experiencing a normal reaction to a series of life events (such as losing her job, being arrested, her boyfriend's breaking up with her, her mother's reluctance to help) or if the onset of her latest depressive episode has nothing to do with those events. This requires the ability to organize and interpret data from the case history in order to better understand Anita's symptom picture. The worker may never know causality, but a competency-based assessment provides the foundation for the worker to fully explore the client's world as well as to look for Anita's strengths in coping with what she describes as a hopeless situation. It is important to discern what can normally happen in a person's life from unfortunate

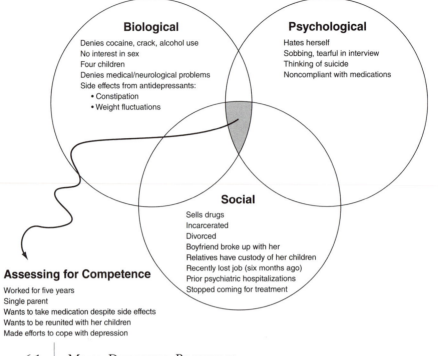

Biological
Denies cocaine, crack, alcohol use
No interest in sex
Four children
Denies medical/neurological problems
Side effects from antidepressants:
• Constipation
• Weight fluctuations

Psychological
Hates herself
Sobbing, tearful in interview
Thinking of suicide
Noncompliant with medications

Social
Sells drugs
Incarcerated
Divorced
Boyfriend broke up with her
Relatives have custody of her children
Recently lost job (six months ago)
Prior psychiatric hospitalizations
Stopped coming for treatment

Assessing for Competence
Worked for five years
Single parent
Wants to take medication despite side effects
Wants to be reunited with her children
Made efforts to cope with depression

FIGURE 6.1 | MAJOR DEPRESSION, RECURRENT

The interactions of the biological, psychological, and social variables in Anita Richards's life.

© Cengage Learning

circumstances—especially losses, humiliation, and social rejection—because they are often followed by depressive symptoms (Monroe, Slavich, & Georgiades, 2009). Anita did not provide evidence to the worker that her depression was related to bereavement issues.

Figure 6.1 illustrates the interactions of the biological, psychological, and social variables in Anita Richards's life.

ANITA RICHARDS'S MULTIAXIAL DSM DIAGNOSIS IS AS FOLLOWS:

Axis I	296.33 Major Depressive Episode, Recurrent, Severe, without Psychotic Features
Axis II	V71.09 (No diagnosis)
	Rule out denial of substance abuse
Axis III	564.0 Constipation Weight Loss
Axis IV	Problems related to interaction with the legal system/crime
	Divorced
	Unemployment
	Problems with primary support group
Axis V	GAF = 20 (on admission)

© Cengage Learning

Advanced
Clinical EP
2.1.10 (b) c

Despite numerous interpersonal difficulties, Anita has shown much strength in coping with recurring major depression. She has been able to maintain employment for a period of time (5 years). Despite the distasteful side effects associated with antidepressant medications, such as constipation and weight fluctuations, Anita realizes the importance of taking them on a regular basis. Perhaps most important, she wants to be reunited with her children, who currently reside with her mother and her former husband.

The following vignette recounts the story of Alice Jackson, who experiences her first episode of depression.

CASE | ## THE CASE OF ALICE JACKSON

Alice Jackson, age 19, gave birth to her second child almost 3 weeks ago, and since then she has been experiencing a "depressed mood" (according to her husband). Mark Jackson brought his wife into the emergency room because "She won't stop crying, and I didn't know what else to do."

I was the social worker on duty, so I introduced myself to Mr. and Mrs. Jackson. He appeared quite upset, and I asked him to have a seat. He slumped into a nearby chair, and I had the impression he had been crying shortly before I saw him. Mrs. Jackson was having her vital signs taken by a nurse in an examining room nearby. I began the interview by asking Mr. Jackson to describe what brought them to the emergency room. He inhaled, ran his hands through his hair and then over his face. Exhaling loudly, he said, "I just don't know what to do with Alice anymore. She's got everything going for her, so I don't know what the problem is. I mean, why would she want to hurt herself? How could she not love our new baby?"

I asked Mr. Jackson to go back and tell me something about the incident or circumstances when he felt his wife first began to experience these problems.

"Well, let's see. We were childhood sweethearts and all that, and she never gave any sign of being anything but rock solid. Sure, we married young—I was 19 and she was 17—but most of our friends married young, too. We both got jobs right outta high school. I got a job working at Sweeny's Auto Repair Shop, and Alice got a job as a cashier at Kmart. Things were going real good for us. We were making good money, rented a nice apartment, and then—bam—our first kid's on the way. Hell, we didn't really care, except maybe it was a little too soon, that's all. Well, I'll tell you what, Alice was beside

herself happy when Ben was born. She fussed and spoilt him like nobody's business. Of course, it was a little rough on her having to adjust to working part-time and staying home with Ben—but you never saw a prouder mother."

I asked Mr. Jackson if his wife had ever exhibited any "baby blues" after Ben was born. He replied, "I didn't notice anything unusual, 'cept maybe she was tired more." He sat and thought for a moment and then continued.

"Everything was going along fine. Ben was growing fat and sassy and was the apple of our eye. We had so much fun showing him off and all. Alice's mother doesn't live too far from us, and she helps out babysitting and stuff every once in awhile, but we try not to trouble her too much 'cause she's got her own problems." When asked to elaborate, Mr. Jackson replied, "Well, I don't like to tell tales outta school you know, but if you think it'll help Alice.... Her mother had some mental problems in the past. I don't know much about it, but she tried to kill herself a few times using some pills and washing it down with a bottle of liquor. Don't that beat all? Damn fool thing to do. She stayed in the hospital for a while. Getting treated for depression or something, Alice said. You know, come to think of it, Alice's two sisters had some trouble like that, too—but I don't know what all that has to do with us."

I asked him to tell me more about Alice. "Well, when Ben was about 6 months old, we found out we were gonna have another one. We were glad, you know, but we knew it was gonna put a big dent in our lives. We had to move to a bigger trailer, and of course the rent went up, so I started working more hours at the body shop. Toward the end of this pregnancy, Alice had some problems carrying the

continued

baby. She gained a lot of weight and her fingers and toes really swole up. She's never been much of a complainer, but she did have lots of aches and pains this time. She had to quit her job, and let her mom take care of Ben most of the day."

"I understand she gave birth just about 3 weeks ago, now," I interjected.

"That's right. His name's Josh, after my Dad. Anyhow, once we got home from the hospital, Alice got so ..." He struggled to name it. "So ... down. She doesn't want to hold the baby or take care of him. She loved nursing Ben, but with Josh she just sits there rocking and crying—with great big tears running down her face. It breaks my heart to see her like that." He looks sad, and afraid for his wife. "She

doesn't want to eat, won't pay any attention to Ben at all, says she's tired, and just wants to go back to bed. I didn't know what else to do but bring her to the hospital. She was never like this before. Alice said she didn't deserve to live any more and was gonna do something about it. I think she needs some help, don't you?"

I asked Mr. Jackson if Alice ever used any type of substances, and he answered with a definitive No—he also indicated that she did not have any other medical problems. She did not exhibit any psychotic symptoms, nor had she had any manic, mixed, or hypomanic episodes. Alice Jackson was admitted to the psychiatric unit at the hospital for observation.

EP 2.1.10 (b) a

ASSESSMENT SUMMARY   In this case vignette, the practitioner is called upon to interpret client data to differentiate the mood disorder diagnosis. Clearly, both Anita and Alice struggle with symptoms of depression, but because Alice has had only one major depressive episode and has never exhibited a manic or hypomanic features, her assessment is major depressive disorder, single episode. Unfortunately, Alice's single episode described in this vignette may very well lead to another occurrence either months or years from now. If (or when) that happens, her assessment will be changed to major depressive episode, recurrent as in the case of Anita Richards.

In summary, the practitioner should consider the following points to make a differential assessment between a single episode of major depression and recurring major depression:

- What are the individual's particular symptoms? Are those symptoms "out of proportion" to the precipitating event?
- What are the duration and intensity of the depressive features?
- Is the individual's mood "reactive" to changes in life—in other words, is the individual likely to "perk up" when something good happens? (Those with a depressive episode are not likely to do so.)
- Is there a family history of major depression?

A wide range of other life problems and /or stressful events are associated with the onset of a major depressive disorder and are important for the practitioner to consider (Hammen, 2005; Monroe, Slavich, & Georgiades, 2009; Monroe & Reid, 2009). In addition, the practitioner must determine whether or not the individual has had episodes of manic-like behaviors, which would indicate a bipolar disorder or cyclothymia. The competency-based assessment helps to carefully examine the multiple influences in a person's life and to distinguish between a depressive episode and a bipolar episode. The competency-based assessment also considers medical conditions (such as epilepsy, cerebrovascular diseases, and certain tumors) that manifest depressive features. Other conditions that complicate making an assessment include psychotic disorders commonly associated with depression such as schizophrenia, obsessive-compulsive disorder (OCD), panic disorder, and personality disorders.

The task of considering Alice Jackson's diagnosis of a major mood disorder, single episode, with postpartum depression may confound the practitioner because the depressive episode occurs shortly after childbirth (about 4 weeks immediately following childbirth) and does not occur at any other times. As we can see in Alice's situation, fathers are not immune to the emotional consequences either. Ramchandani and colleagues (2005) underscore the importance of evaluating the father for depressive symptoms as well.

The practitioner should pay careful attention to situations of postpartum onset because of the increased likelihood of maternal harm to the infant. In Alice's case, her husband Mark reacted quickly to the changes in her behavior, underscoring the importance of collateral contacts.

Schizoaffective disorder can be distinguished from major depression in that it has a defined element of psychosis along with a mood disorder lasting more than 2 weeks. The relative absence of fatigue, loss of interest, and insomnia help the practitioner differentiate between depression and generalized anxiety disorder.

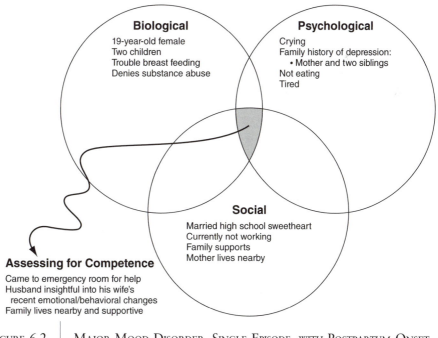

FIGURE 6.2 | MAJOR MOOD DISORDER, SINGLE EPISODE, WITH POSTPARTUM ONSET

The interactions of the biological, psychological, and social variables in Alice Jackson's life.

Those individuals with anorexia nervosa often exhibit depressive features, and the depression occurs around significant weight loss.

The most common emotional change associated with major depression is not the depressed mood per se but rather the *pervasive* loss of interest and pleasure in everyday living. Major depressive episodes are associated with a significant risk of suicide, and individuals suspected of suffering from a mood disorder should routinely be examined for signs that they are contemplating suicide.

Figure 6.2 shows the interactions of the biological, psychological, and social variables in Alice Jackson's life.

ALICE JACKSON'S MULTIAXIAL DSM DIAGNOSIS IS AS FOLLOWS:

Axis I	296.23 Major Mood Disorder, Single Episode, with Postpartum Onset
Axis II	V71.09 (No diagnosis)
Axis III	Childbirth
Axis IV	Deferred
Axis V	GAF = 45 (on admission)

© Cengage Learning

BIPOLAR DISORDER

Bipolar disorders begin more acutely than major depression (Angst & Sellaro, 2000; Johnson, Cuellar, & Miller, 2009). The presence of mania or hypomania defines bipolar disorder. The characteristic feature of the bipolar disorders is the tendency for an individual to experience manic episodes alternating with major depressive episodes. Akin to a roller coaster, the person emotionally moves from the peaks of elation to the depths of despair. Sometimes these moods alternate so quickly that both the highs and lows can be experienced on the same day. **Mania** is defined as a distinct period during which the predominant mood is either elevated, expansive, or irritable with several associated symptoms such as hyperactivity, pressured speech, racing thoughts, inflated self-esteem, decreased need for sleep, distractibility, and excessive involvement in potentially dangerous activity. In addition, the practitioner may observe psychotic symptoms (e.g., delusions or hallucinations and/or other perceptual disturbances). A proposed change to the DSM-5 is to highlight mania by adding persistently increased activity or energy to the "A" criteria for a manic episode. This particular criterion for manic episode currently states, "A distinct period of abnormally and persistently elevated, expansive, or irritable mood lasting at least 1 week (or any duration if hospitalization is necessary)" (American Psychiatric Association, 2000, p. 362).

In mania, the mood disturbance is severe and causes marked impairment in interpersonal functioning; in a **hypomanic episode**, many of the features found in mania may be present, but the mood disturbance is less severe. At times it may be difficult to differentiate severe hypomania from mania. Delusions, hallucinations, and disorganization can be seen during manic episodes and are considered **mood congruent**. The important determinants, it should be noted, are psychotic symptoms or a marked impairment in normal psychosocial functioning. When hospitalization is needed, the condition has crossed an important threshold, that of mania. In conjunction with depression, the term bipolar disorder is a misnomer, in that a single manic episode is enough for the practitioner to make the assessment (i.e., the individual swings from the depressive pole to the manic pole).

EP 2.1.7 b

Competent social workers are knowledgeable about human behavior, but how does the practitioner know when the client's depression is the result of a major depressive disorder or an aspect of bipolar disorder? For most, this distinction is unclear. In other words, major depressive disorder and bipolar disorder overlap, because the depression shows itself in very similar ways in both conditions. In essence, the practitioner takes a critical look at the client's behavior in order to better understand the symptom picture and the interplay with the environment. Luckily for those attempting to make an assessment, only some depressive features are the same; others are quite different. For example:

- Bipolar disorder occurs almost equally in men and women (Asiskal, 2009), whereas major depressive disorder is more commonly seen in women (Kessler et al., 2003; Kessler & Wang, 2009).
- Bipolar disorder seems to occur at about the same rate in childhood and adolescence as in adults (Brent & Birmaher, 2009), and the average age of onset for bipolar I disorder is 15 to 18 years of age and for bipolar II disorder from 19 to 22 years of age (Angst, 2009; Merikangas & Pato, 2009).
- Bipolar disorder, particularly bipolar I disorder (and cyclothymia), is known to occur among people of different cultures (Johnson, 2004; Kawa et al., 2005).
- Bipolar disorder is less affected by psychosocial stressors.
- Bipolar disorder has a greater genetic risk component than major depressive disorder (Garlow, Boone, Li, Owens, & Nemeroff, 2005; Levinson, 2009).

In bipolar disorder, manic episodes can develop within just a few hours' time. However, more typically they emerge over a period of a few days. When a person is experiencing a manic episode, it is not unusual for him or her to go without sleep for several days. The person's speech is often rapid and unremitting, and it has a pressured, urgent quality to it. During a manic episode, the person's judgment tends to be impulsive and poor—for example, the individual may go on an expensive shopping spree that they cannot afford or enter into risky business ventures. Additionally, he or she experiences racing thoughts and is easily distracted. The person develops inflated self-esteem (grandiosity), which can take on delusional dimensions including religious, political, financial, or sexual themes. The individual may even claim to possess exceptional powers, such as having the ability to change the direction of the wind or remain impervious to harm.

PREVAILING PATTERN

EP 2.1.7 b

In order to assess for bipolar disorder, the practitioner takes a discerning look at what is known about his or her client in order to make sense of the symptom picture; specifically, the biological, social, cultural, and psychological development. Environmental factors are also taken into account. Looking at bipolar disorder, the lifetime risk worldwide is estimated to be between 1 percent and 0.8 percent during the past year (Merikangas & Pato, 2009). Despite research, the cause of bipolar disorder remains relatively unclear. We are only now beginning to identify a small group of genes that may be related to this vulnerability, or at least for some types of depression (Bradley et al., 2008; Caspi et al., 2003; Garlow, Boone, Li, Owens, & Nemeroff, 2005; Levinson, 2009). Although bipolar disorder can be seen in young children, it is relatively rare for symptoms to emerge after age 40. A family history of bipolar disorder presents an increased risk for developing a mood disorder in close relatives but not necessarily for a bipolar disorder. It seems that the specific manifestation of a mood disorder is determined by a range of factors, including the person's unique psychological, social, or additional biological factors (Kilpatrick et al., 2007; Rutter, 2010).

As noted earlier, bipolar disorder occurs in episodes or cycles. In between, most individuals experience a "normal" (**euthymic**) interval during which they generally return to their usual state of psychosocial functioning. A first episode may be either depressive or manic. The majority of people do not experience a mixed-manic first episode. The presenting pattern of bipolar disorder is unpredictable—and subsequent episodes, if they occur, remain variable. It would be highly unlikely for the practitioner to find individuals who alternate between manic and depressive episodes.

VARIATIONS OF BIPOLAR DISORDER

Bipolar disorder occurs in the following variations:

Bipolar I—Refers to severe manic symptoms accompanied by one or more periods of major depression.

Bipolar II—Refers to the same pattern of symptoms, but with a major distinction in the degree of severity; typically, this disorder does not lead to psychotic behavior or require hospitalization.

The practitioner considers two additional aspects to identify other key variations in this disorder. They are:

- **Rapid cycling,** which occurs when four or more separate bipolar episodes (in any combination) are experienced within a 1-year period.
- **Seasonal affective pattern,** which applies to those who tend to experience episodes during a particular time of year (e.g., late fall or early winter).

Seasonal affective disorder (SAD) is more prevalent in northern climates than in southern climates because of the difference in the amount of sunlight available during the winter months. Also known as winter depression and popularly called cabin fever, SAD is estimated to affect approximately 2.7 percent of North Americans (Lam et al., 2006). The competency-based assessment pays attention to the client's environmental context. People who live and work in northern regions may complain about winter blues, but such complaints alone are not enough to meet the specific guidelines for bipolar disorder.

Review of the literature suggests that bipolar disorder has a poorer prognosis than major depressive disorder. Comprehensive follow-up studies have shown that 16 percent of individuals with bipolar disorder recover in contrast to 52 percent who experience multiple relapses. One study noted that 8 percent had committed suicide (Angst & Sellaro, 2000). Another longitudinal study indicated higher rates, with 11 percent of those with bipolar disorder who had committed suicide (Angst, Angst, Gerber-Werder, & Gamma, 2005).

Up until the 1980s, the term bipolar II was little known. However, the sequence of mood cycles in bipolar disorder has become the single most important feature in distinguishing it from other mood disorders. Those individuals assessed as having either bipolar I or bipolar II disorder manifest very similar features. An important distinction between the two is the degree of impairment and discomfort in intrapersonal and interpersonal (and especially occupational) functioning. The following case discussion illustrates the shifts in mood common to those who experience bipolar disorder. It is important to note that because Carol Bishop's pattern of symptoms does not lead to psychotic behavior, and because she does not require hospitalization, she is assessed as having bipolar II disorder.

| CASE | THE CASE OF CAROL BISHOP |

I first met 14-year-old Carol when she sometimes stayed in the waiting room while her parents, Frieda and Gerald, came for marriage counseling. I am not sure they ever really had any hope of saving their 15-year marriage—and looking back I guess counseling was really just lip service for them. It was a way to tell themselves, their child, and their respective families, "we tried." About a year after the Bishops stopped coming, they contacted me again.

I have been affiliated with a private practice group made up of other licensed social workers for more years than I want to acknowledge. Several of us old-timers wanted to keep our daytime agency jobs, but also branch out into private work. We decided to share office expenses and subsequently put up our respective shingles. Private practice isn't what it used to be; however, it makes a nice departure from working for someone else. While my private practice doesn't generally necessitate checking telephone messages daily, if a client needs to speak with me or has an emergency, the office can always reach me by beeper or cell phone. The other day, coming in for a regularly scheduled office session, I found a message from Frieda Bishop asking me to call her. She had made a point of saying it was "nothing urgent."

I called Frieda, and after a few minutes of chitchat and catching up on what had been happening, Frieda shared with me that she and Gerald had divorced 2 months ago. He has a girlfriend, the house is up for sale, yadda, yadda. Frieda finally got around to telling me the reason for her call.

"It's Carol, she has been driving me crazy for the last 6 or 8 months. I mean, I don't want to sound like one of those horrible mothers that you see in the movies, but she's really gone off the deep end." Frieda didn't wait for me to say anything before continuing. "Get this, she went to Macy's and charged $3,000 worth of cosmetics and designer purses. Can you imagine how many purses and lipsticks that is?" Sensing that she didn't really expect me to answer, I remained silent.

"What is she going to do with all that stuff?" Frieda asked, rhetorically again. "What could she have been thinking? I told her I wasn't going to give her the money. To top it off, she won't take anything back. How is she going to pay for everything? She only earns minimum wage—I should say she 'used to earn minimum wage.' I found out she just lost her afterschool job. I tried to get her boss to rehire her, but he told me Carol hasn't shown up for work in 3 weeks. He just had to let her go. I guess I can't blame him." Frieda paused, and I could tell she was getting closer to telling me why she called me.

"Carol's boss also told me, 'When she did show up for work, she was either higher than a kite or deader than a doornail.' He said he never knew what to expect when she came to work. He told me he didn't think Carol uses drugs, but he couldn't be sure. He said, 'A lot of the customers complain about Carol because sometimes she talks so fast they can't understand her—either that or she looks like she's falling asleep in the middle of a transaction.'"

continued

Frieda continued, "You know, I feel really guilty now, because I've been so wrapped up in my own troubles that I've ignored what's been going on in Carol's life. I always suspected something wasn't quite right, but I guess I just didn't want to deal with it. Is there any chance that I could bring her in to see you sometime soon?"

An appointment was scheduled for the next afternoon. I was left with the impression that Frieda was terribly overwhelmed. I also realized I hadn't gotten in a word edgewise; that in itself was unusual.

When I did see Carol, I was somewhat surprised by the difference I saw in the youngster I had seen only a year ago. Although she looked more mature, she also appeared to be under a great deal of distress. Initially, I saw Frieda and Carol together and gathered relevant family history. Frieda related that her oldest brother, Henry, has been treated for bipolar disorder since he was 18. She was uncertain as to whether one of his daughters had the same kind of problem. Frieda continued, "When Henry was a kid, he'd do all sorts of wacky stuff. You know, in a way it sounds a lot like what Carol has been up to. As I recall, Henry never needed much sleep. He would talk nonstop and did some wild and crazy things. Then, just like somebody flipped a switch, all the energy would go out of Henry. You couldn't drag him out of bed—all he wanted to do was sleep. My poor parents had a real hard time with him. They were glad when he joined the Army and moved out."

I spent the remainder of the session with Carol. Currently, she is enrolled in the 11th grade and wants to attend a local community college after she graduates. Carol admits that her grades could be a lot better than they are—she "is only failing a couple of classes." She is an attractive young woman, of average height and slender build. My sense of her was that she was restless. I noticed she tapped her fingers on the arm of the chair, and her crossed leg was in a constant motion.

"Carol, why do you think you are here?" I asked.

"I don't know what the problem is," she replied, "because I feel just fine. Maybe the problem is my mother. Now that Daddy is out of the house, she doesn't have anything else to keep her busy, so she's putting her nose into my business. She thinks I have a mental problem, but I don't. Just because I don't need

as much sleep as she does, she gets all bent out of shape. I mean, come on!"

"What about that, Carol? Were you ever so energetic that instead of sleeping you did household chores or worked throughout the night?"

"Sure," she replied. "Look, I just feel happy, that's all. I don't like wasting my time sleeping, all right? Everybody makes such a big deal out of it. I can sleep when I'm old. Right now I'd rather spend my time on the computer. Did you know they have 24-hour chat lines? I mean you can talk to hundreds of people all night long. It's really cool."

I asked, "When you are up all night on the computer, don't you feel tired the next day?"

"Heck no! Even if I don't sleep a wink, I feel GREAT. Why should I worry about sleeping if I don't need it?"

I asked Carol to describe those times when she felt really happy. Her reply was enthusiastic.

"It's the best! It's wonderful! It's great! It's terrific! It's like being on top of the world! I love it because I can do anything and everything." Carol is positively gleeful. "Did I tell you that someday I'm going to be a famous movie star?"

I was very aware of how pressured her speech had become and asked her about it. "Yeah, I've been told I'm pretty talkative—but hey, I guess I just have a lot to say."

I asked Carol if there were times in the past few months or year when she felt the opposite of being happy. "Do you ever feel really sad or tired—or feel like crying? You know, do you ever have feelings that are different from the ones you are describing today?"

Carol appeared thoughtful for a moment, and responded slowly nodding her head. "Yeah, there are some times when I just don't want to get up in the morning. I can't lift my head off my pillow or wake up." Carol looked puzzled. "Sometimes I'm on top of the world—then other times I'm totally down. That's weird, huh?...And for a couple of months I didn't want to eat, so my clothes started to just sort of hang on me. Mom kept bugging me about being anorexic. There were a few times I couldn't wake up for school or work. I didn't care about anybody or anything—but that's all changed now!"

Carol denies using drugs or alcohol. She says she likes to have fun and sometimes spends too much money. She likes to go out and have a good time with her friends. Carol is currently sexually active with four boys, none of whom knows about the others. She admitted she doesn't always use protection but her attitude is, "Nothing bad has happened, so why bother?"

We set up several appointments for the following week, and I gave her a couple of referrals: One is to Dr. John Wojcik, an internist I've worked with before for a medical evaluation to rule out a possible general medical condition such as multiple sclerosis, hyperthyroidism, or AIDS. The other referral is for a psychiatric consultation with Dr. Dylan Macey to consider medication intervention.

EP 2.1.10 (b) a

ASSESSMENT SUMMARY   Professional practice requires the social worker to carefully organize and interpret data from this case vignette illustrating Carol Bishop's symptoms. To begin, a manic episode must always be distinguished from schizophrenia. Although difficult, a differential assessment is possible with a few clinical guidelines. Merriment, elation, and an infectiousness of mood are more commonly seen in manic episodes than in schizophrenia. The practitioner considers the presenting combination of a manic mood, rapid speech, and hyperactivity to tip the scale in the direction of a manic episode. Individuals who are currently undergoing an acute exacerbation of paranoid schizophrenia are able to sit quietly, whereas individuals who present with acute mania are hyperactive and their conversation takes on a pressured quality. Those with catatonic schizophrenia continue to remain self-involved and detached (no matter how agitated their behavior), and they generally maintain limited interaction with others around them (Thaker, 2009). By comparison, those individuals experiencing a manic episode (no matter how fragmented their behavior) want to be involved with others.

In Carol's situation, her mother was the first to notice something unusual. Often, it is a close family member who notices a change in the client's behavior or personality. Carol herself had no insight into her behavior and the difficulties she caused. She explained away her inability to sleep, time spent chatting on the computer, incessant talking, and feelings of invincibility as typical teenage behaviors. The task before the social worker is to differentiate among a manic episode, a hypomanic episode, mixed episode, major depression, or a cyclothymic disorder.

The practitioner assessed Carol's behavior this way. At least one manic and one depressive episode characterized her presentation. Carol exhibited bipolar features by cycling up into a manic episode, returning to her normal behavior, and then cycling down into a depressive episode. Carol's period of major depression, as described in the vignette, was evident when she could not get out of bed to go to work. For a short while after, she "bounced back"—and, if nothing else had occurred, the social worker could probably consider only the presence of major depression. However, common to bipolar disorder, especially in the first episode, is the unexpected arrival of manic features. At this juncture, the social worker pays particular attention to Carol's shopping spree at Macy's and considers bipolar disorder (the shorthand for all mood disorders that include at least one manic episode). Because of the severity of Carol's behavior, the social worker did not consider the diagnosis of cyclothymia. Figure 6.3 illustrates the interactions of the biological, psychological, and social variables in Carol Bishop's life.

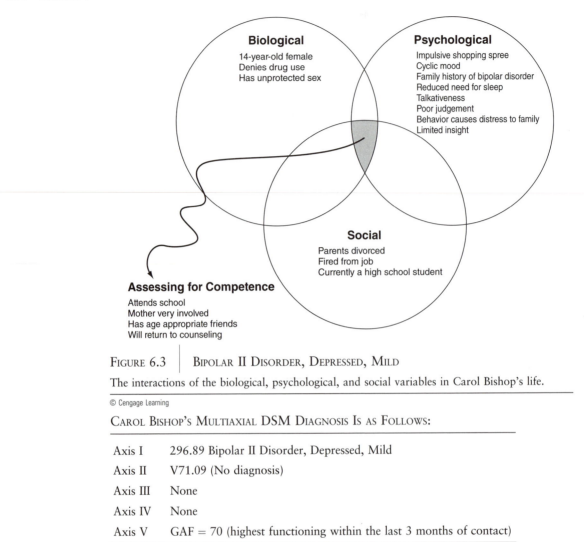

FIGURE 6.3 | BIPOLAR II DISORDER, DEPRESSED, MILD

The interactions of the biological, psychological, and social variables in Carol Bishop's life.

© Cengage Learning

CAROL BISHOP'S MULTIAXIAL DSM DIAGNOSIS IS AS FOLLOWS:

Axis I	296.89 Bipolar II Disorder, Depressed, Mild
Axis II	V71.09 (No diagnosis)
Axis III	None
Axis IV	None
Axis V	GAF = 70 (highest functioning within the last 3 months of contact)

© Cengage Learning

Advanced
Clinical EP
2.1.10 (b) c

The competency-based assessment highlights the many strengths in Carol's context and social support networks. Her mother is concerned about her and very involved. Carol has many friends in school and has been able to work, though sporadically. Finally, Carol followed through with the appointment, has a past positive relationship with the social worker (who knows her family history), and is willing to continue treatment.

THE MINOR MOOD DISORDERS

DYSTHYMIA

Dysthymia is characterized by a relatively low-grade but chronic depression that often lasts for years. The person's symptoms are somewhat milder but remain relatively unchanged. The term **dysthymia** means "ill humored" and was first introduced 25 years ago in the DSM-III (American Psychiatric Association, 1980). Prior to that time, the condition was known as **depressive personality disorder** or **depressive neurosis**—and then (almost 15 years after the term dysthymia was introduced) the name was changed to dysthymic disorder in the DSM-IV (American Psychiatric Association, 1994). The practitioner may encounter individuals with the dysthymic disorder who regard their chronic low mood as "normal." One client remarked, "I don't remember a time when I didn't feel depressed."

These individuals usually have chronic symptoms that seem to pervade their entire past and present existence. Dysthymia shares many of the same symptoms of major depressive disorder. However, the symptoms are considered somewhat milder, and they remain relatively unchanged over a long period of time; sometimes for 20 or 30 years (Angst, 2009; Klein, 2008; Klein, Shankman, & Rose, 2006). It seems that most people suffering from dysthymia eventually experience a major depressive episode. Differences between the two disorders appear to be in their levels of severity and chronicity; dysthymic symptoms are milder but more chronic than those of major depression.

Dysthymia is considered when an individual presents with a chronic depressed mood (or in children and adolescents with an irritable mood) that lasts at least 2 years or more, is evident more days than not, and is not severe enough to fit the picture of someone with a major depressive episode. For the practitioner to consider dysthymia, the person must exhibit two of the following symptoms:

- Increased or decreased sleep.
- Increased or decreased appetite.
- Low energy.
- Low self-esteem.
- Poor concentration or decision-making ability.
- Hopelessness.

In addition, the practitioner should rule out a manic, mixed, or hypomanic episode as well as cyclothymic disorder.

There has been a great deal of discussion within the professional community about whether dysthymia represents a disorder *sui generis* (unique or singular) or whether it is merely a milder form of major depression. A small percentage of individuals with dysthymia never experience a full depressive episode. However, at some point, a large majority of these individuals do experience a depressive episode. The coexistence of dysthymic disorder and major depression is sometimes referred to as **double depression**. Typically, the dysthymic disorder develops first, and then one or more major depressive episodes subsequently occur (Boland & Keller, 2009; Klein, Shankman, & Rose, 2006). It may be important for the practitioner to discern this particular patterning of depression, because it is associated with more severe problems in living and a more problematic future outlook.

PREVAILING PATTERN

Dysthymia typically has an insidious onset beginning in childhood (or adolescent) years. It is less common to find symptoms emerging in adulthood. Dysthymia in children and adolescents can be considered after a 1-year period of a depressed or irritable mood. Those individuals with an onset on or before the age of 21 are characterized as **early onset,** and those after the age of 21 are considered **late onset.** The age when a person first begins to experience the symptoms of dysthymia may influence the course and outcome. Unless the practitioner has known a client for a period of time, dysthymia may be hard to identify. For instance, if the practitioner notices a sudden or gradual worsening of the client's symptoms, then dysthymia might be considered.

A person's mood is characterized as brooding, complaining, sorrowful, gloomy, somber, and nihilistic (having a sense of one's existence as being senseless and useless). Everything seems to be taken very seriously, and life is perceived as a constant struggle that brings little happiness or satisfaction. The biological domain may reflect an assortment of somatic or neuropsychological features, which include fatigue, lack of energy, difficulty thinking, and problems eating and sleeping. The dysthymic disorder is not characterized by episodes but by the perpetual waxing and waning *presence* of symptoms. As a consequence, the individual often feels deficient, unlovable, inferior, and unable to appreciate their value to others. Because of this self-concept, they often experience difficulties in interpersonal domains of their life; for example, marriages and friendships tend to suffer. The combined effects of dysphoria, low sense of self, and poor interpersonal relationships frequently contribute to the individual's vulnerability.

There are no universally accepted precipitants for the etiology of this disorder, but predisposing factors may include a history of childhood psychiatric illnesses, chronic psychosocial stressors, and a family history of major depressive disorder. The following vignette illustrates dysthymia and how it influences Mario Delucca's life. Note that he did not seek help for the symptoms associated with this disorder, but for problems getting along on the job.

| CASE | THE CASE OF MARIO DELUCCA |

Mario Delucca is a 56-year-old married father of three grown daughters. He is a well-respected college professor. Dr. Delucca called my office last week saying he was concerned about how things were going for him at the university. When I saw him, he looked older than his stated age; he carried himself in a stooped and hunched-over manner. While he had what I would characterize as the "rumpled, disheveled, absentminded professor look," there was an air about him that made him look depressed and tired. His gray hair looked to me like a haircut was long overdue—in fact, overall, his personal appearance could be characterized as sloppy: he hadn't combed his hair, and clearly he needed a shave.

He entered my office in a subdued manner and quietly took a seat in the farthest corner possible. I initiated the conversation. "Dr. Delucca, what has been happening that made you decide to come in today?"

He replied, "Things are, well, not so good. I know I should have come in to see you before now, but I got caught up in some family stuff. Well, you know, after awhile things just went downhill. I feel embarrassed just having to talk about it."

"Well, you are here now," I responded, "and that's important." I commented that he appeared tired.

Dr. Delucca sighed and stated, "I just don't seem to have very much free time. When I'm not teaching, I'm grading papers, presenting at conferences, or writing. I guess I don't have many opportunities for leisure." He smiled sadly and continued, "I know I should have come in sooner, but things were going all right for awhile—for about a month—but then everything just went right back to the way it used to be."

I asked Dr. Delucca to elaborate.

"I just feel weary all of the time," he responded. "I never want to do anything, and I'm having some trouble eating and sleeping. I can't say I've lost any weight because my clothes still fit me. I saw my doctor last week for a physical, and she wanted to give me a prescription for some sleeping pills... but I told her I'd rather tough it out. You know, I really can't remember a time when I didn't feel this way. Maybe this's just the way I am—or maybe it's my job. I don't know."

We spoke awhile longer. After he left, I made the following summary of our discussion:

- Manages to work, but is experiencing problems at the university. Should have been promoted to full professor (according to him) 3 years ago (but admits he does not have publications to warrant tenure). Claims his department chair has hinted it's time for him to look for another position elsewhere.

- His third wife (of 5 years)—Rosemary—recently filed for divorce. He says that's more evidence he's a loser. Feels he just can't do anything right.

- Denies having any periods of elevated mood or increased energy.

- Was told by his physician to reduce his stress and salt intake due to hypertension and (mild) congestive heart failure.

- Denies alcohol or drug use—has an occasional beer on the weekends.

- He experiences recurring depressed moods, lasting 1 to 2 months at a time; he only experiences a few weeks in between these episodes that he describes as "normal."

- Denies any psychotic features (no hallucinations, delusions, or bizarre thoughts or ideas).

EP 2.1.10 (b) a

ASSESSMENT SUMMARY   This case vignette offers yet another opportunity to organize and interpret case data to develop the competency-based assessment for Mario Delucca. Looking for differences between dysthymia and major depressive disorder can be very complex, because the symptoms are nearly identical. However, the duration of dysthymia is longer overall, but its symptoms are milder. Dr. Delucca's mood symptoms can be described as chronic versus acute or recurring. He has never been without these features for longer than a few weeks at a time, and they are present more days than not. Dr. Delucca describes a poor self-image, fatigue, decreased appetite, and what could be considered a gloomy outlook on life.

A general state of unhappiness may at times be difficult to differentiate from dysthymia. Many times the practitioner will work with individuals who experience reversals in life, have life-threatening illness, or sustain other misfortunes which, in the context of chronic depression, seem understandable. For most people, however, life is not always filled with misfortune. Through careful questioning the practitioner can usually find a period of time when misfortune did not occur. In the case of Dr. Delucca, even if he did experience a reversal of his misfortunes, he would more than likely still remain sad and gloomy.

Depressive symptoms may occur in individuals with hypochondriasis because they are convinced they have a serious illness, which is considered paramount. However, if depressive symptoms are present in such an individual, they are almost always transitory. In contrast, individuals with dysthymia will accept the physician's affirmation of well-being, but the depressive symptoms continue. In addition, dysthymia can be automatically ruled out at the appearance of any manic episode. Figure 6.4 illustrates the interactions of the biological, psychological, and social variables in Mario Delucca's life.

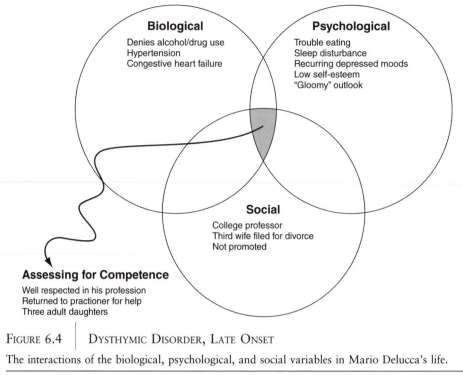

FIGURE 6.4 | DYSTHYMIC DISORDER, LATE ONSET

The interactions of the biological, psychological, and social variables in Mario Delucca's life.

© Cengage Learning

DR. MARIO DELUCCA'S MULTIAXIAL DSM DIAGNOSIS IS AS FOLLOWS:

Axis I   300.4 Dysthymic Disorder, Late Onset

Axis II   V71.09 (No diagnosis)

Axis III   402.91 Hypertensive Heart Disease with Congestive Heart Failure

Axis IV   Employment difficulties

Axis V   GAF = 75 (on initial appointment)

© Cengage Learning

**Advanced
Clinical EP
2.1.10 (b) c**

It might be considered a challenge to look for Dr. Delucca's coping strategies in this case vignette. However, learning about intrapersonal and interpersonal functioning provides a more complete clinical picture of what is going on for Dr. Delucca and helps in identifying competencies within his life that can later be expanded upon in counseling. The emphasis shifts to the positive behaviors and events rather than examining so-called defects. Dr. Delucca's sense of himself is poor, and it would be important to point out the reality that he has had a successful career. Additionally, he is well respected in his profession and needs to focus his concern on ways to achieve tenure and become more productive. His willingness to seek professional help should be viewed as another of his strengths.

Cyclothymia

The second minor mood disorder is cyclothymia, which refers to a chronic or cyclic mood disturbance that has many of the same features found in major depressive episodes. For example, the individual may exhibit low mood, lethargy, despair, problems eating and sleeping, and trouble concentrating. Those with cyclothymia will be in one mood state or the other for years with relatively few periods of a neutral mood (Akiskal, 2009). When considering the diagnosis, this pattern must last for a 2-year period (1 year for children and adolescents) and the individual must not be free of its specific manifestations for more than 2 months. Typically, the person regards his or her chronic low mood as normal or just the way they have always been. Cyclothymia is considered a milder form of bipolar II disorder; that is, the hypomanic phase alternates with mild depressive phases. Cyclothymia often begins early in life and represents a risk factor for the eventual development of bipolar I or bipolar II. Unfortunately, this disorder often goes unrecognized—and the person is simply thought to be high-strung, explosive, moody, or hyperactive (Biederman et al., 2000).

Prevailing Pattern

The symptomatic features of cyclothymia typically alternate in an irregular fashion, lasting for days or weeks. During manic periods, an individual may be described as enthusiastic and cheerful or at times irritable. During the depressive periods, these individuals may be described as ill humored, peevish, or overly sensitive to slights or criticism. Often fatigue and apathy hamper their efforts, and modest changes in their appetite and sleep are seen, with a tendency toward hypersomnia. The following case illustrates the elements of cyclothymia as the client describes her presenting concerns. Carefully look for signs of the mood swings found in bipolar disorder.

CASE	The Case of Othella Prince

Ms. Othella Prince made an appointment at the local community family service center, and during the intake interview claimed her life has been "just like a roller coaster. Sometimes you go up, but then you have to come down." Ms. Prince was assigned to Elaine Pasternak, LCSW, a licensed clinical social worker who made the following presentation at a clinical case staffing:

"I had the opportunity to meet Othella Prince, who is a 33-year-old married woman and the mother of a 4-year-old son. She is an attractive, African American woman. Her medical history reveals that she has had diverticulitis of the colon for the past 10 years. This condition has responded well to dietary restrictions. Currently, Ms. Prince is employed as a waitress at a local deli. The reason she gave for coming to the agency involves her mood swings.

"Ms. Prince complained that over the past 5 years these moods have become more problematic. She related to me that she generally feels pretty well but admitted that from time to time she has difficulty eating and sleeping. According to her, 'That's because I have so many things to do that I can't stop to eat when I'm involved in one of my projects.' She describes herself as usually upbeat but goes on to relate that every few months she experiences a few weeks of not really wanting to do much of anything. She went on to say, and I quote, 'It's just like being on a roller coaster. I don't mean one of those monster things when you go way up and then rush way down. No, it's more like a hill and valley thing.' She denies having medical and/or substance-related problems or suicidal ideation—and has never been hospitalized for these moods."

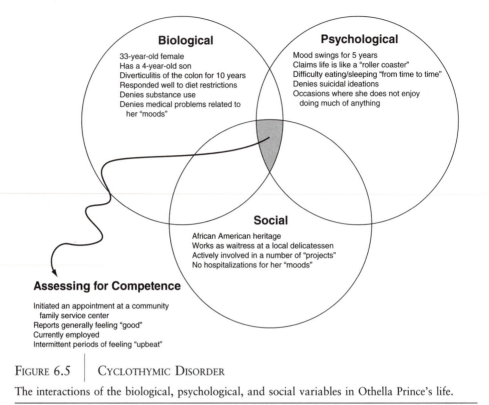

Biological

33-year-old female
Has a 4-year-old son
Diverticulitis of the colon for 10 years
Responded well to diet restrictions
Denies substance use
Denies medical problems related to
　her "moods"

Psychological

Mood swings for 5 years
Claims life is like a "roller coaster"
Difficulty eating/sleeping "from time to time"
Denies suicidal ideations
Occasions where she does not enjoy
　doing much of anything

Social

African American heritage
Works as waitress at a local delicatessen
Actively involved in a number of "projects"
No hospitalizations for her "moods"

Assessing for Competence

Initiated an appointment at a community
　family service center
Reports generally feeling "good"
Currently employed
Intermittent periods of feeling "upbeat"

Figure 6.5　│　Cyclothymic Disorder

The interactions of the biological, psychological, and social variables in Othella Prince's life.

© Cengage Learning

EP 2.1.10 (b) a

Assessment Summary　This case history offers another opportunity for the practitioner to organize and interpret client data to discern the diagnosis of cyclothymic disorder. The vignette illustrates Othella's prevailing mood. Note that the characteristics of cyclothymia include a hypomanic episode that is similar to a manic episode, except that the disturbance is less intense and not severe enough to cause marked impairment in interpersonal functioning. Analogous to a "hill and valley" roller coaster ride, Ms. Prince described a dysphoric mood, but it was not serious enough to qualify as a bipolar disorder. In contrast to bipolar disorder, cyclothymia is characterized by numerous fluctuations (up and down) of hypomanic and depressive features that persist for at least 2 years without intervals in a normal mood range. Figure 6.5 shows the interactions of the biological, psychological, and social variables in Othella Prince's life.

Ms. Othella Prince's Multiaxial DSM Diagnosis Is as Follows:

Axis I	301.13 Cyclothymic Disorder
Axis II	V71.09 (No diagnosis)
Axis III	562.10 Diverticulitis of the Colon, Unspecified
Axis IV	Deferred
Axis V	GAF = 75 (on initial appointment)

© Cengage Learning

SUICIDE RISK AND THE MOOD DISORDERS

EP 2.1.2 b

Of all the complications associated with mood disorders, the risk for suicide is a major concern for the practitioner. All major mental illnesses carry an increased risk for suicide but the affective state of hopelessness, a key feature of major depression, is a powerful predictor (Sudak, 2009). No one really knows why people choose to end their lives—nor does anyone know how to predict those who will try. The social work profession's Code of Ethics is very clear about the practitioner's responsibilities to clients who are at risk of harming themselves. In these instances, the importance of acting in the client's behalf is clearly spelled out in the Code. In particular, "Social workers may limit clients' right to self determination when, in the social workers' professional judgment, clients' actions or potential actions pose a serious, foreseeable, and imminent risk to themselves or others" (National Association of Social Workers, 1999, p. 7). At all times, the practitioner strives to promote clients' well-being and to protect them from harm. Despite this clear professional mandate, the reasons for someone considering suicide are complex, and there are many features for the practitioner to consider.

The competency-based assessment helps to explore those factors that may help identify individuals who have a high risk for suicide. Within the mood disorder cohort, attempted and completed suicide is very common in individuals who experience bipolar I disorder as well as major depressive disorders because of the heightened feelings of hopelessness and helplessness. In 2007, there were 34,598 suicides in the U.S. (American Association of Suicidology, 2011). This translates into 94.8 suicides per day and 1 suicide every 15.2 minutes. The annual suicide rate is 11.5 per 100,000 making suicide the eleventh leading cause of death in the U.S. The actual number may be two to three times higher than reported (Nock et al., 2008).

Sources used to develop the following discussion include the American Association of Suicidology (2003); Kanel (2012); Jacobs et al. (2003); James (2008); and Rudd, Joiner, and Hasan Rajab (2001). We begin with a review of the numerous myths about suicide. It is important for the practitioner to be able to distinguish myth from reality in order to avoid misunderstanding suicidal behavior. Consider the following:

1. *If suicide is discussed with a client, that client will be more likely to attempt suicide.* In practice, it will be a sense of relief for an individual to talk about suicide with someone like the practitioner who is accepting and not judgmental. Simply put, for thoughts about suicide to be addressed, they need to be discussed. This kind of conversation will not cause harm to the individual who is really not suicidal.
2. *Clients who threaten suicide will actually not do it and the practitioner does not need to take them seriously.* A large percentage of people who kill themselves have often previously threatened or disclosed their intent to others beforehand.
3. *Suicide is an irrational act.* If suicide is viewed from the suicidal person's perspective, it makes sense to them.
4. *Individuals who commit suicide are insane.* There is evidence of an association between suicide and mental illness; principally manic depression (or bipolar

disorder), major depression, schizophrenia, or the personality disorders, particularly borderline personality disorder. Comorbidity increases suicide risk, especially the anxiety disorders or panic attacks. A history of alcohol abuse and dependence is commonly found among people who commit suicide, and intoxication at the time of the suicide attempt is an all too common pattern. Unfortunately, most individuals who are suicidal are normal people who are acutely depressed, lonely, hopeless, helpless, newly aggrieved, shocked, deeply disappointed, jilted, or otherwise overcome by an emotionally charged situation.

5. *Suicide is an inherited tendency that tends to run in families.* Although more than one member of a family has been known to commit suicide, the genetic risk for suicide has not been established. However, one may learn self-destructive tendencies, or they may be situational or even linked to depression or other life conditions.

6. *Once a person thinks about suicide, the thought does not go away.* While a person at one point in life may contemplate suicide, he or she may recover from the original threat and related painful feelings that led to the suicidal thought. Additionally, that individual may learn appropriate responses and controls, and go on to live a productive life free of the threat of self-inflicted harm.

7. *When the individual has attempted suicide and moves through it without self-harm, the danger is over.* In reality, most suicides occur within 3 months after the person begins to "improve." A clue the practitioner ought to look for is when the person seems euphoric (or elated) following a depressed or suicidal episode; in essence, the person has everything settled and planned and is at peace with the idea of committing suicide.

8. *One sign of recovery for the person who was suicidal is when he or she shows generosity and shares personal possessions.* Many suicidal individuals begin to give away their most prized possessions once they have enough energy to make a definite (suicide) plan. Giving away personal effects is analogous to acting out a last will and testament.

9. *Suicide is an act that is always impulsive.* There are several types of suicidal acts ranging from impulsive actions to others that are very carefully planned and carried out.

10. *Suicide affects only the wealthy and privileged members of society.* Unfortunately suicide can affect people at all levels of society.

11. *Suicide happens without warning.* Suicide is usually preceded by a warning, and in most cases, the person will show symptoms of suicidal thinking or provide clues to his or her intent.

When considering a person's potential risk for suicide, the following questions are helpful:

- *Is there anything in the client's history that generates the suicidal thoughts/behavior,* such as a family history of a first-degree relative who committed suicide, adverse childhood experiences (parental loss and emotional, physical, and sexual abuse, isolation, and other acute psychosocial stressors)?

- *What precipitated the client's current crisis and is it different from other life events?* Consider, for example, recent adverse life events such as a job loss, financial stress, unemployment and a drop in socioeconomic status, domestic partner violence, separation and divorce, bereavement, poor relationship with family, and family instability. Also ask about current health factors, such as the presence of acute and chronic health problems or diagnoses of conditions like HIV or cancer.
- *What does the client feel during the crisis?* For example, consider feelings of hopelessness, helplessness, despair, or in other words a sense that nothing will ever get better.
- *How does the client think about suicide*; for instance, are they frightened by the idea of self-harm or is this a welcoming thought?
- *What active (or planned) suicidal behaviors have occurred or are occurring?* A suicide plan may include the following: timing, availability of method, setting, and actions made toward carrying out the plan (such as having access to medicines, poisons, rope, or a weapon), choosing and checking out a setting for suicide, and rehearsing the plan. Keep in mind that the more detailed and specific the person's suicide plan, the higher the level of risk for carrying out self-harm through suicide.

EP 2.1.3 a

Social workers are often called upon to apply critical thinking skills to inform their professional judgment about the potential for a client's suicide. In practice, there are a number of evidence-based inventories and research-based questionnaires that are helpful tools to determine a person's suicide risk. Unfortunately because of the emergency nature of suicide, the practitioner often does not have the luxury of time to administer a test, or the client may not be interested in sitting down with a paper and pencil assessment. Therefore the practitioner is usually left to rely on his or her clinical judgment and practice wisdom to assess suicide risk. Each client is different and there is no stereotypical behavioral pattern for people who commit suicide. Although it is beyond the scope of this book to offer specific guidelines for a risk assessment, the following offers a mnemonic for identifying the key warning signs for suicide, called "Is path warm?" They are:

I	Ideation	The person will often express thoughts of suicide or threaten suicide before an attempt. Are they looking for ways to kill themselves by seeking access to firearms, pills, or other means? Are they threatening to hurt or kill themselves? Are they talking (or writing) about death, dying or suicide—and are these actions really out of the ordinary for them?
S	Substance abuse	Is the person suddenly increasing substance use? This includes alcohol, which can sometimes be easily overlooked.
P	Purposelessness	The person may start talking about having no purpose or meaning in life. This may be communicated indirectly, and the practitioner listens for comments like, "Life is not worth living," or "There is no reason to go on."

A	Anxiety	The person may show signs of anxiety or agitation. They might appear to be "on edge" just about all the time. They may be unable to sleep or may sleep all the time.
T	Trapped	The person may feel like there is "no way out" of their situation. They may talk about not seeing any solution to their problem.
H	Hopelessness	Suicidal persons may express feeling hopeless; that is, they may talk about how things will not change and may even seem desperate.
W	Withdrawal	The individual may withdraw from family, friends, and even society. This sense of isolation can be gradual or rather dramatic and sudden. Low self-esteem may be a factor, and the person may feel worthless, guilty, shameful, or unworthy of being around other people.
A	Anger	The person may show signs of rage and uncontrolled anger, and/or seek revenge. Behavior might be erratic and may include hurting others in addition to themselves.
R	Recklessness	The person may engage in high-risk activities or behaviors, seemingly without thinking.
M	Mood changes	Dramatic changes in the person's personality, mood, or behavior are seen.

Additional warning signs the practitioner may look for are:

- Changes in appetite.
- Speaking or moving with unusual speed (or slowness).
- Unusual neglect of one's physical appearance.
- Difficulties concentrating.
- Giving away prized or valued possessions.
- Saying good-bye to family and/or friends.
- Involvement in destructive or abusive relationships.
- Younger children or adolescents may be bullied or bully others.

EP 2.1.1 f

When exploring suicide with a client, the practitioner's goal is to begin to construct alternatives to suicidal behavior and minimize the short-term reinforcements that happen when suicidal ideation and behavior begin to develop. The practitioner initiates the discussion by taking all threats of suicide seriously; does not overreact; is aware of his or her own feelings, especially around the emotional content of suicidal ideation (or countertransference); and remains calm and listens to the client's "story" with empathy (or compassion). The practitioner will:

- Be available and have backup support.
- Obtain consultation or supervision as appropriate.
- Fully explore the client's reasons for considering suicide.
- Minimize opportunities for self-harm.
- Deal with the client's lethality.
- Involve others in the client's life when appropriate.

- Obtain a positive commitment from the client (including a contract agreement, if needed, not to commit suicide).
- Develop a specific plan with the client for continued follow-up care.
- Revisit the client's issues related to suicide, especially as the depression lifts.
- Document the work in the patient's chart.

Antidepressant medications have been linked with suicide. Of interest, people who are taking antidepressants may entertain thoughts of committing suicide about 1 to 2 weeks after starting to take an antidepressant. We now turn to a review of the medications commonly associated with the mood disorders.

MEDICATIONS COMMONLY ASSOCIATED WITH THE MOOD DISORDERS

Unfortunately, many people fail to recognize their depression, figuring that's "just the way it is," but there are a number of biological therapies for treating the mood disorders ranging from medication to electroconvulsive therapy that can dramatically affect brain chemistry. We are only now beginning to better understand the neurobiology of mood disorders. To expand your understanding, we turn to a brief overview of the latest medical approaches beginning with a general idea of how the central nervous system works and the related effects of the four basic types of antidepressants and lithium. We conclude with a synopsis of electroconvulsive therapy, an approach commonly used when medication does not appear to work.

The function of the central nervous system (brain and spinal cord) is to gather and process information, produce responses to stimuli, and coordinate the workings of different cells. This is accomplished by the transmission of messages in the brain—primarily across neurons—through a complicated process of electrical and chemical reactions. The neuron, a basic building block of the nervous system, is an electrically excitable cell that processes and transmits information by electrical and chemical signaling. The synapse is a junction that permits a neuron to pass this electrical or chemical signal to another cell. The neurons do not touch each other but are separated by a very small space, called the synaptic cleft. Responding to a neural impulse, the brain must get its message across the synaptic cleft to another cell. The most uncomplicated explanation is that these messengers are called neurotransmitters. The action, you might say, occurs with these couriers or neurotransmitters Three things can happen to the neurotransmitter. They can:

- bind to a specific site on the postsynaptic cell membrane of the next neuron;
- be reabsorbed into the presynaptic cell to be stored until the next release of transmitter;
- be broken down and metabolized by enzymes (such as monoamine oxidase or acholinesterase).

The neurotransmitters can affect behavior such as mood or emotion through their effect on specific nerve circuits. The better understood neurotransmitters and behaviors suspected to be related to the mood disorders are these (Wade & Tavris, 2010):

- *Serotonin*—Serotonin affects the neurons involved in sleep, appetite, sensory perception, temperature regulation, pain suppression, and mood.
- *Norepinephrine*—Norepinephrine affects the neurons that are involved in increased heart rate, the slowing of intestinal activity associated with stress, and learning, memory, dreaming, waking from sleep, and emotion.

We now turn to the medications commonly associated with treating the mood disorders.

There are four basic types of antidepressant medications; selective-serotonin reuptake inhibitors (or SSRIs), mixed reuptake inhibitors, monoamine oxidase (MAO) inhibitors, and tricyclic antidepressants. The SSRIs are the class of drugs considered the first-line choice of treatment for depression. They work by selectively inhibiting or blocking the presynaptic reuptake of serotonin in the brain. This serves to temporarily increase levels of serotonin at the receptor site. The best-known medication in this class is Fluoxetine (or its brand name of Prozac). There are concerns about the increased risk for suicide when taking this drug, particularly among children and adolescents, and research in this area continues (Baldessarini, Pompili, & Tondo, 2006; Berman, 2009; Fergusson et al., 2005; Hammad, Laughren, & Racoosin, 2006; Olfson, Marcus, & Schaffer, 2006). There are side effects to taking the SSRIs; the most common are physical agitation, sexual dysfunction, low sexual desire, insomnia, and gastrointestinal upset.

The newer antidepressant medications are the mixed reuptake inhibitors. They act in a slightly different manner by blocking reuptake of norepinephrine as well as serotonin. Some of the more common medications are Bupropion (Wellbutrin), Venlafaxine (Effexor), and Duloxetine (Celexia). Nausea, vomiting, insomnia, headaches, and seizure are typical side effects.

The MAO inhibitors work by blocking the enzyme MAO that breaks down neurotransmitters like norepinephrine and serotonin. Because they are not broken down, the neurotransmitters gather in the synapse leading to a down regulation. The MAO inhibitors are known to be slightly more effective than the tricyclics but are used far less often. This is because of the side effects of eating tyramine-rich foods, which can lead to severe hypertensive episodes and even death, such as aged cheese (e.g.: Camembert or Edam), sauerkraut, aged meat, sausages, cold cuts, chocolate, yogurt and sour cream, pickled herring or smoked fish, sardines, anchovies, and yeast extracts (various forms of processed yeast products commonly used as food additives or flavorings), or drinking alcohol (most notably beer and red wine, especially Chianti) as well as caffeinated beverages. Even cold medications are dangerous. Additional side effects include constipation, dizziness, dry mouth, hypotension, insomnia, nausea, sexual difficulties, skin reaction, weakness, and weight gain. The MAO inhibitors tend to be prescribed only when the other antidepressants do not seem to work.

Before the introduction of the SSRIs, the tricyclic antidepressants were more widely used. While researchers do not know exactly how this class of drugs works, it seems they block the reuptake of certain neurotransmitters, allowing them to collect in the synapse, and desensitize or down-regulate the transmission of each particular transmitter—at least initially. That way, less of the neurochemical is transmitted. These drugs seem to have the greatest effect by down-regulating norepinephrine. However, other neurotransmitters are also affected, particularly serotonin. The best-known drugs are Imipramine (Tofranil) and Amitriptyline (Elavil). The side effects are somewhat severe, causing many individuals to stop taking the drug. They include blurred vision, dry mouth, constipation, difficulty urinating, drowsiness, weight gain, and sometimes sexual dysfunction. The SSRIs are preferred because they have fewer side effects (Arroll et al., 2005).

Another common antidepressant is lithium carbonate or lithium, which is considered to be the gold standard for the treatment of bipolar disorder (Thase & Denko, 2008). Those struggling with bipolar disorder tend to respond well, with a reduction in manic symptoms (Goodwin & Jamison, 2007). However, this medication requires careful monitoring to prevent toxicity and lowered thyroid functioning, which might intensify the lack of energy commonly associated with depression. Side effects include vomiting, weakness, cardiovascular and urinary problems, thyroid abnormalities, dizziness, confusion, muscle tremor, and drowsiness. For those who do not respond to lithium, the anticonvulsant valproate (Divalproex) might be prescribed (Johannessen Landmark, 2008). In severe cases of bipolar disorder, another anticonvulsant such as carbamazepine might be used (Sachs & Gardner-Schuster, 2007). The side effects of these mood-stabilizing drugs include digestive problems, muscle tremor and weakness, dizziness, nausea, vomiting, diarrhea, and thrombocytopenia (low blood platelets).

One alternative to antidepressants that has become increasingly popular is the natural herbal extract, St. John's wort (hypericum). It has few side effects and is relatively easy to produce and currently available in health food stores, drugstores, and similar outlets. There is no guarantee that St. John's wort may contain the appropriate ingredients. Different brands may have different concentrations of the active substance. While it is believed to alter serotonin function, the U.S. National Institutes of Health completed a major study finding no benefits from St. John's wort compared to a placebo (Hypericum Depression Trial Study Group, 2002).

In those instances where a person does not respond to medication, electroconvulsive therapy (ECT) may be considered. In this instance, an electric shock is administered directly through the brain for a very brief period of time (less than a second), producing a seizure and a series of brief convulsions. These treatments are usually given once every other day in a series of six to ten administrations, but fewer if the person's mood returns to normal. Side effects include temporary short-term memory loss and confusion that disappears after a week or two. Some individuals may experience longer-term memory problems.

SUMMARY

This chapter reviews the mood episodes that serve as the foundation for the mood disorders, followed by a review of the mood disorders, and concludes with a review of the medications commonly used in treatment. The mood disorders are characterized by serious and persistent difficulty in maintaining an even, productive state. There are four types of mood episodes: (1) major depressive episode, (2) manic episode, (3) mixed episode, and (4) hypomanic episode. According to the DSM (American Psychiatric Association, 2000), a person cannot be diagnosed as having a mood episode, and the manual has no diagnostic code for them.

The mood disorders described in this chapter are the following:

- *Major depression*—Major depression is characterized by the following symptoms: a loss of interest in a person's usual activities, irritability, poor appetite, sleeping difficulties (inability to sleep or excessive sleeping), decreased sexual drive, fatigue, psychomotor agitation, feelings of hopelessness, inability to concentrate, and suicidal ideation. One can experience a "single episode," in which at least four symptoms are present almost daily for more than 2 weeks; alternatively, an individual may have "recurrent episodes" in which the symptoms come and go for intervals of at least 2 consecutive months.

- *Bipolar disorder*—Formerly known as manic-depressive illness, in bipolar disorder one's mood and affect are seen as maladaptive. The symptoms of the manic type of bipolar disorder are hyperactivity, euphoria, distractibility, pressured speech, and grandiosity. The depressive symptoms can include deep sadness, apathy, sleep disturbance, poor appetite, low self-esteem, and slowed thinking. There is a mixed type in which the person shows alternating patterns of manic and then depressed traits. The diagnosis distinguishes between bipolar I and bipolar II disorder.

  a. *Bipolar I disorder* is characterized by a single manic episode or, more commonly, by recurrent manic episodes or hypomanic episodes often immediately preceded or followed by a major depressive episode. (Hypomanic symptoms are identical to the manic episode except that they are not as severe and do not include the possibility of delusions or hallucinations.)

  b. *Bipolar II disorder* is characterized by one or more depressive episodes and at least one hypomanic episode.

- *Dysthymia*—Dysthymia is considered a long-term low-grade depression because the person has a chronically depressed mood for most of each day, on most days, for at least 2 years. Symptoms are sadness, pessimism, dyssomnia (a sleep disorder), poor appetite (or overeating), irritability, fatigue, low self-esteem, and indecisiveness.

- *Cyclothymia*—Cyclothymia is comprised of chronic, fluctuating mood disturbances with numerous periods of hypomanic symptoms and numerous periods of depressive symptoms lasting for at least 2 years in adults (1 year for children and adolescents). This diagnosis is similar to bipolar disorder except that the symptoms are not as severe; for example, there are no major depressive, manic, or mixed episodes.

A visual summary of the differential course of the mood disorders is presented in Figure 6.6.

The DSM-5 has a series of proposed changes to the mood disorders. One recommended change is that the diagnosis Depressive Disorder Not Otherwise Specified (NOS) be subdivided and relabeled as Depressive Conditions Not Elsewhere Classified (CNEC). This might include Subsyndromal Depressive CNEC to address the person who somehow does not meet the formal diagnostic criteria for depression; Major Depressive Disorder Superimposed on a Psychotic Disorder; and Recurrent Brief Depressive Disorder. Another proposed change is the addition of severity dimensions of factors that are currently not a part of the criteria for a specific diagnostic category but can be included with each mood diagnosis. At present, an anxiety dimension as well as a suicide assessment dimension is proposed. A substance abuse severity dimension may also be added. Two depressive disorders not currently listed in the DSM are proposed: Premenstrual Dysphoric Disorder and Mixed Anxiety/Depression. The mixed episodes of Bipolar I Disorder may be removed (or reclassified). There are also proposals to the current specifiers to depression; in particular, the

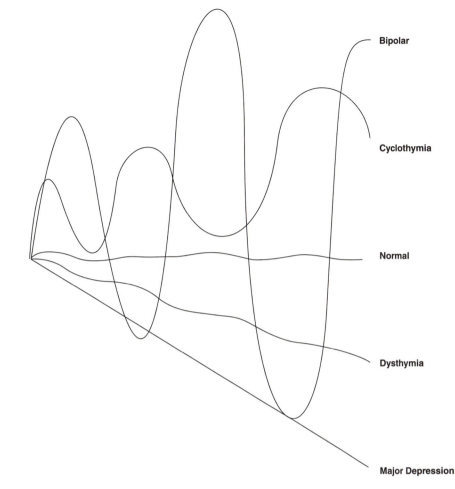

FIGURE 6.6 | A VISUAL SUMMARY OF THE DIFFERENTIAL COURSE OF THE MOOD DISORDERS

© Cengage Learning

addition of "mixed features" and removal of the "chronic" specifier. Finally, three disorders may be removed from the DSM: Bipolar I Disorder—Single Manic Episode; Bipolar I Disorder—Most Recent Episode Mixed; and Mood Disorder Not Otherwise Specified.

PRACTITIONER'S REFLECTIONS

A variety of biopsychosocial factors are correlated with the onset of depression. The competency-based assessment examines all aspects of the client's life. Competent practice takes into account the varying degrees of depression, euphoria, or irritability found in mood disorders. The following activities are aimed at helping us better understand our clients' experiences.

ACTIVITIES

EP 2.1.1 b

1. Persons with a mood disorder present unique challenges for the practitioner. The case of Anita Richards, who struggles with major depression, can evoke many feelings in the practitioner such as incompetence, worry, or anxiety. From the case vignettes presented in this chapter, select a situation reflecting a problem that is (or could be) a potential struggle for you or someone that you know. As a strategy to practice personal reflection and self-correction to assure your continued professional development, ask your supervisor (or a colleague) to role-play the first minute or two of the interview with you. Take turns assuming the role of the client and the social worker, then provide each other with feedback about this experience. Pay attention to the times when your own feelings might potentially get in the way of your therapeutic relationship.

Advanced Clinical EP 2.1.1 b

2. Can you remember a time in your life when you felt down or depressed? Write down in as much detail as you can remember what this experience felt like. For example, consider how you felt during this time, what kinds of thoughts you may have had, your level of energy, whether you experienced any sleep and/or appetite changes, how you related to others who are (or were) important in your life, and what helped you to feel better. Make a list of these insights and discuss with your supervisor how you can use these insights to improve your professional use of self with clients.

Advanced Clinical EP 2.1.10 (b) c

3. Reflect back on the cases presented in this chapter. Consider the interpersonal and/or social obstacles these clients experienced in coping with their mood disorder. Then assess the client coping strategies available to these clients used to reinforce and improve adaptation to living with a mental health diagnosis. Make a list of what else might be needed to improve each client's adaptation to life situations, circumstances, and events related to living with their specific disorder.

EP 2.1.10 (b) a

4. Think back to the clients you have seen in your own clinical practice who were feeling sad or down in the dumps but who you felt did not qualify for assessment as having a mood disorder. What went into making that determination?

EP 2.1.7 b

5. The competency-based assessment determines the influence of contextual situations or events in a person's life and the unique meaning they have to him or her. Interview several people who have shared the same kind of stressful life events (e.g., divorce, serious illness, or a death of a loved one). During these conversations, inquire how they felt about the *event*. Be aware of how each person assigns different meanings to the same type of event.

EP 2.1.10 (b) b

6. Access the CourseMate website at www.cengagebrain.com. There are two case vignettes highlighted. One is the case of Barbara, who typifies someone diagnosed with major depression that is characterized as severe and long lasting. Her feelings of worthlessness, loss of energy, and a marked loss of ability to experience pleasure are prominent in the interview. The second case is about Mary, who is struggling with bipolar disorder. There are illustrations of her in the depressive and manic phases of her diagnosis. The manic phase highlights Mary's symptoms of hyperactivity, pressured speech, racing thoughts, and distractibility. In addition, we see evidence of her psychotic symptoms. As you review each of these client interviews, make a list of each client's strengths as well as their limitations related to their diagnosis.

COMPETENCY NOTES

EP 2.1.1 b: Practice personal reflection and self-correction to assure continual professional development (p. 220): Social workers serve as representatives of the profession, its mission, and its core values.

EP 2.1.1 b: Advanced Clinical—Demonstrate professional use of self with client(s) (p. 220): Advanced practitioners in clinical social work recognize the importance of the therapeutic relationship, the person in-environment and strengths perspectives, the professional use of self with clients, and adherence to ethical guidelines of professional behavior.

EP 2.1.1 f: Use supervision and consultation (p. 214): Social workers commit themselves to the profession's enhancement and to their own professional enhancement.

EP 2.1.2 b: Apply social work ethical principles to guide professional practice (p. 211): Social workers have an obligation to conduct themselves ethically and to engage in ethical decision-making.

EP 2.1.3 a: Distinguish, appraise, and integrate multiple sources of knowledge, including research-based knowledge, and practice wisdom (p. 213): Social workers are knowledgeable about the principles of logic, scientific inquiry, and reasoned discernment.

EP 2.1.7 a: Use conceptual frameworks to guide the processes of assessment, intervention, and evaluation (p. 190): Social workers apply theories and knowledge from the liberal arts to understand biological, social, cultural, psychological, and spiritual development.

EP 2.1.7 b: Critique and apply knowledge to understand person and environment (pp. 190, 220): Social workers are knowledgeable about human behavior across the life course, the range of social systems in which people live, and the ways that social systems promote or deter people in maintaining or achieving health and well-being.

EP 2.1.10 (b) a: Collect, organize, and interpret client data (pp. 193, 196, 203, 207, 210, 220): Social workers have the knowledge and skills to practice with individuals, families, groups, organizations, and communities.

EP 2.1.10 (b) b: Assess client strengths and limitations (p. 220): Social workers have the knowledge and skills to practice with individuals, families, groups, organizations, and communities.

EP 2.1.10 (b) c: Advanced Clinical—Assess client coping strategies to reinforce and improve adaptation to life situations, circumstances, and events (pp. 195, 204, 208, 220): Clinical social work practice involves the dynamic, interactive, and reciprocal processes of therapeutic engagement, multidimensional assessment, clinical intervention, and practice evaluation at multiple levels.

REFERENCES

Akiskal, H. S. (2009). Mood disorders: Clinical Features. In B. J. Sadock, V. A. Sadock, & P. Ruiz (Eds.), *Kaplan and Sadock's comprehensive textbook of psychiatry* (9th ed., Vol I, pp. 1693–1733). Philadelphia: Lippincott Williams & Wilkins.

American Association of Suicidology. (November 2003). Is path warm? Retrieved on July 10, 2011 from: http://www.suicidology.org/web/guest/stats-and-tools/warning-signs

American Association of Suicidology. (2011). Suicide in the U.S.A. Retrieved on July 10, 2011 from: http://www.suicidology.org/c/document_library/get_file?folderId=232&name=DLFE-244.pdf

American Psychiatric Association. (1980). *Diagnostic and statistical manual of mental disorders* (3rd ed.). Washington, DC: Author.

American Psychiatric Association. (1987). *Diagnostic and statistical manual of mental disorders* (3rd ed., revised). Washington, DC: Author.

American Psychiatric Association. (1994). *Diagnostic and statistical manual of mental disorders* (4th ed.). Washington, DC: Author.

American Psychiatric Association. (2000). *Diagnostic and statistical manual of mental disorders* (4th ed., text revision). Washington, DC: Author.

Angst, A., Angst, F., Gerber-Werder, R., & Gamma, A. (2005). Suicide in 406 mood disordered patients with and without long-term medication: A 40 to 44 years' follow-up. *Archives of Suicide Research, 9,* 279–300.

Angst, J. (2009). Course and prognosis of mood disorders. In M. G. Gelder, N. C. Andreasen, J. J. Lopez-Ibor, Jr., & J. R. Geddes (Eds.).

New Oxford textbook of psychiatry (2nd ed., Vol I, pp. 665–669). Oxford, UK: Oxford University Press.

Angst, J., & Sellaro, R. (2000). Historical perspectives and natural history of bipolar disorder. *Biological Psychiatry, 48* (6), 445–457.

Arroll, B., Macgillivray, S., Ogston, S., Reid, I., Sullivan, F., Williams, B., & Crombie, I. (2005). Efficacy and tolerability of tricyclic antidepressants and SSRIs compared with placebo for treatment of depression in primary care. *Annals of Family Medicine, 3,* 449–456.

Baldessarini, R., Pompili, M., & Tondo, L. (2006). Suicidal risk in antidepressant drug trials. *Archives of General Psychiatry, 63,* 246–248.

Barlow, D. H., & Durand, V. M. (2012). *Abnormal psychology* (6th ed.). Belmont, CA: Wadsworth Cengage Learning.

Bech, P. (2009). Clinical features of mood disorders and mania. In M. G. Gelder, N. C. Andreasen, J. J. Lopez-Ibor, Jr., & J. R. Geddes (Eds.). *New Oxford textbook of psychiatry* (2nd ed., Vol I, pp. 632–637). Oxford, UK: Oxford University Press.

Berman, A. L. (2009). Depression and suicide. In I. H. Gotlib & C. L. Hammen (Eds.). *Handbook of depression* (2nd ed., pp. 510–530). New York: Guilford.

Biederman, J., Mick, E., Faraone, S. V., Spencer, T., Wilens, T. E., & Wozniak, J. (2000). Pediatric mania: A developmental subtype of bipolar disorder? *Biological Psychiatry, 48* (6), 458–466.

Blazer, D. G., & Hybels, C. F. (2009). Depression in later life: Epidemiology, assessment, impact and treatment. In I. H. Gotlib & C. L. Hammen (Eds.). *Handbook of depression* (2nd ed., pp. 492–509). New York: Guilford.

Boland, R. J., & Keller, M. B., (2009). Course and outcome of depression. In I. H. Gotlib & C. L. Hammen (Eds.). *Handbook of depression (*2nd ed., pp. 23–43). New York: Guilford.

Bradley, R. G., Binder, E. B., Epstein, M. P., Tang, Y., Nair, H. P., Liu, W., ... Ressler, K. J. (2008). Influence of child abuse on adult depression: Moderation by the corticotropin releasing hormone receptor gene. *Archives of General Psychiatry, 65* (2), 190–200.

Brent, D., & Birmaher, B. (2009). Paediatric mood disorders. In M. G. Gelder, N. C. Andreasen, J. J. Lopez-Ibor, Jr., & J. R. Geddes (Eds.). *New Oxford textbook of psychiatry* (2nd ed., Vol I, pp. 1669–1680). Oxford, UK: Oxford University Press.

Byers, A., Yaffe, K., Covinsky, K. E., Friedman, V. B., & Bruce, M. L. (2010). High occurrence of mood and anxiety disorders among older adults: The National Comorbidity Survey Replication. *Archives of General Psychiatry, 67* (5), 489–496.

Caspi, A., Sugden, K., Moffitt, T. E., Taylor, A., Craig, I. W., Harrington, H., ... Poulton, R. (2003). Influence of life stress on depression: Moderation by a polymorphism in the 5-HTT gene. *Science, 301,* 386–389.

Costello, E. J., Foley, D. L., & Angold, A. (2006). 10 year research update review: The epidemiology of child and adolescent psychiatric disorders: II. Developmental epidemiology. *Journal of the American Academy of Child and Adolescent Psychiatry, 45* (1), 8–25.

Fergusson, D., Doucette, D., Glass, K., Shapiro, S., Healy, D., Herber, P., & Hutton, B. (2005). Association between suicide attempts and selective serotonin reuptake inhibitors: Systematic review of randomized controlled trials. *BMJ, 330,* 396–402.

Fisk, A., Wetherell, J. L., & Gatz, M. (2009). Depression in older adults. *Annual Review of Clinical Psychology, 5,* 363–389.

Garber, J., & Carter, J. S. (2006). Major depression. In R. T. Ammerman (Ed.). *Comprehensive handbook of personality and psychopathology. Volume III: Child psychopathology* (pp. 165–216). Hoboken, NJ: John Wiley and Sons.

Garber, J., Clarke, G. N., Weersing, V. R., Beardslee, W. R., Brent, D. A., Gladstone, T. R., ... Iyengar, S. (2009). Prevention of depression in at-risk adolescents: A randomized controlled trial. *Journal of the American Medical Association, 301* (21), 2215–2224.

Garlow, S., Boone, E., Li, W., Owens, M., & Nemeroff, C. (2005). Genetic analysis of the hypothalamic corticotropin releasing factor system. *Endocrinology, 146,* 2362–2368.

Gelman, D. (1987, May 4). Depression. *Newsweek,* p. 7.

Goodwin, F. K., & Jamison, K. R. (2007). *Manic depressive illness.* New York: Oxford University Press.

Hammad, T., Laughren, T., & Racoosin, J. (2006). Suicidality in pediatric patients treated with antidepressant drugs. *Archives of General Psychiatry, 63,* 332–339.

Hammen, C. (2005). Stress and depression. *Annual Review of Clinical Psychology, 1,* 293–319.

Hasin, D., Goodwin, R., Stinson, G., & Grant, B. (2005). Epidemiology of major depressive disorder. *Archives of General Psychiatry, 62,* 1097–1106.

Hypericum Depression Trial Study Group. (2002). Effect of Hypericum perforatum (St. John's wort) in major depressive disorder: A randomized controlled trial. *Journal of the American Medical Association, 287,* 1853–1854.

Jacobs, D. G., Baldessarini, R. J., Conwell, Y., Fawcett, J. A., Horton, L., Meltzer, H., ... Simon, R. J. (November 2003). *American Psychiatric Association practice guideline for the assessment and treatment of patients with suicidal behaviors.* Retrieved on July 10, 2011 at: http://www.psychiatryonline.com/pracGuide/pracGuideTopic_14.aspx

James, R. K. (2008). *Crisis intervention strategies* (6th ed.). Belmont, CA: Thomson Brooks/Cole.

Joe, S., Baser, R., Breeden, G., Neighbors, H., & Jackson, J. (2006). Prevalence of and risk factors for lifetime suicide attempts among blacks in the United States. *Journal of the American Medical Association, 296,* 2112–2123.

Johannessen Landmark, C. (2008). Antiepileptic drugs in non-epilepsy disorders: Relations between mechanisms of action and clinical efficacy. *CNS Drugs, 22,* 27–47.

Johnson, S. L. (2004). Defining bipolar disorder. In S. L. Johnson & R. L. Leahy (Eds.). *Psychological treatment of bipolar disorder* (pp. 3–16). New York: Guilford.

Johnson, S. L., Cuellar, A. K., & Miller, C. (2009). Bipolar and unipolar depression: A comparison of clinical phenomenology, biological vulnerability, and psychosocial predictors. In I. H. Gotlib & C. L. Hammen (Eds.). *Handbook of depression* (2nd ed., pp. 142–162). New York: Guilford.

Judd, L. (2000). Course and chronicity of unipolar major depressive disorder: Commentary on Joiner. *Child Psychology Science and Practice, 7* (2), 219–223.

Kanel, L. (2012). *A guide to crisis intervention* (4th ed.). Belmont, CA: Brooks/Cole Cengage.

Kawa, I., Carter, J. D., Joyce, P. R., Doughty, C. J., Frampton, C. M., Wells, H. E., Walsh, A. E., & Olds, R. J. (2003). Gender differences in bipolar disorder: Age of onset, course, comorbidity, and symptom presentation. *Bipolar Disorders, 7,* 119–125.

Kessler, R. C., Berglund, P., Demler, O., Jin, R., Koretz, D., Merikangas, K. R., ... National Comorbidity Survey Replication. (2003). The epidemiology of major depressive disorder: Results from the national comorbidity survey replication (NCS–R). *Journal of the American Medical Association, 289,* 3095–3105.

Kessler, R. C., Chiu, W. T., Demler, O., & Walters, E. E. (2005). Prevalence, severity, and co-morbidity of 12-month DSM-IV disorders in the National Comorbidity Survey replication. *Archives of General Psychiatry, 62,* 617–627.

Kessler, R. C., & Wang, P. S. (2009). Epidemiology of depression. In I. H. Gotlib & C. L. Hammen (Eds.). *Handbook of depression* (2nd ed., pp. 5–22). New York: Guilford.

Kilpatrick, D. G., Koenen, K. C., Ruggiero, K. J., Acierno, R., Galea, S., Resnick, H. S., ... Gelernter, J. (2007). The serotonin transporter genotype and social support and moderation of posttraumatic stress disorder and depression in hurricane-exposed adults. *The American Journal of Psychiatry, 164* (11), 1693–1699.

Klein, D. N. (2008). Classification of depressive disorders in the DSM-V: Proposal for a two-dimension system. *Journal of Abnormal Psychology, 117* (3), 552–560.

Klein, D. N., Lewinsohn, P. M., Rhode, P., Seeley, J. R., & Durbin, C. E. (2002). Clinical features of major depressive disorder in adolescents and their relatives: Impact on familial aggregation, implications for phenotype definition, and specificity of transmission. *Journal of Abnormal Psychology, 111,* 98–106.

Klein, D. N., Shankman, S., & Rose, S. (2006). Ten-year prospective follow-up study of the naturalistic course of dysthymic disorder and double depression. *American Journal of Psychiatry, 163,* 872–880.

Lam, R., Levin, A., Levitan, R., Einns, M., Morehouse, R., Michalak, E., & Tam, S. E. (2005). The Can-Sad study: A randomized controlled trial of the effectiveness of light therapy and fluoxetine in patients with winter seasonal affective disorder. *American Journal of Psychiatry, 163,* 805–812.

Levinson, D. F. (2009). Genetics of major depression. In I. H. Gotlib & C. L. Hammen (Eds.). *Handbook of depression* (2nd ed., pp. 165–186). New York: Guilford.

Merikangas, K. R., & Pato, M. (2009). Recent developments in the epidemiology of bipolar disorder in adults and children: Magnitude, correlates, and future directions. *Clinical Psychology: Science and Practice, 16* (2), 121–133.

Monroe, S. M., & Reid, M. W. (2009). Life stress and major depression. *Current Directions in Psychological Science, 18* (2), 68–72.

Monroe, S. M., Slavich, G. M., & Georgiades, K. (2009). The social environment and life stress in depresson. In I. H. Gotlib & C. L. Hammen (Eds.). *Handbook of depression* (2nd ed., pp. 340–360). New York: Guilford.

Morrison, J. (1995). *The DSM-IV made easy.* New York: Guilford.

National Association of Social Workers. (1999). *Code of Ethics.* Washington, DC: Author.

Nock, M. K., Borges, G., Bromet, E. J., Cha, C. B., Kessler, R. C., & Lee, S. (2008). Suicide and suicidal behavior. *Epidemiology Reviews, 30,* 133–154.

Nock, M. K., Hwang, I., Sampson, N. A., Kessler, R. C. (2009). Mental disorders, comorbidity and suicidal behavior: Results from the National Comorbidity Survey Replication. *Molecular Psychiatry, 15,* 868–876.

Olfson, M., Marcus, S., & Schaffer, D. (2006). Antidepressant drug therapy and suicide in severely depressed children and adolescents. *Archives of General Psychiatry, 63,* 865–872.

Ramchandani, P., Stein, A., Evans, J., O'Connor, T., & the ALSPAC Study Team. (2005). Paternal depression in the postnatal period and child development: A prospective population study. *Lancet, 365,* 2201–2205.

Rudd, D. M., Joiner, T., & Hasan Rajab, M. (2001). *Treating suicidal behavior: An effective, time-limited approach.* New York: Guilford.

Rudolph, K. D. (2009). Adolescent depression. In I. H. Gotlib & C. L. Hammen (Eds.). *Handbook of depression* (2nd ed., pp. 444–466). New York: Guilford.

Rutter, M. (2010). Gene-environment interplay. *Depression and Anxiety, 27* (1), 1–4.

Sachs, G. S., & Gardner-Schuster, E. E. (2007). Adjunctive treatment of acute mania: A clinical overview. *Acta Psychiatrica Scandinavica Supplement, 434,* 27–34.

Solomon, D. A., Keller, M. B., Leon, A. C., Mueller, T. I., Lavori, P. W., Shea, T., ... Endicott, J. (2000). Multiple recurrences of major depressive disorder. *American Journal of Psychiatry, 157* (2), 229–233.

Sudak, H. S. (2009). Suicide. In B. J. Sadock, V. A. Sadock, & P. Ruiz (Eds.). *Kaplan and Sadock's comprehensive textbook of psychiatry* (9th ed., Vol II, pp. 2717–2781). Philadelphia: Lippincott Williams & Wilkins.

Thaker, G. K. (2009). Schizophrenia: Phenotypic manifestations. In B. J. Sadock, V. A. Sadock, & P. Ruiz (Eds.). *Kaplan and Sadock's comprehensive textbook of psychiatry* (9th ed., Vol. I, pp. 1541–1547). Philadelphia: Lippincott Williams & Wilkins.

Thase, M. E., & Denko, T. (2008). Pharmacotherapy of mood disorders. *Annual Review of Clinical Psychology, 4,* 53–91.

Wade, C., & Tavris, C. (2010). *Psychology* (10th ed.). Upper Saddle River, NJ: Prentice Hall.

ANXIETY DISORDERS

CHAPTER 7

INTRODUCTION

The **anxiety disorders** are considered the most common and frequently occurring mental disorders. They affect 28.8 percent of Americans at some point in their lives, and slightly over 18 percent over 12 months (Kessler, Berglund, et al., 2005; Kessler, Chiu, Demler, & Walters, 2005). Anxiety is regarded as a warning signal that helps alert a person to impending or imminent danger and enables them to deal with the threat of harm. Fear is a similar warning signal but is markedly different from anxiety. Fear is seen as a response to a definite and/or known hazard, whereas anxiety is a response to an unknown or unspecified threat. The predominant difference between the two is that fear is considered an acute reaction, while anxiety is considered chronic.

The practitioner considers whether or not anxiety is a normal response to something going on in a person's life, or whether the anxiety is excessive or out of proportion. In particular, the competency-based assessment investigates the person's (1) physical resources (physical arousal), (2) cognitive responses and distortions, and (3) coping strategies (Barlow, 2004). An anxiety disorder should be considered if the person's response is exaggerated in at least one of those three areas.

Anxiety is a mood state wherein the person anticipates future danger or misfortune with apprehension. This response causes a markedly negative effect consisting primarily of tension and somatic features (Barlow, 2004). Clients often experience anxiety as a vague feeling of apprehension manifested as worry, unease, or dread. Everyone experiences anxiety from time to time. One might feel a sense of discomfort, "butterflies in the stomach," a rapid heart rate, or "nervous" fidgeting (Barlow & Durand, 2012). Experiencing some anxiety is considered normal, even adaptive, and a certain amount of anxiety can motivate a person toward taking appropriate actions that ward off a threat. Some anxiety is good, but having too much, as we will see in this chapter, is not.

Anxiety is a normal reaction to anything that might be threatening to a person's lifestyle, values, self, or loved ones. Some degree of anxiety can appear when things go wrong—and (perversely) when things go right or change. To illustrate, when you study and prepare yourself for an exam, you are attempting to reduce anxiety in a good way. When you make adequate preparations, you are taking steps to avoid the anxiety you would experience if you did not study and subsequently failed the exam. Your anxiety about taking an exam becomes an "early warning system" that motivates you to take anticipatory action by studying hard to pass the test.

Those who are adversely affected by anxiety are plagued by a sense of having no control over challenging life situations and of being unable to predict them. Anxiety becomes problematic when it begins to significantly interfere with the demands of daily living, particularly in social and occupational functioning. A major problem in understanding anxiety is its subjective nature—anxiety can mean many different things to different people. The competency-based assessment begins by distinguishing between what is considered a normal or adaptive response to life stressors. Anxiety rarely occurs in isolation, and other features such as depression, suicidal ideation, or somatic complaints are commonly noted alongside it (Brown & Barlow, 2009; Clark, 2005; Wilamowska et al., 2010).

The conditions reviewed in this chapter are characterized by anxiety and by behavior calculated to ward it off. Included are those anxiety disorders the social worker commonly encounters in practice: agoraphobia, panic disorder (with and without agoraphobia), specific and social phobias, obsessive-compulsive disorder (OCD), post-traumatic stress disorder (PTSD), acute stress disorder (ASD), and generalized anxiety disorder (GAD).

UNDERSTANDING AGORAPHOBIA

Taken from the Greek language, the term **agoraphobia** literally means "fear of the marketplace." When the practitioner begins to explore the presence of anxiety, what becomes quite apparent is not the fear of being in a particular place or situation but rather the likelihood of suddenly becoming ill, not being able to escape, or not being able to receive immediate help. The person is afraid of being incapacitated or embarrassed.

There is some research supporting the existence of more than one kind of agoraphobia, but the most common type occurs secondarily to **panic disorder** (Perugi, Frare, & Toni, 2007). The research notes a small minority of cases in which people deny ever having a panic attack—they simply experience the dread that "something might happen." In these instances, they are said to have agoraphobia without the resulting panic component (Kikuchi et al., 2005).

When assessing for panic disorder (with or without agoraphobia), the practitioner appraises and integrates multiple sources of knowledge, including research-based knowledge and practice wisdom. The majority of what is known about agoraphobia comes from studies about agoraphobia with panic disorder

EP 2.1.3 a

(Craske & Barlow, 2008). There are not many relevant statistics about agoraphobia without a history of panic, because it is not often seen in clinical practice and it has not garnered the support of empirical research. Interestingly, two-thirds of those who have panic along with agoraphobia are women (Kessler, Berglund, et al., 2005). Somehow it seems more culturally acceptable for women to be fearful and to avoid situations, whereas men, in contrast, are expected to be strong and just tough it out (Wolitzky-Taylor, Castriotta, Lenze, Stanley, & Craske, 2010). In our case presentation of Matilda Suarez, the reader's attention will focus on agoraphobia without panic. In the second case, that of Jada Wu, agoraphobia with panic will be addressed.

PREVAILING PATTERN

The age of onset is typically during the person's early adult life, ranging from mid-adolescence to about 40 years of age, with no reported differences in age of onset or duration between men and women (Kessler, Berglund, et al., 2005). Panic attacks are easily identified in adults, but there is some controversy over how often they occur in young children. Many youngsters are seen by a general medical practitioner with symptoms that resemble a panic attack, such as hyperventilation, but are too young to report other symptoms characteristic of a panic attack; for instance, losing control or a fear of dying (Barlow & Durand, 2012). If left untreated, panic attacks can endure for years with a chronic relapsing course, and remission cannot occur as long as the panic attacks remain. Due to the physical symptoms or discomfort (somatization) that often occurs for those suffering panic attacks, the practitioner may find clients using the health care system frequently.

Most of what is known suggests that agoraphobic avoidance behavior seems to be a complication of severe unexpected panic attacks (Barlow, 2004; Craske & Barlow, 2008). In other words, if someone experiences an unexpected panic attack, they are usually afraid they will experience another one. What the individual wants to do is stay in a place considered safe, just in case another episode occurs. There are a number of situations or places the person with agoraphobia generally avoids, such as being in movie theaters, shopping centers, grocery stores, elevators, subways, airplanes, riding in the backseat of a two-door car, driving in tunnels or over bridges, or even waiting in a line. Some individuals with agoraphobic avoidance also show another cluster of avoidant behaviors known as **interoceptive avoidance** (Wald & Taylor, 2007). In this type of avoidance, the person removes him/herself from situations or activities that might evoke the physiological arousal that resembles the beginnings of a panic attack. For instance, the person might avoid strenuous exercise because it increases their heart rate or they start breathing faster, and this reminds them of panic attacks, which then makes them think this might be the beginning of one.

In extreme situations of agoraphobia without a history of panic disorder, the individual fears being anywhere except in the safety of their own home. For example, the prospect of walking outside to pick up the morning paper may fill the person with debilitating fear. Some people become so incapacitated they refuse to venture out of their homes, which may last for years, as illustrated in the following vignette.

Matilda Suarez, age 58, has not walked outside of her home for the past 15 years. Her parish priest, Father Michael Krane, has referred Ms. Suarez to the Homebuilders' Social Service Agency. He became quite concerned because of her failing health and dwindling financial resources. Father Michael recently learned that Ms. Suarez's apartment complex is going to be demolished to make room for a "neighborhood improvement project." A home visit was scheduled by the social worker, and Ms. Suarez was seen the following week.

Ms. Suarez was born in Havana, Cuba, and immigrated to south Florida during the Mariel boatlift of the early 1980s. She has two daughters, aged 22 and 25, both of whom live in south Florida as well. Ms. Suarez divorced her husband almost 20 years ago and has had no further contact with him. She thinks he may have returned to Cuba.

During the first visit with the social worker, Ms. Suarez indicated that she is quite lonely. "My daughters have their own lives, but I wish they'd visit me more often. Sometimes I don't see anybody for 2 or 3 weeks at a time."

The social worker prompted, "Can you tell me more about why you don't see anyone for weeks at a time?"

Ms. Suarez looked up from under her eyebrows and said, "Well, did Father Michael tell you I haven't been able to leave my house in 15 years?" The social worker nodded to indicate that she knows something about the situation. Ms. Suarez continued, "I mean I don't even go outside to pick up my morning newspaper. The paperboy knows he has to lean the newspaper right up against my front door or else I don't get to read the paper that day. I hate to even open up my front door because I'm afraid I'll get an attack. I know it's no way to live—but what choice do I have?"

The worker asked Ms. Suarez several other questions. The following is a composite of her responses. Ms. Suarez has no contact with anyone other than Father Michael, her daughters, and a visiting nurse. She is completely dependent on her girls to do all shopping and basic household maintenance. She used to do her own errands—not alone, of course, but with at least one of the girls accompanying her. Ms. Suarez says that she is afraid to go out alone, and that she used to get especially nervous if she had to be around a lot of people. She's not so much afraid of the people, but she does not like closed-in spaces. The last time she went to her doctor's office, she walked out because "the waiting room got too crowded and cramped."

A visiting nurse comes to see Ms. Suarez once or twice a year to follow her medical needs. She suffers from varicose veins in her lower extremities, making it difficult for her to walk. She is also monitored for hot flashes associated with being postmenopausal. She denies using alcohol or drugs, and denies depression, hallucinations, delusions, or suicidal ideation. Ms. Suarez earns a living as a medical transcriber, which she is able to do from her home. Ms. Suarez says of her situation, "I have no friends in this world that care about me. I'm a prisoner in my own world." Gesturing expansively, she continues, "My constant companions are these four walls and my television. Year after year, month after month, day after day—nothing ever changes." She sighs. "I can't leave my house because I don't feel safe, and now the County Reclamation Agency is going to tear my world down. Where can I go from here? Don't they understand I can't walk out of my house? What am I going to do?"

ASSESSMENT SUMMARY Because of her anxiety and fears, Ms. Suarez completely avoids going to different places and being in situations where she does not feel safe. Even with a companion, she still feels unable to leave her home. She is not able to explain to the social worker exactly what might happen if she leaves the house, but she is able to recognize that she would feel very afraid.

EP 2.1.10
(b) a

Distinguishing the diagnosis of agoraphobia without a history of panic disorder requires the practitioner to collect, organize, and interpret the data in Ms. Suarez's story. The features illustrated in the vignette are too varied to be **social phobia**. The overriding distinction for assessing agoraphobia is the danger

Ms. Suarez perceives from her environment—social phobia, in contrast, would involve the perception of danger from her relationship with others. She does not have **separation anxiety disorder** because she does not have a problem being left alone. Her diagnosis would not be post-traumatic stress disorder as she does not claim to have experienced any traumatic situations such as being mugged or raped. There are no features suggesting obsessive-compulsive disorder, nor did she show evidence of having a panic disorder. Figure 7.1 illustrates the interactions of the biological, psychological, and social variables in Matilda Suarez's life.

MS. SUAREZ'S MULTIAXIAL DSM DIAGNOSIS AT THIS POINT IS AS FOLLOWS:

Axis I	300.22 Agoraphobia without History of Panic Disorder
Axis II	V71.09 (No diagnosis)
Axis III	454.9 Varicose Veins, Lower Extremities
	627.9 Unspecified Postmenopausal Disorder
Axis IV	Financial difficulties
	Housing problems
	Lack of friends
Axis V	GAF = 65 (on initial appointment)

© Cengage Learning

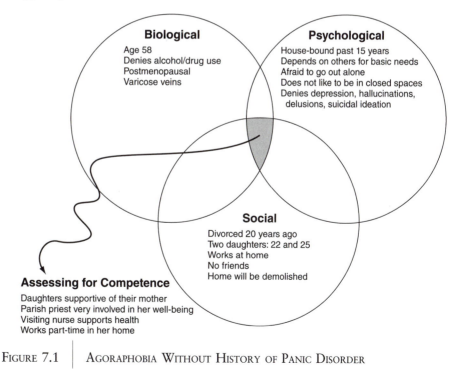

FIGURE 7.1 | AGORAPHOBIA WITHOUT HISTORY OF PANIC DISORDER

The interactions of the biological, psychological, and social variables in Matilda Suarez's life.

© Cengage Learning

The competency-based assessment focuses on coping strategies that reinforce and improve a client's adaptation to life situations, circumstances, and events. Ms. Suarez's coping strategies can be found in two specific areas in life. One is her environment, and the other is related to those intrapersonal issues that support her ability to cope with anxiety. There are four key supports in Ms. Suarez's life: her two daughters, the parish priest, and her visiting nurse. In addition, Ms. Suarez has been able to support herself, though in a limited fashion, by working from home as a medical transcriber.

Now we are going to look at a case example of agoraphobia *with* panic disorder.

CASE | THE CASE OF JADA WU

Jada Wu, a 27-year-old flight attendant, was referred to the social worker at the Employee Assistance Program two weeks ago. The only information known is what Ms. Wu noted in her pre-intake form: "I suffer from feelings of nervousness." This is our first session, and we are meeting in my office near the airport concourse where Ms. Wu is employed.

Jada is a very attractive woman of Chinese descent, who appears to be her stated age of 27. She is of medium height, has a slim figure, and wears her long hair in a braid hanging down her back. She has a ready smile and appeared comfortable meeting me for the first time.

As for her relevant background history, her parents were originally from Beijing and immigrated to south Florida 25 years ago (when Jada was two years old). She remembers growing up in cramped living quarters with several other family members who had also immigrated to the United States around the same time. She says that, although there was not a great deal of money for material things, her family always celebrated traditional festivals and holidays. She remembers especially the Chinese New Year, "sweeping of the grave," and mid-autumn festivals. In addition, her family started one of the first Chinese restaurants in their neighborhood. She has fond memories of helping the family business thrive. She describes herself as being social and gregarious—she waited on tables, took orders, and joked with the customers.

Jada is the first woman in her family to complete college, which seems to have caused a great deal of controversy among family members, because it represents to them a pull away from family unity. In her family, if a child attempts to act independently, he or she is labeled as "inconsiderate, ungrateful, and self-indulgent." The family believes in sticking together.

In addition, when Jada started her job with the airline, she was the first to work outside of the family business. Although they seem proud of her, she senses that her parents simply tolerate her career accomplishments—consequently, Jada says that there is now a certain degree of tension at family gatherings.

When Jada settles in her chair, I ask, "Ms. Wu, why do you think you are here?" After a moment's hesitation, she states, "Please call me Jada.... I guess it's about what's been happening to me lately." She is quiet for a moment and seems to need a bit of direction. I suggest she explain to me what has been happening. Then she continues, "Well, everything was going along just fine until one day I was on a routine flight in-bound from Dallas to San Antonio. All of a sudden—I mean really out of the blue—I know that sounds like a joke," she laughs nervously, "but it wasn't meant to be. Anyway, I began to feel dizzy. One of other attendants sat me down in an empty first-class seat so I wouldn't topple over. I felt nauseous, I was freezing cold, and my heart was beating so fast it felt like it was going to pop out of my chest. I felt short of breath, and I thought I was going to die right there on the plane."

Jada seems to be reliving every sensation as she describes it to me, but she goes on, "The captain made an overhead announcement asking if there was a physician on board. We didn't have a doctor, but the nicest social worker came forward and offered to help. She took one look at me, and asked lots of medical kinds of questions like was I taking any medication, has this ever happened before, did I have a history of heart disease? I told her I had just passed my annual physical examination. As a rule, I've always been a very healthy person. I keep my weight down, I'm a vegetarian—I told her all that sort of stuff. The social worker was really nice. She held my hand, and reassured me that what she thought might be happening was something called a panic attack. She said I'd be all right and suggested I try to breathe into an airsickness bag for about ten minutes. That helped calm me down—but before the social worker left the plane she suggested I seek some counseling and go see my doctor again."

"Do you have any idea what precipitated this incident?" I ask.

Jada responds, "I can't actually tell you."

I ask her a series of questions aimed at exploring whether Jada experiences agoraphobia. "Do any of the following make you feel very fearful, nervous, or anxious? Being away from your home, being in a closed or small room (like an elevator), being on a bridge, or being in a crowd of people like at a concert hall?"

Jada answers right away, "Well, yes, I have had problems leaving my house. You know, for the last several months my sister has started to take me grocery shopping—but I didn't make a connection between that and any problems I've been having." As soon as the words are out of her mouth, she says, "Oh, wait a minute! I just remembered, there were a few times when I felt like I was trapped. I was shopping at the mall. It was really weird, you know, like I needed to escape and get out of there but I couldn't get anyone to help me. Eventually those feelings went away somehow and I managed to get home myself. Since then, I do most of my shopping on the Internet. Did you know you can even get groceries online?"

I comment that it does indeed sound as if she is having episodes of panic, and I ask her how long they've been happening.

Jada replies, "You know, ever since that first time it happened when I was in flight. I've had a lot more. Sometimes they happen every day. They aren't always the same, but they are always terrifying. They start like that," Jada snaps her fingers, "Then they develop really fast—but they are over in 30 or 40 minutes. That doesn't matter, though, because when you are responsible for several hundred people like I am you have to always be ready to help *them,* not the other way around. Several times I had a panic attack when I was walking out of my house to leave for the airport—and twice they happened during a layover when I went out to dinner with the crew. Of course, I didn't tell them anything was wrong with me. I made up a story that I might be getting a fever, and tried to hide it from them. I don't know if they bought my story or if they could see me shaking, breathing hard, and sweating—but no one said anything. You know, it's not a good thing to have a flight attendant who looks like she's falling apart."

When I ask how she is currently doing, she replies, "Well, I'm always worried about when it's going to happen again. It's like I'm constantly worrying. If I have problems leaving my house for work, my mother drives me to the airport—but she can't hold my hand forever, can she? I'm thinking about changing my job. The airline offered me a spot as a reservation clerk, and I'm seriously thinking about it. I'm just too afraid to go through one of these panic attacks while flying. I can hardly think about my life without flying. Flying is my life, and I will really miss traveling."

I ask where she has traveled. She looks down at her hands resting in her lap and replies, "Pretty much everywhere: Mexico, Japan, China, Thailand, Hong Kong, Bali, Australia, Papua New Guinea, Egypt, Israel, Russia, all of Europe and Scandinavia. I guess that's going to be a thing of the past, huh?"

"Not necessarily," I reply, "but I think we have some work ahead of us."

Advanced Clinical EP 2.1.7 c

ASSESSMENT SUMMARY   Jada's panic attack was quite typical; it began suddenly, escalated rapidly, and included heart palpitations, shortness of breath, lightheadedness, and nausea. Jada experienced the same fear that most people do during an attack: that she was going to die. There are times when the practitioner may need to consult with medical professionals to confirm the diagnosis. Although a number of general medical conditions can mimic panic attacks, the social worker should note that Jada recently passed her annual physical examination and was found to be in good health. Making an assessment of specific or social phobia is not likely, because the focus of Jada's anxiety was not directed toward a single situation or to a social situation. Major depressive disorder can accompany panic disorder with or without agoraphobia; however, Jada did not describe a past history of depression.

Advanced
Clinical EP
2.1.10 (b) c

Understanding Jada's functioning on all levels helps provide a more complete clinical picture and helps highlight the coping strategies she can tap into in order to reinforce and improve her adaptation to life situations, circumstances, and events. The competency-based assessment requires the practitioner to discern Jada's medical status and intrapersonal factors as well as the influence that culture plays in her life. The vignette reveals Jada's insight that her problem is interfering with her work, and she has an employer who is supportive. Her family, although only "tolerant" of Jada's moving outside of the family system, are supportive of her independence. When she had fears about going outside, her sister helped with shopping chores. Finally, Jada has followed through on the counseling referral and is motivated to work on her problems. See Figure 7.2 for an illustration of the interactions of the biological, psychological, and social variables in Jada Wu's life.

JADA WU'S MULTIAXIAL DSM DIAGNOSIS AT THIS POINT IS AS FOLLOWS:

Axis I	300.21 Panic Disorder with Agoraphobia
Axis II	V71.09 (No diagnosis)
Axis III	None
Axis IV	None
Axis V	GAF = 75 (current functioning)

© Cengage Learning

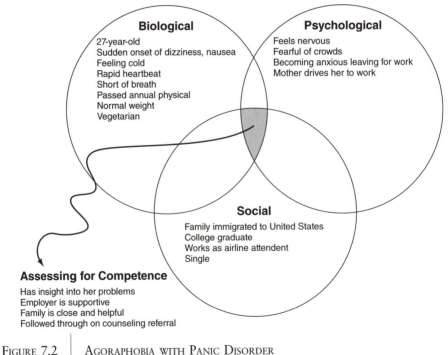

Biological
27-year-old
Sudden onset of dizziness, nausea
Feeling cold
Rapid heartbeat
Short of breath
Passed annual physical
Normal weight
Vegetarian

Psychological
Feels nervous
Fearful of crowds
Becoming anxious leaving for work
Mother drives her to work

Social
Family immigrated to United States
College graduate
Works as airline attendant
Single

Assessing for Competence
Has insight into her problems
Employer is supportive
Family is close and helpful
Followed through on counseling referral

FIGURE 7.2 | AGORAPHOBIA WITH PANIC DISORDER

The interactions of the biological, psychological, and social variables in Jada Wu's life.

© Cengage Learning

UNDERSTANDING SPECIFIC PHOBIA

The term **phobia** is derived from Phobos, the name of the much feared Greek deity whose father, Ares, was the god of war. Thus, we use the word *phobia* to describe an extreme and irrational fear of simple things or social situations. Most of us have the usual kinds of fears that may include ordinary events like going to the doctor or dentist for a checkup. However, these fears do not rule our lives to the point where we completely avoid such activities. Rather, they tend to be considered inconvenient nuisances that we somehow adapt to and try to work around. In contrast, a person who becomes engulfed in a phobic episode usually feels inundated by overwhelming terror that literally obscures almost all other experiences. In its severest form, a phobia becomes extremely incapacitating. Examples of phobic features include profuse sweating, racing heart, a feeling described as choking or smothering, dizziness (or lightheadedness), and trembling, to name a few.

EP 2.1.10
(b) a

A **specific phobia** is defined as any persistent, unreasonable, and irrational fear of a specific object (dogs or cats), activity (driving), or situation (being in an elevator) that causes intense distress. Specific phobias markedly interfere with a person's capability to function well, and they result in the individual's compelling desire to avoid the feared object. More than 100 specific phobias have been identified—and although enumerating them seems to add little to understanding this disorder, it does highlight the extent of the named phobias. The best recognized specific phobias are of four major types (animal, natural environment, blood-injection-injury, and situational) plus one category labeled as "other." This "other" category includes those fears that do not fit into of the four major subtypes; for instance, situations that may lead to choking, vomiting, or even contracting an illness. In practice, the practitioner can expect to see someone who suffers from multiple phobias of different types. Given the number of phobias, the importance of collecting, organizing, and interpreting data from the client's story are key skills for the conducting the assessment of phobia. However, it is more than likely that the separate subtypes will remain in the DSM-5.

The prevalence of fears strong enough to qualify as a phobia during a 1-year period is 8.1 percent of the general population, making this disorder one of the most commonly seen in the United States (Arrindell et al., 2003, Kessler, Berglund, et al., 2005). However, the practitioner should not consider such a diagnosis unless the person is truly impaired by fears and there is marked distress or interference with usual routines, employment, or other areas of interpersonal functioning. While the "other" category does not receive very much attention, parents of toddlers can recognize the viability of its existence. It originates when a child is startled—either by a loud noise (fireworks or marching band) or by a costumed cartoon-type character (familiar or not). The usual scenario involves the child's being very eager to get away from the cause. Even if the character is one of the child's favorites (e.g., Barney or Mickey Mouse), the child becomes quite distressed and fearful—perhaps crying or even screaming in the desire to get away. Children eventually outgrow such reactions—but until they do, parents generally avoid situations that are potentially upsetting.

The following vignettes provide a brief picture of each of the four phobias. In general, remember that the phobias cause a great deal of intrapersonal (or personal) and interpersonal distress for people. The competency-based assessment is helpful for understanding each client's unique source of anxiety and stress.

ANIMAL PHOBIA

Excessive or unreasonable fear of animals and insects defines **animal phobia.** While these are common fears, they are considered to be a phobia when a person's functioning is severely impaired. Young children are especially susceptible to animal phobias, and age of onset usually peaks at 7 years of age (LeBeau et al., 2010), as is illustrated in the following case:

> Kyle Spector, shortly before he turned age 8, was playing in his grandmother's backyard when the dog from next door broke away from his chain restraint and lunged at Kyle, scratching him on the arm. The scratch was not serious, but Kyle's grandmother put a small bandage on it to appease him. For the past 10 years (since the incident), Kyle has not approached another dog, nor has he visited his grandmother's home.

NATURAL ENVIRONMENT PHOBIA

At a very early age some children develop fears of situations or events occurring in nature. These fears are known as **natural environment phobias.** Common examples include heights, storms, and water—and here too, these fears sometimes seem to cluster together (Antony & Barlow, 2002). Here is a brief example of natural environment phobia:

> When Miles Hailey was 6 years old, he accidentally fell out of his family's fishing boat during a camping trip and almost drowned. Miles states, "My dad put his mouth on top of mine and performed CPR. After I was revived, everybody told me I had stopped breathing and had turned blue. I guess you could say I was dead." Since that incident, Miles refuses to go anywhere near a large body of water. His parents recently announced their plans to celebrate their 35th wedding anniversary by taking the family on a cruise to the Caribbean Islands. Miles, who is now 28 years old, absolutely refuses to go.

Fear of water, as described in Miles' story, is only one of the natural environment phobias. Almost any situation or event out of doors that traumatizes a person (e.g., thunderstorms, lightning, quicksand) could potentially become a specific phobia.

BLOOD-INJECTION-INJURY PHOBIA

Those with **blood-injection-injury phobias** almost always differ in their physiological reaction from individuals with other types of phobias. The source of this difference is not known, but the subtype tends to run in families (Hofmann, Alpers, & Pauli, 2009). The average of onset is at about 9 years of age (LeBeau et al., 2010). The following illustrates blood-injection phobia.

> Ralph Tyler, a 29-year-old, Hollywood, Florida, policeman came in for a complete medical examination. Before he was even seated in an exam room, he stated, "I have

been in excellent health my whole life, so I don't need any in-depth tests." Mr. Tyler recently moved to the south Florida area and was told he could not get medical insurance with the police department unless he had a medical examination. Only under great duress had Mr. Tyler agreed to the exam—and he canceled six previously scheduled appointments before showing up today.

His physical health was noted as "unremarkable." When he was escorted into the laboratory area, he asked the technician, "Can I get you to donate some of your blood to substitute for mine? I can't stand the sight of needles. I mean I really freak out. Maybe you don't understand, but I can't stand to even think about blood. My mom is the same way. I can't even watch television shows having to do with medicine. Do you know the doctor program that shows people being treated in the hospital? I think it's called *Dr. House* or something like that. I can't even watch it! Yuk."

After a great deal of reassurance and trying to convince Mr. Tyler that I am the best drawer of blood he was ever going to meet, I jokingly told him that I had won many awards for being south Florida's "most painless lab tech." He finally settled his 6-foot-3-inch, 240-pound frame into one of the lab chairs. I laid out the usual row of tubes, needles, cotton, and alcohol swabs. I tightened the tourniquet on his arm, and began feeling around for a nice juicy vein. As I made preparations to draw his blood, Mr. Tyler said weakly, "I don't feel so good," and then fainted dead away. After he was revived, Mr. Tyler revealed that he always fainted whenever he saw a needle or blood, especially his own. When questioned why he didn't say something to me in the first place, he admitted, "Look at me. I'm supposed to be this big tough cop and look what happens when I see a little tiny needle. Hey, would you tell anybody?"

SITUATIONAL-TYPE PHOBIA

People who have a **situational-type phobia** would have difficulty using public transportation (e.g., buses, trains, and airplanes), or being in enclosed places such as elevators. These features may sound very similar to agoraphobia with panic disorder, but there is a key difference: individuals with situational phobia never experience a panic attack outside the context of their phobic object or situation (Barlow & Durand, 2012). The following vignette is an example of a person with a situational-type phobia:

Upon reporting for jury duty several years ago, the author was sitting in the jury box being asked the typical prospective juror-type questions. "I remember I had just finished answering a series of questions when I happened to glance sideways. I noticed a middle-aged woman in obvious distress. I leaned over and whispered to her, 'Are you alright?'

She whispered back, "I have to get out of here. I mean, I really have to get out of here. Can you see an exit door from here?" I told her I couldn't, and she said, "Oh, I knew this was a bad mistake, this always happens to me." I raised my hand, and a very surprised judge asked, "What seems to be the problem madam?" I suggested that the woman sitting next to me was in need of some immediate attention. The judge quickly took in the situation and ordered a 15-minute recess. After several minutes of discussion among the woman, the attorneys, and the judge, she was excused from jury duty.

As she left the courtroom, she leaned over and said to me, "Thank you so much for helping me out. I always have problems whenever I'm in a place where I can't get out." Then she laughed and added, "You should consider yourself lucky that we weren't in an elevator together."

SOCIAL PHOBIA

Social phobia, also called social anxiety disorder (SAD), is commonly referred to as performance anxiety, a condition in which a person fears performing publicly lest he or she be revealed as inept, foolish, or inadequate, thereby suffering disgrace, humiliation, or embarrassment. Of interest, the term likely to be adopted in the DSM-5 is *social anxiety disorder*. Even though the person who feels this way readily admits the fears are baseless and illogical, he or she nevertheless becomes severely anxious and often goes to great lengths to avoid being in these situations. Several famous stage, screen, and recording artists no longer perform publicly because they fear they will forget song lyrics or their lines in the script, their voice will crack, or they will suffer some other embarrassment. A social phobia is more than a matter of being overly shy. Apparently, it is not the "act" of doing something in and of itself that is feared; rather, it is the "doing of the act" and making a mistake in public that exacerbates the fear (Bogels et al., 2010). However, if the person performs in private, he or she may experience little or no anxiety. In addition to the preoccupation with the fear of embarrassing oneself in public, another symptom is being afraid of offending others with a foul body odor (that is not perceived by others), now called **olfactory reference syndrome.** This latter syndrome has been proposed for inclusion in the DSM-5 Appendix for further study as a possible new disorder (Feusner, Phillips, & Stein, 2010).

Fear of speaking in public is considered the most common form of social phobia (Barlow & Durand, 2012). Other situations that may evoke anxiety are a fear of trembling when writing in public (e.g., signing one's name on a charge receipt in front of a salesperson), worrying about choking on food when eating in a public place, or being unable to urinate when others are present (known as bashful bladder or paruresis). For example, men with this problem often must wait until a stall in a public bathroom becomes available—which can be quite inconvenient, depending on the circumstances. Many persons with a social phobia avoid being in almost all social situations. Sometimes they are able to endure their discomfort and go through with the "performance situation." Other times they may refuse to perform, and in extreme cases, they may have a panic attack. The fear that others will detect their nervousness and see signs of their somatic distress—such as trembling hands or **erythrophobia** (blushing)—adds to the symptom picture.

PREVAILING PATTERN

Undoubtedly, there are a lot more people who are shy but not to the extent of being diagnosed with social phobia. In a given 1-year period, the prevalence of social phobia is 6.8 percent, and may be as high as 12.1 percent, of the general population in the United States (Kessler, Berglund, et al., 2005; Kessler, Chiu, et al., 2005). In other words, more than 35 million people struggle with social phobia. The disorder generally begins during early adolescence, and tends to be more prevalent in young adults (18 to 29 years of age) who are undereducated, single, and of low economic status (Kessler, Berglund, et al., 2005). When making the competency-based assessment, it should not surprise the practitioner to discover interpersonal problems in a client's life—such as problems sustaining employment, suspended educational pursuits, lack of career promotion, and severe social restrictions.

Herb Wilks's story illustrates social phobia.

CASE	## THE CASE OF HERBERT WILKS

I received a referral from a social work colleague who was concerned that a personal friend, Herbert Wilks, was beginning to experience problems whenever he had to speak publicly. The following is a brief description of my first session with Mr. Wilks.

I walked into the waiting room and identified myself to Mr. Wilks. We shook hands and introduced ourselves. I told him, "I like to be called Marilyn," and he said, "I like to be called Herb. My mother is the only one that still calls me Herbert." We made our way down to my office. After a few moments, Herb began to explain the difficulties that brought him in.

"Well, to tell you the truth, this is sort of embarrassing, but I've been having problems doing my job for the past four years," he said. I asked Herb what he does for a living, and he replied, "Well, actually I do several things. To make financial ends meet, I drive an 18-wheel tractor-trailer rig on the weekends, but I only take the short hauls so I can be home with my wife and kids. It's a little different from my other jobs but I like it because I have the chance to just chill and be alone. It's easy money. I also teach a language arts course over at the community college a few days a week, just about every semester. But I guess what you'd call my regular job is being a motivational speaker for big corporations. I've always liked what I do—it's just that, for about the last year or so, I simply can't get up and talk in front of a bunch of people. That's the kiss of death for somebody who has three jobs and two of them involve speaking to big groups of people. It's gotten so bad now, that I'm afraid I'll have to quit those two jobs."

"Let me see if I understand," I ventured. "Is it that you fear being watched or being embarrassed in front of other people?"

Herb replied, "Exactly! That's exactly right! I am just so afraid of being humiliated by giving the wrong answer or not being able to finish my lecture." I asked Herb what happens when this occurs. He continued, "I get all sweaty, my hands shake, sometimes my voice cracks—and a few times I blushed bright red. It's terrible. I worry I'll get tongue-tied. Now mind you, I know this is what you might call an irrational fear, and I've always somehow gotten my words out, but …" Herb pauses, and then continues. "Well, it's gotten to the point where I actually canceled six speaking engagements that were for really high-profile companies. I just couldn't perform." Herb seemed very frustrated with himself. He went on, "A few times, I hid out in the men's room before I had to present. I just didn't want to come out. Several times, I literally had to force myself to do the presentations. I have to tell you, it's just awful. I'm so anxious that, even when I do make it through the talk, my clients aren't getting their money's worth. I'm sure some of them think I'm stupid—they must wonder how in the world I gained a reputation for being such an expert motivational speaker. I can't stand the humiliation." Herb sounded really defeated. "Now I've started canceling some of my classes because I just can't teach feeling this way. Of course, the students are thrilled when the class is canceled, but if news ever gets back to the dean, my job is toast—you know, I'll be finished."

I asked Herb why he thought he had these problems. He shook his head slowly, "You know, I'm a clean and decent fella. I try to help out at my church when I can. I don't use drugs. I don't smoke. I don't drink alcohol. I'm a dedicated family man. I don't think I mentioned my wife. She's a stay-at-home mom…. we were childhood sweethearts … have three great kids." Herb seems truly puzzled. "I have no history of any medical problems. I just don't know how to explain what's going on."

When I asked if there are any other kinds of distress connected to his public speaking, Herb replied, "Yes. I think about this all the time. My wife, Dora, has been giving me a hard time. She tells me just to snap out of it—like I ought to have some control over it. Don't you think I would, if I could? I mean, I realize I'm blowing this out of proportion, but what can I do? Do you think you can help me?"

ASSESSMENT SUMMARY   Herb has some insight into his fears of public speaking and teaching. He did not provide any indication of experiencing panic attacks, nor did he show evidence of anxiety due to a general medical disorder or substance-induced anxiety disorder. Ultimately, Herb's assessment boils down to the differences among the phobias.

None of the features of a specific phobia, agoraphobia, or a personality disorder are manifested in this case. Specific and social phobias could be difficult to ascertain in people who are naturally shy and retiring. Discerning between the two phobias underscores the practitioner's ability to collect, organize, and interpret data from the client's story. Many people worry about or feel uncomfortable when involved in social situations; thus, unless the person is significantly affected occupationally, socially, or in other interpersonal areas, he or she should not be considered as having social phobia. Herb's excessive fears of speaking and teaching certainly fit with a diagnosis of social phobia.

Using the competency-based assessment model, the practitioner is more interested in finding out about what is right about Herb than what is wrong. Questions to Herb about how he manages to get through the day will provide the opportunity to shift the focus away from deficits and toward his own competency. Herb presents himself as a very hardworking, well-educated man. He is married to his childhood sweetheart, and he works very hard at three jobs to keep his family together. He tries to stay active in his church community. His insight and willingness to change—and his decision to seek help—are additional strengths. Figure 7.3 shows the interactions of the biological, psychological, and social variables in Herb Wilks's life.

EP 2.1.10
(b) a

Advanced
Clinical EP
2.1.10 (b) c

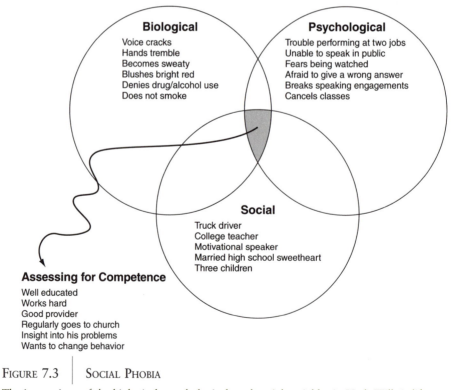

Biological
Voice cracks
Hands tremble
Becomes sweaty
Blushes bright red
Denies drug/alcohol use
Does not smoke

Psychological
Trouble performing at two jobs
Unable to speak in public
Fears being watched
Afraid to give a wrong answer
Breaks speaking engagements
Cancels classes

Social
Truck driver
College teacher
Motivational speaker
Married high school sweetheart
Three children

Assessing for Competence
Well educated
Works hard
Good provider
Regularly goes to church
Insight into his problems
Wants to change behavior

FIGURE 7.3 | SOCIAL PHOBIA

The interactions of the biological, psychological, and social variables in Herb Wilks's life.

Axis I	300.23 Social Phobia
Axis II	V71.09 (No diagnosis)
Axis III	None
Axis IV	Occupational problems
Axis IV	GAF = 75 (during intake)

© Cengage Learning

OBSESSIVE-COMPULSIVE DISORDER

As children, most of us carefully tiptoed down sidewalks in an effort not to step on the cracks. If someone *did* happen to step on a crack, friends joyously chanted, "Stepped on a crack, broke your mother's back." This same process of rituals and superstitions is what drives people with **obsessive-compulsive disorder** (OCD). Even though we weren't sure why we were supposed to avoid "the cracks," we felt that in some way we were protecting our mothers from harm. Most of us can identify with this example, simplistic as it is.

EP 2.1.10
(b) a

What if everyone we know spent their entire lives trying to avoid stepping on cracks—or if they were driven to counting rituals because of being so totally afraid that their every impulse would bring disaster to them or their families? At the very least, it certainly wouldn't feel like a game anymore. In order to distinguish the behaviors representative of obsessive-compulsive disorder, it is important for the social worker to collect, organize, and carefully interpret data from the client's social history. People who are considered obsess*ive* or compuls*ive* are not the same as those who have obsess*ions* or perform compuls*ions*. The difference between the two is more than just the word endings. Obsession is a personality style (with some adaptive features), while "obsessive" represents a mental disorder often considered debilitating.

Persons with obsessive-compulsive disorder are plagued with unwanted, recurrent **obsessions** or **compulsions** (or both). Most of us have experienced, at some time or another, a temporary obsession; for example, when you cannot seem to get the lyrics to a song or an advertising sales pitch out of your mind. It just spins around and around, over and over again. Have you ever gone out for the evening and worried whether you locked your front door or turned off the oven? Sound familiar? Sometimes these thoughts can be initiated by others—say, a coworker asks you the name of an actress in a movie; you know the answer, it's on the tip of your tongue, but you just can't think of it. It starts to bother you. In fact, it bothers you a lot. You might even stop thinking about everything else while you struggle to remember the name of "that" actress. Although you might not recognize it, you are experiencing a mild form of an obsession. The "not knowing" is certainly irritating and bothersome—but after a while you either remember the name of the actress or your need to know diminishes. This is considered perfectly normal because it stops, and does not take over your entire life.

Consider the person who has OCD and fights battles like these every minute of every hour of every day, day after day for most of their lives. Those with clinical obsessions are different from others because they suffer recurrent obsessions and/or compulsions that take over their lives; these obsessions or compulsions are severe enough to be time consuming, cause marked distress, or result in significant impairment in life functioning.

OCD has two components: obsession (which involves thinking, doubts, ideas) and compulsion (which involves doing, acting out, performing), and the disorder is characterized by obsessive, distressing, intrusive thoughts and the related compulsive actions that attempt to neutralize them. At some point, the person realizes that his or her obsessions or compulsions are unreasonable or excessive. The DSM-IV-TR (American Psychiatric Association, 2000) notes that a person's obsessions or compulsions must be time consuming (e.g., taking up more than one hour per day), and they must cause distress or impairment in social, occupational, or school functioning. A diagnosis of OCD requires the presence of *either* obsessions or compulsions alone, or obsessions *and* compulsions together.

Obsession involves the "thinking aspect" or the thoughts and ideas that the person cannot stop thinking about. Obsessions are typically automatic, frequent, distressing for the person, and difficult to control or extinguish. According to the DSM-IV-TR (American Psychiatric Association, 2000, p. 462), obsessions are distinguished by:

- Recurrent and persistent thoughts, impulses, or images that are experienced, at some time during the disturbance, as intrusive and inappropriate and that cause marked anxiety or distress.
- The thoughts, impulses, or images are not simply excessive worries about real-life problems.
- The person attempts to ignore or suppress such thoughts, impulses, or images, or to neutralize them with some other thought or action.
- The person recognizes that the obsessional thoughts, impulses or images are a product of his or her own mind.

There are four major types of obsessions (Mathews, 2009). The most prevalent is associated with symmetry. This includes impulses such as having things aligned in a particular order; for example, pictures on the wall, fringes on a rug, or articles on a desk, or doing something in a specific way. The second most frequent obsession is characterized by forbidden thoughts or actions. This can be seen as repeated ideas such as injuring someone while driving an automobile (e.g., a bump in the road translates into thoughts about running over a body even though it has never actually occurred). There are also aggressive or forbidden obsessive impulses characterized by a fear of shouting obscenities, insults, anti-religious thoughts, or sexual thoughts. The third most commonly occurring obsession is cleaning and a fear of contamination that often leads to washing rituals (Rachman, 2006). Hoarding is the fourth most common obsession (Bloch, Landeros-Weisenberger, Rosario, Pittenger, & Leckman, 2008). Hoarding involves acquiring things. Subsequently the person is afraid to throw something away because it might somehow be important. This could include useless items like old magazines or even used sanitary napkins (Steketee & Frost, 2007a, 2007b). These are the people you hear about in the news where their house is filled from floor to ceiling with junk, leaving just a small path to navigate from room to room. The obsessions are automatic because they come and go on their own accord. Although the person obsesses and may try to resist, ultimately he or she is unable to stop the thoughts (impulses or images) from occurring.

If obsessions are about the thinking, then compulsions are about the doing. Compulsions refer to the specific actions that the person performs, usually repeatedly, in an attempt to try to make the obsession go away. The DSM-IV-TR (American Psychiatric Association, 2000, p. 462) notes that compulsions are defined by:

- Repetitive behaviors or mental acts that the person feels driven to perform in response to an obsession, or according to rules that must be applied rigidly.
- The behaviors or mental acts are aimed at preventing or reducing distress or preventing some dreaded event or situation; however, these behaviors or mental acts either are not connected in a realistic way with what they are designed to neutralize or prevent or are clearly excessive.

The repetitive behaviors that comprise compulsions may include physical or mental acts. This is the hand washing, checking, counting objects a precise number of times, or silently repeating words over and over. The goal of the compulsive behavior is to prevent or reduce anxiety or distress—not to provide the person with pleasure or gratification while performing the act. The lack of pleasure associated with compulsive behavior, and the fact that it is performed in response to obsessive thoughts, help differentiate OCD from other behaviors thought to be compulsive in nature, (e.g., gambling and/or substance abuse).

Compulsions may be manifested in a variety of ways: the person may feel compelled to count, touch, check, wash, buy, hoard (items like newspapers, mail, or string), and/or have everything lined up in perfect symmetrical order. Some compulsions are relatively simple, such as speaking or thinking a word or phrase to protect against an obsessive thought. Other types of compulsions can be exceedingly elaborate—for example, the person may insist on washing in a certain way, dressing in specific clothes, or placing items around the room in exact and complex patterns. These tasks often take many hours to perform, and they can be highly debilitating. People with a contamination obsession and its companion washing compulsion might wash their hands 200 times a day. Hand washing, as shown in the case of Maddy Yarborough (below), has been known to continue even when the skin has been rubbed raw.

If the person manages to resist performing a compulsion (even for a short time), he or she experiences a great deal of anxiety that is relieved only by giving in to the compulsion. Unfortunately, this method of trying to cope becomes a revolving door consisting of obsessions/compulsions that force their way into the person's mind. The process becomes one of thinking = doing = action = relief = thinking = doing = action = relief (on and on and on). The individual experiences extreme distress, especially when these obsessions and compulsions interfere with his or her normal routine, occupation, and other interpersonal activities.

Symptoms of OCD may include:

- A need for both sides of the body to feel even.
- A need to do everything perfectly so that terrible things will not happen.
- A need to prevent contamination (usually by dirt or germs) by repeated hand washing; this cleaning is in lieu of something bad happening.

- A need to hoard things because throwing anything away means something terrible will happen.
- A need for specific counting systems or methods of checking—behaviors generally ruled by magical thinking.
- A strict need for order and symmetry, fueled by superstitions that require, for example, perfectly aligning objects at precise right angles.
- A need to banish sexual thoughts because sex is perceived as "indecent" or as a lewd act; the person may obsess over whether he or she is genuinely aroused by these thoughts.

In summary, the person suffering from OCD generally recognizes the irrational aspect of the obsession as they attempt to quell or suppress these intrusive and tormenting thoughts. In most cases, they recognize their obsessions as a product of their own mind and not something externally imposed—which is an important sign, in that people with delusions *do not* recognize the irrationality of their thoughts and see them as being externally imposed.

PREVAILING PATTERN

EP 2.1.10
(a) b

Onset of OCD ranges from childhood and up to the 30s with a median onset of 19 years of age (Kessler, Berglund, et al., 2005). Keep in mind that all of us have had intrusive or strange thoughts, but they are generally passing worries. The importance of carefully collecting, organizing and interpreting data to distinguish behaviors considered normal and adaptive is underscored. Steketee and Barlow (2002) identified some of the thoughts that people without OCD have had, particularly when they were bored, such as hoping someone doesn't succeed, urges to do something over and over until it feels "just right", thoughts of "unnatural" sexual acts, the thought of blurting something out in church, a fear of offending God, the idea of leaving the curling iron on, or the idea of having left the car unlocked despite knowing it is locked, just to list a few. Unfortunately for those who do develop OCD, the disorder tends to follow a chronic course (Steketee & Barlow, 2002). When engaging with clients, empathy is a key skill in relationship building. In other words, imagine what it is like to live with these thoughts repeating over and over and over.

The lifetime prevalence of OCD is about 1.6 percent for the general US population (Kessler, Berglund, et al., 2005). In a given 1-year period, the prevalence is 1 percent (Kessler, Chiu, et al., 2005). OCD causes considerable distress to those who suffer from it, and those same individuals may also be affected by other mental disorders which could include:

- Body dysmorphic disorder,
- Depression,
- Substance abuse,
- Eating disorders,
- Bipolar disorder,
- Personality disorders,
- Another anxiety disorder,
- Tourette's disorder.

The following case discussion illustrates someone with obsessive-compulsive disorder.

| CASE | THE CASE OF MADDY YARBOROUGH |

I had a message to return the call of Nelson Roberts, M.D., a board-certified dermatologist who often referred clients to me. The following is an account of our telephone conversation.

"Hi, Dr. Roberts, I got the message that you called."

"Hey, I'm really glad you called me back so quickly. The reason for my call is I have a very interesting patient I would like to refer to you. Your social work expertise is always right on target. Her name is Maddy Yarborough. She's 22, and a single mother of two small children. I first saw her about a month ago for a severe case of excoriation (denuding the skin) that was complicated by a superficial infection. She had come in to see me complaining that her hands, knuckles, and elbows were raw and bleeding. Apparently, this young woman has been washing—no, I take that back—she wasn't washing, she was scouring her hands and arms with surgical soap and scrub brushes, sometimes more than 100 times a day. Maddy told me that she sometimes spends six hours a day washing. She's afraid of being contaminated by some antibiotic-resistant flesh-eating bacteria she heard about on television."

All I could think of to say was, "Oh … my … God."

Dr. Roberts went on, "I treated her with a course of topical antiseptic ointment for ten days, but that didn't really help. I saw her back in the office after that, and she had even more inflammation, with an early cellulitis. I started her on oral antibiotics and saw her back in the office about a week later, only to find a persistent and progressive cellulitis. I realized that if I didn't get her to stop washing her hands so much, she would continue to get even worse. So at that point I applied an occlusive dressing to both of her hands." Dr. Roberts took a deep breath. "Finally, I saw signs of significant improvement by the next visit—now she's back with the same symptoms. That's why I'm calling you. I don't think the antibiotic medication treating her skin infection alone is going to make a significant difference. I hope you can help her. She's going to need more help than I can give her."

I told him I'd do my best and thanked him for the referral. I met with Maddy a few days later. She appeared to be in obvious distress about something.

I had barely introduced myself when she blurted out, "I can't remember if I locked the front door of my house."

I asked if she had ever actually left home without locking her front door before. She answered, "Well, I haven't—yet—but I know I did this time. I can't stop worrying about it until I get home and can check on it."

I mentioned that I had spoken with Dr. Roberts, and asked her, "How does it feel when you have these worries?"

"Oh, I can't stop thinking about getting diseases from people," she replied. "That's why I wear a surgical mask and gloves all the time. I took them off just before coming in. Didn't want to scare you. Anyway, that's why I wash my hands all the time, too. I can't stop worrying about germs. I know all about how antibiotics can't treat infections anymore because the germs are mutating so fast that everything is becoming resistant to bacteria. Pretty soon we are going to have a plague on our hands, like the one that caused millions of deaths back in the Middle Ages." The whole time we had been talking, Maddy had been looking around my office and fidgeting. At this point, she leaned over and began to straighten up some books lying on top of my desk. Then she moved on to tidying up my pencils and errant social work journals. Our eyes met, and she smiled sheepishly.

"Sorry. I'm always doing that, and I don't even realize it. My mom is always telling me our kitchen floor is cleaner than a hospital operating room." I asked her to tell me more about that. "Oh, ever since I was, what, maybe 15 or 16, I've been a cleaning nut. I just can't help it. I don't like it when anything is out of place. I guess part of it is because I don't like to throw anything away, so I have to keep it neat. My mother is constantly nagging me to throw away my stacks of magazines. She tells me they are a fire hazard in the house, but I just can't seem to throw them away."

I asked Maddy a series of questions to explore the difficulties she has been experiencing—questions like:

What does she do to get rid of these thoughts in order to put them out of her mind?

continued

Does she try to ignore the thoughts?

Are these her own thoughts, or does she believe they're put in her head by someone or something outside of herself?

Are there any other things she worries about?

Changing the focus slightly, I asked Maddy if she was employed. She replied, "I used to work as a restaurant hostess at a really nice place, but sometimes I had to pitch in and bus tables when it got busy. I guess one of the customers was freaked out by the scabs on my hands and complained to the manager.... and then there were a few times when a line formed at the hostess desk while I was in the ladies' room washing my hands. That job only lasted a couple of days, thank goodness. Arrgh, I was disgusted having to handle some stranger's dirty dishes—ugh, nasty, nasty job!"

I asked Maddy to tell me more about her washing—whether it was a ritual that she always had to do in a particular order. When she described the sequence of her ritual, I also explored what happened if the order of washing was changed. Would she have to start all over again? Maddy looked surprised and said, "Yes. How did you know that?"

After a bit more discussion, I asked again about her employment status, in particular if she had any other jobs in addition to the work as a restaurant hostess. She replied, "I once worked as a salesperson, but the manager wouldn't let me wear gloves when I handled money. The stupid manager told me [mimicking a singsong voice] 'Maddy, you spend entirely too much time rearranging the money drawer and all the clothes on display. You are supposed to *sell* clothes, not fuss over whether they're hanging straight on the hanger.'" Shifting back to her natural voice, she continued, "After that, I looked for jobs where I didn't have to have direct public contact. The only one I've found so far is telemarketing. It meets all my needs, and I don't have to put up with anybody telling me what to do or when to do it. Hey, I'm not getting rich, but it's putting food on my table."

When I asked Maddy about her friends, she answered, "I don't have much time or money to party with people. I'm really lucky that my best friend from high school, Melissa, still hangs out with me. Sometimes, though, she can be just like my mother—constantly nagging me not to be so clean." Maddy looks down at her hands and picks idly at a thread on her bandage. She continued softly, "I think I'm a nice person, but some people see me as strange. I used to have a boyfriend, but he got fed up because he said I always spent more than half our date in the bathroom washing my hands."

"What do you think might happen if you didn't wash your hands?" I asked.

Maddy replied, "Well, first of all, something bad might happen to him. See, he didn't understand that if I didn't wash my hands I couldn't protect him. I know it probably sounds crazy to you—and in a way it sounds crazy to me—but I get so unstrung if I don't wash." Maddy paused for a moment and then added a little testily, "Why does anybody care if I do this? It's not like I'm hurting anybody."

I asked if her difficulties had affected her children at all. She replied, "Did I tell you both of my babies were potty trained before they were a year old? Thank goodness, I live with my mother—I couldn't stand changing dirty diapers, so she took care of that job. Yuk!" With a look of complete distaste, she continued. "I have a hard time just touching my babies—never mind actually holding them—the only way I can do it is if mom does 'the cleansing ritual' first. Otherwise, forget it. They're dirty, you know?"

I asked if she knew why she felt compelled to wash her hands. Maddy looked pensive for a moment and answered, "I know it sounds really strange, but a part of me just has to wash all the time; otherwise, the pressure just builds up inside me until I have to wash—I wash, I feel better—but it only lasts for a little while. Then the thoughts start up again, and, well, you know ... I end up at Dr. Roberts' office."

Maddy denied depression, suicidal ideation, and eating or sleeping problems.

ASSESSMENT SUMMARY   Maddy Yarborough experiences some short-lived relief from obsessive tension but finds no pleasure or gratification from the hand washing ritual itself. She recognizes her obsessive thoughts as somewhat irrational and senseless (unlike someone with schizophrenia who has delusional thoughts). For Maddy, her rigidity around washing seems quite reasonable to her.

The terms *obsessive-compulsive disorder* and *obsessive-compulsive personality disorder* sound similar, but there are several notable distinctions between the two conditions. People with obsessive-compulsive personality disorder (refer to the chapter on the personality disorders) rigorously defend following rules and regulations—but their rigid compulsive perfectionism gets in their way; things have to be done so correctly that they rarely get tasks completed to their total satisfaction. Although there once may have been a degree of perfectionism that was adaptive or encouraged by parents or teachers, the pattern now has become self-defeating.

The person with obsessive-compulsive personality disorder shows behaviors that are punctual, precise, dependable, and conscientious. At the same time, their behavior often wears friendships thin because of the compulsive rigidity. In contrast, Maddy never attempts to justify her behavior, nor does she adhere to the rigidity that influences those with obsessive-compulsive personality disorders. The likelihood that Maddy has social or specific phobias, however, must be considered because of her (almost phobic) concern about contamination. The fear of humiliation in those with social phobias and the need to avoid particular things in those with specific phobias constitute significant differences from OCD. The patterns of the phobias do not hold true in Maddy's situation.

The practitioner's struggle is in shifting the lens away from Maddy's pathology. The competency-based assessment considers all of the various environmental influences in Maddy's life. Despite what could be a potentially debilitating condition, she is coping relatively well. Maddy followed through on the physician's referral, and she complies with medical treatment recommendations. Similarly, she works cooperatively with the social worker. Maddy's mother and Melissa (Maddy's high school friend) provide a support system. In addition, Maddy has found gainful employment that allows her to work at home—a rather clever way to cope with her fear of germs in the workplace. Figure 7.4 illustrates the interactions of the biological, psychological, and social variables in Maddy Yarborough's life.

MADDY YARBOROUGH'S MULTIAXIAL DSM DIAGNOSIS IS AS FOLLOWS:

Axis I	300.3 Obsessive-Compulsive Disorder
Axis II	V71.09 (No diagnosis)
Axis III	682.9 Cellulitis
Axis IV	None
Axis V	GAF = 70 (at intake)

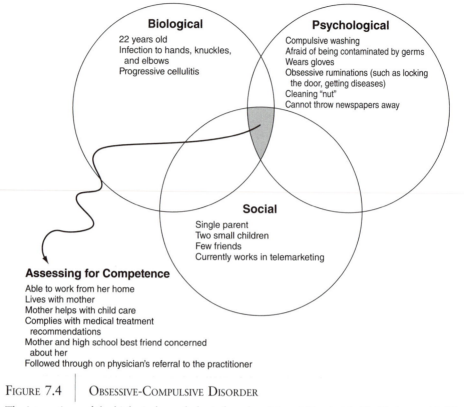

Biological
22 years old
Infection to hands, knuckles,
 and elbows
Progressive cellulitis

Psychological
Compulsive washing
Afraid of being contaminated by germs
Wears gloves
Obsessive ruminations (such as locking
 the door, getting diseases)
Cleaning "nut"
Cannot throw newspapers away

Social
Single parent
Two small children
Few friends
Currently works in telemarketing

Assessing for Competence
Able to work from her home
Lives with mother
Mother helps with child care
Complies with medical treatment
 recommendations
Mother and high school best friend concerned
 about her
Followed through on physician's referral to the practitioner

FIGURE 7.4 | OBSESSIVE-COMPULSIVE DISORDER

The interactions of the biological, psychological, and social variables in Maddy Yarborough's life.

© Cengage Learning

POST-TRAUMATIC STRESS DISORDER

The major reference points for **post-traumatic stress disorder (PTSD)** include the reaction to catastrophic events, such as:

- Witnessing a homicide or suicide.
- Traffic accidents.
- Combat.
- Natural disasters.
- Sexual assault.
- Victimization (such as sexual molestation, robbery, aggravated assault).
- Survivors of holocausts.
- Life events such as domestic violence or a diagnosis of HIV.

EP 2.1.6 b

Keep in mind that close exposure to the trauma seems to be a main aspect of developing PTSD (Friedman, 2009). Combat experiences and sexual assault are the most common traumas associated with PTSD (Barlow & Durand, 2012). The research evidence about who is likely to develop PTSD helps to inform the practitioner about what to look for in the client's history. For example, the plight of war veterans and the after-effects of their experiences suggest that certain types of war events are empirically connected with longer-term problems. Among Vietnam veterans, 18.7 percent developed PTSD, with prevalence rates related to combat exposure in which the soldier experienced the horrors of dying, death, and direct attack (Dohrenwend, Turner, & Turse, 2006). Another example is the now infamous 9/11 tragedy. Among those who lived close to the site of the World Trade Center, 20 percent were diagnosed with PTSD (Galea et al., 2002) We now know that post-traumatic stress disorder can affect not only the "survivors" but also their families, significant others, and society as a whole.

PTSD is a specific set of symptoms that develop after an individual experiences an extreme traumatic stressor (Barlow, 2004). The person reacts to the trauma in several different ways—namely with unmitigated fear, helplessness, feelings of reliving the event, and/or trying to avoid being reminded of it (American Psychiatric Association, 2000). The development of symptoms subsequent to the event is the hallmark of PTSD. The features include exposure to some form of extreme trauma, the intrusive recollection and re-experiencing of the trauma, avoidance of events similar to the traumatic event or circumstance, numbing of general responsiveness, hyperarousal or hypervigilance, changes in aggression, and experiencing persistent symptoms, distress, and impairment in most areas of life.

EP 2.1.7 a

The competency-based assessment takes into account each person's individualized response to overwhelming stress. Some people can simply walk away from a terrible automobile accident in which they have been pried out with the "jaws of life." They never give the incident another thought, other than perhaps the details about getting their car replaced. Others re-experience the automobile accident in their dreams and waking thoughts (daydreaming), endure a numbing of responsiveness, and evade or shun everything that reminds them of the accident. Their lives may become centered exclusively on the traumatic event and accompanied by somatic complaints and chronic anxiety to the extent that difficulties arise in interpersonal functioning. Some people may not react until years afterward; why this happens is not yet clear.

Those suffering from PTSD may not make the connection between the traumatic event and feeling depressed and/or anxious, abusing substances, cognitive difficulties (memory problems or poor concentration), domestic violence, or marital problems. The competency-based assessment provides a conceptual framework to guide the assessment, including specific questions about either a traumatic event or a series of traumatic events experienced over time.

For an assessment of PTSD, symptoms must last for more than 1 month and significantly affect important interpersonal areas of the person's life such as family interaction and employment. The competency-based assessment should take into account coping strategies and adaptations to stressful life events. When there is a history of trauma such as physical battering or child sexual abuse, the pain from the abusive experience may surface later in life as an additional or different disorder such as:

- Borderline personality disorder,
- Addictive disorders,
- Severe mental illness (i.e.: schizophrenia),
- Depression or bipolar disorder,
- Dissociative disorder.

EP 2.1.10
(b) a

PTSD can occur at any time and to anyone. For diagnostic specificity, onset is subdivided into acute and chronic. Acute is indicated when the symptom picture emerges 1 to 3 months after the traumatic event happened. When PTSD continues for longer than 3 months, the specifier chronic is added to the diagnosis. Sometimes those exposed to a traumatic event may not exhibit PTSD features until years afterward (as in the following case of Buddy Jackson). When that happens, the diagnosis is specified with a delayed onset. These specifiers point to the importance of carefully collecting, organizing, and accurately interpreting the client's data.

PREVAILING PATTERN

Interest in returning war veterans helped focus clinical research efforts on trauma, leading to the emergence of the post-traumatic stress disorder diagnosis, which was first named in the DSM-III (American Psychiatric Association, 1980). Historically, social workers have recognized the impact of stressful life events and the challenges they place on a client's life (Gitterman & Germain, 2008). Longitudinal studies suggest PTSD can become a chronic problem, often persisting for decades and sometimes lasting a lifetime (Op Den Velde, Deeg, Hovens, Van Duijn, & Aarts, 2011).

The National Comorbidity Survey Replication (NCS-R), conducted between February 2001 and April 2003, indicated the lifetime prevalence of PTSD was 3.6 percent among men and 9.7 percent among women (National Comorbidity Survey, 2005). Within a 12 month period, prevalence was 1.8 percent among men and 5.2 percent among women. Looking at the rates of PTSD among adolescents between the ages of 12 and 17, Kilpatrick and colleagues (2003) found that the 6-month prevalence was estimated to be 3.7 percent for boys and 6.3 percent for girls. The relationship between gender and post-traumatic stress disorder suggests women tend to be more vulnerable to traumatic events than men.

Among the general population, the prevalence rate of PTSD is 6.8 percent (Kessler, Berglund, et al., 2005), and 3.5 percent during the past year (Kessler, Chiu, et al., 2005). Often, the onset of PTSD is triggered only when the person is in a situation closely resembling the original traumatic event, as we will see in the following case.

| CASE | THE CASE OF BUDDY JACKSON |

"I just don't know where to begin. I mean everything in our lives has been turned upside down. I'm at a loss as to where to go from here," said a tearful Margaret Jackson. I asked her to start at the beginning so I could understand what had happened to bring her to my office.

"I guess I should start by telling you something about Buddy and me," she began again. "We met in 1945, at the USO. I don't imagine you know what I'm talking about, because you seem much too young. But there were literally hundreds of these service clubs in the states and around the world during the war. Servicemen went there for food, dancing, and you know, R & R. The fellas really loved the USOs because, no matter where they were transferred, just about, they knew there would be a place

for them to go and relax and meet people—especially young ladies, I guess. Well, my girlfriends and I attended the club in Philly, where I lived then. My cousin, Wynne, and I went at least once a month."

I could tell by the look on her face that Mrs. Jackson was remembering a magical time in her life.

"You know it's kinda funny, but I remember the night I met Buddy as if it were yesterday. I saw him from across the room; he was so handsome in his Navy uniform. So tall, so ... I don't know, I guess it was love at first sight for me. Anyway, he was due to be discharged soon, and one thing led to another. He found a job as a bookkeeper for a small company in Philadelphia, and the rest is history. We were married a year later, and then the kids started coming. I used to laugh that our life was just like that rhyme from grade school: 'First comes love, then comes marriage, then comes Maggie with a baby carriage.'" Mrs. Jackson smiled broadly and stared into the distance, transported.

"We had three boys. We named the boys after the saints—you know, Christopher, Patrick, and Anthony. Buddy thought the names would help keep the boys out of trouble, but it didn't work. I don't know, maybe Buddy was too strict with them. Oh, he didn't abuse them or anything like that, but he did have a heavy hand sometimes. Once in a while he used to take a belt to them, just to keep them in line. I'm sure you can imagine what a handful three boys can be." Mrs. Jackson sat quietly for a moment before continuing.

"Looking back, I guess you might say Buddy was kind of isolated from the boys. Don't get me wrong, he was always a good father, and a good husband and provider—but every once in a while he'd go on what I'd call a bender. I kinda feel bad telling you this, but Buddy really liked to tie one on every now and then. He never missed much work or anything— he'd just go on what I would call a lost weekend. It was just alcohol, you know. Back then, nobody had heard of all these drugs and things they have now."

I asked Mrs. Jackson where her boys are now.

"Oh, the boys are all grown and out of the house. I guess they are doing as well as can be expected. Christopher, our oldest, has had his fair share of setbacks in his life. He's divorced twice and has a lot of financial troubles. His ex-wife never lets up on him about making alimony payments. Did you know that Saint Christopher is the patron saint of travelers but then later lost his sainthood status? Well, almost. Seems back in the late 1960s, the church started to raise questions about whether he really even existed in the first place. In spite of all that, St. Christopher hangs in there. I guess it's all somehow fitting when I tell you more about my Christopher." Mrs. Jackson seemed oblivious to the non sequitur and continued, "Somehow our Christopher seems to have gotten lost in life—and Patrick, the middle son, unfortunately has been in and out of jail since he was a teenager. I don't know what Patrick's problem is. Buddy has just about stopped letting Patrick come visit me at the house. It's not always Patrick's fault—his boss stole money and blamed the whole thing on Pat. What a scoundrel! ... the boss, I mean."

Mrs. Jackson brightened a little. "Our youngest son, Anthony, is a good boy. He's never been married, and we call him the playboy of the family. He's got a good job, but he lives in California, so we never see him. I'm still waiting to be a grandmother, but I don't think it's going to happen anytime soon." I remained silent, curious to see where the conversation would go next. After a moment, she went on.

"Anyway, this year Buddy and I have been married 50 years. Some of our friends went to Hawaii to celebrate their anniversary, and they suggested we do the same. Buddy and I have never really traveled anywhere past Teaneck, New Jersey. I guess we're just two country bumpkins. I know Buddy didn't want to go to Hawaii, so I told him the trip was free— actually, I lied and told him I won the trip in the San Pedro church raffle. I had some money set aside, and I really wanted to go."

I couldn't help but admire her feisty spirit, but she didn't wait to hear whether or not I was going to pass judgment on her. Instead, she asked if she could have a glass of water. After a rather long swallow, she continued. "The trip was supposed to be the thing dreams are made of. You know ... a second honeymoon?" I nodded my head encouragingly; she proceeded. "Hawaii in December, what could be better? Well, maybe I'm getting ahead of myself. I guess I should go back and tell you that Buddy was stationed in 1941 at Pearl Harbor, on December 7th. You know, people call it The Day of Infamy—but, in 50 years' time, Buddy never talked about that day, or about the war, for that matter. It was an unwritten rule in our house; you just didn't talk about Pearl Harbor or what happened in the war. Even when our boys were growing up, they weren't allowed to ask him any questions. If a documentary came on television about the war, Buddy either turned it off or walked out of the room. After a while, we just got used to the way he was about it. All I ever knew was that Buddy was hospitalized for a few weeks after Pearl Harbor with some kind of shrapnel injury. He has this big old scrape on the side of his body. But he never talked about it, and I didn't want to be too nosy, you know—so I really don't know for sure what happened."

Maggie was quiet for what seemed like a long moment. I asked how she was doing. "Oh, I'm alright. It's just difficult to tell you about this part," she replied.

continued

"I can understand that," I said.

She blew her nose and began once more. "Well, there we were in Oahu. We couldn't have asked for a nicer flight over to Hawaii, nicer weather, or a nicer hotel. In fact, we met several couples on the airplane who were flying to Hawaii for their wedding anniversaries, too. Anyway, Buddy and I met this one couple, Gert and Abe, sitting next to us on the plane. Get this, Abe was a gunnery officer in Pearl Harbor—such a small world, isn't it? Well, Gert told me all about how Abe shot down some enemy airplanes and earned a Bronze Star. She said they planned this trip so Abe could have a reunion with the guys he served with. When I realized that our trip coincided with the 55th anniversary of Pearl Harbor, well you could have knocked me over with a feather. Imagine, of all the lousy timing. I had been so caught up in the idea of Hawaii and luaus and leis—I never once thought about Pearl Harbor even being there! Now, with it being the 55th anniversary, how could we not go?" Maggie had become somewhat tearful and she reached for several more tissues. After another sip of water, she continued.

"I can't remember when I've talked so much about this. I can't seem to stop now that the floodgates are opened. Are you sure you're okay listening to me go on and on?"

I replied, "It sounds as if you have a lot to say."

Maggie looked surprised and said, "Why, yes, I guess I do. Well, we did some sightseeing and everything was fine—or I should say I *thought* everything was fine. I found Buddy walking the floor at night at the hotel. When he did sleep, he seemed so restless and agitated, almost like he was having a bad dream. I figured he might be feeling the effects of jet lag, you know, the difference in time? Me, I'm fine. No problems eating, sleeping, or anything. I'm soaking up the sun and having lots of fun. I'm busy being a tourist and having a ball. Buddy was more quiet than usual, but I didn't think much of it. I noticed he took a few extra blood pressure pills, but he said not to worry about it." I noticed that Mrs. Jackson was beginning to "worry" the tissue she was holding. But she went on.

"One day we met Abe and Gert leaving the hotel. They were on their way to visit the Pearl Harbor Naval Shipyard. On the spur of the moment, Abe asked us if we wanted to go with them. They were going to visit the memorial dedicated to the *USS Arizona* battleship. I said yes right away, but Buddy was quiet a long time. He asked Abe if he'd be willing to wait an extra minute so he could get something from our hotel room. Everybody got cozy in the taxicab, and we're waiting for Buddy to join us. Well, out of the front door of the hotel comes Buddy, and he's wearing a flak jacket—something I never saw before. It looked burned in several places and was ripped up pretty good, too." She looked up at me and said with a kind of wonder, "You know what I thought? All that went through my mind was that that jacket could use a really good cleaning."

I couldn't help laughing out loud, but she continued with her story.

"Buddy settled into the taxi, and everything seemed to be all right. When we got to the Memorial Visitor Center, Abe and Buddy sort of wandered off together, and Gert and I got interested in one of the National Park Service rangers detailing the battle that took place. We saw a 20-minute film documenting some of the actual footage of the attack, went through a small library, and found a few things to buy in the gift shop. I thought the memorial was a wonderful tribute to the men and women who died there, and it was done in really nice taste. Gert and I got to see some dioramas that explained exactly what happened that day. So many of our people were killed—and so many ships and planes were destroyed. I remember thinking about how the ex-servicemen, like Buddy and Abe, were dealing with the Japanese visitors who were also there. I started to wonder what it must have been like at that day for Buddy.

"Well, anyway, when the 'boys' came back, we took a shuttle boat out to where the *USS Arizona* sank after it was hit. The tour people pointed out all the interesting areas like Battleship Row and Ford Island—that's where the beginning battle took place. Did you know that seven of those enormous battleships were destroyed? I remember, I kept peeking over at Buddy to see if he was okay. He didn't acknowledge me. He seemed like he was in his own world."

She went on, "One thing that impressed me was how quiet everyone was when we were riding over to the *USS Arizona*. It was so eerie. You could hardly believe there was a bustling city not more than ten minutes away. Anyway, we walked up the gangplank, and, I have to tell you, I had heard people complain about the memorial being too plain. Well, I don't agree—it isn't plain—I thought it was a perfect balance between respect, serenity, and dignity. We were really lucky because when we got there the earlier crowds had already thinned out, and only about 30 people were walking around taking pictures. Buddy immediately walked away from me, and I guessed he wanted to be alone. I drifted over to the memorial railing, you know, to look over the side. It's true what they say; you can still see evidence of an oil slick floating on top of the water. Imagine that—after all these years. Anyway, I was wearing the lei the hotel gave me when we first arrived. I was so touched about being there that I took the lei off, dropped it in the water, and said a prayer for the dear souls who had died that day. I watched my lei float off on the oil slick and the current."

"That was a nice thing to do," I offered.

"I realized that it must be very hard for people to come back here and deal with what happened during the war. I started thinking that maybe I should be with Buddy, so I started looking around for him. He was at the far end of the memorial in what's called the Shrine Room. I could see he was reaching up to touch some of the names of people who died. I started to walk over to him, when all of a sudden a loud commotion happened exactly where I last saw him. I thought Oh, Lord, no! But I felt in my bones that something was wrong with Buddy. It could not have been more than 20 seconds, but by the time I got to him I had to push my way through a small crowd of people. He was lying on the floor, sort of wrapped into a tight ball. He was rocking side to side, and screaming, 'Get down, hurry up, and get over here! The planes are coming, hurry, hurry, hurry! John, Harry, Paul, Billy, get over here. Help me with this. We've got to undo the ties on the planes or they'll be destroyed just sitting on the field. Hurry, hurry, hurry. No! No! No! Get away from there. No! No! Nooooooo! Oh, noooooooooo!'"

As tears trickled down her cheeks, Maggie said, "I can still hear Buddy's tormented screams. One of the Service Park rangers gently asked me if Buddy had seen military action here. I told him, yes, that Buddy had been at Pearl. The ranger said he'd seen this reaction a lot of times over the years. He said it's post-traumatic stress disorder, and of course I'd heard of it with the boys from Vietnam and that Desert Storm war—but how on earth could it happen after more than 50 years? The ranger didn't know much about that, but he told me, 'Ma'am, your husband should get some kind of counseling once you get him home.'"

Maggie reached for more tissues and kept going. "Somehow we got Buddy stabilized, but he refused to leave the ship, saying he had something he had to do. Buddy took two small boxes from the pocket of his flak jacket. When he opened up the boxes, I saw two beautiful Purple Heart medals nestled in the white silk lining. He walked over to the railing of the memorial and silently dropped each medal into the water. I saw him salute, turn on his heel, and we walked away. He never once looked back. We left for home the next day."

"He hasn't talked much about what happened at Pearl Harbor, except to say that he saw his four best friends die—and he was stranded for hours guarding their dead bodies. Apparently, he saved the lives of several people when he erected a temporary shelter from flying debris. He also saved a man's leg by tying off a severed artery." Mrs. Jackson dabbed at her eyes and looked at me. "You think you know somebody after 50 years, but I guess you never know. Buddy was a war hero, and no one knew about it. It just breaks my heart to think how scared he must have been—just a 20-year-old boy in the middle of a raging battle. Buddy just hasn't been the same since we returned from our trip. Do you think you can help him?"

I was a little overwhelmed by how much Mrs. Jackson had to say. It seemed like she'd been holding all of this in for a long time—but the significant facts of Buddy's PTSD seemed pretty clear to me. In an effort to reassure her, I looked squarely at Ms. Jackson and said, "Let's begin with your husband's reactions to the war memorial. Later we can work on how all of this has affected the family. How does that sound?"

EP 2.1.10
(b) a

ASSESSMENT SUMMARY   In general, post-traumatic stress disorder must be differentiated from other mental disorders through careful questioning by the practitioner about the presence of previous traumatic experiences. The key assessment skills of collecting, organizing, and interpreting client data are highlighted in this vignette. Mrs. Jackson shares a great deal of information about her life story, and the practitioner's challenge is to listen for the indicators of Buddy's diagnosis of PTSD. Of course the diagnosis of PTSD will not be formally assigned until the practitioner sees Buddy first hand. Although the 50-year delay of Buddy Jackson's symptoms is quite atypical, his traumatic episode is typical. The fact that Buddy experienced the severe trauma of combat and the death of several of his closest friends, coupled with his avoidance of talking about these experiences, contributes to the diagnosis of PTSD. There is no evidence to suggest Buddy was experiencing an anxiety or mood disorder, because his life history is not consistent with those symptoms. Adjustment disorder was not considered a factor because it is more often associated with ordinary stressors, such as the impending birth of a child, a divorce, or even going back to graduate school.

PTSD may go undetected because substance abuse frequently masks the debilitating symptoms, as seen in Buddy's situation (Sadock, Sadock, & Ruiz, 2009). Acute stress disorder (ASD) can be considered when all the elements of PTSD are present, but for less than 1 month. If symptoms persist beyond that time, the disorder is no longer considered acute. The practitioner begins by listening for the full spectrum of symptoms that last much longer, as seen with Buddy Jackson. In Buddy's situation, a true war trauma occurred. He attempted to deal with his experiences by not talking about them—so, when he and his wife visited the site of the trauma, his memories emerged.

In contrast to people with PTSD or ASD, those with malingering disorder cannot sustain their symptoms when there is no secondary material gain (e.g., insurance or disability claims). The avoidant behavior seen in people with phobias may be similar to that seen in PTSD. However, people with phobias usually acknowledge the senselessness of their behavior—Buddy Jackson's behavior was readily understandable. It is noteworthy that those with malingering disorder or a factitious disorder may present a history compatible with PTSD. (If needed, refer to the glossary for definitions of terms not yet covered in detail.)

Advanced
Clinical EP
2.1.10 (b) c

Assessing Buddy's condition solely in terms of whether or not he meets the DSM criteria fails to appreciate the ways in which he has coped with life's challenges. Competency-based practice emphasizes the importance of investigating Buddy's coping strategies that serve to reinforce and improve his adaptation to life situations, circumstances, and events. This approach to the assessment focuses on Buddy's assets rather than his defects. Buddy has had a long-term and stable marriage, and his wife is very devoted to him. Additionally, he made an effort to be a parent to his sons and sustained long-term employment. Though troubled by the symptoms of PTSD, he is very proud of his military service record. In fact, he proved himself a war hero at a very young age. Figure 7.5 shows the interactions of the biological, psychological, and social variables in Buddy Jackson's life.

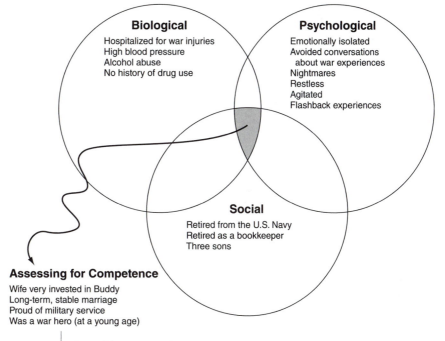

Biological
Hospitalized for war injuries
High blood pressure
Alcohol abuse
No history of drug use

Psychological
Emotionally isolated
Avoided conversations
  about war experiences
Nightmares
Restless
Agitated
Flashback experiences

Social
Retired from the U.S. Navy
Retired as a bookkeeper
Three sons

Assessing for Competence
Wife very invested in Buddy
Long-term, stable marriage
Proud of military service
Was a war hero (at a young age)

FIGURE 7.5 | POST-TRAUMATIC STRESS DISORDER
The interactions of the biological, psychological, and social variables in Buddy Jackson's life.

© Cengage Learning

BUDDY JACKSON'S MULTIAXIAL DSM DIAGNOSIS IS AS FOLLOWS:

Axis I	309.81 Post-traumatic Stress Disorder, Delayed Onset
Axis II	V71.09 (No diagnosis)
Axis III	Rule out alcohol abuse
	History of war injury
Axis IV	Problems with his children
Axis V	GAF = 70 (at intake)

© Cengage Learning

ACUTE STRESS DISORDER

Aspects of **acute stress disorder (ASD)** were identified in the DSM-I under the category entitled "gross stress reaction." Specific characteristics of this disorder were initially covered under the diagnosis of PTSD in the DSM-III (American Psychiatric Association, 1980). Being relatively new to the DSM-IV-TR, the symptom picture of ASD looks a lot like PTSD. The only difference is the emphasis on the severe reaction that some people have within the first month immediately following a trauma. There is some debate over whether the diagnostic criteria (especially its emphasis on dissociation) accurately reflect the aftereffects of someone's traumatic experience (Harvey & Bryant, 2002). The inclusion of ASD was not accompanied by extensive research, and the research that has been done is still in its early stages.

EP 2.1.3 a

The practitioner's skill in distinguishing and evaluating multiple sources of knowledge, including research-based knowledge and practice wisdom, is a key part of the diagnosis of ASD. For instance, there have been studies identifying the presence of ASD in survivors in several different types of events such as motor vehicle accidents, typhoons, industrial accidents, violent assaults, burn victims, or those who have experienced a robbery or mass shootings, to list a few (see, for example, Elklit, 2002; Holeva, Tarrier, & Wells, 2001). The practitioner must determine that the symptom picture emerges shortly after the trauma and dissipates within a month for a diagnosis of ASD. If the person does not recover within that 1-month time frame, then the diagnosis changes to PTSD. The individual with ASD is more likely to have the enduring symptoms associated with PTSD when the traumatic event evokes feelings of intense fear, helplessness, or horror.

While we cannot predict when a traumatic event will happen, we can predict that there will be an emotional impact. For some people, simply learning that such a traumatic event has happened to a loved one or close friend can cause problems. Likewise, just witnessing a horrific event may trigger symptoms. It has become clear that the effects of trauma are not limited to the people directly affected by the experience—**secondary traumatization** has the potential to affect others as well (Marcus & Dubi, 2006). Secondary traumatization is defined as "the cumulative transformation in the inner experience" that comes about as a result of empathic engagement with another's trauma (Pearlman & Saakvitne, 1995, p. 31). Frequently, rescue workers and health care professionals (including social workers) who are involved in caring for trauma survivors are affected by secondary traumatization. These helpers may experience physical symptoms and emotional reactions analogous to those exhibited by the trauma survivor (Hesse, 2002). In essence, professionals who extend themselves to trauma survivors are included into a secondary circle of trauma (Inbar & Ganor, 2003). Symptoms are nearly identical to those of PTSD except exposure to the traumatic event is through "witnessing, hearing, and connecting—time and time again—with the painful material of others" (Knight, 2004, p. 82).

Much like ASD, sleeplessness, irritability, anxiety, emotional withdrawal, avoidance of certain tasks, isolation, feelings of helplessness and inadequacy, and even flashbacks are among the symptoms. Those who seem to be the most affected are closest to the survivors (Morrissette, 2004). This includes family members, rescue workers, and other helpers. Clearly, those who work with people suffering from the aftermath of traumatic events suffer themselves because of the work. Secondary trauma is commonly referred to as **compassion fatigue** (Figley, 2002). This reaction is a major risk for those helpers who are reluctant to identify themselves as suffering from the symptoms of secondary trauma. They tend to see themselves as "supports" for the survivors and fail to admit (or even realize) they need help for themselves—despite hearing and seeing tragic stories of suffering and loss for days, weeks, or months at a time during disaster recovery work (Fullerton, Ursano & Wang, 2004).

By definition, disasters are public tragedies with dramatic media coverage that captures the attention of people far beyond those directly affected. The recent natural disasters all over the world have focused attention on compassion fatigue as well as the traumas associated not only with loss of life but also with the physical and economic destruction of entire communities. An earthquake beneath the Indian Ocean near Sumatra on December 26, 2004, resulted in a devastating tsunami in Thailand and other countries as far away as the west coast of Africa. The disasters continue as seen by the 2010 catastrophic earthquake in Haiti just outside the capital city of Port au Prince. Here, thousands of people died or were injured, and approximately 1 million were left homeless (CBS News, 2010). The earthquake that took place in China early March 2011 adds to the list. As a result of this latter disaster, 26 people died and over 300 were injured; a third were seriously injured (Yan, 2011). Aftershocks caused extensive damage, and approximately 127,000 people were forced to evacuate. Ironically, the earthquake struck one day before a much larger earthquake struck the Pacific coast of Japan that also generated a tsunami. The resulting damage caused a number of nuclear incidents, primarily, the meltdown at three nuclear power plants causing the evacuation of at least 600,000 surrounding residents (Branigan, 2011).

In the United States the 2004 Atlantic hurricane season proved to be one of the deadliest and most costly events ever—at least 3,132 deaths occurred as a result of the flooding rains or winds, and the physical damage ran to approximately $42 billion dollars (National Climactic Data Center, 2004). Four hurricanes (named Charley, Frances, Ivan, and Jeanne) made landfall in the southeastern United States within a 6-week period of time in 2004. Hurricane Charley came ashore near Port Charlotte, Florida, on August 13. Frances moved onto the coast of Florida in the early hours of September 5, eventually striking the Florida panhandle. Ivan initially landed near Gulf Shores, Alabama, and then reorganized and crossed into south Florida on September 21. Jeanne officially hit at Hutchinson Island on Florida's east coast on September 25. Frances and Jeanne hit nearly the exact same location within three weeks of each other, and floodwaters were brought to near-record levels.

Adding to the stress of these storms, studies have shown that the number and strength of hurricanes tend to follow a 50- to 70-year cycle (Knutson & Tuleya, 2004). The following year, hurricanes Katrina, Rita, and Wilma struck the southeastern United States, distinguishing the 2005 hurricane season by both its early beginning and the number of intense storms. For the first time since the current naming system was introduced in 1952, all 21 names on the year's list were used, and the National Hurricane Center named six later storms with Greek letters. Millions of people were affected by being displaced or left entirely homeless (American Red Cross, 2005). Katrina holds the record as the deadliest and the most costly storm in the United States since 1928 (National Climactic Data Center, 2006). Katrina alone caused more than 1,300 deaths, and on final count will probably cost more than $100 billion dollars. Coordinating efforts to provide relief challenged the entire nation. Thousands worked to provide the basic necessities of food, water, shelter, health care, and critical relief supplies as well as financial donations (American Red Cross, 2005). The early spring of 2011 found deadly storms pounding the Midwest, extending from the great lakes southward to the Texas Gulf Coast, causing a deadly path of floods and tornadoes (Environment News Service, 2011).

Extreme distress, no matter what its source, is associated with adjustment problems for both survivors and helpers (Halpern & Tramontin, 2007). Growing recognition of transient and normative stress reactions has paved the way for the conceptualization of ASD and its ultimate inclusion in the DSM. Our country's recent experiences with disasters, both natural and manmade, have further highlighted acute stress disorder, which is the most common psychiatric problem following a traumatic event (Bryant & Harvey, 2000). A person has a greater risk of developing problems when faced with human-caused trauma. For example, the terrorist attacks in New York City and Washington, DC, on September 11, 2001, injured and killed thousands, and many more felt their traumatic impact. This tragedy will forever be a part of a nation's memory and is characterized as a day of violence and disaster. For numerous individuals and their families, life will never be the same.

PREVAILING PATTERN

Acute stress disorder and PTSD share many of the same symptoms (American Psychiatric Association, 2000), including:

- Re-experiencing the trauma through recurrent dreams (or nightmares) of the event or flashbacks and intrusive memories.
- Unrest in situations that bring back the painful memories of the trauma.
- Avoidance of things associated with the event including not wanting to talk about the event or experience.
- Loss of emotion (emotional numbing).
- Reduced interest in others and the outside world.
- Persistent increased arousal (e.g., constant watchfulness, irritability, being easily startled, outbursts of rage, insomnia, problems concentrating, problems falling or staying asleep).

PTSD is very much like ASD but develops weeks to months (maybe even years) after a disaster. Acute stress disorder occurs within the first month after a disaster and lasts from 2 days to 4 weeks. ASD is also distinguished from PTSD by a greater emphasis on distressing dissociative symptoms. The diagnosis can only be made within the first month after a traumatic event. A person with ASD may experience three or more of the following dissociative symptoms (American Psychiatric Association, 2000):

- A sense of numbing, detachment, or absence of emotional responsiveness. (The person may have a diminished ability to experience pleasure; anxiety and irritability are common.)
- A reduced awareness of one's surroundings, often reported as being in a daze.
- Derealization (the external environment feels remote and unreal).
- Depersonalization (a feeling that one's body is unreal, changing, or dissolving).
- Dissociative amnesia (cannot remember an important part of the trauma).

The person suffering from either of these disorders also shows a marked avoidance of the stimuli (thoughts, feelings, conversations, activities, specific places or people) that arouse recollections of the trauma. The disturbance is severe enough to cause impairment in at least one of the following areas:

- Ability to cope with marked distress from the symptoms.
- Social, occupational, or personal functioning.
- Ability to seek help (legal and/or medical) or ability/willingness to share the experience with family or close friends.

The prevalence of ASD is unknown, but a fair assumption is that it is proportionate to both the severity of the trauma and the extent of exposure to the trauma. Symptoms may affect any sex or age group, and the onset usually starts during or immediately after the trauma. Those who have been exposed to prior trauma, have had a previous diagnosis of PTSD, or have experienced other psychiatric difficulties, such as depression or a history of psychiatric treatment, are at greater risk for ASD (Bryant & Harvey, 2000). Many people recover as soon as they are removed from the traumatic situation and given appropriate support (i.e., understanding, empathy, the opportunity to talk about what happened and their reactions to it). Often the retelling of "the story" in itself is beneficial. The author recalls hosting a dinner party several years ago for close friends who experienced Hurricane Jeanne. One couple brought along pictures of their destroyed home. Although my friends tried very hard to engage in small talk at the dinner table, the conversation kept drifting back to their experiences with the storm. The telling and retelling of their encounters with the storm seemed to help them to let go of some of the feelings associated with their loss.

The following case of Louise Ann Brown illustrates acute stress disorder.

CASE | THE CASE OF LOUISE ANN BROWN

Louise Ann Brown is a single mother of two children, and she was feeling "blessed." After Hurricane Katrina, Louise Ann, her daughter Vernika, age 14, and son Darius, age 11, had lost a lot ... the house, her job and ... well, everything. Even the kids' school was gone, destroyed in the storm. She felt very lucky to relocate to Paris, Tennessee, a small town in the western part of the state due north of Memphis. Everybody there was so helpful. Louise Ann admitted that she missed the familiar sights, smells, and sounds of her home in New Orleans. She especially remembers the smell of chicory-roasted coffee ... and those beignets! She smiled to herself remembering how one of her new neighbors had called them "big nets." Paris is the home of the world's biggest fish fry, so she reckons she'll have to get used to the local delicacies. "Whatever," she thought. "I feel safe here, and folks are just so nice." The warm welcome offered by the people of Paris made missing home just a little easier.

After all, her memories of the storm were not particularly pleasant. Louise Ann and Darius had gone out for last minute-hurricane supplies, so they were not even at home when Vernika was rescued. As Louise Ann went out the front door, she remembered turning to wave at her daughter, who was talking on her cell phone with her best friend. No one anticipated how fast the water would come up—and the flooded streets made it impossible to get back to the house.

When Vernika tells the story of how she was rescued, her fingers absentmindedly fiddle with strands of her braided hair. She remembers going up to the attic, and when the water continued to rise she climbed out a small window on the side of the house. Somehow she managed to get up on the roof. Vernika tried to get her cell phone to work so she could call her mother. All she got was a busy signal. "Next thing you know," Vernika said, "two men came floating by my house in a boat. That was so weird, seeing somebody float by the roof of your house. One of the men had a hatchet, and he had to cut a hole in the side of the house to reach me," she added. "I kept hearing a voice calling, 'Vernika,

continued

Vernika' over and over, and finally I realized that the other man in the boat was one of our neighbors—it was him, calling to me." Vernika seemed as if she were simply recalling a dream. "He's a fireman, and somehow he knew where Mama and Darius were, so he took me right over to them. I didn't realize how lucky that was until I saw all the news later on about missing people and stuff." She kept wrapping one of her braids around her finger. "Mostly, we just hung out on the streets with the folks from our church. It was *so* hot—that's what I remember—how hot it was. No electricity, no water, and piles of junk and garbage everywhere! The hard part was not being able to bathe and not having food and water unless we went out hunting for it."

Vernika went on to explain that, while all this was happening to her, her best friend was also trapped on the roof of her house. "I heard she's in Springfield now with 12 of her aunts, uncles, and cousins, all in one house." Vernika pauses. "I feel lucky that me and Mama and Darius can be in our own apartment instead of being crammed in with relatives. Some people from our church knew this family, here in Paris, who had a place where we could stay." Vernika had overheard Louise Ann telling somebody that they were able to stay rent-free in the apartment until they could get settled. "I didn't know folks could be so nice, but I guess you pull together when something like this happens," added Vernika. "To tell you the truth, I usually zoned out at church when the preacher was giving his sermon—but now, after how good people have been to us, I think I finally know what he means about doing good works."

Louise Ann had taken small steps to get her little family relocated to Tennessee. "Making a game plan and being proactive really helped," she stated proudly. Her first item of business was to enroll the kids in school. She worked hard to keep to a regular daily routine with normal times for sleeping and eating—that way she felt she could cut down on the stress of relocating for the kids. She also found a wonderful church community at Fairview Baptist, and the members there were a great support. Next, she wanted to get Darius registered to play baseball. He had been on a team back home, so Louise Ann thought it would be important for Darius to be able

to keep doing something he enjoyed. She marveled at Vernika's adjustment—her daughter loved her new school and made several new friends right away. "Planning for our future and taking small steps made things so much easier for us," Louise Ann remarked.

The best part of living in Paris was Louise Ann's new job. She had worked for a bank in New Orleans, but her new position was a step up, to head teller. The benefits were great and the pay raise sure came in handy. Actually, she had been at her new job just about a week when the tornado hit.

"It was Tuesday, November 15, 2005—but I remember it like it was yesterday. Well, I remember parts of the day really well—other parts are just a blur," said Louise Ann. "I was busy helping with the cash tally, and before I knew what was happening, it hit. It was such a surreal moment. My hand was shaking so much I could hardly hold on to things. All at once, there was a huge roar outside and the wind really started blowing. The windows creaked and rattled. Then the building actually started to groan. I was so scared." Louise Ann was almost rigid in her chair as she recounted the experience. "I had almost lost Vernika in Katrina, and this time I didn't think I was going to get out. All I could think about was that I would never see my kids again. It was so hard to wrap my brain around what was happening. The tornado watches were issued throughout the morning, and on the news they talked about how dangerous tornadoes are—but they also said how unusual tornadoes are for mid-November, so I just didn't think much about it." Louise Ann looked down and shook her head slowly. "You know, you can prepare for a hurricane. It's on the news for days ahead ... but a tornado? It hits all of a sudden. I don't know which is worse. I guess it's a tornado 'cause you never know when it will hit. I tried to stay calm through it all—and at the time everybody applauded me for handling the situation—but after that I just couldn't cope. Heck, I can't even remember how I got home that day."

Even though the event ended safely for Louise Ann, physically at least, she no longer felt competent or able to return to work. She couldn't seem to shake the emotional burden precipitated by her close involvement in the tornado. The bank building she was in survived intact—but at least 30 nearby houses were completely destroyed, and severe damage was widespread throughout the surrounding area. There were constant reminders of the storm everywhere. "Even the Henry County emergency management center took a direct hit from one of the tornadoes and was forced to relocate," Louise Ann recalled.

After the tornado, Louise Ann no longer wanted to visit friends, constantly felt on the alert, experienced distress whenever she tried to return to work, and was convinced that her family was in danger even after the incident was over. Just before the tornado hit, she remembered hearing on the radio at work that some high school sports games were canceled that day, but the seriousness of it all didn't seem to hit until a few days later. She stopped watching the news on TV altogether. When Louise Ann saw all the devastation caused by the tornado, she just couldn't believe this really had happened to her. All of the feelings seemed to go out of her, and Louise Ann just felt numb. Then she began to have trouble concentrating—but the nights were the worst; after the kids were in bed and asleep, the trembling started.

For the first few days after the tornado, she would sleep for only two hours a night because, "my heart was pounding, thump, thump," she recounted. "I kept remembering the tornado." All Louise Ann could think about was her narrow miss with the tornado.

Luckily, within the first three weeks following the tornado, a conscientious human resources manager at the bank recognized the symptoms of acute stress disorder and referred Louise Ann to the Employee Assistance Program for crisis counseling. Louise Ann subsequently saw a social worker who specialized in the treatment of the emotional aspects of trauma. "I thought I'd try it out—and I found it really useful. I had only one really long session with the social worker, and then I spoke to her on the phone a couple of times as well. She told me my response is normal. She said strong reactions are common during and in the days and even weeks following these kinds of disasters. When she told me that I had good reasons to be upset, I really felt a lot better—that was encouraging. It wasn't a magical cure or anything like that, but it was really helpful." Louise Ann has made a full recovery and is once again back on the job and enjoying her new life in Paris, Tennessee.

ASSESSMENT SUMMARY   Prior to the tornado, Louise Ann enjoyed a close relationship with her kids, her new friends, and colleagues at work. She was enjoying success at her job and was involved in her church community. You could characterize Louise Ann as "well adjusted," especially considering that she had just been through the displacement caused by Hurricane Katrina. Under the circumstances, her response to the tornado was an understandable (and common) reaction to an abnormally disturbing event. Louise Ann had no prior history of substance use or depression, nor had she taken any medications for a medical condition that could better explain her symptoms.

For an accurate assessment for ASD, symptoms must develop within 1 month of a traumatic event. In this situation, Louise Ann's symptoms emerged almost immediately—her hands started shaking uncontrollably, and she had difficulty grasping the enormity of the event. As she said, "It was so hard to wrap my brain around what was happening." She worried about never seeing her children again and began to feel numb. She hardly remembers driving home after the storm. Shortly thereafter, Louise Ann experienced difficulty concentrating, felt unable to cope with work, and was not sleeping well. She refused to watch the news on TV, and her thoughts were preoccupied with memories of the tornado. Fortunately, her symptoms abated within a month's time, thus confirming the diagnosis of ASD.

Advanced
Clinical EP
2.1.10 (b) c

The competency-based assessment looks to a client's coping strategies to reinforce and improve adaptation to life situations, circumstances, and events. Fortunately, Louise Ann's employer was able to recognize the symptoms of acute stress and made a timely referral to an appropriate practitioner. In addition, Louise Ann

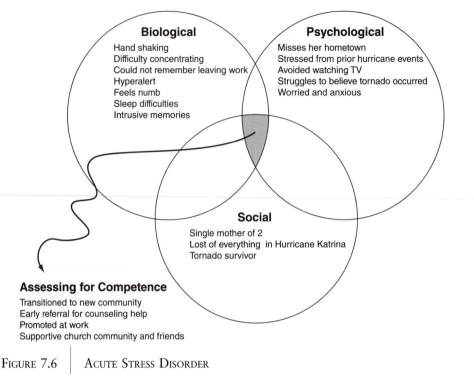

FIGURE 7.6 | ACUTE STRESS DISORDER

The interactions of the biological, psychological, and social variables in Louise Ann Brown's life.

© Cengage Learning

had survived Hurricane Katrina and was making a smooth transition to a new community. She was also attentive to helping her children make the transition from a familiar home in New Orleans to her new community in Tennessee. Figure 7.6 summarizes the interactions of the biological, psychological, and social variables in Louise Ann Brown's life.

LOUISE ANN BROWN'S MULTIAXIAL DSM DIAGNOSIS IS AS FOLLOWS:

Axis I	308.3 Acute Stress Disorder
	Rule out PTSD
Axis II	V71.09 (No diagnosis)
Axis III	None
Axis IV	None
Axis V	GAF = 65 (at intake)

© Cengage Learning

GENERALIZED ANXIETY DISORDER

In contrast to people with the anxiety disorders already discussed, individuals with **generalized anxiety disorder (GAD)** do not focus on any particular object, situation, or person. Rather, the anxiety they suffer pervades their entire lives and significantly interferes in all aspects of life functioning. Most of us understand that experiencing some worry is part of the normal human condition, but those with generalized anxiety disorder are considered incessant worrywarts—they worry about everything, even when there is nothing obvious going on in their lives to provoke their concerns. This uncontrollable worry is the most salient feature of generalized anxiety disorder.

PREVAILING PATTERN

Slightly over 3 percent (or 3.1 percent) of the United States population meets the criteria for generalized anxiety disorder during a given 1-year period (Kessler, Chiu, & Walters, 2005). At some point in their lifetime, 5.7 percent will be affected making it one of the most common anxiety disorders (Kessler, Berglund, Demler, Jin, & Walters, 2005). GAD refers to what used to be termed **free-floating anxiety**, or the kind of anxiety experienced but not attached to any specific situation. If you were to ask someone with GAD, "Do you find yourself worrying a lot about minor things?" do not be surprised by a "yes" answer. In essence, the person with GAD focuses his or her anxiety and worry on minor everyday events as well as major life events. The focus of these worries differs with age (Albano & Hack, 2004; Ayers, Thorp, & Weatherell, 2009; Furr, Tiwari, Suvey, & Kendall, 2009). Typically, children worry whether they are competent in sports, academics, or social skills. Adults center their worries on potential misfortunes that may happen to their children, health, and job responsibilities, as well as minor problems such as being on time for appointments. As might be expected, older adults focus on health concerns. The etiology of GAD is not clear, and unfortunately little is known about its cause and predisposing features. Since worry is such a central component of GAD, one proposal for the upcoming DSM-5 is to rename the disorder to generalized worry disorder (Andrews et al., 2010). In addition, the DSM-5 proposes including muscle tension as the principle physical symptom.

Individuals with the symptoms of generalized anxiety disorder generally tough it out on their own—if help is sought, it is usually from a primary care physician rather than a social worker or other mental health practitioner. Although GAD can occur at any age, it is most prevalent among those who are under the age of 30. The following case vignette illustrates the symptoms and effects of generalized anxiety disorder on an individual's life.

CASE | THE CASE OF BARBARA "BARBIE" CHAPMAN

Barbara Chapman is a 34-year-old married woman with two daughters (ages 5 and 7). Barbie (as she is called) and her husband Jeffrey have come for marital counseling because her excessive anxiety, worry, and physical complaints are "destroying their 12-year marriage."

This is their first session, so I am seeing them together (as is typical). I begin by asking them what

brought them to my office. Barbie answers first. "Jeffrey overstates the problem. He thinks I worry too much—he calls me a worrywart, and Mrs. Misgiving. I guess I do tend to worry a little, but he calls me names—and, well, it does cause tension between us."

Jeffrey rejoins. "Barbie understates the problem. She is in fact overly concerned about absolutely everything. Now, I'm not just talking about being

continued

CASE | THE CASE OF BARBARA "BARBIE" CHAPMAN *continued*

worried if it will rain, for example, and whether or not she should take an umbrella to work. I'm talking about worrying that she'll get the girls to school late, have an accident along the way, run a yellow light, run out of gas, or maybe the windshield wipers won't work—I mean, I could go on and on, but you get the picture."

Barbie breaks in, "Hey, it's not a crime to take care of your family's safety, is it?"

Jeffrey responds, "Yeah, but you are always restless and edgy. You have trouble falling asleep, and when you wake up you're always tired. It's because you worry so much. You know, I could recite a litany of things that you worry about. You worry about something bad happening to you, to the girls, or me; you worry about your job, you worry about driving, the weather, your mother's health, the Brazilian rain forest, and—just absolutely everything. You even call me ten times a day to make sure I'm okay. Your own mother put in caller ID just so she could screen out your calls. You worry about things even before they happen. Do you remember that presentation you had to do at work? You fretted about that for weeks and weeks beforehand."

I ask if Barbie is generally a nervous person.

She responds, "Well, I guess I do tend to ruminate about stuff, but I can't seem to stop, no matter how hard I try. I get so nervous. Maybe I *am* just a worrywart like Jeffrey says. You know, I try to maintain a tight control over all aspects of my life. If I can stay alert to anything that could go wrong, then I can prevent mistakes."

I inquire if Barbie ever experiences any physical problems.

She replies, "Well, I do feel fidgety and jittery, you know, like I'm keyed up or something. I mean, this has been going on for years. It's nothing new. Sometimes my mind goes blank, and I have trouble concentrating. That's not so good when you're making a presentation in front of your boss. I sometimes worry so much that I can't fall asleep, so of course I wake up tired. I always seem to have neck and back aches, and I just about live on Tylenol because of muscle tension. I tried using a heating pad, you know, for the muscle aches. But then I worried the heating pad would short out and cause an electrical fire and burn the house down."

I ask, "Barbie, how have these worries changed your life?"

"Oh man, it's affected my job performance," she replies, "my relationship with Jeffery and the girls, and our social life. With all my worrying, we only have one couple who are still our friends—that's Kenny and Sue. We try to go to a movie with them at least once a month, but we don't see much of our other friends anymore."

EP 2.1.10
(b) a

ASSESSMENT SUMMARY   Generalized anxiety disorder is difficult to assess, because worry is a part of everyone's life. Although worry and physical tensions are very common experiences for most, the kind of severe anxiety experienced by Barbie is above and beyond what would be considered normal. Her worry is chronic and excessive, and it greatly diminishes the overall quality of her life.

Distinguishing the symptom picture of generalized anxiety disorder calls on the practitioner's skills to collect, organize, and interpret data from the client's story. Unlike acute stress disorder, which lasts about a month, generalized anxiety disorder is often pervasive and does not diminish over time. Individuals with phobias worry, but the quality of Barbie's worrying is very different. Those with panic disorder may develop anticipatory anxiety, but the anxiety in panic disorder is over the anticipation of having another attack. The focus of Barbie's worries is her husband, her children, and her job performance. If the target of her concerns revolved around a fear of becoming contaminated, the practitioner might begin thinking about obsessive-compulsive disorder. This vignette does not illustrate any struggles with depression, so a mood disorder would not be a viable consideration. Barbie

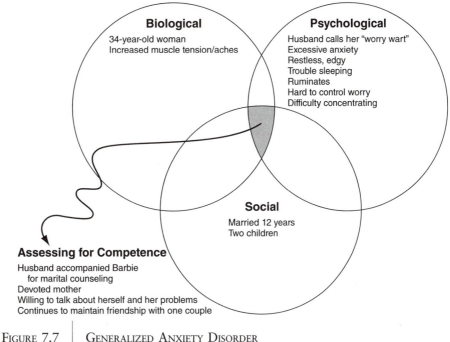

Biological
34-year-old woman
Increased muscle tension/aches

Psychological
Husband calls her "worry wart"
Excessive anxiety
Restless, edgy
Trouble sleeping
Ruminates
Hard to control worry
Difficulty concentrating

Social
Married 12 years
Two children

Assessing for Competence
Husband accompanied Barbie
  for marital counseling
Devoted mother
Willing to talk about herself and her problems
Continues to maintain friendship with one couple

FIGURE 7.7 | GENERALIZED ANXIETY DISORDER

The interactions of the biological, psychological, and social variables in Barbie Chapman's life.

© Cengage Learning

experiences no worries about her health or about having a serious illness. Therefore, the practitioner would not consider the presence of hypochondriasis or somatization disorders.

A competency-based assessment looks at the wide range of factors influencing Barbie's life. Among them, the practitioner inquires about medications or drugs Barbie is taking because they could produce side effects that might mimic generalized anxiety features (e.g., taking certain antidepressants can cause similar symptoms). Generalized anxiety disorder is far more problematic than the symptoms found in an adjustment disorder; in the latter, symptoms tend to be milder. **Adjustment disorder** is distinguished from the stresses one normally encounters in daily life, but its symptoms are not sufficient to cause clinically significant impairment and warrant a diagnosis of a mental disorder.

On the surface, Barbie's concerns about her family, husband, and job might not warrant professional intervention, but her husband describes a much different scenario. He experiences his wife's multiple excessive worries and her inability to control them as problematic. Additionally, her ongoing physical complaints have now become a burden for him. As illustrated in the vignette, family members tend to feel the brunt of Barbie's worries, but they remain supportive of her. In addition, this couple is able to maintain a relationship with another couple and socializes with them on a regular basis. Figure 7.7 shows the interactions of the biological, psychological, and social variables in Barbie Chapman's life.

BARBIE CHAPMAN'S MULTIAXIAL DSM DIAGNOSIS IS AS FOLLOWS:

Axis I	300.02 Generalized Anxiety Disorder (GAD)
Axis II	V71.09 (No diagnosis)
Axis III	Muscle Tension
Axis IV	None
Axis V	GAF = 75 (at intake)

© Cengage Learning

SUMMARY

The core emotions of anxiety and fear serve as an alarm to escape danger or harm. They warn the person to take extra precautions or to galvanize protective behaviors; for example, a student who wants to pass a difficult test must study hard. The student's efforts are partially motivated by a fear of failure. Anxiety is a symptom found in almost all mental disorders. However, when anxiety is the main symptom that requires the practitioner's help, it then is considered in a class by itself.

The behaviors a person uses to manage his or her anxiety will show in very different ways. The competency-based assessment helps the practitioner to tease out those critical differences. In sum:

- *The phobias*—Social phobias are those in which people fear they will embarrass themselves in front of others or attract negative attention (as in the case of Herb Wilks). Specific phobias show behaviors reflecting a persistent fear of objects or situations (as in Ralph Tyler's fear of blood).

- *Agoraphobia with panic disorder*—Panic disorders consist of intense attacks of anxiety and/or worries that an unexpected attack will occur. (Jada Wu's fear of flying and her concerns about being in places from which there is no escape cause her great distress.)

- *Agoraphobia without panic disorder*—This disorder restricts the person's life by causing severe impairments in almost all aspects of intrapersonal and/or interpersonal functioning. (As seen in Matilda Suarez's fears about

leaving her home, she depends on others for her basic needs, is afraid to go out alone, and does not like being in crowded places.)

- *Obsessive-compulsive disorder*—Maddy Yarborough illustrates the unwanted thoughts, images, and urges that compel a person to engage in repetitive behaviors in order to help reduce anxiety.

- *Post-traumatic stress disorder*—Buddy Jackson's experiences in combat during World War II precipitated his traumatic reaction 50 years after the event. His struggles around re-experiencing this early trauma were manifested through flashbacks, insomnia, increased heartbeat (physiological reactions), and feelings of detachment.

- *Acute anxiety disorder*—Acute anxiety disorder is distinguished from post-traumatic stress disorder by the emergence of symptoms within days to weeks after a trauma and by their duration of less than 1 month. If symptoms are longer lasting, then a diagnosis of PTSD is considered.

- *Generalized anxiety disorder*—GAD can overlap with other conditions such as panic disorder. However, the central feature, as in the case of Barbie Chapman, is one of overriding worry and concern. Her complaints revolved around feeling restless and keyed up, experiencing sleep disturbance and sleep deprivation, having difficulty concentrating, and having increased muscle tension—all of which caused problems in the intrapersonal and interpersonal domains of her life.

Looking to the DSM-5, one proposal is to change the name of *obsessive-compulsive disorder* to *anxiety and obsessive-compulsive spectrum disorders*. The rationale for this proposal is based on the person's presenting symptoms; that is, anxiety is one of the primary defining characteristics of OCD, and individuals with the diagnosis are highly anxious about their obsessive and compulsive symptoms. In addition, the diagnoses of *panic disorder with agoraphobia* and *panic disorder without agoraphobia* may ultimately be classified as panic disorder. However, agoraphobia will possibly be maintained as a separate condition but minus the addition of the terms, *without history of panic disorder*.

PRACTITIONER'S REFLECTIONS

Most people function every day with some form of anxiety generated by life stresses, upheavals, or challenges. Anxiety is considered a normal part of one's internal signaling system that alerts us to changes in our bodies and the world around us. Anxiety may be either adaptive or maladaptive.

Some degree of anxiety is experienced not only when things go wrong in life but also when things simply change or happen unexpectedly. The purpose of the following activities is to help the practitioner differentiate among normal anxiety and the various types of anxiety disorders.

ACTIVITIES

EP 2.1.10 (b) a

1. Reflect back on the cases presented in this chapter. Select one of them, and find a partner to role-play the details of the case with you. Assume the role of either the client or the social worker. After you have finished the role-play, identify the point in the exchange when you determined the presence of an anxiety disorder. Keep in mind that the focus is to practice collecting, organizing, and then interpreting client data in order to ascertain the client's diagnosis and related competence. Then describe how you were able to distinguish between normal worry and the client's symptoms.

Advanced Clinical EP 2.1.10 (b) c

2. Rent the popular, award-winning film *As Good as It Gets* featuring the actors Jack Nicholson and Helen Hunt. Describe how his compulsive behaviors affected the everyday life of Nicholson's character. Pay particular attention to how he was able to cope, and notice those interpersonal and social factors in his environment that provided support.

3. Discuss (with another colleague or with your supervisor) how superstitions are perceived in our society versus how compulsions are viewed. Describe how you would engage a superstitious client as an informant to help you to learn more about their cultural beliefs in order to make the distinction between superstitions and the compulsions found in obsessive-compulsive disorder.

EP 2.1.4 d

4. Access the CourseMate website at www.cengagebrain .com. The case vignette of Chuck is highlighted here. He is someone who describes himself as "a little bit compulsive." For example, once he has a thought, he can't put it out of his head. He's also a "checker," meaning that he has to repeatedly check things. Another case vignette introduces Steve, who is diagnosed with agoraphobia with panic disorder. He talks about his panic attacks and how they have changed his behavior in a way that indicates the distress that these attacks have caused him. Imagine that either one (or both) of these individuals was assigned as your client. Describe how you would develop empathy for their behaviors and concerns.

EP 2.1.10 (a) b

COMPETENCY NOTES

EP 2.1.3 a: Distinguish, appraise, and integrate multiple sources of knowledge, including research-based knowledge and practice wisdom (pp. 226, 254): Critical thinking requires the synthesis and communication of relevant information.

EP 2.1.4 d: Social workers view themselves as learners and engage those with whom they work as informants (p. 265): Social workers understand how diversity characterizes and shapes the human experience and is critical to the formation of identity.

EP 2.1.6 b: Use research evidence to inform practice (p. 246): Social workers use research findings to improve practice, policy, and service delivery.

EP 2.1.7 a: Use conceptual frameworks to guide the process of assessment, intervention, and evaluation (p. 247): Social workers apply theories and knowledge form the liberal arts to understand the client's biological, social, cultural, psychological, and spiritual development.

EP Advanced Clinical 2.1.7 c: Consult with medical professionals, as needed, to confirm diagnosis and/or to monitor medication in the treatment process (p. 231): Advanced practitioners understand how to synthesize and differentially apply the theories of human behavior and the social environment (biological, developmental, psychological, social, cultural, and spiritual).

EP 2.1.10 (a) b: Use empathy and other interpersonal skills (pp. 242, 265): Social workers have the knowledge and skills to practice with individuals, families, groups, organizations, and communities. This involves the dynamic and interactive process of the skill of engagement.

EP 2.1.10 (b) a: Collect, organize, and interpret client data (pp. 228, 233, 238, 239, 247, 252, 262, 265): Social workers have the knowledge and skills to practice with individuals, families, groups, organizations, and communities.

EP Advanced Clinical 2.1.10 (b) c: Assess client coping strategies to reinforce and improve adaptation to life situations, circumstances, and events (pp. 230, 232, 238, 252, 259, 265): Clinical social work practice involves the dynamic, interactive, and reciprocal processes of therapeutic engagement, multidimensional assessment, clinical intervention, and practice evaluation at multiple levels.

REFERENCES

Albano, A. M., & Hack, S. (2004). Children and adolescents. In R. G. Heimberg, C. I. Turk, & D. S. Mennin, (eds.)., *Generalized anxiety disorder: Advances in research and practice*, (pp. 383–408). New York, NY: Guilford.

American Psychiatric Association. (1980). *Diagnostic and statistical manual of mental disorders*, (3rd ed.). Washington, DC: Author.

American Psychiatric Association. (2000). *Diagnostic and statistical manual of mental disorders*, (4th ed., text revision). Washington, DC: Author.

American Red Cross. (2005). Facing a record-breaking hurricane season. Retrieved on May 18, 2006 from http://www.redcross.org/news/ds/hurricanes/2005/index.html

Andrews, G., Hobbs, M. J., Borkovec, T. D., Beesdo, K., Craske, M. G., Heimberg, R. G., ... Stanley, M. A. (2010). Generalized worry disorder: A review of DSM-IV generalized disorder and options for DSM-V. *Depression and Anxiety*, 27 (2), 134–147.

Antony M. M., & Barlow, D. H., (eds.) (2002). *Handbook of assessment and treatment planning for psychological disorders*. New York: Guilford Press.

Arrindell, W.A., Eisemann, M., Richter, J., Oei, T. P. S., Caballo, V. E., van der Ende, J., ... Hudson, B. L. (2003). Phobic anxiety in 11 nations. Part I: Dimensional constancy of the five-factor model. *Behavior Research and Therapy*, 41, 461–479.

Ayers, C. R., Thorp, S. R., & Weatherell, J. L. (2009). Anxiety disorders and hoarding in older adults, In M. M. Antony & M. B. Stein, (eds.)., *Oxford handbook of anxiety and related disorders*, (pp. 625–635). New York, NY: Oxford University Press.

Barlow, D. H. (2004). *Anxiety and its disorders: The nature and treatment of anxiety and panic*, (2nd ed.). New York, NY: Guilford Press.

Barlow, D. H., & Craske, M. G. (2007). *Mastery of your anxiety and panic: Workbook (Treatments that work)*, (4th ed.). New York, NY: Oxford University Press.

Barlow, D. H., & Durand V. M. (2012). *Abnormal psychology*, (6th ed.). Belmont, CA: Wadsworth Cengage Learning.

Bloch, M. H., Landeros-Weisenberger, A., Rosario, M. C., Pittenger, C., & Leckman, J. F. (2008). Meta-analysis of the symptom structure of obsessive-compulsive disorder. *American Journal of Psychiatry*, 165 (2), 1532–1542.

Bogels, S. M., Alden, L., Beidel, D. C., Clark, L. A., Pine, D. S., Stein, M. B., ... Voncken, M. (2010). Social anxiety disorder: Questions and answers for the DSM-V. *Depression and Anxiety*, 27 (2), 168–189.

Branigan, T. (March 13, 2011). Tsunami, earthquake, nuclear crisis—now Japan faces power cuts. *The Guardian* (London). Retrieved on July 10, 2011 from: http://www.webcitation.org/5xDAT05x0

Brown, T. A., & Barlow, D. H. (2009). A proposal for a dimensional classification system based on the shared features of the DSM-IV anxiety and mood disorders: Implications for assessment and treatment. *Psychological Assessment*, 21 (3), 256–271.

Bryant, R. A., & Harvey, A. G. (2000). *Acute stress disorder: A handbook of theory, assessment, and treatment*. Washington, DC: American Psychological Association.

CBS News (March 9, 2010). Red Cross: 3 M Haitians affected by quake. Retrieved on July 10, 2011, from: www.cbsnews.com/stories/2010/01/13/world/main6090601.shtml?tag=cbsnewsSectionContent.4

Clark, L. A. (2005). Temperament as a unifying basis for personality and psychopathology (Special Issue). *Journal of Abnormal Psychology, 114*, 505–521.

Craske, M. G., & Barlow, D. H. (2008). Panic disorder and agoraphobia. In D. H. Barlow, (ed.), *Clinical handbook of psychological disorders: A step-by-step treatment manual* (4th ed., pp. 1–64). New York, NY: Guilford Press.

Dohrenwend, B. P., Turner, J. B., & Turse, N. A. (2006). The psychological risks of Vietnam for U. S. veterans: A revisit with new data and methods. *Science, 313*, 979–982.

Elklit, A. (2002). Acute stress disorder in victims of robbery and victims of assault. *Journal of Interpersonal Violence, 17*, 872–887.

Environment News Service. (April 27, 2011). Tornadoes, floods wrack U.S. southeast and northwest. Retrieved on July 9, 2011 from: http://www.ens-newswire.com/ens/apr2011/2011–04–27–091.html

Feusner, J., Phillips, K., & Stein, D. (2010). Olfactory reference syndrome: Issues for DSM-V. *Depression and Anxiety*, 27 (6), 592–599.

Figley, C. R. (Ed.) (2002). *Treating compassion fatigue*. Philadelphia, PA: Brunner/Mazel.

Friedman, M. J. (2009). Phenomenology of post-traumatic stress disorder and acute stress disorder. In M. M. Antony and M. B. Stein, (eds.)., *Oxford handbook of anxiety and related disorders*, (pp. 65–72). New York, NY: Oxford University Press.

Fullerton, C. S., Ursano, R. J., & Wang, L. (2004). Acute stress disorder, post-traumatic stress disorder, and depression in disaster or rescue workers. *American Journal of Psychiatry, 161*, 1370–1376.

Furr, J. M., Tiwari, S., Suvey, C., & Kendall, O. C. (2009). Anxiety disorders in children and adolescents. In M. M. Antony and M. B. Stein, (eds.)., *Oxford handbook of anxiety and related disorders*, (pp. 636–656). New York, NY: Oxford University Press.

Galea, S., Ahern, J., Resnick, H., Kilpatrick, D., Bucuvalas, M., Gold, J., Vlahov, D. (2002). Psychological sequelae of the September 11 terrorist attacks in New York City. *New England Journal of Medicine, 346* (13), 982–987.

Gitterman, A., & Germain, C. B., (2008). *The life model of social work practice: Advances in theory and practice*, (3rd ed.). New York: Columbia University Press.

Halpern, J. & Tramontin, M. (2007). *Disaster mental health: Theory and practice*. Belmont, CA: Brooks/Cole Thomson Learning.

Harvey. A. G., & Bryant, R. A. (2002). Acute stress disorder: A synthesis and critique. *Psychological Bulletin, 128* (6), 886–202.

Hesse, A. (2002). Secondary trauma: How working with trauma survivors affects therapists. *Clinical Social Work Journal, 30*, 293–309.

Hofmann, S. G., Alpers, G. W., & Pauli, P. (2009). Phenomenology of panic and phobic disorders. In M. M. Antony & M. M. Stein, (eds.)., *Oxford handbook of anxiety and related disorders*, (pp. 34–46). New York, NY: Oxford University Press.

Holeva, V., Tarrier, N., & Wells, A. (2001). Prevalence and predictors of acute stress disorder and PTSD following road traffic accidents: Thought control strategies and social support. *Behavior Therapy, 32*, 65–83.

Inbar, J. & Ganor, J. (2003). Trauma and Compassion fatigue: Helping the helpers. *Journal of Jewish Communal Services, 79*, 109–111.

Kessler, R. C., Berglund, P. Demler, O., Jin, R., Merikangas, K., & Walters, E. E. (2005). Lifetime prevalence and age of onset distributions of DSM-IV disorders in the National Comorbidity Survey Replication. *Archives of General Psychiatry, 62*, 593–602.

Kessler, R. C., Chiu, W. T., Demler, O., & Walters, E. E. (2005). Prevalence, severity, and comorbidity of 12-month DSM-IV disorders in the National Comorbidity Survey Replication. *Archives of General Psychiatry, 62*, 617–627.

Kikuchi, M., Komuro, R., Oka, H., Kidani, T., Hanaoka, A., & Koshino, U. (2005). Panic disorder with and without agoraphobia: Comorbidity within a half-year of the onset of panic disorder. *Psychiatry and Clinical Neurosciences, 59*, 639–643.

Kilpatrick, D. G., Ruggiero, K. J., Acierno, R., Saunders, B. E., Resnick, H. S., & Best, C. L. (2003). Violence and risk of PTSD, major depression, substance abuse/dependence, and comorbidity: Results from the National Survey of Adolescents. *Journal of Consulting and Clinical Psychology, 71* (4), 692–700.

Knight, C. (2004). Working with survivors of childhood trauma: Implications for clinical supervision. *The Clinical Supervisor, 23* (2), 81–105.

Knutson, T. P., & Tuleya, R. E. (2004). Impact of CO_2-induced warming on simulated hurricane intensity and precipitation: Sensitivity to choice of climate model and convective parameterization. *Journal of Climate, 17* (8), 3477–3495.

LeBeau, R. T., Glenn, D., Liao, B., Witchen, H. U., Beesdo-Baum, K., Ollendick, T., & Craske, M. (2010). Specific phobia: A review of DSM-IV specific phobia and preliminary recommendations for DSM-V. *Depression and Anxiety, 27* (2), 148–167.

Marcus, S., & Dubi, M. (2006). The relationship between resilience and compassion fatigue in counselors. *Vistas: Compelling perspectives on counseling 2006*, (pp. 223–225). Alexandria, VA, US: American Counseling Association.

Mathews, C. A. (2009). Phenomenology of obsessive-compulsive disorder. In M. M. Antony & M. B. Stein, (eds.)., *Oxford handbook of anxiety and related disorders*, (pp. 56–64). New York, NY: Oxford University Press.

Morrissette, P. J. (2004). *The pain of helping: Psychological injury of helping professionals*. New York, NY: Brunner/Routledge.

National Climactic Data Center. (2004). Climate of 2004 Atlantic hurricane season. Retrieved May 18, 2006, from http://www.ncdc.noaa.gov/oa/climate/research/2004/hurricanes04.html

National Climactic Data Center. (2006). Climate of 2005 Atlantic hurricane Season. Retrieved May 18, 2006, from http://www.ncdc.noaa.gov/oa/climate/research.2005/hurricanes05.html

National Comorbidity Survey. (2005). NCS-R appendix tables: Table 1. Lifetime prevalence of DSM-IV/WMH-CIDI disorders by sex and cohort. Table 2. Twelve-month prevalence of DSM-IV/WMH-CIDI disorders by sex and cohort. Retrieved July 17, 2011, from: http://www.hcp.med.harvard.edu/ncs/publications.php

Op Den Velde, W., Deeg, D. J., Hovens, J. E., Van Duijn, M. A., Aarts, P. G. (2011). War stress and late-life mortality in World War II male civilian resistance veterans. *Psychological Reports 108* (2), 437–448.

Pearlman, L., & Saakvitne, K. (1995). *Trauma and the therapist: Countertransference and vicarious traumatization in psychotherapy with incest survivors*. New York: W. W. Norton.

Perugi, G., Frare, F., & Toni, C. (2007). Diagnosis and treatment of agoraphobia with panic disorder. *CNS Treatment, 21*, 741–764.

Rachman, S. (2006). *Fear of contamination*. New York, NY: Oxford University Press.

Sadock, B. J., Sadock, V. A., & Ruiz, P., (eds.). (2009). *Kaplan and Sadock's comprehensive textbook of psychiatry*, (9th ed.). Philadelphia, PA: Williams and Wilkins.

Steketee, G. & Barlow, D. H. (2002). Obsessive-compulsive disorder. In D. H. Barlow, *Anxiety and its disorders: The nature and treatment of anxiety and panic*, (2nd ed., pp. 516–550). New York, NY: Guilford Press.

Steketee, G., & Frost, R. O. (2007a). *Compulsive hoarding and acquiring: Client workbook*. New York, NY: Oxford University Press.

Steketee, G., & Frost, R. O. (2007b). *Compulsive hoarding and acquiring: Therapist guide*. New York, NY: Oxford University Press.

Wald, J., & Taylor, S. (2007). Efficacy of interoceptive exposure therapy combined with trauma-related exposure therapy for posttraumatic stress disorder: A pilot study. *Journal of Anxiety Disorders, 21*, 1050–1060.

Wilamowska, Z. A., Thompson-Hollands, J., Fairholme, C. P., Ellard, J. K., Farchione, T, J., & Barlow, D. H. (2010). Conceptual background, development, and preliminary data from the unified protocol for transdiagnostic treatment of emotional disorders. *Depression and Anxiety*, 27 (10), 882–890.

Wolitzky-Taylor, K. B., Castriotta, N., Lenze, E. J., Stanley, M. A., & Craske, M. B. (2010). Anxiety disorders in older adults: A comprehensive review. *Depression and Anxiety*, 27 (2), 190–211.

Yan, J. (March 22, 2011). Death toll from SW China earthquake rises to 26. Xinhua News Agency. Retrieved on July 17, 2011 from: http://news .xinhuanet.com/english2010/china/2011–03/22/c_ 13790890.htm

CHAPTER 8

SOMATOFORM, FACTITIOUS, AND MALINGERING DISORDERS

INTRODUCTION

In the days of Hippocrates and in the Egyptian era before him, the word *hysteria* implied that the source of certain disorders (occurring in women) could be traced to a "wandering uterus." Centuries later, Greek physicians still believed that this condition resulted from the uterus being displaced so that it would float about the body, dislocating other vital organs and causing multiple physical symptoms. The treatment for this unfortunate condition consisted of attracting and redirecting the wayward uterus to its proper place, by using aromatic substances placed near the vagina.

In the ninth century, hysteria was considered a purely physical disorder—but by the Middle Ages, the perspective had shifted away from conceiving of hysteria as a medical condition to thinking of it as a spiritual disorder emerging from evil and demonic possession, as in the case of witchcraft. Hysteria applied to a state of mind characterized by unmanageable fear or emotional stress. The fear often centered on one part of the body. In the seventeenth century, Thomas Sydenham, an English physician, observed that hysteria could disguise almost any medical disease. Because hysteria was thought of as a disease for so long, its various definitions became blurred over time. For example, a century after Sydenham, Dr. William Cullen adapted the term *neurosis* to describe a type of "nervous energy" or "nervous force" that he thought played an important part in the etiology of certain illnesses having medical, neurological, or psychiatric underpinnings.

In 1859, the noted French physician Pierre Briquet studied 430 of his patients for more than a decade and was able to provide the first formal description of somatoform disorders. Briquet focused on describing people who had seemingly endless lists of complaints that did not have a supporting medical basis. His observations advanced the notion that individuals were usually afflicted early in life, and their symptoms were manifested by recurrent, unexplained, somatic complaints noted in many organ sites. Women were primarily affected. The disorder seemed to be incurable; individuals would return time and again with a new batch of symptoms. The most common complaints noted by Briquet's patients included vomiting, **aphonia** (inability to create sounds or speak), painful limbs, muscle weakness, dizziness, painful menstruation, a burning sensation in reproductive organs, and paralysis. Because of his initial observations, this "hysterical" disorder became known as Briquet's syndrome, and remained so named for more than 100 years. In 1980, the disorder was renamed **somatization disorder** and was included for the first time in the DSM-III (American Psychiatric Association, 1980).

During the latter part of the nineteenth century, the emerging field of psychiatry began to become more differentiated, and so did certain disorders, including hypochondriasis, hysteria, and **neurasthenia** (unexplained fatigue and lassitude) that came to be regarded more as psychological disorders than organic disorders.

ESSENTIAL FEATURES OF SOMATOFORM DISORDERS

Somatoform disorders generally involve a cluster of illnesses that comprise physical symptoms but do not seem to be caused by a medical condition. These somatic complaints are serious enough to cause the person significant emotional distress and/or diminish his or her interpersonal functioning, especially in social or occupational roles. The social worker should not underestimate the genuine discomfort experienced by the client and should recognize the person's need to address somatic complaints. Maynard (2003) suggests that it is helpful to acknowledge that the person's symptoms are real and distressing. Instead of talking about what is physically wrong with the client, focus the conversation on how symptoms limit functioning.

When considering the various etiologic factors applicable to the somatization process, one must also appreciate the distinction between the concepts of illness and disease. The term **disease** broadly refers to any condition that impairs normal function. It is often understood to be a medical condition associated with specific signs, symptoms, and laboratory findings peculiar to it (Venes, 2005). In addition, a disease exhibits objectively measurable anatomic deformations and pathophysiologic states presumably caused by such varied factors as degenerative processes, traumas, toxins, and infectious agents. **Illness** refers to those experiences associated with disease that ultimately affect the person's state of being and social functioning. When describing illness, most people would agree that it includes more than just the notion of a state of being sick. The practitioner takes into account the uniquely personal nature of each individual's suffering, his or her inability to fully participate in activities, and the decreased capacity for interpersonal relationships, all of which significantly affect quality of life. The major distinction between disease and illness is that illness is a highly individual or subjective experience. A person may have a serious disease, for example, hypothyroidism, but experience no feelings of pain or suffering, and thus no illness. Conversely, a person may be extremely ill, as with a somatization disorder, but have no evidence of disease that can be measured by pathological changes in the body.

People who have somatoform disorders are not deliberately faking their symptoms (as they would be in the case of factitious disorder), nor are they consciously pretending to be ill with a clear motive (as would be in the case of malingering disorder). The people with somatoform disorder really believe they have something seriously wrong with them, and this often causes enormous anxiety, distress, and impairment.

There are five somatoform disorders: (1) *somatization disorder*, (2) *conversion disorder*, (3) *pain disorder*, (4) *hypochondriasis*, and (5) *body dysmorphic disorder*. Two additional categories will be briefly addressed in this chapter. The first is *undifferentiated somatoform disorder*; this includes those persons who do not "fit" or fall below threshold somatization disorder behaviors because their symptoms are perceived as less severe. The second is *somatoform disorder not otherwise specified*; this is considered a catchall category for those who do not meet specific criteria for any of the somatoform disorders listed above.

The central feature signaling the presence of somatoform disorders is the individual who is pathologically concerned about the functioning or appearance of his or her body. In the assessment process, these somatoform disorders are divided into three different groups based on the specific focus of the individual's beliefs or concerns regarding physical symptoms, physical illness, and/or physical appearance:

1. If the focus of attention and/or concern is on the individual's physical symptoms, then somatization disorder, undifferentiated somatoform disorder, pain disorder, and conversion disorder should be considered.
2. If the focus is on the belief that the individual has a serious or life-threatening physical illness, then hypochondriasis should be considered.
3. If the individual believes and is convinced they have a serious defect in their physical appearance (while appearing normal to others), then body dysmorphic disorder should be considered.

All of the somatoform disorders share two important features—they involve predominately somatic complaints (or bodily preoccupation), and they are based on the idea that the focus on the body cannot be fully explained by any known medical disease or substance use. This is the individual who engages in somatization, or the tendency to communicate distress through physical symptoms and to seek out medical help for these symptoms (Hurwitz, 2004). Kirmayer and Taillefer (1997) suggest, "as illness behavior, somatoform disorders can be best typified and understood in terms of dimensions rather than categories, processes rather than symptoms and signs, and social contexts rather than isolated behaviors" (p. 334). They further note, "this social approach not only fits the research data better than the individual psychopathology oriented perspective, [but] it also has very useful implications for clinical assessment and treatment" (p. 334). The competency-based assessment is a way to help practitioners rethink the category of somatoform disorders. This assessment model encourages the practitioner to avoid some of the invalidating, negative attitudes, and stigmatization that affect clients with somatoform disorders. From the competency-based perspective, the assessment pays attention to the client's biological domain and calls upon the practitioner to consider the presence of four pain symptoms, two gastrointestinal symptoms, one sexual symptom, and one pseudoneurological symptom when assessing for somatoform disorders. We will review each of the major somatoform disorders and provide an illustrative example for each.

SOMATIZATION DISORDER

Somatization, considered an uncommon disorder, represents a polysymptomatic disorder that begins early in life, typically during adolescence, and affects mostly women (Creed & Barsky, 2004). It is characterized by recurrent, multiple bodily or physical somatic complaints. It goes without saying that those with somatization disorder will overuse and misuse the health care system (Barsky, Orav, & Bates, 2005). One study showed that 19 percent of people with somatization disorder were on disability (Allen, Woolfolk, Escobar, Gara, & Hammer, 2006). Unlike most of the other groups of disorders we have discussed so far, somatoform disorders are not anchored together by common etiologies, family histories, or other associated factors.

Most of us have endured annoying physical symptoms or ailments at one time or another. We have all probably suffered from headaches, nausea, muscle aches, or just feeling blah—and, when we do, we usually try to "tough it out" or ignore the discomfort. For the individual with somatization disorder, this is generally not true. For almost every ache or pain, the person will seek medical attention, which may include an office visit to a physician (with a workup that involves extensive laboratory tests, X-rays, or other diagnostic procedures) and will more than likely emerge with prescriptions to "cure" the medical complaint. It is incumbent upon the practitioner to be mindful of the client who describes a pattern of recurring, multiple, clinically significant physical complaints.

The practitioner should listen carefully when the client talks about his or her medical history. It may be helpful to ask about the extent to which someone who is suffering from somatization *wants* to get better—and what it would mean to give up the physical symptoms that are sometimes used to control or manipulate others, hold on to a relationship, or divert attention from other problems (Gray, 2006). The individual tends to be somewhat inaccurate, vague, and uncertain about when symptoms first started. They may also tend to exaggerate or dramatize symptoms. For example, a backache is never described as "a mild ache that will pass." I can remember a client with somatization disorder who described her backache as "the worst backache anyone in the entire world could possibly have—it feels like red-hot pokers jammed up inside my spine."

Some individuals may assume an opposite emotional stance, showing inappropriate indifference in the face of seemingly tragic and overwhelming medical events, known as **la belle indifference** (Stone, Smyth, Carson, Warlow, & Sharpe, 2006). This blasé attitude toward illness is sometimes shown by people with actual physical disorders, as well. Practitioners should be cautioned, however, that neither the presence nor absence of *la belle indifference* is an accurate measure of whether the individual has somatization disorder.

After repeatedly recounting descriptions of complaints, the individual with somatization disorder might begin to reinvent or create changes regarding the intensity, duration, severity, or the level of impairment in his or her health and medical problems. Ultimately, these symptoms become a never-ending way of life. If the person manages to gain some relief, there are always new complaints waiting to emerge. The person's symptoms may come and go, but the accompanying sick role and related complaints seem to provide meaning and organization to an otherwise chaotic life.

EP 2.1.10
(b) a

As a part of the assessment process, the practitioner carefully collects, organizes, and interprets client data. Certain red flags in a client's medical history should alert the practitioner to begin thinking about somatization disorder. Often, the first clue is the medical history itself—it is complicated and fraught with multiple diagnoses, failed treatments, and voluminous medical records. Hardly a year will pass without the person experiencing some intense physical discomfort, and the medical story is further complicated by other features, such as a history of multiple allergies or medication intolerance. None of these signs by itself is **pathognomonic** (indicative of a disease). However, each is important to consider when combined with other signs and symptoms. They include complaints for which no well-integrated structural or pathophysiologic models are known, or for which the individual does not fit the definition of the syndrome. **Pathophysiology** refers to the study of how normal physiological processes are altered by disease. Examples include:

- Irritable bowel syndrome.
- Burning tongue or burning mouth.
- Bodily sensations.
- Nonanginal chest pain (pain despite normal angiogram).
- Pseudoseizures.
- Pseudocyesis (false pregnancy).
- **Dysphagia** (difficulty swallowing).
- Chronic fatigue syndrome.
- Fibromyalgia.
- Myofascial pain syndrome.
- Interstitial cystitis.
- **Dyspareunia** (painful coitus).
- **Dysmenorrhea** (painful menses).
- Hysterical paralysis.
- Tension headache.
- **Syncope** (fainting).
- Premenstrual syndrome.

As mentioned earlier, an important area for the practitioner to explore is the extent to which a person who is suffering from a somatoform disorder wants to get better versus what it would entail to give up his or her physical symptoms. People with somatization disorder sometimes use their symptoms to control, manipulate, hold on to a relationship, or divert attention away from other problematic aspects of their lives. Other individuals may experience **alexithymia**, which is the inability to identify and articulate their feelings and needs, or to experience and express emotions except through physical symptoms.

The symptom picture of somatization disorder is frequently nonspecific, and the diagnostic criteria have been clarified to a great extent by requiring the presence of at least eight symptoms. For those reporting fewer than eight somatic complaints, undifferentiated somatization disorder may apply. We will discuss assessment differentiation in greater detail later in the chapter.

When considering somatization disorder, the assessment includes:

1. Onset before the age of 30 and a history of many physical complaints occurring over several years.
2. Symptoms either were treated, or they resulted in significant impairment in social, occupational, or other important areas of interpersonal functioning.
3. The course of the disturbance must have involved all of the following individual symptoms at some time. (These symptoms do not have to be concurrent.)
   - *Pain symptoms* (four or more) that are related to different sites or functions (e.g., head, abdomen, back/spine, joints, extremities, chest, rectum) or are related to bodily functions (e.g., sexual intercourse, menstruation, or urination).
   - *Gastrointestinal symptoms* (two or more, excluding pain), such as nausea, bloating, vomiting (other than during pregnancy), diarrhea, or intolerance of certain foods.
   - *Sexual symptoms* (at least one, excluding pain), including indifference to sex, difficulties with erection or ejaculation, irregular menses, excessive menstrual bleeding, or vomiting throughout an entire pregnancy.
   - *Pseudoneurological symptoms* (at least one), a history suggesting a neurological condition, including poor balance or poor coordination, paralysis or localized weakness, difficulty in swallowing or feeling a lump in the throat, loss of voice, urinary retention, hallucinations, loss of touch or pain sensation, double vision, blindness, deafness, or seizures or other dissociative symptoms (i.e., amnesia or loss of consciousness, other than fainting). Pain in itself in any of these areas is not enough to assess the presence of a pseudoneurological symptom.
4. For each of the symptoms noted in item #3, *one* of the following conditions must also be met:
   - Appropriate physical or laboratory examination determines that symptoms cannot be fully explained by a general medical condition or by the use of substances (e.g., a drug of abuse or a medication).
   - When a related general medical condition does exist, the impairment or physical complaints experienced exceed what would be expected, based on the person's history, physical examination, or laboratory findings.
5. The individual must not be consciously feigning or intentionally producing the symptoms, as in factitious disorder (maintaining the sick role for his or her secondary gain) or as in malingering (to achieve some material gain) (American Psychiatric Association, 2000).

PREVAILING PATTERN

Although somatization is a discrete (or single) disorder, the practitioner may also recognize it as a continuum of physical disturbances. Individuals with this disorder have a number of both medical and physical complaints. Individuals considered to be primarily emotionally distressed frequently utilize medical services instead of using mental health services. For instance, the median prevalence in samples of a large number of patients in primary care settings was 16.6 percent (Creed & Barsky, 2004).

Advanced
Clinical
EP 2.1.7 c

It seems that a fine line exists between those who have psychologically related concerns and those who struggle with somatic complaints. In practice, those with somatization disorder tend to be shuffled back and forth between medical and mental health settings. It is not unusual for practitioners to consult with medical professionals, as needed, in order to confirm a client's diagnosis. When taking somatization disorder into account, consider recommending a thorough physical examination to identify those physical symptoms that cannot be explained by the accompanying physical findings.

Medically unexplained physical symptoms seem to be fairly common worldwide. However, it is not always easy to rule out the medical causes of somatic complaints in developing countries where parasitic and other diseases associated with poor nutrition are common and are not always easy to diagnose (Gureje, 2004). In addition, cultural factors and beliefs may affect prevalence rates as well as the kind of symptoms reported.

In the United States, women who are unmarried and from lower socioeconomic groups are most likely to be assessed as having somatization disorder (Creed & Barsky, 2004). Somatization may be a way disenfranchised women can express their discontent or disappointment with their social situation without incurring the negative consequences of acting out in other, more inappropriate ways. Further, those who lack social support may be driven to seek out medical or clinical attention as a substitute for the lack of a social network. Although these individuals tend to focus on physical complaints, they also report wide spectrum of psychological symptoms and are often assessed with mood and anxiety disorders. For example, as many as 76 percent of patients suffering from major depressive disorder have reported somatic symptoms, such as headaches, stomach pain, back pain, and poorly localized pain (Denninger et al., 2006). Phobias and panic disorders are often present, as is a history of suicide attempts.

DIFFERENTIAL ASSESSMENT

The competency-based assessment provides insight into the somatization disorder by directing the practitioner's attention to a better understanding of biopsychosocial factors. Several findings point to a **biological predisposition**. Studies have shown an increased incidence of somatization disorder and hypochondriasis in first-degree relatives, implying a possible inheritable predisposition (Escobar, 2009). Somatization disorder is strongly correlated to a familial predisposition for antisocial personality disorder. (Refer to the chapter on personality disorders for a more detailed discussion.)

EP 2.1.7 b

Somatization disorder promotes a critical assessment of the way in which the person's social environment influences the symptom picture. In particular, some researchers have suggested that the familial association between somatization disorder and antisocial personality disorder is a gender-based expression of the same underlying biological predisposition. Specifically, somatization occurs chiefly in women, while antisocial personality disorder (ASPD) occurs primarily in men. These two disorders are linked through several distinctive and overlapping features; that is, both begin early in life, follow a chronic course, and are complicated by marital discord, substance abuse, and suicidal behavior (Mai, 2004). On the surface, these disorders seem to be quite different, but the influence of gender differences underscores the value of using the competency-based approach to the assessment process by putting together what is known about a client and looking to the interplay among the social and interpersonal aspects of a person's life, the illness experience, and the stigma of medically unexplained symptoms.

Another interesting point is that individuals with an antisocial personality disorder (mostly males) do not seem to experience anxiety. They are often seen as taking what they want and are indifferent to the concerns of others. These are people who are characterized as doing whatever they can to further their own goals. Lying and cheating is second nature. Aggressive intrapersonal tendencies are common themes for those with antisocial personality disorder. Gene researchers are looking for the genetic differences that may influence the person's relative lack of anxiety or fear (van Goozen, Fairchild, Snoek, & Harold, 2007). Among women, however, a different calculus seems to be at work. The frequent development of new somatic symptoms, the lack of aggression, and notable dependence often garner women immediate sympathy and attention, even though this eventually dissipates. Women with a somatization disorder exhibit a variety of somatic complaints and psychological problems *in lieu of* being aggressive.

These findings raise some interesting questions. Is it possible that gender roles and societal attitudes toward gender socialization play a large role in the profound differences found between men and women in the expression of the same biological vulnerability? Could these gender differences suggest that, while society is more forgiving of aggression in men, it does not accept a similar response in women? Those behavioral characteristics of antisocial personality disorder that include problems with law enforcement, persistent lying, problems with money and finances, poor interpersonal relationships, occupational difficulties, and physical aggression toward others are seen as more acceptable for men. If women exhibit these same behaviors, they are most often viewed as being "disturbed."

Somatization disorder is rare, and making the diagnosis requires the presence of eight symptoms. Along with physical complaints, individuals may have a variety of psychological complaints, usually, the anxiety of mood disorders (Lieb, Zimmerman, Friis, Holler, Tholen, & Witchen, 2002). The practitioner may also see a history of suicide attempts, but they seem to be more of an attempt to manipulate rather than a true attempt at death (Chioqueta & Stiles, 2004). Thus while individuals with somatization disorder will more than likely be seen in the health care system, it is inaccurate to view people who somatize as having predominately physical symptoms.

EP 2.1.7 a

The competency-based assessment provides a conceptual framework to assess the influence of interpersonal variables in a person's life when considering the diagnosis of somatization disorder. Those with somatization disorder often describe childhood experiences that include pain or serious illness in a family member. Women with somatization disorder are more likely to report a history of childhood sexual and/or physical abuse than other females who have somatic complaints. Interestingly, it may be that women who suffered childhood abuse establish some sort of paradoxical communication patterns that include hiding their feelings and reality on one hand, while seeking acknowledgment of their current suffering from medical intervention on the other hand. Given the challenges in making an accurate diagnosis of somatization disorder, few studies of its causes have been conducted, but an earlier work by Brodsky (1984) identified six important family factors to be considered when assessing for somatization disorder:

1. Raised in a family that has a history of multiple physical complaints.
2. Nurtured by parent(s) who were seen as demanding and unrewarding when the child was healthy, but seen as caring and loving when the child was sick.
3. Grew up in a home environment where one or both parents suffered from multiple illnesses.
4. Developed in an environment where other coping mechanisms for handling or dealing with psychosocial crises were unavailable.
5. Cultivated a repertoire of reactions used to withdraw from usual life activities or to engage, manipulate, or punish others.
6. Fabricated and invented an illness in order to obtain something of value, gain a benefit, or avoid punishment.

Somatization disorder generally begins before the person is 30 years old. While a person's symptoms may come and go, the disorder and the associated sick-role behavior is chronic and often continues into old age. The most common symptoms associated with somatization disorder include chest pain, palpitations, feeling bloated, shortness of breath (without exertion), dizziness, headaches, feelings of weakness, and fatigue. The following vignette illustrates how someone who has a somatization disorder might come to see a social worker.

CASE | THE CASE OF HELENE MARTIN

Helene Martin, 24, is a single, attractive African-American woman. She came into the emergency room with her best friend, Jessica Leah, because she was "having trouble breathing." She thought she might be starting to have a heart attack. Helene also complained to the emergency room physician that she was experiencing terrible swelling in her knees.

Helene and Jessica have been friends since grade school and have shared many troubles together. Their friendship is extremely important to Helene. During the physical examination, Helene related that she had had many health problems over the years. She always considered herself to be a sickly child, but she started having "serious" physical problems when she was a teenager. (According to Helene, her mother was sickly as a child, too.) She related that she was raised in a family who was usually demanding and critical—unless she was ill. Then, her parents seemed to be loving and caring.

As a part of her medical history, Helene revealed that her father tended to rule the family with an iron hand and a heavy belt. The physician noted in the

medical history that Helene was overly dramatic when talking about herself, had a strong need to be the center of attention, and expressed emotion in a shallow and rapidly shifting way. In addition, Helene described an excessive concern with her physical appearance, and that her relationships with men were fraught with sexually provocative behavior.

The physician considered Helene to be very bright, yet she never finished high school. Helene stated that she wants to go back to night school to earn her GED. Her lack of formal education seemed to keep her locked into low-paying and menial jobs, causing feelings of discontent and disappointment. Before the physician could go further in her examination, Helene took out a large sheaf of papers, and handed them over.

"Here," she stated. "Instead of me rattling off all the problems I've had, I'll give you a copy of my records. It'll save you some time figuring everything out."

Helene's personal 300-page health diary documented 10 years of her past medical history. The following highlights a partial, limited accounting of her most recent and current problems:

January 10 (3:30 P.M.) I had a terrible period, with lots of horrible cramps and bleeding. I stayed in bed 4 days; had to miss work. I saw Dr. Able, and she gave me a prescription, but it didn't help very much.

January 31 (3:00 A.M.) I had pain during intercourse (again). I went to see Dr. Baker today, but she wasn't very helpful. She told me to "relax more." What a joke!

February 9 I had a urinary tract infection, and it burned a lot when I tried to pee. I saw Dr. Carter, but he wouldn't give me a prescription (said it wouldn't help). He said that I complained about urinary burning three times last year, and I didn't have anything wrong then, and I didn't have anything wrong today. I won't go back to him again!

March 7 I had another seizure. I was admitted to the hospital, but the EEG didn't show anything. I was hospitalized at Mercy Baptist for 2 days and had lots of tests. Dr. Dankin said, "There is really good news, you don't have a brain tumor." I told him that I felt really dizzy a lot this week and lost my balance four times. He told me not to worry about anything and said my problems would probably disappear if I forgot about them.

April 11 (8:00 P.M.) My knee and hip joints are really painful and swollen. I lost 3 days of work because I can hardly sit or walk. Mom came over to cook dinner. Dr. Evans was on vacation, but her associate (I don't know her name) was on emergency call. The doctor said that since she didn't know me well enough, she couldn't give me a prescription over the telephone. She told me to go the emergency room and she would meet me there to examine me. I don't think I'm gonna use Dr. Evans anymore.

May 21 I had several really bad episodes of diarrhea, bloating, and vomiting the past few days. I went in for an appointment with Dr. Frankel, and he admitted me to the hospital. He said that I needed a complete workup. I had every test you could think of (upper and lower barium enema, sigmoidoscopy, colonoscopy, X-rays of my stomach, MRI, lots of blood work). Dr. Frankel called it the VIP treatment.

After all that, he said, "Absolutely nothing is wrong with you," and suggested that maybe "it was just an upset stomach." Dr. Frankel added that I should watch my diet for a couple of days after I got home. He also suggested that I make an appointment to see a social worker. I think he wants to blame this on a mental condition, but he's wrong.

May 25 I had terrible diarrhea again at midnight; also think I'm allergic to eggs, because I had a serious case of heartburn.

June 1 The diarrhea is finally gone, but now I'm so constipated I feel very bloated. My rectum is swollen and it hurts to have a bowel movement. Being constipated has irritated my hemorrhoids into acting up. I called Dr. Graystone, but she's no longer in practice, so I guess I'll find another doctor (someone who can finally help me). I went to the emergency room, and they agreed with me that I was constipated. I wanted a prescription for my condition, but they told me to go out to the drug store and buy some milk of magnesia. They promised it would work.

June 15 I have both a terrible headache and backache, but I don't have the money to go see a doctor, so I used some of the medicine I once got from Dr. Carter, but it didn't help. I'm in a tremendous amount of pain. I have to miss work again.

June 17 (2:00 A.M.) My headache and backache continue to cause me terrible pain. I finally went to the emergency room, and they admitted me for observation. I had several tests, but the doctors think that whatever I had went away, and that I shouldn't have any more trouble. The ER doctor gave me the name of some social worker, but I told him, "I'm not a head case." They are just trying to pass me off because they can't find out what's wrong with me.

July 15 I'm having a lot of trouble swallowing. I saw a new doctor, Dr. Herrold, and he referred me to Dr. Isaac, an ear, nose, and throat specialist. Dr. Isaac stuck some tubes down my throat, and said he couldn't find anything wrong. He told me not to think about it, and that it would go away. I got a peek at my insurance form, and saw that the doctor called my swallowing trouble, "Globus hystericus." I looked up that diagnosis as soon as I got home.

continued

I think that Dr. Isaac doesn't know what he's talking about. Globus hystericus doesn't sound like "nothing" to me. In the meantime, mom prepares soft foods and milk shakes for me to eat.

August 13 I can't tolerate eating any dairy products because I have had lots of stomach bloating recently. I found out from my mom that when I was a teenager I had lots of "intolerances to foods and certain medications."

September 22 I'm having burning when I urinate. I went to see Dr. Jankowski and she told me, "Helene, you don't have any evidence of a urinary tract infection. There is nothing to treat you for." I don't agree with her. Later in the day, I made an appointment to see Dr. Kaye (who came highly recommended by another secretary who used her). Dr. Kaye said she thought I might have a bladder problem. I had all sorts of "procedures" done. She told me, "Your laboratory tests were unremarkable and didn't support any findings that would lead me to believe that you have any kind of urinary or bladder problem going on right now." She told me to drink more fluids.

October 5 (11 P.M.) I'm feeling really very, very nauseated. I know that I'm not pregnant (have my period, too). I threw up lots of times. I don't know what's wrong. Fred went to get me

something from the drug store. I didn't work yesterday or today.

November 15 I went to see Dr. Baker (again). My period is causing me a lot of discomfort. She said that if I still have problems by tomorrow, she'll do another D&C, but she said she was not happy to be performing a fourth procedure on me. She said I should go to a specialist after this.

November 22 Today, I went to the outpatient facility for a D&C. The doctor said that maybe I should seek out some counseling. I told her I'd think about it, but I really won't. How come they don't realize how much pain I'm in?

December 15 (6:00 A.M.) I'm really having problems breathing. I can't catch my breath or take a deep breath. I'm worried that I might be having a heart attack because my heart feels like its fluttering. Jessica's coming to take me to the emergency room. Maybe they can help me.

On December 16, Helene was hospitalized because of her cardiac symptoms and breathing complaints. During the current hospitalization, she had both a comprehensive physical and medical examination, and laboratory tests (to rule out any viable medical condition). Helene was given a clean bill of health and subsequently referred to a social worker for counseling and support.

ASSESSMENT SUMMARY   Irrespective of the underlying motives, all possible explanations for somatization encourages a thorough medical examination and an inquiry into Helene's biopsychosocial history. Helene's behavior should be explored in the context of existing medical complaints and the extent to which her symptoms might be helping to resolve her life problems or represent psychological conflicts. The extent of Helene's complaints, the degree to which she suffers, and her inability to engage in her usual level of activities are noteworthy.

Individuals with major depressive disorder, generalized anxiety disorder, and schizophrenia might present somatic complaints, but eventually their symptoms override the somatic complaints. Although there is a strong association between panic attacks and somatization disorders, the person diagnosed with panic disorder is generally not bothered by somatic symptoms between panic attacks. In factitious disorder, the person derives great satisfaction from being considered ill. In malingering disorder, the symptoms are intentionally produced to avoid some task or legal action, or to obtain material and/or financial goods. In contrast, Helene's physical discomfort is genuine, in that she truly believes she is ill. She also exhibits a long-standing pattern of excessive emotionality and attention-seeking behavior that seeps into all areas of her life. She needs to be the center of attention in two main ways: (1) she puts her own interests at the forefront of all of her relationships, and (2) her behavior, including speech, constantly calls attention to herself. This supports an Axis II diagnosis of histrionic personality disorder.

Advanced Clinical EP 2.1.7 c

In beginning to understand Helene's total functioning, the practitioner must first make an assessment that includes all aspects of her life history and life experiences. Helene's worker, first and foremost, must rule out nonpsychiatric medical conditions that may offer an alternative explanation of her symptoms. In a case like Helene's, it is not unusual for the practitioner to consult with other medical professionals, when needed, to better confirm the diagnosis of somatization disorder. Unlike individuals with hypochondriasis, who excessively "doctor shop" and who are preoccupied with the false belief that they have a specific disease or have a fear of a specific disease, Helene focuses more heavily on the *symptoms of disease*. In conversion disorder (discussed later in this chapter), symptoms are usually limited to only one, typically involving the central nervous system—for example, the individual becomes "blind," "paralyzed," or "mute." Pain disorder (also discussed in this chapter) is limited to one or two complaints of pain symptoms, such as low back pain. In contrast, Helene's health diary reveals a wide variety of symptoms occurring over a period of time. When one complaint is addressed, another one emerges.

Advanced Clinical EP 2.1.10 (b) c

The competency-based assessment provides a framework for assessing Helene's strengths. In particular, an assessment of interpersonal factors notes that she has a good relationship with her mother. She also has a close childhood friend who is supportive of her. Additionally, Helene wants to return to school for her GED. Figure 8.1 shows the interactions of the biological, psychological, and social variables in Helene Martin's life.

HELENE MARTIN'S CURRENT MULTIAXIAL DSM DIAGNOSIS IS AS FOLLOWS:

Axis I	300.81 Somatization Disorder
Axis II	301.50 Histrionic Personality Disorder
Axis III	None
Axis IV	None
Axis IV	GAF = 60 (at time of examination)

© Cengage Learning

CONVERSION DISORDER

The symptoms of **conversion disorder**, a type of somatoform disorder, have been described since antiquity. The affected individual experiences a loss or change in physical functioning that suggests the presence of a physical disorder but cannot be explained on the basis of any known physiologic mechanism. In other words, this loss or change does not exist outside the individual's own personal experience.

Sigmund Freud believed the anxiety that was the product of unconscious conflicts needed to find expression and was somehow "converted" into physical

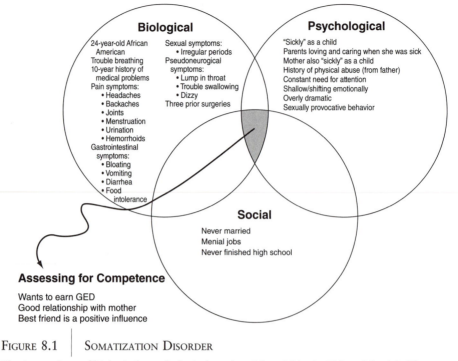

FIGURE 8.1 | SOMATIZATION DISORDER

The interactions of biological, psychological, and social variables in Helene Martin's life.

© Cengage Learning

symptoms. He believed that this transformation, or conversion, allowed the individual to "get rid" of some anxiety without actually having to experience it as such (Barlow & Durand, 2012). Freud is credited with coining the term *conversion* in conjunction with one of his most famous cases, that of Anna O (Freud, 1894). However, he was not the actual originator of the term—he borrowed it from the Middle Ages.

Conversion disorder is one of the most intriguing types of behavior a practitioner will encounter in his or her entire professional practice. What could possibly account for a person going blind when the optic functions are perfectly normal? What could cause a person to experience a seizure when there is no viable neurological explanation? Consider the following historical account from the 1677 Bargarran witchcraft trial:

> Seven people were condemned in Paisley, Ireland, for allegedly using witchcraft against Christina, favored daughter of the powerful Laird of Bargarran. As the story unfolds, 7 months after several disgruntled servants placed a "spell" on Christina, she began having bizarre seizures. During these episodes, she claimed to see the devil. She believed that invisible assailants forced strange and foreign materials into her mouth, and she herself had no real understanding of why she experienced fits [seizures] or why she ate strange things. The notable Glasgow physician, Matthew Brisban, was consulted, and he later gave evidence at the trial against the servants. Dr. Brisban admitted he could

find no natural explanation for Christina's seizures or for her eating strange substances.

Christina subsequently recovered, and later married a minister from Kilmours. After her husband's untimely death (no information is known about what happened), Christina established a highly prosperous spinning business that later led to the beginning of the famous Paisley cotton industry. (McDonald & Thom, 1996)

The case of Christina is a good example of pseudoneurological symptoms. Her conversion symptoms resemble genuine sensory or motor symptoms but do not conform to anatomical patterns expected for a condition with a well-defined physical cause—and they developed suddenly, after what anyone would agree was a stressful event (being cursed by disgruntled servants).

PREVAILING PATTERN

If Christina found herself in similar circumstances today, she would likely be diagnosed with a conversion disorder, the essential feature of which is the presence of symptoms that affect voluntary motor or sensory function, suggesting a neurological or other general medical condition (Gray, 2006). The assessment criteria for conversion disorder are:

- One or more symptoms affecting voluntary motor or sensory function, suggesting a neurological or another general medical condition.
- Symptoms whose onset (or exacerbation) can be associated with psychological factors resulting from preceding interpersonal conflicts or other social stresses.
- Symptoms are not consciously produced or feigned (as is the case in factitious or malingering disorders).
- A general medical condition, medication, the effects of a substance, or culturally sanctioned behaviors cannot fully explain these symptoms.
- Symptoms are not limited to pain or sexual dysfunction.
- Symptoms do not occur solely for the duration of somatization disorder, and no other medical disorder better explains them.
- Symptoms are serious enough to produce at least one of the following:
  - Distress that is clinically important.
  - Distress that warrants medical evaluation.
  - Distress that impairs social, occupational, or personal functioning.
- Symptoms or deficits that can be *specified* from among the following four types:
  1. Motor symptoms or deficits (e.g., difficulty swallowing (lump in throat), poor balance or gait, paralysis or weakness in arms or legs, loss of voice, and urinary retention).
  2. Sensory symptoms or deficits (e.g., loss of touch or pain sensation, blindness, double vision, and deafness).
  3. Seizure-like symptoms or convulsions.
  4. A mixed presentation of symptoms (American Psychiatric Association, 2000).

Although the symptoms of conversion disorder are temporarily disabling, they differ significantly in a number of ways from those disabilities caused by actual neurological disorders. In conversion disorder, the symptoms ebb and flow depending on the person's activity level. The symptoms typically do not conform to known anatomical pathways, disease processes, or physiological mechanisms. Conversion disorder is characterized by the occurrence of certain signs and symptoms that are clearly inconsistent with what is actually known about human anatomy and pathophysiology. In other words, the individual's understanding (or misunderstanding) and their own conceptualizations (or misconceptions) of anatomy, diseases, and physiology help shape the symptoms they present. The individual who is actually paralyzed cannot move certain parts of his or her body, whereas in conversion disorder the individual is able to move his or her "paralyzed" arm if needed to scratch an annoying itch. However, the person does not realize that movement is possible. This is not to say that these symptoms are consciously constructed or intentionally faked. For the individual who suffers from conversion disorder, the intent and construction of symptoms are an unconscious process. The proposal for the DSM-5 is to change the name to functional neurological disorder because the current term, conversion disorder, suggests that there is a specific cause for a person's symptoms when there is no (or insignificant) supportive evidence. Including the term *functional* is intended to add more clarity by characterizing symptoms as lacking an organic cause (Stone, LaFrance, Levenson, & Sharpe, 2010).

Conversion symptoms are called pseudoneurological because they resemble actual sensory or motor symptoms. They usually do not correspond to the anatomical pattern that would be expected for a condition with a well-defined physical cause. Actual manifestations of symptoms are quite varied. In some cases, the disorder mimics neurological problems, wherein symptoms presented range among poor balance, poor coordination, paralysis, or an inability to see. Others experience symptoms of weakness in their limbs or have difficulty swallowing. Sometimes, conversion disorders appear as tics or tremors. At other times, there may be sensory symptoms or deficits that include double vision, tunnel vision, blindness, deafness, hallucinations, or the absence of touch or pain sensation. When the practitioner explores a person's medical history, most individuals with conversion disorder will describe only one motor or neurological symptom—most commonly, one of the following: blindness, paralysis, seizures, tunnel vision, coordination disturbances (previously known as *astasia-abasia*), **ataxia** (defective muscle coordination), **globus hystericus** (lump in throat), syncope (fainting), **dyskinesia** (inability to perform voluntary movements), **paresthesia** (sensation of numbness, prickling, or tingling), **tonic-clonic pseudoseizures** (muscular spasms), **anosmia** (absent sense of smell), **hemiplegia** (paralysis on one side of the body), deafness, anesthesia (absence of feel), or **akinesia** (complete or partial loss of muscle movement).

When conversion anesthesia occurs in a hand (or foot), the syndrome might accompany the so-called **stocking-glove anesthesia** (Aybek, Kanan, & David, 2008). The individual experiences loss of sensation or numbness in a hand (or foot), in an area typically covered by a glove (or stocking), which ends abruptly in a sharply demarcated line like a bracelet around the wrist (or ankle). The actual disbursement pattern of the nerves (or "wiring" that occurs in the hand or foot) is in reality very different. If a true paralysis occurred, it would run the entire length of the hand or foot, and not end in such a sharply demarcated line.

Although conversion disorder can appear at any age, most individuals experience their first symptoms during adolescence or early adulthood. In most cases, the actual onset is abrupt and typically follows a major stress event in a person's life.

Other important features associated with conversion disorder of which it is important for practitioners to be aware include:

- *Primary gain*—Individuals can achieve primary gain by keeping internal conflicts outside of their awareness, and they have low levels of insight about what is going on in their lives.
- *Secondary gain*—Individuals accumulate discernible advantages from their symptoms and behaviors as a result of being in the sick role. For instance, they may be excused from confronting or dealing with difficult life situations, they may be able to control other people, or they might receive support and help that might not otherwise be given.

There is some risk of actual physical and long-term impairment if certain conversion symptoms persist over an extended period of time. Those who do not regularly use their muscles often experience muscle atrophy (or damage). This disuse of muscles may also result in the demineralization of the skeletal system.

DIFFERENTIAL ASSESSMENT

Advanced Clinical EP 2.1.7 c

Conversion disorder generally refers to some type of physical problem without any underlying physical pathology. Hurwitz (2004) points to a psychodynamic explanation wherein a person experiences a trauma that is too difficult to bear and, as a consequence, the distress is converted into a sensory motor disability that is easier to tolerate. Conversion disorders have an uncanny resemblance to neurological problems. Formulating a differential assessment is critical, and the practitioner should refer the client to a medical professional in order to rule out neurological diseases and confirm the diagnosis. The following case represents the symptom picture of conversion disorder.

CASE | THE CASE OF JENNY WEBBER

Jake Webber rushed his wife, Jenny, to the emergency room of a rural hospital that was two towns away from their home. During the 75-mile drive, he was extremely worried about his wife. Jenny Webber is 34 years old and the mother of three children. She has been employed as a secretary for the past 8 years at a local accounting firm. She is involved in her church, where she teaches Sunday school—and through work and church she has cultivated many friends.

In the emergency room, Jake tells the resident physician on duty, "We were just standing in line buying some soda at Duncan's General Store when all of a sudden some guy pulls out a gun and says, 'This is a holdup.' Then he tells us to get down on the floor." He continues, "The robber grabs some money out of the cash register, runs to a waiting car, and heads for the hills. I mean, the whole thing didn't take more than 15 seconds. The next thing I know, the police are all over the place, and they're asking people to

continued

describe the thief. One of the cops comes over to Jenny and me and asks us if we'd come downtown to the station and go through some mug shots. Of course, I said sure, anything to help out," Jake said. "But the next thing I know, Jenny stumbles and falls—she's in a panic, telling me she can't see anything."

The physician began his physical examination. He noted that, although Mrs. Webber complained of blindness, her pupils constricted when he directed his penlight in her eyes. And when he made a sudden movement toward her face, she blinked involuntarily.

Mrs. Webber was examined for signs of neurological or other general medical conditions that may account for her inability to see. Her laboratory results indicated that she was not under the influence of drugs or alcohol. The physician consulted the other (more senior) doctor in town, who suggested treatment with a placebo. The emergency room physician assured Mrs. Webber that the "special injection" he was going to administer would restore her vision back to normal. Within ten seconds of having this special shot, Mrs. Webber's vision returned, much to her delight. She was discharged from the hospital with a follow-up referral to evaluate the risk for any longer-term adjustment problems at the North Bismark Mental Health Center.

ASSESSMENT SUMMARY   In contrast to somatization disorder, which is chronic and poly-symptomatic (involving many organ systems), Jenny Webber's conversion disorder was spontaneous and monosymptomatic. Her frightening experience of witnessing the general store holdup set the foundation for a symbolic relationship between the underlying psychological struggle to cope with her fears and the associated loss of sight—her blindness occurred suddenly, just when the police officer asked her and her husband to come to the station to look at mug shots of potential suspects.

The Webbers were unwilling participants in this criminal and potentially violent event, yet she manifested none of the features of acute stress disorder (e.g., poor concentration, hypervigilence, or an exaggerated startle response) as discussed earlier (refer to the chapter on anxiety disorders). Jenny claimed she could not see, yet her eyes reacted to light. When the physician moved toward her, she blinked reflexively in response to his sudden movement.

When given a placebo injection, Jenny experienced a spontaneous remission of her blindness and a complete recovery. In fact, prompt recovery is the rule with treatment of conversion disorder, and especially when the individual, like Jenny Webber, is surrounded by supportive family members. It is not uncommon for the practitioner to see someone similar to Jenny in an ambulatory or emergency room setting where the individual responds to almost any therapeutic intervention that offers the suggestion of a cure. The key strategy for recovery is to identify and attend to the person's traumatic life event. Hypnosis and cognitive behavior therapy are also effective intervention strategies (Moene, Spinhoven, Hoogduin, & van Dyck, 2003).

Advanced
Clinical EP
2.1.10 (b) c

Although the relevant information in this case focuses on deficits and blindness, the competency-based assessment provides a framework for the practitioner to look at the whole person and take into consideration Jenny's strengths as an integral part of the assessment. Figure 8.2 shows the interactions of the biological, psychological, and social variables in Jenny Webber's life. For example, she is very active in her rural community and committed to church functions. A number of

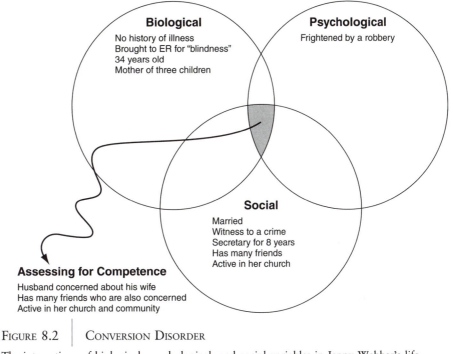

Biological

No history of illness
Brought to ER for "blindness"
34 years old
Mother of three children

Psychological

Frightened by a robbery

Social

Married
Witness to a crime
Secretary for 8 years
Has many friends
Active in her church

Assessing for Competence

Husband concerned about his wife
Has many friends who are also concerned
Active in her church and community

FIGURE 8.2 | CONVERSION DISORDER

The interactions of biological, psychological, and social variables in Jenny Webber's life.

© Cengage Learning

friends seem to care about Jenny. In addition, she has worked in the same position for 8 years, and lastly, her husband, Jake, is very devoted to her. The social worker's focus was short term and crisis oriented, but she also considers the possibility of risk factors that may potentially affect Jenny's longer-term recovery. The referral to the mental health center for further evaluation was made as a preventative measure to further ensure Jenny's continued recovery.

JENNY WEBBER'S MULTIAXIAL DSM DIAGNOSIS WOULD BE AS FOLLOWS:

Axis I	300.11 Conversion Disorder
Axis II	V71.09 (No diagnosis)
Axis III	None
Axis IV	None
Axis IV	None
Axis V	GAF = 60 (on admission) 90 (at discharge)

© Cengage Learning

UNDERSTANDING PAIN DISORDER

The assessment of **pain disorder** can be made when pain is the client's "predominant focus of clinical attention" *and* when psychological factors are present that may play a significant role in causing or maintaining the pain. This disorder has been known by a number of different names in the past, including somatoform pain disorder, psychogenic pain disorder, idiopathic pain disorder, and atypical pain disorder.

Pain disorder is assessed when both psychological and medical factors are present. The psychological factors play a role in the onset, severity, exacerbation, and/or maintenance of the person's pain. For example, a person may sustain a hand injury that causes excessive pain at the time of injury. In spite of treatment, the individual may continue to seek a disproportionate amount of medical attention based on the conviction that there is a health professional out there who can "cure" the pain. Some practitioners have been known to diagnose pain disorders only on the basis of psychological features, such as a previous diagnosis, evidence of past somatization, prominent guilt, or a history of physical or emotional abuse by either a parent or spouse. However, these "soft" findings, even taken along with negative laboratory or physical findings, do not automatically imply that the pain presented is attributable to mental or emotional factors.

A valid assessment of this disorder requires that pain occur in one or more anatomic sites, with an etiology dominated by psychological factors, particularly anxiety focused on the experience of pain (Asmundson & Carleton, 2009). The defining feature is the preoccupation with pain that cannot be accounted for by any known medical or neurological condition. Pain disorder shares a noteworthy feature with conversion disorder, in that they are the only two conditions noted in the DSM-IV-TR whose criteria consist of intrapersonal factors playing the primary role in the development and/or maintenance of symptoms. One proposal for the DSM-5 is to make pain disorder part of a larger category called complex somatic symptom disorder.

EP 2.1.10
(b) a

Diagnosing pain disorder can be problematic because it renders the social worker's assessment to one shaped by subjectivity—that is, what is important to one practitioner may seem irrelevant to another. A second problem is that pain itself is also subjective and difficult to measure with any validity. As the practitioner collects data about the client's pain experience, the emphasis is to carefully organize and interpret this data. It is commonly agreed that people experience pain differently and, for that reason, it becomes important for the practitioner to use the competency-based assessment as a tool for separating out emotional reactions associated with chronic or excruciating pain.

Pain disorder can occur at any age, but most often it becomes apparent during adolescence or early adulthood. Symptoms usually emerge after an unexpected acute stressor, and they can last weeks or months. Factors that influence a person's recovery from pain disorder include an acknowledgement of pain, giving up unproductive efforts to control pain, returning to regularly scheduled activities, and a mind-set of not allowing the pain to become a determining factor in one's lifestyle. However, if the person envisions or anticipates secondary gain, the pain might persist or continue indefinitely. Much like those with somatization disorder, these people are known to physician shop; undergo unnecessary examinations, procedures, and tests; become ingrained in maintaining the sick role; restrict their social and occupational functioning (often because they are bedridden); and abuse medications, especially analgesics. Assuming the sick role suggests that "being sick" helps to release someone from their usual personal and family obligations while absolving them of any blame for their sick condition. The sick role can also function as a way to obtain love, to punish one's own failures, to compensate for guilt, or to atone for an innate sense of badness.

Pain can assume many forms, but it is most frequently manifested in three areas: the head, the pelvis, and the lower back. The pain presented can be traumatic, **neuropathic** (disease of nerves), neurological, and/or **iatrogenic** (seen as the inadvertent or adverse physical condition caused by side effects of surgical or medical treatment). Pain is the primary motivator for people to seek medical attention. But individuals have different thresholds for tolerating pain—some can grin and bear it while others become severely immobilized and incapacitated.

There is very little information about the prevalence of pain disorder. What we do know is that up to 56 million American adults, or 28 percent of the adult population, experience chronic pain, making it a fairly common condition (Brennan, Carr, & Cousins, 2007). Chronic pain accounts for 10 to 20 percent of primary care visits (Marcus 2005). The total US direct and indirect cost of chronic pain is almost $50 billion per year and is associated with millions of days of lost work (Burgoyne, 2007).

Curiously, aspirin, commonly taken for pain, is consumed by Americans by as much as 50 million tablets every day, making that about 18 billion pills a year.

PREVAILING PATTERN

The assessment for pain disorder includes the following features:

- Pain that occurs in more than one anatomical site, is the presenting problem, and is the predominant focus of clinical attention; the pain is severe enough to warrant clinical attention.
- The pain causes distress that impairs occupational, social, or other important areas of functioning.
- Intrapersonal factors are considered important in the onset, severity, and exacerbation of pain (or support maintaining the pain).
- The individual does not consciously feign the pain symptoms (as seen in malingering or factitious disorder).
- The pain is not explained by a mood, anxiety, or psychotic disorder, and it does not meet the criteria for dyspareunia (pain that occurs during or after sexual intercourse).

If a person's pain lasts less than 6 months, it is considered acute; if it lasts longer, it is considered chronic. It is important to consider not only intrapersonal factors but also medical or biological conditions when exploring onset, intensity, exacerbation, and maintenance of pain. The following vignette describes Aleta Austin's pain disorder.

CASE | THE CASE OF ALETA AUSTIN

Aleta Austin is a 26-year-old woman who was seen by a social worker during her first clinic visit. When asked what brought her in, Aleta explained, "I work as an aide in a nursing home, and I was lifting a patient up from a chair to her wheelchair. Well, anyhow, all of a sudden I felt this terrible and very painful snap in the back of my neck. I lost my balance and fell on the floor. As I was falling, I hit my arm real

continued

bad, too. The next thing I knew, I was in the hospital, and they were doing some X–rays and an MRI. The doctors said I sprained my neck, and I might have a hairline fracture of my arm. They put some kind of neck brace on me and said I had to wear it for 2 weeks. I didn't need to have a cast on my arm, but I was supposed to be real careful."

Aleta continued, "I wasn't allowed to work for 6 weeks, so I got workmen's comp—but the checks stopped when the doctors said I could go back to work. It has been 4 months, and they say that's too long to have pain for the injury I got. So now I have money problems on top of everything else, but I don't care what they say, I still hurt." Apparently without realizing it, Aleta was rubbing her neck while she was talking. She went on, "After being discharged by those doctors, I went to see several new ones. I thought, you know, maybe the first ones didn't know what they were talking about."

The social worker asked what other doctors Aleta had seen.

"Well, over the past 3 months," she replied, "I saw two orthopedic surgeons, one neurologist, two chiropractors, and a massage therapist. I was given lots of different medicines and treatments, but I still didn't get much relief. One of the doctors said I should see a shrink. He thought my problems were all in my head. Can you beat that?" Aleta sounded very annoyed. "That really steamed me—doesn't he realize I really want to go back to work and see all my friends again? Not only that, does he think I *like* being in constant pain? Does he think I *like* taking all this medicine and not getting any relief from any of it?"

The practitioner asked Aleta about the medications she is currently using.

She answered, "In the beginning, they gave me some pain pills that helped some, but the doctors won't prescribe anything for me now. They think I'm getting too used to all the pills. Now I can only take over-the-counter stuff like, you know, aspirin, Aleve, Tylenol, Motrin—but they don't do much good. Nothing seems to help nowadays."

When asked how she spent her days, she replied, "I pretty much stay inside the house all day long. I have a hard time finding a comfortable place to sit or lay down. My brother, Chad, brought over his favorite recliner chair for me to use, and that does help some. Most of the time I watch TV, sleep, or play with my dogs." Aleta volunteered that she and her husband are "in the middle of getting a divorce after being married 5 years." She stated, "It was his idea, but I guess it's all for the best. During the time we were married, I realized that I am a lesbian, so ... I always felt different from other women and a little confused about this. I tried really hard to just bury these feelings—my family sort of freaked out. It's so hard to come to terms with this.... But I can't believe he wants a divorce after all the time we've been together. He doesn't know about me being gay, and he told me he isn't seeing anyone else—he just said he was tired of me being sick all the time. I don't believe him." Aleta studied her fingernails for a moment. "Well, like I said, maybe it's for the best. He's absolutely no use to me now."

The practitioner asked Aleta to say a little more about that. As it happens, Aleta's parents had moved into her home 3 months ago, "so they could help out while I was recovering," she explained. "My dad works full-time, as a barber, but he finds the time to mow the grass, run errands, and do the house repairs. I'm starting to get a little behind on my bills, and dad tries to help out a little in that department, too." Aleta repeatedly stated she wanted to go back to work; however, she also said, "It's kinda nice to have mom and dad around the house right now. Mom fixes all my favorite foods—[laughing] I know I'm gonna gain ten pounds before she leaves to go back home!"

"You know, my mom told me that when she was younger, she had problems like me. I guess when she was a teenager she had problems with pain in her back for a really long time. Isn't that weird? Mom said when she was around 20 she had trouble with really bad headaches and something with her breathing—she doesn't like to talk about it much." Aleta related that she once asked her Aunt Dolly (her mother's oldest sister) about it, and she had just said, "Oh, it's just something the Walker women get when they are young'uns."

When asked if she had experienced any previous psychological problems such as hallucinations, delusions, depression, suicidal ideation, or anxiety, Aleta laughed, and said, "My lord, no. Aside from this neck and arm pain, my health has been somewhat good." She described herself having frequent bouts of low back pain, headaches, and "sometimes my jaw hurts real bad, off and on," she offered, "but overall I don't have any serious medical problems."

During the relating of her past medical history, the social worker observed that Aleta's train of thought had been derailed somehow. Sure enough, she interrupted herself, "You know, I've been thinking about the question you just asked, the question about psychological problems. Does sibling rivalry count as a psychological problem?" She continued, "When Chad, my brother, and I were growing up, we fought like we were mortal enemies. I mean we hated each other." I always felt like Chad was mom's favorite, so I grew up feeling like a 'Secondhand Rose.' It was awful."

The session continued along these lines for another 15 minutes or so. When the time was up and Aleta was walking out the door, she said to the social worker, "You know, it's really great to have all of my mother's attention right now because I'm in so much pain."

ASSESSMENT SUMMARY The dramatic presentation of Aleta's pain sounds extreme at first, but the practitioner cannot take this symptom alone to qualify for making the assessment of pain disorder. In this situation, the pain has not only impaired Aleta's ability to work, but it has also caused problems in her relationships with her husband, family, and coworkers. The pain must be distinguished from other somatoform disorders, despite the fact that some can and do coexist. For example, pain complaints may be discernible in those with conversion disorder; however, by definition, conversion disorder includes other symptoms along with pain, and the associated discomfort is seen as short-lived. Although the diagnosis of hypochondriasis does not include actual pain, the person's concerns, fears, or worries about having a serious illness can be confused with a pain disorder; additionally, those with hypochondriasis have many more fluctuating symptoms than do individuals with pain disorder. Malingering is connected with clearly recognizable benefits and advantages (in litigation, for example, where the individual invents symptoms in order to fraudulently receive financial gain). Aleta's suffering is real to her, and she gives no indication that her pain changes depending on whether she is at home or at work. A differential assessment is the only way to distinguish those who falsify their symptoms from someone like Aleta, who truly believes her pain is genuine, is the result of an actual medical condition (a sprained neck and hairline fracture of her arm), and it continues for 4 months after the incident at work. Although the increased attention Aleta is receiving from her parents may resemble secondary gain, her main concern is always feeling like she was not the favored child when she was growing up.

EP 2.1.7 b

Practitioners may be tempted to diagnose first and then ask questions to support that clinical picture. The competency-based assessment helps to stifle that impulse by encouraging an exploration of the multiple influences in the client's life—i.e., intrapersonal issues, patterns of interpersonal relationships, social context, and support networks. The core elements of this assessment framework encompass knowledge about human behavior across the life span, the social systems in which the client lives, and the ways social systems affect health and well-being. Figure 8.3 illustrates the interactions of the biological, psychological, and social variables in Aleta Austin's life.

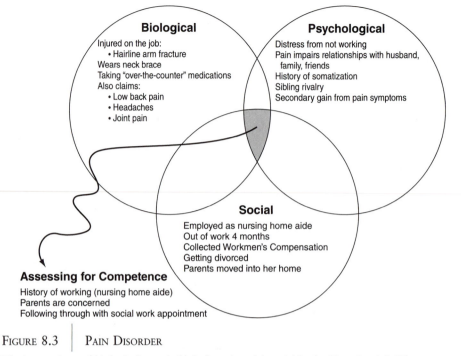

FIGURE 8.3 | PAIN DISORDER

The interactions of biological, psychological, and social variables in Aleta Austin's life.

© Cengage Learning

ALETA AUSTIN'S MULTIAXIAL DSM DIAGNOSIS IS AS FOLLOWS:

Axis I	307.89 Pain Disorder Associated with Psychological Factors and a General Medical Condition, Acute
Axis II	V71.09 (No diagnosis)
Axis III	Hairline Fracture of Arm
Axis IV	Divorce
	Unemployed 4 months
	Financial problems
Axis V	GAF = 65 (current)

© Cengage Learning

DIFFERENTIAL ASSESSMENT

As discussed earlier, the distinguishing feature of pain disorder is when a person experiences chronic and constant pain and the pain is often so severe that it interferes with work, social, or personal functioning. Pain disorder, by definition, is a syndrome having three dimensions; biological, psychological, and social (Disorbio, Bruns, & Barolat, 2006). However, it is the psychological factors that are important in the onset, maintenance, and severity or worsening of the pain. The competency-based assessment is organized around each of these three dimensions, offering insight into differentiating pain disorder from other disorders. A person's cognitive processes and personality may impact on both the perception of pain and how he or she adjusts to it. When the cause of the continued pain is not clearly understood, both the individual and the practitioner may become frustrated, and this complicates the assessment. It is important to remember that the person still feels the pain, whether there is a physical basis or not.

EP 2.1.10
(b) a

As a part of organizing and interpreting this data in order to distinguish pain disorder from other diagnoses, the practitioner collects as much data as possible about a person's experience with pain. It is important to look for the symptoms of mood, anxiety, or other psychotic disorders that may better account for the person's pain. To further complicate the assessment, some disorders have similar or even the same symptoms of pain disorder; for example, **osteoporosis** (a decrease in bone mass causing bones to become fragile), **osteoarthritis** (a form of arthritis involving the deterioration of the cartilage that cushions the ends of bones within joints), or **fibromyalgia** (a chronic disorder characterized by widespread pain in muscles and soft tissues surrounding joints, accompanied by fatigue). It is important to discern whether the person's pain is entirely accounted for by a general medical condition. If so, the diagnosis of pain disorder does not apply. Though people with chronic pain are often presumed to be overanxious and fearful, the idea of a "pain-prone personality" is not well supported by research (Szalavitz, 2005). However, there are a number of personality attributes, such as introversion/extraversion, optimism, perceived locus of control affect, and personality disorders, that affect patients' ability to cope with pain (Gatchel & Weisberg, 2000).

UNDERSTANDING HYPOCHONDRIASIS

The person with **hypochondriasis** is characterized as having physical complaints that are without a clear cause. These physical symptoms become an overwhelming and unrelenting preoccupation that is deeply rooted in some unrealistic, apocalyptic interpretation or **somatosensory amplification**; that is, the tendency to experience bodily sensations as being unusually intense, aversive, and distressing. This is the individual who not only strongly suspects but also actually believes he or she is suffering from a very serious and life-threatening condition. Often the hypochondriasis process begins when the person notices a lump, bruise, or blemish. From that humble beginning, he or she starts to assume, with a great degree of certainty and considerable anxiety, that a serious illness has taken root—as they continue to ruminate about it, the lump becomes a tumor, the bruise becomes hemophilia, and the blemish becomes skin cancer. As the process unfolds, the individual begins to constantly fret about "the illness," often to the point that normal occupational activities and relationships with others are dramatically disrupted. The world of the hypochondriac becomes filled with unrealistic and dire interpretations of disease symptoms and his or her subsequent reactions to them. They remain steadfast in their concern for themselves, and they are convinced that something is very wrong with them.

The person with hypochondriasis takes a better-safe-than-sorry approach to dealing with even a minor physical symptom by getting it checked out as soon as possible. A central feature of this disorder is the person's faulty interpretation of physical signs and sensations as evidence of having an actual physical illness. The anxiety and mood disorders, especially with panic disorder, often co-occur with hypochondriasis (Creed & Barsky, 2004). Since anxiety or the fear that one has a serious disease characterizes hypochondriasis, the DSM-5 may consider the possibility that many with hypochondriasis might be more appropriately diagnosed as having an anxiety disorder (Taylor & Asmundson, 2009). The person's expression of anxiety, however, is different from that of the other anxiety disorders. Someone struggling with hypochondriasis is preoccupied with bodily symptoms and sees them as indications of a serious illness despite reassurance from others that they are fine. Any relief they might get from being reassured about their medical condition is generally short-lived. In time, they once more begin to focus on their symptoms, and the cycle of worry begins anew. This kind of anxiety that is primarily focused on the possibility of disease or illness is referred to as a disease conviction (Woolfolk & Allen, 2011). The preoccupation with minor symptoms, the persistent conviction that they suffer from a deadly disease, and the futile inadequacy of medical reassurance can cause friendships to wear thin, especially when the sufferer's every ache or pain is recounted in minute detail. Easy access to medical and diagnostic information via the Internet has spawned a mutation of this phenomenon known as **cyberchondria** (Gray, 2006).

PREVAILING PATTERN

The true prevalence rate of hypochondriasis in the general population currently remains unknown; however, what is known is that men and women are equally at risk. Hypochondriasis may begin any time between the adolescent years through to older adulthood, but peak onset occurs during the 20s and 30s (Springhouse, 2008).

Historically considered one of the hysterical disorders (and therefore unique to women), the actual gender ratio between men and women for hypochondriasis is about 50:50 (Kirmayer, Looper, & Taillefer, 2003). When looking at occurrence in psychiatric and medical clinics, prevalence rates change. Feinstein and Fallon (2003) point out women are found to have hypochondriasis 3 to 4 times more often than men.

The clinical course of hypochondriasis is lifelong and chronic, with symptoms waxing and waning over months or years. Often symptoms flare up during times of stress. The individual's conclusion is always on the side of having a grave, life-threatening condition, versus a transient or minor disease.

Hypochondriasis includes the following features:

- The individual misinterprets bodily symptoms and therefore becomes preoccupied with the fear and the idea that he or she has a serious or grave illness.
- The individual's preoccupation persists despite receiving appropriate medical investigation, examination, and/or reassurance.
- These ideas are not considered delusional (as would be seen in delusional disorder), and the ideas are not restricted to concern about appearance, as is seen in body dysmorphic disorder.
- This preoccupation causes clinically significant distress or impairment in the performance of occupational, social, or interpersonal functioning.
- Symptoms persist for at least 6 months.
- This preoccupation of ideas cannot better be explained by generalized anxiety disorder, obsessive-compulsive disorder, major depressive episode, panic

disorder, separation anxiety, or other somatoform disorders (American Psychiatric Association, 2000).

If, during most of the episode, the individual does not recognize that his or her preoccupation is excessive or unreasonable, then that person is deemed to have poor insight.

DIFFERENTIAL ASSESSMENT

EP 2.1.10
(b) a

When organizing and interpreting data collected about the client's symptoms, the most important diagnostic consideration for the diagnosis of hypochondriasis is the presence of an underlying medical condition and the person's persistent preoccupation with his or her medical status—despite appropriate medical evaluation and/or reassurance. Somatic symptoms are more commonly found in children (e.g., stomach pain) and would be diagnosed as hypochondriasis if the child is concerned about having a more serious illness than a stomachache. Some people with a major depressive episode may be preoccupied about their health. Hypochondriasis in not considered if these health concerns occur only during the major depressive episode. When depression occurs secondarily to hypochondriasis, then the more appropriate diagnosis would be hypochondriasis.

As a part to the diagnostic picture for hypochondriasis, the person constantly seeks reassurance about his or her medical condition. This preoccupation may resemble symptoms of an obsessive-compulsive disorder; however, the diagnosis would be obsessive-compulsive disorder only when the obsessions or compulsions include concerns other than those related to illness (e.g., the person is also concerned if he or she left the house and the door is unlocked). The diagnosis of panic disorder is considered when recurrent unexpected panic attacks are also present. For those struggling with body dysmorphic disorder, the concern is limited to the individual's personal appearance. Specific phobia is considered when the person is fearful of developing or being exposed to a disease in contrast to hypochondriasis, wherein the person is preoccupied with the idea that they actually have the disease. For those with hypochondriasis, the conviction that they have a disease does not reach the delusional proportions found in the psychotic disorders. The following vignette illustrates Carl Beacher's struggles with hypochondriasis.

CASE | THE CASE OF CARL BEACHER

Carl Beacher is a 53-year-old white male. He has been married to his high school sweetheart, Sally, for 30 years. Although they have no children of their own, the couple is involved actively in the lives of their many nieces, nephews, and godchildren.

Carl's initial complaint was of anxiety and stress due to his high-pressure job as a manager in used car sales. During our first contact, it didn't take long for me to realize that his principal concern is about

health issues. Whenever he experiences some minor physical problem, say, a cough or headache, Carl immediately concludes that the coughing symptoms are lung cancer, or a headache means a malignant brain tumor. When experiencing other (benign) physical sensations, he quickly transforms them into life-threatening medical conditions.

With considerable frustration, Carl relates, "Going to all these doctor appointments cuts into

continued

my commissions and my time off. I really can't afford to be away from work anymore. As it is, the big bosses are starting to watch me like hawks. I don't know how long I can keep doing this. Even Sally has started calling me her disease-of-the-month husband—which, I might add," he says testily, "I don't really appreciate. You know, I don't think she takes my medical concerns seriously."

He admits that his constant worrying about having a serious disease has caused a lot of tension, not just in his relationship with Sally, but with other family members as well. "They don't want to listen to me anymore." Carl says he finds himself absorbed by reading medical books or medical journals. In fact, he admits to subscribing to several of them. "Sometimes, when I have a problem I look up my physical symptoms—that's when I really start worrying." Interestingly, Carl brags about having an extensive and valuable collection of vintage medical books and antique surgical instruments purchased at local flea markets.

"He lives in fear of being diagnosed," Sally confirms. "Just in the last 6 months alone, Carl has complained of chest pain, stomach problems, dizziness, muscle spasms, bruises on his arm—I could go on and on."

Carl adds somewhat defensively, "Even hearing about a friend or family member's illness is enough to incapacitate me for days." He explains that his fears developed about 5 years ago, around the time he was trying to start up a new trucking business. "I had a bad cough that just wouldn't go away, so first I went to our family doctor, Dr. Vasquez, who couldn't find anything wrong with me. Dr. Vasquez sent me to a specialist, but he couldn't find anything wrong with me either." Carl had continued to see a succession of physicians despite the fact that each one assured him that he was in excellent health. "So, after all this time, I still haven't found out what's really going on with me," he concluded.

I ask Carl how it feels to be constantly reassured that no medical condition exists. He answers, "The doctors just keep missing it—but somebody's going

to figure it out. I know they will." When asked if he ever felt a sense of relief when reassured that he didn't have cancer, Carl said, "At first, I feel some relief, but it only lasts a few days. When my symptoms start up again, I start worrying all over again."

The next question, I ask somewhat cautiously. "Carl, when the doctors tell you that they haven't found anything wrong, can you say what it is that gets in the way of you believing them?"

He answered with complete conviction, "You know, laboratories are always making mistakes. They aren't infallible. Suppose they mixed up my results with somebody else's? Can you absolutely tell me that that doesn't happen? Well, I say it's hard to feel reassured when so many people have the opportunity to mess up."

I ventured a step further and asked him if he thought it was at all possible that he didn't have cancer.

"Absolutely not!" he replied. "The only reason they haven't diagnosed me yet is because they have to do a few more tests. The last time I had a workup was 6 months ago. I'm sure between then and now something has had time to develop."

I asked Carl about his car sales job—whether this was having any impact on his ability to work (other than the time he takes off to visit doctors).

He allowed that his concerns about his medical "condition" sometimes takes his mind away from business at the office. "I get so distracted that every once in a while I lose a customer. I won't lie to you, things could be better in the money department," he said.

Carl denies thoughts about suicide, says he doesn't have delusions or hallucinations, and he shows no symptoms of a major depressive episode. His appetite and sleep habits are no cause for concern, except for every once in a while, "when I can't stop worrying about my cancer." He denies a history of problems related to alcohol or recreational drug use. Although he has experienced quite a lot of anxiety about having cancer, he has never had symptoms suggestive of a panic disorder.

ASSESSMENT SUMMARY The distinction between hypochondriaşis and somatization disorder essentially rests on age of onset and the number of symptoms individuals are likely to report. Carl's complaints are typical of the person experiencing hypochondriasis—that is, his initial concerns started when he was in the stage of older adulthood, or 48 years of age. In contrast, somatization tends to surface in people who are 10 to 15 years younger. The individual with hypochondriasis readily seeks out constant medical attention because they truly believe they are afflicted with a serious disease despite a lack of supportive findings. In this case, Carl continues to question his physicians' expertise. His world is filled with anxiety and constant worry. He is absolutely convinced that it is not a matter of *if* he is going to be diagnosed with cancer, a tumor, or a serious disease, but *when* he is going to be diagnosed. To Carl, every symptom is the precursor of a life-threatening condition.

The individual with somatization disorder complains because it hurts when he or she coughs. However, when Carl coughs, he concludes it is another sign that he has cancer; this time it might be lung cancer. Phobic individuals who are afraid they might develop a disease usually take steps to avoid being in situations exposing them to risks. People with panic disorders might fearfully overreact to physical symptoms, but their reaction is generally confined to the experience of having a panic attack—and they do not consult physicians to verify or disprove their health status. In contrast, Carl consults physicians, one after the other, hoping to find the right one, the one who will confirm his "disease." Carl truly believes he experiences these physical symptoms, rather than inventing or maintaining them, as found in persons with factitious and malingering disorders. Figure 8.4 summarizes the biopsychosocial features in Carl's life.

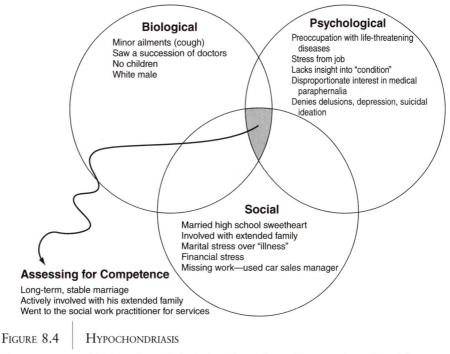

FIGURE 8.4 | HYPOCHONDRIASIS

The interactions of biological, psychological, and social variables in Carl Beacher's life.

CARL BEACHER'S MULTIAXIAL DSM DIAGNOSIS IS AS FOLLOWS:

Axis I	300.7 Hypochondriasis
Axis II	V71.07 (No diagnosis)
Axis III	None
Axis IV	Financial problems
Axis V	GAF = 70 (at intake)

© Cengage Learning

Advanced Clinical EP 2.1.10 (b) c

Rather than sustaining the focus on Carl's "illness," the competency-based assessment includes opportunities for the social worker to identify his coping strategies, some of which may serve to improve his adaptation to life situations. Paying attention to coping and adaptation serves a preventive function in that Carl learns to anticipate (and thereby prevent) further problems from arising. He has a long-term and stable marriage, is actively involved in the lives of extended family members, and is seeking counseling.

UNDERSTANDING BODY DYSMORPHIC DISORDER

The initial formulation of the clinical category of dysmorphophobia (which literally means fear of being ugly) resulted from a term coined by Enrico Morselli during the late nineteenth century. Dysmorphophobia referred to specifiable behaviors that described having an "attitude" toward parts of oneself and/or one's body and often referred to as an imagined ugliness. Dysmorphophobia disorder has been depicted for more than a century and has been reported to exist around the world. This concept was commonly referenced in European literature during the 1960s and 1970s but was not formally introduced in the United States until its appearance in DSM-III-R (American Psychiatric Association, 1987). As an interesting aside, the DSM-IV editors felt the term *dysmorphophobia* is somewhat misleading and inaccurately suggests the presence of phobic avoidance. Consequently, they decided to relabel dysmorphophobia as **body dysmorphic disorder (BDD)** in order to avoid any clinical confusion.

A central feature to remember about body dysmorphic disorder is the person's preoccupation about some imagined defect in their body. Virtually any body part can be the focus of concern. The individual is greatly preoccupied with the notion that something is very wrong with the shape, size, or appearance of some part of his or her body. Many people with BDD become fixated on mirrors, frequently checking for some presumed ugly feature to see if any change has taken place, or they might avoid reflective surfaces altogether (Veale & Riley, 2001). If there happens to be some slight physical defect present, the concern is grossly exaggerated and well in excess of what is considered normal. Although the individual with BDD is continually distressed about his or her appearance, he or she appears perfectly normal to others. This preoccupation with physical appearance includes extreme self-consciousness and embarrassment, excessive importance given to appearance in self-evaluation, avoidance of activities, body camouflaging, and a pattern of constant body checking. Keep in mind that body dysmorphic disorder does not refer to persons who are grossly disfigured or have a deformed appearance and realistically need multiple plastic surgeries (Anderson, 2003).

PREVAILING PATTERN

Body dysmorphic disorder includes the following features:

- The individual is preoccupied with an imagined defect in their appearance or is excessively concerned about a slight physical anomaly.
- The individual's preoccupation causes significant distress or impairs several important areas of interpersonal functioning (e.g., family, social relationships, or at work).
- The individual's preoccupation is not better explained by another disorder (e.g., anorexia nervosa) (American Psychiatric Association, 2000).

The most common symptoms of body dysmorphic disorder social workers will encounter in practice involve facial flaws such as wrinkles, spots and/or the texture of the skin, excessive facial hair, and the shape of certain features (e.g., the nose, jaw, mouth, eyes, or eyebrows). It is common for individuals to be concerned about four different body areas, but the focus on a particular "flawed" body part will sometimes change from one site to another. For example, someone who is worried about wrinkles on their face may have plastic surgery and afterwards "discover" that his or her lips are not full enough and therefore appear grotesque. They may also go to great lengths to camouflage a "flawed" appearance by using excessive amounts of makeup, clothing, or hats. Still others can be found tanning themselves excessively to hide skin defects (Phillips, Menard, Fay, & Weisberg, 2005). In sum, their lives are significantly affected, as they tend to withdraw from most social and occupational activities. In severe cases, the person may become housebound to hide the perceived deformity. To give an idea of the desperation those who struggle with BDD have about their perceived distorted appearance, Veale (2000) describes several cases in which individuals had performed "DIY" surgery wherein they attempted by their own hand to alter their appearance dramatically after they were either turned down for or could not afford surgery. For instance, one man was so concerned about the loose skin around his face that he took a staple gun to both sides of his face to tighten his skin. Needless to say, the results were disastrous. The staples fell out after a couple of minutes and he almost damaged a facial nerve. Another woman who was unable to afford liposuction for what she saw as ugly parts of her body cut open her thighs and attempted to squeeze out the fat.

DIFFERENTIAL ASSESSMENT

EP 2.1.10
(b) a

The practitioner carefully organizes data collected about a client's symptoms in order to interpret the diagnostic picture, especially in light of recent research that suggests that body dysmorphic disorder is comorbid with a wide range of disorders—from obsessive-compulsive disorder to social phobia, generalized anxiety disorder, or panic disorder. Depression and substance abuse are commonly seen (Phillips et al., 2010). The practitioner must carefully assess a client's thoughts about him- or herself and how those perceptions influence interpersonal relationships.

Gender differences occurring in body dysmorphic disorder are just beginning to emerge, and several studies have noted some interesting findings about the way physical defects are seen. Women tend focus on more varied areas of the body such as the size of their hips and the texture of their skin, and they are more likely to be diagnosed with an eating disorder. Women also pay significant attention to their breast size and shape of their legs. Men are found to be significantly preoccupied about their genitals, body height or build, and either excess hair or thinning hair (Pope et al., 2005). Men are also more focused on "correcting" muscle defects by body-building, known as **muscle dysmorphia**. These individuals may spend many hours in the gym working out in lieu of both social and occupational pursuits. Although it is rarely recognized, this disorder may afflict a substantial number of people, often causing severe subjective distress and creating the potential for abuse of anabolic steroids or other body-building substances (Pope & Brower, 2009). Most often, both men and women seek out plastic surgery or dermatological interventions—but these procedures, while physically and clinically successful, are not able to change perceptions about the defect.

The following vignette introduces Barry Roger and describes his concern about his thinning hair. This case can help practitioners recognize the pathologic state associated with body dysmorphic disorder.

| CASE | The Case of Barry Roger |

"Oh, please, whoever you are, just shut that door. You're letting in all the light."

I started to poke my head inside my office, when the voice once again demanded, "Please, just come on in and close that door."

Somewhat taken aback, I said to the voice, "I know I'm in the right room, because this is my office."

The voice said, "Who are you looking for?"

"I have an appointment to see Barry Roger," I replied. "Is that you?"

The voice answered somewhat wearily, "Yeah, that's me all right. I guess the staff was pretty freaked out when they saw me walk into the waiting room."

"Oh? Why is that?" I inquired.

Mr. Roger replied, "Well, you have to admit I'm pretty ugly looking. Hey, I don't blame anybody getting grossed out when they see my ugly and grotesque baldness. I mean, come on, I can't even look. Yuk! Anyway, that's why your staff hustled me in your office real quick because they didn't want me scaring the other people. Don't get me wrong or anything— they were real nice to me, but I could see 'that look' in their eyes."

By a bit of dim light afforded me from a small separation between the window shades, I was able to see Mr. Roger sitting on a chair in the corner of my office. When I approached, he turned his face away, apparently trying to hide from my gaze. I was able to see that he had covered the top part of his head with something that looked like a cross between a baseball cap and something worn by the French Foreign Legionnaires.

As I sat down in my usual spot, I asked Mr. Roger why he had made an appointment to come see me.

He replied, "I want to have another hair transplant."

I pointed out that as a social worker, "I'm not allowed to do hair transplants."

"Very funny," he retorted. "I used to go to old Doc Connolly," he said, getting down to business. "But he retired last year. So I found this new plastic surgeon, Dr. Frick. He told me that I wasn't bald, and he refused to do any more surgery because he said I didn't need it. I don't know what his problem is. He told me that I was lucky because I had a nice full head of hair—he said I might have the slightest bit of thinning but that that was normal for a guy 27 years old. Personally, I think he needs glasses."

I noted that Mr. Roger's overall health was excellent except for episodic hemorrhoid inflammation. I gently reminded him that he hadn't answered my question about his reasons for coming to the agency.

"Dr. Frick told me I didn't have a hair problem," he said rather petulantly, "but a problem about the way I see myself. He said he absolutely wasn't going to do a hair transplant, and that I should go talk to a professional."

"I see," I said before asking my next question. "Well, could you describe for me what you think you look like?"

He responded with a deep sigh. "Yeah, it's obvious that I look gross, ugly, and disfigured. I mean look at this." He snatched his hat off. "What do you think about this, huh?"

I was a bit startled, but managed to answer, "Well, actually I see a very full head of hair."

He responded quietly, "That's what everyone says."

After a moment, I continued. "I was wondering— may I call you Barry?" He nodded, and I went on. "I was wondering how much time you spend thinking about your hair?"

"Oh, all the time," he said. "I can't seem to get my mind off my baldness. If only I didn't have this problem, everything else would be terrific."

"Have you discussed this with anyone in your family or perhaps with your friends?" I asked.

He replied, "Yeah, but all they do is say the same thing that you just did. They don't see what I'm talking about. You know, it's funny—well, not really funny—but my girlfriend, Sharon, broke up with me a few months ago. She told me she was damn tired of always hearing about my hair. I mean, what's her problem? If she doesn't love me enough, well then,

good riddance to her. It just proves how ugly I really am without much hair." When I asked how long he's been troubled by his "baldness," he said, "I can't really say exactly when I started worrying about my hair. Maybe it started 3 years ago when I was 24. I started to notice that I was picking more and more hairs out of my hairbrush. Whenever I asked my family or friends if they noticed I am going bald, they just told me I had enough hair on my head for three people."

I asked Barry if his "baldness" caused him any difficulties other than feeling ugly.

He responded, "I can't leave my house or do anything outside. I know I disgust people because I can see it in their eyes. I notice it more when I don't wear my hat, because people point at me and laugh. I *hate* living like this. I'm a salesman, and I have to be able to interact with people—but I can't do it as a bald man."

Barry admitted that he felt unhappy but denied feeling depressed or having any thoughts about suicide. He stated he was eating and sleeping well and felt no loss of energy. I asked if there were other parts of his body that concerned him. He reported that when he was a teenager he had a few plastic surgeries, including a rhinoplasty, having his ears flattened, and a "huge" mole removed from the right side of his nose.

He continued, "I had a hard time convincing my parents to let me have those surgeries. You know how parents are. They always think their child looks perfect, even when they are ugly and deformed."

He admitted to regularly working out at a gym near his home. Last year he opted to have bilateral chest muscle implants "because my chest looked so sunken in." He insists, "I know my life would be absolutely perfect if I could only get another hair transplant. Is that so terrible?"

ASSESSMENT SUMMARY   The interactions of the biological, psychological, and social variables in Barry Roger's life are illustrated in Figure 8.5. If we look at Barry Roger's difficulties in relation to other types of disorders, we see that people with a narcissistic personality disorder always have excessive concerns about maintaining a flawless appearance; hypochondriacal individuals (like Carl Beacher) might be overly concerned about having blotches or blemishes on their body, but their primary fear is one of being diagnosed with a serious disease. Those with anorexia nervosa are characterized by a pervasive concern with the shape and size of their bodies—their goal is to be successful in the pursuit of absolute thinness rather

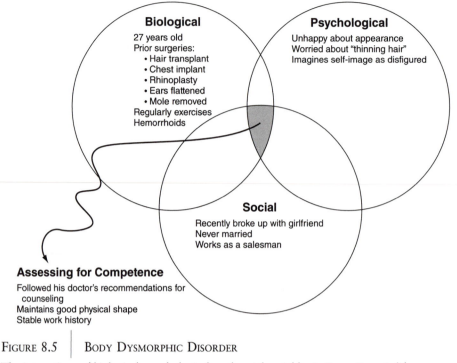

Biological

27 years old
Prior surgeries:
 • Hair transplant
 • Chest implant
 • Rhinoplasty
 • Ears flattened
 • Mole removed
Regularly exercises
Hemorrhoids

Psychological

Unhappy about appearance
Worried about "thinning hair"
Imagines self-image as disfigured

Social

Recently broke up with girlfriend
Never married
Works as a salesman

Assessing for Competence

Followed his doctor's recommendations for
 counseling
Maintains good physical shape
Stable work history

FIGURE 8.5 | BODY DYSMORPHIC DISORDER

The interactions of biological, psychological, and social variables in Barry Roger's life.

than in the quest to maintain a normal weight. A notable difference for Barry Roger, however, is that he sees himself as ugly in an interpersonal world that does not view him in the same way. He is generally satisfied in other aspects of his life, but Barry's thinning hair, and the "gross" appearance he imagines it creates, cause him a great deal of distress.

In contrast to Barry's body dysmorphia, some people develop **monohypochondriacal paranoia** (delusional disorder, somatic type) and harbor delusional beliefs in which one particular part of their bodies play a part. (For example, a person might think his or her eyes are grossly deformed or distorted.) In body dysmorphic disorder, the individual is not seen as being delusional—he or she is simply unwilling to acknowledge the possibility that the perceived defect (that others may consider as ordinary) is minimal.

Advanced
Clinical EP
2.1.10 (b) c

Focusing on deficiencies is an especially unhelpful approach for a practitioner to use with the client who has BDD. Concentrating on negative characteristics often reinforces the client's belief in the defect, and it may encourage him or her to continue picking out negative qualities—not only in him- or herself, but also in life and in significant others. It is helpful to assess the client's coping strategies and to reinforce and improve adaptation to life situations, circumstances, or events. It is of utmost importance that Barry Roger be helped to identify and focus on his positive assets, which include following up on the referral for counseling and maintaining a healthy lifestyle.

Barry Roger's Multiaxial DSM Diagnosis Is as Follows:

Axis I	300.7 Body Dysmorphic Disorder
Axis II	V71.09 (No diagnosis)
Axis III	455.6 Hemorrhoids
Axis IV	Recently broke up with girlfriend
Axis V	GAF = 75 (at intake)

© Cengage Learning

UNDERSTANDING OTHER SOMATOFORM DISORDERS

Understanding the somatoform disorders requires the practitioner to appreciate the biological or medical aspects of the individual's symptomatic behavior, even though referrals to the social worker are generally made to provide support for the client's emotional underpinnings. In order for practitioners to make careful assessments of those client behaviors that do not quite meet the categories described earlier—and to avoid stigmatizing or stereotyping clients—a separate category called undifferentiated somatoform disorder is included in this discussion. There is also a category called somatoform disorder not otherwise specified (NOS) that is included in this chapter to help the practitioner consider those persons with characteristics suggestive of somatoform disorder but who do not meet the intensity or duration assessment criteria.

EP 2.1.4 c

There may be some instances in which making an assessment is not clear-cut. It is during those times that the practitioner must be especially savvy about the multiple factors influencing the client's life, and especially about the cultural influences that play an important role in understanding a person's manifestation of physical illness. Vague complaints (often labeled as an unconscious psychological conflict) may in fact be culturally acceptable and adaptive behavior. For example, neurasthenia is more common in eastern Asia than in the West and is used to describe a symptom picture of fatigue, anxiety, headache, neuralgia, depressed mood, and related vague somatic complaints more commonly seen in upper-class professionals with sedentary employment (Schwartz, 2002). From a Western perspective, these symptoms are considered to be related to stress rather than to pathology.

Unfortunately, minimal published data is available on these two categories of somatoform disorders, and therefore, little can be said about their history, genetic composition, familial patterns, epidemiology, and treatment predictability.

UNDIFFERENTIATED SOMATOFORM DISORDER

Undifferentiated somatoform disorder was almost eliminated from the DSM-IV but was kept in the DSM-IV-TR because of its significance in primary health care settings (Gray, 2006). The assessment of **undifferentiated somatoform disorder** is an appropriate category for those clients who meet the following criteria:

1. The client has one or more physical complaints that cannot be explained by any known general medical condition or pathophysiologic mechanism, or has symptoms that grossly exceed the expected complaints of a medical condition.
2. The client is below the threshold for meeting the diagnostic criteria for a specific somatoform disorder (American Psychiatric Association, 2000).

Often with the passage of time, some individuals will develop additional somatic complaints—if they eventually meet the specific criteria for somatization disorder, they are reclassified. Isolated somatic symptoms do not really predict very much of anything. In order to consider the presence of an undifferentiated somatoform disorder, the symptoms must be present for at least 6 months, and they must cause significant emotional distress or seriously impair the person's social or occupational functioning. Additionally, undifferentiated somatoform disorder includes neurasthenia ("nervous exhaustion"), and chronic fatigue syndrome, as well as other functional somatic symptoms and syndromes that are without widely accepted medical explanations.

There are two types of symptom patterns that are seen in those individuals with undifferentiated somatoform disorder: (1) those involving the autonomic nervous system or involving the respiratory, gastrointestinal, and/or urogenital systems; and (2) those involving sensations of fatigue, weakness, or being unable to perform everyday activities due to feelings of exhaustion.

Undifferentiated somatoform disorder includes the following features:

- The individual has at least one physical complaint, such as painful urination, fatigue, or gastrointestinal complaints.
- The individual's symptoms meet *one* of the following two conditions:
  1. After an appropriate investigation, the symptoms presented cannot be fully explained by the presence of a recognized general medical condition or by the use of substances (including medications and alcohol).
  2. When a general medical condition is present, the physical complaints or resulting social or occupational impairment far exceed what would typically be expected, based on the person's history, physical examination, or laboratory findings.
- The symptoms cause clinically significant distress or have a negative effect on work (or school), social, or interpersonal functioning.
- The disturbance lasts longer than 6 months.
- Another mental disorder (such as mood, anxiety, sleep, or psychotic disorder) or the diagnosis of a sexual dysfunction does not better explain the disturbance.
- The individual does not intentionally produce or fake symptoms for material gain (malingering) or willingly seek secondary gain by occupying the sick role (factitious disorder).

Because of their close resemblance to somatization disorder, undifferentiated somatoform disorder and somatoform disorder not otherwise specified (NOS) do not warrant separate case studies. However, the following discussion of somatoform disorder not otherwise specified (NOS) is provided to help understand the complete picture of somatoform disorders. With this information, the practitioner will be better able to discern among the various clusters of symptoms and better grasp their impact on the individual's life picture.

SOMATOFORM DISORDER NOT OTHERWISE SPECIFIED (NOS)

This residual or catchall category includes people who have some symptoms suggestive of a somatoform disorder but who do not meet the specific diagnostic criteria for any of the other specific somatoform disorders, including the undifferentiated type (American Psychiatric Association, 2000). This category primarily addresses clusters of symptoms that include:

- **Pseudocyesis**—a false belief of being pregnant without supporting objective physical signs and clinical manifestations of pregnancy, such as an enlarged abdomen, nausea, amenorrhea (absence of menstruation), breast engorgement, fetal movements, and labor pains at the approximate "due date." Although there may be evidence of endocrine changes, a general medical condition that causes these endocrine conditions (as in a hormone-secreting tumor) is not found.

- **Transient hypochondriac states (nonpsychotic)**—presents symptoms that would meet criteria for hypochondriasis except that they do not last for the required 6 months.

- **Environmental illness** (or total environmental allergy syndrome)—a relatively new phenomenon that is a polysymptomatic disorder considered by some to be associated with immune system dysfunction and allergy-like sensitivity to many compounds found in chemicals, food, clothing, perfumes, and airborne substances. Individuals with this disorder claim to be allergic to almost everything they come in contact with, sometimes isolating themselves from these chemical toxins by staying indoors and at other times using extreme protective measures (such as wearing a gas mask out in public).

- A disorder involving unexplained physical symptoms that last less than 6 months and with symptoms not caused by another psychological disorder (American Psychiatric Association, 2000).

RELATED DISORDERS: MALINGERING AND FACTITIOUS DISORDER

There are two notable conditions related to the somatoform or somatic disorders, in that people with these conditions exhibit symptoms having no evidentiary physical cause, and their symptoms are collectively viewed as being manifested unconsciously. They are briefly discussed in this chapter because, historically, practitioners have thought of them as having common threads, with similar symptoms and processes.

UNDERSTANDING MALINGERING DISORDER

Malingering involves a pattern of behavior similar to that seen in someone who has a genuine medical disorder. It occurs mostly frequently in males, but it can also occur in females. Instead of actually having a medical problem, the person deliberately and consciously pretends to be suffering from "something" that is nonexistent in order to arouse sympathy, avoid criminal prosecution or military duty, obtain drugs, or receive financial rewards. An example of malingering would be those individuals who pretend to make a slow recovery from an illness or a previously sustained work-related injury in order to continue receiving benefits from workmen's compensation or an insurance settlement. The "illness" may also provide opportunities for a temporary escape from harsh situations, such as being incarcerated or being in other unpleasant settings. Here is a transcript of a conversation between a client and a social worker that illustrates the kind of questioning a practitioner might use when considering an assessment of malingering disorder.

CASE | The Case of Brad Jones

"Ow, ow, that hurts, oh my gosh, ow, my neck hurts something terrible," said Brad Jones as he was easing himself into a chair. He had been referred to our clinic by Mr. James Martino, a well-known personal injury attorney. When asked what brought him here, Mr. Jones stated he had been involved in a rear-end collision and subsequently missed a great deal of work. He added, "You know, I'm enduring a tremendous amount of pain. I have constant neck pain and terrible headaches. I feel dizzy most all the time, and I don't sleep a wink at night. If that isn't bad enough, my chest hurts when I try and take a deep breath, and I really feel lousy. You know, I'm not asking for anything special. I just want some kind of restitution from the woman who rear-ended me—she destroyed my car, ruined my health, and cost me my job."

The social worker was trying to recall the specifics of an article she just happened to read in a journal not too long ago. The piece was about malingering disorder and the type of questions a practitioner can ask when trying to make a competency-based assessment. Luckily, she had made some notes on the article, so she remembered more of the questions than she might have otherwise.

SOCIAL WORKER: *Mr. Jones, can you tell me about what is currently going on for you?*

BRAD JONES: *I can't begin to tell you how much pain this accident has caused me. I mean, I can't do anything for myself anymore. I had to move into a limited nursing care facility. Do you know anything about what they are like?*

SW: *Could you tell me?*

BJ: *Well, it's a place you live where they cook your meals, do your laundry, and clean your room—I didn't want to move into a place like that, but Mr. Martino, that's my lawyer, told me that I wouldn't have to strain myself having to do all this stuff for myself. He thought it would be best, especially since I'm in so much pain.*

SW: *Where did you live before the accident?*

BJ: *I lived here and there. You know, sometimes with friends, and sometimes with family*

members. *Hey, aren't we here to talk about how much pain I'm having?*

SW: *Yes, could you tell me more about that?*

BJ: *Well, yeah, I ran up a lot of financial costs as a result of that nitwit smashing into my car. Now I'm taking lots of medicine, but none of it seems to help. I was wondering if maybe one of the docs here could give me something to help me relax—you know, for my muscle spasms and all?*

SW: *Mr. Jones, have you ever been involved in any kind of lawsuit before this one?*

BJ: *What do you mean, like a slip and fall accident or something like that?*

SW: *Well, yes—or something like that.*

BJ: *You probably won't believe this, but I did fall down once when I was walking out of a department store. It was really storming something fierce. The exit ramp was very slippery. I wrenched my neck and back, and broke my glasses. I had to wear a neck brace and walked with a cane for 6 months. Oh, wait a minute. I just remembered there was one other time. I was working at a diner over on West Street, as a short-order cook, you know? My arm got burned when I was cooking some eggs in hot grease. But it was really nothing like this.*

SW: *What do you make of what has happened?*

BJ: *Oh, I get it. You're just like all the rest of them, aren't you?*

SW: *What do you mean?*

BJ: *You know, suggesting that I just want to make some money off of this accident.*

SW: *Why, has someone accused you of that?*

BJ: *Yeah, and I don't like it one bit. It's not like I'm trying to get away with something. You know what? I'm outta here! Send the bill to Martino.*

Mr. Jones abruptly stood up, prematurely ending the session. Interestingly, he showed no indication of having the debilitating physical pain so much in evidence earlier.

ASSESSMENT SUMMARY   Malingering is very often confused with factitious disorder. The single most notable difference between these two disorders is the impetus or incentive for maintaining symptoms. In malingering disorder, symptom continuance is externally motivated (i.e., individuals obtain something they want or desire, such as money, drugs, or shelter). In factitious disorder, these external incentives are not present, but the individual maintains the sick role.

Making the distinction between malingering and conversion disorder can be more difficult. The malingerer exhibits the same pattern of behavior as someone with conversion disorder, but the malingerer deliberately and intentionally produces symptoms in order to obtain appreciable rewards or incentives, or to avoid some unpleasant situation. The person with conversion disorder, as in the case of Aleta Austin, does not intentionally produce her symptoms. Malingerers can voluntarily control the symptoms of illness, often switching back and forth between normal and abnormal physical behavior. In addition, they are able to stop their symptoms when considered no longer profitable or when the danger of being "discovered" becomes too great. In the case of Brad Jones, he chose to leave the interview session abruptly. (As a postscript, the social worker followed up with a letter inviting him to return, but unfortunately there was no further communication between them.)

Malingering is easy to suspect—it is much harder to prove even in the face of overt documentation, such as surveillance videos. The practitioner should strongly suspect malingering if any combination of the following features is noted:

- If there is legal litigation or a medical context that overshadows the symptoms presented, especially when there is an opportunity for financial gain, such as receiving cash or a free hospital room and board.
- If the client's history suggests the presence of an antisocial personality disorder (American Psychiatric Association, 2000).
- If a lack of client cooperation is noted during diagnostic efforts and evaluation *and* if there is a lack of compliance with a prescribed medical regimen.
- If there are marked discrepancies between the individual's claimed clinical presentation and objective findings.

Careful documentation is essential to the accurate assessment of malingering disorder, to prevent iatrogenic conditions, and to rule out actual medical disorders. In some situations, the individual diagnosed with malingering disorder has a history of substance abuse.

UNDERSTANDING FACTITIOUS DISORDER

Another puzzling set of conditions is **factitious disorder;** something that is not real, genuine, or natural. Here, the person displays physical and psychological symptoms that are intentionally produced and are completely under the person's voluntary control (as with malingering), *but* there is no obvious reason for voluntarily producing the symptoms except, possibly, to take on the sick role and receive increased attention. As a part of the competency-based assessment, the practitioner will find it helpful to explore the person's level of social and occupational functioning. Clues to this disorder include records of hospitalizations, medical appointments, and being sick—all of which may impair relationships and job performance. These individuals often have distorted perceptions of justice as well as a sense of entitlement, which further justify their sick role. They are also prone to see themselves as victims.

A prototypical factitious disorder is Munchausen syndrome. In the eighteenth century, Baron Karl Friedrich Hieronymous von Munchausen, a German cavalry officer, had a reputation for being a colorful raconteur who spun outrageous stories and wandered about the countryside to find audiences. (As a character, he was committed to history in Raspe's (1948) book, *Baron Munchausen's Narrative of His Marvelous Travels and Campaigns in Russia*.) There is no evidence that the real Baron von Munchausen ever believed the stories he fabricated, tried to deceive his listeners, or sought out unneeded medical treatment. Nevertheless, his name continues to be linked to a term that represents a syndrome considered the most extreme example of factitious disorder. In 1951, Richard Asher, an English physician, wrote an article entitled "Munchausen's syndrome" in *The Lancet*. The first sentence in his article stated, "Here is described a common syndrome which most doctors have seen, but about which little has been written" (Asher, 1951, p. 339). He borrowed Munchausen's name and applied it to people who demonstrated a triad of features: (1) the recurrent simulation of disease, (2) pathological lying (pseudologia fantastica), or (3) wandering (peregrination). The individual so afflicted will travel extensively in order to receive medical care where his or her previous medical history is unknown. It has been suggested that if Asher had been less self-effacing, the syndrome might have been named after him. However, Asher's article served to bring the syndrome to public attention. The disorder has been called various names, including polysurgical addiction, hospital addiction, and professional patient syndrome.

The literature available for understanding this disorder is still evolving. IsHak and colleagues (2010) recommend large descriptive and longitudinal studies with adequate diagnostic workups, including medical, neurologic, neuropsychological, and personality testing evaluations, aimed at developing a clearer understanding of factitious disorder. Unfortunately these kinds of studies are difficult due to the reality that those struggling with factitious disorder try not to be discovered. These are the clients who will provide misleading information about themselves. It is not clear which subtypes of factitious disorder are most common, but the prevalence of physical symptoms seems higher than for psychological symptoms (Krahn, Li, & O'Connor, 2003). Individuals with the psychological subtype are predominantly males with a history of hospitalizations beginning in adolescence. Women outnumber men for non-chronic factitious disorder by about 3 to 1.

Munchausen by proxy is a variant of the factitious disorder, but this disorder occurs within the context of a relationship between the parent and child. Those involved with Munchausen by proxy tend to be mothers who are married, educated, middle-class women in their early 20s. Females who are employed in medical fields, such as nursing or medical technology, where there are opportunities to learn about diseases and easy access to equipment to produce them (such as syringes or chemicals), have a high incidence of factitious disorder (Todd & Ahmed, 2001). It is briefly presented here to complete the discussion of factitious disorder.

This condition occurs when the parent or caregiver deliberately falsifies the child's (i.e., their proxy's) medical history and subjects the child to unnecessary medical procedures (including unnecessary surgeries) and unneeded hospitalizations.

| CASE | THE CASE OF NAN FINKELHORN |

Nan Finkelhorn is a 27-year-old female who is currently in her 35th hospital admission. She works as a nurse in the dialysis unit of the hospital, and her supervisor is wondering if Nan may have some kind of rare infection. Recently, Nan was diagnosed with chronic fatigue, and since that time her job performance has been sporadic. It has been difficult for the supervisor to know how to respond because Nan is vague about the details of her condition. It seems that when the unit is hectic and there is much work to be done, Nan loudly announces to her coworkers that she needs a coffee break. As a result, there is growing tension between Nan and her supervisor concerning performance expectations.

Nan's presenting problems during this current admission include chronic headaches, fevers, lupus-like symptoms, vomiting, inability to walk, and numbness in her left hand and her right foot. She came to the emergency room last evening asking for narcotic medication for pain. During her examination by the attending physician on duty, Nan doubled over and said she felt a terrible pain in her left kidney area. The physician felt it was prudent to admit Ms. Finkelhorn for observation. Nan's reaction was, "I hate hospitals, especially this one—my mother died here, and no one ever bothered to take care of her."

After a complete set of laboratory tests and additional physical examinations, Nan was given a clean bill of health. Just a few minutes after she was discharged and declared fit to return to her full responsibilities at work, Ms. Finkelhorn began to complain loudly. "Are you people nuts? I am an extremely ill person. All of you doctors are incompetent—I'm going to report all of you, and my stupid supervisor, to Employee Assistance. Looks like that's the only way I'll ever get any justice from this place." As she continued down the corridor, Nan muttered, "When I end up dead, it'll be on your heads."

Similar to the goal of assuming the sick role in factitious disorder, the motivation behind this behavior is the parent's psychological need to assume the sick role, albeit indirectly. The deception can involve contaminating laboratory samples, providing false medical history, initiating an injury, or actually causing sickness (e.g., by poison) of the child. Munchausen by proxy is considered a form of child abuse and is mandated by law reportable if suspected. Detection of this disorder is extremely difficult.

In all types of factitious disorder, the client displays feelings of victimization, a sense of entitlement, and usually some self-righteous indignation. The following vignette illustrates how a client with factitious disorder might present his or her concerns to a practitioner.

CLOSING OBSERVATIONS ABOUT NAN FINKELHORN   There is no assessment summary discussion for the case presentation of Nan Finkelhorn because the primary intention is to show how clients with a diagnosis of factitious disorder might present themselves to the practitioner. The important distinction when making this diagnosis is that Nan's symptoms are not better explained by a true general medical condition or by an apparent mental disorder. Instead, Nan describes a vague set of symptoms, such as headaches, fevers, lupus-like symptoms, vomiting, inability to walk, and numbness in her left hand and her right foot, that bring her to the emergency room for some kind of relief. On the face of it, none of these complaints seems to justify her request for a narcotic medication. While the attending physician is examining her, Nan inexplicably doubles over in pain. However, the physical examination and related lab tests do not support her physical complaints.

EP 2.1.1 d

Interestingly, when Nan's job gets hectic and much work needs to be done, she announces that she needs a coffee break, creating tension with her supervisor. Nan's vague illnesses, self-righteous indignation, and veiled threats about getting justice certainly shift the focus away from her work performance. As a matter of fact, her supervisor is beginning to wonder if Nan might have some kind of rare infection that might better explain her behavior. Clients like Nan can be difficult to work with and can certainly challenge the practitioner's ability to maintain a professional demeanor and to communicate respectfully in the face of such overt hostility.

SUMMARY

This chapter has reviewed the various somatoform disorders with a focus on the most prevalent diagnoses. Somatization disorders have earned a reputation of being very difficult to assess. As a practitioner, remember that, even though the client is faking an illness, he or she is still ill. The client's concerns must be taken seriously rather than dismissed. The competency-based assessment facilitates an emphasis on the client's concerns by:

- Evaluating symptom presentation in the context of both current and past interpersonal, social, cultural, and environmental factors.
- Encouraging the practitioner to include in each session a conversation about how well clients are functioning in terms of their interpersonal relationships and their social and family support systems.
- Keeping the focus on intrapersonal, interpersonal, and/or social problems, not the physical or somatic symptoms. (This is not to say that new signs or symptoms are not carefully evaluated.)
- Reminding the practitioner that, to the clients, their symptoms are very real and quite distressing.
- Recognizing early on the need for a comprehensive medical evaluation, especially for those individuals who have chronic symptoms, severe psychological consequences, or morbid types of illness behavior.

From the competency-based perspective, the practitioner:

- Questions the client thoroughly about his or her medical history.

- Provides reassurance to the client that he or she does not have a serious illness.
- Suggests to the client that symptoms will eventually resolve themselves.
- Encourages the client to return to normal activities.
- Follows the client for a period of time and inquire about medical status on subsequent visits.

In the DSM-5, body dysmorphic disorder (BDD) may be moved from the somatoform disorders into a new category of anxiety and obsessive-compulsive spectrum disorders. The second proposed change related to this shift is to add the specifier *muscle dysmorphia* (that is, the person has the obsession that his or her body is either too small or insufficiently muscular). Another proposed change is to combine four of the somatoform disorders—hypochondriasis, somatization disorder, undifferentiated somatoform disorder, and pain disorder—into a new diagnosis called complex somatic symptom disorder (CSSD). Subtle differences exist among the three disorders, and the DSM-5 proposals would allow for further specification. When considering the presence of CSSD, if a person presents solely with health-related anxiety in the absence of somatic symptoms, the individual may be more appropriately diagnosed as having an anxiety disorder. The fears experienced by those with what is currently characterized as hypochondriasis would then be called health anxiety. Conversion disorder would remain as a separate somatoform disorder.

PRACTITIONER'S REFLECTIONS

This chapter outlines the primary features found in somatoform, factitious, and malingering disorders. The development of somatoform disorders centers around an individual's excessive preoccupation with his or her health—even when there are no identifiable medical conditions to support his or her complaints. Factitious disorders are characterized by the intentional feigning of physical symptoms to assume the sick role. This contrasts to the malingering disorder, which includes external motivations for sustaining such behavior (for example, seeking economic gains through litigious actions). The following activities are intended to help practitioners better understand these disorders.

ACTIVITIES

Advanced Clinical EP 2.1.1 d

1. This activity focuses on personal reflection to advance your understanding of the symptom picture of hypochondriasis. Hopefully, you will be better able to develop, manage, and maintain the therapeutic relationship with someone struggling with hypochondriasis within the person-in-environment and strengths perspectives.
   a. Keep a log of your bodily sensations for 3 or 4 days. Be as detailed as you can in your recording. Include, for example, headaches, backaches, muscle aches, stomach grumblings, perspiration, fatigue, and so forth.
   b. Reflect back on your log and compare how your own body sensations differ from those in the case of Carl Beacher. Be as specific as you can.
   c. Imagine for a moment that you are having a conversation with Carl Beacher. How would he respond to your listing of your body sensations?
   d. Remember the last time you had a common cold? Write down your experiences. Be sure to include how you felt, how long it lasted, and what you had done (if anything) to minimize your discomfort.
   e. Look over this list, and imagine how a person diagnosed with hypochondriasis would describe his or her own experience with having a cold.

Advanced Clinical EP 2.1.1 d

2. Describe a person with a factitious disorder and what their experiences of a common cold would be like. What challenges can you identify that would affect your ability to develop, manage, and maintain a therapeutic relationship within the person-in-environment and strengths perspectives?

EP 2.1.2 a

3. Develop a list of the advantages and disadvantages of undergoing plastic surgery. Taking your own personal values into consideration as a means to acknowledge the professional values to guide practice, imagine how a person with body dysmorphic disorder would critique your listing.
4. Considering the increase of cosmetic surgeries, how do you feel about individuals who have multiple surgical procedures to improve "defects" that no one else can see? Develop a list of the ethics related to having a "perfect" body.
5. In many instances, the practitioner's first contact with a client is over the telephone, which (because of the lack of visual stimuli) can help the practitioner to better focus on the client's concerns. This activity is designed to help you learn to focus, as sharply as possible, on the client's concerns. Review the case of Barry Roger.

a. With a colleague or your supervisor, role-play how you would proceed in the first 5 minutes of conducting a telephone interview with him. Imagine this is your first contact. Make an effort to screen out all visual stimuli (e.g., sit in a darkened room, wear a blindfold when playing the role of the practitioner, or sit with your back to your partner).

b. After you have completed the role-playing exercise, exchange with each other the "cues" you were able to pick up on that helped you recognize you were speaking with someone with body dysmorphic disorder.

c. Ask yourself the following questions: At what point did you begin to consider that Mr. Roger is someone with body dysmorphic disorder? When did you decide that he met the criteria for body dysmorphic disorder? How does he cope? What strengths does Mr. Roger have?

6. Persons with body dysmorphic disorder tend to focus their attention on the defects found with their breasts, face, neck, or genitals. Using the format described above, conduct a role-play of someone who is concerned about a mole on his or her chin (or use another example), but who does *not* have a body dysmorphic disorder.

COMPETENCY NOTES

EP 2.1.1 d: Demonstrate professional demeanor in behavior, appearance, and communication (p. 310): Social workers commit themselves to the profession's enhancement and to their own professional conduct and growth.

EP Advanced Clinical 2.1.1 d: Develop, manage, and maintain therapeutic relationships with clients within the person-in-environment and strengths perspectives (p. 311): Advanced practitioners in clinical social work recognize the importance of the therapeutic relationship, the person-in-environment and strengths perspectives, the professional use of self with clients, and adherence to ethical guidelines of professional behavior.

EP 2.1.1 f: Use supervision and consultation (p. 312): Social workers commit themselves to the profession's enhancement and to their own professional conduct and growth.

EP 2.1.2 a: Recognize and manage personal values in a way that allows professional values to guide practice (p. 311): Social workers have an obligation to conduct themselves ethically and to engage in ethical decision-making.

EP 2.1.4 c: Recognize and communicate an understanding of the importance of difference in shaping life experiences (p. 303): Social workers understand how diversity characterizes and shapes the human experience and is critical to the formation of identity.

EP 2.1.7 a: Use conceptual frameworks to guide the process of assessment, intervention, and evaluation (p. 277): Social workers apply theories and knowledge from the liberal arts to understand the client's biological, social, cultural, psychological, and spiritual development.

EP 2.1.7 b: Critique and apply knowledge to understand person and environment (pp. 276, 291): Social workers are knowledgeable about human behavior across the life course, the range of social systems in which people live, and the ways social systems promote or deter people in maintaining or achieving health and well-being.

EP Advanced Clinical 2.1.7 c: Consult with medical professionals, as needed, to confirm diagnosis and/or to monitor medication in the treatment process (pp. 276, 281, 285): Advanced practitioners understand how to synthesize and differentially apply the theories of human behavior and the social environment (biological, developmental, psychological, social, cultural, and spiritual).

EP 2.1.10 (b) a: Collect, organize, and interpret client data (pp. 274, 288, 293, 295, 299, 312): Social workers have the knowledge and skills to practice with individuals, families, groups, organizations, and communities.

EP Advanced Clinical 2.1.10 (b) c: Assess client coping strategies to reinforce and improve adaptation to life situations, circumstances, and events (pp. 281, 286, 298, 302): Clinical social work practice involves the dynamic, interactive, and reciprocal processes of therapeutic engagement, multidimensional assessment, clinical intervention, and practice evaluation at multiple levels.

REFERENCES

Allen, L. A., Woolfolk, R. L., Escobar, J. I., Gara, M. A., & Hammer, R. M. (2006). Cognitive-behavioral therapy for somatization disorder: A randomized controlled trial. *Archives of Internal Medicine, 166* (14), 1512–1518.

American Psychiatric Association. (1980). *Diagnostic and statistical manual of mental disorders*, (3rd ed.). Washington, DC: Author.

American Psychiatric Association. (1987). *Diagnostic and statistical manual of mental disorders*, (3rd ed. revised). Washington, DC: Author.

American Psychiatric Association. (2000). *Diagnostic and statistical manual of mental disorders*, 4th ed. text revision. Washington, DC: Author.

Anderson, R. C. (2003). Body dysmorphic disorder: Recognition and treatment. *Plastic Surgical Nursing, 23*, 125–129.

Asher, R. (1951). Munchausen's syndrome. *Lancet, 1*, 339–341.

Asmundson, G. J., & Carleton, R. N. (2009). Fear of pain. In M. M. Antony & M. B. Stein, (eds.), *Oxford handbook of anxiety and related disorders*, (pp. 551–561). Oxford, UK: Oxford University Press.

Aybek, S., Kanan, R. A., & David, A. S. (2008). The neuropsychiatry of conversion disorder. *Current Opinion in Psychiatry, 21*, 275–280.

Barlow, D. H., & Durand, V. M. (2012). *Abnormal psychology*, (6th ed.). Belmont, CA: Wadsworth Cengage Learning.

Barsky, A. J., Orav, E., & Bates, D. (2005). Somatization increases medical utilization and costs independent of psychiatric and medical comorbidity. *Archives of General Psychiatry, 62*, 903–910.

Brennan, F., Carr, D. B., & Cousins, M. (2007). Pain management: A fundamental human right. *Anesthesia and Analagesia, 105* (1), 205–221.

Brodsky, C. M. (1984). Sociocultural and interactional influences on somatization. *Psychosomatics, 25*, 673–680.

Burgoyne, D. S., (2007). Prevalence and economic implications of chronic pain. *Managed Care Magazine, 16* (2 suppl 3), 2–4.

Chioqueta, A., & Stiles, T. (2004). Suicide risk in patients with somatization disorder. *Crisis: The Journal of Crisis Intervention and Suicide Prevention, 25* (1), 3–7.

Creed, F., & Barsky, A. (2004). A systematic review of the epidemiology of somatization disorder and hypochondriasis. *Journal of Psychosomatic Research, 56*, 391–408.

Denninger, J. W., Papakostas, G. I., Mahal, Y., Merens, W., Alpert, J. E., Nierenberg, A. A., Yeung, A., & Fava, M. (2006). Somatic symptoms in outpatients with major depressive disorder treated with fluoxetine. *Psychosomatics, 47*, 348–452.

Disorbio, J. M., Bruns, D., & Barolat, G. (2006). Assessment and treatment of chronic pain. *Practical Pain Management, 5* (7), 1–10.

Escobar, J. I. (2009). Somatoform disorders. In B. J. Sadock, V. A. Sadock, & P. Ruiz, (eds.), *Kaplan and Sadock's comprehensive textbook of psychiatry*, (9th ed., Vol. I, pp. 1927–1948). Philadelphia, PA: Lippincott Williams and Wilkins.

Feinstein, S., & Fallon, B. (2003). Don't be fooled by hypochondriasis. *Current Psychiatry, 2* (9). Retrieved on August 21, 2011 at: http://www.current psychiatry.com/toc.asp?FID=129&issue= September %202003&folder_description= September% 202003%20(Vol.%202,%20%20No.%209)

Freud, S. (1894, 1962). The neuropsychoses of defense. In J. Strachey, (ed.), *The complete psychological works*, Vol. 3, (pp. 45–62). London: Hogarth Press.

Gatchel, R. J., & Weisberg, J. N. (2000). *Personality characteristics of patients with pain*. Washington, DC: American Psychological Association.

Gray, S. W. (with Zide, M. R.) (2006). *Psycho-pathology: A competency-based treatment model for social workers*. Pacific Grove, CA: Brooks/Cole Thomson Learning.

Gureje, O. (2004). What can we learn from a cross national study of somatic distress? *Journal of Psychosomatic Research, 56*, 409–412.

Hurwitz, T. A. (2004). Somatization and conversion disorder. *Canadian Journal of Psychiatry, 49*, 172–178.

IsHak, W. W., Rasyidi, E., Saah, T., Vasa, M., Ettekal, A., & Fan, A. (2010). Factitious disorder: Case series with variations of psychological and physical symptoms. *Primary Psychiatry, 17* (9), 40–43.

Kirmayer, L. J., Looper, K. J., & Taillefer, S. (2003). Somatoform disorders. In M. Hersen and S. M. Turner, (eds.), *Adult psychopathology and diagnosis*, (4th ed., pp. 420–475). New York: John Wiley & Sons.

Kirmayer, L. J., & Taillefer, S. (1997). Somatoform disorder. In S. M. Turner & M. Hersen, (eds.), *Adult psychopathology and diagnosis*, (2nd ed., pp. 333–383). New York: John Wiley & Sons.

Krahn, L. E., Li, H., & O'Connor, M. K. (2003). Patients who strive to be ill: Factitious disorder with physical symptoms. *American Journal of Psychiatry, 160* (6), 1163–1168.

Lieb, R., Zimmerman, P., Friis, R. H., Holler, M., Tholen, S., & Witchen, H. U. (2002). The natural course of DSM-IV somatoform disorders and syndromes among adolescents and young adults: A prospective longitudinal community study. *European Psychiatry, 17,* 321–331.

Mai, F. (2004). Somatization disorder: A practical review. *Canadian Journal of Psychiatry, 49,* 652–662.

Marcus, D. A. (2005). Practical approach to the management of chronic pain. *Comprehensive Therapy, 31* (1), 40–49.

Maynard, C. K. (2003). Assess and manage somatization. *The Nurse practitioner, 28,* 20–29.

McDonald, S. W., & Thom, A. (1996). The Bargarran witchcraft trial—a psychiatric reassessment. *Scottish Medical Journal, 41* (5), 152–158.

Moene, F. C., Spinhoven, P., Hoogduin, K. A., & van Dyck, R. (2003). A randomized controlled clinical trial of a hypnosis-based treatment for patients with conversion disorder, motor type. *International Journal of Clinical and Experimental Hypnosis, 51*(1), 29–50.

Phillips, K. A., Menard, W., Fay, C., & Weisberg, R. (2005). Demographic characteristics, phenomenology, comorbidity, and family history in 200 individuals with body dysmorphic disorder. *Psychosomatics, 46,* 317–325.

Phillips, K. A., Wilhelm, S., Koran, L., M., Didie, E., Fallon, B., Feusner, J., & Stein, D. K. (2010). Body dysmorphic disorder: Some key issues for DSM-V. *Depression and Anxiety, 27* (6), 573–591.

Pope, C., Pope, H., Menard, W., Fay, C., Olivardia, R., & Phillips, K. (2005). Clinical features of muscle dysmorphia among males with body dysmorphic disorder. *Body Image, 4,* 385–400.

Pope, H. G., & Brower, K. J. (2009). Anabolic-androgenic steroid related disorders. In B. J. Sadock, V. A. Sadock, & P. Ruiz, (eds.), *Kaplan and Sadock's comprehensive textbook of psychiatry*, (9th ed., Vol. I, pp. 1419–1431). Philadelphia, PA: Lippincott Williams and Wilkins.

Raspe, R. E. (1948). *Singular travels, campaigns, and adventures of Baron Munchausen.* London: Cresset Press.

Schwartz, P. Y. (2002). Why is neurasthenia important in Asian cultures? *The Western Journal of Medicine, 176* (4), 257–258.

Springhouse. (2008) *Professional Guide to Diseases,* (9th ed.). Ambler, PA: Lippincott Williams & Wilkins.

Stone, J., LaFrance, W. C., Levenson, J. L., & Sharpe, M. (2010). Issues for DSM-5: Conversion disorder. *American Journal of Psychiatry, 167,* 626–627.

Stone, J., Smyth, R., Carson, A., Warlow, C., & Sharpe, M. (2006). La belle indifference in conversion symptoms and hysteria: Systematic review. *British Journal of Psychiatry, 188,* 204–209.

Szalavitz, M. (2005). The pleasant truths about pain. *Psychology Today.* Retrieved on August 20, 2011 from: http://www.psychologytoday.com/articles/200508/the-pleasant-truths-about-pain

Taylor, S., & Asmundson, G. J. (2009). Hypochondriasis and health anxiety. In M. M. Antony & M. B. Stein, (eds.), *Oxford handbook of anxiety and related disorders*, (pp. 525–540). Oxford, UK: Oxford University Press.

Todd, E., & Ahmed, I. (2001). Factitious disorder. *eMedicine Journal, 2*(1). Retrieved from: http://emedicine.medscape.com/article/291304-overview#showall

van Goozen, S. H. M., Fairchild, G., Snoek, H., & Harold, G. T. (2007). The evidence for a neurobiological model of childhood antisocial behavior. *Psychological Bulletin, 133,* 149–182.

Veale, D. (2000). Outcome of cosmetic surgery and "DIY" surgery inpatients with body dysmorphic disorder. *Psychiatric Bulletin, 24* (6), 218–221.

Veale, D., & Riley, S. (2001). Mirror, mirror on the wall, who is the ugliest of them all? The psychopathology of mirror gazing in body dysmorphic disorder. *Behavior Research and Therapy 39,* 1381–1393.

Venes, D. (Ed.) (2005). *Taber's cyclopedic medical dictionary*, (20th ed.). Philadelphia: F. A. Davis.

Woolfolk, R. L., & Allen, L. A. (2011). Somatoform and physical disorders. In D. H. Barlow, (ed.), *The Oxford handbook of clinical psychology*, (pp. 334–358). New York, NY: Oxford University Press.

Dissociative Disorders

CHAPTER 9

INTRODUCTION

When the DSM-I was first published in 1952, only one dissociative disorder, the dissociative psychoneurotic reaction, was described (American Psychiatric Association, 1952). Fifteen years later, the second edition noted two dissociative disorders: depersonalization neurosis and dissociative type of hysterical neurosis (mentioning multiple personality disorder as a symptom). The DSM-III (American Psychiatric Association, 1980) and the later revised version DSM-III-R (American Psychiatric Association, 1987) included four dissociative disorders: psychogenic amnesia, psychogenic fugue, depersonalization disorder, and multiple personality disorder. In the DSM-IV (American Psychiatric Association, 1994), all of these dissociative categories underwent a name change, and the role dissociation plays in each disorder was highlighted. Currently, the existing categories are (1) dissociative amnesia, (2) dissociative fugue, (3) depersonalization disorder, and (4) dissociative identity disorder (American Psychiatric Association, 2000).

All of these conditions have in common a dysfunction in the memory and/or awareness processes. What happens when we cannot remember why we are in a certain place or who we are? What happens if we lose our sense that our surroundings are real? These are examples of disintegrated experience—of alterations in our relationship to our self, to our world, and/or to our memory processes (Gleaves, May, & Cardena, 2001). Many of us experience minor sensations of dissociation that may temporarily help to handle stress by keeping it at an arm's length. However, once we are feeling calmer and able to adjust to the stressful situation, the dissociation usually goes away. For instance, you might be faced with taking the licensure exam, and just as you sit down in the testing room, you might have the sensation that the whole situation is unreal (or you dissociate from your surroundings). However, once you start the test and feel good about your answers to the first few questions, your confidence returns and you begin to work on completing the test. You are back on task and in touch with what's going on around you. Keep in mind that you are at a higher risk for this kind of dissociative experience if you stayed up all night cramming for the exam and if you were tired or did not get enough sleep beforehand (Giesbrecht, Smeets, Leppink, Jelicic, & Merckelbach, 2007). The dissociative disorders are quite different. The person's separation from self can be severe. This class of disorders is quite controversial, and most practitioners find them difficult to understand. Could a person be faking these symptoms or pretending to be more troubled than they really are? This question becomes particularly relevant in situations where a person is charged with a serious crime, and he or she pleads not guilty by reason of insanity.

EP 2.1.10
(b) a

The causes of the dissociative disorders are not really known, but if a person experiences a traumatic event, between 31 and 66 percent will experience dissociation (Keane, Marx, & Sloan, 2011). Dissociative experiences seem to be triggered by unexpected trauma or severe emotional threats—however, the connection between trauma and dissociation is controversial (Giesbrecht, Lynn, Lilienfeld, & Merckelbach, 2008). The fact is that the majority of people who have experienced trauma *do not* suffer a dissociative disorder—which underscores the importance of a competency-based assessment in avoiding premature conclusions about what happens in the client's life, along with carefully collecting, organizing, and interpreting assessment data. Often, the most salient points in a client's life history reside in what is *not* said. The person may have large gaps of time for which he or she cannot account—or the individual may relate many inconsistencies about his or her past. Rather than acknowledge these discrepancies, the person may try to make up the details or shift the subject away from a conversation about him- or herself. As practitioners attempt to determine the presence of dissociative disorder, they may use a set of questions that draw on the competency-based assessment, such as those presented in Table 9.1.

Barlow and Durand (2012) review several variables that are related to a person's vulnerability to a dissociative disorder. They are:

1. Childhood trauma—A history of physical and/or sexual abuse as a child is involved.
2. Suggestibility—Considered a personality trait; some people are more suggestible than others. In particular, people who are suggestible may use dissociation to defend against extreme trauma. However, the exact nature of this intrapersonal process and its relationship to the etiology of dissociative disorders remains unclear.
3. Biological factors—Traits that are inherited, such as tension and responsiveness to stress, may increase a person's vulnerability to the dissociative disorders. Head injury, seizure disorders, and sleep deprivation increase the likelihood of dissociative experiences.

Dissociation is defined as a "disruption in the usually integrated functions of consciousness, memory, identity, or perception of the environment" (American Psychiatric Association, 2000, p. 822) that is distressing or impairs an individual's basic areas of functioning. The term is generally used to describe an alteration of

TABLE 9.1	QUESTIONING PROTOCOL FOR PRESENCE OF DISSOCIATIVE DISORDER USING THE COMPETENCY-BASED ASSESSMENT MODEL

Interpersonal Relationships:
- Do others seem to know you, and yet you do not know them?
- Are you unable to figure out how you got from one place to another?

Social Environment:
- Have you ever found things and not known how you happened to have them?
- Have you ever had things missing and you have no idea how this happened?

[After the therapeutic relationship has been established and the presence of alters is suspected]

Intrapersonal Domain:
- Are you unable to remember significant periods of time?
- Are there periods of time in your life (especially during early childhood) that you cannot remember?
- Do you sometimes hear voices when no one else is physically present?
- Are there other people who are inside of you and who take charge of you at times?
- Do you think that one of the individuals (inside of you) takes charge for any particular period of time?
- Do any of these people have a special occupation, behavior, or social relationship that the others (inside of you) do not?
- Are all of the persons (inside of you) of the same age or gender?
- Do these people have names?
- How often do you notice these changes in your personality?

© Cengage Learning

consciousness characterized by estrangement from the self or the environment, and a mechanism of defense to ward off the emotional impact of traumatic or abusive events and memories. To qualify as a dissociative experience, discrepancies in the person's experiences cannot be the product of other forms of conscious deception (e.g., in the case of malingering, where the person intentionally attempts to produce symptoms). In other words, dissociation allows the mind to separate or compartmentalize selected memories or thoughts from normal consciousness. These "split-off" mental contents are not erased from the person's mind—they may resurface spontaneously or be triggered by something in the person's environment. Dissociation refers to a state in which one group of normal mental processes becomes separated from the rest; that is, the person's sense of identity changes along with a particular set of memories, feelings, and perceptions. The individual experiences a loss in connections—parts of his or her identity are relegated to a separate compartment (or buried)—but they may reemerge suddenly and unexpectedly. Some individuals experience a sudden onset with temporary symptoms, whereas others experience a gradual onset and a chronic course.

Advanced Clinical EP 2.1.10 (b) c

There has been a resurgence of interest in dissociative disorders, especially in view of its association with post-traumatic stress disorder and its correlation with severe childhood sexual abuse. Unfortunately, the bulk of the published literature in the field consists of anecdotal experience, poorly conceived studies (suffering from lack of adequate controls, selection bias, and/or unwarranted conclusions from data), and controversial arguments. What we do know is that social and cultural factors strongly influence the dissociative disorders (Barlow & Durand,

2012). The competency-based assessment, which considers all of the systems affecting the client's life, is most helpful in understanding the client's experience of traumatic life events, and how each person struggles to make sense of these events, while concurrently looking for those strengths that enable them to cope with life situations and events. This shifts the emphasis away from a standardized description of dissociation toward those skills integral to assessing each person's unique response to trauma.

Not all dissociative experiences are pathological, and to some extent, most of us have experienced dissociative events at one time or another. Daydreaming is a common experience of how people can switch states of consciousness. To do this, a person's sets of memory and attitudes must also switch. We all know (all too well) what it is like to be listening to a lecture or presentation, and suddenly become aware that we have "tuned out" what is being said. To others, it appears that we are still listening intently, when in fact we are on automatic pilot. Usually these incidents are brief and do not interfere with normal functioning.

The **dissociative disorders** entail a more complicated process wherein people forget who they are, where they are, and what they have been doing. One might begin to think of these disorders as the "elsewhere disorders"; that is, part of the person's present memory or identity is elsewhere and not available. In dissociative states, people "lose" their identity. For example, they may wander away from their home (as seen in a fugue state) or lose their memory without wandering away from their home (as seen in amnesia). In extreme cases of dissociation, people may acquire one or more distinct identities, each of which is typically referred to as an **alter** (the shorthand term for a different identity or personality). Each one of these alternate identities represents a cohesive character with his or her own unique memories, attitudes, habits, facial expressions, gestures, and personal histories that are clearly different and apart from the "host" individual they share. Typically, these personalities differ from each other along any number of dimensions, including race, gender, age, and intelligence. As an alter emerges, the host individual appears to become a different person.

Because all humans are capable of experiencing dissociation, there is a dissociative continuum on which we are all placed. The normal end of this dissociative continuum includes daydreaming and culture-specific manifestations, while the dysfunctional end of the spectrum is represented by the dissociative disorders. For instance, people in many different cultures have dissociative experiences in the course of religious or other group ceremonies that induce a trancelike state. The essential feature of a dissociative disorder is disruption in the client's intrapersonal domain—specifically of the mental functions of consciousness, identity, perception of the environment, and memory. The dissociative disorders share several common features: they generally end suddenly, a profound disturbance of memory is noted (except in depersonalization disorder), and episodes are precipitated by psychological conflicts. There are five key symptoms found in most dissociative disorders:

1. **Amnesia**—The loss of memory of one's own identity or the loss of periods of time in one's past. (It is more than simple forgetfulness, such as where the car is parked.)
2. **Depersonalization**—Feeling detached from oneself or as an outside observer of one's own self.

3. **Derealization**—Sensing that objects in one's world are strange, unreal, or have suddenly changed dimension, appearance, or location (e.g., one's own home feels unfamiliar).
4. **Identity confusion**—Being unsure of one's own identity, who one is.
5. **Identity alteration**—Behaving in a way that suggests one has assumed a new identity.

Dissociative disorders were previously thought to be extremely rare, but in a survey by Johnson and colleagues (2006), the prevalence of dissociative identity disorder (DID) was found to be 1.5 percent in a non-clinical community setting. When the dissociative episode does occur, it is transient in nature and disappears within a few hours or days. As a result, most practitioners have few opportunities to witness an episode first hand. Relying on client accounts of their experiences complicates understanding the dissociative disorders. The two most common dissociative disorders are dissociative amnesia and depersonalization disorder, but dissociative identity disorder, formerly known as multiple personality disorder (MPD), attracts the most research and clinical attention. On the dissociative continuum, dissociative identity disorder is considered the most severe.

CULTURAL PERSPECTIVES AND DISSOCIATION

EP 2.1.4 c

Practitioners must take into account the individual's social and cultural context when considering the dissociative disorders. The practitioner's skill in recognizing and communicating his or her understanding of the importance of (cultural) difference in shaping the person's experiences is underscored when attempting to assess for pathology associated with dissociation. Throughout history and across many cultures, examples of dissociation have been described. Dissociative experiences such as trance states, speaking in tongues, or spirit possession are widely accepted and practiced in many present-day cultures—and such experiences are not considered to be disorders within the culture. Specific characteristics of these dissociative experiences are generally determined by the culture within which they occur. The symptoms may appear to outsiders as evidence of dissociation, but insiders view the personality changes as attributable to a spirit or some other aspect of their belief system.

Within the environmental or cultural context, trances or possession states are not just culturally sanctioned; they are seen as normative and adaptive. For example, in regions of Thailand, Phii Pob (a common type of spirit possession) temporarily takes over a person's body. Afterward, the individual has no memory of what took place during the event. Other cultures have shamans or healers who induce trance-like states in order to communicate with spirits or with the "other world." In the highland region of Papua New Guinea, dissociative states are an intrinsic part of religious ceremonies. Only men participate in ceremonies in the spirit house (a place of worship), where they speak with their ancestors through the "crocodile spirit" who intercedes and interprets ancestors' responses. Women are expressly forbidden to enter a spirit house or practice any form of "ancestor" religion.

In light of these types of cultural differences, practitioners must systematically review a person's cultural background before making the diagnosis of dissociative disorder (Eriksen & Kress, 2005). The role of culture in the expression of symptoms and level of dysfunction is evaluated with attention to:

- *Cultural identity of the individual*—Explore the individual's ethnic or cultural orientation.
- *Cultural explanations of the person's illness*—Pay attention to the predominant phrases or behaviors through which symptoms are communicated (i.e., do not automatically assume the presence of a dissociative disorder).
- *Cultural and psychosocial environment*—Look for all culturally relevant explanations of the person's level of functioning and the influence of social stressors, and/or available supports.
- *Cultural aspects of the relationship between the individual and the practitioner*—Consider the impact culture may have on formulating a diagnosis, noting that some behaviors unfamiliar to the practitioner are regarded as normative in a different culture.

A **culture-bound syndrome** denotes "recurrent, locality-specific patterns of aberrant behavior and troubling experience that may or may not be linked to a particular DSM-IV diagnostic category" (American Psychiatric Association, 2000, p. 898). In particular, this non-normative behavior has a unique set of symptoms, the progression of which tends to be specific to a particular geographic, ethnic, or cultural group.

The types of culture-bound syndromes that would be consistent with a diagnosis of dissociative disorder are numerous. One example is **amok**, a trance syndrome—common in Southeast Asia—characterized by a sudden outburst of unrestrained violent and aggressive behavior, usually of a homicidal nature, preceded by a period of anxious brooding and followed by exhaustion. Similar patterns of behavior are found in Puerto Rico (where it is referred to as *mal de pelea*), and among the Navajo (who call it *iich'aa*). Amok is often accompanied by ideas of persecution, automatism, amnesia, and exhaustion, but following the episode the person returns to his or her premorbid level of functioning.

Another culturally accepted dissociative experience is **ataques de nervios**, a commonly noted response to acute stress in Latin American and Hispanic cultures. Features include uncontrollable crying, screaming, shouting, seizure-like behaviors, and a failure to remember the episode afterward. The event is usually brief, leaves no evidence of any residual difficulties, and is perceived within the culture to be a beneficial and adaptive way to cope with and relieve distress. Lopez and Guarnaccia (2000) characterize *ataques de nervios* as not really "a cultural syndrome or clinical entity that resides within individuals, but as a common illness that reflects the lived experience largely of women with little power and disrupted social relations" (p. 581). **Latah**, primarily thought of as a Malay-Indonesian syndrome, is another set of trancelike symptoms that occur in response to startling stimuli. It is characterized by the person's attention becoming highly focused, along with increased anxiety and trancelike behaviors (e.g., violent body movements, striking out, dropping objects, or mimicking others' movements). Again, the competency-based assessment dictates that the individual's cultural context be taken into account, which may result in the practitioner finding that this client's "dissociation" is actually adaptive.

Falling out (blacking out) is characterized by the individual's collapsing, sometimes without warning, in a trance. The person's eyes are usually open, but the individual claims an inability to see. It can be preceded by feelings of dizziness or a sensation of swimming in the head. The person is not able to move, yet they are able to hear and understand what is going on around them. This culture-bound syndrome occurs primarily among Caribbean groups or in the southern United States. A similar syndrome, called **indisposition**, occurs in Haitians. Here, too, the person falls to the ground in a trance—the difference is that they are not able to understand anything that is said or done around them.

Pibloktoq, sometimes called arctic hysteria, is a Polar Eskimo trance syndrome described as "an abrupt dissociative episode accompanied by extreme excitement of up to 30 minutes' duration and frequently followed by convulsive seizures and coma lasting up to 12 hours" (American Psychiatric Association, 2000, p. 901). Before the attack, the person may be irritable or withdrawn for several hours or days. During the episode, the person may rip off his or her clothes and go running into the snow or across the ice, shout obscenities or scream incoherently, eat feces, become violent, or do something seen as dangerous or irrational. The individual has no memory of his or her actions. Interestingly, this behavior has also been described as resulting from the sexual exploitation of Inuit women by explorers. Although this syndrome is seen primarily in arctic and subarctic Eskimo communities, it can also be found among the Miskito Indians of Central America, where it is referred to as **grisi siknis**.

A Korean syndrome known as **shin-byung** involves initial feelings of anxiousness and somatic complaints (such as weakness, dizziness, fear, anorexia, insomnia, or gastrointestinal problems) followed by dissociation and possession by ancestral spirits. **Zar**, another term that refers to the experience of spirits possessing an individual, is found in Ethiopia, Somalia, Egypt, Sudan, Iran, and other North African and Middle Eastern societies.

DISSOCIATIVE IDENTITY DISORDER

Dissociative identity disorder (DID) is considered the most severe of all the dissociative disorders because the most common and fundamental alteration includes the presence of more than one discrete identity. Most research studies indicate the average number of personalities exhibited by those who suffer from DID as 15 (Ross, 1997). However, some question the presence of multiple personalities and describe them as differences in representations of different emotional states (Merckelbach, Devilly, & Rassin, 2002). However, DID is a viable diagnosis and could benefit from a clearer definition of symptoms (Gleaves, May, & Cardena, 2001). Unfortunately, once the disorder is established, it tends to last a lifetime (in the absence of treatment). It is usually traceable to traumatic events that occurred during childhood.

A competency-based assessment that pays attention to life situations, circumstances, and events will set the stage for the practitioner's skill in uncovering environmental factors that lead to the development of dissociative identity disorder. The client's life history, in at least one aspect, contains terrible and frequently indescribable instances of physical or sexual abuse, most often incest. In the author's practice experiences, all too often, clients relate childhood incidents of being locked in basements or closets, brutally tortured, burned, cut, beaten, or tormented in a variety of ways far too horrible to recount in detail here. In all such cases, the important thing to remember is that the individual learns as a young child to survive by fleeing into the dissociative process. This process includes a psychobiological mechanism that allows the mind to escape what the body is experiencing; that is, the child exists in a fantasy world where these brutal experiences are blunted. Each time the child endures an abusive episode, he or she "learns" better how to escape by recreating the haven of safety and "switching" into his or her fantasy world. On some level, the child learns there is no limit to the variety of identities he or she can construct for protection from the abusive situation.

The process of switching seems to decrease with age, and over time one of the personalities becomes more dominant than the others. Although the use of dissociation as a defense mechanism begins in childhood, the presence of a dissociative identity disorder is often undetected until adulthood. By this time, the dissociation is well entrenched as a way of coping.

The developmental disruptions that accompany child sexual abuse and neglect set into motion events that increase the likelihood of future maladaptation. It should be pointed out that not all children who experience maltreatment will later develop serious problems in living. However, they are at a much greater risk for problems—for example, aggression and violence, chronic impairment in self-concept and self-esteem, emotional and behavioral self-regulation, and depression and post-traumatic stress disorder. In adulthood, the developmental impairments stemming from those childhood experiences often lead to more pervasive and chronic intrapersonal and interpersonal difficulties such as panic disorders, eating disorders, personality disorders, and sexual problems.

There is emerging opinion that dissociative identity disorder is a very extreme subtype of post-traumatic stress disorder (PTSD) (Barlow & Durand, 2012). In both conditions, strong emotional reactions are commonly associated with experiencing a severe trauma. When post-traumatic stress disorder was first identified, the specific reference points were catastrophic events—for example, war, rape, torture, natural disasters (hurricanes or floods), and disasters of human origin (airline or train crashes). A distinction should be made between trauma and other extremely stressful life events such as a family breaking up due to a divorce. The traumatic experiences associated with post-traumatic stress disorder are likely to exceed and overwhelm the person's abilities in coping. Interestingly, children who experience sexual abuse show many of the same symptoms previously identified in adults who experienced combat situations, torture, or natural disasters; that is, what they share in common is nightmares, fears, and panic attacks for many years following the traumatic experiences. Although it happened in 1992, the author vividly remembers Hurricane Andrew, in which as many as 30 percent of the children who experienced this natural disaster were reported to have severe levels of PTSD symptoms for almost 2 years afterward (La Greca, Silverman, Vernberg, & Prinstein, 1996).

PREVAILING PATTERN

Most people with dissociative identity disorder are generally not forthcoming about their various personalities, even when they learn that they have them. They often fear they will be regarded as an exhibitionist or worse, as a freak. The various personalities tend to be distinctive and dominate or control the behavior of the person;

often there is a sense of struggle for dominance among the alters. Sometimes there may be a shifting importance in the role of each personality over time, which is reflected in the amount of time spent in each identity.

The "host" identity, that is, the person who comes in (or is referred) for counseling, is usually overwhelmed by efforts to hold various fragments of these personalities together. The person may not be aware of the presence of these alters and may be confused about what is happening. A prevailing question is whether these fragmented identities are real or if the individual is just faking symptoms to avoid some responsibility or get relief from stress. Similar to conversion disorder, this question is very difficult to answer. Evidence indicates that those diagnosed with DID tend to be suggestible (Giesbrecht et al., 2008). Another possibility is that the person's alters may be created in order to respond to leading questions from practitioners. For instance, the practitioner who believes that a history of childhood abuse is a primary cause of dissociative identity disorder will probably be more likely to ask clients leading questions and to use interview techniques that encourage a report of symptoms that might not otherwise be offered. Admittedly, although some individuals may enact dissociated identities, and some practitioners may reinforce these enactments, not all cases of dissociative identity disorder are fabrications (Kluft, 1996). Both the practitioner and the client are best served if the practitioner completes a competency-based assessment that carefully explores all domains of the client's life—and remains open-minded to all manner of possibilities that explain client behavior.

DIFFERENTIAL ASSESSMENT

EP 2.1.10
(b) a

Dissociative disorder symptoms can resemble other diagnoses and highlight the practitioner's skill in collecting, organizing, and interpreting the client's story. For example, dissociative disorder must be differentiated from other general medical conditions, particularly, neurological conditions and the effects of psychoactive substances that can lead to impaired memory. Individuals with certain neurological disorders, especially seizure disorders, experience an increase of dissociative features (Barlow & Durand, 2012). Dissociative features must also be distinguished from other diagnoses such as the substance use disorders. For example, a person may experience memory loss associated with substance intoxication (e.g., blackouts), and behave in a way that is very uncharacteristic. Although the person may have no memory of the blackout, he or she maintains the same identity during that episode. Thus, a neurological examination is essential to rule out other factors that might produce symptoms of dissociation. With malingering disorder, any reasons the client might have for inventing other personalities must be ruled out, and the practitioner has to be alert to any type of gain, financial or otherwise, that a person might obtain by virtue of having these symptoms.

The dissociative disorder is often misconstrued as being a thought disorder similar to schizophrenia (in which the individual exhibits delusions, hallucinations, bizarre behavior, and/or disorganized speech). However, dissociative identity disorder is the result of switching back and forth between one personality entity and another. The symptoms are usually transient and related to a cycling of personality entities as they struggle for control over the person's core identity. Dissociative amnesia, fugue, and depersonalization are not characterized by the experience of multiple, discrete identities. People suffering from dissociative identity disorder may initially be misdiagnosed as having an affective disorder because the mood swings found in affective disorders are confused with the switching personalities in DID. However, the individual with DID usually does not feel depressed for any length of time—and, if mood swings exist, they are typically of short duration.

The following case introduces Emily Samuels, who suffers from dissociative identity disorder.

CASE | THE CASE OF EMILY SAMUELS

Emily Samuels was referred by one of the authors' colleagues for a consultation. The colleague called and said, "Susan, I've seen Emily three times, and I'm more confused than ever. While she presents herself in sessions with some depression, I'm not sure what is going on for this young woman. I only know it might be something very serious. Could you please see her for me?"

The first thing I noticed about Emily was how she entered my office. She was very subdued and approached the session in a tentative, hesitant manner. I felt she was watching and waiting for me to make the first move. Her voice was barely above a whisper as she introduced herself. Once she was settled, I asked her why she thought she was referred to me.

Emily responded, "Well, I don't want you to think I'm crazy or anything, but sometimes I get into trouble using my MasterCard."

Her answer took me a little by surprise, so I asked her to elaborate on what she meant by that.

"Well, I know it sounds really strange, but the MasterCard company claims I've charged over $22,000 this year on three different cards." Emily was looking directly at me now, and her voice was a little louder than the whisper she started out with. "I don't know anything about that. I think they are a bunch of crooks trying to rip me off. I wanna know one thing. If I spent that much money, where is all the stuff I'm supposed to have bought? They don't want to tell me anything. They are taking me to court in 2 months. They said I applied for three different credit cards in three different names and now I have to pay up. Where would I get that kinda money? Besides, I can prove I didn't spend that money. Those cards aren't in my name, and on top of it all the handwriting on the charge receipts isn't mine either."

I asked her, "Has anything else happened like this before where you didn't remember things?"

"Sometimes, people I don't even know call me by other names," she replied. "Like last week, I was in Wal-Mart, and this lady I've never laid eyes on was calling me 'Harriet.' She just about ran me down yelling, 'Yoo-hoo, Harriet, Harriet where are you going? Why didn't you answer me?' I was so humiliated because she was creating such a scene."

I asked Emily, "What did you think about that?"

She shrugged her shoulders to indicate she was not sure, and looked slightly uncomfortable. "She's the one who made an idiot out of herself."

"No," I said, "I meant what did you think about her mistaking you for someone else?" I thought I saw a momentary look of fear in her eyes, but then she averted her gaze away from mine. I continued, "Has this ever happened to you before?"

She responded, "Well, yeah. Now that you mention it, some guy I didn't know before called me 'Beth Ann' when I was grocery shopping. I thought he was a nut job, you know, a stalker or something. I complained to the store manager, and he said he'd take care of it. Only he came back and told me that that guy claimed to be my husband." Emily's face flushed with embarrassment. "I guess that's why Mary Jo asked you to see me. I don't think she's ever heard of anything like this before."

I asked Emily, "What do you think happened to you when you were in the grocery store?"

She sort of giggled and said, "The lighting musta been bad, and I didn't recognize my husband, that's all." She refused to answer any further questions along that line.

I asked Emily a series of questions regarding her interpersonal experiences as a child—specifically about school and whether she had any difficulties with her peer group or with her family. She acknowledged problems with poor grades, truancy, and having only a few friends. She also mentioned her parents were very strict with her; she was their only child. She said she had never been hospitalized for anything other than having her tonsils out. Emily also said that she doesn't take any medications.

At this point in the interview, she looked pensive. After a moment, she quietly asked, "When you say hospitalized, is that the same as being in a mental institution?"

"Well, that depends on how you think about it," I answered cautiously.

Emily cleared her throat. "My parents put me in a mental hospital a coupla times when I was a kid 'cause I used to have terrible nightmares all the time. I would try to stay awake all night. I guess I was afraid to go to sleep." When asked about what happened at this time in her life, she replied, "I don't really remember much except that I had these terrible, terrible dreams that somebody was really hurting me."

After some gentle prodding, Emily recounted that the nightmares usually had a pattern and that they were connected to her father coming into her room at night and touching her in secret places. "I told my mother about my dreams," she continued, "but she just laughed and said, 'Emily, you *do* have a vivid imagination. You know I'd never let anybody hurt you.' She used to tell me, 'That's why we put you in a mental institution—because you remembered things that never happened.' I wish she would have believed me." Emily denied currently feeling depressed or suicidal.

Shifting the subject, I asked Emily if she ever found items of clothes, jewelry, or other things that she didn't recognize.

She looked at me as if to say, How did you know that? She replied, "Yeah, once I found some motorcycle stuff in my closet at home. It was really weird stuff, too." Gently, I asked her to elaborate. "Well, you know, some of the stuff looked like it shoulda belonged to a guy. It sure didn't belong to me."

She sounded a bit scared and uncertain at this point. Then she went on, "I mean, what would I be doing with a pair of black leather pants, boots, and some bracelets with those spikey things sticking out? The only thing I can think of is, I musta found them

and brought them home or something," she replied, twisting in her chair.

I decided to ask Emily a series of questions about time and memory. I asked, "Have you ever experienced any gaps in time? You know, time that you just could not account for?" and "Have there been large periods of time when you were growing up that you could not remember?"

Quite abruptly, Emily sat up and began to stare at me in a way that she had not done before. I observed almost immediately that her posture, facial expressions, and mannerisms also changed. Her voice became gruff and raspy.

"Hey, bitch, you leave the kid alone. You hear what I'm saying? She's had enough trouble from you shrinks, so back off."

I responded that I had been asking Emily about time gaps in her life. Then I decided to take a direct approach. "What did I say that brought about such a change?"

"Well, first of all, I ain't Emily, I'm Rick. I bet you weren't expecting me, huh?" I began to wonder about several inconsistencies in what Emily had told me earlier. I replied, "Okay, Rick, I wonder if you could tell me something about who you are."

"Emily doesn't know about us, but we know all about her. We don't get in her face too often, but every once in a while we like to get out and have fun. She's much too fussy, you know what I mean? Anyway, there are four of us and...," she continued.

"Hey, Bozo, you don't have to talk for me, I can talk for myself. I'm Frenchy, and I love sex." She laughs hysterically. *"That Emily's always been such a rigid little piece of work. She used to really freak out when her old man made her do him. You know,"* mockingly, *'Boo hoo, Daddy, don't. It hurts. Boo, hoo, hoo.' So I take over for her—'cause I don't care. It don't bother me as much, so it don't hurt, right?"* The interview continued.

"Where was I?" continued Rick, **"Oh yeah, I was telling you how we protect Emily—always have. So butt out."**

At this point, Emily flexed her neck and head from side to side, and looked at me in the way I first remembered meeting her. She smiled shyly, raised her eyes, and asked, "Did something happen I should know about?" Before answering her, I immediately remember thinking that I needed to call Mary Jo and discuss this interesting turn of events.

ASSESSMENT SUMMARY   The most striking feature about Emily is her sudden shift during our session among three distinct personalities: Emily (the host), Rick, and Frenchy. It should be pointed out that the phenomenon of "switching" is rare and a relatively unusual occurrence in practice. Each distinct personality struggles for dominance, and this shift from one to another can initially confuse the practitioner. As Emily's story unfolds, she is relating to me as a shy, soft-spoken, and demure young woman. Then I notice there are some indications of other personalities. Rick emerges in the interview at a time when I am beginning to explore potentially sensitive material, specifically, whether or not Emily ever experiences blocks of time she can't explain. It turns out that Rick, who is a different gender, seems quite protective of Emily. He is brusque and controlling. Then Frenchy emerges as I attempt to understand Rick and his relationship to Emily. It is Frenchy who functions as Emily's protector, and becomes clear as the content of childhood sexual abuse is again introduced. (The first reference to abuse is made when Emily talks about being institutionalized in a mental hospital.)

Emily is considered the host personality, and it is the host who usually seeks help from a practitioner. Although Emily is unaware of her alters, they are aware of each other—however, they only revealed themselves one at a time during the interview. The transition from one personality to another occurred during stressful points in the session. Both alters expressed protectiveness toward Emily, especially during the most stressful times in Emily's life.

Emily's history of childhood sexual abuse by her father set the stage for the development of her dissociative identity disorder. This fantasy world is, in fact, very closely associated with post-traumatic stress disorder in that both are strong reactions to the experience of childhood trauma. Emily's escape into the dissociative realm blunted her physical and emotional pain.

Assessment conversations should always involve the client, no matter what the source of the referral. During the initial meeting, I encouraged Emily to share personally relevant material, and helped her to explore situations of concern, their meanings, and related feelings. Sometimes people will immediately bring up topics for discussion, and at other times, like Emily, they are reserved and hesitant. Figure 9.1 illustrates the interactions of biological, psychological, and social variables in Emily Samuels's life.

EMILY SAMUELS'S MUTIAXIAL DSM DIAGNOSIS IS AS FOLLOWS:

Axis I	300.14 Dissociative Identity Disorder
Axis II	V71.09 (No diagnosis)
Axis III	None
Axis IV	Childhood sexual abuse
Axis V	GAF = 55 (at interview)

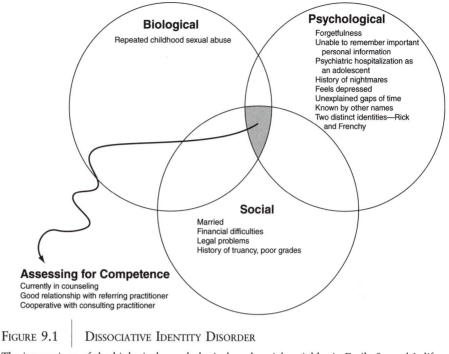

Biological
Repeated childhood sexual abuse

Psychological
Forgetfulness
Unable to remember important
   personal information
Psychiatric hospitalization as
   an adolescent
History of nightmares
Feels depressed
Unexplained gaps of time
Known by other names
Two distinct identities—Rick
   and Frenchy

Social
Married
Financial difficulties
Legal problems
History of truancy, poor grades

Assessing for Competence
Currently in counseling
Good relationship with referring practitioner
Cooperative with consulting practitioner

FIGURE 9.1 | DISSOCIATIVE IDENTITY DISORDER

The interactions of the biological, psychological, and social variables in Emily Samuels's life.

© Cengage Learning

DISSOCIATIVE AMNESIA DISORDER

Dissociative amnesia disorder was formerly known as psychogenic amnesia. This is a completely reversible amnesia that is associated with some form of emotional, traumatic, or psychological stress. While the person's generalized fund of life knowledge remains intact, he or she cannot remember important personal information, such as his or her name, age, or marital status. This cannot be attributed to ordinary forgetfulness or absentmindedness.

There are several different patterns of dissociative amnesia:

1. **Localized (or circumscribed) amnesia**—The person is unable to recall events that occurred during a particular time or following a profoundly disturbing event, such as combat.

2. **Selective amnesia**—The person can bring to mind patchy recollections of an event, but other portions of time are forgotten (for example, a woman might not remember giving birth to her child, but she might remember various aspects of being in labor, or events after the actual birth). This failure to recall specific events occurring during a specific period of time is very common during war (Cardena & Gleaves, 2003).

3. **Generalized amnesia**—This is a disorder that encompasses all of the experiences during a person's entire lifetime. The person cannot remember

anything from infancy to the present, including his or her name and other identifiers.

4. **Continuous amnesia**—This type of amnesia refers to a person's inability to remember all events from a given time up to and including the present time, while retaining memory prior to that given time.

5. **Systematized amnesia**—The person loses memory pertaining only to certain categories of information, such as information related to his or her family or work.

These latter three types of amnesia are less common than the first two, and the behaviors associated with them may eventually lead to a more complex diagnosis of dissociative identity disorder.

Dissociative amnesia has been poorly studied and consequently not much is known about family prevalence, demographic data, or etiology. Dissociative amnesia can occur among any age group, but it is most commonly reported in young women and is usually preceded by severe stress. The symptoms disappear as suddenly as they appear; amnesia events can range from minutes to years. In fact, most often symptoms of amnesia resolve without intervention, and the individual does go on to remember what was forgotten (Barlow & Durand, 2012). In rare instances, the amnesia can recur. In fact, dissociative amnesia can be downright unpredictable. For instance, a person may remember what he or she had for breakfast but not recall his or her name. In contrast, those with Alzheimer's-type dementia usually remember their names, but not what they ate for breakfast. Memory loss associated with abusing substances, taking medications, or a general medical condition (such as seizures) should be distinguished from the symptoms of dissociative amnesia.

PREVAILING PATTERN

A single episode of dissociative amnesia is the most common pattern; however, multiple episodes are possible in situations where there are repeated experiences of extreme stress or trauma (e.g., being the victim of a crime). The person who suffers from dissociative amnesia experiences at least one episode where he or she is either partially or completely unable to retrieve important memories and personal information. The information usually is about the trauma or stress, and the amnesia is more extensive than what could be explained by ordinary forgetfulness. These symptoms cause significant distress and interpersonal difficulties, including, for example, problems with employment and in social relationships. They do not occur solely during dissociative fugue, acute stress disorder, post-traumatic stress disorder (PTSD), dissociative identity disorder, or somatization disorder. The symptoms are not caused by a general medical condition or the use of alcohol and/or drugs (including prescribed medications).

Advanced Clinical EP 2.1.10 (b) c

The assessment is not made if the loss of recall is only around childhood memories; it must involve events that are more current, usually those following a psychologically traumatic event. The correlation between dissociative amnesia and traumatic events is not clear, and the practitioner is encouraged to proceed cautiously when evaluating the onset of dissociative amnesia in a client's life. However, individuals who have had one episode of dissociative amnesia may be more vulnerable to developing amnesia in reaction to a subsequent trauma (Barlow & Durand, 2012). A competency-based assessment that thoroughly explores the interactions of biological, psychological, and social factors in a person's life greatly decreases the possibility of coming to the wrong conclusion about how a person copes with and adapts to traumatic life events.

DIFFERENTIAL ASSESSMENT

In contrast to those who experience the middle-age onset of **transient global amnesia,** a type of amnesia involving a sudden temporary episodes of short-term memory loss, people with dissociative amnesia usually suffer their first bout of amnesia at a young age—but, most importantly, they are eventually able to recall what happened. Dissociative amnesia is not assessed if the person's memory gaps occur exclusively during dissociative fugue states (which involve unexpected travel and confusion about personal identity). Feigned dissociative amnesia indicates either malingering or factitious disorder.

The following vignette introduces Margarethe Jean-Baptiste, whose case depicts dissociative amnesia as it is typically encountered by practitioners.

| CASE | THE CASE OF MARGARETHE JEAN-BAPTISTE |

[Voice from the hospital intercom system] "Paging Doctor Gray. Doctor Susan Gray, please call operator number three."

I grabbed the nearest house telephone and asked for operator three. "This is Susan Gray, you're looking for me?"

The voice on the other end of the line responded, "Hi, Susan, it's Terry in the ER. Look, I don't have time to go into a lot of detail, but could you please come down here right away?"

"Sure, I'm on my way," I replied and headed into the stairwell for the two-flight descent. Terry Holcomb, an ER nurse on duty in admitting, was waiting for me. "Terry, what's up?"

"Well, we have a situation here," she said as she gestured me into a quiet corner. "Did you hear about the group of Haitian rafters the Marathon Police picked up this morning?" I shook my head no. She continued, "Well, it's the same old story—the police found five men and two women beached in what was left of a homemade wooden raft out near the Seven Mile Bridge. One of the men told me that ten of them set out 8 days ago, but they started having trouble with the raft almost right away. There was a bad squall, and three people were swept overboard, along with most of their water and supplies. It's nothing short of a miracle that the rest of them made it at all—and they're not in too bad shape. You know, aside from exhaustion and sunburn."

"So, you want me to check for ASD, PTSD, or what?" I asked.

"No, I need you to talk with a young woman—they call her Margarethe Jean-Baptiste—but you couldn't prove it by her. She can't remember anything about the last 8 days. We asked her the usual questions, you know, 'Who are you? Where are you? What's today's date? yadda, yadda … nothing! It's like time just stopped for her. Margarethe does not remember what happened to the other people, and it's my guess she experienced some pretty bad emotional stuff on that raft—more than likely, one of those who didn't make it was a family member, or something. She doesn't know where she is, even though I've reminded her several times that she's safe and sound in the hospital here in the Florida Keys."

I asked Terry, "What about her physical exam?"

She responded, "Everything checks out fine. Margarethe doesn't appear to be suffering from any kind of problem other than being sunburned and having some mild dehydration. She's some lucky lady, considering what she's been through. Just to cover all my bases, I brought in Malcolm Renaldo. Do you know him? No? Well, he just started his neurology rotation here from the University of Miami and seems like a sharp fellow. Anyway, I spoke to him before I called you. On his physical exam he found no evidence of any head trauma or anything else that could explain her memory loss. Margarethe's labs just came back—nothing

continued

remarkable there either, you know, like drugs or whatever. So it appears, medically at least, she's all right. I guess, the next look-see is in your department. I'll be waiting to hear from you."

I introduced myself to Margarethe through an interpreter who spoke Creole and asked what I could do to be of help. Her English was pretty good, but I used the interpreter as a backup. I also wanted to reduce any additional stresses in our conversation, with English being Margarethe's second language.

"I want to call my family back home and let them know I'm all right," she replied. "They will be worried about me." I sensed that Margarethe was a bit uneasy at this point and gently inquired about how she managed to survive the last few days. Tears welled up in her eyes as she spoke to me. She said (sobbing softly), "I remember leaving my country to make a new life. Since the storm, I, I, I … I do not know the rest."

I reassured Margarethe that I would try to help. After a few days in the hospital, Margarethe was discharged with a referral to the Middle Keys Guidance Clinic and another to legal aid, to deal with her immigration status.

ASSESSMENT SUMMARY   Margarethe Jean-Baptiste's amnesia was the chief concern for hospital staff. Aside from being sunburned and dehydrated, she was in good overall medical health. Nonetheless, she was experiencing a great deal of physical exhaustion and emotional stress from a tortuous and traumatic boat trip, which could have provided the stimulus for her dissociative amnesia. When found, Margarethe was brought to the local hospital, where she received a complete medical evaluation. The findings of her tests and examination were all within normal limits and provided no basis to support any biological cause for her state of amnesia. There was no indication of head trauma, epilepsy, or substance abuse, and it would seem that Margarethe's health was generally good before the boat trip. Ultimately, her dissociative amnesia was attributed to the traumatic experience of leaving her country and the resulting voyage.

The competency-based assessment looks at environmental factors as well as intrapersonal ones that include a person's thoughts and feelings about what happened to them. In Margarethe's case, her immigration from Haiti was complicated by a perilous boat journey that ended in the death of several of her companions. This traumatic incident was the capstone of events causing her memory loss. Figure 9.2 shows the interactions of the biological, psychological, and social variables in Margarethe Jean-Baptiste's life.

MARGARETHE JEAN-BAPTISTE'S MULTIAXIAL DSM DIAGNOSIS IS AS FOLLOWS:

Axis I	300.12 Dissociative Amnesia
Axis II	V71.09 (No diagnosis)
Axis III	Sunburn Dehydration
Axis IV	Illegal immigrant
	No social support
	Death of friends
Axis V	GAF = 55 (on admission) 70 (on discharge)

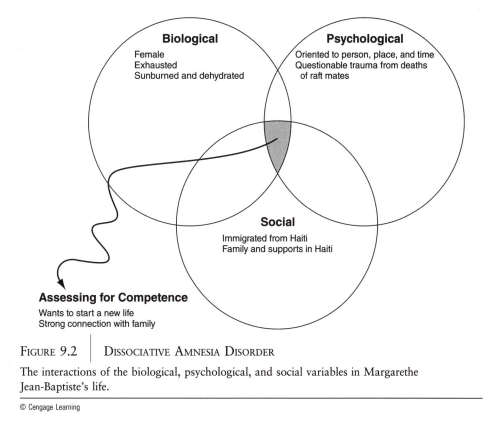

FIGURE 9.2 | DISSOCIATIVE AMNESIA DISORDER

The interactions of the biological, psychological, and social variables in Margarethe Jean-Baptiste's life.

© Cengage Learning

DISSOCIATIVE FUGUE DISORDER

People with **dissociative fugue disorder,** formerly called psychogenic fugue, experience sudden, unexpected travel away from their home or work, suffer an inability to recall their past, assume a new identity, and cannot remember important personal details about their past. Mostly, the person with this curious disorder just takes off and loses the ability to recall his or her entire previous identity. While in a fugue state, the person does not remember his or her prior life—after the fugue, the episode may or may not be remembered. The stimulus for a fugue state usually involves the individual leaving behind some kind of difficult and troubling situation that (on some level) he or she finds intolerable. For example, traumatic memories, financial crises, and/or marital problems have triggered fugue states. In some cases, the individual assumes an entirely new identity along with traveling to another geographical location.

PREVAILING PATTERN

Fugue states usually do not appear until early adolescence, and more commonly occur in adulthood. Symptoms rarely appear for the first time after the age of 50 but once they do appear, they usually continue well into old age (Barlow & Durand,

2012). The duration of the fugue state may range from a few hours to several days, and it usually ends abruptly. Once the person returns home, he or she may recall some of what happened during the fugue.

DIFFERENTIAL ASSESSMENT

EP 2.1.10
(b) b

Dissociative fugue is far more common in movies and television programs than in clinical practice. The person with this disorder usually comes to the practitioner's attention as a John or Jane Doe who is lost or confused about who he or she is and where he or she comes from. A competency-based assessment helps practitioners avoid being overly vigorous in assigning pathology and looks to strengths and coping mechanisms. This orientation to the assessment helps the practitioner to discern the more serious conditions with similar symptoms (such as dissociative identity disorder, dementia, delirium, substance-related disorders, or schizophrenia).

The symptoms associated with dissociative fugue are the same as those for dissociative amnesia except for the sudden travel component. Other diagnostic categories to consider are manic or schizophrenic episodes accompanied by traveling; organic, nonepileptic factors such as brain tumors; and alcohol- and drug-related memory loss accompanied by wandering. Before making an assessment of dissociative fugue, the practitioner should also consider assessments for delirium, dementia, malingering, factitious disorder, and dissociative identity disorder.

The following case illustrates someone who experiences a dissociative fugue.

CASE | THE CASE OF "ELVIS GARFIELD LANCASTER SMITH"

"I'll tell you boys once again, my name is Elvis Garfield Lancaster Smith, but my friends call me Elvis. Now that we've gotten through that, I'd like to get back to the shelter and get something to eat. That is, if y'all don't mind."

Mr. Smith was brought to the emergency room after getting into a physical scuffle with another man also seeking a meal and a shower at the Salvation Army Shelter.

The police brought Mr. Smith (who appeared to be middle-aged) to the hospital because he sustained a head wound during the physical altercation. When the emergency room physician asked Mr. Smith for some identification or proof of insurance, the staff quickly determined that he carried no personal papers or identification of any kind on him.

On physical examination, the physician noted, "The patient has very recently sustained severe body trauma, and shows evidence of multiple slash-type wounds."

Mr. Smith commented when viewing his injuries, "Man, sure looks like somebody beat me up pretty good—I just don't remember nothing about it."

As the interview progressed, Mr. Smith offered that he was new to the Miami area, and he could not recall where he had worked or lived before he came here. He was unable to provide the names of friends or family members who could be contacted to help. The police began an investigation to see if they could find out anything further about Mr. Smith, who was kept overnight for observation.

During the night, the police were able to piece together his identity and what had happened to him. Mr. Smith, as it turned out, was really Mr. Edgar Edelstein, who lived in Orlando. Three days before the physical altercation at the homeless shelter, Mr. Edelstein was involved in an automobile accident that killed his wife, Margie, and his mother-in-law, Sheila. The Orlando police had been looking for Mr. Edelstein, who apparently wandered away from the scene of the accident.

ASSESSMENT SUMMARY   The competency-based assessment serves as a tool to organize the data collected. This case is a classic example of dissociative fugue in that "Mr. Smith" Edelstein was confused about his identity. He traveled away from home and set about seeking shelter. There is no evidence that Mr. Edelstein switched to any other personality entities, which rules out making the assessment of dissociative identity disorder—dissociative fugue and dissociative identity disorder cannot coexist. There is no evidence in Mr. Edelstein's history of a cognitive disorder (other than the obvious amnesia) that would support an assessment of dementia.

Figure 9.3 shows the interactions of the biological, psychological, and social variables in Mr. Smith's (Edgar Edelstein's) life.

EDGAR EDELSTEIN'S MULTIAXIAL DSM DIAGNOSIS IS AS FOLLOWS:

Axis I	300.13 Dissociative Fugue Disorder
Axis II	V71.09 (No diagnosis)
Axis III	Sustained severe body trauma
Axis IV	Death of wife and mother-in-law 3 days ago Police investigation of accident
Axis V	GAF = 60 (current)

© Cengage Learning

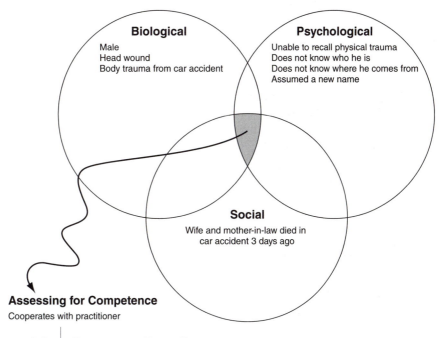

FIGURE 9.3 | DISSOCIATIVE FUGUE DISORDER

The interactions of the biological, psychological, and social variables in Mr. Smith's (Edgar Edelstein's) life.

DEPERSONALIZATION DISORDER

The people with **depersonalization disorder** experience themselves as strange or unreal in some way. They feel detached from their surroundings, as if someone else is "in control" or as if they are living in a dream or moving in slow motion. The depersonalization experience is highly subjective. The individual reports feeling detached from his or her body. Although the individual remains in touch with reality, his or her symptoms may be persistent, recurrent, or may seriously impair functioning—only then should an assessment of depersonalization disorder be considered.

Depersonalization seems to be one of those disorders that capture the imagination of filmmakers and tabloid headline writers. Consider the popular comic-book character, Superman, who adopts a different personality to hide his true self from the world. On the one hand, there is the invincible persona who flies around wearing a cape and doing good; on the other hand, there is the meek and mild-mannered news reporter, Clark Kent. Other popular characters—like Spider Man and the Incredible Hulk—also capture people's imaginations because they suggest the idea that an individual may harbor more than one personality. Steinberg and Schnall's (2001) popular book, *Stranger in the Mirror,* explores the extent of dissociation in society. In reality, depersonalization remains poorly studied and is rarely seen in clinical practice. It is included in this chapter to remind the practitioner that, even though they are unlikely to encounter a client who has these experiences, a competency-based assessment will help to ensure that premature or incorrect conclusions are not reached about the person's biopsychosocial history.

PREVAILING PATTERN

Often the first episode of depersonalization occurs during late adolescence or early adulthood and generally begins without warning. The person finds him- or herself "detached" but able to continue doing what he or she was already doing (e.g., eating, working, or talking). The individual seems to be observing things rather than actually participating in them. One client described the experience as, "I'm on automatic pilot and watching myself looking at seeing myself from outside my body." The following case discussion illustrates how these symptoms may emerge in the therapeutic conversation.

CASE | THE CASE OF JEAN REDHORSE OSCEOLA

"Listen, I don't want to be here. I want to go home. I don't want somebody to lock me up and tell me that I'm crazy or something," Jean Redhorse cried.

She had come to the attention of the school social worker when it was reported that the 17-year-old Native American told one of her teachers she "felt like a robot," and "I can see myself standing outside my body." Jean Redhorse's mother was called at work and was asked to come to the school immediately.

"My daughter had this thing several times before," Mrs. Osceola said, "but it doesn't amount to much of anything. It's just her crazy talk—I have way too much to do at work to be wasting my time coming down to school when she gets into one of her spells. I just wish she would eat a good breakfast, ya know?"

The social worker replied, "Can either you or Jean Redhorse tell me anything more about this?"

"Well," Jean Redhorse replied, "sometimes it looks like my arms and legs get really big or really small. Sometimes I feel like I'm floating up in the air—you know, like floating outside my body and above my head. It's not like I'm crazy or anything, because I know it's happening ... but the first time it was so weird. Now, it's getting a little scary. I feel like I have no control over it. It just sorta happens."

Jean Redhorse denies experiencing any blackout spells, convulsions, headaches, dizziness, or trauma to her head. She also denies hearing voices or having hallucinations. She denies feeling that other people plot against her, and never feels suicidal or depressed. She claims she is alcohol- and drug-free—and, though some of her friends tried pot once or twice, she never did.

Mrs. Osceola interjected with a note of pride in her voice, "It is unacceptable for us Navajos to drink."

Jean Redhorse had just undergone a physical examination by their family physician. Other than her spells, nothing appears to be wrong with Jean Redhorse Osceola.

ASSESSMENT SUMMARY

Jean Redhorse appears to be a typical teenager in every way except for the "spells" she experiences. These episodes are typical depersonalization experiences wherein Jean Redhorse reports feeling as if a part of her body is detached from the rest of her. Doctors have found no physical or neurological bases for these sensations. Although Mrs. Osceola dismisses them as teenage exaggerations, Jean Redhorse seems to be increasingly concerned by their recurrence.

Advanced Clinical EP 2.1.9 a

The practitioner in this case is not Native American. Therefore, in order to make an accurate competency-based assessment, the worker needs to have a better understanding of the client's cultural environment. This approach to the assessment process underscores the importance of being able to assess the quality of a client's interactions within their social contexts. For instance, when Mrs. Osceola comments that the Navajo do not use alcohol, the worker notes this as a reflection of her culture's beliefs about drinking. When considering depersonalization disorder, the practitioner should not be confused by the presence of their client's culture and its interplay with coping behaviors. In other words, individuals need to be placed in their sociocultural context before their behavior can be judged to be pathological. Another example can be found among the Hindu Yogis who, through yogic meditation, experience a voluntary form of depersonalization. This deliberately induced trance practice should not be confused with depersonalization disorder.

Figure 9.4 illustrates the interaction of the biological, psychological, and social variables in Jean Redhorse Osceola's life.

JEAN REDHORSE OSCEOLA'S MULTIAXIAL DSM DIAGNOSIS WOULD BE AS FOLLOWS:

Axis I	300.6 Depersonalization Disorder
Axis II	V71.09 (No diagnosis)
Axis III	None
Axis IV	None
Axis V	GAF = 70 (current)

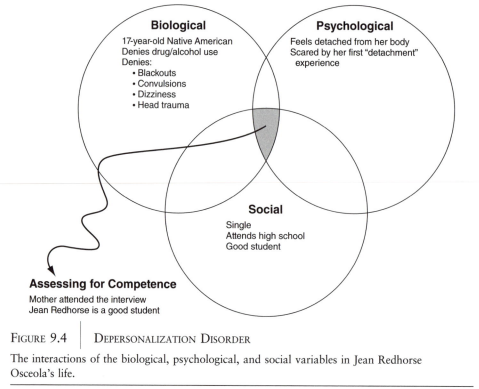

Biological

17-year-old Native American
Denies drug/alcohol use
Denies:
  • Blackouts
  • Convulsions
  • Dizziness
  • Head trauma

Psychological

Feels detached from her body
Scared by her first "detachment"
  experience

Social

Single
Attends high school
Good student

Assessing for Competence

Mother attended the interview
Jean Redhorse is a good student

FIGURE 9.4 | DEPERSONALIZATION DISORDER

The interactions of the biological, psychological, and social variables in Jean Redhorse
Osceola's life.

© Cengage Learning

SUMMARY

The competency-based approach to assessment explores the full spectrum of a client's life. In this way, the practitioner not only considers the overt, troublesome, or difficult behaviors but also pays attention to the influence of interpersonal and sociocultural factors underpinning the dissociative experience. The dissociative disorders continue to be mired in controversy. The symptoms are not easily seen, and many people do not seek counseling help. Many have another disorder. Mueller and colleagues note that about 17 to 25 percent of people with another psychiatric disorder also have a dissociative disorder, most commonly depersonalization disorder (Mueller, Moergeli, Assaloni, Schneider, & Rufer, 2007). We can say with a great degree of confidence that dissociative disorders are more common than they used to be, affecting about 2 to 3.4 percent of the American population (Maaranen et al., 2005).

There are a number of proposed changes to the dissociative disorders for the upcoming DSM-5. One proposal is for dissociative fugue to become a subtype of dissociative amnesia. Another change revolves around dissociative trance disorder, currently listed in Appendix B as a disorder for further study. In order to provide more cross-cultural generalizability, the symptom of the pathological possession trance component may be subsumed into dissociative identity disorder. The pathological trance component, however, would remain in dissociative disorder NOS. Aimed at reducing the use of the diagnosis dissociative identity disorder NOS, the DSM-5 proposes better clarification of the language, including indicating that different states can be reported or observed (Spiegel et al., 2011).

PRACTITIONER'S REFLECTIONS

Depersonalization is a common phenomenon, and it is not necessarily considered pathological. The practitioner must listen carefully to the client's story, especially when the individual experiences alterations in his or her perception and a temporary loss of reality—which *is* generally viewed as pathological. By paying close attention to the client's symptoms, the practitioner can distinguish dissociative disorders from other, less serious, disorders or normal behavior.

ACTIVITIES

Practitioners often encounter clients who come from different cultural backgrounds, as evidenced in the cases of Margarethe Jean-Baptiste and Jean Redhorse Osceola. This exercise is aimed at helping you increase your sensitivity to a client's cultural background while integrating that sensitivity into developing a full understanding of his or her presenting concerns.

Advanced Clinical EP 2.1.9 a

1. Imagine that you are the social worker assigned to Margarethe or Jean Redhorse. Briefly summarize your knowledge about the language, customs, and values found in the Haitian and Native American cultures.

   a. What could be some of Margarethe's motives for coming to the United States illegally?

   b. What immigration problems will she encounter?

   c. What difficulties might she have in locating other family members who live here while she gets settled?

   d. Describe some of the residuals of either Margarethe's or Jean Redhorse's culture that they may try to maintain, such as family traditions, religious ceremonies, or folklore sayings.

2. Sometimes dissociation is a normal experience (e.g., tuning out a boring lecture or conversation). Reflect back on those situations where this may have happened to you. How does your experience compare with someone who has a dissociative disorder?

3. Rent the video (or read the book) *The Three Faces of Eve*. How closely does this portrayal fit the classification of dissociative identity disorder?

COMPETENCY NOTES

EP 2.1.4 c: Recognize and communicate understanding of the importance of difference in shaping life experiences (p. 319): Social workers understand how diversity characterizes and shapes the human experience and is critical to the formation of identity.

EP Advanced Clinical 2.1.9 a: Assess the quality of clients' interactions within their social contexts (pp. 335, 337): Advanced practitioners are knowledgeable about how relational, organizational, and community systems may impact their clients.

EP 2.1.10 (b) a: Collect, organize, and interpret client data (pp. 316, 323): Social workers have the knowledge and skills to practice with individuals, families, groups, organizations, and communities.

EP 2.1.10 (b) b: Assess client strengths and limitations (p. 332): Social workers have the knowledge and skills to practice with individuals, families, groups, organizations, and communities.

EP Advanced Clinical 2.1.10 (b) c: Assess client coping strategies to reinforce and improve adaptation to life situations, circumstances, and events (pp. 317, 328): Clinical social work practice involves the dynamic, interactive, and reciprocal processes of therapeutic engagement, multidimensional assessment, clinical intervention, and practice evaluation at multiple levels.

REFERENCES

American Psychiatric Association. (1952). *Diagnostic and statistical manual of mental disorders.* Washington, DC: Author.

American Psychiatric Association. (1980). *Diagnostic and statistical manual of mental disorders,* (3rd ed.). Washington, DC: Author.

American Psychiatric Association. (1987). *Diagnostic and statistical manual of mental disorders,* (3rd ed. -revised). Washington, DC: Author.

American Psychiatric Association. (1994). *Diagnostic and statistical manual of mental disorders,* (4th ed.). Washington, DC: Author.

American Psychiatric Association. (2000). *Diagnostic and statistical manual of mental disorders,* (4th ed. -text revision). Washington, DC: Author.

Barlow, D. H., & Durand, M. V. (2012). *Abnormal psychology,* (6th ed.). Belmont, CA: Wadsworth Cengage Learning.

Cardena, E., & Gleaves, D. H. (2003). Dissociative disorders: Phantoms of the self. In M. Hersen, & S. M. Turner, (eds.), *Adult psychopathology and diagnosis,* (4th ed., pp. 476–505). New York: John Wiley & Sons.

Eriksen, K. & Kress, V. E. (2005). *Beyond the DSM story: Ethical quandaries, challenges, and best practices.* Thousand Oaks, CA: Sage.

Giesbrecht, T., Lynn, S. J., Lilienfeld, S., & Merckelbach, H. (2008). Cognitive processes in dissociation: An analysis of core theoretical assumptions. *Psychological Bulletin, 134* (5), 617–647.

Giesbrecht, T., Smeets, T., Leppink, J., Jelicic, M., & Merckelbach, H. (2007). Acute dissociation after 1 night of sleep loss. *Journal of Abnormal Psychology, 116* (3), 599–606.

Gleaves, D. H., May, M. C., & Cardena, E. (2001). An examination of the diagnostic validity of dissociative identity disorder. *Clinical Psychology Review, 21,* 377–608.

Johnson, J. G., Cohen, P., Kasen, S., & Brook, J. S. (2006). Dissociative disorders among adults in the community, impaired functioning, and Axis I and Axis II comorbidity. *Journal of Psychiatric Research, 40,* 131–140.

Keane, T. M., Marx, B. P., & Sloan, D. M. (2011). Trauma, dissociation, and posttraumatic stress disorder. In D. H. Barlow, (ed.), *Handbook of clinical psychology,* (pp. 359–386). New York, NY: Oxford University Press.

Kluft, R. P. (1996). Treating the traumatic memories of patients with dissociative identity disorder. *American Journal of Psychiatry, 153* (Suppl. 7), 103–110.

La Greca, A. M., Silverman, W. K., Vernberg, E. M., & Prinstein, M. J. (1996). Symptoms of post-traumatic stress in children after Hurricane Andrew: A prospective study. *Journal of Consulting and Clinical Psychology, 64,* 712–723.

Lopez, S. R., & Guarnaccia, P. J. J. (2000). Cultural psychopathology: Uncovering the social world of mental illness. *Annual Review of Psychology, 51,* 571–598.

Maaranen P., Tanskanen, A., Honkalampi, K., Haatainen, K., Hintikka, J., & Viinamaki, H. (2005). Factors associated with pathological dissociation in the general population. *Australian and New Zealand Journal of Psychiatry, 39,* 387–394.

Merckelbach, H., Devilly, G. J., & Rassin, E. (2002). Alters in dissociative identity disorder: Metaphors or genuine entities? *Clinical Psychology Review, 22,* 481–497.

Mueller, C., Moergeli, H., Assaloni, H., Schneider, R., & Rufer, M. (2007). Dissociative disorders among chronic and severely impaired psychiatric outpatients. *Psychopathology, 40,* 470–471.

Ross, C. A. (1997). *Dissociative identity disorder.* New York, NY: John Wiley.

Spiegel, D., Loewenstein, R. J., Lewis-Fernandez, R., Sar, V., Simeon, D., Vermetten, E., Cardena, E., & Dell. P. F. (2011). Dissociative disorders in DSM-5. *Depression and Anxiety, 28,* 824–852.

Steinberg, M., & Schnall, M. (2001). *Stranger in the mirror.* New York: Harper Collins.

EATING DISORDERS

CHAPTER 10

INTRODUCTION

Eating disorders have been recognized throughout history, beginning with the ancient past, through the early Christian era, the Dark and late Middle Ages, early Renaissance, the twentieth century, and now continuing into the twenty-first century. Each historical period has influenced the frequency and appearance of eating disorders, and cases of bulimia have been described for thousands of years (Parry-Jones & Parry-Jones, 2002). For example, incidents of bingeing (or excessive eating) and purging (vomiting) of food were considered socially acceptable during the Roman era—when banquets serving 20 or more different courses were a common occurrence. Societal, cultural, or religious beliefs have always affected people's eating patterns. During the Dark Ages, a person could rid themselves of sin and/or sexual desire through acts of purging. During the Middle Ages, according to well-documented accounts, women known as "the sainted women" starved themselves for their religious beliefs; such episodes of starvation as these are referred to as *anorexia mirabilis* or holy anorexia. At the time, this practice was not considered pathological because the women's fasting practices were seen as culturally accepted expressions of their religious devotion.

In 1689, Dr. Richard Morton described a self-starving 18-year-old woman who looked like a "skeleton only clad with skin." He referred to her condition as "nervous consumption" (Hersen, Turner, & Beidel, 2007; Kilgus, Maxmen, & Ward, 2009). Other examples of starvation involved the notorious fasting girls of the sixteenth and seventeenth centuries. Certain young women adopted this eating pattern as a visible demonstration of their virtuous lifestyle and zealous commitment to the church. Some societies allowed or sanctioned starvation, while others encouraged women to have a well-fed or plump appearance to indicate that a father or husband was a good provider and could afford to feed his family well.

Anorexia nervosa, as it is currently recognized, was first described in the early 1860s and 1870s by the French physicians Marcé (1860) and Lasegué (1873) and by the English physician Sir William Gull (1873). Gull characterized this disorder of eating as a "want of appetite," which he saw as being characteristic of a "morbid mental state." Marcé eloquently describes the ravages of starvation and the curious mental state that often accompanies it:

> Whatever the duration of their abstinence, they experience a distaste for food which the most pressing want is unable to overcome.... Deeply impressed, whether by the absence of appetite or by the uneasiness caused by digestion, these patients arrive at a delirious conviction that they cannot or ought not to eat. In one word, the gastric nervous disorder becomes cerebro-nervous. (pp. 264, 266)

Lasegué notes the frustration encountered by families and caregivers:

> The delicacies of the table are multiplied in the hopes of stimulating the appetite, but the more the solicitude increases, the more the appetite diminishes. What dominates in the mental condition of the hysterical patient is, above all, the state of quietude.... Not only does she not sigh for recovery, but she is not ill-pleased with her condition. (pp. 385, 403)

The age-old question of what drives so many into a dangerous and life-threatening eating pattern of semistarvation or purging remains unanswered. Being overweight, dieting, and dissatisfaction with one's body, and status in a higher social class seem to be increasingly recognized as the primary risk factors for developing an eating disorder (Polivy & Herman, 2002; Stice, Ng, & Shaw, 2010).

AN OVERVIEW OF THE EATING DISORDERS

Because of the pandemic proportions of eating disorders over the last century, the DSM-IV (American Psychiatric Association, 1994) included them for the first time as a separate group, within which two major eating disorders are identified.

1. **Anorexia nervosa,** wherein the individual severely limits food intake, resulting in substantial weight loss and dangerously low body weight.
2. **Bulimia nervosa,** where the individual's "diet" results in out-of-control binge eating episodes followed by purging behaviors whereby food is eliminated by vomiting or other means.

Although anorexia and bulimia are the most thoroughly studied eating disorders, the most common eating disorder is **binge eating disorder (BED)** (American Psychiatric Association, 2000; Barlow & Durand, 2012). This disorder is characterized by recurrent binge eating, but without the inappropriate weight control behaviors that are part of the bulimic picture.

Anorexia nervosa and bulimia nervosa are both characterized by the individual's overemphasis on body image, but there are several important distinctions between these two disorders. The individual diagnosed with anorexia nervosa must have an abnormally low body weight, and, in the case of women, must miss at least three consecutive menstrual cycles (**amenorrhea**). The person with bulimia nervosa generally has a normal or slightly above-normal weight. They exhibit a pattern of sequential binge eating in addition to inappropriate compensatory weight loss responses that include self-induced purging (vomiting), misuse of laxatives or enemas, and excessive exercise. Although the majority of eating disorders are first noticed during late childhood and early adolescence, they often continue well into adulthood. An in-depth examination of childhood eating disorders is beyond the scope of this discussion; however, the reader is referred to *Eating Disorders in Childhood and Adolescence* by Bryan Lask and Rachel Bryant-Waugh as an excellent resource on childhood psychopathology.

There are several significant coexisting disorders associated with eating disorders, including major depressive disorders, particularly depression and obsessive tendencies; anxiety disorders; personality disorders; substance abuse, including both alcohol and drugs; and suicide (Agras, 2001; Hudson, Hiripi, Pope, & Kessler, 2007). Underlying traits of emotional instability and novelty seeking are also found in some individuals (Wade, Bulik, Prescott, & Kendler, 2004).

Advanced
Clinical EP
2.1.10 (a) a

Looking at all the psychological disorders, both anorexia and bulimia are not specific to a certain culture. For instance, Anderson-Frye (2009) noted that these disorders can found in a number of immigrant populations who have recently moved to Western countries, including the United States (Goel, McCarthy, Phillips, & Wee, 2004). While eating disorders can be found around the world, they seem more prevalent in Western cultures, in contrast to those countries where food is scarce. When looking to dissatisfaction with one's body, African American adolescent girls are found to have fewer concerns about their weight, and a more positive self-image compared to Caucasian adolescent girls (Celio, Zabinski, & Wilfley, 2002). This could be related to the cultural norm whereby African American women are socialized to be more independent and self-reliant than other women of color, thus making the former less susceptible to the thin ideal promoted by popular media (Grabe & Hyde, 2006). These differences underscore the importance of developing a culturally responsive therapeutic relationship.

ANOREXIA NERVOSA

ESSENTIAL FEATURES

Individuals with eating disorders manifest abnormal attitudes about their body shape as well as maladaptive attempts to control their body weight. The assessment criteria for anorexia nervosa include:

- Refusal to maintain weight at or above a minimally normal weight for age and height (e.g., a woman who should weigh 100 pounds according to age and height criteria weighs less than 85 pounds).
- Desperately fearful of gaining weight or becoming "fat," even though already severely underweight.
- Disturbance in the perception of body weight or body shape, or denial that present low weight is seriously dangerous.
- In women of postmenarche status, absence of at least three or more consecutive menstrual cycles (amenorrhea).

SUBTYPES OF ANOREXIA NERVOSA

EP 2.1.10
(b) a

Anorexia nervosa is divided into two subtypes, based on the method used to limit calorie intake. They are referred to as the restricting type and the binge eating/purging type, and they have significantly different clinical presentations and characteristics. Distinguishing between these subtypes highlights the importance of carefully organizing and interpreting the client data collected.

During an episode of the **restricting type of anorexia nervosa**, the individual severely limits caloric intake but *does not* regularly engage in binge eating or purging behavior. These individuals are described as highly controlled, rigid, and obsessive. They use various techniques that help enhance their control over food intake; for example, they might eat very slowly, make their food less attractive, or garnish their food with unappetizing spices. They often feel a great deal of satisfaction about controlling or regulating their calorie intake.

Individuals with the **binge eating/purging type of anorexia nervosa** regularly engage in weight control behaviors such as self-induced vomiting and/or misuse of laxatives, enemas, or diuretics. They alternate between periods of perfectionism (with rigid control) and impulsive eating behavior (American Psychiatric Association, 2000). **Binge eating** is defined as an episode in which the individual eats "out of control" and is unable to resist the temptation to consume certain foods.

A **binge** is seen as ingesting a much larger amount of food than most people would eat under similar circumstances in a limited period of time (Kearney & Trull, 2012). Although there can be a wide variation in the quantity of calories ingested, a very large amount of food is consumed during a binge episode. Some binges occur in time-limited situations such as over the lunch hour; while others can take up most of the day, where the individual eats small amounts of food almost continuously. The latter is sometimes referred to as **grazing**. On the average, binge episodes last about two hours. Binge eating is usually performed in private because the individual does not want to be discovered or interrupted.

Binge episodes should be distinguished from those overeating incidents that occur during special occasions, such as birthday celebrations or holiday events. Perhaps the most notable culturally sanctioned time for overeating for Americans is the Thanksgiving holiday dinner.

Binge eating is often followed by depressive moods, feelings of guilt, and self-deprecating thoughts. However, when overeating is sanctioned (along with little or no long-lasting guilt for eating a large meal), the person does not have the sense of "losing control," and to him or her, the amount of food eaten more closely resembles a normal meal than the quantity of food consumed during a binge.

Purging is defined as any activity aimed at ameliorating the perceived negative effects of a binge on body shape and weight. This includes **self-induced purging** (vomiting); the misuse of laxatives, enemas, or diuretics; and/or excessive exercise. When exercise and diet are used for weight loss rather than to counteract the effects of a particular episode of excessive bingeing, they should be regarded as *compensatory behaviors*—but with eating disorders, the individual continues to use weight loss techniques or purging in the desperate hope that they will somehow "work."

Prevailing Pattern

The development of anorexia nervosa seems related to several factors, with no single identifiable event that could be considered as the cause of the person's eating difficulties (Austrian, 2005). Although many women diet to control their weight, few individuals will go on to develop the extreme weight loss and clinical symptoms of anorexia. The primary intrapersonal characteristics that indicate the presence of anorexia nervosa include an unreasonable fear of gaining weight, perceptual disturbance regarding body shape or size, and the relentless pursuit of wanting to be thin no matter what the consequence (American Psychiatric Association, 2000).

In essence, individuals with anorexia nervosa have two faulty perceptions regarding their own body: (1) the way they view their body—or **body image distortion (BID)**, and (2) body image concerns involving a delusional misperception, referred to as "body dysmorphophobia." The key feature in each of these views is the *mis*perception of body size and shape. Body image, or the overinvestment in the way one appears, is primarily a perceptual phenomenon (Grabe & Hyde, 2006). Those with body dissatisfaction are more than just concerned about their weight (Thompson & van den Berg, 2002).

There are a number of risk factors that can play a role in an individual's judgments about his or her body, such as cognitive, affective, cultural, and attitudinal variables (Hill, 2006; McGee, Hewitt, Sherry, Parkin, & Flett, 2005; Sassaroli et al., 2008; Stice, 2002; Utter, Neumark-Sztainer, Wall, & Story, 2003). These influences underscore the importance of applying a competency-based assessment that thoroughly examines all aspects of an individual's life. Some of the broad social factors that can potentially influence the eating disorders include a cultural emphasis on the desirability of being thin as well as concerns with attractiveness, self-concept, body concept, and sexuality. The practitioner's competency-based assessment also carefully evaluates the possible coexistence of other mental disorders (e.g., anxiety, affective, or personality disorders).

DIFFERENTIAL ASSESSMENT

EP 2.1.10
(b) a

Anorexia is most often seen in adolescent girls (American Psychiatric Association, 2000). Between 90 and 95 percent of all reported cases are females who start to diet in the belief that they are excessively fat, whether or not in reality this is true. In general, most individuals with an eating disorder do not exhibit a prodromal phase—that is, they are usually characterized as being normal and healthy prior to the actual onset of the eating disorder. Making the distinction between normal eating habits and the onset of disordered eating requires the practitioner to carefully collect, organize, and interpret client data. Occasionally, going off to college, experiencing a death in the family, or some other major life cycle event will immediately precede the onset. At other times, the precipitating factor may be so integrated into a "decision to begin dieting" that the onset seems almost immaterial. For example, in the following case discussion, Joy Walker wanted to lose weight so she could fit into her prom dress. Joy began to diet simply by reducing her total daily food intake and only later began to restrict all high-calorie foods. Eventually, her eating pattern became so severely limited that she ingests very few foods. She dreaded being fat, but her weight loss did not alleviate this fear. In addition, she underestimates the extent of her thinness—she believes she is "fat and ugly"—when in reality, she appears skeletal to her family and friends.

The most striking feature of anorexia is the marked distortion in the way the individuals experience their body size and shape. Often they have no concept of how they appear to others and distort what they see in the mirror; even though they are emaciated, they often complain of feeling fat and express concerns about gaining weight. One of the authors recalls a conversation with a client diagnosed with anorexia nervosa: she remarked, "Every time I looked in the mirror I hated my body. My reflection only exposed my imperfections." This client would elaborate her fears of developing a double chin and seeing fat cells "just about everywhere," despite her gaunt, wasted appearance. These individuals are generally dissatisfied with their weight; losing weight every day and for months on end is seen as satisfactory. Although the person is usually hungry and preoccupied with thoughts of food, they will not eat because of their relentless obsession to be thinner.

Work has been done to prevent the prevalence of disordered eating behaviors, unhealthy dieting practices, and distorted body image, but with mixed success (Stice, Shaw, & Marti, 2007). In general, the eating disorders are seen as motivated by peer pressure, media influence, and the perception that extreme dieting strategies are harmless. These realities underscore the importance of looking at the whole person and exploring variables in their social context. The competency-based assessment expands the practitioner's thinking and considers the influence of the multiple social and environmental factors found in a person's life.

By the time individuals with anorexia nervosa come to the attention of a practitioner, they usually weigh even less than the 15 percent below normal that is specified by the DSM criteria (American Psychiatric Association, 2000). By the time these individuals seek help, they often weigh between 25 percent and 30 percent below their normal weight. Unfortunately, there is no clear boundary between the "thinness" of anorexia nervosa and that of an individual who is considered naturally slender, so careful evaluation of the multiple influences in a person's life is important when considering an eating disorder. Many individuals are naturally thin, and others diet to remain slim, while still others are in occupations where low body weight is mandated, such as a jockey, fashion model, or ballet dancer (Tiggerman & Slater, 2001). The difference between someone who is of low weight and someone with anorexia nervosa revolves around intrapersonal factors whereby the individual *refuses* to maintain a normal body weight and is *extremely fearful* of becoming fat.

The lifetime prevalence rates for the presence of anorexia nervosa in women ranges from 0.5 to 3.7 percent (American Psychiatric Association, 2006). The prevalence rate for men is approximately one-tenth that of women. Unfortunately, we know relatively less about why eating disorders are less prevalent in men. However, some interesting findings have emerged. For instance, eating disorders are found to be on the rise among male athletes, especially where a lean appearance may lead to a competitive advantage, such as in wrestling, rowing, boxing, and possibly ski jumping (Glazer, 2008; Sudi et al., 2004).

While child maltreatment is not necessarily specific to the eating disorders, many people with a major mental disorder report significantly higher rates of child abuse or trauma (Jacobi, Hayward, deZwan, Kraemer, & Agras, 2004; Stice, 2002). Those who have experienced such abuse are more likely to have more serious and chronic eating disorder symptoms (Carter, Bewell, Blackmore, & Woodside, 2006).

As mentioned earlier, anorexia nervosa typically develops during adolescence; the average age of onset ranges between 14 and 18, with a mean age of 17

(American Psychiatric Association, 2000). The DSM suggests that the onset of this disorder in females is relatively rare for postmenopausal women. A study by Scholtz, Hill, and Lacey (2010) found that when the eating disorders are seen in older age, the symptoms are clinically and diagnostically challenging. The authors noted lifelong disability and enduring deficiencies in quality of life, even despite weight restoration in some cases. This highlights the devastating longer term impact of eating disorders. Eating disorders can and do happen late in life, and practitioners should pay attention to those associated intrapersonal factors as a part of their competency-based assessment—in particular, bereavement issues or perceptions about body image.

Causal factors associated with anorexia nervosa include a woman's perception regarding ideal body size, which is greatly influenced by television commercials, magazines, and/or beauty pageants. For reasons that are unclear, the incidence of anorexia nervosa has increased substantially in North America during the last half of the twentieth century (American Psychiatric Association, 2000). The media, which promotes being thin as the ideal standard for beauty, can partially explain this rise in anorexia nervosa. As a corollary, many impressionable young women (and men) hold unreasonable expectations about how thin they should be in order to be attractive (Andrist, 2003).

BIOLOGICAL FACTORS ASSOCIATED WITH ANOREXIA NERVOSA

One of the unfortunate aspects of this eating disorder is that it is entirely possible for an individual to starve to death in the midst of plenty. As the person stops eating, her body tries to conserve resources, and amenorrhea (cessation of monthly menstruation) commonly occurs (Crow, Thuras, Keel, & Mitchell, 2002). This is considered perhaps the most characteristic medical complication. From the standpoint of biology, it works like this: abnormally low levels of the estrogen hormone are found, which in turn diminishes pituitary secretions of follicle-stimulating hormone (FSH) and luteinizing hormone (LH); diminished levels of FSH and LH turn off the mechanism for generating the menstrual cycle, thus causing amenorrhea. When considering an assessment of anorexia nervosa, practitioners should keep in mind that amenorrhea is a significant requirement of and a defining feature for this eating disorder. The biological component, an integral part of the competency-based assessment, helps serve as an objective physical index of the degree of food restriction.

There are a number of additional medical complications associated with the starvation that characterizes the advanced state of anorexia, including osteoporosis (caused by loss of calcium from the bones), constipation, and swollen joints (Rome & Ammerman, 2003). When purging behaviors are suspected, the practitioner should be mindful of a number of cardiovascular or renal problems that may be present, including **hypotension** (chronically low blood pressure), **bradycardia** (slow heartbeat), **cardiac arrhythmia** (irregular heartbeat), and an increased risk of kidney failure. In addition, purging often depletes essential body-sustaining minerals such as potassium, sodium, magnesium, phosphate, and chloride, creating concern about the development of **hypokalemic alkalosis** (a condition caused by the kidneys' reaction to an extreme lack or loss of potassium, which may be caused by some diuretic medications).

Purging behaviors may also cause fatigue and weakness, a mild cognitive disorder, or seizures. Other purging complications include infection of the parotid or salivary glands, which sometimes gives the face a puffy or "chipmunk" appearance. Frequent vomiting also takes a tremendous toll on teeth, causing severe dental erosion and tooth decay. The front teeth are especially vulnerable and may appear "moth-eaten." Most people who purge become quite adept at inducing vomiting at will and can do so without any extraneous methods such as the use of emetics. However, there are those who consume large amounts of **ipecac** (solution that induces vomiting); this practice occasionally causes death from overdose toxicity.

Those who suffer from anorexia nervosa tend to be secretive, and it behooves the practitioner to look for clues to disturbances in eating patterns. Just by observation, practitioners may detect the following signs of the disorder:

- Skin that is dry or scaly (yellowed) in texture.
- **Lanugo** ("peach fuzz" or baby-fine hair found on the trunk, face, and extremities).
- Intolerance of cold temperatures or hypothermia. (It is not uncommon to find a person wearing a heavy sweater on a hot summer day.)
- Extensive weight loss that has affected the skeletal structure. When there is a tremendous loss of body fat and muscle mass, the individual takes on a stooped or hunched-over appearance.
- Dull, lifeless hair, a pale complexion, poor posture, and extreme thinness hidden under loose, baggy clothing.

Advanced Clinical EP 2.1.3 a

The combination of medical complications and psychological clues to an eating disorder necessitates the practitioner to synthesize multiple sources of knowledge, including what we know from the research data and practice experience. As a part of the competency-based assessment, the practitioner might explore biological issues by asking about the individual's target weight; dieting, nutritional, or exercise patterns; and use of laxatives. Nonverbal communication should be observed carefully by the practitioner when asking about a client's eating habits—some individuals may withhold information or minimize the extent of their disturbed eating behaviors. Using a courteous but direct approach, the practitioner should ask questions that will specifically explore the following areas:

- Has there ever been a time when people (either friends or others) have given you a hard time about being too thin or losing too much weight?
- Have you ever weighed a lot less than others thought you should weigh? [If the answer is *yes* to either question, follow with:]
- How old were you when this first happened?
- Is this still true?
- What was the lowest amount you have ever weighed?
- What do you weigh right now? How do you feel about that?
- What do you think about your body size and shape?
- What do you think about how much you weigh?
- Are you on a diet right now?
- Do you ever feel the urge to binge or purge? What happens when you do?

- How often do you diet?
- Have either you or anyone in your family ever had a history of anorexia, bulimia, or obesity?

The course and outcome of anorexia nervosa varies; some individuals recover after a single episode, whereas others continue to vacillate between trying to restore their normal weight and/or relapsing. Those who struggle with a fluctuating pattern may require hospitalization to reinstate their weight and address fluid and electrolyte imbalances. Anorexia nervosa is considered a potentially fatal disease, with a mortality rate that ranges somewhere between 5 percent to 10 percent (American Psychiatric Association, 2000; Keel, Dorer, Eddy, Franko, Charatan, & Herzog, 2003; Zipfel, Lowe, Deter, & Herzog, 2000). The mortality rate from the eating disorders, and particularly anorexia, is the highest of any psychological disorder (Vitiello & Lederhendler, 2000). The cause of death is usually associated with starvation, suicide (Sadock, Sadock, & Ruiz, 2009), infection, or electrolyte imbalance.

The following vignette describes Joy Walker's struggle to lose weight and illustrates some of the eating patterns typical of a person with anorexia nervosa.

CASE | ## THE CASE OF JOY WALKER

Joy Walker started with a diet to lose weight but almost lost her life instead. At the age of 17, she weighed 130 pounds (considered normal for her height and build). She was asked to go to the senior prom by her boyfriend, Kenneth, but he warned her in advance, "You'd better lose some weight, because I don't want to be seen dancing with a fat blimp."

Joy made up her mind to lose some weight and started by skipping breakfast. A few days later, she stopped eating lunch. Dinner time with her family became problematic, because she did not eat anything. She was served regular portions, but she ended up moving the food around on her plate to make it appear she was eating. She told her parents that she ate "a huge lunch" so she was not very hungry.

Most of the time, Joy secretly dropped food to the family dog who conveniently positioned himself under the table. Other times, she would hide food in her pockets and throw it away later. Within a month, Joy lost almost 30 pounds. She began to receive a lot of positive attention, especially from her boyfriend, and compliments on how nice she looked. By now her daily food intake included eating some lettuce

leaves or an apple, but nothing more. Her hair began to thin and then started falling out in clumps. Her fingernails started to split, and she began to have problems with constipation, cold intolerance, and painful swelling of her fingers, knees, and elbows.

After 5 months of dieting, Joy weighed 85 pounds. She had gone from a size nine to a size zero. Her friends started telling her that she looked "like a skeleton" and was "way too thin." Joy's response was, "I just want to lose a few more pounds because my thighs are way too fat, and my stomach pouches out too much." She added, "I'm so disgusting." Joy hadn't had a normal menstrual period for the past 3 months, which pleased her.

While dancing with Kenneth at the senior prom, Joy fainted. She was taken by ambulance to a nearby emergency room, where the attending physician expressed shock at Joy's physical condition and state of emaciation. The doctor immediately contacted Joy's parents and explained that their daughter was in serious trouble. Joy was admitted to the hospital and diagnosed with anorexia nervosa. The hospital social worker spoke to Joy and referred her and her family to the eating disorder clinic.

EP 2.1.10
(b) a

ASSESSMENT SUMMARY   The differential assessment of anorexia nervosa requires the practitioner to collect, organize, and interpret client data. The assessment in Joy's case is complicated by her denial of symptoms and an unwillingness to seek help. In addition, she has been extremely secretive about her eating patterns and methods of weight control. Joy's caloric intake, consisting of an apple or lettuce leaves, is typical of someone with anorexia nervosa. Even though Joy is 35 percent underweight, she continues to express unrealistic concerns about being fat. She has a distorted view of her body (also characteristic of those with anorexia nervosa), seeing her thighs as too fat and her stomach as bulging.

Some individuals are humiliated or embarrassed when seen eating food in public, as in *social phobia*. Although Joy obsessed about her food intake, she did not show obsessions and compulsions in other areas of her life, as commonly is seen in persons with obsessive-compulsive disorder (OCD). OCD might be considered if Joy shows obsessions and compulsions unrelated to food, such as repeatedly washing her hands. Those with body dysmorphic disorder are preoccupied with an *imagined* defect in their body appearance—but this assessment would only apply here if the details of Joy's distortion were unrelated to body size and shape. Joy's main concerns do revolve around her body image.

Weight fluctuations, vomiting, and eccentric food handling might occur in some somatization disorders; however, the symptoms related to somatization are not considered as severe as Joy Walker's eating habits. Further, those with somatization disorder do not have the morbid fear of becoming fat.

Schizophrenia might look very similar to anorexia, especially if the person refuses to eat. However, upon closer examination, the person with schizophrenia (though perhaps exhibiting bizarre eating patterns) is rarely concerned about caloric content. People with schizophrenia are neither preoccupied with the fear of becoming fat nor do they perceive body distortions. Those with major depressive disorder, in the absence of anorexia, may eat very little and profess to have little or no appetite. However, peculiar attitudes about eating (such as Joy's tendency to push food around her plate, feed it to the dog, or hide it in her pockets, the pursuit of being thin, and the increased level of physical activity) are absent.

Advanced
Clinical
EP 2.1.7 c

The practitioner consults with medical professionals, as needed, to confirm a diagnosis. Joy's case highlights the need for a referral to a physician to determine whether or not there are other processes going on that can better account for the weight loss—for example, hyperthyroidism, diabetes mellitus, Crohn's disease, acquired immunodeficiency syndrome (AIDS), neoplasms, or tuberculosis. The important distinction between the eating disorder illustrated in the Joy Walker vignette versus a general medical condition is that individuals with general medical conditions usually do not have a **distorted body image (DBI)**, or the desire for further weight loss. Figure 10.1 illustrates the interplay of the biological, psychological, and social variables in Joy Walker's life.

Advanced
Clinical EP
2.1.10 (b) c

Although the case vignette does not address Joy's familial picture and related interpersonal processes, the competency-based model looks at the full range of factors affecting Joy's life—for example, how she copes with life challenges, and the supports that are available to her that would reinforce and improve her adaptation to life situations, circumstances, and events. This perspective says: The person is not the problem, but the problem is the problem. What is known is that Joy lives

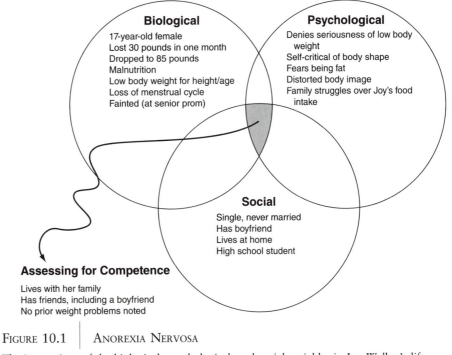

Biological

17-year-old female
Lost 30 pounds in one month
Dropped to 85 pounds
Malnutrition
Low body weight for height/age
Loss of menstrual cycle
Fainted (at senior prom)

Psychological

Denies seriousness of low body
 weight
Self-critical of body shape
Fears being fat
Distorted body image
Family struggles over Joy's food
 intake

Social

Single, never married
Has boyfriend
Lives at home
High school student

Assessing for Competence

Lives with her family
Has friends, including a boyfriend
No prior weight problems noted

FIGURE 10.1 | ANOREXIA NERVOSA

The interactions of the biological, psychological, and social variables in Joy Walker's life.

© Cengage Learning

at home with her family who are concerned about her, she has many friends, and she has not experienced prior eating difficulties.

JOY WALKER'S MULTIAXIAL DSM DIAGNOSIS IS AS FOLLOWS:

Axis I	307.1 Anorexia Nervosa, Restricting Type
Axis II	V71.09 (No diagnosis)
Axis III	263.0 Malnutrition, Moderate
Axis IV	None
Axis V	GAF = 55 (on admission)

© Cengage Learning

BULIMIA NERVOSA

ESSENTIAL FEATURES

Bulimia nervosa is characterized by repeated dietary restriction alternating with uncontrollable binge eating and desperate measures to prevent weight gain. Individuals with purging type bulimia counteract the effects of eating either by vomiting or using compensatory methods (e.g., using large amounts of laxatives to purge their bowels) in the struggle to control their weight. Those who use excessive exercise and fasting to control their weight are considered nonpurging types. The use of fasting is often a misguided method for controlling a binge—the process usually backfires, causing increased hunger and leading to greater overeating.

The characteristic feature of bulimia nervosa is eating a larger amount of food (typically junk food such as potato chips, candy bars, doughnuts, or cookies) than most people would or could eat under similar circumstances (Fairburn, Cooper, Shafran, & Wilson, 2008). However, the actual caloric intake varies from person to person (Franco, Wonderlich, Little, & Herzog, 2004).

Bulimia nervosa is a disorder that was introduced comparatively recently in the DSM-III (American Psychiatric Association, 1980). It occurs more frequently than anorexia nervosa (American Psychiatric Association, 2000) but tends to be under-assessed, perhaps because the symptoms are less obvious and discernible than the starving symptoms of anorexia or perhaps because most individuals suffering from it are normal or only slightly overweight in appearance. Bulimia nervosa is known to occur among individuals considered moderately or morbidly obese, but this is an uncommon pattern.

An important distinction between anorexia nervosa and bulimia nervosa is that the person with bulimia does not have the extreme distortion of self-image characteristic of those with anorexia. A majority of individuals with bulimia have never had anorexia. However, it is not uncommon to find a history that includes many anorexic features. The assessment criteria for bulimia nervosa include:

- Recurrent episodes of binge eating, which are characterized by *both* of the following:
  1. Eating occurs during a discrete period of time (e.g., within two hours).
  2. The amount of food eaten is definitely larger than most other individuals would eat during a similar period of time and under similar circumstances.
- The individual experiences a lack of control over eating during the episode.
- They cannot stop eating or control what they are eating.
- Recurrent, inappropriate compensatory methods are used to prevent weight gain (e.g., self-induced vomiting, fasting, excessive exercise, and misuse of laxatives, enemas, diuretics, or other medications).
- Both the binge eating and inappropriate compensatory methods must occur, on average, at least twice (or more) a week for 3 months.
- Body shape and weight unduly influence the way a person sees her- or himself.
- The disturbance does not occur exclusively during an episode of anorexia nervosa.

SUBTYPES OF BULIMIA NERVOSA

EP 2.1.10
(b) a

Bulimia nervosa is divided into two subtypes based on the method used to limit weight gain: (1) the purging type and (2) the nonpurging type. Distinguishing these subtypes calls for the practitioner to collect, organize, and interpret the data found in the client's struggle with bulimia.

The *purging type* involves the individual regularly engaging in self-induced vomiting or the misuse of laxatives, diuretics, or enemas. The *nonpurging type* involves the individual using other inappropriate compensatory behaviors, such as fasting or excessive exercise, but *not* regular inducement of vomiting or misuse of laxatives, diuretics, or enemas (American Psychiatric Association, 2000). The non-purging type is considered rare, accounting for only 6 percent to 8 percent of people with bulimia (Striegel-Moore et al., 2004). Generally, for practitioners who struggle with this diagnosis, it is helpful to remember that the major features of this disorder tend to cluster together (Fairburn et al., 2003; Franco, Wonderleich, Little, & Herzog, 2004; Gleaves, Lowe, Snow, Green, & Murphy-Eberenz, 2000; Keel, Mitchell, Miller, Davis, & Crow, 2000).

PREVAILING PATTERN

The person with bulimia nervosa is usually a young woman. The lifetime prevalence of women who meet the assessment criteria ranges between 1 percent and 4 percent; the rate of occurrence in males is approximately one-tenth of that found in females (Kearney & Trull, 2012). Bulimia may or may not begin in the context of another disorder (e.g., depression, obsessions, or substance abuse). The onset of symptoms occurs fairly innocuously during late adolescence or the early 20s when an attempt to diet is closely followed by purging behaviors. At first, purging may serve as a convenient method of overeating without gaining the resultant weight, but it quickly becomes a destructive process that cannot be easily controlled. Over time, the binge/purge cycle escalates and becomes more dominant in the individual's thoughts and behaviors, often causing a multitude of difficulties, such as impaired interpersonal relationships, which then leads to isolation, shame, helplessness, and lowered self-esteem.

Bulimia appears to run a chronic and episodic course whereby the occurrence of binge eating may either have a gradual or acute presentation. Sometimes the individual can sense a binge starting, whereas other times he or she has no fore-warning. They may or may not report feeling hungry preceding a binge, and a binge is often precipitated by the simple presence of something to eat. Psychologically stressful circumstances can often trigger a binge because for that individual, food becomes a temporary fix to soothe and reduce emotional tensions.

The individual often reports episodes in which they eat large amounts of food in a short period of time, once or twice a week or several times a day. Generally, high-calorie sweets are the food of choice, but once a binge begins it is very difficult to control, and the person eats everything within reach. Most often, binges last upward of one hour, and the eating continues well past the point when the sensation of being hungry has been quelled.

An episode of binge eating is followed by the physical discomfort of abdominal distension (bloating) caused by the amount of food eaten. There is also the emotional distress of how much was consumed—the person often feels helpless, disgusted, depressed, and fearful about becoming fat. He or she usually feels very guilty and anxious about the amount of food consumed, and the planning to get rid of it begins almost immediately. The most common and favored action is vomiting (whereby the individual sticks their finger or fingers down their throat to bring about regurgitation). Some individuals become so proficient that they do not need any other catalyst measures—they can vomit at will.

Like those with anorexia nervosa, individuals with bulimia are very secretive about their eating behaviors. It is helpful for the practitioner to look for telltale visual signs of repeated purging behaviors. Chronic bulimia (with purging) has a number of medical consequences that the practitioner may look for when considering the diagnosis (Pomeroy, 2004). These perceptible clues consist of skin lesions, abrasions, small lacerations, or raised calluses found on the dorsal (top) surface of fingers and knuckles. These dorsal lesions, known as **Russell's signs**, are the by-products of repeated and constant friction of fingers being scraped back and forth across incisor teeth to induce vomiting. Not all individuals use finger manipulations to induce vomiting—instead, they use emetics such as ipecac. Sometimes, diuretics such as furosemide are used as a cathartic for weight control. Other maneuvers used for purging include laxatives or (less often) enemas to empty the bowel. Still other techniques involve using coat hangers, wadded paper, or pens that are stuck down the throat.

BIOLOGICAL FACTORS ASSOCIATED WITH BULIMIA NERVOSA

As noted in the previous discussion of anorexia nervosa, purging behaviors can produce negative health complications. The chemical stimulation of vomiting by ingesting ipecac can lead to serious heart damage. Excessive laxative abuse often causes constipation or permanent damage to the colon. Perhaps one of the most serious medical complications is electrolyte abnormalities (low potassium levels), which not only can disrupt signals to the heart, causing irregular conduction, but also can cause kidney failure.

DIFFERENTIAL ASSESSMENT

EP 2.1.10
(b) a

Impulsivity is a personality feature associated with bulimia nervosa, and persons with bulimia nervosa are more likely to engage in impulsive behaviors such as shoplifting and/or substance abuse (Stice, 2002). In addition, the eating disorders may co-occur with personality disorders—for example, borderline personality disorder or avoidant personality disorder. Depression and anxiety disorders can also co-occur with bulimia. These characteristic behaviors and co-occurring disorders highlight the importance of collecting, organizing, and interpreting the data found in the client's story.

Similar to anorexia, bulimia has been associated with a history of sexual and physical abuse. Childhood sexual abuse appears to be more strongly associated with bulimic disorders, especially purging behaviors, than with the restricting type of anorexia (Carter, Bewell, Blackmore, & Woodside, 2006). However, the brutality of the person's history of abuse does not appear to correlate with the severity of the bulimia. Family variables, interpersonal skills, and emotional reactions following sexual abuse serve to buffer the negative effects of these adverse life events. A past history of sexual abuse is not a specific risk factor for an eating disorder, but rather a risk factor for intrapersonal (or personal) difficulties in general. However, as a part of the competency-based assessment, consider the possibility of prior sexual or physical abuse when an eating disorder is diagnosed. Those individuals who report recent episodes of abuse tend to show greater body image disturbance.

The tragic pull of a binge/purge episode is depicted in the following vignette describing Mary McDaniel's struggles with her eating disorder.

This case focuses on a typical day of bingeing and purging rather than on the full range of intrapersonal, interpersonal, and sociocultural variables that may be in play.

CASE | THE CASE OF MARY McDANIEL

"I eat a tremendous amount of food—and I don't even care what the food is. You know, like milk and orange juice usually sour the stomach? I don't care about anything like that. I eat whatever is in the pantry. The best way I can explain it is that it's sorta like a feeding frenzy. I gulp food down, and most of the time I don't even taste it."

Mary continues, "A typical day for me starts after my kids go off to school and my husband leaves for work. I usually have an extra hour before I have to leave the house. During that time, I usually eat anything I can stuff in my mouth. I start with some ice cream, and when I'm done with that, I munch on bags of cookies. They are much easier to put in my mouth while I'm getting dressed. I always try and eat soft things, because they're easier to vomit up. I don't like to eat stuff like pretzels or hard candies. I also don't like to eat spicy stuff, you know, hot peppers, garlic, and onions. They are terrible to bring up!

"Before I leave for work, I have just enough time to vomit up everything I just ate. I'm pretty good at it—most of the time, I don't even need to stick my fingers down my throat anymore. All I have to do is just start thinking about throwing up, and the next thing I know, I start gagging and I just vomit. I usually vomit within 20 minutes after I've eaten, because after that it's started digesting, and then it's too late. The food is already being absorbed.

"When I'm driving to work, I always have a bag of M&Ms or cookies in the car, or else I stop and buy a dozen Dunkin Donuts. You know, it's stuff I can eat without taking my eyes off the road. Usually, I throw up before I get to work—I always keep a couple of mason jars under the front seat of my car for that. I prefer not to do it that way because it smells up everything, and I can't always rinse my mouth out right afterward. I do keep a can of air freshener in the glove compartment, though.

"When I'm at work, I don't eat much in front of other people. They mean well, I guess, but they're always so critical of me. They'll say things like, 'You eat like a bird, but you never lose any weight on all your different diets.' I always eat lunch by myself—and most of the time, I go out. I either get a couple of hamburgers, fries, and a large shake, or I'll find a drive-in fast-food place to get something. I always eat in my car, and I always throw up before I go back to work. If things are rushed at work and I don't have a full lunch hour, I'll grab a bunch of laxatives. Only problem with that is going to the bathroom all afternoon. Good thing my office is away from everybody and down the hall near the restrooms.

"After work, I eat stuff in the car on the way home, but as soon as I get home I hit some of my secret stashes—I have 'em all over the house. There's food hidden in the bottom of the laundry hamper. That's a great hiding place 'cause you know nobody but me is going to be emptying it out to do the wash! I have candy stuffed inside my shoes and shoeboxes ... inside the pockets of my winter clothes ... under my mattress. I used to hide food under the kid's cribs, but they sleep in beds now. Once, I put a huge bag of M&Ms in the dog's dry food bin, and my husband found it. I had a hard time explaining that one. So I stopped putting stuff in there. Now, I have to get real creative, like when I wrap up ice cream bars in aluminum foil so they look like frozen hamburger patties. I'm always saving empty cereal boxes so I can put food back inside them and then put them back in the pantry."

"My husband complains sometimes about our food bills, but he doesn't know why we go through so much. I tell him that prices are really terrible, but most of the time I clip coupons to help with the cost. During dinner I eat like everybody else. But then as soon as dinner is over I start eating again right up until the time I go to bed. I usually can put away half of an apple pie and a quart of ice cream, but I have to be quiet when I throw up because everybody is home and they might hear me. Sometimes, when it's late at night and everyone is in bed, I'll treat myself to a nice enema.

"Most of the time I eat in the bathroom, because it's the only place that gives me any privacy. Did you know that mothers only get about 42 minutes a day to themselves? I've got to be creative. The hard part is throwing up so no one hears me. I usually run the shower to hide my gagging noises.

"I used to pride myself on being a nice person, but now I'm just this horrible pig. I feel terrible, but I don't know how to stop. I've tried stopping so many times. I just can't give up the food—and if I don't vomit, use laxatives, or enemas, I start putting on the pounds. This is no way to live."

Advanced
Clinical EP
2.1.7 b

ASSESSMENT SUMMARY   The physical complications associated with bulimia highlight the importance of consulting with medical professionals, as needed. Consistent with bulimia nervosa, Mary McDaniel's behaviors leave little doubt that she has all the salient features, including binge/purge cycles, use of laxatives, diuretics, and enemas, and no control over how much she eats. If Mary's binge eating and purging occurred during periods of anorexia nervosa, then her diagnosis of bulimia nervosa would be noted as co-morbid with anorexia nervosa. Despite feeling unhappy about herself, Mary is unable to stop her eating pattern; in fact, she believes she has no control over this behavior. For Mary, her struggles around food are never ending. It is an all or nothing perspective; she is either completely in control or completely out of control. Likewise, food is seen as either all good or all bad. With this pattern, the practitioner might begin to be on the lookout for **somatic complaints**.

THE ROLE OF OBESITY

While not physically healthy, obesity is *not* considered a psychiatric disorder (American Psychiatric Association, 2000); however, it is generally lumped together with eating or weight disorders. Unfortunately, this only serves to stigmatize those who are portly. As researchers continue to examine the role of biological influences, particularly neurotransmitters and genetic predisposition, perhaps society will begin to view obesity differently—that is, as a complex metabolic disorder, rather than explain it as an emotional or behavioral problem. It would seem that as our society advances technologically, we are simply getting fatter (Henderson & Brownell, 2004). People are constantly exposed to what is considered to be a toxic environment: easy availability of inexpensive fatty foods that have low nutritional value combined with an increasingly inactive life style (Schwartz & Brownell, 2007). The promotion of an inactive, sedentary lifestyle and consuming a high-fat diet seem to be the major contributors to obesity (Caballero, 2007; Levine et al., 2005).

Nevertheless, being overweight and obese does pose major public health challenges. These conditions place a person at a higher risk for various cardiovascular diseases, hypertension, and high blood cholesterol (National Center for Health Statistics, 2005). The prevalence of obesity or a body mass index (BMI) of 30 or greater among adults of all gender, age, and racial/ethnic groups in the United States in 2000 was 30.5 percent of the general population and steadily increased to 33.8 percent in 2008 (Flegal, Carroll, Ogden, & Curtin, 2010). While this increase seems to be leveling off, the problem of obesity in our society continues. Flegal and colleagues (2010) note that 5.7 percent of the adult population have a BMI over 40, or 10 million people in the United States alone. The numbers for children and adolescents are even worse. Obesity rates for children ages 2 to 19 years of age (or above the 95th percentile for sex-specific BMI for their age) increased from 13.9 percent in 2000 to 16.9 percent in 2008 (Ogden, Carroll, Curtin, Lamb, & Flegal, 2010).

The term *obesity* does not appear in the DSM-IV-TR because a consistent association has not been established between obesity and a psychological or behavioral syndrome (American Psychiatric Association, 2000). The DSM reads, "When there is evidence that psychological factors are of importance in the etiology or course of a particular case of obesity, this can be indicated by noting the presence of Psychological Factors Affecting Medical Condition" (American Psychiatric Association, 2000, p. 583). The DSM notes that obese individuals *may* develop eating disorders (a small percentage of individuals with bulimia nervosa are obese, and still more obese individuals engage in binge eating behaviors). Binge eating has two main characteristics: first, the consumption and the amount of food eaten is unquestionably greater than most people would eat during a similar period of time or under the same circumstances; and second, the individuals feel they are eating "out of control" and cannot stop.

THE MAJOR FEATURES OF BINGE EATING DISORDER

EP 2.1.7 b

Binge eating disorder (BED) has been called by a variety of other names, including bulimia, nonpurging bulimia nervosa, and compulsive overeating. The syndrome is most like bulimia, except that there is no self-induced vomiting or laxative misuse (Barlow & Durand, 2012). Therefore, binge eating disorder involves none of the medical complications attributable to purging behaviors. However, the practitioner may consult with medical professionals, as needed, to confirm the diagnosis.

Binge eating disorder is currently listed in the appendix of the DSM-IV-TR as a potential new disorder that calls for further study (American Psychiatric Association, 2000); therefore, any discussion about the syndrome at this point in time should be considered tentative. The available research is simply insufficient to support the clear set of diagnostic criteria needed for inclusion in the body of the DSM. The areas that require further research include indications that individuals with BED do not regularly engage in purging, and the criteria for BED do not specify any weight range. What *is* known is that most people who binge eat have varying degrees of obesity and are generally considered overweight (American Psychiatric Association, 2000). However, individuals with BED have some of the same concerns about their body shape and weight as those with a diagnosis of anorexia nervosa and bulimia (Wilfley, Schwartz, Spurrell, & Fairburn, 2000). In contrast to findings about bulimia, early studies indicate that BED occurs predominately in individuals who are obese (Spitzer et al., 1991).

In a pattern similar to that of bulimia, individuals with BED alternate between episodes of binge eating and efforts to restrict their food intake. While people with BED consume large quantities of food, they also report disorganized and even chaotic eating habits. Interestingly, although the presentation appears comparable to that of bulimia, there are two distinctive differences: (1) the person comes for treatment later in life, and (2) the individual usually seeks methods of weight reduction. The criteria for diagnosis of binge eating disorder include:

- Recurrent episodes of binge eating, in which:
  - Eating occurs during a discrete period of time (e.g., within 2 hours).

- The amount of food consumed is much larger than most people would be able to eat in similar circumstances and in the same amount of time.
- The individual experiences a lack of control and feels he or she cannot stop what or how much is eaten.
- Binge eating episodes are usually characterized by *three or more* of the following:
  - Consuming food more rapidly than would be considered normal.
  - Eating until one feels uncomfortably full or overstuffed.
  - Eating large quantities, even when not physically hungry.
  - Eating in private because of embarrassment about the quantity of food eaten.
  - Feeling disgusted or guilty after overeating.
- The eating binge results in marked distress such as unpleasant feelings during and after binge episodes or concerns about the long-term effects on body weight and shape.
- Binge eating occurs, on average, twice a week over a period of at least 6 months.
- Binge eating does not occur in conjunction with regular use of inappropriate alleviative behaviors (e.g., fasting), and does not occur solely during the course of either anorexia or bulimia (American Psychiatric Association, 2000).

Current investigative clinical trials are being conducted to determine whether or not binge eating disorder or BED should eventually become a DSM category. Although controversial, it is expected to almost certainly be included as a disorder in its own category in the DSM-5 (Wonderlich, Gordon, Mitchell, Crosby, & Engel, 2009). While some critics note it may be premature to single out a particular subgroup of eating disorders, not otherwise specified (EDNOS), there is growing evidence that supports the BED distinction in that some persons have different patterns of heritability compared to other eating disorders (Bulik, Sullivan, & Kendler, 2000). There is increasing evidence that some individuals who meet the preliminary criteria for BED can often be seen in weight control programs (Fairburn, Cooper, Doll, Norman, & O'Connor, 2000). In addition, the diagnostic category of eating disorders is proposed to be renamed "feeding and eating disorders" in the DSM-5 publication.

Individuals with BED seem to differ in a variety of ways from people with other eating disorders as well as from obese people who do not engage in binge behaviors. For example, there is a greater likelihood of BED occurring in males and with a later age of onset (Bulik, Sullivan, & Kendler, 2000). In addition, there is a greater chance for remission, and the person tends to show a better response to treatment than with the other eating disorders (Striegel-Moore & Franko, 2008; Wonderlich, Gordon, Mitchell, Crosby, & Engel, 2009).

In essence, individuals with the eating pattern referred to as binge eating disorder exhibit different eating behaviors from those exhibited by Mary McDaniel in the earlier vignette. Those with BED do not attempt to compensate for gaining weight by vomiting, using laxatives, or exercising excessively. Although no weight range is currently noted for diagnostic purposes, these individuals do tend to be obese.

SUMMARY

Individuals with anorexia nervosa differ in one very important way from those with bulimia—they are (much to their detriment) extremely successful at losing weight. Granted, the individual with bulimia is not trying to achieve low weight—his or her motivating force is to avoid becoming fat. The anorexic's desire is to be extremely thin. Although these two conditions frequently coexist, the individual with bulimia usually does not meet the criterion for those with anorexia of being at least 15 percent underweight. (Refer to Table 10.1

for a summary of the major features of anorexia nervosa and bulimia nervosa.)

Binge eating may occur in those with anorexia, but some confusion still exists as to when the collateral assessment of bulimia should apply. While anorexia is less common than bulimia, there is a great deal of overlap between the two disorders. Fairburn and colleagues (2008) observe that many individuals with bulimia have a history of anorexia. These individuals report a history of having used fasting as a way to reduce

TABLE 10.1 | AN OVERVIEW OF THE MAJOR FEATURES OF ANOREXIA NERVOSA AND BULIMIA NERVOSA

	Anorexia Nervosa	Bulimia Nervosa
Characteristics	• Ego-syntonic • Malnutrition/starvation • Refusal to maintain minimal weight • Intense fear of gaining weight • Loss of menstrual cycle • Distorted body image • Perfectionism • Somatic complaints • Denial about weight condition • Compliant and accommodating • Very deceptive • Infantile, demanding, negative • Manipulative • Hair loss and/or lanugo	• Ego-dystonic • Binge/purge cycle • Purging: self-induced vomiting, laxatives, diuretics, exercise • Weight fluctuation • Fear of being fat • Fear of loss of control
Medical Complications	• Sudden death • Loss of normal muscle and fat • Low insight/misinterprets body image • Secondary gain about appearance • Decreased sexual interest • Irregular heartbeat • Osteoporosis • Digestive/gastrointestinal problems	• "Chipmunk" cheeks • Teeth yellow, eroded ("moth-eaten") • Sore throat from purging • Russell's signs (knuckles have callous formation) • Acute electrolyte imbalance • Abnormalities of renal and reproductive systems • Esophageal tears • Gastrointestinal systems (heartburn, abdominal pain, cramps, and bloating) • Irregular menstrual cycle • Constipation (rebound from laxatives) • Poor hair texture • Dehydration

their body weight below desirable levels. The practitioner should begin by evaluating how often the individual engages in the purging/bingeing behaviors. An important rule of thumb for assessment of these disorders is the individual assessed with anorexia who experiences only a few binges scattered throughout a year should *not* be considered for bulimia—but an individual with anorexia who binges several or more times a week would appear to have both disorders concurrently (Barlow & Durand, 2012).

During the past 20 years, attention on eating disorders has increased substantially, and research efforts have scrambled to keep up with this burgeoning interest. Unfortunately, there are some serious methodological problems in many of the studies referenced in the literature; namely, diagnostic criteria vary greatly, there are low numbers of individuals included in the studies, and there are inadequate comparison groups. Nevertheless, some tentative conclusions can be drawn:

- Eating disorders are primarily conditions found in females from the ages of 15 through early 20s.
- Medical complications associated with both anorexia and bulimia are often serious and can be life threatening without appropriate intervention.
- Individuals with anorexia and bulimia show evidence of significant cognitive distortion (about themselves and their bodies), along with a variety of other psychological problems, such as depression.
- The literature finds limited support for theories concerning the etiology of eating disorders.

Future research, it is hoped, will lead to a significant increase in the factual knowledge concerning these eating disorders.

PRACTITIONER'S REFLECTIONS

This chapter outlined the major characteristics of the eating disorders, including anorexia nervosa, bulimia nervosa, and binge eating disorder (BED). Anorexia nervosa refers to an individual's refusal to eat anything but minimal amounts of food, resulting in extremely low body weight. Those with bulimia nervosa engage in uncontrolled binge eating episodes followed by self-induced purging. Both disorders involve an overwhelming desire to be thin. Individuals with binge eating disorder, while experiencing marked distress due to their binge eating, do not engage in extreme compensatory behaviors. In each of these eating disorders, because of the individuals' tendency to hide their patterns of eating, the practitioner must learn to listen and look for clues.

ACTIVITIES

Advanced Clinical EP 2.1.10 (a) a

1. There are cultural differences in attitudes about ideal body weight, and in some groups a heavy body type is valued. Imagine that you are overweight and comfortable with your body image. If you were assigned to work with a client diagnosed with an eating disorder, describe how you would develop a culturally responsive therapeutic relationship; be sure to be attentive to your own cultural beliefs and those of your client.

2. Negative stereotypes are often perpetuated in the media.

EP 2.1.10 (b) a

   a. Browse through a popular magazine and identify the number of advertisements that portray individuals whom you consider to be thin and those with a heavier body frame. How many are portrayed as thin and how many have more body weight?
   b. Next, identify how many are female and how many are male.

c. Finally, identify how many are ethnic minorities.

d. Describe how refining your understanding of negative stereotypes found in the media will influence how you will go about collecting, organizing, and interpreting client data when assessing a client with an eating disorder.

EP 2.1.4 b

3. This activity is designed to begin to sensitize you to what it might be like to have an eating disorder and how all-consuming thoughts about food and weighing oneself can be. Keep a diary for 1 week and record everything that you eat, the time of day you ate, whether or not you were hungry, whether or not the food satisfied you, whether or not you had cravings for certain foods, and whether or not you thought about food more often than you regularly do. In addition, weigh yourself every time you eat something. How will this level of self-awareness about your own eating habits help you to eliminate the influence of your personal biases and values in working with clients who struggle with an eating disorder?

EP 2.1.10 (a) c and Advanced Clinical EP 2.1.10 (b) b

4. Review the case of Joy Walker. Refer to the following list of topics to answer the questions below:

Feelings about her appearance.

Things she likes to eat and what she does not like.

Her "ideal" appearance, and what that would look like.

Concerns that she may have had with her appearance in the past.

Current health problems (e.g., feeling weak or dizzy, heart palpitations, sore throat, hair loss, and so on).

Possible long-range worries about health issues.

Past medical problems.

Attempts to keep healthy, fit, and attractive (e.g., her exercise regimen and diet).

a. Which topics do you think Joy would feel comfortable discussing with you?

b. Which topics do you imagine would be the most difficult for her to talk about?

c. Assume that you are the practitioner assigned to work with Joy, and illustrate through a role play with a colleague or your supervisor how you would go about developing a mutually agreed-on focus for working together.

d. Based on what you know about Joy, how would you assess her readiness for change?

5. Access the CourseMate website at www.cengagebrain.com. Read the case of "Susan," someone who struggles with anorexia. Listen as she talks about her fears of not being "skinny enough." Although she weighs only 96 pounds, she does not want to eat because she is afraid of gaining weight. She describes her urge to either purge or to take a laxative.

EP 2.1.10 (a) b and Advanced Clinical EP 2.1.3 b

a. Provide an example of how you would express empathy for her concerns about her weight.

b. Identify Susan's strengths and vulnerabilities.

COMPETENCY NOTES

EP 2.1.3 a: Distinguish, appraise, and integrate multiple sources of knowledge, including research-based knowledge and practice wisdom (p. 346): Social workers are knowledgeable about the principles of logic, scientific inquiry, and reasoned discernment.

EP Advanced Clinical 2.1.3 b: Identify and articulate clients' strengths and vulnerabilities (p. 359): Advanced practitioners understand and differentiate the strengths and limitations of multiple practice theories and methods, clinical processes, and technical tools, including differential diagnosis.

EP 2.1.4 b: Gain sufficient self-awareness to eliminate the influence of personal biases and values in working with diverse groups (p. 359): Social workers understand how diversity characterizes and shapes the human experience and is critical to the formation of identity.

EP 2.1.7 b: Critique and apply knowledge to understand person and environment (p. 355): Social workers apply theories and knowledge from the liberal arts to understand biological, social, cultural, psychological, and spiritual development.

EP Advanced Clinical 2.1.7 b: Use bio-psycho-social-spiritual theories and multiaxial diagnostic classification systems in formulation of comprehensive assessments (p. 354): Advanced practitioners understand how to synthesize and differentially apply the theories of human behavior and the social environment (biological, developmental, psychological, social, cultural, and spiritual).

EP Advanced Clinical 2.1.7 c: Consult with medical professionals, as needed, to confirm diagnosis and/or to monitor medication in the treatment process (p. 348): Advanced practitioners understand how to synthesize and differentially apply the theories of human behavior and the social environment (biological, developmental, psychological, social, cultural, and spiritual).

EP 2.1.10 (a) b: Use empathy and other interpersonal skills (p. 359): Social workers have the knowledge and skills to practice with individuals, families, groups,

organizations, and communities. This involves the dynamic and interactive process of the skill of engagement.

EP 2.1.10 (a) c: Develop a mutually agreed-on focus of work and desired outcomes (p. 359): Social have the knowledge and skills to practice with individuals, families, groups, organizations, and communities.

EP Advanced Clinical 2.1.10 (a) a: Develop a culturally responsive therapeutic relationship (pp. 341, 358): Advanced practitioners have a theoretically informed knowledge base so as to effectively practice with individuals, families, and groups.

EP 2.1.10 (b) a: Collect, organize, and interpret client data (pp. 341, 343, 348, 350, 352, 358): Social have the knowledge and skills to practice with individuals, families, groups, organizations, and communities.

EP Advanced Clinical 2.1.10 (b) b: Assess client's readiness for change (p. 359): Advanced practitioners have a theoretically informed knowledge base so as to effectively practice with individuals, families, and groups.

EP Advanced Clinical 2.1.10 (b) c: Assess client's coping strategies to reinforce and improve adaptation to life situations, circumstances, and events (p. 348): Advanced practitioners have a theoretically informed knowledge base so as to effectively practice with individuals, families, and groups.

REFERENCES

Agras, W. S. (2001). The consequences and costs of eating disorders. *Psychiatric Clinics of North America, 24,* 371–379.

American Psychiatric Association. (1980). *Diagnostic and statistical manual of mental disorders* (3rd ed.). Washington, DC: Author.

American Psychiatric Association. (1994). *Diagnostic and statistical manual of mental disorders* (4th ed.). Washington, DC: Author.

American Psychiatric Association. (2000). *Diagnostic and statistical manual of mental disorders* (4th ed.-text revision). Washington, DC: Author.

American Psychiatric Association. (2006). *Treatment of patients with eating disorders* (3rd ed.). Washington, DC: Author.

Anderson-Frye, E. (2009). Cross-cultural issues in body image among children and adolescents.

In L. Smolak & J. K. Thompson (Eds.). *Body image, eating disorders, and obesity in youth: Assessment, prevention, and treatment* (2nd ed. pp. 113–133). Washington DC: American Psychological Association.

Andrist, L. C. (2003). Media images, body dissatisfaction, and disordered eating in adolescent women. *American Journal of Maternal Child Nursing, 28,* 119–123.

Austrian, S. G. (2005). *Mental disorders, medications, and clinical social work* (3rd ed.). New York: Columbia University Press.

Barlow, D. H. & Durand, V. M. (2012). *Abnormal psychology* (6th ed.). Belmont, CA: Wadsworth Cengage Learning.

Bulik, C. M., Sullivan, P. F., & Kendler, S. K. (2000). An empirical study of the classification of eating disorders. *American Journal of Psychiatry, 157* (6), 886–895.

Caballero, B. (2007). The global epidemic of obesity: An overview. *Epidemiologic Review, 29,* 1–5.

Carter, J. C., Bewell, C., Blackmore, E., & Woodside, D. B. (2006). The impact of childhood sexual abuse in anorexia nervosa. *Child Abuse and Neglect, 30* (3), 257–69.

Celio, A. A., Zabinski, M. F., & Wilfley, D. E. (2002). African-American body images. In T. F. Cash & T. Pruzinsky (Eds.). *Body image: A handbook of theory, research, and clinical practice* (pp. 234–242). New York, NY: Guilford.

Crow, S. J., Thuras, P., Keel, P. K., & Mitchell, J. E. (2002). Long-term menstrual and reproductive function in patients with bulimia nervosa. *American Journal of Psychiatry, 159,* 1048–1050.

Fairburn, C. G., Cooper, Z., Doll, H. A., Norman, P. & O'Connor, M. (2000). The natural course of bulimia nervosa and binge eating disorder in young women. *Archives of General Psychiatry, 37,* 659–665.

Fairburn, C. G., Cooper, Z., Shafran, R.,& Wilson, G. T. (2008). Eating disorders: A transdiagnostic protocol. In D. H. Barlow (Ed.), *Clinical handbook of psychological disorders: A step-by-step treatment manual* (4th ed., pp. 578–614). New York, NY: Guilford.

Fairburn, C. G., Stice, E., Cooper, Z., Doll, H. A., Norman, P. A., & O'Connor, M. E. (2003). Understanding persistence in bulimia nervosa: A 5-year naturalistic study. *Journal of Counseling and Clinical Psychology, 71,* 103–109.

Flegal, K. M., Carroll, M. D., Ogden, C. L., & Curtin, L. R. (2010). Prevalence and trends in obesity among US adults, 1999–2008. *Journal of the American Medical Association, 303* (3), 235–241.

Franco, D. L., Wonderlich, S. A., Little, D., & Herzog, D. B. (2004). Diagnosis and classification of eating disorders. In J. K. Thompson (Ed.), *Handbook of eating disorders and obesity* (pp. 58–80). New York: John Wiley & Sons.

Glazer, J. L. (2008). Eating disorders among male athletes. *Current Sports medicine Reports, 7,* 332–337.

Gleaves, D. H., Lowe, M. R., Snow, A. C., Green, B. A., & Murphy-Eberenz, K. P. (2000). Continuity and discontinuity models of bulimia nervosa: A taxo-metric investigation. *Journal of Abnormal Psychology, 109* (1), 56–68.

Goel, M. S., McCarthy, E. P., Phillips, R. S., & Wee, C. C. (2004). Obesity among U.S. immigrant subgroups by duration of residence. *Journal of the American Medical Association, 292,* 2860–2867.

Grabe, S. & Hyde, J. S. (2006). Ethnicity and body dissatisfaction among women in the United States: A meta-analysis. *Psychological Bulletin, 132,* 622–640.

Gull, W. W. (1873). Anorexia hysterical (Apepsia hysteria). *British Medical Journal, 2,* 527.

Henderson, K. E., & Brownell, K. D. (2004). The toxic environment and obesity: Contribution and care. In J. K. Thompson (Ed.) *Handbook of eating disorders and obesity* (pp. 339–348). New York, NY: John Wiley and Sons.

Hersen, M., Turner, S. M., & Beidel, D. C. (2007). *Adult psychopathology and diagnosis.* Hoboken, NJ: John Wiley and Sons.

Hill, A. J. (2006). Motivation for eating behavior in adolescent girls: the body beautiful. *Proceedings of the Nutrition Society, 65,* 376–384.

Hudson, J. I., Hiripi, E., Pope, H. G., & Kessler, R. C. (2007). The prevalence and correlates of eating disorders in the national comorbidity survey replication. *Biological Psychiatry, 61,* 348–358.

Jacobi, C., Hayward, C., deZwan, M., Kraemer, H. C., & Agras, W. S. (2004). Coming to terms with risk factors for eating disorders: Application of risk terminology and suggestions for a general taxonomy. *Psychological Bulletin, 130,* 19–65.

Kearney, C. A., & Trull, T. J. (2012). *Abnormal psychology and life: A dimensional approach.* Belmont, CA: Wadsworth Cengage Learning.

Keel, P. K., Dorer, D. J., Eddy, K. T., Franko, D., Charatan, D. L., & Herzog, D. B. (2003). Predictors of mortality in eating disorders. *Archives of General Psychiatry, 60,* 179–183.

Keel, P. K., Mitchell, J. E., Miller, K. B., Davis, T. L., Crow, S. J. (2000). Predictive validity of bulimia nervosa as a diagnostic strategy. *American Journal of Psychiatry, 157* (1), 136–138.

Kilgus, M. D., Maxmen, J. S., & Ward, N. G. (2009). *Essential psychopathology and its treatment* (3rd ed.). New York, NY: W. W. Norton.

Lasegué, C. (1873). L'anorexia hysterique. *Archives generales de medicine, 1,* 385–403.

Lask, B., & Bryant-Waugh, R. (2007) *Eating disorders in childhood and adolescence* (3rd ed.) New York, NY: Routledge.

Levine, J. K., Lanningham-Foster, L. M., McCrady, S. K., Krizan, A. C. Olson, L. R., Kane, P. H., Jensen, M. D., & Clark, M. M. (2005). Interindividual variation in posture allocation: Possible role in human obesity. *Science, 307,* 584–586.

Marcé, L. V. (1860). On a form of hypochondriacal delirium occurring consecutive to dyspepsia, and characterized by refusal of food. *Journal of Psychological Medicine and Mental Pathology, 13,* 264–266.

McGee, B. J., Hewitt, P. L., Sherry, S. B., Parkin, M., & Flett, G. L. (2005). Perfectionistic self-presentation, body image, and eating disorder symptoms. *Body Image, 2,* 29–40.

National Center for Health Statistics. (2005). Chart book on trends in the health of Americans. *Health, United States.* Hyattsville, MD: Public Health Service.

Ogden, C. L., Carroll, M. D., Curtin, L. R., Lamb, M. M., & Flegal, K. M. (2010). Prevalence of high body mass index in US children and adolescents, 2007–2008. *Journal of the American Medical Association, 303*(3), 242–249.

Parry-Jones, B., & Parry-Jones, W. L. (2002). History of bulimia and bulimia nervosa. In K. D. Brownell & C. G. Fairburn (Eds.), *Eating disorders and obesity: A comprehensive handbook* (2nd ed., pp. 145–150). New York, NY: Guilford Press.

Polivy, J. & Herman, C. P. (2002). Dieting and its relation to eating disorders. In K. D. Brownell & C. G. Fariburn (Eds.), *Eating disorders and obesity: A comprehensive handbook* (2nd ed., pp. 83–86). New York, NY: Guilford.

Pomeroy, C. (2004). Assessment of medical status and physical factors. In J. K. Thompson (Ed.), *Handbook of eating disorders and obesity* (pp. 81–111). New York: John Wiley & Sons.

Rome, E. S., & Ammerman, S. (2003). Medical complications of eating disorders: An update. *Journal of Adolescent Health, 33* (6), 418–426.

Sadock, B. J., Sadock, V. A., & Ruiz, P. (Eds.) (2009). *Kaplan and Sadock's comprehensive textbook of psychiatry* (9th ed.). Philadelphia, PA: Lippincott, Williams and Wilkins.

Sassaroli, S., Romero Lauro, L. J., Maria Ruggerio, G., Mauri, M. C., Vinai, P., & Frost, R. (2008). Perfectionism in depression, obsessive-compulsive disorder and eating disorders. *Behaviour Research and therapy, 46,* 757–765.

Scholtz, S., Hill, L. S., & Lacey, H. (2010). Eating disorders in older women: Does late onset anorexia nervosa exist? *International Journal of Eating Disorders, 43* (5), 393–397.

Schwartz, M. B., & Brownell, K. D. (2007). Actions necessary to prevent childhood obesity: Creating the climate for change. *Journal of Law, Medicine, and Ethics, 35,* 78–79.

Spitzer, R. L., Devlin, M. J., Walsh, B. T., Hasin, D., Wing, R., Marcus, M. D., ... Nonas, C. (1991). Binge-eating: To be or not to be in DSM-IV. *International Journal of Eating Disorders, 10,* 627–629.

Stice, E. (2002). Risk and maintenance factors for eating pathology: A meta-analytic review. *Psychological Bulletin, 128,* 825–848.

Stice, E., Ng, J., & Shaw, H. (2010). Risk factors and prodromal eating pathology. *Journal of Child Psychology and Psychiatry and Allied Disciplines, 51* (4), 518–525.

Stice, E., Shaw, H., & Marti, C. N. (2007). A meta-analytic review of eating disorder prevention programs: Encouraging findings. *Annual Review of Clinical Psychology, 3,* 207–231.

Striegel-Moore, R. H., Cachelin, F. M., Dohm, F. A., Pike, M., Wilfley, D. E., & Fairburn, C. G. (2004). Comparison of binge eating disorder and bulimia nervosa in a community sample. *International Journal of Eating Disorders, 29,* 157–165.

Striegel-Moore, R. H., & Franko, D. L. (2008). Should binge-eating disorder be included in the DSM-V? A critical review of the state of the evidence. *Annual Review of Clinical Psychology, 4,* 305–324.

Sudi, K., Ottl, K., Payerl, D., Baumgard, P., Tauschmann, K., & Miller, W. (2004). Anorexia athletica. *Nutrition, 20,* 657–661.

Thompson, J. K., & van den Berg, P. (2002). Measuring body image attitudes among adolescents and adults. In T. F. Cash & T. Pruzinsky (Eds.), *Body image: A handbook of theory, research, and practice* (pp. 142–154). New York: Guilford.

Tiggerman, M., & Slater, A. (2001). A test of objectification theory in former dancers and non-dancers. *Psychology of Women Quarterly, 25,* 57–64.

Utter, J., Neumark-Stainzer, D., Wall, M., & Story, M. (2003). Reading magazine articles about dieting and associated weight control behaviors among adolescents. *Journal of Adolescent Health, 32,* 78–82.

Vitello, B., & Lederhendler, I. (2000). Research on eating disorders: Current status and future prospects. *Biological Psychiatry, 47,* 777–786.

Wade, T. D., Bulik, C. M., Prescott, C. A., & Kendler, K. S, (2004). Sex influences on shared risk factors for bulimia nervosa and other psychiatric disorders. *Archives of General Psychiatry, 61,* 251–256.

Wilfley, D. E., Schwartz, J. N. B., Spurrell, B., Fairburn, C. G. (2000). Using the eating disorders examination to identify the specific psychopathology of binge eating disorder. *International Journal of Eating Disorders, 27,* 259–269.

Wonderlich, S. A., Gordon, K. H., Mitchell, J. E., Crosby, R. E., & Engel, S. G. (2009). The validity and clinical utility of binge eating disorder. *International Journal of Eating Disorders, 42* (8), 687–705.

Zipfel, S., Lowe, B., Deter, H. C., & Herzog, W. (2000). Long-term prognosis in anorexia nervosa: Lessons from a 21-year follow-up study. *Lancet, 355,* 721–722.

CHAPTER 11 | THE PERSONALITY DISORDERS

INTRODUCTION

Hippocrates (460–377 B.C.), traditionally considered the father of Western medicine, suggested that disease, mainly brain disease or head trauma, was responsible for mental problems. He believed that most were due to an imbalance in four essential fluids, or "humors," that circulated throughout the body. These humors, blood, black bile, yellow bile, and lymph, were somehow responsible for characterizing an individual's worldview. In his work *Hippocratic Corus* (Maher & Maher, 1985), Hippocrates advanced the idea that the psychological disorders could be treated like any other disease. Indeed, Hippocrates described several mental disorders that are familiar to contemporary practitioners, including mania, melancholia, and paranoia.

Two thousand years later, DSM-I described 27 personality disorders and organized them into five specific headings: (1) personality pattern disturbance, (2) personality trait disturbance, (3) sociopathic personality disturbance, (4) special symptom reactions, and (5) transient situational personality disorders (American Psychiatric Association, 1952).When DSM-II made its appearance, the subheadings were subsequently eliminated and the number of personality disorders was reduced from 27 to 12 categories (American Psychiatric Association, 1968). The professional community did not endorse these as positive changes because they were considered too limited. The next round of diagnostic revisions began in 1974, leading to the publication of the DSM-III in 1980 (American Psychiatric Association, 1994). This manual introduced the concept of Axis II; for the first time, the personality and developmental disorders were separated from the clinical syndromes noted on Axis I. This Axis II stipulation ensured the personality disorder designation would not be overlooked. DSM-III-R, published in 1987, described 11 personality disorders subdivided into three clusters, with each cluster representing disorders related by their symptomology. (The clusters and their corresponding disorders are discussed in detail later in this chapter.)

Although there are many schools of thought, Freudian psychodynamic theory has historically influenced the way practitioners conceptualize personality and pathology. (An in-depth discussion of psychoanalytic theory is beyond the scope of this book; however, for a thorough review, the reader is directed to Goldstein, Miehls, and Ringel [2009], and Teyber and McClure [2011].) Briefly, adult personality is viewed as the accumulation of early childhood experiences. Individuals generally learn to solve their own emotional problems during various stages of childhood development. These characteristic ways of interacting help determine adult personality traits. Freud has been credited for noticing that the emotional problems of childhood are resolved by the development of defense mechanisms aimed at decreasing anxiety (as cited in Corey, 2009). Defenses were conceptualized as unconscious processes originating within the **ego**, or the executive function of the individual's personality structure.

The term *personality* implies the manner in which a person interacts with his or her environment and other people. Personality disorder characterizes those individuals who usually respond poorly to changes, exhibit deficiencies in their capacity to form relationships, and have interpersonal problems in a variety of arenas, such as employment or school. Problems occur when traits—those features that make up a personality—remain inflexible, thus impairing individuals' ability to interact within their social environment and with others.

Each person has a unique and individualized repertoire of **defense mechanisms** geared to maintaining balance between their internal drives and the external world. This repertoire is seen as personality—a set of characteristics defining the behaviors, thoughts, and emotions of each individual. These characteristics become ingrained and usually dictate the person's worldview, lifestyle, and life choices. An individual's **personality** can be defined as those emotional and behavioral traits that characterize day-to-day living under normative conditions; an individual's personality is relatively predictable (Sadock, Sadock, & Ruiz, 2009).

A **personality disorder** is seen as a variant of character traits going far beyond the normative range found in most people. When these traits are extremely inflexible and maladaptive, and cause significant functional impairment or subjective distress, they constitute a personality disorder. Individuals characterized by a personality disorder exhibit deeply ingrained, inflexible, rigid, problematic, and maladaptive patterns of relating to others and in perceiving themselves. Although the individual's interactional style generally creates no distress for him or her, it may adversely affect others; that is, the person's behavior is considered **ego-syntonic**. This might present a major problem for the practitioner, especially when trying to foster the therapeutic relationship and develop collaborative efforts aimed at change.

The DSM-IV defines a personality disorder as "an enduring pattern of inner experience and behavior that deviates markedly from the expectations of the individual's culture, is pervasive and inflexible, and has an onset in adolescence or early adulthood, is stable over time, and leads to distress or impairment" (American Psychiatric Association, 2000, p. 685). The competency-based assessment expands this definition by considering the influence of the full range of biological, psychological, sociocultural, and environmental factors that affect the individual's life.

UNDERSTANDING PERSONALITY DISORDERS

We all have notions about personality: Juan, for instance, can be described as gregarious, Walter as fun-loving, and Richard as quiet and introspective. In fact, personality goes beyond the way people *think* or *behave*. Each of us has probably behaved at times in ways that can be characterized as gregarious, fun-loving, and quiet and introspective—but behavior is seen as being part of an individual's personality only if it cuts across many situations and events (Barlow & Durand, 2012). This chapter will examine characteristic ways of behaving as they relate specifically to personality disorders, which as mentioned earlier originate in childhood and continue well into adulthood (Phillips, Yen, & Gunderson, 2003).

The Clusters

The DSM-IV noted ten distinct personality disorders, plus one nonspecific category, "which warrant(s) additional future investigation" (American Psychiatric Association, 1994, pp. 732–733). These disorders are grouped into three clusters—A, B, and C—with the following designations:

> *Cluster A: Odd and eccentric*—Includes individuals who have paranoid, schizoid, and schizotypal personality disorders.
>
> *Cluster B: Emotional, dramatic, or erratic*—Includes individuals with antisocial, histrionic, borderline, and narcissistic personality disorders.
>
> *Cluster C: Anxious, fearful*—Includes individuals with avoidant, dependent, and obsessive-compulsive personality disorders.

Table 11.1 shows each cluster along with the major characteristics of each included personality disorder.

The DSM-IV-TR (American Psychiatric Association, 2000) acknowledges that "the clustering system ... has serious limitations and has not been consistently validated" (p. 686). Nonetheless, this method of organization is a helpful framework for the competency-based assessment, which looks at the influence of the wide range of factors affecting client behavior and attempts to identify the impact of those factors on the client's biopsychosocial world. The personality disorders are seen as long-term, stable patterns of unusual and inflexible personality characteristics leading to pervasive impairment or interpersonal distress throughout a person's life (Sadock, Sadock, & Ruiz, 2009). The pattern of impairment is evident in two (or more) of the following areas.

> *Cognition*—Ways of perceiving and interpreting oneself, other people, and events.
>
> *Affectivity*—The range, intensity, and appropriateness of emotional response(s).
>
> *Interpersonal functioning*—The instability of and inability to maintain relationships; poor self-image or self-esteem.
>
> *Impulse control*—The ability to withhold inappropriate verbal or motor responses while completing a task; individuals who act or speak without anticipating the repercussions of their behavior or without learning from

TABLE 11.1 | OVERVIEW OF PERSONALITY DISORDERS

Cluster A: Odd and eccentric

Paranoid	*Schizoid*	*Schizotypal*
Suspicious and distrustful of other's motives as malevolent	*Socially restricted*	*Perceptual disturbances; interpersonal deficits*
• Others seek to harm them • Preoccupied with unjust doubts about loyalty • Reluctant to confide in others • Reads hidden meanings • Bears grudges • Counterattacks or reacts angrily • Recurrent suspicion about fidelity of partner	• No desire for close friendships • Chooses solitary activities • No interest in sex • Takes little pleasure in activities • Lacks friends • Indifferent to praise or criticism • Cold, detached, or flat affect	• Ideas of reference • Odd beliefs • Unusual perceptions • Odd thinking and speech • Suspicious or paranoid ideation • Behavior appears odd, eccentric • Inappropriate affect

Cluster B: Emotional, dramatic, or erratic

Antisocial	*Borderline*	*Histrionic*	*Narcissistic*
Violent, blatant disregard for other; behavior present before 15 years old; must be 18 before diagnosed	*Unstable relationships; poor self-image; marked impulsivity*	*Excessive emotionality; attention seeking*	*Requires excessive admiration*
• Failure to conform to social norms • Dishonest for own profit and purposes • Irritability and/or aggressiveness • Impulsivity • Reckless disregard for self or others • Irresponsible • Lack of remorse	• Frantic efforts to avoid being abandoned • Unstable, chaotic relationships • Impulsive spending, sex, substance abuse • Suicidal • Feeling "empty" • Inappropriate, intense, or poorly controlled anger • History of mutilating	• Uncomfortable when not center of attention • Provocative behavior • Uses physical attraction to draw attention to self • Self-dramatization • Rapidly changes shifting emotions • Highly suggestible	• Grandiose • Fantasizes about unlimited success, power • Striking sense of entitlement • Lacks empathy • Believes self "special" and others ordinary • Interpersonal relationships exploited; others manipulated • Envious of others and thinks others jealous of them • Arrogant

Cluster C: Anxious, fearful

Avoidant	*Obsessive-Compulsive*	*Dependent*
Inhibited; feels inadequate	*Order; perfection; inflexible*	*Needs to be taken care of; clinging behavior*
• Avoids meaningful relationships with others • Unwilling to get involved unless "guaranteed" they will be liked • Shows restraint because they fear shame or ridicule • Preoccupied with criticism or rejection • Feels inadequate • Views self as inept, inferior • Reluctant to take risks, might be embarrassed	• Preoccupied with rules, regulations • Perfection interferes with completion of tasks • Over-conscientious • Hoards objects • Rigid and stubborn • Reluctant to delegate tasks	• Difficulty making everyday decisions • Desires others to assume responsibility for them • Lacks initiative • Excessive lengths to obtain support from others • Feels uncomfortable or helpless • Preoccupied with fears of being left alone

undesirable consequences of their previous behavior that it is appropriate to delay an action are seen as having poor impulse control.

Most individuals are able to adapt their behavior to a variety of different situations. For example, someone who is considered talkative is able to be quiet during an important speech or a religious service. Individuals with a personality disorder, however, exhibit personality traits so out of proportion or inflexible that they often cause problems for themselves and those around them. These difficulties continue over an extended period of time (Kearney & Trull, 2012). It is possible that earlier in the individual's life, these traits were effective in coping with conditions in his or her family of origin.

To identify the presence of a personality disorder, the individual must exhibit *four or five* of the following characteristics:

- Almost always inflexible across a wide range interpersonal and intrapersonal situations.
- Behavior leads to significant distress or impairment in social, occupational, or other important areas of interpersonal functioning.
- Behavior is stable and of long duration; onset can usually be traced back to early adolescence (or earlier).
- Behavior is not the result of another mental disorder.
- Behavior is not due to the direct physiological effects of a substance (e.g., a drug of abuse) or a general medical condition (American Psychiatric Association, 2000).

The 10 personality disorders described in this chapter are certainly not the "final word," but they do arise from historical traditions of dividing the domain of personality disorders. These categories can cause assessment dilemmas when an individual's behavior pattern comes very close to what is considered normal behavior versus abnormal behavior. Identifying the boundary between one specific personality disorder and another also poses a challenge. The main point for the practitioner to recognize is that these personality disorders are considered no more than behavioral prototypes with indistinct boundaries.

EP 2.1.7 a

The competency-based assessment underscores the uniqueness of each individual. In addition, when the influence of biopsychosocial factors is considered, an individual's life story is clearly far more complex than any listing of behavior patterns. The DSM should not be used as a "recipe" for understanding behavior. However, an awareness of the DSM guidelines for differential assessment will help practitioners approach the competency-based assessment process in a systematic way. The competency-based framework is intended to enhance, not to replace, the central role of the practitioners' clinical judgment, empirical evidence to formulate a clinical diagnosis, and the wisdom of accumulated practice experience. Merging the DSM format with the competency-based assessment model provides a framework for practitioners to fully explore a client's life history and the impact of biological, psychological, and social variables. This approach to the assessment helps the practitioner to better understand clients and their environment. For example, the dramatic personality disorders (Cluster B) are found to be highly co-morbid with social problems such as unemployment, poverty, violent death, incarceration, recidivism such as parole violations, and significant relationship instability (Fountoulakis, Lecht, & Kaprinis, 2008).

In what follows, descriptions of the 10 personality disorders noted in the DSM-IV-TR will be provided. While these descriptions tap into the basic features of each personality disorder, it is important to understand that these are only abbreviated characterizations. In practice, the social worker attends to the whole person and their unique life history.

CLUSTER A: ODD AND ECCENTRIC

PARANOID PERSONALITY DISORDER

In **paranoid personality disorder**, the individual's behavior is characterized by pervasive, groundless suspiciousness and an inherent distrust of others (Meissner, 2001; Phillips, Yen, & Gunderson, 2003). This person is often described as hostile, irritable, or angry, and they refuse to take responsibility for their own actions and feelings. As the name suggests, these individuals generally interpret innocent remarks as insults or threats. They often believe their personal character and reputation are being attacked when, in fact, these perceived injuries are wholly unintended. Because of the fear of exploitation, they generally do not confide in or trust others. Central characteristics of the paranoid personality include:

- *Suspicion*—Although the individual has no real basis or evidence of another person's malfeasance, they tend to be preoccupied assuming others are somehow betraying or being unfaithful to them.
- *Holding grudges*—These individuals do not forgive insults, slights, or injuries; are predisposed to blame others for their problems; and often have a history of being litigious.
- *Paranoia*—The prominent characteristics are permanent and unshakeable suspiciousness and persecutory delusions in a person who is otherwise clear-thinking. These individuals have a tendency to be chronically tense, and they constantly mobilize themselves against perceived threats from others in their social environment. This worldview generally begins by early adulthood.
- *Problems with intimacy*—The individual has difficulty being intimate with others, and is generally distrusting.
- *Centrality*—These individuals perceive themselves as the focus of other people's interest or attention.
- *Censure*—The person has a strong tendency to blame others. He or she thinks of others as ill-intentioned or hostile, and therefore is hypervigilant. The individual is supersensitive to issues regarding rank, class, and power, and resents those who have things he or she does not.

Individuals with paranoid personality disorder are prone to see insult where none exists and quick to take offense when none was intended (Sadock, Sadock, & Ruiz, 2009). They are convinced that most people cannot be trusted (Tyrer & Davidson, 2000). Their personality can be described as chronically sarcastic, argumentative, angry, irritable, and querulous—in short, they have "chips on their shoulders." It is not unusual for the individual to bear a grudge for an excessively long time, and he or she pursues "insults" with a righteous, moralistic tenacity. Relationships with neighbors or coworkers can be described as tense. For example, the paranoid individual views a barking dog as the neighbor's deliberate attempt to annoy him or her.

There exists a profound negativistic, bitter, and cynical attitude, which often pervades the person's perception of life. They are cold and humorless, extremely self-protective of their own interests, jealous, controlling, and possessive in whatever relationships they secure. The practitioner should not be surprised to see such individuals fascinated with weapons, survivalist organizations, or with extremist political groups.

PREVAILING PATTERN   As many as 1 in 10 adults in the United States may have a diagnosable personality disorder (Lenzenweger, Lane, Loranger, & Kessler, 2007). These individuals rarely seek help on their own, but rather are referred to treatment by others in their social environment, such as a spouse or an employer. This disorder appears to be more common in men than women and does not seem to have a familial pattern. Currently, there have been no systematic long-term studies conducted; but it *is* known that these individuals have lifelong problems in living and working with others.

EP 2.1.10
(b) a

DIFFERENTIAL ASSESSMENT   Paranoid schizophrenia may *mimic* many aspects of paranoid personality disorder. Integral to the assessment process, the practitioner interprets the data found in the client's story to determine an accurate assessment. For those with schizophrenia, the practitioner notes the presence of chronic delusions or hallucinations and detects a greater degree of incoherence and illogical speech. These characteristics are not found in people with a paranoid personality disorder. The persecutory subtype of delusional disorder may resemble paranoid personality disorder—however, the major distinction is the chronic delusions present in the persecutory subtype. Delusions experienced by those with a paranoid personality disorder are transient or may not occur at all. Individuals with paranoid personality disorder display constant **hypervigilance** (wherein the person is obsessively concerned, defended, or watchful) or pervasive mistrust, which are not seen in delusional disorder. Yet another differentiating factor is that, on closer examination, those with a paranoid personality disorder desperately want relationships with others, whereas, for someone with borderline personality disorder (characterized as chaotic, fractured, and difficult), relationships are extremely problematic.

The following vignette about Ben Rogers illustrates the characteristics of someone with a paranoid personality disorder.

CASE   THE CASE OF BEN ROGERS

Ben Rogers is a 77-year-old retired pharmacist, and is being seen by a social worker at a senior citizens center for an evaluation of health care needs for himself and his 75-year-old bedridden wife, Franne. Mr. Rogers states that he is a relatively healthy individual, except for angina and high blood pressure. He has been the sole caretaker for his wife and was recently urged by their only child, Myra Schwartz, to seek help because his wife's condition is deteriorating. His responsibilities in caring for Franne have become a tremendous physical drain on him. Getting help for her dad was not easy for Myra. She explains, "I just put dad in the car, drove up to the senior center, and told him I wasn't going to budge until he got out and went inside. I told him he didn't have to have a smile on his face—he just had to go in the door of the center and ask for some help. I felt so guilty," Myra confides, "but I was desperate. This was one of the most awful things I've had to do—but I knew it was the only thing that would work with dad."

Because Myra was the catalyst in getting her father involved with the senior citizens center, the social worker set some time aside to talk with her and get an idea of what is happening in the Rogers's home. Myra tells the social worker that her parents have been married for 55 years. Her father, who retired about 15 years ago to care for her mother full time, used to have a moderately successful business as a pharmacist. Myra confides that her parents' relationship has always been somewhat rough. "Mother was the only person my father ever showed any tender feelings for," she said. She also reveals that, except for her mother, "My father never trusted anyone—his attitude has always been that people can't be trusted. They are always out to get you.... He refuses offers of help from anybody in the family and from our friends because he thinks they just want a chance to 'get something on him' that they can use against him later."

Myra shakes her head slowly, and with a wry smile offers, "My father probably has earned a place in the *Guinness Book of World Records* for holding a grudge longer than anyone else on earth. He has never, ever, forgiven an insult." When asked if her father exhibited evidence of mood swings or psychosis, she responds, "No, he's not crazy or anything like that, he's just nasty."

According to his daughter, Ben Rogers's personality issues have been fairly stable. "Oh, dad's always acted this way—as long as I can remember, anyway.... You know, now that I'm an adult and I look back on my relationship with him, I don't really know him very well at all. He's hard to have a relationship with." Myra is quiet for a moment and then continues. "Don't get me wrong, I love my father, but it's like I always have to walk on eggshells whenever I try to talk with him. I mean, he questions my every motive."

Advanced Clinical EP 2.1.10 (b) c

ASSESSMENT SUMMARY   Exploring the interaction of the biopsychosocial factors in Ben Rogers's life makes it appear that his wife's deteriorating health condition has intensified his paranoid beliefs. Franne continues to decline physically, and his ability to care for her becomes increasingly demanding and emotionally draining. Circumstances are conspiring; they seem to force Ben, someone who usually refuses help, to reach out to others and to depend on them for assistance. As Myra points out, "Dad has a long history of not trusting people." He is suspicious of everyone and is known to hold a grudge for a long time. He expects other people will take advantage of him and sometimes reads hidden meanings into others' innocent remarks.

The competency-based assessment focuses on strengths and positives in the client's situation. This includes a focus on the client's coping strategies and how they contribute to how he adapts to his life that includes a diagnosis of paranoid personality disorder.

Ben Rogers has had a moderately successful career as a pharmacist, an occupation in which it was necessary for him to interact with others—and, despite evidence of interpersonal difficulties, he has maintained a 55-year marriage. His daughter acknowledges that he has always demonstrated tender feelings for his wife.

Ben has been in relatively good health in the past, but the physical demands of being the sole caretaker for his wife are beginning to take their toll on his own health status; he is currently taking medication for hypertension and angina. Though one might suspect it is difficult, Ben has been attending the senior citizens center once or twice a week after being urged by his daughter to seek help.

From the information available in this case presentation, Ben has come to the practitioner's attention because of interpersonal family issues, and he has not sought help on his own. This pattern of access to services is not inconsistent with people who experience intense interpersonal conflicts. Further, Ben lacks the insight to understand that his behavior creates relational difficulties with others;

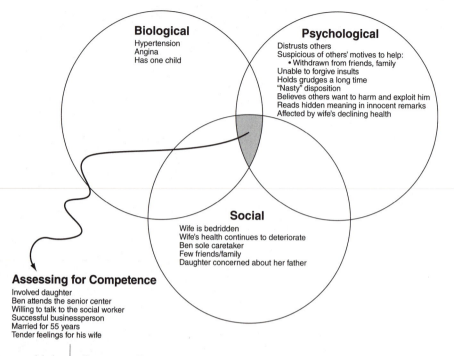

Biological
Hypertension
Angina
Has one child

Psychological
Distrusts others
Suspicious of others' motives to help:
    • Withdrawn from friends, family
Unable to forgive insults
Holds grudges a long time
"Nasty" disposition
Believes others want to harm and exploit him
Reads hidden meaning in innocent remarks
Affected by wife's declining health

Social
Wife is bedridden
Wife's health continues to deteriorate
Ben sole caretaker
Few friends/family
Daughter concerned about her father

Assessing for Competence
Involved daughter
Ben attends the senior center
Willing to talk to the social worker
Successful businessperson
Married for 55 years
Tender feelings for his wife

FIGURE 11.1 | PARANOID PERSONALITY DISORDER

The interactions of the biological, psychological, and social factors in Ben Rogers's life.

© Cengage Learning

personality traits that produce such behavior are considered **ego-syntonic**. It is important for the practitioner to be attentive to the features of this personality disorder, as this characteristic way of relating will influence the helping relationship. Figure 11.1 illustrates the interactions of the biological, psychological, and social variables in Ben Rogers's life.

BEN ROGERS'S MULTIAXIAL DSM DIAGNOSIS IS AS FOLLOWS:

Axis I	V71.09 (No diagnosis)
Axis II	301.0 Paranoid Personality Disorder
Axis III	413.9 Angina Pectoris
	402.91 Hypertensive Heart Disease, with Congestive Heart Failure
Axis IV	Wife bedridden and in poor health
Axis V	GAF = 70 (on intake)

© Cengage Learning

SCHIZOID PERSONALITY DISORDER

Persons with **schizoid personality disorder** display a lifelong pattern of social withdrawal; that is, they tend to be introverted and remain isolated from others by choice. Often, their lifestyles are described as bland and solitary (Austrian, 2005), with very little human interaction. Eccentric, lonely, and ill at ease in the company of others—these are the typical ways of describing their behaviors. However, the individual with schizoid personality disorder does not exhibit the disordered thinking so apparent in those with schizophrenia. Gathering information about the individual's childhood may reveal a history of having been a loner, or of being sensitive to the teasing of other children during early school years.

The outstanding characteristics of schizoid personality disorder include:

- *No penchant for social relationships*—Although some with this disorder may form stable relationships with family members (or others), they lack the ability to *sustain* close relationships in general.
- *Little or no sex drive*—These individuals rarely date or marry; men are more likely to remain single than women (perhaps due to problems in initiating courtship).
- *Preference for solitary activities*—Typically, the individual retains low-level jobs requiring limited interpersonal contact (e.g., they might be employed as a night security worker, janitor, or computer technician). Interestingly, they often succeed at solitary jobs others might find difficult to endure.
- *Limited range of emotions*—These individuals have a confined range of emotions in social settings and are often described as cold and detached. The person appears indifferent to both compliments and/or criticisms, and takes little or no pleasure in life. His or her discomfort with relationships is noteworthy.

Do you know someone you consider a loner? Someone who would rather stay home to watch television than accept an invitation to join a party? Magnify this preference for isolation many times over, and you begin to grasp the impact on someone with a schizoid personality disorder. These individuals give the impression of being reserved, indifferent, or detached from everyday events. They lead quiet, distant, reclusive, and unsociable lives with remarkably little need or desire for emotional ties to others (Sadock, Sadock, & Ruiz, 2009). The person is characterized as eccentric, isolated, detached, or lonely. These are individuals who may daydream excessively and/or become attached to animals. They usually do not marry or even form long-lasting romantic relationships. Sadly, beneath the surface of their indifference there often exists a deep loneliness and a desire for close relationships.

PREVAILING PATTERN Knowledge about this disorder remains incomplete. However, over the past several decades research has pointed to the role of biological influences in combination with poor family socialization and early learning or relationship problems (Wolff, 2000). The onset typically occurs during early childhood years, and this disorder may affect between 1.7 percent to 4.9 percent of the general population in the United States (Lenzenweger, Lane, Loranger, & Kessler, 2007). Childhood shyness is reported as a warning sign of this diagnosis in adults (Phillips, Yen, & Gunderson, 2003).

Review of the individual's biopsychosocial history may reveal solitary interests and noncompetitive, remote, or secluded types of employment such as working the graveyard shift. Additionally, the person may not be able to express his or her anger directly. Perhaps because of their lack of close friendships and inability to form close connections with others, people with this diagnosis are prevalent among the homeless population (Rouff, 2000).

DIFFERENTIAL ASSESSMENT   Many similarities are shared between individuals with the schizoid personality disorder and those with paranoid personality disorder. This underscores the importance of collecting and carefully organizing data from the client's story in order to accurately formulate the competency-based assessment. What differentiates them is that those with the paranoid personality are more socially connected, and show a greater tendency to project their feelings onto others. Those with avoidant personality disorders are also characterized by isolation, but they show a strong desire to participate in activities, something that is absent in those with the schizoid personality disorder. Also absent are the oddities of perception, thought, behavior, and communication seen in schizotypal personality disorder (which is more similar to schizophrenia).

The following case discussion of Tyrone White, a young man brought to a mental health clinic by a concerned relative, illustrates what the life of someone with schizoid personality disorder might look like.

CASE | THE CASE OF TYRONE WHITE

His cousin, Sabrina, referred Tyrone White to the XYZ Mental Health Clinic. With concern in her voice, she said, "Tyrone is such a lonely boy and needs someone to talk to about his troubles."

As I entered the waiting room, the first thing I noticed about Tyrone was that he seemed oblivious to those around him. His face was hidden in a movie star magazine. I went over to greet him and invite him into my office. When Tyrone entered my office, it was quite apparent to me that he did not regard the appointment as much of an event. His physical appearance said the same thing; his shorts were torn, his T-shirt tattered, and he was barefoot. My initial impression was that he was dressed for washing his car instead of going to an office appointment.

When he sat down, Tyrone continued to leaf through his magazine. I waited for about a minute for him to say something, but he did not even seem to notice that I was sitting there. As our interview began, he continued looking at his magazine.

"Hello, I'm Marilyn Zide, one of the social workers here. I understand your name is Tyrone. Is that what other people call you?"

He nodded his head in agreement.

"Most people call me Marilyn, and if you'd like, you can also. May I call you Tyrone?"

He nodded affirmatively.

"How are you doing?" I asked.

"Fine," he replied.

"Do you know why you are here today?" I asked.

"Nuh huh," he replied. (I waited again.)

"Well, what I know about why you are here is that your cousin Sabrina is worried about you and thought you might need someone to talk to. What do you think?"

"I'da know," he replied, still reading his magazine.

I asked (trying again), "Did Sabrina tell you why she was so worried about you?"

"Nuh huh," he replied.

Most of my interview with Tyrone followed this same pattern, so I will try to summarize what transpired. If I asked Tyrone a direct question, he answered but did not elaborate or volunteer additional data. He sat quietly reading his magazine throughout the interview, and I noticed no evidence of abnormal or eccentric behavior. When asked, he was appropriately oriented to time, place, and date, and he denied any drug or alcohol use. I asked if he had ever heard any voices that other people did not hear or saw things that other people did not see. His usual reply was, "Nuh huh."

Tyrone is African American, and somehow through our convoluted conversation I was able to learn that he is 27 years old and the youngest of eight children. He revealed that his father died 10 years ago from some kind of surgical complications. He volunteered no other details. His mother recently remarried, and, he added, "I don't see my family very often." He lives alone in a small apartment in the same neighborhood as his cousin, Sabrina. He supports himself as a movie projectionist. Tyrone did not finish high school, and he has held this job for the past 7 years. He has gotten several raises over the years, and was even asked to become a manager, but Tyrone replied that he does not want to "attend all those meetings with all those people." He went on, "Besides, once you're in the union, nobody can push you into something you don't want. I like that!" He stated, "I like my job a lot because I can look at movie stars all day, and nobody bothers me." He considers himself to be an "average guy" and doesn't really want friends or family around because he "likes my own good company." Tyrone does not have a history of dating nor has he been sexually active.

In speaking with his cousin, Sabrina, after the session, she commented to me that Tyrone has always been "a loner," even when he was a child. Tyrone corroborated this, saying, "I was a street kid." He never spent much time with his family and does not remember very much time spent doing family things. Tyrone stated that the neighborhood kids "picked on me because I was so small," but he insists, "I never cared." In school, his progress was noted as "nothing special."

When asked, "What makes you happy?" he replied, "I just like being left alone." When the session was over, Tyrone stood up, carefully turned down the corner of the page he had been reading, tucked the magazine under his arm, and walked out of my office without a backward glance, never to return.

Advanced Clinical EP 2.1.10 (b) c

ASSESSMENT SUMMARY   Tyrone relates to the practitioner in a stilted but passively cooperative manner. His behavior challenges the practitioner's ability to assess how he copes. Although Tyrone responds to the interviewer, for example, he provides little information beyond superficial data, which further complicates the practitioner's task to determine what might be done to improve his circumstances. Tyrone seems more comfortable answering questions than initiating conversation. He appears to be poorly prepared for his session, reflected not only in his casual, almost shabby attire but also in his insistence that he is unaware of his cousin Sabrina's concerns about him. Tyrone appears to be oriented to his surroundings (time, place, and date) and denies hearing voices and seeing things that others do not.

Tyrone's affect during the interview, while seeming appropriate on the surface, has an underlying detached quality. Tyrone shows a greater interest in reading a magazine than in talking to the social worker. He denies having any problems, giving the impression that he would not seek counseling on his own.

Tyrone is in good health and denies alcohol or drug use. His family interactions are limited; his father died 10 years ago, and his mother recently remarried—he gave the impression she plays no part in Tyrone's current life. Tyrone's social context is constricted, and he has few environmental resources (he lives alone and professes he does not want friends or family around). His choice of job further limits any opportunity for developing social contacts.

Tyrone's biopsychosocial history reveals a pattern of being a loner from early childhood and being singled out for ridicule because of his small size while growing up. Although he is the youngest of eight children, very little is known about his older siblings. His academic performance was not exceptional, and he did not complete high school. Being left alone seems to be a source of pleasure for Tyrone; he is single, does not date, lives by himself, and works alone. Tyrone does not seem interested in job promotions, primarily because the additional responsibilities would require more interaction with others.

Tyrone White tends to turn inward, and he moves away from interpersonal connections with the outside world. This inner-directed reality does not exhibit the

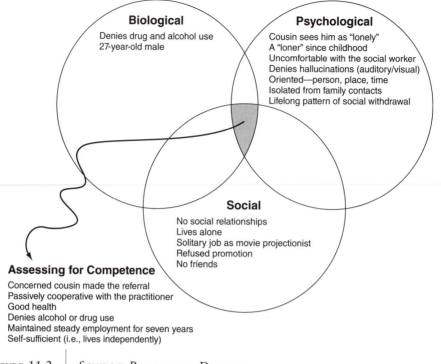

Biological
Denies drug and alcohol use
27-year-old male

Psychological
Cousin sees him as "lonely"
A "loner" since childhood
Uncomfortable with the social worker
Denies hallucinations (auditory/visual)
Oriented—person, place, time
Isolated from family contacts
Lifelong pattern of social withdrawal

Social
No social relationships
Lives alone
Solitary job as movie projectionist
Refused promotion
No friends

Assessing for Competence
Concerned cousin made the referral
Passively cooperative with the practitioner
Good health
Denies alcohol or drug use
Maintained steady employment for seven years
Self-sufficient (i.e., lives independently)

FIGURE 11.2 | SCHIZOID PERSONALITY DISORDER

The interactions of the biological, psychological, and social factors in Tyrone White's life.

© Cengage Learning

disordered pattern of thinking commonly associated with those who have schizophrenia. As demonstrated in the interview, he has a constricted emotional range—Tyrone is a man who is unsociable, distant, indifferent, and reclusive. Based on the way he approaches interpersonal relationships, a practitioner can expect him to relate more like an observer rather than an active participant in the therapeutic relationship.

The medical model might accentuate the negatives in looking at Tyrone's behavior. The competency-based assessment pays attention to the associations between behaviors and the various positive external factors. (Refer to Figure 11.2 for the interactions of the biological, psychological, and social variables in Tyrone White's life.) Tyrone has worked steadily for the past 7 years; he is self-sufficient; he pays his own rent; he receives routine raises; and he has been offered opportunities for job advancement. Although Tyrone is socially isolated, his cousin Sabrina seems concerned enough to bring him to the clinic for help. And somehow she got his cooperation in coming.

TYRONE WHITE'S MULTIAXIAL DSM DIAGNOSIS IS AS FOLLOWS:

AXIS I	V71.09 (NO DIAGNOSIS)
Axis II	301.20 Schizoid Personality Disorder
Axis III	None
Axis IV	None
Axis V	GAF = 65 (highest level past year)

© Cengage Learning

SCHIZOTYPAL PERSONALITY DISORDER

Individuals with **schizotypal personality disorder** exhibit strikingly odd or strange mannerisms in addition to having a very active fantasy life. This may include **magical thinking** (an irrational belief that one has powers that defy laws of nature and physics and thus can cause or prevent events), **illusions** (perceptual disturbances in which things appear differently from what they actually are in reality), **derealization** (loss of one's sense of reality in the external world), and **ideas of reference** (in which everything everyone else does somehow relates back to them). Interpersonally, they are described as loners, much like Tyrone White, who was described in the previous vignette and diagnosed with a schizoid personality disorder. However, their solitary pursuits and social isolation may stem from strained social anxiety that does not diminish with familiarity.

The major characteristics of schizotypal personality disorder are summarized as follows:

- *Extreme discomfort in social relationships*—even when people are familiar to them. They are rarely able to form intimate relationships, and it is usually impossible for them to sustain employment that requires extended social contact. When left alone, they may be able to perform simple tasks; however, the peculiarities of their thoughts often sidetrack them.
- *Restricted close relationships*—They rarely have close friends or confidants.
- *Odd appearance and thinking*—They have unusual perceptual experiences, such as illusions and sensing the presence of a force or person not actually there. Generally described as being unkempt, they also show unusual mannerisms or may talk to themselves (without loosening of association). Their speech is characterized by vagueness, digressions, excessive abstractions, limited vocabulary, or an unusual pattern of words.
- *Paranoid ideas*—They are very suspicious and believe others are talking about them; however, their affect is more likely to be characterized as anxious rather than hostile. They may perceive references to themselves in others' conversations.

Delineation of schizotypal personality disorder in the DSM evolved from attempts to clarify the boundary between schizophrenia and borderline personality disorder. Schizotypal personality disorder is associated with schizophrenia in a number of important ways. Individuals with schizotypal personality disorder experience subtle distortions of their environment similar to those experienced by individuals with schizophrenia, but the latter have the fully developed syndrome that includes hallucinations or delusions and loss of contact with reality. Under stress, individuals with schizotypal personality disorder may decompensate and display psychotic symptoms, but these lapses are usually of brief duration. In severe instances, **anhedonia** (inability to experience pleasure) and severe depression may also be present.

The notion that there is a relationship between schizotypal personality disorder and schizophrenia arises in part from how people with these two disorders behave. For example, symptoms such as ideas of reference, illusions, and paranoid thinking are similar, yet those with schizotypal personality disorder have somewhat better interpersonal skills and are more connected to their social environment (Gabbard,

2001). Ongoing research into these two disorders seems to support a genetic component in each disorder. Several theorists suggest that individuals with a diagnosis of schizotypal personality can be influenced by their environment (Barlow & Durand, 2012). However, there is growing support for the biological theories of schizotypal personality disorder (Voglmaier et al., 2000).

From an early age, individuals with schizotypal personality disorder are unable to have long-lasting interpersonal relationships, which leave them severely isolated and reduce their capacity for ever maintaining connections with others. They often feel anxious with strangers and cannot banter or make small talk. They exhibit distortions in their thinking, eccentric perceptions, and magical thinking, which make them appear unusual or odd to others. Often, these individuals manifest unusual perceptual experiences, such as feeling as if another person is in the room when they are in fact alone. Their behavior is influenced by associated odd beliefs or by magical thinking inconsistent with cultural norms, including superstitions and belief in telepathy. Frequently, they believe they have special powers of thought and insight.

PREVAILING PATTERN   Schizotypal personality disorder occurs in approximately 0.6 percent to 3.3 percent of the general population (Lenzenweger, Lane, Loranger, & Kessler, 2007). Practitioners need to thoroughly explore the client's family history for evidence of schizophrenia because of the greater incidence of schizotypal personality disorder found among first-degree biological relatives of people with schizophrenia.

EP 2.1.10
(b) a

DIFFERENTIAL ASSESSMENT   Oddities in behavior, thinking, perception, and communication (in addition to a strong family history of schizophrenia) distinguish those individuals with schizotypal personality disorders from the general population as well as from those with other personality disorders. In addition, these individuals exhibit two sets of qualities: (1) they experience intense discomfort in interpersonal relationships and an impaired ability to form close relationships, and (2) they often manifest cognitive or perceptual distortions, and eccentric behavior.

Tyrone White, as described in the earlier vignette, is distant from others and is pictured as a loner. Unlike those individuals with schizophrenia, Tyrone has not lost total contact with reality. Ben Rogers, someone with a paranoid personality disorder, is characterized as hostile and suspicious, whereas Tyrone's affect is typified as anxious. This distinction underscores the importance of collecting and organizing client data in order to interpret the accurate diagnosis. Schizotypal personality disorder can be distinguished from schizophrenia by the absence of psychosis (but, if psychotic symptoms are present, they are brief and fragmentary). The following case describes Juan Enrique Martinez, who has been assessed with schizotypal personality disorder.

CASE | THE CASE OF JUAN ENRIQUE MARTINEZ

Juan Enrique Martinez, a 35-year-old single (never married) Mexican-American man, has been urged to attend our community mental health center's activities program by his mother. Mrs. Martinez seems somewhat older than her stated age of 58 and looks really tired. She sounds worried as she tells the social worker that her son "just needs a little help making friends."

When the social worker asks for more details, Mrs. Martinez adds that Juan has had a lifelong pattern of social isolation. She can't remember a time when her son had some "real" friends—he usually spends hours "doing nothing."

Mrs. Martinez says it all started when Juan was about 13, and he lost interest "in just about everything." During that time, she took him to her parish priest, who assured her, "Juan will grow out of it; it's just a stage he's going through."

"Well, he never grew out of it," Mrs. Martinez adds ruefully. "He hasn't been able to keep a bunch of jobs, including his last one as a postal worker." Apparently, Juan did not show up for work on multiple occasions and could not deal with the close public contact. She stated, "I'm worried that Juan will lose his room in the boarding house because he has no way to pay the rent now ... and he was picked up by the Metro Dade police. They charged him with disorderly conduct and said he was drinking. I know my son and he is not a drinker."

Mrs. Martinez confides that Juan's appearance is becoming "more strange." When asked to explain what she means, she says, "He's been getting a lot of tattoos, and now he's talking about wanting to get some body piercing done." She frowns, looks momentarily distracted, and then asks for the social worker's opinion about the health risks associated with body piercing. Mrs. Martinez admits that her main concern—the real reason she wanted Juan to come to the mental health center was because "he is acting really weird." By that she means he believes he

can sense forces around him. "He is so sure these forces exist and that they are somehow against him," Mrs. Martinez relates. She also indicates that Juan is highly suspicious about other people. "These suspicious thoughts are what caused Juan's problems in his last job—but he also does not get along with people he has known for years."

Mrs. Martinez sighs heavily and goes on to say that it is harder and harder for her to communicate with her son. She adds, "I worry that he will turn out to be just like my brother, Lorenzo, who was sent away to a mental hospital when he was 17. Everybody thought he was crazy. He used to hear voices and see things that no one else did. I remember during one visit that the doctor wanted me to convince Lorenzo to take his medicine. I asked the doctor what this medicine was for and the doctor looked at me so surprised. He told me, 'I thought you knew! Lorenzo is schizophrenic.'" Mrs. Martinez begins to cry, "I don't want that to happen to my little Juan."

When the social worker meets with Juan, he is distant and conveys a high level of distrust. He describes in intricate detail his somewhat uneventful everyday life. He tells the practitioner that he really doesn't like people and he does not want to join any group here at the center where he will have to "talk to people." Juan then stands up, and with an almost forced air of bravado, walks out of the office saying, "If my mother wants to talk, she can join your group."

Advanced Clinical EP 2.1.10 (b) c

ASSESSMENT SUMMARY Juan's interpersonal pattern of relating shows that he is unable to form relationships or respond to others in a meaningful way. His sense of "forces" around him, suspiciousness, and paranoia keep him socially isolated. The practitioner's conversation with Juan is difficult because of his peculiar communication style; for instance, he goes into intricate detail about his day, which in reality was uneventful. Although his communication (and his appearance) can be characterized as "odd" and his perception of his social environment is subtly distorted, Juan does not show evidence of hallucinations or delusions characteristic of those with schizophrenia. Mrs. Martinez's concerns were clear to the social worker and seem to have increased over time. Unfortunately (but not surprisingly), Juan is indifferent to his mother's worries.

Despite a close community, Juan is withdrawn from his social environment, and his recent job loss has further increased his isolation. In this case illustration, his isolation can be traced back to early adolescence, a time when peer influence is important—and yet it was during this period that Juan began to lose interest "in just about everything" according to his mother. She characterizes him now as a socially isolated young man. Participation in the community mental health center's activities group might decrease Juan's social isolation, but his abrupt departure from the interview suggests this may be a frightening prospect for him. Mrs. Martinez

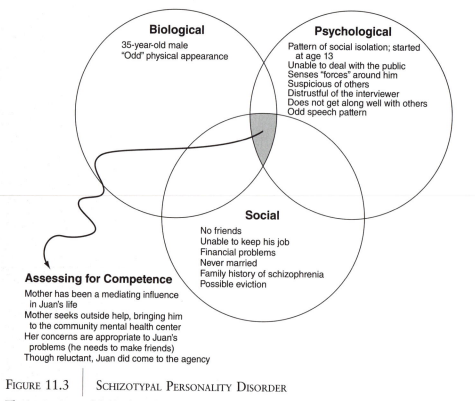

Biological
35-year-old male
"Odd" physical appearance

Psychological
Pattern of social isolation; started
   at age 13
Unable to deal with the public
Senses "forces" around him
Suspicious of others
Distrustful of the interviewer
Does not get along well with others
Odd speech pattern

Social
No friends
Unable to keep his job
Financial problems
Never married
Family history of schizophrenia
Possible eviction

Assessing for Competence
Mother has been a mediating influence
   in Juan's life
Mother seeks outside help, bringing him
   to the community mental health center
Her concerns are appropriate to Juan's
   problems (he needs to make friends)
Though reluctant, Juan did come to the agency

FIGURE 11.3 | SCHIZOTYPAL PERSONALITY DISORDER

The interactions of the biological, psychological, and social factors in Juan Enrique Martinez's life.

© Cengage Learning

points out that Juan tends to wander around doing nothing, and, although Juan's behaviors and appearance might be unusual, they are not provocative.

The practitioner's challenge is to assess how Juan copes in order to reinforce and improve his adaptation to life situations, circumstances, and events. The involvement of significant others, for example, is important. As in Juan's situation, this is what led him to the mental health center. Juan's mother has been a mediating influence in his social environment as seen in the biological, psychological, and social influences in his life (refer to Figure 11.3). For example, she is the person in his social environment who brings him to the center for help with socialization or to make friends. Though reluctant, Juan did come into the agency, and perhaps with time he would feel more comfortable participating in activities there.

JUAN ENRIQUE MARTINEZ'S MULTIAXIAL DSM DIAGNOSIS IS AS FOLLOWS:

Axis I	303.00 Rule Out Alcohol Intoxication
Axis II	301.22 Schizotypal Personality Disorder
Axis III	None
Axis IV	Housing problems
	Financial problems
	Unemployment
Axis V	GAF = 60 (at intake)

© Cengage Learning

CLUSTER B: EMOTIONAL, DRAMATIC, OR ERRATIC

NARCISSISTIC PERSONALITY DISORDER

Narcissistic disorder is not recognized around the world but may be a reflection of our modern Western culture that displays a number of criteria reflective of the narcissistic personality disorder; in particular, it is seen in a society that is self-centered, materialistic, and less centered on familial or interpersonal bonds (Foster, Campbell, & Twenge, 2003). A heightened sense of self-importance and unrealistic, inflated self-worth, often disguising an underlying fragile sense of self, characterize the individual with **narcissistic personality disorder**. As the name implies, individuals with this personality disorder tend to be self-absorbed, self-important, and grandiose. They see themselves as unique and special, deserving of extraordinary treatment. Their sense of entitlement is striking. Others in their social environment might describe them as arrogant and boastful. The major characteristics of this disorder include:

- *Feelings of grandiosity*—These individuals not only feel superior to others, but they also believe they are unique and special. They are convinced they are entitled to "special handling" just because of who they are. Although they may envy others, their belief is that others envy them even more. Their accomplishments, physical attributes, and talents are often self-exaggerated. They easily criticize others, but have a very difficult time receiving criticism.
- *Constant desire or need for admiration*—The person invariably seeks out adulation, admiration, and compliments from others. They are overly sensitive to what others think about them.
- *Lack of empathy for others*—The individual has good social skills, especially when it comes to initiating relationships with others. They can be very charming in securing others' admiration, but, because they are so focused on themselves, they often are incapable of empathizing with others. Relationships tend to wear very thin over time. As ultrasensitive as they are about their own feelings, they have poor insight regarding the emotional needs of others, often feigning empathy when none exists.
- *"Fantasy world" preoccupation*—These individuals have an active fantasy life, and maintain that they experience the best of everything, even when this is not true. For example, a narcissist might own a car just short of making it to the junk yard, but he or she bills it a classic.
- *Possess overly high expectations*—If the person does not attain the unrealistic goals they have set for themselves, they will react with a strong sense of failure that brings about feelings of shame and worthlessness.

Most of us know people who think very highly of themselves, perhaps even a little beyond their actual abilities. However, individuals with narcissistic personality disorder possess this tendency to extremes. They exhibit an exaggerated sense of self-importance and a tremendous preoccupation with gaining attention from others. They have a lifelong pattern of needing admiration, and truly believe they are unique and special. The person considers their accomplishments to be far greater than they are in reality.

Essential features include "a pervasive pattern of grandiosity, a need for admiration, and a lack of empathy that begins by early adulthood and is present in a variety of contexts" (American Psychiatric Association, 2000, p. 714). They tend to have a very rich inner life, entertaining fantasies of masterminding their next venture, which will of course bring them fame and fortune. Interpersonal exploitation is very common among people with narcissistic personality disorder. Although this feature is not part of the DSM criteria, underneath this individual's grandiosity and excessive need for admiration is a very vulnerable person with a fragile sense of self-esteem.

PREVAILING PATTERN   This personality disorder is somewhat uncommon; it occurs in less than 1 percent of the general population (Trull, Jahng, Tomko, Wood, & Sher, 2010). Because of the individual's flair for being the center of attention, this is the kind of client who will be easily remembered. Information about this disorder's etiology is somewhat limited, but it does appear more frequently in males than in females (Lynam & Widiger, 2007). The disorder has a tendency to be chronic and is difficult to treat because the individuals must consistently struggle with looking at the impact of their behavior or its interplay with their life experiences. The person is prone to bouts of depression, handles the aging process poorly, and is more vulnerable to midlife crises than others.

The following case illustrates the major features of someone with a narcissistic personality disorder.

CASE | THE CASE OF LAWRENCE SHULL

"Hello, is this Dr. Susan Gray?" a voice on the telephone asked.

"Why, yes," I replied. "Can I help you?"

"Well, you don't know me, but my name is Lawrence Shull, and I've just moved to South Florida from New York."

"So how did you come across my name, Mr. Shull?" I asked.

"Well, first I called the Dade County Mental Health Association, then I checked with the National Association of Social Workers, then I went to *Who's Who of Social Work Digest*, and, finally, I asked several local leaders 'Who is the best social worker in town?' That's how I got your name."

"That's very flattering, Mr. Shull," I replied. "What can I do for you?"

"Well, I want to make an appointment," he responded.

Our session took place three days later. Mr. Shull presented himself as a very refined-looking gentleman. He was extremely well groomed, and what I would consider a natty dresser. Although it was a typically warm tropical day, he wore a brown suit, matching tie, and expensive-looking dress shoes. He confessed to me that he is 55 years old but added, with a wink, "I had a little surgical help from the 'top doc' in Manhattan. Everybody says I look 10 years younger." He is 6 feet tall, 200 pounds, and looks as if he works out and takes extremely good care of himself. His nails are buffed and manicured, and he had not a hair out of place. Although he had said he is new to the South Florida area, he sported a bronzed, suntanned appearance. He looked as if he spent a lot of time at the beach.

After our initial greeting and when we were settled, I asked, "What brings you here, Mr. Shull?"

He responded saying, "Please call me Lawrence, and by the way, may I call you Susan?" (I nodded yes.) "Well Susan, dear, it's quite a long and involved story, but the bottom line is: I'm quite miffed at having to relocate because of my job. You see, I'm an underwriter for a very well-known national tire chain. The problems all started when one of the managers there got jealous of my productivity level. You see, I sold lots of tires, shock absorbers, and brakes … actually, I sold more than all the other service writers put together." He was silent for a moment, and I prompted him to continue.

"The store manager is such a jerk! No, he's more than a jerk! He's a nitwit. He doesn't know how to run a business. I've been on the job for 3 months, and I already know more than he does. I can't believe he disapproved of my selling style. Me! I was the best they ever had. He told me that I was unfair to the rest of the guys because I made deals for prices the store wouldn't support and that customers had problems with my enthusiasm for selling." Mr. Shull's face was becoming flushed. He continued, "Can you believe that! I was too enthusiastic?" (He shook his head slowly.) "They are just envious of my success. So it was suggested I relocate to South Florida. I took a big salary hit, and was demoted to, get this, [chuckling] an assistant service writer." He paused and then added, "You know Susan, they'll be sorry when I end up being the CEO and owning the damn company. They can't stop me!"

Farther along in our discussion, Mr. Shull abruptly stated that he broke up with his girlfriend of 6 months.

"She was very dependent on me, and I don't need that extra baggage to carry around. I need someone who is my intellectual equal, someone who complements me," he stated. "I'm still looking for the right woman. So far, nobody's been able to meet my needs." Mr. Shull stopped talking for a moment, smiled at me, and continued, "You know Susan, I just realized all I've been talking about is me, me, me, and me. Why don't you tell me what you think about me and my problems? Do you think you can see me five times a week?"

When our session was over, I scheduled another appointment for Mr. Shull for the following week.

Advanced Clinical EP 2.1.10 (b) c

ASSESSMENT SUMMARY   Narcissistic personality disorder often coexists with antisocial, histrionic, and borderline personality disorders, thus complicating the process of assessment. Lawrence Shull exhibits less anxiety and his life is less chaotic than someone with borderline personality characteristics. His presentation of the symptoms of narcissistic personality disorder is also different from those with antisocial personality disorder. People with an antisocial personality disorder behave somewhat differently; in addition to being arrogant, they almost always exploit others for financial power or material gain, tend toward impulsive behavior and alcohol or other substance abuse (Laub & Vaillant, 2000), and tend to have frequent problems with law enforcement. For Lawrence Shull, financial gain is not considered a key issue. Instead, he is forced to relocate and take a cut in pay, which he mentions only in passing, but continues to nurse the idea of being the company's next CEO. His sense of personal glory and entitlement is the central focus of his life. People who have a histrionic personality disorder are also seen as self-absorbed and eager to be the center of attention, but they are usually more willing to connect with others. This contrasts with Lawrence Shull, who apparently without a backward glance abruptly ended a 6-month relationship with his girlfriend. Another complication in assessment of histrionic versus narcissistic personality disorder is that individuals with histrionic personality disorders show qualities of exhibitionism and interpersonal manipulativeness very similar to those associated with narcissistic personalities.

Those with an obsessive-compulsive personality disorder also complicate the assessment process for narcissistic disorder. In both types of clients, the practitioner sees evidence of an air of superiority and marked condescension toward others masking very vulnerable, fragile individuals underneath. The difference between the two lies in the methods used to express contempt or hostility. The person with a narcissistic personality disorder does not settle for smugness and a superior attitude, but rather gravitates toward malicious (passive-aggressive) counterattacks in response to any criticism (real or perceived) that is directed toward him or her

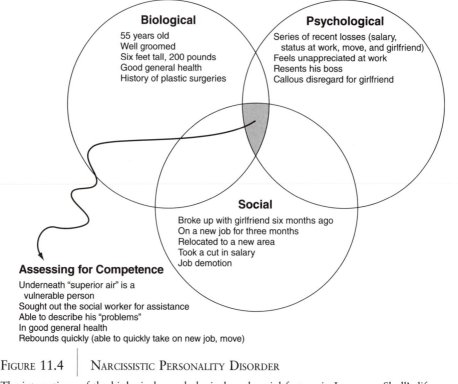

Biological

55 years old
Well groomed
Six feet tall, 200 pounds
Good general health
History of plastic surgeries

Psychological

Series of recent losses (salary,
  status at work, move, and girlfriend)
Feels unappreciated at work
Resents his boss
Callous disregard for girlfriend

Social

Broke up with girlfriend six months ago
On a new job for three months
Relocated to a new area
Took a cut in salary
Job demotion

Assessing for Competence

Underneath "superior air" is a
  vulnerable person
Sought out the social worker for assistance
Able to describe his "problems"
In good general health
Rebounds quickly (able to quickly take on new job, move)

FIGURE 11.4 | NARCISSISTIC PERSONALITY DISORDER

The interactions of the biological, psychological, and social factors in Lawrence Shull's life.

© Cengage Learning

(Miller, Campbell, & Pilkonis, 2007). Lawrence Shull, for instance, undercut the prices of his coworkers at the tire company in order to succeed, and then he perceived his boss as being envious of his success.

Understanding all of the various aspects of Lawrence Shull's functioning helps to provide a more complete clinical picture and to identify his areas of competency—in particular, how Lawrence copes so that the practitioner has a starting place to reinforce and improve his adaptation to life situations, circumstances, and events (see Figure 11.4). Within this framework, the difficulties that he brings to the interview are related to how he approaches problem solving. However, he is articulate in describing his problems and seeks out the social worker on his own. He also seems to have resilience (the ability to bounce back) despite his job demotion (Gitterman, 2001).

LAWRENCE SHULL'S MULTIAXIAL DSM DIAGNOSIS IS AS FOLLOWS:

Axis I	V71.09 (No diagnosis)
Axis II	301.81 Narcissistic Personality Disorder
Axis III	None
Axis IV	Employment problems
Axis V	GAF = 80 (at intake)

© Cengage Learning

HISTRIONIC PERSONALITY DISORDER

An individual with histrionic personality disorder is not to be confused with those persons whose behavior can be characterized as being "hysterical"; the person with a histrionic personality has far greater problems relating to others. The individual with **histrionic personality disorder** is often described as colorful, dramatic, extroverted, excitable, and emotional. Underneath this flamboyant presentation is a deep-seated inability to maintain strong, reciprocal, and long-lasting friendships. These individuals attempt to acquire attention in inexplicable and unusual ways. A basic characteristic is a pattern of extreme attention seeking and highly expressive emotions. They tend to incessantly involve others in their life drama, while keeping themselves at the center of attention. Others frequently describe them as superficial, disingenuous, and unconvincing. Although all of these characteristics are (mercifully) not found in everyone with histrionic personality disorder, they do serve as a means for assembling an initial basis for making an assessment. The major characteristics of histrionic personality disorder include:

- *Excessive emotionality*—These individuals often have rapid shifts of emotion that may seem artificial to others. They are also quite manipulative, using strong emotional outbursts to get their own way.
- *Attention-seeking behavior*—They intensely crave attention from others and feel uncomfortable when they are not the center of attention. These individuals dress in extravagant, lavish, and provocative styles, and women especially use makeup, hairstyles, and clothes to attract further attention.
- *Easily influenced and susceptible*—These individuals are very impressionable, become enthusiastic about the latest fads, and base their convictions on very little evidence.
- *Self-centered/self-absorbed*—They tend to be unusually vain and self-absorbed. Other people barely register as blips on their radar. Relationships with others are apt to be superficial, as evidenced by speech and emotional expression that lack genuine feeling or concern.
- *Concerns with presentation*—The individual with a histrionic personality may change his or her presentation depending upon the circumstances as they attempt to engage whoever is present.

EP 2.1.4 a

These individuals have a long-standing pattern of excessive emotionality and attention seeking, which seeps into most areas of their lives. They are often described as being provocative and sexually seductive. They are always overly concerned with their physical attractiveness. These features are characteristic of the American culture's stereotypical female and may lead to over-diagnosis of histrionic disorder among women (Sprock, 2000). When formulating the competency-based assessment, it is important for the practitioner to recognize the extent to which culture plays a role, sometimes further oppressing or marginalizing the client. Consider histrionic disorder only if the person's emotional expression is excessive within her cultural group and causes distress or impairment (Anderson, Sankis, & Widiger, 2001). The need for approval can be so excessive at times that they will call attention to themselves through their speech, dress, behavior, and extreme emotions. Of those with histrionic personality disorder, the women tend to dress and act seductively, whereas the men act tough or macho. Relationships (in both genders) are inclined to be stormy and short-lived, as the person becomes easily bored with others; conversely, others may become fed up with *their* behavior and leave. These individuals rarely maintain stable, enduring, and meaningful relationships. They are often described as shallow, lacking in substance, and incapable of having reciprocal, meaningful relationships with others.

PREVAILING PATTERN   This is a lifelong pattern of behavior, although symptoms generally tend to be modulated by the aging process. It remains unclear whether these individuals tend to burn out due to the amount of energy required to maintain their character throughout the years (Douglas, Vincent, & Edens, 2006). What we do know is that the personality disorders originate in childhood and continue into the adult years, drawing the attention of others (Cloninger & Svakic, 2009). When researchers have been able to follow a person's progress over the years, problems associated with the disorder continue (Ferguson, 2010). These are the individuals who may get into trouble with the law, abuse substances, and act promiscuously.

EP 2.1.10
(b) a

DIFFERENTIAL ASSESSMENT   Making the distinction between histrionic and borderline personality disorders is admittedly difficult. This highlights the practitioner's task of collecting, organizing, and carefully interpreting data from the client's story. Both disorders may be assessed for the same individual, but the two should be noted separately. Histrionic traits do occur in a number of other personality disorders, and the overlap has caused some to question whether the histrionic personality disorder should be reclassified in the DSM-5 (Bakkevig & Karterud, 2010). However, there are certain specific differential points that help clarify making a correct assessment:

- Individuals with a narcissistic personality may be quite self-aggrandizing, constantly searching for praise, and needing to be the center of attention—but they usually lack the intense emotion seen in histrionic individuals.
- Individuals with borderline personality may be characterized as flamboyant and self-destructive; however, they have an enduring sense of emptiness and loneliness. In contrast, histrionic individuals are seen as shallow and lacking substance.
- Those with antisocial personality disorder tend to be highly impulsive, as are the histrionic; however, histrionic individuals become dependent or deeply attached to others, unlike the antisocial person.

The following case illustrates many of the features of someone with histrionic personality disorder.

| CASE | THE CASE OF MS. TAMIKA BROWN |

During a routine physical examination, Tamika Brown, a 43-year-old African American single parent, suddenly started crying and blurted out to her doctor that she was thinking about committing suicide. She said she had been playing with a razor and making marks on her arms. Tamika stated that she used to do this when she was a teenager to get her mother's attention. The physician immediately made an emergency referral to a nearby county mental health center.

The social worker at the center noted Ms. Brown's appearance as soon as she walked in. She was almost six feet tall and had what could be considered a naturally graceful style, but the most striking thing was Ms. Brown's unusual hair. It was braided but had what looked like spikes accentuating her forehead and was partially shaved in the back. Her clothes could be characterized as dramatic; everything was black, accented with animal prints, and extremely tight fitting. She wore about a dozen gold bracelets on each arm and a large, heavy gold chain around her neck. The first three or four buttons of her shirt were left unbuttoned, revealing her bra (also black) and showing extensive cleavage. Her overall appearance could best be described as distracting. The social worker asked why she had been referred for an evaluation.

Ms. Brown laughed and said, "I know something about psychotherapy, and I'm hoping to find a special therapist who understands me and will really help me. I promise to be your most interesting patient. You know, [chuckling] been there, done that?"

During the interview, Ms. Brown described a tortured childhood that included an abusive alcoholic father, an absent mother, and being picked on by other children for being a "fat butt." When she became an adolescent she lost weight and began a dedicated workout regimen. Boys began to be attracted to her, but she completely ignored them. Instead, she continued to exercise and study hard in school so she could "get out" of the neighborhood and as far away as possible from her family.

Tamika confided that she wants to be a model. In her early 20s, she had breast implants, lip augmentation, and surgical tightening of the buttock muscles to further accentuate her figure. Although she is currently working, the nature of her job is somewhat vague and mysterious. She happened to bring along her portfolio and offered to show it to the social worker. Tamika's professional photo book included several seductive poses in bikini bathing suits, lingerie, and semi-nude shots. As she put her portfolio away, she explained that she belongs to a gym where some very famous movie and television stars are also members. She stated, "It's just a matter of time until I get discovered. My body is way better than some of those cows," she sneered. "I can't believe they still haven't asked me to work out with them. Well, I know it's because they are jealous. They can't compete with me."

Tamika makes Herculean efforts to be seen around the hot spots in town. She dines in only the trendiest South Beach restaurants, always arriving in a super-deluxe stretch limousine. She makes a dramatic entrance because she loves to wear the most revealing clothes she can find. "If ya got, flaunt it!" she says as she bobbles her head and grins. The South Beach location is important to her because that's the area known for attracting celebrities. Tamika went on to say that she routinely sends photographs of herself doing the town "big time" to several of the local newspapers.

When asked about the other people in her life, Tamika recounted multiple relationships that were short-lived and unsatisfying to her. She concluded, "I don't have a boyfriend right now. I dumped the last one, Geoffrey Halesander, 'cause he was so shallow—and besides, he didn't meet any of my needs. I like to be taken out and pampered, but all he wanted to do was sit around the house and watch television. How boring!"

The social worker's primary objective as the session ends is to assess the potential of Ms. Brown's suicidal ideation.

Advanced Clinical EP 2.1.10 (b) c

ASSESSMENT SUMMARY   People with histrionic personality disorder are differentiated from the other personality disorders by their attention-seeking behaviors. Tamika Brown reflects this characteristic way of relating to her social environment by being overly dramatic in her emotional displays, her attempts to be the center of attention, and her inability to be ignored. She is self-centered and appears unable to develop any degree of intimacy. Tamika has no insight about what went wrong with Geoffrey Halesander, her former boyfriend. In actuality, her ability to connect in a meaningful way had always been short-lived. As a consequence of her very strong need to be the center of attention, Tamika has few enduring friendships.

Tamika initially presented herself to the practitioner as an engaging, yet highly emotional, woman. Upon closer examination, it became apparent that those emotions were shallow, and she lacks the ability to sustain meaningful relationships. When the practitioner began the interview, Tamika connected readily and seemed

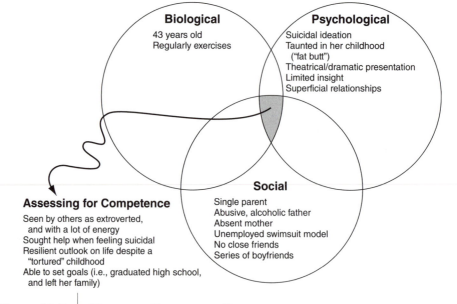

Biological
43 years old
Regularly exercises

Psychological
Suicidal ideation
Taunted in her childhood
   ("fat butt")
Theatrical/dramatic presentation
Limited insight
Superficial relationships

Assessing for Competence
Seen by others as extroverted,
   and with a lot of energy
Sought help when feeling suicidal
Resilient outlook on life despite a
   "tortured" childhood
Able to set goals (i.e., graduated high school,
   and left her family)

Social
Single parent
Abusive, alcoholic father
Absent mother
Unemployed swimsuit model
No close friends
Series of boyfriends

FIGURE 11.5 | HISTRIONIC PERSONALITY DISORDER

The interactions of the biological, psychological, and social factors in Tamika Brown's life.

© Cengage Learning

eager to please with her responses. However, she was not in touch with her real feelings and was very vague about the details of her suicide attempt.

Using the competency-based model enables the practitioner to work collaboratively with Tamika in order to mobilize her strengths and coping abilities, locate resources, and begin to explore opportunities within her environment that may help pave the way for this client to achieve success (refer to Figure 11.5). Despite a miserable childhood with an abusive, alcoholic father, she maintains a resilient outlook on life and has set some realistic future goals for herself. Tamika reports that she does not abuse drugs or alcohol.

TAMIKA BROWN'S MULTIAXIAL DSM DIAGNOSIS IS AS FOLLOWS:

Axis I	V71.09 (No diagnosis)
Axis II	301.50 Histrionic Personality Disorder
Axis III	None
Axis IV	None
Axis V	GAF = 50 (at initial appointment)

© Cengage Learning

ANTISOCIAL PERSONALITY DISORDER

EP 2.1.7 a

The person with **antisocial personality disorder** is characterized by continual asocial or criminal acts, but being antisocial is not synonymous with criminality. These individuals tend to have a long and involved history of lying, theft, substance abuse, illegal activities, rejection of social norms, and lack of remorse for any hurtful actions directed toward others. These behaviors initially surface in childhood and intensify during adolescence. It is important to note the developmental nature of antisocial behavior in that many adults with antisocial personality disorder had the diagnosis of a conduct disorder as children (Salekin, 2006). Clearly, this behavioral pattern underscores the value of using the competency-based assessment framework to guide the assessment process. Rather than to solely focus on the negative behavioral characteristic, the competency-based assessment includes a parallel exploration of strengths and resources.

Because antisocial personality disorder results in a variety of problems with law enforcement, the legal system, and within families, it has been the subject of more clinical interest and research than any other personality disorder. Unfortunately, the studies have revealed that the future is pessimistic for those with antisocial personality disorder (Meloy, 2001).

The essential features of this disorder include a pervasive pattern of disregard for and violation of the rights of others, usually beginning in earnest after the age of 15, with evidence of conduct disorder before age 15 (American Psychiatric Association, 2000). As youngsters, they often acquire a reputation in the neighborhood for being a bully toward younger children and for being cruel toward animals. Overall, these are individuals who behave in ways that most of us would find unacceptable, such as stealing from friends and family or being deceitful, irresponsible, and impulsive (DeBrito & Hodgkins, 2009). As youngsters, these individuals appear out of control, and most efforts to discipline them have little or no lasting effect. Nothing seems to have an impact on them or be able to touch them. They remain unmoved by any kindness shown, steal and destroy property for the pleasure of it, and habitually lie even when telling the truth is just as convenient. Although many of these individuals have a childhood marked by incorrigibility, school problems, and/or running away from home, there are a number of complex biological, psychological, and cultural factors that combine in intricate ways for someone to develop antisocial personality disorder (Gelhorn, Sakai, Price, & Crowley, 2007). Therefore it is important for practitioners to reserve this assessment for individuals who are over the age of 18 and who have a history of conduct disorder before the age of 15 (American Psychiatric Association, 2000; Meloy, 2001). The major characteristics of antisocial personality disorder include:

- *Lack of remorse or empathy*—These individuals have no feelings or remorse for those they harm. They rationalize reasons for hurting or taking advantage of others (e.g., "they should have known better than to trust me"), and often blame the victim for making them act in a harmful manner because they consider themselves smart enough to "get away with it."
- *Defiance*—They do not feel they should obey societal norms or laws, instead favoring making their own rules.
- *Self-absorbed*—They are most often concerned with their own needs, wants, and desires, and do not allow anyone or anything to get in the way of getting what they want.
- *Irresponsible*—Those with antisocial personality disorder have problems fulfilling commitments such as those to family and employers, and may have difficulty meeting financial obligations. Their marriages tend to be troubled, violent, and short-lived. Being faithful in a relationship whether there is a

marriage or not is a matter of convenience, and children are often viewed as being a burden.

- *Deceitful*—Being truthful is also considered a matter of convenience; if a lie proves more useful, then that is what will be used. These individuals have no qualms about using different aliases, changing occupations, and moving from location to location—especially if they are trying to elude the law. They are excellent at running confidence schemes for their own profit, pleasure, or power.
- *Irritable and aggressive*—Reckless, violent, and cruel behavior is common among those who are antisocial. They are irritable when dealing with authority but seem comfortable using aggression against others. Frequently they are involved in physical assaults and confrontations; for example, there is a high incidence of reported domestic violence and child abuse, showing little or no concern for the safety of themselves or others.

A veneer of charm and a smooth and ingratiating seductiveness may mask the antisocial person's interest in exclusively meeting their own needs. They often present themselves as fascinating, disarming, and beguiling; they are the ultimate con artists. At the same time, they are undependable, impetuous, and dishonest. They do things others find particularly offensive (e.g., stealing from family members or friends). Dr. Robert Hare (1993) has conducted extensive studies of those with psychopathic personalities and he eloquently describes these individuals in his book *Without Conscience: The Disturbing World of the Psychopaths among Us:*

> [They are] social predators that charm, manipulate, and ruthlessly plow their way through life, leaving a broad trail of broken hearts, shattered expectations, and empty wallets. Completely lacking in conscience and in feelings for others, they selfishly take what they want and do as they please, violating social norms and expectations without the slightest sense of guilt or regret. (p. xi)

Persons who struggle with antisocial disorder are often described as having a long history of being rebellious problem children, and during their adolescent years continue a pattern of activities harmful to, and violating the rights of, others (American Psychiatric Association, 2000; Austrian, 2005). Many come to the practitioner's attention through a mandate of the court system. They generally recount extensive histories filled with arrests for fraud, theft, embezzlement, alcohol (DUIs) and drug use, physical violence, and disregard for alimony and/or child support payments. Although most tend to have poor employment records, many do display a high degree of success in the business or corporate world. It is a mistake to assume that they reside in poor neighborhoods, ride motorcycles, wear torn T-shirts, or any other stereotypical description—they can be anyone.

PREVAILING PATTERN The prognosis for antisocial personality disorder is variable at best. These individuals are at increased risk for substance abuse, alcoholism, vagrancy, suicide, criminal activity, repeated incarceration, and death by violence. Their antisocial disposition, tendencies, and attitudes are usually chronic and life-long; however, this pattern can shift over time in some individuals. As they reach age 30 and beyond, many of them burn out, and gradually the frequency of their antisocial acts decreases. Often, the antisocial behaviors are replaced with somatic behaviors (e.g., hypochondriasis). This is a serious disorder, and overall the long-term outcome is generally considered to be poor, regardless of the person's gender (Colman et al., 2009). It is considered as the diagnosis of last resort. Very early on, Stoudemire (1994) observed, "In the psychiatric setting, antisocial personality disorder is viewed as one of the most difficult personalities to treat" (p. 187).

The following vignette describes some of the behaviors considered typical of antisocial personality disorder.

| CASE | THE CASE OF LUKE ROSSEY |

"I want to divorce my brother Luke," said Sara Rossey, weeping. "Isn't there anything I can do? Legal aid? The court system?" The social worker prompted her to continue.

Sara took a deep breath, and went on, "Luke is 23 and works as a cable installer—at least that's what he's doing this week. He's had at least 20 different jobs, but he can't keep any of them. It's not that he's stupid or anything. In fact, when he was in school they tested his IQ, and it was somewhere up in the 160s! Anyway, what he did last week was the last straw for me and my family, no matter how smart he is."

"What happened?" asked the practitioner.

Sara continued, "He was caught threatening an elderly woman at knifepoint at a neighborhood ATM!"

"Tell me a bit more about Luke," the social worker said as she leaned forward.

"Oh, god, I don't even know where to start, 'cause it seems like he's always been in trouble one way or another," Sara began again. "Well, when he was little, all the other kids used to pick on him because he was smaller than them. I guess he got fed up, and one day he killed a couple of their dogs and drowned a kitten. They left him alone after that—mostly, I think, because their parents told them to stay away from Luke." She stared at a spot on the rug as if she were transported back in time. "Now that I think about it, I guess that's when he first started to be mean ... I mean *really* mean. He would pick out some little kid and beat him up real bad for no reason. Luke was suspended lots of times from school, and even when he wasn't suspended he sometimes just didn't go. I remember there were weeks at a time when he missed school. I don't think the school really cared, because when he was there he would

steal from classmates, threaten teachers, and damage school property."

She continued, "My poor mother really had her hands full with him. In her heart, I think she had a hard time believing Luke could be so mean. Our dad died when Luke was six—dad was an alcoholic and I think maybe he used some drugs, too. So mom raised the two of us by herself. She just couldn't control Luke. He joined a gang when he was about 13 and right after that he was sent to juvenile hall for assault and battery of a police officer ... who was just doing his job breaking up a fight Luke was in the middle of. I think it was some kind of gang initiation rite. Luke got some shrink who told the judge that Luke was a victim of conduct disorder or something like that. They just slapped his wrists, and sent him to some country-club youth ranch, where he got time off for good behavior. I don't know how he fooled them, but as soon as he got out, he went right back to his old ways and his gang buddies.

"He started boozing it up nonstop and using every drug he could get his hands on. I learned a whole new language. Have you ever heard of 'shrooms'? Anyway," Sara continued, "when Luke was 16, they sent him to the state youth program for 9 months. That didn't do him any good, either. As soon as he was back home, he got busted for selling drugs to an undercover cop. They sent him up again, and after he was released they made him go to some kind of drug rehab program. Some rehabilitation!" Sara exclaimed, disgusted. "That's where I think he learned more ways of messing up. He would relapse and then was just sent away again. Eventually, mom didn't want him to live at home anymore. She felt like a prisoner in her own home. Mom had to put a lock on every door—if she didn't, Luke would steal everything that wasn't nailed down and sell it for money to

continued

---

buy drugs or booze. Luke even hocked mom's wedding ring—it was an heirloom—for ten lousy bucks. He got just enough for dad's pocket watch to buy a bottle of booze. He doesn't care about anyone but himself. That's why I want to divorce him."

The social worker responded, "It sounds as if things have been pretty rough for you and your mom."

"That's not even the half of it," she sighed, and then continued. "When Luke was 19, he joined the Army, and mom and I thought maybe he'd finally get straightened out. Three months later he was court-martialed and thrown out on his ear. He beat

up a captain who caught him selling drugs in the barracks. Luke came home after that. He wasn't home more than 2 weeks when his old girlfriend sued him for support of her baby. She had named him as the father, but Luke wouldn't even bother to go for genetic testing. He just denied the baby was his. When I tried to talk to him about the situation, Luke told me, 'Alyssa is a stupid bitch who wants me to support someone else's brat.' Can you believe that? I think he probably used to beat her up, too."

When the social worker asked if Sara had ever seen any evidence of psychotic behavior, she replied, "No, he's only a mean son-of-a-...."

Advanced Clinical EP 2.1.10 (b) c

ASSESSMENT SUMMARY   The roots of Luke's problems are recognized in his early childhood behavior, which included hurting animals, truancy from school, and stealing things from his parents with no remorse. As Luke's sister talked about her brother when they were growing up, she presented a history of his rebellious, problematic childhood and adolescence. The practitioner listens to the client's life story and pays attention to the possibility for those co-occurring diagnoses commonly associated with antisocial personality disorder—for example, substance abuse and dependence (Kessler et al., 1997). Other co-morbid diagnoses are the borderline, narcissistic, histrionic, and schizotypal personality disorders (Becker, Grilo, Edell, & McGlashan, 2000; Marinangeli et al., 2000). In Luke's situation, we find evidence of substance abuse. People with antisocial personality disorder may run into other social problems—and in this case we find that Luke has a history of legal charges.

EP 2.1.1 c

The practitioner is cautioned to consider all aspects of a client's life before making a diagnosis. If someone does have a criminal record, no matter how long, this does not of itself serve as a qualification for a diagnosis of antisocial personality disorder. The DSM makes a distinction between individuals diagnosed with adult antisocial behavior and those with antisocial personality disorder—that is, the former manifest activities of a career criminal but these activities *do not* pervade all aspects of their lives; those with antisocial personality disorder exhibit pervasive egocentricity, selfishness, reckless exploitation, lack of remorse, and failure to conform to social norms. Clients like Luke Rossey challenge the practitioner's ability to sustain appropriate conduct. Maintaining the professional role might be a challenge when working with Luke. Without a doubt, it would be easy to dislike him. Luke would be a very difficult client to work with, and his behaviors are quite complex. He is likely not to have a great deal of insight into his problems. In addition, Luke is not motivated to come in, and he has not indicated that he thinks there is a problem with his behavior. As far as he is concerned, everyone else is the problem. There is the remote possibility that Luke might come in for counseling at the demand of

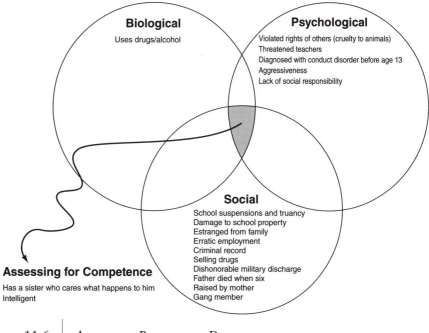

FIGURE 11.6 | ANTISOCIAL PERSONALITY DISORDER

The interactions of the biological, psychological, and social factors in Luke Rossey's life.

© Cengage Learning

others, such as an employer, the court system, or a spouse. However, it is very unlikely that he will seek out intervention on his own behalf or follow through with appropriate treatment. If Luke were to seek help, the competency-based assessment would be invaluable because it relies on observation and systematic exploration rather than on unsupported personal reactions by the practitioner. This objectivity would be essential to drawing any conclusions about how the client's behavior is being influenced in all areas of his life. Figure 11.6 shows the interactions of the biological, psychological, and social variables in Luke Rossey's life.

LUKE ROSSEY'S MULTIAXIAL DSM DIAGNOSIS IS AS FOLLOWS:

Axis I	305.00 Alcohol Abuse
	304.30 Cannabis Dependence
	304.20 Cocaine Dependence
Axis II	301.7 Antisocial Personality Disorder
Axis III	None
Axis IV	Criminal record
	Estranged from family
	Unemployed
Axis V	GAF = deferred

© Cengage Learning

Borderline Personality Disorder

Borderline personality disorder is one of the most common personality disorders (Cloninger & Savkic, 2009). An unstable mood, extremely poor relationships with others, and low self-image alternating between extremes of idealization and devaluation (commonly referred to as "splitting") characterize the person with a borderline personality disorder. These individuals are considered very intense, often going from strong feelings of anger to depression in a very short period of time. Some will engage in self-injurious behaviors, such as cutting themselves to reduce tension (Bohus et al., 2000).

These individuals frequently complain of an empty feeling, and they are sometimes characterized as chronically bored. They might have difficulty with their own identity (Wilkinson-Ryan & Westen, 2000). One of the core features of this disorder is dysfunction in the area of emotion; these individuals often engage in behaviors that are suicidal, self-mutilative, or both, cutting, burning, or punching themselves (Linehan & Dexter-Mazza, 2008). The term **borderline personality disorder** was not widely researched until it appeared in the DSM-III in 1980, and since then it has been used too frequently, and inaccurately, to describe any observed form of personality disorder. Before this disorder was added to the DSM-III, borderline individuals often were diagnosed with schizophrenia, latent type. The term was also subjected to a wide range of definitions and continues to be one of the most controversial personality disorder diagnoses.

Although the disorder has been well described in the professional literature, there is still no consensus concerning its etiology or even the meaning of its most notable features (Distel, Trull, & Boomsma, 2009). There is a confusing hodgepodge of hypotheses suggesting that the borderline individual is trying to conceal his or her *rage* directed toward the mother figure; is manifesting *depression* over loss of his or her mother; or is spending his or her life energy ambivalently pursuing, seeking, and rejecting relationships resembling the original mother-child bond. Others suggest that this disorder results from a lack of "fit" between the mother and her infant.

There is agreement that this disorder is characterized by a history of ambivalence, very unstable and intense relationships and moods, erratic and often self-destructive behaviors, feelings of boredom, poor self-esteem, poor impulse control, and a fear of abandonment (Phillips, Yen, & Gunderson, 2003). Individuals may also have short-lived psychotic episodes (noted as micropsychotic episodes) when under severe stress, rather than a psychotic break. These symptoms are almost always transient and fleeting. The major characteristics of borderline personality disorder include:

- *Poor interpersonal relationships*—The person's primary fear (real or imagined) is of being abandoned and left alone. He or she will make heroic efforts searching for companionship yet at the same time struggle against being engulfed in a relationship.
- *Unstable self-image*—The person's life has been marked by uncertainty in major life issues (e.g., occupation, education, values, and relationships with others).
- *Unstable emotions*—The individual's emotional state frequently fluctuates between extremes, dramatically going from euphoric mood to intense anger and rage in a matter of moments.
- *Marked impulsivity*—These individuals are capable of reckless and self-destructive behaviors.

PREVAILING PATTERN   Assessing for a borderline personality disorder can usually be made by early adulthood when the individual has exhibited a pervasive pattern of unstable interpersonal relationships; frantic efforts to avoid real or imagined abandonment; alternated between extremes of idealization and devaluation; experienced identity disturbance; engaged in recurrent suicidal behavior, gestures, or threats; complained of chronic feelings of emptiness; exhibited inappropriate and intense anger or difficulty coping; and been impulsive in at least two areas, such as spending money, sexual encounters, and/or substance abuse (American Psychiatric Association, 2000). The behaviors that make up this disorder are fairly stable and do not change very much over time. Although this is considered a chronic disorder, most individuals experience a lessening of symptoms as they reach their middle years (Zanarini, Frankenburg, Hennen, Reich, & Silk, 2006).

Approximately 1 percent to 2 percent of the general population may qualify for the designation of borderline personality disorder (Cloninger & Svakic, 2009). It is one of the most common personality disorders seen in clinical practice settings and applies to a far greater proportion of clients who seek out mental health care than those who are not seen in the mental health arena. Molly Layton's (1995) earlier characterization still holds true when she states:

> In the minds of many therapists, the borderline diagnosis has come to be a code word for trouble. The diagnosis signals a kind of impossible case—long, grueling work with the client often challenging the therapist's equanimity over and over, withdrawing in a sulk or attacking in a rage, creating melodramatic scenes, threatening suicide, demanding more and more of the therapist's love and time, while the shaken therapist feels used, abused and manipulated, thinking he or she is often making no difference at all. (p. 36)

The borderline personality is characterized by gross impairment in behavior, cognitive and emotional styles, and interpersonal relationships. These deficits can be described as follows:

- *Behavior*—These individuals perform physically self-damaging acts, such as suicidal gestures, self-mutilation, or inciting fights.
- *Cognitive style*—They experience their world and relate to others in terms of black and white. The individual is often described as inflexible and impulsive. Their inflexibility and impulsivity are characteristic of "splitting" (the inability to integrate contradictory qualities). The person tends to view others as "all good" or "all bad." The defense mechanism of projective identification is also associated with these individuals. By externalizing inner, unacceptable aspects of themselves, they select relationships with people who conform to these projected perceptions. In this way, the person with a borderline personality disorder is able to relate to those who now own these externalized perceptions rather than endure what would otherwise be very painful self-castigation (i.e., face the aspects of themselves they see as unacceptable).
- *Emotional style*—The person's mood is characterized by *marked* shifts ranging from normal (euthymic), to dysphoric, to anger, and to intense rage. At the other extreme are feelings of emptiness, boredom, or experiencing a deep void.
- *Interpersonal*—They develop relationships rather quickly and intensely, while their social adaptiveness remains superficial. The person is extraordinarily intolerant of being left alone and goes to great lengths in seeking the company

of others (e.g., making late-night telephone calls to people they barely know or having indiscriminate multiple sexual affairs).

EP 2.1.10 (b) a

DIFFERENTIAL ASSESSMENT   Clinical attention should be drawn to the possible coexistence of a mood, substance abuse, or eating disorder (Grant et al., 2008; Trull, Sher, Minks-Brown, Durbin, & Burr, 2000; Zanarini, Reichman, Frankenburg, Reich, & Fitzmaurice, 2010). The possibility of a client struggling with multiple co-morbid diagnoses underscores the value of carefully collecting, organizing, and interpreting client data. As an example, consider the individual with histrionic personality disorder who also shows extreme emotions but does not exhibit chronic feelings of emptiness or loneliness, self-destructive behaviors, or intensively impaired relationships seen in those with a borderline personality disorder. Differentiation between schizophrenia and a borderline personality disorder includes differences between prolonged psychotic episodes (in the former) and the presence of a major thought disorder (in the latter). A relatively stable self-image and relative lack of self-destructiveness, impulsivity, and abandonment concerns distinguish paranoid and narcissistic personality disorders from the borderline personality disorder. The antisocial personality disorder is characterized by manipulative behavior motivated by the desire for power, control, or material gain, versus the person with a borderline personality's desire for nurturance. The person with a dependent personality disorder has abandonment concerns, but they appease and submit in interpersonal relationships, unlike in a borderline personality disorder.

The following case portrays a young woman whose behaviors are consistent with those commonly seen in borderline personality disorder.

CASE | THE CASE OF SUZIE HUTCHFIELD

When Suzie Hutchfield called the community mental health center, she asked for an appointment by saying, "I need someone to help me." An appointment was made for later that week.

"You know it's really hard to make something of yourself when your own father tells you that you're never gonna make much of yourself," Suzie told me. "Do you know what he told me when I was 14 years old? I had just run away from home, 'cause he always smacked me around. When the police brought me home, my dad told me that I'd better learn to be good making money on my back because that's all I'll ever be good for."

She continued, "He was such a dumb shit. You know men have always been jerks, starting with him. He was no Prince Charming. He used to beat me and my younger brother up real good, and then

he'd go plant his fat butt in front of the television set and drink his booze. Oh, and he had a girlfriend too, but I bet my mother didn't care."

Suzie is currently employed as a waitress in a delicatessen. However, she admits that she has had a series of jobs, none of which lasted very long. She adds, "I've been married three times, and once I married the same man twice. Did I confuse you? Did you understand what I said?" I nodded my head, indicating that I understood. "Anyway, I can't seem to get it right, even though I'm 42 years old. You know, I'm a single mom—I've got two girls—and even at home I can't get things right. My oldest daughter, Candy, she's 16 and a real piece of work. She should be making As, but skips school a lot. One of these fine days some goody-two-shoe social worker is gonna haul me to jail because that kid's always truant." Suzie went on, "Now my little girl, Heather, she's the best. She's 11 years old, cute as a button, and a better kid you never saw." She added, "Don't that beat all? I got one good kid and one bad one.

"What did you ask? Oh yeah, I remember now. My boyfriend. Well, Bob just moved in with us, but I'm not so happy about it already. I think he's been cheating on me, but he tells me he's not. Twice last week I followed him after he left for his motorcycle repair shop. Anyway, he drove right over to his ex-girlfriend's house, and stayed there for 2 hours! When he came home, I confronted him, and he told me some cock-and-bull story that she needed some 'house maintenance' done. Some maintenance! I've been through this with him before, many, many times. I throw him out, and then he swears this is the last time, but it never is, and I still take him back." She said, "You know there's nothing I hate more than being alone, and if it means taking that bum back, well at least I know what I have, ya know? It's not that I need him. I've had lots of men in my life. I always have a man waiting in the wings. You never know what can happen. I really just don't want to ever be alone."

Suzie leaned toward me and continued in a softer voice, "Can you keep a secret?" I nodded in the affirmative. "I met this orderly last week when I was in the hospital, you know for the cutting and the cocaine?"

It should be pointed out that Suzie has been hospitalized several times for suicide attempts by cutting her wrists.

"Anyway, I think he loves me," she confided, "but he's not exactly a rocket scientist, if you know what I mean. We found a broom closet when I was in the hospital and made out a coupla times. We even made a date for after I got out.

"You know, sometimes I just feel empty, so I'll do something really exciting for fun. My old social worker said I do these crazy things for attention. She's so stupid! Not like you—you seem to be real smart and I bet you can help me. What do you think?

"I once spent $2,000 at Payless Shoes. They're still waiting for me to pay." Suzie explained that she bought all different sizes in men's, children's, and women's shoes. The store manager told her that they had a no-return policy and stamped her receipt to that effect. Despite this, Suzie still tried to return the shoes because she was worried that her credit card was charged over the limit. In fact, as a result of this incident, her credit card was canceled. Suzie also admits to long-term problems using alcohol and drugs, "But I'm not a drug addict or nothing like that. I just wanna smoke a little weed, drink a little wine, have a good time—I don't hurt anybody."

Advanced Clinical EP 2.1.10 (b) c

ASSESSMENT SUMMARY   Suzie's interpersonal relationships have always been unstable, chaotic, and intense. This pattern of interacting with others underscores the importance of looking to coping strategies that may be in place in her life to reinforce and improve her adaptation to life situations, circumstances, and events. Unfortunately, she has a very poor self-image, a fear of being abandoned by others, and a tendency to engage in self-destructive behavior. Confronted with evidence that her boyfriend is cheating on her, she still tries to maintain this flawed relationship by meeting someone else when she was hospitalized for a suicide attempt. Suzie exhibits **mood reactivity** (a depressed mood that can brighten readily at a positive turn of events) related to her poor impulse control (demonstrated by spending $2,000 on useless shoes), multiple suicide attempts, and alcohol and drug use. Figure 11.7 summarizes the major interactions of the biological, psychological, and social factors particular to Suzie's life. It is important to note that the multiaxial assessment concludes that Suzie's symptoms are severe, by virtue of her many attempts at suicide.

Historically, people with borderline personality disorder have been stereotyped as being very difficult, demanding, impatient, and prone to acting out. You might have even encountered a practitioner who has avoided working with someone like Suzie and may have even characterized the client by his or her diagnosis rather than those factors that make him or her unique. The competency-based assessment is concerned with individual differences and is sensitive to the factors that influence

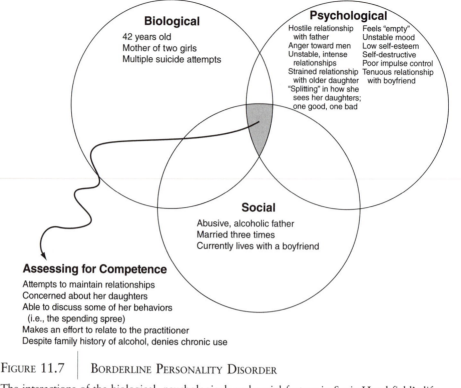

Biological

42 years old
Mother of two girls
Multiple suicide attempts

Psychological

Hostile relationship   Feels "empty"
  with father   Unstable mood
Anger toward men   Low self-esteem
Unstable, intense   Self-destructive
  relationships   Poor impulse control
Strained relationship   Tenuous relationship
  with older daughter   with boyfriend
"Splitting" in how she
  sees her daughters;
  one good, one bad

Social

Abusive, alcoholic father
Married three times
Currently lives with a boyfriend

Assessing for Competence

Attempts to maintain relationships
Concerned about her daughters
Able to discuss some of her behaviors
  (i.e., the spending spree)
Makes an effort to relate to the practitioner
Despite family history of alcohol, denies chronic use

FIGURE 11.7 | BORDERLINE PERSONALITY DISORDER

The interactions of the biological, psychological, and social factors in Suzie Hutchfield's life.

© Cengage Learning

Suzie in her social environment. For instance, Suzie does convey to the practitioner some sense of wanting to make changes in her life.

SUZIE HUTCHFIELD'S MULTIAXIAL DSM DIAGNOSIS IS AS FOLLOWS:

Axis I	305.00 Alcohol Abuse
	304.30 Cannabis Dependence
Axis II	301.83 Borderline Personality Disorder, Severe
Axis III	968.5 Cocaine Overdose
	Old lacerations to both wrists
Axis IV	History of childhood neglect
	Occupational problems
Axis V	GAF = 45 (at intake)

© Cengage Learning

CLUSTER C: ANXIOUS, FEARFUL

AVOIDANT PERSONALITY DISORDER

The category of **avoidant personality disorder** was introduced in the DSM-III (American Psychiatric Association, 1980), and thus it has a shorter history in the psychiatric literature than most of the other personality disorders. Its appearance was marked by considerable controversy, as some clinicians argued that there was too little distinction among the avoidant, the schizoid, and the dependent personality disorders (Phillips, Yen & Gunderson, 2003). The DSM-III advanced criteria emphasizing features considered at that time typical of the avoidant personality disorder: pervasive and generalized timidity, inhibition, and avoidance. DSM-III-R (American Psychiatric Association, 1987) reflected some variation in perspective and attempted to demarcate this disorder more clearly from its close neighbors. Trait criteria such as "desire for acceptance" and "low self-esteem," initially considered central to the formulation, were removed, and new guideline parameters were added, for example, "fear of being embarrassed by blushing" and "fear of saying something inappropriate." These additions were considered fundamental to the core of the avoidant personality disorder construct. The current DSM criteria have been modified to differentiate between the avoidant and dependent personality disorders.

The prevalence of the avoidant personality disorder ranges between 5 to 5.2 percent of the general population (Lenzenweger, Lane, Loranger, & Kessler, 2007). No information is available about familial patterns or the proportion of men to women with the disorder. The literature on avoidant personality disorder is sparse, but there is some evidence that it is related to other schizophrenia-related disorders—that is, occurring more often in relatives of those who have schizophrenia (Fogelson et al., 2007).

People diagnosed with this disorder are often confused with individuals described as "being shy." As the name suggests, people with avoidant personality disorder are highly sensitive to the opinions of others and therefore avoid most social relationships (Barlow & Durand, 2012). Because of their heightened sensitivity toward criticism and censure by others, they have a propensity to be self-effacing and eager to please. These qualities often lead to marked social detachment. Additional features include feelings of low self-esteem, being standoffish or introverted, fear of closeness to and rejection by others, social awkwardness, and a chronic fear of being embarrassed. These characteristics persist throughout adulthood, affecting nearly all aspects of daily life.

Individuals with this disorder have a chronic, lifelong pattern of social withdrawal grounded in the anticipation of being rejected. They would like to have a relationship with others; however, the person is extremely sensitive to any form of criticism, making it nearly impossible for them to develop any relationships unless there is a strong guarantee of uncritical acceptance.

The main characteristics of avoidant personality disorder are constant feelings of inadequacy and ineptitude, especially in social situations. The features of the disorder can be summarized as follows:

- *Avoids social situations*—Individuals may ardently avoid social situations yet at the same time desire social relationships.
- *Disengages from social situations*—They are almost always detached from others, afraid of being embarrassed, criticized, or ridiculed (so that they withdraw from social situations whenever possible). This disengagement sets up a vicious cycle wherein the individual appears aloof and distant to others who mirror similar restraint toward him or her.
- *Desires relationships with others*—Although the person is inhibited and overly cautious, he or she longs for affection and social acceptance and is quite distressed by its absence.

- *Feels inadequate*—They view themselves as socially undesirable. Although these individuals want to be involved with others, low self-esteem and fear of rejection keep them from becoming involved.
- *Overly sensitive to negative criticism*—They worry about embarrassing themselves and consequently do not try anything new or different.

PREVAILING PATTERN   These individuals are inhibited and overly cautious. They fear that new situations will throw them a curve for which they are not prepared. Many are able to function as long as they stay protected in a "closed" or safe environment. Some individuals with avoidant personality disorder do marry and have families; being surrounded by familiar relationships and life circumstances that do not demand spontaneity is helpful. In the workplace, these individuals will often accept subordinate jobs, thus removing them from the realm of having increased responsibilities and increased contact. These individuals are hypervigilant about being rejected, and they seek constant reassurance that others will like them. They tend to avoid occupations requiring social interactions, and generally do not attain very much personal advancement; they are instead seen as demure and eager to please. If forced into a social encounter, they are usually very timid, inhibited, and afraid at every step of making a mistake that will bring the rejection they are sure is forthcoming.

EP 2.1.10
(b) a

DIFFERENTIAL ASSESSMENT   Compared to those with schizoid personality disorder who want to be left completely alone, the individual with avoidant personality disorder longs for social interaction and affection. He or she is not considered as querulous, irritable, irascible, or unpredictable as those with borderline or histrionic personality disorders. The differential picture between the avoidant and dependent personality disorders is difficult to tease out and underscores the value of collecting, organizing, and interpreting client data. The individual with the dependent personality has a greater fear of being abandoned or not loved than does the person with the avoidant personality disorder. For the practitioner, the clinical picture may be virtually indistinguishable. The individual with social phobia has problems around specific social situations (such as a speaking engagement), versus the personal relationship difficulties the avoidant individual experiences; however, the two disorders can coexist.

The following vignette portrays a young woman diagnosed with avoidant personality disorder.

| CASE | THE CASE OF MABEL HUMPHRIES |

Mabel, a 33-year-old single woman, has been referred to the employee assistance program by her supervisor. The major complaint centers around Mabel's unwillingness to change her working hours from nights to days; currently, she works the 11 P.M. to 7 A.M. shift in the hospital morgue.

As the social worker assigned to interview Mabel, I can report that my first impression of her was that she likes being alone. She expressed herself in the following way:

"Listen, it don't take much to keep me satisfied. As long as everybody stays outta my way, we'll get along just fine. I don't know what my supervisor told you, or what her problem is, but I don't want to work days. I like the peace and quiet of working the graveyard shift. That way I do my job and nobody's in my face. I guess I'm set in my ways. You see what I'm saying? I don't tell nobody my business and keep to myself. Always have, always will."

I took a wild guess and asked, "Mabel, do you try to avoid the type of work that requires a lot of contact with people?"

"Well, it's true I don't care to be around a lot of people," she answered, "but mostly it's because they might not like me, you know."

I thought this was a pretty brave admission on Mabel's part. So, I decided to go with some more relationship-oriented questions like:

Have you ever turned down a promotion because you were worried other people would be critical of you?

Do you worry about being rejected?

Do you find yourself having trouble carrying on a conversation with someone you just met?

Do you often feel inadequate in work or social situations?

Do you usually feel like you are not as interesting or as much fun as other people are?

Having answered yes to all of my questions, Mabel tried to explain. She said, "I was raised by a deadbeat alcoholic mother who never cared about anybody, including me. My mother always had trouble with people, especially men. Somewhere along the way, I remember somebody said she had borderline something-or-other. If that means One Tough Bitch, then that'd be about right."

Mabel didn't seem at all sentimental as she recounted this. She was just saying what was. After a moment, she continued, "She used to beat the hell out of me and tell me I was no good. Didn't take long for her to convince me—I mean a mother wouldn't lie, would she?" At that point, Mabel's eyes suddenly filled, so I asked if she would like a drink of water or a tissue. "No, don't waste anything on me, I'm fine," she replied.

I asked Mabel if she had any friends.

She tried to laugh but was struggling now to keep her composure. "Nobody wants to be friends with a loser," she replied. "It's not like I haven't tried. But, let's face it, I don't have a lot to offer other people. Like I said before, I'm pretty much of a loner. I don't like to go out and stuff like that, so I guess that's one reason I don't make any friends. The way I figure it, they won't like me, so why bother? And besides, what would I talk about? I don't do anything except wheel dead people around in the morgue." Mabel smiled a little and said, "Hey, I do have lots of friends, but they're all dead." Before Mabel left at the end of our session, she added, "I sure hope you can get my supervisor off my back so I can get back to work."

Advanced Clinical EP 2.1.10 (b) c

ASSESSMENT SUMMARY   Mabel desires social interaction with others, and is distressed by its absence, but goes to great lengths to try and hide that—she describes herself as a loner, but she also struggles with wanting to have some interpersonal relationships. People with avoidant and schizoid personality disorders spend most of their time alone and isolated. The discrete difference is that Mabel is unhappy with her lack of social interaction, whereas Tyrone White (described earlier to illustrate schizoid personality disorder) *prefers* having no social contacts with others.

Perhaps the more difficult differential assessment exists between avoidant and dependent personality types. Mabel, who is avoidant, approaches interpersonal relationships with reluctance motivated by her fear of saying something foolish and looking inept. In contrast, Walter Pearson (introduced in the upcoming vignette on dependent personality disorder), is socially isolated because of a clinging, submissive relationship with his mother.

The competency-based assessment serves as a guide to the types of information to obtain. This approach to the assessment provides a framework for assessing how clients cope and sets the stage to reinforce and improve adaptation to life situations, circumstances, and events. Figure 11.8 shows the interactions of the biological, psychological, and social variables in Mabel's life. It is important for the practitioner to be knowledgeable about the many factors related to a client's presenting issues. In this way, Mabel's problems can be better understood, and the

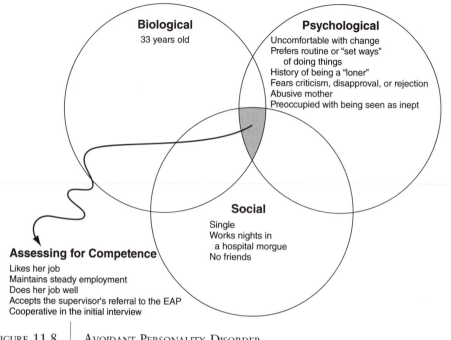

FIGURE 11.8 | AVOIDANT PERSONALITY DISORDER

The interactions of the biological, psychological, and social factors in Mabel Humphries's life.

© Cengage Learning

diagnostic label has the potential to provide additional insight into what is a complicated symptom picture. On the surface, it may appear that Mabel has problems getting along with her boss, but a thorough assessment reveals her underlying reasons for wanting to stay on the night shift. At the same time, the practitioner comes to appreciate the strengths in Mabel's personality and life situation. For instance, fearful as she is of criticism, she is willing to discuss "what's wrong" with the practitioner.

MABEL HUMPHRIES'S MULTIAXIAL DSM DIAGNOSIS IS AS FOLLOWS:

Axis I	V71.09 (No diagnosis)
Axis II	301.82 Avoidant Personality Disorder (Principal Diagnosis)
Axis III	None
Axis IV	None
Axis V	GAF = 75 (at intake)

© Cengage Learning

DEPENDENT PERSONALITY DISORDER

In 1952, the DSM-I included dependent personality disorder as a subtype of the passive-aggressive personality disorder. The category of dependent personality disorder received a great deal of criticism for presenting an overly narrow definition and for perpetuating possible gender bias toward women.

Dependent personality disorder describes a pervasive pattern of extreme inability to act independently of others. For example, people with dependent personality disorder allow others to take responsibility for their lives and to make decisions for them, feel helpless when alone, subjugate their needs to those of others, endure mistreatment in order to maintain a relationship, and are unable to function when self-assertiveness is required. These individuals' dependency needs are so great that they will often tolerate almost any kind of behavior on the part of others who seem to meet their needs. During the assessment, it is clinically relevant to ask if clients have experienced abuse or battering, either past or present.

Individuals with a dependent personality disorder go to great lengths to avoid undertaking or assuming positions of responsibility or leadership. Instead, they prefer to perform tasks under someone else's direction. It is important to discern that these individuals have a problem that is more than just being indecisive. The disorder is more than being unable to choose between the tuna salad and the hamburger for lunch. What is so striking is the individual's inability to expedite decision-making without exorbitant amounts of advice and reassurance. They want others to make decisions for them in all areas of their lives, including, for example, their occupation, where to live, how to dress, or even how to act. They cling tenaciously to others and make excessive sacrifices to win the slightest sign of appreciation. At first blush, this dependency might seem like a compliment to the person being depended upon; however, the excessive demands for reassurance eventually become so bothersome and irritating that most people are driven away. The tendency to be dependent on people is pervasive—which, not surprisingly, makes the mental health system, the agency, and the practitioner prime targets for dependence.

To summarize, the central characteristics of dependent personality disorder include:

- *Difficulty in making decisions*—The individual relies on excessive advice and reassurance from others, and avoids, at all costs, having to rely only on him- or herself.
- *Excessive need for reassurance*—The individual is filled with feelings of self-doubt, passivity, pessimism, and helplessness, and is uncomfortable when alone. The person often remains in relationships even when it is detrimental to his or her well-being.
- *Fear of rejection and abandonment*—The person is very reluctant to disagree with others out of fear of losing support and approval; it is not uncommon for this individual to live with someone who is controlling, domineering, overprotective, and infantilizing.

PREVAILING PATTERN   Dependent behavior begins by early adulthood and is present in a variety of contexts; for example, these individuals have difficulty expressing disagreement, go to excessive lengths to obtaining nurturance and support from others, are uncomfortable and helpless when alone, are incapable of making everyday decisions, and have difficulty initiating projects. In clinical settings, a dependent personality disorder is more commonly diagnosed in women than in men (American Psychiatric Association, 2000). However, little is known about the overall course of this disorder. What we do know is that individuals tend to exhibit impaired occupational functioning and show little or no ability to act independently and without close supervision. Social relationships are apt to be limited to those they "depend" on—as a consequence, the individual may endure mental or physical abuse as long as he or she remains unassertive and passive.

**EP 2.1.10
(b) a**

DIFFERENTIAL ASSESSMENT The differential assessment is a complicated process, because features of dependence are found in the other personality disorders as well as in other conditions, such as somatization disorder and agoraphobia. Dependence is a factor in histrionic and borderline personality disorders; however, the individual with the dependent personality disorder usually has a long-standing relationship with one main person on whom they are dependent, versus a series of persons. This distinction is illustrated in the following vignette about Walter Pearson, which shows how his story unfolds. This data establishes the base for organizing and interpreting Walter's history in order to formulate the DSM diagnosis.

CASE | THE CASE OF WALTER PEARSON

Walter Pearson has been referred to the employee assistance program (EAP) for an evaluation. His boss at the bank where he works complains, "Walter requires too much direction and guidance, and he's always wasting his coworkers' time trying to get some reassurance about what he's doing. It really interferes with his job responsibilities."

Walter is a 38-year-old African American single male. He is an only child and was raised by his single-parent mother. "My momma has always spoiled me rotten," he relates proudly. At Walter's request, Mrs. Pearson has come along to his interview. She jokingly tells the social worker, "As a baby, Walter just hated when I had to drop him off at the day-care center. Oooo wee, could that little feller cry! He had problems when he started elementary school, too—I guess he just wanted his momma!"

Walter interjects, "Momma, do you remember when they sent me home from sleep-away camp? I cried so much and was so homesick, they put me on the first train that was coming in this direction." Walter and his mother chuckle at the memory. Then Walter continues, "As a youngster all the kids in the neighborhood made fun of me and called me Momma's Boy, but I didn't care. I guess because it was true."

He finished high school and was accepted to a small liberal arts college, where he earned his degree. Immediately after graduation, he came home because, as he says, "Momma needed me to help her with the business." At this point, Walter looks at his mother expectantly. The social worker has the impression

that he's looking for his mother's approval. Almost imperceptibly, Mrs. Pearson smiled and nodded approvingly in Walter's direction. Walter currently lives at home with his mother. Although he tried renting an apartment of his own nearby, he commented, "I didn't like the location, and it wasn't safe—so I moved home after about 3 months."

Walter has done some dating, but hasn't found anyone special, or anyone that his mother particularly liked. He said, "Momma is very picky—she won't like anyone I date, I know that. I used to see a really nice girl, named Debbie McPhrew, but Momma complained about how talkative Debbie is." He smiles at his mother and continues, "After a while, I started to think she was right. Debbie *did* talk a blue streak. I know I'm an adult, but Momma does have my best interests at heart. Anyhow, my judgment hasn't always been the greatest. I've made lots of mistakes in my life."

Mrs. Pearson sat quietly by his side with a reserved but noticeable smile on her face. Periodically, she would nod in agreement as if to reinforce Walter's comments about how much he needed her. He went on to say, "When Momma helps me make decisions, things just seem to work out better."

Walter has worked as a bank teller for the past 5 years. "Momma knew the manager, so he helped me get the job." Walter recently turned down a promotion because his mother thought it would be too much responsibility for him. "I was worried that I couldn't do a good job, and that I'd make lots of mistakes. It's better that I stay in my present position," Walter concluded.

Advanced Clinical EP 2.1.10 (b) c

ASSESSMENT SUMMARY   Walter's story is an example of someone with a dependent personality disorder, wherein we see a middle-aged man who continues to be bound in one way or another to someone else; in this situation, it is his mother. The vignette suggests that Walter lacks the initiative to make decisions or assert himself. His dependency needs are so great that he accepts most suggestions his mother offers—even if they are not in his best interest. He accepts this advice without question in order to avoid being rejected or criticized. In fact, he has become convinced that his judgment is not "the greatest" except when his mother intercedes on his behalf.

On closer examination, Mrs. Pearson seems to want to keep Walter close to home. She discouraged any attempts he may have made in developing other relationships, such as with a girlfriend. On some level, it appears that Walter fears being separated from his mother and left to shift for himself. He maintains a submissive, clinging role in order not to be abandoned. He looks to his mother for approval. His dependence on others has now surfaced as a problem at work, so much of a problem that his supervisor has referred him to the EAP office for help. Interestingly, Walter's mother accompanies him to the appointment.

The client's history provides opportunities to assess coping strategies that can be reinforced to improve the client's adaptation to life situations, circumstances, and events. An important social work value relates to appreciating human worth and respecting human dignity. The profession is committed to helping those who are oppressed and disempowered. In Walter's situation, his "oppression" is not related to any of the various forms of discrimination but arises from his dependence on his mother for her approval and advice—and that oppression is just as debilitating as any other would be. A competency-based assessment examines Walter's present functioning in relationship to past events, while considering biopsychosocial factors as well as environmental systems. This thorough examination adds clarity to the way Walter relates to his world. By focusing on his strengths rather than deficits, the practitioner has the opportunity to build on his eagerness to please others and foster a new relationship built on mutual respect and collaboration around problem solving. Figure 11.9 illustrates the interactions of the biological, psychological, and social variables in Walter's life.

WALTER PEARSON'S MULTIAXIAL DSM DIAGNOSIS IS AS FOLLOWS:

Axis I	V71.09 (No diagnosis)
Axis II	301.6 Dependent Personality Disorder
Axis III	None
Axis IV	None
Axis V	GAF = 70 (current)

© Cengage Learning

OBSESSIVE-COMPULSIVE PERSONALITY DISORDER

Individuals with **obsessive-compulsive personality disorder** do not have obsessions or compulsions in the same sense that they do in obsessive-compulsive disorder (OCD); rather, the energy of their entire personality is channeled into perfectionism. These individuals are rigid, orderly, and inflexible, and they are emotionally constricted. They often have difficulties making decisions, and appear excessively moralistic.

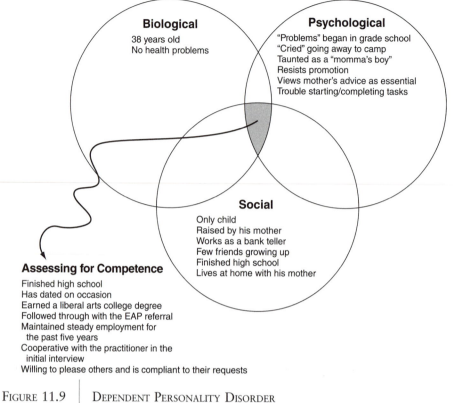

Biological
38 years old
No health problems

Psychological
"Problems" began in grade school
"Cried" going away to camp
Taunted as a "momma's boy"
Resists promotion
Views mother's advice as essential
Trouble starting/completing tasks

Social
Only child
Raised by his mother
Works as a bank teller
Few friends growing up
Finished high school
Lives at home with his mother

Assessing for Competence
Finished high school
Has dated on occasion
Earned a liberal arts college degree
Followed through with the EAP referral
Maintained steady employment for
  the past five years
Cooperative with the practitioner in the
  initial interview
Willing to please others and is compliant to their requests

FIGURE 11.9 | DEPENDENT PERSONALITY DISORDER

The interactions of the biological, psychological, and social factors in Walter Pearson's life.

© Cengage Learning

They are frequently characterized as headstrong and preoccupied with doing things the right way. This personality disorder is commonly found among gifted children whose quest for perfection can be debilitating (Nugent, 2000). This disorder is often confused with OCD, but OCD is distinguished by thinking obsessions and performing compulsions. With obsessive-compulsive disorder, the practitioner encounters individuals who spend a great deal of time performing ritualized behaviors such as checking, counting, or washing. In contrast, the major characteristics of obsessive-compulsive personality disorder include:

- *Perfectionism*—These individuals have inflexible ethical standards that they believe everyone should follow. They do not delegate work to others because they fear things will not be done to their own exacting standards. To all outward appearances, they seem to stride through life with meticulous, regimental thoroughness.
- *Difficulty discarding worthless objects*—The individual is known to hoard and accumulate seemingly useless or worn-out possessions. They are often described as "pack rats" and being stingy.
- *Difficulty with interpersonal control*—These individuals overanalyze things, which has the effect of distancing and detaching them. The alternative, emotional spontaneity, is too threatening to tolerate.

PREVAILING PATTERN   These individuals are more apt to seek intervention on their own than are people with other personality disorders. Although they often have stable relationships and marriages (especially if the spouse is passive), people with obsessive-compulsive personality disorder usually have few close friends, and their lives tend to be constricted and joyless. Routines are rigidly adhered to, and their occupational lives are usually formal.

These individuals tend to become lost in details and are completely immobilized by indecision. Projects are ultimately left uncompleted. They feel more comfortable exercising control over other people and greatly resist attempts at being controlled. Individuals with this disorder appear to be supersaturated with upholding the highest level of scruples and are inflexible regarding moral and ethical matters. Consequently, they are often described as cold, insensitive, single-minded, stubbornly rigid, frugal, parsimonious, and miserly to the point of being unwilling to part with any material possessions. Although obsessive-compulsive personality disorder tends to be chronic, there is some suggestion that cognitive-behavioral therapy might be effective for helping people to manage their symptoms (Svartberg, Styles, & Seltzer, 2004).

EP 2.1.10
(b) a

DIFFERENTIAL ASSESSMENT   The competency-based assessment provides a framework for the practitioner to collect, organize, and interpret client data. Other disorders that should be ruled out when making an assessment of obsessive-compulsive personality disorder include major depressive disorder, dysthymic disorder, and obsessive-compulsive disorder (OCD). Individuals with obsessive-compulsive disorder have true obsessions and compulsions that are not found in persons with obsessive-compulsive personality disorder. However, that is not to say that the person might not eventually develop OCD. Individuals with a narcissistic personality disorder, albeit concerned with perfection and correctness, are focused on seeking adulation, versus maintaining these behaviors out of fear and guilt. The following vignette illustrates the most salient features of obsessive-compulsive personality disorder.

CASE | THE CASE OF GEOFFREY HALES

Geoffrey Hales is 45, married and has two children: a boy who is 11, and a girl who is 9. He is employed as an electrical engineer for a nationally known company. Geoffrey and his wife Irene have come in (at Irene's insistence) because of marital problems. Here is a synopsis of their initial interview.

After greetings and introductions, when everyone is seated, Irene blurts out, "Marilyn, my husband is driving me crazy! No, I take that back—he's driven me crazy already! You gotta help him."

I laugh and ask them both to tell me about what has brought them to my office. They exchange a quick glance, and Irene goes ahead. "Where do I

start? He's never home, he's always working, we haven't been on a vacation in the 15 years we've been married. He's overworked, and he never seems to sleep. He always brings work home with him and stays up until 3 A.M. most mornings working on the computer." She took a breath, and then continued, "Everything has to be just letter perfect—but it rarely is, because he's constantly changing his work so nothing is ever finished. He can't even keep a secretary for more than 3 months—they can't stand his perfectionism either. He doesn't have time for the kids or for me. We never go out because he's too involved with his work. I mean, how many times can he rewrite a

continued

report? His current secretary calls him 'Mr. Four-Rs.' It stands for rules, rigidity, regulation, and regimen. Boy! She sure pegged Geoffrey!"

Geoffrey finally spoke up. "Irene, you know other people just don't do things the way I want them done."

I asked if other difficulties were affecting their relationship. Irene replied, "The house looks like we're ready to move out. He's got boxes scattered all around the place, and no one is allowed to touch anything. He says he is saving important information that he's going to use, but he never does. I jokingly call him a 'pack rat,' but it's not funny anymore. He can't throw anything away. We've got newspapers dating back 10 years sitting in a corner of the living room! What's he going to do with all that junk?"

Geoffrey shrugged and answered, "I guess I am a collector, but I think of it as 'waste not, want not.' Actually, I think it's Irene who has the problem, not me. Why don't we talk about how disorganized she is around the house? She doesn't even know how to balance a checkbook."

Geoffrey went on to say that he runs his life by meticulous planning and making lists. As he describes the processes he uses in minute detail, I notice that he is totally absorbed, as if he must make me see the rightness of his approach. "I know that other people think that I'm a perfectionist but that's the only way you get things done in this world."

Irene retorted, "You might see yourself that way, but everyone else sees you as indecisive, preoccupied with details, and a procrastinator who never gets the job done." She went on to say, "One of the reasons I insisted you come for help is that I've put up with your behavior for 15 years, and now it's time to stop. I'm tired of your 'it's my way or the highway' attitude."

Geoffrey looked somewhat chastened, and he replied tentatively, "I guess I am inflexible sometimes, and I know I turn people off—but it's only because I want things done right. I can't stand it when people bend the rules and try to cut corners."

Irene turned to me and asked, "Do you think there is any hope for our marriage?"

ASSESSMENT SUMMARY   Figure 11.10 provides a summary of the major biological, psychological, and social features of Geoffrey Hales's life. Although his wife is quite unhappy and dissatisfied with his behaviors, Geoffrey is unaware of the extent of her discontent and continues to defend his need for orderliness and perfectionism. He is always working, and when he finishes a project he then feels the need to rework the details. As a matter of fact, getting the job done "correctly" seems to irritate his coworkers, as indicated by his secretary's comments. Aside from an already troubled marriage, he seems to have no friends or interests outside of his job. In addition, Geoffrey Hales's preoccupation at getting things done properly comes at the expense of spending time with his family—never mind a family vacation.

Advanced Practice EP 2.1.1 b

Geoffrey's demeanor changed when he described the minutiae of his daily routine to the social worker—he became quite preoccupied. This kind of observation by the practitioner can prove to be very helpful. In the relationship with a practitioner, clients tend to replicate the preoccupations that dominate their lives. It is important to recognize this parallel process, as it can provide clinical insight into the characteristic patterns that these individuals follow in relating to their social world. The practitioner demonstrates the professional use of self with clients to advance the work. It is not surprising that Irene is seeking out counseling—people with personality disorders are often unaware of the impact their behavior has on others.

Clients do not exist in a vacuum. There is more to Geoffrey than his life story and a description of symptoms. The competency-based assessment helps to individualize Geoffrey while exploring the full range of factors affecting his life.

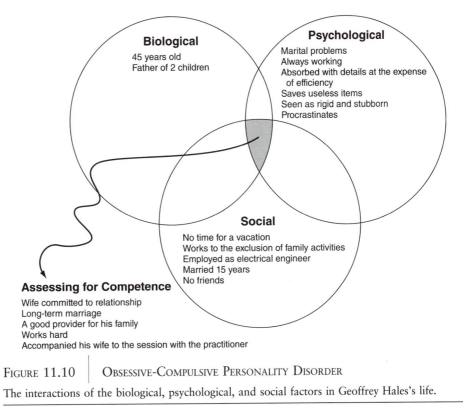

Biological

45 years old
Father of 2 children

Psychological

Marital problems
Always working
Absorbed with details at the expense
of efficiency
Saves useless items
Seen as rigid and stubborn
Procrastinates

Social

No time for a vacation
Works to the exclusion of family activities
Employed as electrical engineer
Married 15 years
No friends

Assessing for Competence

Wife committed to relationship
Long-term marriage
A good provider for his family
Works hard
Accompanied his wife to the session with the practitioner

FIGURE 11.10 | OBSESSIVE-COMPULSIVE PERSONALITY DISORDER

The interactions of the biological, psychological, and social factors in Geoffrey Hales's life.

© Cengage Learning

He is very committed to his family and is being a good provider. Since personality disorder features are ego-syntonic, Geoffrey has been genuinely unaware of the distress his behavior creates for his family.

GEOFFREY HALES'S MULTIAXIAL DSM DIAGNOSIS IS AS FOLLOWS:

Axis I	V71.09 (No diagnosis)
Axis II	301.4 Obsessive-Compulsive Personality Disorder, Moderate
Axis III	None
Axis IV	None
Axis V	GAF = 75 (current)

© Cengage Learning

SUMMARY

Individuals with a personality disorder relate to others and to their social environment in rigid and inflexible ways. As they attempt to cope with stress or respond to problems in their usual ways, matters only become worse. Unfortunately, the individual is largely unaware of the difficulties these behavioral patterns may pose and fails to recognize the connection to their personality. As a result, they generally do not seek out counseling on their own. If they do come to the practitioner's attention, it is usually through a referral or coercion by others in their social environment.

The ego-syntonic nature of their behavior makes change difficult, and they are largely unmotivated to give up this characteristic disposition. The individual's behavior frequently elicits the kind of response from others that reinforces their maladaptive traits. It is helpful for the practitioner to be aware of those distinctive ways that individuals with a personality disorder relate because this process will more than likely emerge in the counseling relationship. The case vignettes in this chapter demonstrate that individuals with a personality disorder are very different from one another—not just in terms of their symptoms but in the various strengths they have developed to cope with their life situations. Figure 11.11 provides

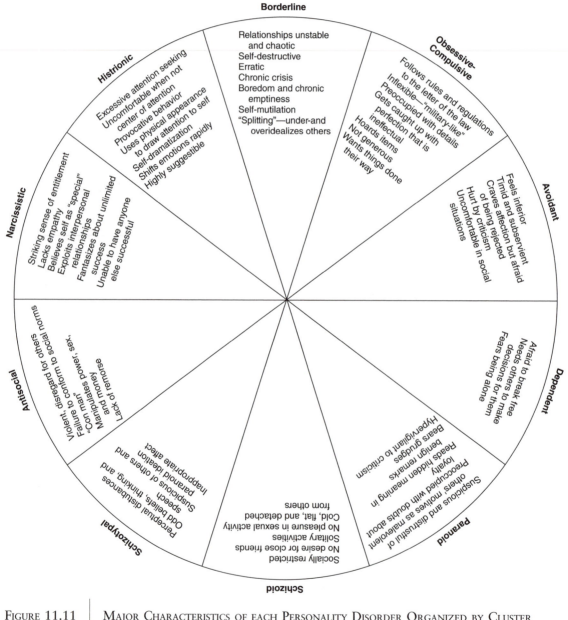

FIGURE 11.11   MAJOR CHARACTERISTICS OF EACH PERSONALITY DISORDER ORGANIZED BY CLUSTER

© Cengage Learning

an overview summarizing the major features of personality disorders.

The personality disorders have consistently presented diagnostic challenges for the practitioner, and this classification system will more than likely represent the most significant changes in the forthcoming DSM-5. First, the definition of what a personality disorder is, in general, is expected to change. The proposed revision suggests that instead of a pervasive pattern of thinking/emotionality/behaving, a personality disorder will indicate a person's adaptive failure involving impaired sense of self-identity or failure to develop effective interpersonal functioning. Every one of us has a set of personality features, but they will be considered as a personality disorder when there is a pervasive failure to adapt to the demands of everyday life. In addition, instead of ten personality types, DSM-5 has attempted to simplify the system by cutting them down to just five. The proposed types are: antisocial/psychopathic, avoidant, borderline, obsessive-compulsive, and schizotypal personality types. Eliminated will be the paranoid, schizoid, histrionic, narcissistic and dependent personality disorders. Each personality type will come with a narrative paragraph description. Practitioners will review a short summary of each type and then rate on a scale of 1 to 5 how much a person matches each category (with 4 or 5 being the threshold for diagnosis). Shaped around the widely used five-factor model of personality (Digman, 1990), the third aspect of the proposed system for diagnosing a personality disorder will be a series of six personality "trait domains." The six domains will include: negative emotionality, **introversion**, antagonism, disinhibition, compulsivity, and schizotypy. Practitioners will then be asked to rate each of the six domains on a 0–3 scale, depending on how descriptive each is of the client. The DSM-5 will provide subset of adjectives, or facets, for each of the six domains. Finally, two new personality disorders are expected to be included under the appendix for further study. They are depressive personality disorder (which includes self-criticism, dejection, a judgmental stance toward others, and a tendency to feel guilt) and passive-aggressive (negativistic) personality disorder (characterized by passive aggression in which people adopt a negativistic attitude to resist routine demands and expectations).

PRACTITIONER'S REFLECTIONS

Perhaps the greatest challenge for a practitioner trying to assess for personality disorders is to distinguish among those features that may be helpful and those that may get in the way of coping with and adapting to life's problems. The following activities are designed to encourage further reflections about the diagnostic categories of personality disorders.

ACTIVITIES

Advanced Clinical EP 2.1.1 b

1. People with a personality disorder generally do not come to the practitioner without some kind of external catalyst. Problem-solving behaviors, though troublesome to others, are ego-syntonic, and the person's motivation for change is often limited. Looking back on the cases discussed in this chapter, select one and imagine for a moment that the client in the vignette is coming to your agency or office for the first time. Role play with a colleague or your supervisor how you would conduct yourself in the interview. To highlight your ability to identify as a social work professional in the face of what potentially could be seen as a challenging client, consider the following:
   a. How would you start the initial interview?
   b. What strengths can you identify?
   c. What might potentially get in the way of developing a therapeutic relationship with this client (and their family)?

d. What is going on in this client's life that may be helpful in forming a therapeutic relationship?

2. Imagine that you have been assigned to work with Mr. Shull after his social worker, Dr. Gray, left the agency. This is your first interview with him, and he says abruptly, "You know, Dr. Gray was the greatest, and she knew everything about me. I just don't think you and I will be able to get along as well. My situation is so unique."

a. Role play with a colleague or your supervisor how you would respond to Mr. Shull.

b. Describe how you would go about developing, managing, and maintaining the therapeutic relationship with Mr. Shull.

c. Considering the competency-based assessment, looking to Mr. Schull's environment, what strengths noted in his case

vignette would influence your response?

3. Access the CourseMate website at www.cengagebrain.com. The case of "George" is highlighted on the Web site. His social history reveals a pattern of drug use beginning when he was about 9 or 10 years old. He talks about his anger and describes his long history of violating people's rights so often found in antisocial personality disorder.

a. As you review George's story, identify the professional strengths, limitations, and challenges you might encounter if George was your client.

b. What concerns would you discuss with your supervisor to advance your professional clinical social work practice skills?

COMPETENCY NOTES

EP 2.1.1 c: Attend to professional roles and boundaries (p. 392): Social workers commit themselves to the profession's enhancement and to their own professional conduct and growth.

EP Advanced Clinical 2.1.1 b: Demonstrate professional use of self with clients (pp. 408, 411): Advanced practitioners in clinical social work recognize the importance of the therapeutic relationship, the person-in-environment and strengths perspectives, the professional use of self with clients, and adherence to ethical guidelines of professional behavior.

EP Advanced Clinical 2.1.1 c: Understand and identify professional strengths, limitations and challenges (p. 412): Advanced practitioners in clinical social work recognize the importance of the therapeutic relationship, the person-in-environment and strengths perspectives, the professional use of self with clients, and adherence to ethical guidelines of professional behavior.

EP Advanced Clinical 2.1.1 d: Develop, manage, and maintain therapeutic relationships with clients within the person-in-environment and strengths perspectives (p. 412): Advanced practitioners in clinical social work recognize the importance of the therapeutic relationship, the person-in-environment and strengths perspectives, the professional use of self with clients, and adherence to ethical guidelines of professional behavior.

EP 2.1.4 a: Recognize the extent to which a culture's structures and values may oppress, marginalize, alienate, or create or enhance privilege and power (p. 385): Social workers understand how diversity characterizes and shapes the human experience and is critical to the formation of identity.

EP 2.1.7 a: Critique and apply knowledge to understand person and environment (pp. 368, 388): Social workers are able to apply theories and knowledge from the liberal arts to understand biological, social, cultural, psychological, and spiritual development.

EP 2.1.10 (b) a: Collect, organize, and interpret client data (pp. 370, 374, 378, 386, 396, 400, 404, 407): Social workers have the knowledge and skills to practice with individuals, families, groups, organizations, and communities.

EP Advanced Clinical 2.1.10 (b) c: Assess client's coping strategies to reinforce and improve adaptation to life situations, circumstances, and events (pp. 371, 375, 379, 383, 387, 392, 397, 401, 405, 408): Advanced practitioners have a theoretically informed knowledge base so as to effectively practice with individuals, families, and groups.

REFERENCES

American Psychiatric Association. (1952). *Diagnostic and statistical manual of mental disorders* (1st ed.). Washington, DC: Author.

American Psychiatric Association. (1968). *Diagnostic and statistical manual of mental disorders* (2nd ed.). Washington, DC: Author.

American Psychiatric Association. (1980). *Diagnostic and statistical manual of mental disorders* (3rd ed.). Washington, DC: Author.

American Psychiatric Association. (1987). *Diagnostic and statistical manual of mental disorders* (3rd ed.-revised). Washington, DC: Author.

American Psychiatric Association. (1994). *Diagnostic and statistical manual of mental disorders* (4th ed.). Washington, DC: Author.

American Psychiatric Association. (2000). *Diagnostic and statistical manual of mental disorders* (4th ed.-text revision). Washington, DC: Author.

Anderson, K. G., Sankis, L. M., & Widiger, T. A. (2001). Pathology versus statistical infrequency: Potential sources of gender bias in personality disorder criteria. *Journal of Nervous and Mental Disease, 189,* 661–668.

Austrian, S. G. (2005). *Mental disorders, medications, and clinical social work* (3rd ed.). New York: Columbia University Press.

Bakkevig, J. F., & Karterud, S. (2010). Is the Diagnostic and Statistical Manual of Mental Disorders, fourth edition, histrionic disorder category a valid construct? *Comprehensive Psychiatry, 51* (5), 462–470.

Barlow, D. H., & Durand, V. M. (2012). *Abnormal psychology: An integrative approach* (6th ed.). Belmont, CA, CA: Wadsworth Cengage.

Becker, D. F., Grilo, C. M., Edell, W. S., & McGlashan, T. H. (2000). Comorbidity of borderline personality disorder with other personality disorders in hospitalized adolescents and adults. *American Journal of Psychiatry, 157* (12), 2011–2016.

Bohus, M., Haaf, B., Stiglmayr, C., Pohl, U., Bohme, R., & Linehan, M. (2000). Evaluation of inpatient dialectical behavioral therapy for borderline personality disorder—A prospective study. *Behavior Research and Therapy 38* (9), 873–887.

Cloninger, C. R., & Svakic, D. M. (2009). Personality disorders. In B. J. Sadock, V. A. Sadock, & P. Ruiz (Eds.), *Kaplan and Sadock's comprehensive textbook of psychiatry* (19th ed., Vol II, pp. 2197–2240). Philadelphia, PA: Lippincott Williams and Wilkins.

Colman, L., Murray, J., Abbott, R., Maughan, B., Kuh, D., Croudace, T.... Jones, P. B. (2009). Outcomes of conduct problems in adolescence: 40 year follow-up of national cohort. *British Medical Journal, 338,* a2981.

Corey, G. (2009). *Theory and practice of counseling and psychotherapy* (8th ed.). Belmont, CA: Thomson Brooks/Cole.

DeBrito, S. A., & Hodgkins, S. (2009). Antisocial personality disorder. In M. McMurran & R. C. Howard (Eds.), *Personality, personality disorder and violence: An evidence based approach* (pp. 133–154). New York, NY: Wiley and Sons.

Digman, J. M. (1990). Personality structure: Emergence of the five-factor model. *Annual Review of Psychology, 41,* 417–440.

Distel, M. A., Trull, T. J., & Boomsma, D. I. (2009). Genetic epidemiology of borderline personality disorder. In M. H. Jackson & L. F. Westbrook (Eds.), *Borderline personality disorder: New research* (pp. 1–31). Hauppage, NY: Nova Science Publishers.

Douglas, K. S., Vincent, G. M., & Edens, J. R. (2006). Psychopathy and substance use disorders. In C. J. Patrick (Ed.), *Handbook of psychopathy* (pp. 533–554). New York, NY: Guilford.

Ferguson, C. (2010). Genetic contributions to antisocial personality and behavior: A meta-analytic review from an evolutionary perspective. *The Journal of Social Psychology, 150* (2), 160–180.

Fogelson, D. L., Nuechterlein, K. H., Asarnow, R. A., Payne, D. L., Subotnik, K. L., Jacobson, K. C., … Kendler, K. S. (2007). Avoidant personality disorder is a separable schizophrenia spectrum personality disorder even when controlling for the presence of paranoid and schizotypal personality disorders: The UCLA family study. *Schizophrenia Research, 91,* 192–199.

Foster, J. D., Campbell, W. K., & Twenge, J. M. (2003). Individual differences in narcissism: Inflated self-views across the lifespan and around the world. *Journal of Research in Personality, 37,* 469–486.

Fountoulakis, K. N., Lecht, S., & Kaprinis, G. S. (2008). Personality disorders and violence. *Current Opinion in Psychiatry, 21,* 84–92.

Gabbard, G. O. (2001). *Treatments of psychiatric disorders* (3rd ed.). Washington, DC: American Psychiatric Press.

Gelhorn, H. L., Sakai, J. T., Price, R. M., & Crowley, T. J. (2007). DSM-IV conduct disorder criteria as predictors of antisocial personality disorder. *Comprehensive Psychiatry, 48,* 529–538.

Gitterman, A. (2001). *Handbook of social work practice with vulnerable and resilient populations.* New York: Columbia University Press.

Goldstein, E. G., Miehls, D., & Ringel, S. (2009). *Advanced clinical social work practice: Relational principles and techniques.* New York: Columbia University Press.

Grant, B., Choi, S., Goldstein, R., Huang, B., Stinson, F., Saha, T., … Pickering, R. P. (2008). Prevalence, correlates, disability, and comorbidity of DSM-IV borderline personality disorder: Results from the Wave 2 National Epidemiologic Survey on Alcohol and Related Conditions. *The Journal of Clinical Psychiatry, 69* (4), 533.

Hare, R. D. (1993). *Without conscience: The disturbing world of the psychopaths among us.* New York: Pocket Books.

Kearney, C. A., & Trull, T. J. (2012). *Abnormal psychology and life: A dimensional approach.* Belmont, CA: Wadsworth Cengage Learning.

Kessler, R. C., Crum, R. M., Warner, L. A., Nelson, C. B., Schulenberg, J., & Antony, J. C. (1997). Lifetime co-occurrence of DSM-III alcohol abuse and dependence with other psychiatric disorder in the National Comorbidity Survey. *Archives of General Psychiatry, 54* (4), 313–321.

Laub, J. H., & Vaillant, G. E. (2000). Delinquency and mortality: A 50-year follow-up study of 1,000 delinquent and nondelinquent boys. *American Journal of Psychiatry 157,* 96–102.

Layton, M. (1995). Emerging from the shadows. *Family Therapy Networker,* May/June, 35–41.

Lenzenweger, M., Lane, M., Loranger, A., & Kessler, R. (2007). DSM-IV personality disorders in the National Comorbidity Survey Replication. *Biological Psychiatry 62* (6), 553–564.

Linehan, M. M., & Dexter-Mazza, E. T. (2008). Dialectical behavior therapy for borderline personality disorder. In D. H. Barlow (Ed.), *Clinical handbook of psychological disorders: A step-by-step treatment manual* (4th ed., pp. 365–420). New York: Guilford Press.

Lynam, D. R., & Widiger, T. A. (2007). Using a general model of personality to understand sex differences in the personality disorders. *Journal of Personality disorders, 21,* 583–602.

Maher, B. A., & Maher, W. B. (1985). Psychopathology: I From ancient times to the eighteenth century. In G. A. Kimble & K. Schlesinger (Eds.), *Topics in the history of psychology* (pp. 251–294). Hillsdale, NJ: Erlbaum.

Marinangeli, M. G., Butti, B., Scinto, A., Di Cicco, L., Petruzzi, C., Daneluzzo, E., & Rossi, A. (2000). Patterns of comorbidity among DSM-III R personality disorders. *Psychopathology, 33* (2), 69–74.

Meissner, W. W. (2001). In G. O. Gabbard (Ed.). *Treatment of psychiatric disorders,* Vol. 2 (3rd ed., pp. 2227–2236). Washington DC: American Psychiatric Press.

Meloy, J. R. (2001). Antisocial personality. In G. O. Gabbard (Ed.), *Treatment in psychiatric disorders,* Vol. 2 (3rd ed., pp. 2251–2272). Washington, DC: American Psychiatric Press.

Miller, J. D., Campbell, W. K., & Pilkonis, P. A. (2007). Narcissistic personality disorder: Relations with distress and functional impairment. *Comprehensive Psychiatry, 48,* 170–177.

Nugent, S. A. (2000). Perfectionism: Its manifestations and classroom-based interventions. *Journal of Secondary Gifted Education, 11,* 215–221.

Phillips, K. A., Yen, S., & Gunderson, J. G. (2003). Personality disorders. In R. E. Hales & S. C. Yudofsky (Eds.), *Textbook of clinical psychiatry* (4th ed., pp. 804–832). Washington, DC: American Psychiatric Press.

Rouff, L. (2000). Schizoid personality traits among the homeless mentally ill: A quantitative and assessment. In C. J. Patrick (Ed.), *Handbook of psychopathy* (pp. 389–414). New York, NY: Guilford.

Sadock, B. J., Sadock, V. A., & Ruiz, P. (2009). *Kaplan and Sadock's comprehensive textbook of psychiatry* (9th ed.). Philadelphia, PA: Lippincott, Williams and Wilkins.

Sprock, J. (2000). Gender-typed behavioral examples of histrionic personality disorder. *Journal of Psychopathology and Behavioral Assessment, 22,* 107–122.

Stoudemire, A. (1994). *Clinical psychiatry for medical students.* Philadelphia: J. B. Lippencott.

Svartberg ,M., Styles, T. C., & Seltzer, M. H. (2004). Randomized, controlled trial of the effectiveness of short-term dynamic psychotherapy and cognitive therapy for cluster C personality disorders. *American Journal of Psychiatry, 161,* 810–817.

Teyber, E., & McClure, F. (2011). *Interpersonal process in psychotherapy: An integrative model* (6th ed.). Belmont, CA: Brooks/Cole Cengage.

Trull, T. J., Jahng, S., Tomko, R. L., Wood, P. K., & Sher, K. J. (2010). Revised NESARC personality disorder diagnoses: Gender, prevalence, and comorbidity with substance dependence disorders. *Journal of Personality disorders, 24,* 412–426.

Trull, T. J., Sher, K. J., Minks-Brown, C., Durbin, J., & Burr, R. (2000). Borderline personality disorder and substance use disorders: A review and integration. *Clinical Psychology Review, 20,* 235–253.

Tyrer, P., & Davidson, K. (2000). Cognitive therapy for personality disorders. In J. G. Gunderson & G. O. Gabbard (Eds.). *Psychotherapy for personality disorders* (pp. 131–149). Washington, DC: American Psychiatric Press.

Voglmaier, M. M., Seidman, L. J., Niznikiewicz, M. A., Dickey, C. C., Shenton, M. E., & McCarley, R. W. (2000). Verbal and nonverbal neuropsychological test performance in subjects with schizotypal personality disorder. *American Journal of Psychiatry, 157,* 787–793.

Wilkinson-Ryan, T. A., & Westen, D. (2000). Identity disturbance in borderline personality disorder: An empirical investigation. *American Journal of Psychiatry, 157,* 528–541.

Wolff, S. (2000). Schizoid personality in childhood and Asperger syndrome. In A. Kline, F. R. Volkmar, &S. S. Sparrow (Eds.), *Asperger syndrome* (pp. 278–305). New York: Guilford Press.

Zanarini, M. C., Frankenburg, F. R., Hennen, J., Reich, D. B., & Silk, K. R. (2006). Prediction of the 10year course of borderline personality disorder. *American Journal of Psychiatry, 163,* 827–832.

Zanarini, M. C., Reichman, C. A., Frankenburg, F. R., Reich, D. B., & Fitzmaurice, G. (2010). The course of eating disorders in patients with borderline personality disorder: a 10-year follow-up study. *International Journal of Eating Disorders, 43* (3), 226–232.

Assessing for Competency in Psychopathology

The following questions are designed to test your competency in psychopathology. Some items require you to apply what you know to a case study involving a hypothetical client. Other questions ask you to remember information about the various diagnostic categories. The section heading indicates the chapter where the answer can be found. You may want to answer these questions before reading the book in order to test your understanding of psychopathology. Alternatively, you might try to answer the questions after reading the book and then review those chapters where you had the most incorrect answers. All in all, I hope this quiz will better prepare you for knowing about psychopathology. Good luck with the questions!

CHAPTER ONE–AN INTRODUCTION TO THE COMPETENCY-BASED ASSESSMENT MODEL

1. The DSM, or *Diagnostic and Statistical Manual*, is considered the:
   a. Classification system for general medical disorders
   b. Psychological evaluation measurement
   c. Handbook to the treatment of mental illness
   d. Standard reference used to diagnose all mental disorders
2. The multiaxial system does not record:
   a. Clinical disorders
   b. General medical conditions
   c. Personality disorders and other conditions that may be a focus of clinical attention
   d. Cultural background
3. Social workers in the mental health field are often encouraged to fully evaluate each client utilizing the DSM's five axes. What information is listed on the third axis?

    a. General medical conditions
    b. Psychosocial and environmental problems
    c. The presenting clinical problem
    d. Personality disorders and/or mental retardation

4. Axis II is used to code all of the following *except*:
    a. Mental retardation
    b. Schizotypal personality disorder
    c. Obsessive-compulsive personality disorder
    d. Schizophreniform disorder

5. Axis I is used to record all of the following *except*:
    a. Cognitive disorders
    b. Anxiety disorders
    c. Mental retardation
    d. Schizophrenia and other psychotic disorders

CHAPTER TWO–DISORDERS OF INFANCY, CHILDHOOD, OR ADOLESCENCE

6. Six-year-old Christina has been telling her brothers about her field trip to the zoo with her Girl Scout Brownies troop. She was fascinated with petting zoo and what she fed the goats that day. This behavior would come as a surprise to her teachers in school who never heard her talk. Christina's diagnosis would be:
    a. Childhood disintegrative disorder
    b. Selective mutism
    c. Tourette's disorder
    d. Disruptive behavior NOS

7. Paul's behavior is typified by uncontrollable squeals, odd grunting sounds, and sniffing. His diagnosis is:
    a. Selective mutism
    b. Attention deficit hyperactivity disorder hyperactive-impulsive type
    c. Rumination disorder
    d. Tourette's disorder

8. One of the defining characteristics of children with _____ disorder is that they do not develop the types of social relationships expected for their age.
    a. Autistic disorder
    b. Asperger's disorder
    c. Pica
    d. Conduct disorder

9. One of the symptoms shown in children with this disorder is the consistent violation of others. This disorder is called:
    a. Oppositional defiant disorder
    b. Conduct disorder
    c. Rett's disorder
    d. Childhood disintegrative disorder

10. Children with this disorder may have problems with symptoms of inattention, hyperactivity, and impulsivity. This disorder is:

a. Attention deficit hyperactivity disorder predominately inattentive type
b. Attention deficit hyperactivity disorder predominately hyperactive-impulsive type
c. Attention deficit hyperactivity disorder combined type
d. Attention deficit hyperactivity disorder NOS

CHAPTER THREE–COGNITIVE DISORDERS: DELIRIUM AND DEMENTIA

11. Dr. Johnson, a physician, referred his 73-year-old patient, Abner Smith, to you for a consultation. Mr. Smith has been having difficulty remembering and concentrating for the last 3 years. He came to the interview with his son, Jake. Abner Smith admitted to feeling depressed and anxious. His wife of 48 years died several years ago, and since that time he has lived alone in their house. Jake Smith added that his father seems to have changed over time; his father leaves food cooking on the stove unattended, was found wandering around the neighborhood as if he was lost, and forgets the names of family members. These symptoms support the diagnosis of:
    a. Dementia
    b. Delirium
    c. Paranoid personality disorder
    d. Schizophrenia, paranoid type

12. Kenny Grayson accepted a new job in another town several hundred miles away, and he is worried about leaving his 72-year-old father behind. Kenny's father lives alone, is very confused, and is bowel- and bladder-incontinent. In addition, the senior Grayson suffered a mild stroke several years ago, which left a number of areas in his brain damaged. He is now showing signs of neurological impairment. What is the most likely DSM-IV diagnosis for Kenny's father?
    a. Dementia due to a general medical condition
    b. Dementia of the Alzheimer's type
    c. Dissociative fugue
    d. Vascular dementia

13. The clinical picture of dementia, Alzheimer's type, includes all of the following symptoms, *except*:
    a. Sudden onset
    b. Individual gets lost in familiar places
    c. Night restlessness and difficulty falling asleep
    d. Short-term memory loss

14. The majority of people who experience an episode of delirium:
    a. Tend to progress rapidly to dementia without recovery
    b. Usually recover within several days or weeks after the causative factor is eliminated
    c. Do not recover unless treated with a carbamazepine protocol
    d. Should have psychosocial rehabilitation to support social and functioning skills that the individual may have lost in the earlier phase of the episode

15. Edna Trybus states that her mother, Hilda Walker, 75 years old, has become increasingly irritable and reclusive over the last 4 or 5 years. Mrs. Walker

accuses her children of plotting to steal her house and her life savings. Mrs. Walker has been unable to care for herself; for example, she cannot cook her own meals, dress herself, or clean her home. Mrs. Walker is often confused in that she cannot remember her home address, her phone number, or her children's names. What DSM-IV diagnosis best describes Mrs. Walker's signs and symptoms?
   a. Agoraphobia, without panic disorder
   b. Delirium
   c. Pick's disease
   d. Dementia, Alzheimer's type

CHAPTER FOUR–SUBSTANCE-RELATED DISORDERS

16. The substance use disorders are:
    a. Substance dependence and abuse
    b. Substance intoxication and withdrawal
    c. Polysubstance dependence
    d. All of the above

17. If a person is on agonist therapy, this means that they:
    a. Are in a great deal of pain
    b. Are taking certain medications that can cause delirium
    c. Are taking a substance that "tricks" the body into reacting as if the endogenous chemical were present
    d. Are in an environment where access to substances is restricted

18. _____ occurs when a person uses a drug without a legitimate medical need to do so.
    a. Dependence
    b. Abuse
    c. Intoxication
    d. Withdrawal

19. _____ is defined as specific behavioral patterns and symptoms (including cognitive impairment, emotional lability, belligerence, impaired judgment, and poor social or occupational functioning) due to recent use of a drug, alcohol, medication, or toxin.
    a. Dependence
    b. Abuse
    c. Intoxication
    d. Withdrawal

20. When assessing for substance use, it is helpful to explore:
    a. Route of administration
    b. Duration of effects
    c. Use of multiple substances
    d. All of the above

21. The following is considered the most commonly used drug in the United States and is legal for adults over the age of 21:
    a. Sedatives
    b. Anxiolytics

    c. Alcohol

    d. Nicotine

22. The following drugs are usually prescribed for short-term relief of severe and debilitating anxiety and may cause dependence when not used as directed:

    a. Benzodiazepines

    b. Barbiturates

    c. Opioids

    d. Sedatives

23. These drugs, also known as speed or pep pills, are central nervous system stimulants that are usually synthetically made in illegal labs.

    a. Cocaine

    b. Amphetamines

    c. Opioids

    d. Hallucinogens

24. A hallucinogen persisting perception disorder is commonly referred to as:

    a. Flashbacks

    b. Snorting

    c. A "bad trip"

    d. A hangover

25. _____ are a chemically diverse group of psychoactive substances that includes a variety of substances found in common household products.

    a. Hallucinogens

    b. Inhalants

    c. Phencyclidines

    d. Green hornets

CHAPTER FIVE–SCHIZOPHRENIA AND OTHER PSYCHOTIC DISORDERS

26. Mrs. Stacy Hill contacted the XYZ Mental Health Center because she is concerned about her 24-year-old daughter, Violet, who lives at home and is displaying several symptoms that seem to be cause for concern. Violet's symptoms include persecutory delusions, auditory hallucinations, incoherence, and loosening of associations. According to Mrs. Hill, her daughter was just fine until 3 months ago when this "strange behavior suddenly developed." There is some family history of schizophrenia. What would your diagnosis be?

    a. Schizophrenia, paranoid type

    b. Schizophreniform disorder

    c. Schizoid personality disorder

    d. Brief psychotic disorder

27. Sarah, age 23, gave birth to her first child 3 days ago. Her initial complaints consisted of insomnia, restlessness, and emotional lability that progressed to confusion, irritability, delusions, and thoughts of wanting to harm her baby. What is the most correct diagnosis?

    a. Brief psychotic disorder, postpartum onset

    b. Autoscopic psychosis

    c. Cotard's syndrome

    d. Induced delusional disorder

28. A delusional system shared by two or more persons was previously known as induced paranoid disorder and *folie à deux*. Persecutory delusions are most common, and the key presentation is the sharing and blind acceptance of these delusions between two (or more) people. What is the name of this disorder according to the DSM-IV?
    a. Pseudomentia
    b. Shared psychotic disorder
    c. Capgras disorder NOS
    d. Schizophreniform disorder

29. Mario Walters believes that he has developed a major plan that would end all hunger, homelessness, and crime in the world. In addition, he believes the President of the United States, the Queen of England, and various important heads of state support his plan. This is an example of:
    a. Delusions of persecution
    b. Tangential thought
    c. Delusions of grandeur
    d. Neologism

30. Luther Ortega once met the criteria for schizophrenia. However, he no longer has the pronounced symptoms of disorganized speech or behavior, delusions, or hallucinations. Luther does occasionally exhibit odd beliefs and peculiarities of behavior. What would be the correct diagnosis?
    a. Schizophrenia, disorganized type
    b. Schizoaffective disorder, not otherwise specified
    c. Schizophrenia, residual type
    d. Schizophreniform disorder

31. This disorder is a delayed effect of taking long-term antipsychotic medication. The signs and symptoms of this disorder consist of abnormal, involuntary, irregular movements of the muscles in the head, limbs, and the trunk of the body. The most common symptoms include the twisting, chewing, and protruding thrusting movements of the tongue. This disorder is known as:
    a. Huntington's disease
    b. Gorsion dystonia
    c. Sydenham's chorea
    d. Tardive dyskensia

32. Echopraxia is:
    a. The pathological imitation of another person's movements
    b. Difficulty finding the correct name for an object (or objects)
    c. A condition in which the individual's speech is halting, laborious, and inaccurate
    d. Pathological persistence of an irresistible feeling that cannot be eliminated

33. The pathological repeating (over and over) of the same word or phrase just spoken by another person is called:
    a. Verbigeration
    b. Anologism
    c. Echolalia
    d. Hebephrenia

CHAPTER SIX–MOOD DISORDERS

34. John Sanford constantly worries about his health, finances, job security, and the stability of his marriage. He worries about absolutely everything. Often, his worries keep him awake at night, causing him to be so fatigued at work that he cannot perform his duties adequately. His wife, Sharron, is becoming frustrated with him because he is so preoccupied with his worries that he is unable to do his chores around the house or help care for their children. What is John's most likely diagnosis?
    a. Panic disorder
    b. Simple phobia
    c. Generalized anxiety disorder
    d. Obsessive-compulsive disorder
35. Which of the following list of symptoms is the first sign of the beginning of a manic episode?
    a. Racing thoughts
    b. Hallucinations
    c. Hypergraphia
    d. A change in sleeping patterns
36. Which of the following symptoms is not apparent in a manic episode?
    a. The person is more talkative than usual or evidences pressured speech
    b. Distractibility—attention too easily drawn to irrelevant stimuli
    c. Excessive sleeping
    d. Excessive involvement in pleasurable activities
37. One subtype of bipolar mood disorder is characterized by four or more episodes a year with mania and depression following each other. Which type is this?
    a. Seasonal affective disorder
    b. Double depression
    c. Rapid cycling
    d. Cyclothymia
38. _____ was formerly known as depressive neurosis and was considered less severe than major depressive disorder. This disorder is more common in women than in men and is chronic. Its onset is insidious and occurs more often in persons with a history of long-term stress or sudden loss. This disorder often coexists with other psychiatric disorders (e.g., substance abuse, personality disorders, and obsessive-compulsive disorder). This diagnosis requires the presence of at least two of the following symptoms: poor appetite, overeating, sleep problems, fatigue, and/or low self-esteem. What is this disorder?
    a. Panic disorder
    b. Dysthymic disorder
    c. Schizoaffective disorder
    d. Post-traumatic stress disorder
39. Which of the following would not be present during a major depressive episode?
    a. Changes in sleep and/or appetite habits
    b. Anxiety
    c. Anhedonia
    d. Grandiosity

40. Maria Gonzalez was agitated and screaming when her family brought her to the emergency room of a local hospital. The previous week, Maria had learned that her former husband had remarried in their home country, the Dominican Republic. Since then, she has become increasingly agitated, has developed insomnia, and is unable to eat—and by the time she arrived at the emergency room, she alternated between being mute and mumbling unintelligibly in both Spanish and English. She was admitted to the psychiatric unit and was given a small dose of an antipsychotic medication with no response. The social worker reported that Ms. Gonzalez had outbursts of bizarre behavior, had ideas of reference, complained of headaches, and felt "out of control." In addition, she cried, pulled her hair, rocked back and forth, and could not be consoled. Over a period of 3 days, Maria's family assured her that she and her children would be well cared for, and the psychotic-like symptoms resolved, at which time she was released from the hospital. Ms. Gonzalez's diagnosis would be:
    a. Ataque de nervios, a culture-bound syndrome
    b. Hysterical conversion disorder
    c. Panic disorder without agoraphobia
    d. Bipolar II disorder
41. Euphoria, boundless optimism, inflated self-esteem, and grandiosity are characteristic symptoms of:
    a. Bipolar disorder, manic type
    b. Schizophrenia, catatonic type
    c. Delusional disorder
    d. No mental disorder is present

CHAPTER SEVEN–ANXIETY DISORDERS

42. Ilene has a tremendous fear of public speaking, and she makes every effort to avoid formal speeches in front of others. This symptom may indicate:
    a. Specific phobia
    b. Nonspecific phobia
    c. Phenophobia
    d. Social phobia
43. Agoraphobia is defined as the fear and avoidance of:
    a. Anxiety-provoking events and situations
    b. Situations and places from which escape might be difficult or embarrassing
    c. Interactions with anxiety-provoking individuals
    d. Performing in public
44. Three basic types of panic attack are identified in the DSM-IV. These include all of the following *except*:
    a. Situationally bound
    b. Free floating
    c. Unexpected
    d. Situationally predisposed

45. A panic attack may be characterized by all of the following *except*:
    a. An abrupt experience of intense fear or discomfort
    b. Heart palpitations
    c. Sweating
    d. Elevated mood

46. Post-traumatic stress disorder may arise after any of the following events *except*:
    a. A traumatic wartime experience
    b. An earthquake, flood, or hurricane
    c. An allergic medication reaction
    d. Sudden death of a loved one

47. Dylan is extremely afraid of snakes. He makes every effort to never be in the presence of them or even to look at pictures of snakes. His phobia is considered:
    a. Social phobia
    b. A complex phobia
    c. Agoraphobia
    d. A specific phobia

CHAPTER EIGHT–SOMATOFORM, FACTITIOUS, AND MALINGERING DISORDERS

48. The following symptoms are all necessary for a DSM-IV diagnosis of hypochrondriasis *except*:
    a. Preoccupation with the fear of acquiring a serious or life-threatening disease
    b. Preoccupation with suing one's doctor for not finding a serious or life-threatening disease
    c. A misperception of one's own bodily symptoms
    d. Significant distress in one's everyday functioning

49. Kenny Marks, a third-year medical student, returned to the student health services for the fifth time with complaints of diarrhea. After a thorough medical workup that included a barium enema and various other procedures, Kenny was told that there was no organic disease present. Despite this reassurance from several doctors, Kenny continued to test his stool for blood, and remained convinced that the doctors missed making the correct diagnosis. Kenny is exhibiting:
    a. Malingering disorder
    b. Hypochondriasis
    c. Body dysmorphic disorder
    d. Conversion disorder

50. Malingering disorder differs from factitious disorder in the following way:
    a. "Clanging" is more prominent in the factitious disorder than in malingering
    b. In malingering, there is an identifiable external gain
    c. There is evidence of displacement of anxiety left over from the oral stage
    d. Malingering is similar to factitious disorder but with fewer symptoms

51. Josette Saint-Jean, age 27, recently experienced an episode of blindness following a physical assault that occurred while she was walking home from work. Upon physical examination in a local emergency room, her eyes were found to exhibit normal dilation when exposed to light. Josette related that her blindness developed spontaneously when the police officers at the scene asked her to come down to the station and go through mug shots. What is your diagnosis?
    a. Dissociative disorder, not otherwise specified
    b. Depersonalization disorder
    c. Dissociative fugue
    d. Conversion disorder

52. _____ is characterized by the voluntary production of signs, symptoms, or disease for no other apparent goal than to be cast in the role of being "sick." What is this disorder called?
    a. Conversion disorder
    b. Malingering disorder
    c. Factitious disorder
    d. Munchausen syndrome by proxy

53. Which of the following disorders was originally known as Briquet's syndrome?
    a. Dissociative identity disorder
    b. Somatization disorder
    c. Body dysmorphic disorder
    d. Hypochondriasis

54. Hope Udall is a shy, anxious-looking 29-year-old homemaker who was hospitalized after an overdose of Valium washed down with some vodka. While in the hospital, Hope met with the social worker in a darkened room and insisted on wearing a scarf that covered her hair, and nose. When the social worker asked what had happened to bring Hope in, she replied, "I have no friends, and my husband just left me. It's just so hard to talk about. I don't know if I can, it's too embarrassing." After some discussion, she revealed that the overdose was because of her nose, which she described as "grotesque and deformed." She related to the social worker that her nose has "huge pock marks and ugly bumps." The social worker did not note any such appearance and, in fact, saw a lovely young woman of normal appearance. According to the DSM-IV criteria, what would Hope's diagnosis be?
    a. Narcissistic personality disorder
    b. Body dysmorphic disorder
    c. Histrionic personality disorder
    d. Generalized anxiety disorder

55. The essential feature of this disorder is an individual's intentional production of an illness; that is, grossly exaggerating physical and/or psychological symptoms motivated by external incentives such as obtaining financial compensation through litigation or disability status or to avoid military duty. This criterion meets which diagnosis?
    a. Malingering disorder
    b. Neuropsychiatric organizational disorder
    c. Hysterical conversion disorder
    d. Somatothymic disorder

CHAPTER NINE–DISSOCIATIVE DISORDERS

56. Nathan Roberts's complaints include: "My perception of my environment often feels distorted or strange. Like, sometimes I have a sudden overwhelming sense of being detached from my own body. During some of these episodes, I can't understand people when they talk to me. The best way I can describe it is that I feel like a robot—or like I'm really outside of my body." Mr. Roberts says that he has been experiencing these episodes since he was a teenager and that they are often accompanied by feelings of anxiety, panic, or depression. What is your beginning assessment?
    a. Dissociative fugue
    b. Depersonalization disorder
    c. Dissociative amnesia
    d. Dissociative identity disorder

57. Ling Wong is a 34-year-old woman who recently survived the sinking of a ferryboat on the Mississippi River. She claims she has no memory of the events surrounding this disaster, including how she got ashore. Her physical examination was unremarkable, and her cognitive ability is intact. She is very distraught about the unknown fate of her husband, who was also aboard the ferry. She can remember everything but the event. Which of the following is Ling's diagnosis?
    a. Amnesia due to transient cerebral anoxia
    b. Dissociative amnesia
    c. Dissociative fugue
    d. Derealization disorder

58. Which of the following factors contributes to the difficulty in assessing dissociative identity disorder?
    a. These individuals are difficult to hypnotize because it is impossible to gain access to each of the separate "alters"
    b. Some of the presenting symptoms may appear similar to symptoms of schizophrenia
    c. Few individuals report gaps in memory
    d. The different personalities are usually in conflict with each other

59. Which of the following is true of dissociative identity disorder?
    a. The separate identities are always fully developed
    b. There are rarely more than two separate identities
    c. It was previously known as multiple personality disorder (MPD)
    d. Each of the identities is completely aware of the others

60. In almost all cases of dissociative identity disorder, an apparent cause is found in the client's history, which includes:
    a. An overactive imagination
    b. Lack of social support
    c. Severe physical and/or sexual abuse during childhood
    d. Familial predisposition

CHAPTER TEN–EATING DISORDERS

61. Which of the following is a feature found in both bulimia nervosa and anorexia nervosa?
    a. Excessive concern with body weight
    b. Excessive fear of being fat
    c. Bingeing
    d. Weight loss

62. Which of the following is considered the most severe medical complication associated with bulimia?
    a. Dental erosion
    b. Irregular heartbeat
    c. Electrolyte imbalance
    d. Hypertension

63. Which of the following is *not* considered an eating disorder by the DSM-IV?
    a. Binge eating disorder (BED)
    b. Obesity
    c. Anorexia nervosa
    d. Bulimia nervosa

64. Twarla Jones is just less than 5 feet tall and weighs 80 pounds. She has always been involved in her school's cheerleading, swim team, and gymnastics. When she turned 16 several months ago, she became extremely fearful about gaining weight. Twarla initially began to limit her food and caloric intake. In addition, she began exercising excessively in order to prevent herself from gaining weight. Twarla calls herself "a blimp." However, her parents, teachers, and friends all reassure her that she is quite thin. Twarla's diagnosis is probably:
    a. Bulimia nervosa, purging type
    b. Anorexia nervosa, restricting type
    c. Eating disorder, not otherwise specified
    d. Bulimia nervosa, nonpurging type

65. _____ refers to self-induced vomiting or laxative misuse to influence body weight.
    a. Purging
    b. Excessive exercise
    c. Restricting
    d. Binge eating

66. Each of the following medical complications, *except* _____, is associated with anorexia nervosa.
    a. Dry yellowish skin
    b. High blood pressure
    c. Bradycardia (slow heartbeat)
    d. Electrolyte imbalance

CHAPTER ELEVEN–THE PERSONALITY DISORDERS

67. Perry Max lives his life following a very strict schedule everyday. Perry must have everything perfect, in its place, and organized. He is devoted to his job as a plant manager, and he insists on following all rules and regulations without deviation. Perry has not taken a vacation in 10 years. Although he loves his job, Perry has tremendous difficulty completing projects and getting his reports done in a timely fashion. Which of the following best characterizes his personality type?
    a. Paranoid
    b. Obsessive-compulsive
    c. Dependent
    d. Avoidant

68. Jamie is a 19-year-old man who was mandated to therapy by the court and assigned to you for an intake appointment. Reviewing the background materials, you notice that the client has exhibited significant signs of conduct disturbance since the age of 14. He has a history of lying, stealing, and selling drugs—he physically attacked his mother on several occasions. He shows no remorse and is indifferent to others' suffering. In session, the client seems surly and irritable. He blames others for his problems with the law. The best diagnosis for this client is:
    a. Cluster A personality disorder
    b. Antisocial personality disorder
    c. Oppositional defiant disorder
    d. Borderline personality disorder

69. Nancy has recently been assigned to you because her prior worker left the agency. You note from the psychosocial history in her file that she has a tendency to sexualize all relationships and displayed irrational emotional outbreaks to her previous worker. She likes to be the center of attention. Nancy also shows a tendency toward suggestibility, dramatization, and chaotic behavior. Her diagnosis would be:
    a. Schizoid personality disorder
    b. Histrionic personality disorder
    c. Borderline personality disorder
    d. Narcissistic personality disorder

70. According to his family, Barry, 28 years of age, has always been shy. He did not do well in grade school and dropped out of high school before graduating. He is described as being isolated, having no friends, and showing no interest in dating or sexual activity. Despite adequate intelligence, Barry has never been able to keep a job. He lives at home with his father—he is so unmotivated and so isolated that he has never bothered to obtain a driver's license. He plays computer games all day. Beyond Barry's reclusive nature and emotional aloofness, he has no desire to change and refuses to go for counseling. What is Barry's diagnosis?
    a. Avoidant personality disorder
    b. Borderline personality disorder
    c. Schizoid personality disorder
    d. Dependent personality disorder

71. According to the DSM-IV, the ten personality disorders are divided into _____ clusters that are based on certain descriptive characteristics.
    a. 1
    b. 2
    c. 3
    d. 4

72. Cluster _____ personality disorders are characterized by odd and eccentric behaviors.
    a. A
    b. B
    c. C
    d. D

73. A pervasive distrust and suspiciousness of others characterize _____ personality disorder, such that the motives of others are interpreted as malevolent, and hidden meanings are read into benign remarks.
    a. Paranoid
    b. Schizoid
    c. Dependent
    d. Histrionic

74. Which of the following personality disorders is most closely related to schizophrenia?
    a. Borderline
    b. Antisocial
    c. Schizotypal
    d. Schizoid

75. This personality disorder is characterized by excessive expression of emotion and attention seeking.
    a. Obsessive-compulsive
    b. Histrionic
    c. Narcissistic
    d. Schizotypal

76. Which of the following personality disorders is best characterized by feelings of inadequacy, extreme sensitivity to negative remarks, and social inhibition?
    a. Avoidant
    b. Schizoid
    c. Dependent
    d. Borderline

77. Cluster C personality disorders are characterized by _____ behaviors.
    a. Aggressive and hostile
    b. Dramatic, emotional, and erratic
    c. Odd and eccentric
    d. Anxious and fearful

78. Persons with this personality disorder are described as having a preoccupation with orderliness, perfectionism, and mental and interpersonal control at the cost of being flexible and efficient.

    a. Narcissistic
    b. Histrionic
    c. Obsessive-compulsive
    d. Dependent

79. Cheyenne is described as having a tremendous amount of instability in inter-personal relationships, a poor self-image, marked impulsivity, and self-destructive behaviors. Her personality disorder would most likely be which of the following?
    a. Narcissistic
    b. Borderline
    c. Antisocial
    d. Paranoid

80. Cluster B personality disorders include all of the following *except* _____.
    a. Antisocial
    b. Borderline
    c. Histrionic
    d. Paranoid

ANSWER KEY

1. (d) Standard reference used to diagnose all mental disorders
2. (d) Cultural background
3. (a) General medical conditions
4. (d) Schizophreniform disorder
5. (c) Mental retardation
6. (b) Selective mutism
7. (d) Tourette's disorder
8. (a) Autistic disorder
9. (b) Conduct disorder
10. (c) Attention deficit hyperactivity disorder combined type
11. (a) Dementia
12. (d) Vascular dementia
13. (a) Sudden onset
14. (b) Usually recover within several days or weeks after the causative factor is eliminated
15. (d) Dementia, Alzheimer's type
16. (d) All of the above
17. (c) Taking a substance that "tricks" the body into reacting as if the endogenous chemical were present
18. (b) Abuse
19. (d) Withdrawal
20. (d) All of the above
21. (c) Alcohol
22. (a) Benzodiazepines

23. (b) Amphetamines
24. (a) Flashbacks
25. (b) Inhalants
26. (b) Schizophreniform disorder
27. (a) Brief psychotic disorder, postpartum onset
28. (b) Shared psychotic disorder
29. (c) Delusions of grandeur
30. (c) Schizophrenia, residual type
31. (d) Tardive dyskensia
32. (a) The pathological imitation of another person's movements
33. (c) Echolalia
34. (c) Generalized anxiety disorder
35. (a) Racing thoughts
36. (c) Excessive sleeping
37. (c) Rapid cycling
38. (b) Dysthymic disorder
39. (d) Grandiosity
40. (a) Ataque de nervios, a culture-bound syndrome
41. (a) Bipolar disorder, manic type
42. (d) Social phobia
43. (b) Situations and places from which escape might be difficult or embarrassing
44. (b) Free floating
45. (d) Elevated mood
46. (c) An allergic medication reaction
47. (d) A specific phobia
48. (b) Preoccupation with suing one's doctor for not finding a serious or life-threatening disease
49. (b) Hypochondriasis
50. (b) In malingering, there is an identifiable external gain
51. (d) Conversion disorder
52. (c) Factitious disorder
53. (b) Somatization disorder
54. (b) Body dysmorphic disorder
55. (a) Malingering disorder
56. (b) Depersonalization disorder
57. (b) Dissociative amnesia
58. (b) Some of the presenting symptoms may appear similar to symptoms of schizophrenia
59. (c) It was previously known as multiple personality disorder (MPD)
60. (c) Severe physical and/or sexual abuse during childhood
61. (a) Excessive concern with body weight
62. (c) Electrolyte imbalance

63. (b) Obesity
64. (b) Anorexia nervosa, restricting type
65. (a) Purging
66. (b) High blood pressure
67. (b) Obsessive-compulsive
68. (b) Antisocial personality disorder
69. (b) Histrionic personality disorder
70. (c) Schizoid personality disorder
71. (c) 3
72. (a) A
73. (a) Paranoid
74. (c) Schizotypal
75. (b) Histrionic
76. (a) Avoidant
77. (d) Anxious and fearful
78. (c) Obsessive-compulsive
79. (b) Borderline
80. (d) Paranoid

GLOSSARY

Introduction to Glossary

The reader will no doubt recognize many familiar terms throughout this book. Occasionally the same word will have a different or very specialized meaning. In some instances, you may be unfamiliar with some of the vocabulary used in mental health practice. Highlighted are those that may need further clarification. You will find them defined here.

Active or acute phase in schizophrenia, the phase of the disease course in which psychotic symptoms are present; the active phase of schizophrenia is preceded by the prodromal phase and followed by the residual phase

Acute stress disorder an anxiety disorder that occurs within 1 month of encountering a distressing situation and results in recurrent thoughts, dreams, flashbacks, and upset when the person is reminded of the stressor; the person develops anxiety symptoms (such as sleeplessness, poor concentration, restlessness, exaggerated startle response) and dissociative symptoms (such as numbing and emotional detachment, feeling dazed), depersonalization, derealization, and an inability to remember aspects of the trauma

Adaptations the continuous, change-oriented, cognitive, sensory-perceptual, and behavioral processes people use to sustain or improve the fit

between themselves and their environment

Addiction a term used interchangeably with substance dependence

Adjustment disorder a maladaptive response of no more than 6 months' duration to a specific psychosocial stressor, such as divorce or loss of a job; the response occurs within 3 months of the onset of the stressor event and impairs life functioning

Affect observable manifestation of a person's mood or emotion; one of the "four A's" used to identify the splitting of external reality in schizophrenia, such as when affect is expressed by diminished emotions

Affectivity the range, intensity, and appropriateness of a person's emotional responses

Agonist a substance that acts to trick the body into reacting as if the endogeneous chemical were present

Agoraphobia anxiety about being in situations or places from which escape might be difficult (for example, in a crowded elevator)

Agnosia loss of recognition of familiar objects

Akinesia complete or partial loss of muscle movement

Alcoholic dementia problems with memory and cognitive skills as a result

of excessive drinking over a period of years

Alexithymia inability to identify and articulate feelings or needs, or to experience and express emotion except through physical symptoms; a common feature found in post-traumatic stress disorder and somatoform disorders

Alogia a speech disturbance in which a person talks very little and responds to questions in brief, mostly concrete answers; this negative symptom of schizophrenia is sometimes referred to as impoverishment of speech

Alters additional identities that a person assumes within a dissociative state; alters are distinct personalities with cohesive characters, unique memories, attitudes, habits, facial expressions, and personal histories that are clearly different and apart from the host individual

Alzheimer's-type dementia a chronic progressive disorder that begins with mild memory loss, progressing to deterioration of intellectual functioning, personality changes, and speech and language problems; this type accounts for more than 50 percent of all dementias

Ambivalence positive and negative values that often exist simultaneously; can refer to uncertainty about taking a particular direction or frequent vacillation between two different perspectives or courses of action; one of the "four A's" used to identify the splitting of the external reality in schizophrenia

Amenorrhea the absence of three or more consecutive menstrual cycles; one of the signs used to assess anorexia nervosa

Amnesia is the loss of memory of a person's identity or the loss of periods of time

Amnestic disorders disorders characterized by prominent memory disturbances, in levels of alertness, or other cognitive complications that are found in delirium or dementia; associated features include disorientation, confabulation, emotional blandness, and apathy; amnestic disorders may be due to a general medical condition, be substance-induced, or due to multiple etiologies

Amok a culture-bound syndrome found in Southeastern Asia, it is a trance-like state characterized by a sudden outburst of unrestrained violent or aggressive behavior, usually of a homicidal nature, preceded by a period of anxious brooding and ending with exhaustion; a similar pattern of behavior is found in Puerto Rico (where it is referred to as *mal de pelea*) and among the Navajo (who call it *iich'aa*)

Amphetamines otherwise known as "speed" or "pep pills"; central nervous system (CNS) stimulants frequently synthetically made in illegal labs

Amyloid cascade hypothesis belief that deposits of amyloid proteins cause cell death in the brain; associated with Alzheimer's disease

Amyotrophic lateral sclerosis (ALS) a rare illness involving progressive muscle atrophy that develops slowly over a period of months or years

Anhedonia an emotional state in which the person lacks the full capacity to experience pleasure in situations that do seem pleasurable to others

Animal phobia a subtype of specific phobia (formerly known as simple phobia) characterized by a fear of animals or insects

Anorexia nervosa a major eating disorder in which affected individuals severely limit food intake, resulting in substantial weight loss and dangerously low body weight; there are two subtypes of anorexia nervosa, the *restricting type* in which caloric intake is severely restricted, and the *binge eating/purging*

type in which binge eating is followed by self-induced vomiting and/or misuse of laxatives, enemas, or diuretics

Anosmia absence of the sense of smell

Antisocial personality disorder a Cluster B personality disorder characterized by a long and involved history of lying, theft, substance use, illegal activities, rejection of social norms, and lack of remorse for any hurtful actions directed toward others; this disorder exhibits itself in a disregard for the rights of others; onset may be as early as age 10

Anxiety a mood state wherein the person apprehensively anticipates future danger or misfortune

Anxiety disorder a chronic or recurring state of tension, worry, fear, and uneasiness that can come from unknown or unrecognized perceptions of danger or conflict

Aphasia impairment in the ability to formulate or comprehend language in any of its forms (reading, writing, or speaking) due to brain disease or injury

Aphonia inability to create sounds or speak

Apraxia impaired movement

Arrangers persons with obsessive-compulsive disorder who are ruled by magical thinking and superstitions that fuel their need for extreme orderliness and symmetry; arrangers compulsively and repetitively arrange particular items in a specific order

Associations (loosening of) illogical and disturbed thought processes; one of the "four A's" used to identify the splitting of external reality found in schizophrenia

Ataques de nervios is a culture-bound syndrome or a culturally accepted dissociative experience featuring uncontrollable crying, shouting, screaming, and seizure-like behaviors in which the person does not remember the episode afterward; it lasts for a brief period of time and is perceived to be adaptive

Ataxia impairment in control of voluntary muscle coordination

Auditory hallucinations hearing voices that do not exist within the environmental context; the most common psychotic feature of schizophrenia, the voices typically talk about, and to, the affected individual

Autism a disorder of neural development characterized by impaired social

interaction and communication, and by restricted and repetitive behavior that begins before 3 years of age

Autism spectrum disorders (ASD) one of a distinct group of congenital-neurological conditions that are characterized by a constellation of symptoms; they are also referred to as pervasive developmental disorders (PDD) or sometimes the autistic disorders

Asperger's disorder an autism spectrum disorder that is characterized by significant difficulties in social interaction together with restrictive and repetitive patterns of behavior and interests; physical clumsiness and atypical use of language are frequently seen

Attention deficit hyperactivity disorder one of the most well-recognized childhood developmental disorders characterized by inattention, hyperactivity, and impulsiveness; the individual may also show behavior and/or learning problems

Avoidant personality disorder a Cluster C personality disorder characterized by a pervasive pattern of social inhibition, hypersensitivity to criticism, and feelings of personal inadequacy; though individuals with this disorder desire relationships with others and are distressed by the lack of them, avoidance of social interactions and situations pervade their lives

Avolition a negative symptom of schizophrenia that is characterized by lack of interest in and inability to initiate or sustain goal-directed activity

Bashful bladder a condition sometimes found in social phobia in which the affected person fears being unable to urinate when others are around such as in a public restroom

Binge an episode that involves ingesting much larger amounts of food or drink than most people would ingest under similar circumstances

Binge eating an eating episode where the individual eats "out of control" and is unable to resist the temptation to consume certain foods

Binge eating disorder (BED) a disorder characterized by recurrent binge eating, but without the inappropriate weight control behaviors (e.g., purging) that are a part of the bulimic picture

Binge eating/purging type of anorexia nervosa a condition in which a person regularly engages in impulsive eating behavior followed by weight control behaviors such as self-induced vomiting and/or misuse of laxatives, enemas, or diuretics; the person between periods of perfectionism (with rigid control) and impulsive (out of control) eating behavior

Biological predisposition biological factors passed on from one generation to the next that increase the likelihood of an individual developing a certain disorder

Biomedical model a model or paradigm that delineates and describes diagnostic criteria to explain human behavior from a medical perspective

Biopsychosocial framework a perspective for examining an individual that validates the potential importance of biogenetic, psychological, social, and environmental factors in understanding human behavior

Bipolar disorder a major mood disorder with a distinct period during which the predominant mood is elevated, expansive, or irritable, accompanied by symptoms such as hyperactivity, pressured speech, racing thoughts, inflated self-esteem, decreased need for sleep, distractibility, and excessive involvement in potentially dangerous self-destructive activity

Bipolar I disorder refers to severe manic symptoms accompanied by one or more periods of major depression

Bipolar II disorder refers to the same patterns of symptoms found in bipolar I, but without the same degree of disability; bipolar II disorder is less severe, does not lead to psychotic behavior, and typically does not require hospitalization

Bizarre behavior patterns of conduct or demeanor far removed from normal and expected experience

Blood-injection-injury phobia a subtype of specific phobia (formerly known as simple phobia) characterized by the fear of seeing blood, looking at an injury, or receiving an injection (or any other invasive medical procedure)

Body dysmorphic disorder (BDD) disorder characterized by the affected individual's preoccupation about some imagined defect in his or her body, causing extreme self-consciousness, embarrassment, avoidance of activities, and body camouflaging

Body image distortion (BID) a distortion in the way individuals view their bodies within the context of an eating or weight disorder

Borderline personality disorder a Cluster B personality disorder characterized by marked impulsivity, poor and unstable interpersonal relationships, and disturbances in affect and self-image

Bradycardia slow heartbeat

Brief psychotic disorder a psychotic disorder that includes one or more positive symptom(s) of schizophrenia (such as hallucinations, delusions, disorganized speech or behavior) lasting more than 1 day but less than 1 month; this disorder often occurs following a severe life stressor

Bulimia nervosa a major eating disorder in which the affected person's diet leads to out-of-control episodes of binge eating followed by purging behaviors; there are two subtypes of bulimia nervosa: purging type and nonpurging type

Cannabinoids the psychoactive compounds found in the marijuana plant

Cardiac arrhythmia irregular heartbeat

Cataplexy stupor or motor immobility

Catatonia a state of mental disorder in which a person seems detached from reality and oblivious to environmental stimuli and whose behavior alternates between immobility and excited agitation; these symptoms are diagnosed as catatonic-type schizophrenia

Catatonic posturing semi-stiff poses or postures assumed by people with catatonic-type schizophrenia; this posturing or posing can be remain fixed for hours or days

Catatonic-type schizophrenia a type of schizophrenia characterized by unusual posturing, mutism or incoherent chatter, and/or facial grimacing

Censure within paranoid personality disorder, the tendency of affected individuals to blame others and to believe others are ill intentioned or hostile toward them; this tendency results in hypervigilance against the hurtful intentions of others

Centrality within paranoid personality disorder, the belief of affected individuals that they are the center of people's interest or attention

Checkers people with obsessive-compulsive personality disorder who are ruled by magical thinking and superstitions that fuel their strict need for orderliness and symmetry; checkers repetitively check and recheck particular items or situations in their environment, such as making sure a door is locked or the iron is turned off

Childhood disintegrative disorder a condition in which a child develops normally until age 3 or 4, and then over a few months the child loses language, motor, social, and other skills that had already been learned

Chipping a term used to describe a pattern of drug use in which the user is not physically dependent and is able to control his or her use of a drug (e.g., someone who uses drugs for relaxation, not for escape)

Chronic tic or chronic motor tic disorder involves quick uncontrollable movements or vocal outbursts (but not both)

Clanging a characteristic of disorganized speech in which the affected person primarily uses rhymes or puns to communicate with others

Clouding of consciousness the inability to focus, sustain, or shift attention, which makes the affected individuals appear confused, bewildered, or alarmed

Cluster A a DSM grouping of personality disorders in which individuals are seen as odd and eccentric; this cluster includes paranoid, schizoid, and schizotypal personality disorders

Cluster B a DSM grouping of personality disorders in which individuals appear highly emotional, dramatic, or erratic; this cluster includes antisocial, histrionic, borderline, and narcissistic personality disorders

Cluster C a DSM grouping of personality disorders in which individuals are seen as fearful and anxious; this cluster includes avoidant, dependent, and obsessive-compulsive personality disorders

Cognition refers to the mental processes involved in individuals' perceiving and interpreting themselves, other people, and events

Comorbid the simultaneous existence of two or more diseases or syndromes within a single affected person

Compassion fatigue a term used to describe an experience of mental health workers (or other caregivers) who experience a gradual lessening of compassion over time; a growing sense that caring for clients seems like a chore

Competency-based assessment model a framework for understanding human behavior that includes not only intrapersonal factors but also social, cultural, and environmental influences on the individual; the model seeks to understand human behavior from a multidimensional and dynamic ecological systems perspective, with the goal of identifying the individual's strengths to be used as a resource for resolving dysfunction

Competency-based practice a framework for practice that focuses on client strengths, resilience, and coping abilities and identifying social environmental supports

Compulsions repetitive behaviors (e.g., hand washing, checking, or counting) intended to prevent or reduce anxiety or distress, not to provide the affected person with pleasure; compulsions are performed to extinguish obsessional thoughts

Conduct disorder a childhood behavior disorder characterized by aggressive and destructive activities that cause disruptions in the child's natural environment such as home, school, church, or neighborhood; a central feature of this disorder is the repetitive and consistent pattern of behaviors that violate societal norms and the rights of other people

Confabulation a tactic used by individuals who are memory impaired in which they unconsciously make up false answers or stories in an attempt to hide their memory loss; most often seen in cognitive disorders

Continuous amnesia a rare type of dissociative amnesia in which the affected individual cannot remember anything from a given time in the past up to and including the present

Conversion disorder a type of somatoform disorder in which the affected individual experiences a loss or change in physical functioning that suggests the presence of a physical disorder but cannot be explained by any physiologic mechanism

Coping measures any efforts by an individual to regulate negative feelings about changes in his or her environment

Counters people with obsessive-compulsive personality disorder who are ruled by magical thinking and superstitions that fuel their strict need for orderliness and symmetry; counters repetitively and compulsively count

objects (or items of any sort) a precise number of times in a ritualistic fashion

Creutzfeldt-Jakob disease a fatal disease of the central nervous system known to cause degenerative, progressive brain deterioration; often confused with dementia; precipitated by an organism known as a prion (an infectious particle)

Culture-bound syndrome a recurrent pattern of aberrant behavior or troubling experience whose unique symptoms and their progression are specific to a particular geographic, ethnic, or cultural group (e.g., ataques de nervios or zar); these aberrant behaviors may or may not be linked to a particular DSM-IV diagnostic category

Cyberchondria a type of hypochondriasis that is fed by easy access to medical and diagnostic information via the Internet

Cyclothymia a minor mood disorder characterized by chronic or cyclic mood disturbance that lasts at least 2 years and has many of the same features found in a major depressive episode; "up and down" fluctuating periods of hypomanic and depressive features occur over a long period of time

Defense mechanisms mental strategies that operate unconsciously to maintain balance between internal drives and the external world; according to psychoanalytic theory, defense mechanisms are used by the ego to reduce anxiety and mediate conflicting demands among the id, ego, and superego

Delirium a syndrome characterized by temporary but prominent disturbances in alertness, confusion, and disorientation

Delusion a psychotic symptom involving a false or fixed belief based on incorrect deductions or misrepresentations of reality; these beliefs are not normative within the person's cultural or religious group; the false beliefs persist despite incontrovertible, obvious proof of their falsity

Delusional disorder a disorder involving fixed, false beliefs, contrary to reality (delusion); this disorder does not involve other features seen in schizophrenia, (e.g., hallucinations, affective flattening, and additional symptoms of a thought disorder)

Delusions of grandeur irrational belief that one is special, famous, or important

Delusions of persecution irrational belief that others intend harm to the individual

Delusions of reference affected individuals have an irrational belief that they are the object of discussion among others or that messages broadcast through the media are intended for them

Dementia a progressive and degenerative condition in which a broad range of cognitive abilities slowly deteriorate; involves prominent memory disturbances and central nervous system damage over a protracted period of time

Dementia praecox a term coined by Belgian psychiatrist Benedict Augustin Morel in the mid-1800s to describe the disorder now known as schizophrenia

Dependent personality disorder a Cluster C personality disorder characterized by a pervasive pattern of being unable to act independently of others; the individual exhibits submissive, clinging behaviors and will maintain relationships despite mistreatment and neglect; affected individuals are unable to assert themselves when needed

Depersonalization a feeling of extreme detachment such that the individual feels like an outside observer of his or her own behavior; characteristic of dissociative disorders

Depersonalization disorder a dissociative disorder in which the affected person remains in touch with reality, but experiences the self as strange or unreal; recurrent feelings of detachment from one's own body and surroundings, as if someone else is in control; some affected individuals report feeling as if they are observing themselves from the outside

Depressant a chemical agent that diminishes the function or activity of a specific part of the body

Depression a condition characterized by feelings of sadness, discouragement, despair, pessimism about the future, reduced activity and productivity, sleep disturbance (or excessive fatigue), and feelings of inadequacy, self-effacement, and hopelessness; some individuals have symptoms that are only mild, intermittent, and undetectable by observers while others have constant and intense symptoms

Depressive neurosis also called dysthymic disorder; is characterized by sadness, pessimism, dyssomnia (sleep disorder), poor appetite or overeating, irritability, fatigue, low self-esteem, and indecisiveness; symptoms occur most of each day, on most days, and for at least 2 years

Depressive personality disorder *see* depressive neurosis or dysthymic disorder

Derailment a characteristic of disorganized speech in which the affected person randomly leaps from topic to topic

Derealization loss of one's sense of reality in the external world; affected persons may experience familiar objects or persons as strange and odd

Differential assessment a consideration of a comprehensive range of diagnostic possibilities in the practitioner's evaluation and assessment process; the process of identifying markers of one disorder versus another in order to reach an accurate diagnosis

Disease a condition in which a system (or a portion of it) is not functioning properly; also referred to as a disorder

Disorder of infancy, childhood or adolescence not otherwise specified (NOS) a residual diagnostic category that is used for children when it is clear that some childhood disorder ought to be diagnosed, but the practitioner does not have enough information about the child's difficulties to assign a more specific diagnosis; as more information becomes available the NOS is discarded and a more specific diagnosis can be made

Disorganized behavior involves physical actions that do not appear to be goal directed (e.g., maintaining unusual body positions, pacing excitedly, or taking off one's clothes in public)

Disorganized speech a style of speaking seen in individuals with schizophrenia that includes mimicking, disconnected or incoherent speech patterns, and/or the invention of new words

Disorganized type of schizophrenia a condition whose features include disrupted speech and behavior, fragmented delusions and hallucinations, and flat or silly affect

Dissociation an alteration of consciousness characterized by estrangement from the self or the environment; is often a mechanism of defense to ward off the emotional impact of traumatic or abusive events and memories

Dissociative amnesia disorder formerly known as psychogenic amnesia; a reversible amnesia (not attributed to ordinary forgetfulness) associated with some form of emotional, traumatic, or psychological stress wherein affected individuals retain their generalized fund of life knowledge, but cannot remember important personal information such as their own name, age, or marital status

Dissociative disorder a group of disorders precipitated by psychological conflicts featuring a disruption in the client's intrapersonal domain, specifically consciousness, identity, perception of the environment, and memory

Dissociative fugue disorder formerly known as psychogenic fugue; affected individuals experience confusion about their identity in which important personal details cannot be recalled; characteristically involves sudden travel to a different geographical location away from home and work

Dissociative identity disorder (DID) formerly known as multiple personality disorder; a form of dissociative disorder in which the individual has two (or more) distinct personalities; the individual may not be aware of the existence of these other personalities; the alternative identities are often experienced as taking control, supplanting the prior identities, or being in conflict with one another; the change from one identity to another may happen in seconds or can occur gradually over a longer period of time

Distorted body image (DBI) an irrational perception that one's body shape and size is defective

Dizygotic twins a dual birth resulting from two separately fertilized ova (i.e., fraternal twins); because there are two ova and two sperm, the resulting twins are no more genetically related than ordinary siblings

Dopamine a catecholamine neurotransmitter that helps to regulate cognition, sensory processes, and mood

Double depression coexistence of dysthymic disorder and major depressive disorder

Drug high a state induced by an addictive substance; the user experiences a brief rush of euphoria called a high

DSM-IV the fourth edition of the *Diagnostic and Statistical Manual* (published by the American Psychiatric Association); is the standard tool for assessing psychopathology, by virtue of its categorical classification of mental disorders by type and diagnostic criteria

Dyskinesia an inability to control voluntary movements

Dysmenorrhea pain associated with menstruation

Dysmorphia *see* body dysmorphic disorder (BDD)

Dyspareunia pain that occurs during or after sexual intercourse; painful coitus

Dysphagia difficulty swallowing

Dysphoric mood also known as dysphoria; is a general dissatisfaction with life and feelings of unhappiness, exhibited as anxiety, hypersensitivity, anger, and/or depression

Dysthymia a minor mood disorder characterized by a relatively low-grade, but chronic depression often lasting for years; dysthymia differs from major depression in that symptoms are milder but more chronic

Early onset refers to the presentation of a disorder or syndrome prior to the expected age of onset

Echolalia pathological repetition or mimicry of spoken words of others

Echopraxia pathological repetition or mimicry of physical gestures and movements of others by a person with catatonic-type schizophrenia

Ecological perspective a framework emphasizing dynamic interaction between individuals and their environments; within this framework, "goodness of fit" between individuals and their surroundings is achieved through mutual interaction, negotiation, and compromise

Ego referred to as the self in psychoanalytic theory; is the part of the mind that mediates between the demands of the body and the realities of the environment, consisting of cognition, perception, defense mechanisms, memory, and motor control

Egocentricity a personality trait exhibited as showing no regard for the thoughts, attitudes, or feelings of others; the irrational belief that the affected individual is the center or focus of interest and importance above all else and all others

Ego-dystonic traits of personality, behavior, thought, or orientation, considered to be unacceptable, repugnant, or inconsistent with the person's perceptions (conscious or unconscious) about him- or herself; a synonym for ego alien

Ego-syntonic traits of personality, thought, behavior, and values that are incorporated by a person who considers them acceptable and consistent with his or her overall sense of self

Electrolyte abnormalities low potassium levels that can disrupt signals to the heart (causing irregular conduction) and cause kidney failure

Encopresis a diagnosis that describes the repeated involuntary passage or leaking of feces in a child over 4 years of age in places other than a toilet (for example in their underwear) that continues for at least 1 month

Enuresis a diagnosis characterized by the involuntary discharge of urine either during the day or at night

Environmental illness a newly identified phenomenon also called total environmental allergy syndrome; a polysymptomatic disorder associated with immune system dysfunction and allergy-like sensitivity to many compounds found in chemicals, foods, clothing, perfumes, and substances found in the air

Erythrophobia persistent, irrational, and pathological dread of blushing in public

Euthymic a description of mood characterized as normal (without depression or expansiveness)

Excoriation denuding of the skin; often seen in those who engage in compulsive hand washing

Executive functioning refers to the personality traits related to judgment, impulse control, and the ability to analyze, understand, and adapt to new situations

Factitious disorder a condition in which an individual maintains the sick role for secondary gain; the individual derives satisfaction from being considered ill

Falling out also called blacking out; a culture-bound syndrome occurring primarily among Caribbean groups or in the southern United States; characterized by the individual collapsing, sometimes without warning, in a trance; the person's eyes are usually open, but the individual claims an inability to see; can be preceded by feelings of dizziness; the person is not able to move, yet is able to hear and understand what is going on around him or her

Fibromyalgia a chronic disorder characterized by widespread pain in muscles and soft tissues surrounding joints, accompanied by fatigue

Flat affect the observable absence of (or minimal presence of) facial expression as if the person is unaffected by the contextual environment that surrounds him or her

Folie à deux also known as shared psychotic disorder, communicated insanity, infectious insanity, or double insanity; the main features include the gradual development of delusions resulting from the excessively close relationship between two people, one of whom is dominant over the other

Free-floating anxiety pervasive tension not attached to any specific threats, situations, or ideas

Full-blown episode a stage in the disease process in which the affected individual experiences the full spectrum of symptoms for that disease

Generalized amnesia a rare form of dissociative amnesia encompassing a loss of memory that includes all the experiences during the person's entire life from infancy to present time

Generalized anxiety disorder (GAD) formerly known as free-floating anxiety; a disorder featuring pervasive and non-specific anxiety (anxiety not attached to any particular situation) that interferes in all aspects of life functioning

Globus hystericus the sensation of having a lump in one's throat when swallowing

Grazing a pattern of binge eating in which affected individuals consume large amounts of food almost continuously throughout the day

Grisi siknis a culture-bound syndrome found among the Miskito Indians of Central America; an abrupt dissociative episode accompanied by extreme excitement of up to 30 minutes' duration and frequently followed by convulsive seizures and coma lasting up to 12 hours; also found in arctic and subarctic Eskimo communities where it is referred to as *pibloktoq*

Hallucinations experiences of sensory events in the absence of actual environmental stimulation; tactile, olfactory, visual, and/or auditory hallucinations may be experienced during a psychotic episode

Hallucinogen persisting perception disorder a condition occurring after an individual has stopped taking an hallucinogen involving flashbacks or re-experiencing one or more perceptual symptoms experienced while intoxicated with the hallucinogenic substance (e.g., geometric hallucinations, false perceptions of movement in the peripheral visual fields, flashes of color, intensified colors, trails of images of moving objects, positive afterimages, halos around objects, macropsia, and micropsia)

Hallucinogens a broad class of natural and synthetic compounds that alter a person's perception and consciousness

Hebephrenia a type of psychosis characterized by silly and immature emotionality; also known as disorganized schizophrenia

Hemiplegia paralysis on one side of the body, which may be a presenting condition in conversion disorder

Hepatic encephalopathy an altered mental state secondary to liver failure

Histrionic personality disorder a Cluster B personality disorder characterized by excessive emotionality, extreme attention-seeking behaviors, self-centeredness, self-absorption, and susceptibility; affected individuals demonstrate an inability to maintain strong, reciprocal, and long-lasting friendships and are often described as colorful, dramatic, extroverted, excitable, and emotional

Hoarders individuals with obsessive-compulsive personality disorder who cannot throw anything away because of an irrational belief that if they do something terrible will happen to them or to those they care about; hoarders feel compelled to save even worthless items such as newspapers or string

Huntington's chorea an autosomal-dominant disorder; the onset of which may feature personality changes, inability to adapt to one's environment, depression, and psychosis

Huntington's disease a progressive and degenerative disease that causes difficulties in cognition, emotion, and movement

Hypersomnia a sleep disturbance in which the affected individual sleeps too much

Hypertension high blood pressure

Hypervigilance the quality of being obsessively concerned, defended, or watchful (e.g., an individual with paranoid personality disorder is hypervigilant to perceived insults or harmful personal exploitation)

Hypnotizability the ease with which someone can be hypnotized; research has shown links between hypnotic suggestibility and increased risk of resorting to hypnotic-like dissociation in anxiety-provoking situations

Hypochondriasis a disorder of cognition and misperception of bodily symptoms, lasting at least 6 months; affected individuals are preoccupied with fears of having a serious or life-threatening illness despite the lack of medical substantiation

Hypokalemic alkalosis a condition caused by the kidneys' reaction to an extreme lack or loss of potassium which may be caused by some diuretic medications

Hypomanic episode symptoms of at least four days' duration that are less extreme and less disruptive than that of a full-blown manic episode

Hypotension low blood pressure

Iatrogenic the adverse mental or physical condition(s) caused by surgical or medical treatment

Ideas of reference delusions in which the affected individual believes the actions and speech of others relate or refer back to them

Identity alteration within dissociative states, a condition in which an affected individual behaves in ways that suggest he or she has assumed a new identity

Identity confusion within dissociative states, a condition in which an affected person is unsure of his or her own identity

Illness refers to the experiences associated with disease that ultimately affect the person's overall state of being and social functioning; illness is highly individual in that a person may have a serious disease but experience no feelings of pain or suffering (and thus no illness); conversely, a person may be extremely ill (as with a somatization disorder), but have no evidence of disease that can be measured by pathological changes in the body

Illusions perceptual disturbances in which things appear different from their objective reality

Impulse control an individual's ability to withhold inappropriate verbal or motor responses while completing a task; people are said to have poor impulse control when they act or speak without anticipating the repercussions of their behavior, without learning from undesirable consequences of their previous behaviors, or without delaying an action when it would be appropriate to do so

Indisposition a culture-bound syndrome occurring in Haitian culture; the affected person falls to the ground in a trance and is not able to understand or hear anything that is said around him or her

Inhalants a chemically diverse group of psychoactive substances found in volatile solvents, making them available for a person to breathe directly into the lungs

Insomnia the most common sleep complaint, which involves difficulty maintaining or initiating sleep; a disturbance in an individual's regular sleep pattern

Interoceptive avoidance emotional evasion of subjective perceptions of panic and fear

Interpersonal functioning characteristic ways of establishing and maintaining relationships with significant others; ways in which one communicates and interacts with others

Interprofessional collaboration an effective interpersonal process—enacted through teamwork or group efforts with professionals from other disciplines (i.e., nurses, physicians, neurologists, psychiatrists, psychologists)—that facilitates the achievement of goals that cannot be reached by one practitioner working alone

Ipecac also known as syrup of ipecac; a solution used to induce vomiting

Korsakoff psychosis an amnestic disorder caused by damage to the thalamus as a result of chronic, heavy alcohol use

La belle indifference a term used to describe an unrealistic degree of indifference or apathy in the face of one's own symptoms (as seen in the conversion reaction)

Lanugo also known as "peach fuzz," the baby-fine hair found on the trunk, face, and extremities of individuals who have an eating disorder

Latah a culture-bound syndrome found primarily in Malaysia and Indonesia characterized by an extreme response to a startling stimuli; the affected person's attention becomes highly focused and anxious, and he or she exhibits violent body movements, striking out, dropping objects, or mimicking others movements as if in a trance

Late onset refers to the presentation of a disorder or syndrome beginning after the expected age of onset

Life stressors within the ecological perspective, the difficult social or developmental transitions, traumatic life events, or other issues that disturb the existing "fit" between an individual and his or her environment

Localized amnesia also known as circumscribed amnesia, a type of dissociative amnesia in which the affected individual is unable to recall events that occurred during a particular time or following a profoundly disturbing event

Loosening of associations incoherent speech in which connections among ideas are absent or obscure; commonly found in schizophrenia

Macropsia a perceptual distortion that makes objects look larger than they actually are

Magical thinking the irrational belief that one has powers defying laws of nature and physics that can cause or prevent events in the external world; magical thinking is seen as pathological in adults, but is a normal part of the childhood development process

Major depression also referred to as a major depressive episode; characterized by depressed mood with related functional changes in behavioral, physical, and cognitive areas lasting at least 2 weeks

Major depressive episode also known as major depression; depressed mood with related functional changes in behavioral, physical, and cognitive areas lasting at least 2 weeks

Malingering the conscious and intentional maintaining of the sick role for some material or financial gain; symptoms are intentionally produced by the individual to avoid some task, for advantage in legal actions, or to obtain disability status

Mania a period of abnormally elevated or euphoric mood; associated with bipolar disorder

Manic depression now known as bipolar disorder, characterized by extreme euphoria or heightened mood occurring either alone or in combination with depressive episodes

Manic episode extreme mood elevation or irritability with related functional changes in behavioral, physical, and cognitive areas lasting at least 1 week

Medical model a conceptual framework that views an individual's problems as being "inside" of the person and resulting from a variety of causative factors such as genetic predisposition, internal conflicts, early traumatic experiences, and/or metabolic factors

Mental retardation a term used when a person has subnormal intellectual development and is characterized by any of various cognitive insufficiencies including impaired learning, social, and vocational ability

Mental status exam the initial evaluation of a client by a practitioner to determine the client's overall mental condition (including orientation to person, place, time; insight and judgment; mental and emotional state)

Micropsia a perceptual distortion in which objects look smaller than they are in reality (analogous to how objects appear in the rear view mirror of a car)

Mixed manic episode a condition in which the affected person experiences both elation and depression or anxiety at the same time

Monohypochondriacal paranoia a form of a delusional disorder that occurs in the absence of any other psychiatric illness; the affected person harbors delusional beliefs involving his or her body

Monozygotic twins a dual birth resulting from a single fertilized ovum that splits, thus producing genetically identical twins

Mood a pervasive and sustained emotion that affects every aspect of a person's life

Mood congruent a determination that an individual's emotions are normative to or in sync with the situation he or she faces

Mood disorders also known as affective disorders; a group of emotional disturbances characterized by serious and persistent difficulty maintaining an even, productive emotional state

Mood reactivity a depressed mood that can brighten readily at a positive turn of events

Morbid obesity a condition in which an individual is 30 percent or more above the average weight for a person of the same age, height, and gender

Munchausen by proxy a variant of factitious disorder characterized by the deliberate falsification by a caregiver of another's medical history and by manipulation of the medical community in a way that causes the charge to be subjected to unnecessary medical procedures and hospitalizations; the caregiver acts on the unconscious psychological need to maintain the sick role, even though the sick role is experienced only indirectly

Muscle dysmorphia a very specific type of body dysmorphic disorder in which a person becomes obsessed with appearing more muscular; some individuals have implants to enhance their musculature

Narcissistic personality disorder a Cluster B personality disorder characterized by a heightened sense of self-importance and inflated self-worth that often mask a fragile sense of self; affected individuals show a marked grandiosity, need for admiration, and sense of superiority to others; they see themselves as unique and special and show a marked lack of empathy

Natural environment phobia a subtype of specific phobia (formerly known as simple phobia) characterized by a fear of situations or events that occur in the natural environment (e.g., storms, heights, or water)

Negative symptoms also known as second-rank symptoms in schizophrenia; those characteristics that are notably absent in the affected person but are usually present in a person's experience (e.g., appropriate self-care, full range of affect)

Negativism disturbance of volition found in schizophrenia and characterized by a stubborn refusal to follow any course of action suggested or expected by others

Neologism a type of thought disturbance in which the affected person creates and utters nonsensical words or phrases to which he or she has assigned a symbolic meaning

Neurasthenia unexplained fatigue and lassitude

Neurons cells that conduct electrochemical signals in the central nervous

system and are considered the basic unit of the nervous system; also referred to as nerve cells

Neuropathic describing or referring to any disease of the nervous system

Neurotransmitter dopamine neurotransmitters are chemical messengers in the nervous system, and dopamine affects neurons involved in voluntary movement, learning, memory, emotion, pleasure or reward, and, possibly, response to novelty

Neurotransmitters chemical substances, such as epinephrine or dopamine, that transmit nerve impulses across synapses to act on the target cell, either inhibiting it or exciting it

Obsessions recurrent thoughts (such as becoming contaminated by shaking hands), impulses (such as having to align things in a particular order), or fears that automatically occur, despite resistance from the affected person

Obsessive-compulsive disorder (OCD) a disorder characterized by recurrent thoughts and irresistible urges that are severe enough to be time consuming and cause the affected person marked distress or significant impairment; the most common obsessions are repeated thoughts (e.g., of being contaminated by germs); the most common compulsions are hand washing, checking, or counting

Obsessive-compulsive personality disorder a Cluster C personality disorder characterized by extreme orderliness, rigidity, and inflexibility accompanied by emotional restriction; affected individuals are often described as perfectionists and have difficulty with interpersonal control

Olfactory reference syndrome a fear of offending others with a foul body odor currently proposed for inclusion in the DSM-5 appendix for further study

Onset refers to the beginning phase of a disease or syndrome

On the nod a drug-induced state in which the affected person goes back and forth between feeling alert and feeling drowsy

Opioids also called narcotics; a class of drugs that depress the central nervous system (widely used for relief of pain)

Oppositional defiant disorder (ODD) a childhood disorder characterized by a pattern of disobedient, hostile, and defiant behavior toward authority figures; the absence of a serious violation of the basic rights of others distinguishes this disorder from conduct disorder

Osteoarthritis a type of joint inflammation that involves deterioration of the cartilage that cushions adjoining bones within the joints

Osteoporosis a decrease in bone mass that causes bones to become brittle and fragile

Overcontrolled behaviors a personality prototype in disorders of infancy, childhood, or adolescence that tends to create more problems for the child than for others such as internalizing anxious or depressive behaviors

Pain disorder a condition in which pain itself is the primary clinical focus and in which the pain is maintained by psychological factors; the affected individual is preoccupied with pain that cannot be accounted for by any known medical or neurological condition; also known as somatoform pain disorder, psychogenic pain disorder, idiopathic pain disorder, and atypical pain disorder

Pain prone personality a person who uses the experience of pain to assuage long-standing feelings of guilt and worthlessness and who views pain as punishment or as a way of atoning for past misdeeds

Panic attack sudden intense fear for which there is no logical explanation; the affected person experiences physiological symptoms (e.g., racing heart, increased rate of breathing, profuse sweating) accompanied by thoughts of dying or losing control

Panic disorder a condition in which the affected person has recurrent, intense, and unpredictable episodes of extreme anxiety for which there are no rational explanations

Paranoia a condition characterized by groundless mistrustfulness and suspiciousness of others along with a tendency to view others as malevolent

Paranoid personality disorder a Cluster A personality disorder characterized by an enduring and pervasive pattern of baseless suspiciousness and inherent distrust of others; affected individuals are usually seen by others as hostile, irritable, and angry

Paranoid type of schizophrenia a type of schizophrenia in which the affected individual experiences hallucinations

with persecutory or grandiose content and delusions of persecution, while his or her speech, motor, and emotional behavior remain relatively unimpaired

Parasthesia a skin sensation of numbness, prickling, or tingling

Parkinson's disease a slowly progressing neurological disorder resulting in tremors, postural instability, and impairment in fine motor movements

Pathognomonic a sign or symptom that is so indicative of one disease that its presence is interpreted as a diagnosis

Pathophysiology the study of how normal physiologic processes are altered by disease

Pedantic speech a style of speech often found in children with Asperger's disorder characterized as academic, or a bookish type of speech

Persecutory delusions in paranoid-type schizophrenia, the affected person holds fixed beliefs that he or she is the target of others' ill will; these beliefs remain unchanged, despite overwhelming evidence to the contrary

Perseveration a characteristic of disorganized speech in which the affected person repeats the same word, phrases, or sentences over and over

Personality a set of defining behaviors, thoughts, and emotions that become ingrained to the extent that they dictate the person's worldview, lifestyle, and life choices; emotional and behavioral traits that characterize day-to-day living under normal conditions

Personality disorder a condition in which the affected individual's pervasive and enduring character traits are extremely inflexible and maladaptive, causing significant functional impairment or subjective distress; characterized by an individual's impaired interactions within his or her social environment and with others

Person: environment fit a measure of the compatibility between an individual's (or group's) needs and his or her surroundings; a concept within the ecological perspective used in client assessment

Phencyclidine a class of hallucinogenic drugs that produce feelings of depersonalization and detachment from reality

Phii Pob a culture-bound syndrome found in Thailand referring to a

common type of possession by a spirit or ghost; these spirits temporarily take over a person's body, thereby gaining power over other human beings

Phobia a common disorder in which a particular stimulant, object, or situation (e.g., heights, snakes, spiders) prompts overwhelming terror and obscures all other experiences; a phobic episode may feature profuse sweating, racing heart, dizziness, and trembling; specific phobias may include fear of animals (animal type), fear of bodies of water (natural environment type), fear of medical procedures (blood-injection-injury type), or fear of being trapped in an elevator (situational type)

Physical substance dependence a condition in which regular substance use accustoms the body to its effects, resulting in the need to continue the substance use just to feel normal

Pibloktoq also called arctic hysteria, a culture-bound syndrome occurring among Polar Eskimos and involving a trance-like state; the person affected becomes extremely excited for up to 30 minutes' duration followed by convulsive seizures and coma lasting up to 12 hours; before the attack, the person may be irritable or withdrawn for several hours or days; also known as grisi siknis among the Miskito Indians of Central America

Pica a disorder characterized by an appetite for nonnutritive substances; for example metal, clay, coal, dirt, sand, soil, feces, chalk, pens, and pencils, to list a few

Pick's disease a degenerative disease of the brain similar to Alzheimer's disease; differences include marked changes in personality early in the disease course, but less memory impairment than is usually seen in Alzheimer's disease

Polysubstance dependence a diagnosis made when a person is using (or abusing) at least three groups of substances (excluding caffeine and nicotine)

Positive symptoms also known as first-rank symptoms in schizophrenia; refers to characteristics that are notably present but normally absent in people's experience (e.g., delusions and hallucinations)

Postpartum blues also known as baby blues; a temporary and nonpathological state of emotional disturbance characterized by sadness and general dysphoria following childbirth

Postpartum depression a serious psychiatric condition requiring clinical intervention that occurs within 4 weeks of childbirth; characterized by the mother's severe depression, apathy, thoughts of harming the newborn and/or herself, and delusions

Postpsychotic depressive disorder a major depressive episode that is superimposed on and occurs during the residual phase of schizophrenia

Post-traumatic stress disorder (PTSD) a specific set of symptoms developing after an individual experiences an extremely traumatic event; symptoms may include intrusive recollection and re-experiencing of the trauma, avoidance of triggers that remind the person of the trauma, numbing of general responsiveness, hyperarousal or hypervigilance, and impairment in life functioning

Pressured speech speech with a rapid, unremitting, urgent quality; a symptom of bipolar disorder

Prodromal phase the interval between the onset of the earliest symptoms of a disease and the appearance of the disease itself

Projective identification a defense mechanism in which a person projects unacceptable aspects of his or her own personality onto another person (group or organization) and then induces that person (or others) to behave in accordance with the projected attitudes

Protodeclarative point or pointing to show something such as when a child points his finger to show his dad an airplane

Pseudocyesis a false belief of being pregnant

Pseudoneurological symptoms signs resembling sensory and motor symptoms but lacking clinical or medical foundation

Psychodynamic model a framework for explaining human behavior that focuses on symptoms, behaviors, and underlying processes

Psychological substance dependence a condition that develops when the habitual use of a drug results in emotional reliance on its effects either to elicit pleasure or to relieve pain

Psychomotor agitation a notable increase in physical restlessness as a result of inner tension; the activity is usually meaningless and repetitive (e.g.,

hand wringing, fidgeting, and foot tapping)

Psychomotor retardation an observable decrease or slowing down of motor activity; a common symptom of major depression

Psychosis the loss of reality testing and the impairment of mental functioning manifested by delusions, hallucinations, confusion, impaired memory, and the inability to function within the interpersonal domain

Psychotropic medications drugs designed to alter the mental state as treatment for individuals affected by mental illnesses (e.g., Resperdal is prescribed in the treatment of psychosis)

Purging any activity aimed at ameliorating the perceived negative effects of an eating binge on body shape and weight (e.g., self-induced vomiting or use of laxatives)

Rapid cycling a term used to describe the occurrence of four or more separate bipolar episodes (in any combination) within a 1-year period

Reactive attachment disorder sometimes referred to as attachment disorder, wherein the child has not bonded to an adult and has difficulty forming lasting relationships

Receptors the binding site of neurotransmitter molecules; much like a key fits a lock, neurotransmitter molecules are released into the synaptic cleft between two neurons and then bind to these sites or receptors

Residual phase also called residual type, the "filler" category in the disease formulation of schizophrenia; characterized by improvement to the extent that schizophrenic features can no longer be ascertained; the residual phase follows the active phase in the disease process

Residual type of schizophrenia a category reserved for individuals who have had at least one episode of schizophrenia but no longer display schizophrenic features; some evidence of bizarre thoughts and/or social withdrawal remain

Restricting type anorexia nervosa a condition in which a person severely limits his or her caloric intake, but *does not* regularly engage in binge eating or purging behavior; the affected person uses various techniques that help enhance his or her control over food intake (e.g., eating very slowly, making

food less attractive, or garnishing food with unappetizing spices)

Rett's disorder a childhood neurodevelopmental disorder considered part of the autism spectrum disorders wherein the child shows normal development during the first 6 to 18 months of life followed first by a period of stagnation and then by rapid regression in motor and language skills; girls only are affected

Rumination a preoccupation with distressful thoughts or worries

Rumination disorder a diagnosis involving bringing up food from the stomach into the mouth (regurgitation) and chewing the food

Russell's signs dorsal lesions caused by repeated and constant friction of fingers being scraped back and forth across incisor teeth to induce vomiting

Schizoaffective disorder a psychotic disorder featuring symptoms of both schizophrenia and a major mood disorder

Schizoid personality disorder a Cluster A personality disorder characterized by social withdrawal and/or odd or strange mannerisms; symptoms include magical thinking, ideas of reference, illusions, and derealization

Schizophrenia a severe psychotic disorder characterized by hallucinations, delusions, disordered thought processes, and bizarre behaviors; characterized by the presence of psychotic, disorganized, and negative factors

Schizophreniform disorder a psychotic disorder with symptoms similar to but less severe than those found in schizophrenia; this disorder must last less than 6 months (in contrast to symptoms in schizophrenia, which last more than 6 months) and must have prodromal, active, and residual phases

Schizotypal personality disorder a Cluster A personality disorder characterized by behavioral eccentricities, extreme discomfort with and reduced capacity for interpersonal relationships, and cognitive and perceptional distortions

Seasonal affective disorder (SAD) a mood disorder characterized by depression related to a season of the year, especially winter

Seasonal affective pattern bipolar episodes that tend to occur during a particular time of the year (e.g., late fall or early winter)

Secondary gain accumulated discernable advantages gained from symptoms and behaviors related to being in the sick role

Secondary traumatization the cumulative transformation in the inner experience that is the result of empathic engagement with another's trauma; a phenomenon frequently experienced by rescue workers such as police, paramedics, and other emergency workers

Selective amnesia a type of amnesia found in dissociative disorders; the affected person has only patchy recollections of an event

Selective mutism a disorder is characterized by the child's inability to speak in certain settings where speaking is expected while they are able to speak in other settings

Self-induced purging forced vomiting (e.g., through the misuse of emetics such as ipecac or by self-triggering the gag reflex); characteristically found in some eating disorders

Separation anxiety disorder a condition characterized by excessive anxiety, fear, and distress when a major attachment figure (such as a parent) is absent; a condition commonly seen in children

Serotonin a neurotransmitter that plays a part in neurological processes such as memory and sleep; also plays a role in some mood disorders

Shared psychotic disorder also known as communicated insanity, infectious insanity, double insanity, and *folie à deux*; refers to the slow development of a delusion as a result of being in a symbiotic relationship in which the subordinate party develops the delusion held by the dominant party

Shin-byung a Korean culture-bound syndrome in which the affected person initially feels anxious and experiences somatic complaints such as weakness, dizziness, fear, anorexia, insomnia, or gastrointestinal problems followed by dissociation and possession by ancestral spirits

Sign affective, behavioral, and emotional manifestations of conditions that are objectively observed by the clinician for diagnostic use

Simple deteriorative disorder also referred to as simple schizophrenia; a progressive development over a 1-year

period of the following symptoms: marked decline in academic or occupational functioning, increasingly flattened affect, reduced quantity and quality of speech and activity, poor interpersonal rapport, and social withdrawal

Situational-type phobia a subtype of specific phobia (formerly known as simple phobia) characterized by fear that is cued by a specific situation (e.g., public transportation, tunnels, bridges, elevators, flying, driving, or enclosed places)

Social phobia also known as performance anxiety; characterized by an enduring and irrational fear of public embarrassment or of a poor showing in performance-based or social situations; the affected individual is significantly and adversely impacted by attempts to avoid such activities

Somatic complaints preoccupation with illness or with bodily and physical symptoms

Somatic hallucinations *see* tactile hallucinations

Somatization disorder one of the somatoform disorders; characterized by the person's long history of complaints about symptoms that are not caused by physical disease, injury, or drugs; symptoms include being "sickly" for much of one's life, gastrointestinal symptoms, pseudoneurological symptoms, psychosexual symptoms, pain, palpitations, shortness of breath, and reproductive disorders

Somatoform disorder a polysymptomatic presentation that begins early in life and is characterized by multiple bodily or physical complaints

Somatoform disorders a cluster of illnesses with physical symptoms that cannot be fully accounted for by a general medical condition

Somatoform disorder not otherwise specified (NOS) a residual category for individuals who have some symptoms suggestive of a somatoform disorder but who do not meet the specific diagnostic criteria for any of the other specific somataform disorders, including the undifferentiated type

Somatosensory amplification a condition in which affected individuals experience their own bodily sensations as being unusually intense, aversive, and distressing

Specific phobia once called simple phobia, one of the anxiety disorders; characterized by marked and persistent fear of a clearly identifiable object or situation

Specifiers terminology used to refine the diagnosis of a disorder (e.g., in disorders involving substance use, a specifier such as "early partial remission" clarifies the diagnostic picture)

Splinter abilities a condition in which people with developmental disorders have one or more areas of expertise

Splitting a defense mechanism involving alternation between extremes of idealization and devaluation; seen in borderline personality disorder

Stereotyped behaviors preconceived and relatively fixed impressions of an individual based on superficial characteristics or overgeneralizations of traits observed in some people

Stereotypic movement disorder a disorder distinguished by the child's repeated, rhythmic, purposeless movements such as nail biting, head banging, or body rocking

Stereotypy purposeless repetitive movements often seemingly driven and nonfunctional (e.g., folding a piece of paper along the same crease until it disintegrates)

Stocking-glove anesthesia found in conversion disorder; characterized by the loss of sensation in the hand or foot, with the location of the loss of sensation approximating the presence of a stocking or a glove

Strengths perspective an orientation to the assessment that draws attention to the attributes, capacities, experiences, and resources in a person's life that contribute to a positive and satisfying life and effective social functioning

Stress a response to life events; characterized by anxiety, guilt, anger, fear, depression, helplessness, or despair

Substance abuse the excessive or inappropriate (not medically intended) use of a drug

Substance dependence a condition involving the continued use, craving for, and other cognitive, behavioral, and physiological symptoms that accrue from the use of certain drugs, alcohol, medications, and toxins; symptoms of dependence include preoccupation about the substance, taking greater amounts than intended, persistent efforts to control its use, reducing occupational or social activities, and continued use (despite recognition of recurrent physical, psychological, or social problems); the term *addiction* is used interchangeably with dependence

Substance-induced disorders a diagnostic category characterized by intoxication and withdrawal; symptoms include mood changes and sleep-related problems directly related to maladaptive patterns of using drugs and/or alcohol

Substance intoxication the affected person experiences impaired judgment, mood changes, and lowered motor ability (e.g., problems walking or even talking); features of this state depend on the drug taken, how much is ingested, and the individual's biological reactions

Substance tolerance a condition with two aspects: the need for markedly increased amounts of the substance to achieve intoxication (desired effect) or a markedly diminished effect with continued use of the same amount of the substance

Substance use disorders a diagnostic category of those disorders associated with the pathologic use of psychoactive substances; the affected person shows maladaptive behavioral changes

Substance withdrawal significant patterns of physical discomfort and emotional distress, cognitive impairment, emotional lability, belligerence, impaired judgment, and poor social or occupational functioning due to reduced or discontinued use of a specific drug, alcohol, medication, or toxin

Suicidal ideation thoughts of killing oneself

Sui generic the unique or singular aspect of a disorder

Sundowning the exacerbation of symptoms during the early evening hours experienced by individuals with delirium

Switching within dissociative disorder, the retreat of the affected person into a fantasy world in order to escape or blunt some abuse or memory of abuse; in dissociative identity disorder (DID), switching specifically refers to the movement among various alters (alternative identities)

Symptom a subjective, behavioral and/or emotional manifestation of a condition experienced by an individual and reported to the clinician for diagnostic use

Synapse the site where transmission of a nerve impulse from one nerve cell (or neuron) to another occurs; included are the axon terminal, the synaptic cleft, and receptor sites in the membrane of the receiving cell

Syncope fainting

Syndrome signs and symptoms that occur together often enough to suggest a direction for potential diagnostic and treatment formulations

Systematized amnesia a rare type of dissociative amnesia in which the affected person loses memory pertaining only to certain categories of information (e.g., relating to family or to work)

Systems theory a framework for viewing human behavior through three distinct frames of reference, or systems—biological, psychological, and social; systems theory does not attempt to explain human behavior

Tactile hallucinations the feeling of bodily sensations or objects that are not actually present in the environment

Tardive dyskinesia (TD) a particular set of side effects resulting from extended high doses of antipsychotic medications; characterized by involuntary movements such as lip smacking, chin wagging, tongue thrusting, hand tremors, and unsteady gait; Cogentin may be prescribed to relieve these side effects

Thought broadcasting an irrational belief held by the affected person that his or her thoughts can be heard by other people without the use of written or verbal communication

Thought insertion an irrational belief held by the affected person that thoughts have been purposely placed inside his or her mind by another person

Tic sudden, recurrent, and involuntary movements of the face, neck, head, or body; may also involve sudden, recurrent, involuntary vocalizations

Tic disorder NOS a diagnosis assigned when tics are present but do not meet criteria for any of the more specific tic disorders

Tic disorders disorders characterized by the persistent presence of tics, seen as sudden, recurrent, and involuntary movements of the face, neck, head, or body; may also involve sudden, recurrent, involuntary vocalizations

Tolerance *see* Substance tolerance

Tonic-clonic pseudoseizures muscular spasms

Tourette's disorder a tic disorder involving multiple involuntary movements or vocalizations; onset usually occurs before the age of 21

Transient global amnesia a type of amnesia involving a sudden temporary episode of short-term memory loss, usually non-recurrent and lasting a few hours without other signs or symptoms of neurological impairment; the cause is usually unknown

Transient hypochondriac states (non-psychotic) a condition characterized by the same symptoms found in hypochondriasis, but lasting less than 6 months

Transient tic a tic disorder that consists of multiple motor and/or phonic tics (or both) lasting at least 4 weeks but less than 12 months

Trichotillomania compulsive pulling of hair characterized by the repeated urge to pull out scalp hair, eyelashes, eyebrows or other body hair

Undercontrolled behaviors a personality prototype in disorders of infancy, childhood, or adolescence where the child lacks or has insufficient control over his or her behavior (such as externalizing aggressive, hyperactive, or noncompliant behaviors)

Undifferentiated somatoform disorder a condition in which affected individuals have one or more physical complaints not explained by any known general medical condition or pathophysiologic mechanism, grossly exceed the expected complaints of a medical condition, and do not meet the diagnostic criteria for a specific somatoform disorder

Undifferentiated-type schizophrenia a condition characterized by the major features of schizophrenia without meeting full assessment distinctions for the paranoid, disorganized, or catatonic types of the disease

Uremic encephalopathy an altered mental status secondary to kidney failure

Vascular dementia also known as multi-infarct dementia; is caused by a stroke

Vegetative features bodily symptoms often seen in conjunction with mood disorders (e.g., insomnia, poor appetite, and low energy)

Washers individuals with obsessive-compulsive personality disorder who fear contamination, usually by dirt or germs, and are compelled to clean to keep something bad from happening to them or their families

Waxy flexibility the semi-stiff quality of poses or postures made by a person with catatonic-type schizophrenia

Wernicke encephalopathy a deficiency in the vitamin thiamine arising from its poor metabolization in heavy alcohol abusers; symptoms include confusion, loss of muscle coordination, and unintelligible speech

Wilson's disease an autosomal recessive disorder that results in liver dysfunction and has symptoms of depression, irritability, psychosis, and dementia

Withdrawal *see* Substance withdrawal

Zar a culture-bound syndrome (resembling the Korean *shin-byung*) that refers to the experience of spirits possessing an individual; found in Ethiopia, Somalia, Egypt, Sudan, Iran, and other North African and Middle Eastern societies

Name Index

Subject Index

Note: Figures are indicated by f and tables by t following the page reference.